Literature and Revolution in England, 1640–1660

Literature
and Revolution
in England
1640–1660

Nigel Smith

Yale University Press
New Haven and London · 1994

Set in Goudy Old Style by SX Composing Ltd., Rayleigh, Essex
Printed and bound in Great Britain by Biddles Ltd., Guildford and Kings Lynn

Library of Congress Cataloging-in-Publication Data

Smith, Nigel.
    Anglia Rediviva : Literature and Revolution in England.
  c. 1640–c. 1660 / Nigel Smith.
      p.   cm.
    Includes bibliographical references and index.
    ISBN 0-300-05974-4
    1. Great Britain—History—Puritan Revolution, 1642–1660.
  2. English literature—Early modern, 1500–1700—History and
criticism. 3. Politics and literature—Great Britain—History—17th
century. 4. Literature publishing—England—History—17th century.
5. Religion and literature—History—17th century. 6. England—
Church history—17th century. 7. England—Civilization—17th
century. 8. Rhetoric—1500–1800. 9. Literary form. I. Title.
DA406.S63 1994
941.06′3—dc20   94–11191
                                          CIP

A catalogue record for this book is available from the British Library.

for G.F.N.

Contents

List of Illustrations

Preface

IN THE SUMMER of 1985, Robert Baldock suggested that I write a book for Yale University Press on literature during the period of the English (or British) Civil War and the revolution that followed. This seemed a very good idea. Despite the continued interest in that turbulent episode in history, there was no general book on Civil War literature for the specialist, the undergraduate, or the general reader. Indeed, the common view was that the 1640s and 1650s were a literary dead end: lyric poetry went into a decline, the theatres were shut, Milton was writing pamphlets; only the poetry of Marvell and Vaughan (and perhaps Lovelace) amounted to a serious contribution. Anyone wishing to teach the Civil War through its literature had to turn to the works of historians for help.

As with all good ideas, I soon discovered that I was not venturing into a lonely field. I have benefited greatly from the work of Lois Potter, Tom Corns and Gerald MacLean. I seem to have crossed swords pretty fiercely with Jim Holstun, but even if we cannot agree, the stimulation afforded by his attitude should not go unnoticed. Steven N. Zwicker's *Lines of Authority: Politics and English Literary Culture 1649–1689* (Ithaca, N.Y., 1993) appeared too late for me to make use of its many insights. The same is true of Blair Worden's important new work on republicanism.

What I have tried to do is to write a broad and genuinely inter-disciplinary account of the career of literature between 1640 and 1660, a period as crucial for the future of English literature as it was for all aspects of the nation's culture. I hope that students of literature will be able to use this book as an introduction to more detailed exploration of authors and texts, and that students of history will be able to assimilate the arguments and materials offered here into their grasp of other interpretations of the period in political, religious and social history. Specialists in both disciplines will find, I am sure, that they dispute as much as they are able to approve in the following pages. The very nature of the book has required sustained acts of compression, and there are countless instances where more detailed, specialist exploration is fighting to escape from the text. I have tried to provide a framework which encourages debate: difference is, after all, the essence of the 1640s. Above all, I hope that the general reader will simply be attracted to a series of remarkable writings produced at a remarkable time.

Seventeenth-century historical scholarship is infamously controversial, to an extent that literary criticism in the same period is not. I have tried to maintain, where appropriate, a balanced approach. Some of the issues touched upon in political and religious ideas are about to be the subject of yet another revolution in our understanding of the Interregnum: I have tried to catch a sense of the moment of revision. Most traditional literary history of the period has been undeniably royalist in sympathy. Studies of puritanism and radicalism have ploughed their own furrows. By giving a cross-cultural perspective (and indeed by fitting my own earlier work on radicalism inside the wider scene), this book offers a corrective to that view; and a provocation. I have not dealt with the popular literature of ballads and chapbooks except where they interact with or were part of the literature that is the central subject of this book.

Several people and institutions (among many others) deserve thanks by name for the help they have given me with this project. An award from the British Academy enabled me to visit U.S. libraries during the early stages of research. Tom Corns, David Norbrook, Frank Romany, John Morrill and an anonymous Yale reader provided highly useful and often deeply insightful comments on earlier versions of the completed study. Alan Rudrum gave his expert opinion with regard to religious lyrics; I am grateful to Joad Raymond for discussions on newsbooks, Ian McClellan for thoughts on romance, Susan Wiseman and Nancy Maguire for help with the drama, and Roger Pooley for responses to Richard Overton. Further help came from conversations with Ian MacLean, Andrew Ball, Scott Mandelbrote, Sue Owen, Anna Beer, Paul Hammond and Nick Ward-Lowery. Candida Brazil has been a truly heroic copy-editor, and I am extremely grateful for her guidance. My graduate students have been loyal and stimulating sounding boards: Ben Faber, Alison Shell, Chris Orchard, Madeleine Forey, Hero Chalmers, Jim Rigney and Tim Morton. All of my undergraduate students at Keble and The Queen's Colleges (and elsewhere in Oxford) have had some measurable impact on the following pages. As ever, I must acknowledge the example and strong friendship of John Carey, Geoffrey Nuttall and Neil Keeble. Kate Flint has reined in my prose and offered surpassing intelligent and affectionate companionship. As ever, blame for all shortcomings rests with me.

Keble College
December 1993

Abbreviations

Textual Note

For ease of reference, and where necessary, short titles have been used. In all quotations, punctuation and spelling remain as in the originals. Unless stated otherwise, the place of publication is London. Where a work is named and discussed at length in the text, page or line references are given in brackets in the text. In all other cases, references are contained in the endnotes.

BDBR   *A Biographical Dictionary of British Radicals in the Seventeenth Century*, 3 vols (Brighton, 1982–4), edd. R.L. Greaves and R. Zaller
BIHR   *Bulletin of the Institute of Historical Research*
BL   British Library
Bodl.   Bodleian Library
CJ   *Journal of the House of Commons*
CPW   *The Complete Prose Works of John Milton*, ed. D.M. Wolfe *et al.*, 8 vols (New Haven, 1953–82).
DNB   *Dictionary of National Biography*
DRD   *Divine Right and Democracy: An Anthology of Political Writings in Stuart England*, ed. David Wootton (1986)
EHR   *English Historical Review*
ELR   *English Literary Renaissance*
Folger   Folger Shakespeare Library, Washington, D.C.
HJ   *Historical Journal*
JBS   *Journal of British Studies*
JEH   *Journal of Ecclesiastical History*
JMRS   *Journal of Medieval and Renaissance Studies*
LJ   Journal of the House of Lords
NLH   *New Literary History*
P & P   *Past and Present*
PBA   *Proceedings of the British Academy*

PL   *Puritanism and Liberty, Being the Army Debates (1647–49)*, ed. A.S.P.
          Woodhouse (1938, 1986)
POW   Sir Robert Filmer, *Patriarcha and Other Writings*, ed. Johann P.
          Sommerville (Cambridge, 1991)
PQ   *Philological Quarterly*
RES   *Review of English Studies*
RPECW   *Revolutionary Prose of the English Civil War*, edd. Howard Erskine-Hill
          and Graham Storey (Cambridge, 1983)
SEL   *Studies in English Literature*
TRHS   *Transactions of the Royal Historical Society*
WWW   *The Writings of William Walwyn*, edd. Jack R. McMichael and Barbara
          Taft (Athens, Georgia, 1989)
YES   *The Year's Work in English Studies*

I am not ignorant, or insensible, from what *Precipice*, and into what *Gulf* I am falling; Not like one in a Dream, who starts at the *horrour* of the *Object*, which his own *imagination* creates: But deeply affected with those serious and reall impressions, which *Time* and *Experience* (the two great *Luminaries* of *Reason*) have fixt upon me. Methinks I see the various, cloudy, and sad distracted Fancies of these *Times* (that flutter up and down betwixt the *Twi-light* of *Ignorance* and *Self-conceitednesses*) bandy themselves against this *Work*, led on by *Prejudice*, which they muster up and gather together, happily from the *drosse* of those *Fragments*, or *vapours* of *Story*.

        Arthur Wilson, *The History of Great Britain* (1653), Sig. A2r.

INTRODUCTION

Dissent Refracted:
Text, Genre and Society 1640–60

AT THE START of the Restoration of the monarchy in 1660, at the end of the period with which this study is principally concerned, the Act of Indemnity and Oblivion attempted to enforce political unity, so that 'all names and terms of distinction may . . . be put to utter oblivion'. Anyone who 'shall presume maliciously to call or allege of, or object against any other person or persons any name or names, or other words of reproach tending to revive the memory of the late differences or the occasions thereof' would be punished with fines.[1] As usual with governmental attempts to regulate language, the legislation did not work, not least because it was rarely enforced. Yet this section of the Act reflected with particular intensity the fears of Charles II's ministers, especially Edward Hyde, Earl of Clarendon, of a recurrence of the momentous phenomenon of the previous twenty years.

The argument of this study is that the literature of mid-seventeenth-century England underwent a series of revolutions in genre and form, and that this transformation was a response to the crises of the 1640s: the Civil War and the political revolution which followed. It is also my contention that literature *was* part of the crisis and the revolution, and was at its epicentre. Never before in English history had written and printed literature played such a predominant role in public affairs, and never before had it been felt by contemporaries to be of such importance: 'There had never been anything before to compare with this war of words. It was an information revolution.'[2]

The administrations of James I and Charles I had attempted to control, and in some cases stifle, the expansion of the means of communication in the 1620s and 1630s, especially where such means were used to voice criticism of the regime. The sinews of communication made the Civil War possible, and, beyond the level of brute force, communication and authority were fought over and disputed until the end of the century. Moreover, 'as the most fixed and daunting structures of the external world – monarchy, Lords, Church – crumbled, so the internal pillars of thought crumbled. Men were freed to think hitherto unthinkable thoughts.'[3] More communication and more ideas meant

1

that public opinion – a body of views belonging to literate people with
varying degrees of influence – had been born, and its consent had to be
sought.

What began as a belated rebellion of the nobility, and ended in the
establishment of a republic, was accompanied by a series of expansions or
dilations in various spheres of political, religious and cultural practice.
Put in summary form, the 'subject' was understood to have more liberty,
godliness was seen to involve a greater degree of interior personal
awareness and self-determination, and discovery, lifted from its literal
sense of new world exploration, was redeployed as an image describing
the revealing of the rich mines of knowledge and experience within the
old world. Without literature to articulate these openings-up of the
collective imagination, the 'English Revolution' as we know it could not
have been. And since these 'discoveries' and 'new lights' emerged
through a civil conflict, cultural polarisation was endemic; literature was
one of the major ways by which the disease of division spread.

The effect of social instability upon literary institutions (the places and
habits which enabled literary production, such as the public theatres)
was to shake them up, and the consequence was a remarkable period of
disruption, dividing and reforming of literary types. The function of
literature itself was reconsidered. The literary innovations of the 1640s
were different from the innovations of the 1590s, a decade usually seen as
one of the most excitingly original in the history of English literature.
The great achievements of the 1590s – Spenser's *The Faerie Queene*,
Shakespeare's histories and comedies, Sidney's *Arcadia*, Donne's *Songs
and Sonets* – all succeed by the internal accumulation of literary
components. They 'overgo' the classical, native and continental
materials that are their models and that help to form them. In terms of
the theory of genre which I will shortly set out, we can say that the 1590s
was a period when cultural capital was achieved – at long last, the
English Renaissance was capable of realising in some density, and not
without anxieties, the cultural ideals it had for so long sought.[4]

If we then go to another famous literary decade, and this time a
revolutionary one, the 1790s, we find neither the splendid accumulation
of the 1590s nor the dividedness of the 1640s, but a replaying in some
measure of the innovations of the 1590s in terms of the concerns and
possibilities established in the 1640s. England experienced revolution in
the 1790s only vicariously (the real action was in France), and English
literature responded by replaying its own earlier revolution as a memory
and an accumulation – in particular through the use of Miltonic poetics.
Elsewhere in this period, generic invention (such as we see in Gothic
fiction and the radical novel) functions as a means of experiencing
(French) revolutionary excitement, while simultaneously keeping its
dangerous import well at bay. Only the most revolutionary and visionary

of the poets – the young Wordsworth, Blake and later on, Shelley – were capable of making revolution their form.[5]

But the 1640s were about war, and its literature, from the simplest to the most complex forms, was all to do with that. Genres fell to bits in the 1640s; they failed to achieve their aims, and circumstances prevented individual works being completed. While many authors were discomforted by such disturbances, others, like Milton, revelled in the artistic and civic freedom of different and various possibilities. The disruptions of the 1640s caused new forms to emerge, and reconstructions and renovations of suddenly outdated modes. The literature devoted to the republic and the Protectorate has been almost entirely neglected as a significant and interrelated aesthetic achievement, and it is one of my aims to end that neglect. Nevertheless, the failure of the republic and the Protectorate to impose their stamp upon the nation meant that what emerged was no unified art of a non-monarchical state.

How can we best understand these movements in the history of literature? Most of us want to, and do, see literature and society as interconnected. We also acknowledge that society and literature are to some extent separate, if parallel, worlds. On the one hand, people write texts, they are reproduced and circulated, other people read them, and others still try to stop some texts being read at all; in this way texts are of course part of lived, social reality. On the other hand, texts are constellations of linguistic signs, tied together by grammar rules and other systems of signification. The world of a text always has the potential to act on the real world because its contents may affect, perhaps greatly affect, a reader. That reader might do something unusual, socially transformative even, because of what he or she has read, or heard. The texts available to mid-seventeenth-century English people were vital components in how they understood themselves and their society, and they played a central role in the disturbed world of the 1640s and the 1650s. At the same time, the nature of those texts was also transformed by events – by immediate needs and circumstances. The text then is a dynamic vehicle of individual and collective human intelligibility and agency.

The connection between the two realms of text and society is in genre, its practice, and where relevant, its theory. A genre is nothing more nor less than a 'bag' or 'sack' of words (however large or small), the totalised identity of all the linguistic, rhetorical and narrative elements by which we recognise a particular speech act or text. It 'performs' when it is uttered or published and this itself is of course related to the assumptions which underlie its composition. As such, 'genre' is to do with human actions and the relationships of social difference and exchange which occur within texts and between texts and the people who use them.

Genres matter in the most simple of ways. Mikhail Bakhtin treated conversation as a series of genres (the most obvious are forms of greeting), all of which are, he said, susceptible to linguistic analysis.[6] The relationship between the conversational genres and complex literary genres is not explored (it should be), but we are left in no doubt that genre is to do with identity, and the play of identities within the dynamics of a society. For Bakhtin, genres are the motors of cultural revolution:

> In familiar speech, since speech constraints and conventions have fallen away, one can take a special unofficial, volitional approach to reality. This is why during the Renaissance familiar genres and styles could play such a large and positive role in destroying the official medieval picture of the world.[7]

The linguistic disorder which contemporaries complained of so frequently in the 1640s is an example of the situation Bakhtin has in mind. It is the 'buzz' of a destabilised society. We can disagree with Bakhtin's historical formulation (his 'familiar genres and styles' were often not the spontaneous invention of the people so much as recovered classical forms), but his picture of a society energised by opposed and interactive speech and writing is irresistible. Genres and forms are crucially bound up with those great themes of the Civil War and the Commonwealth – liberty, freedom, authority, tyranny, salvation, deliverance – because they gave them shape and intelligibility, and, therefore, an inevitable role in the social process. In doing so, genres, with their capacity for transformation as well as representation, define the parameters of public debate, the nature of change, and the means for comprehending that change.

Before the late eighteenth century, 'kind' or 'species' were the terms used in England instead of 'genre', and little explicit thought was given to any social or historical dimension.[8] Even very recently, mid-seventeenth-century English literature has been seen as generically eclectic, turning Bakhtin's idea of dialogue away from society towards an emphasis upon a timeless imaginative richness.[9] Yet even though Aristotle treats genre as a mode of classification on the same terms as natural *genera*, in practice genre is not simply a means of categorisation.[10] Unlike the myths which structural anthropologists regard as an 'escape' from history for primitive minds (a view which deserves to be challenged), genres are always engaged in the social relations in which they originate.[11] The earliest genres seem to have been tomb poems left behind by Egyptian officials in which their sense of identity is wholly determined by their function for the king. We could go further back (or

out) and argue that the marks which tribal people make on their bodies
to signify their tribal identity and the myths of that tribe are also
genres.[12] To speak or write a literary work in early modern England
usually meant expressing part of a national and a social identity. Most
literary forms in early modern England also involve more than one genre,
and their interaction in the reading or performance of the text
constitutes a dynamic play of power relationships.[13] Pastoral is usually
also either romance, complaint or elegy, or it incorporates one of these,
and their interaction facilitated social, political, religious and
philosophical statement. Richard Helgerson writes of late sixteenth-
century genres and forms: 'Like chivalric romance, every form . . .
depended for its meaning and its effect on its difference from some openly
or latently competing form.'[14] In other words, generic interaction is the
literary counterpart or surrogate of social and political difference, and
often it represents or even effects that difference.[15] Because satire
generates hostile images of a supposed enemy or 'other', it has often been
acknowledged as a force in the emergence of party politics in the
seventeenth century.[16] In this way, identity, politics and genre are bound
together.

In his bibliography of seventeenth-century studies, John Morrill has a
section on literature in which he wonders why no one asks why people
actually wrote poems and plays.[17] Why *did* people write poetry in early
modern England? Partly because it was in various ways an extension of
being – for some of being a gentleman of course, but also of being
civilised or being a Christian. You *are* your genres, in so far as genre is a
refraction of identity and a means through literary structure of exploring
potentials and acknowledging limitations in relation to the world. Hence
the large degree of generic inventiveness and eclecticism among women
authors between 1640 and 1700: they were discovering for themselves the
voices of authorship.[18] Writing and publishing a text is also a form of
acting which should be considered alongside any other individual and
collective human act, as 1640s commentators on public events were only
too well aware. In a similar way, texts have a power in their circulation,
interpretation and use, not necessarily connected with the circumstances
of their production.

Richard Helgerson gives a neat formulation of the interaction of
people, books and society:

> To be like the Greeks, to have the kingdom of one's own language, to
> base one's identity and the identity of one's country on a project of
> imitative self-transformation is precisely to adopt the 'English strain', as
> Drayton defines it. Self and nation are here caught in a mutually self-
> constituting process, just as text and nation were. Indeed, it is about texts
> and their form that both Drayton and Spenser are writing. Text, self, and

nation are 'true images' of one another. And the three are 'ever in
motion, still desiring change.'[19]

This formulation is too tidy: in any particular instance it might leave us
with a 'chicken and egg' problem with regard to causal explanation. But
it does define the terms of cultural interaction that are our concern. And
if the gentry and the top end of the middling sort were the chief
beneficiaries of the Commonwealth (many of them profited from land
redistribution and office-holding), the possibilities of literary production
went considerably down the social scale. In that all but the poorest now
had the possibility of authorship, we can say that the English Revolution
was more thoroughgoing in the extension of the possession and use of
words than it was in property redistribution.

There have been impressive attempts recently to explain large-scale
literary transformation through generic as well as social transformation.
Michael McKeon's huge study of the origins of the English novel argues
that between 1600 and 1740 instability in generic and social categories
ultimately resulted in the rise of the novel. Generic instability is a
function of epistemological uncertainty, and social instability 'registers a
cultural crisis in attitudes toward how the external social order is related
to the internal, moral state of its members'.[20] A variety of responses in
representation were the consequence, and the result, a number of
different narrative conventions which settled in the mid-eighteenth
century and became widely accepted as the novel. There is a problem
with the definition of genre here (surely McKeon needs 'form' as well as
genre to do justice to the complexity of the situation; in places McKeon's
'ideology' seems to mean the same as 'genre' too), but while this study
shares McKeon's interest in the relationship between genre and society,
the focus is deliberately more chronologically limited. For all its range
and inventiveness, *The Origins of the English Novel* restates in a
sophisticated way the old thesis associating the rise of the novel with the
consolidation of middle-class economic pre-eminence.[21] In this study,
readers will find a different and more historically attentive account.

Take an example. Nearly every major work by Milton, and a good
number of his minor ones, involve some kind of generic transformation.
The 'politics' of the works are communicated to the reader by a process in
which the text remakes its genre as it is read. *Lycidas* (1637) painfully
induces prophetic pastoral while acknowledging and then rejecting
pastoral elegy, and all in the cause of confessing puritan commitment
(among other things) while lamenting Edward King's untimely death.
Milton also makes genres leap out of high literature into the world of
politics, war and pamphlets. In the anti-episcopal tracts, the poet is
figured as epic hero and national saviour, and, more adventurously still,
in the *Defences*, the English people are described as the true 'epic'.

Such features are in part a consequence of Renaissance literary theory, but they are also especially typical of mid-seventeenth-century England, and precisely an effect of the impact of the national crisis on the activities of writing and publication. They link Milton with his past, with what has formed his capacity to write; they are the means of a response to a current predicament, and they are also the key to our interpretation of Milton's intervention in history. Milton's importance is not a little to do with the fact that he read the national literary predicament so well, and put it at the centre of everything he wrote. His enormous influence upon succeeding generations is related to the skill with which he dismantled and then reassembled the literary past under the pressure of his experience and understanding of the English Revolution.

A less rarefied alternative example of a different kind would be the sermon. Few historians would disagree that puritan sermons were not responsible for motivating people to active discontent in the 1630s and 1640s.[22] The trope of exodus, by which the English people were imaged as the ancient Israelites on the journey out of exile to the promised land of Canaan, was popularly transmitted through the sermon to give a powerful unifying sense of national destiny – a final and lasting reformation. The sermon's remarkable emotive powers of exhortation were embedded in its rhetorical formation. The situation we have to imagine is one where people are motivated, often to considerable degrees of intensity, by the sense and the sound of the words of the Bible, as they were re-arranged and selected by the art of preaching.[23] The effects of preaching in the New Model Army are well documented: having heard the Word, soldiers carried it into battle on banners and on their tongues. Differences between sermons formed part of the politics of religious difference in the period: between, on the one hand, the ornate and highly learned episcopal sermon, and on the other, simple puritan 'plain style' (and the gestural styles of preaching that accompanied sermon delivery). But in a very intense way in the 1640s and 1650s, the sermon leapt out of the control of trained ministers and into the possession of untrained lay 'mechanic preachers'.[24] The literature of the sects was much less regulated than that of the established church: the sermon became swallowed up in the broader category of prophecy, and was seen by non-sectaries as much more socially threatening. The clergy, although aware of the benefits of pious reading, also persistently complained of the bad effects of printed book circulation (because reading encouraged dissent and private opinions) whereas a preached sermon (so they felt) kept the listeners in the thrall of the preacher.

There are exceptions to these stories of change. Precisely because it was such an obviously transparent form, the fable was more or less untouched as a genre during the mid-seventeenth century, while almost

every other genre was. Its opaqueness and its comparative
unconnectedness with specific social relations meant that it did not need
to be restructured. The translations of Aesop published during the 1640s
and 1650s were specifically directed at public affairs and were assumed to
be proper vehicles for advising rulers, as they had been, it was thought,
in antiquity.[25] Fable remained the same as a form, although the stories
were often changed in order to suit events.[26] Leonard Willan claimed
that his translations of Aesop had been transformed by the war, but an
examination of his verse does not confirm the claim. Willan's tendency is
to opt for a generalised and vague symbolism in each fable. Sir John
Ogilby's translations of Aesop are by contrast an extended veiled analysis
of how the royalist cause came to grief, and yet how it possessed an
unanswerable superiority to the Commonwealth.[27]

Milton's allusion to fable in his regicide tracts serves as an occasion to
ridicule the Royalists. Fable had non-monarchical usages in history
before and after the Civil War, but by 1650, it was, by and large, and
with very few exceptions, about kings and frightful opposition to them.[28]
Andrew Marvell framed his fabular passages in 'Upon Appleton House'
(*c.* summer 1651) so that the evocative power and political identity of the
unmistakably royalist tree fable is compromised – pecked down by the
woodpecker or 'hewel' (sts 68–70). There is a surprise that the hewel
could fell such a mighty tree, but then we learn that the oak has been
internally weakened by a worm. Marvell lets the fable do its work, as the
worm suggests not sin but internal corruption – disorganisation, evil
counsel, and so on – but then the jarring fall of the oak fits not the
context (although it does go with the easy execution in Marvell's 'An
Horatian Ode' (June–July 1650)):

> And yet that worm triumphs not long,
> But serves to feed the hewel's young,
> While the oak seems to fall content,
> Viewing the treason's punishment. (ll. 557–60)

The destruction of the tree signals also the eradication of fable: for
republicans, it was simply an insufficient vehicle.

Michel Foucault resisted the categories of literary genre because they
did not seem to him to represent the divisions in the discourses of
knowledge by which man and the cosmos were defined.[29] But if genres
bear within them the marks of identity and the means by which those
marks change – the very means by which civilisation knows itself and
changes its understanding of itself – it is surely significant that genres
(not fixed categories, but interacting *foci* of intelligibility) became
overwhelmingly important during a civil war. There is, for instance,
evidence to suggest the creative interaction of scientific discourse and

political or religious expression in these years. John Saltmarsh caught the
sense of religious discovery in the mid-1640s in these terms:

> *new revealed truths*; if such be offered clearly from heaven by the hands of
> men, we finde that in Arts & Sciences the *Sistemes* are not such as will
> admit of no advancement: the profoundest agents in nature are led daily
> on to new *experiments*, and the *Aristotelian magistrality* hath been found no
> little hindrance to young travellers in the *regions* of *nature*.[30]

'Discourse' and genre are not separate categories, but part of the same
process.

Political and religious pamphleteering is generic too – alternating
between the parliamentary speech, the newsbook, the printed sermon
and printed controversy. These genres (and genre-mixtures within single
discourses) are not as unified as conventional and complex literary
genres: their circumstances of usage require that their internal
components be more mutable and fragmentary. The metaphorical
inventiveness which Conal Condren sees at work in Hobbes and his
lesser-known controverter George Lawson is precisely that kind of
generic embattlement and transformation which we have already seen in
more conventional 'literary' genres, and similar features are at work, as
we shall see, in shorter, more ephemeral publications.[31] It is not just that
publications in this realm were 'rhetorical', as opposed to 'logical' or
'philosophical' – using arguments simply to prove a case in a particular
context, as opposed to developing a theory in an exhaustive fashion, or a
narrative with closure. The education and forms of expression behind
different pamphleteers provided the dynamic by which they were
understood or misunderstood. Radical religious pamphlets appeared to
many contemporaries as incredible or incomprehensible because of their
unorthodox metaphorical organisation.[32] The hostile fictions which
pamphleteers were able to project of their enemies were an effective
means of political and religious action.[33] By the same token, to argue
that some radical pamphlets obeyed a broad Protestant consensus or a
concern with 'practical Christianity' looks only partially true when
Walwyn the Leveller uses Menippean satire or Montaignian scepticism,
or when Sexby the ex-Leveller uses a form of inverted patronage address
to urge Cromwell to offer himself as a sacrifice for the state.[34] It greatly
diminishes the importance of the often-made claim that there was no
republicanism before 1649 when the orator who speaks in *Areopagitica*
(1644) is clearly addressing a Senatised House of Commons, and when
the Leveller-associated *Vox Plebis, Or, The People's Out-cry* (1646)
repeatedly talks of a 'Republick' and of raising up the 'English Roman
spirit' while successively citing examples of political analysis from
Machiavelli's *Discorsi* (60). By naming republican institutions in this

way, the author is in a sense bringing them to life. It has been argued that one cause of constitutional conflict prior to 1640 was the 'jumping' of one kind of discourse from its conventional location (for instance, divine right theory as a branch of theology) into another arena (divine right theory applied to current politics equals dynamite).[35] The invasion of absolute prerogative concepts of sovereignty into common law discourse destabilised the way in which the relationship between king and subjects was seen to be founded. Charles I did not help himself by misusing the idioms of political and legal expression. What we have here is an example of literary displacement; such cases abound in the 1640s.

The ways in which political and religious institutions were represented inside and between genres were changeable, and make the analogy between institution and genre come alive. The process by which a concern or no concern at all with parliamentary sovereignty in the 1640s developed into a series of imaginative experiments in the expression of what a political community could possibly be (in Hobbes, Harrington, Winstanley, Baxter, and so many others) is well known. Where poetic genres tend to be concerned with personal states (although not always), other genres investigated the collective. The fascination with Parliament itself and its own murky history provoked increasing and broader examination of similar representative institutions in other (earlier) societies – senates, ecclesias, Sanhedrins. The intellectual dust-gathering of Coke (echoed by Prynne) gave way to the more comprehensive gatherings of Selden, or the speculations of Thomas May on the English constitution in relation to republican models.[36] As we will see, historical writing (from Polybius and Tacitus, through Guicciardini, Contarini, Machiavelli, and Ralegh, to May and Clarendon) is the generic link between personal agency (as it is found, say, in tragedy) and the constitutional arguments of controversial pamphlets.

Republicanism, no less than royalism, was especially literary in its sources. Partly because of its life largely inside literary form and literary memory, early English republican propaganda is almost inherently tragic in the sensibility it offers.[37] This is not only the case because *literati* like Milton and John Hall were major figures in the propaganda effort: the same is true of the lawyer and regicide John Cook, who mesmerically represents the time of revolutions as a ticking clock, while an irresponsible Charles I amuses himself with Shakespeare and Jonson, as opposed to reading the truth on kingship in the Bible.[38] All forms of royalist apology foregrounded elegy at some point, and while they too acknowledged tragedy as a response to the regicide, tragi-comedy entered the royalist frame, as much to ridicule the free state as to indicate hopes of a Stuart restoration. The two most enduringly generic but also generically indeterminate works produced in the seventeenth century were Hobbes's *Leviathan* (1651) and Harrington's *Oceana* (1656): also the two most important works of political theory of the period.

With these shifts came a series of central literary transformations which had a lasting impact on the nature of literary activity. 1) Royal censorship came to an end and the level of publication rose – providing the possibility of fully-fledged pamphlet war. Modes of reportage coincident with the rise of the serial newsbook provided models for historians so powerful that we are only just beginning to escape from them. 2) The theatres were closed down and the performing of plays suppressed. 3) The theatrical migrated into pamphlets and newsbooks, with playwrights becoming journalists and actors sometimes soldiers, even Levellers. 4) 'Cavalier' court culture, as it had been known in the 1630s, came to an end. With the embattlement of, and final defeat of a Royalist party, the lyric became embittered and textually fragmentary as the libertine ethos of the Cavalier was disgraced in literal military defeat. Yet some lyric forms remarkably prevailed and the lyric would become transformed by puritan and republican ideals. 5) The genre supposed to flourish most in time of war became unwritable in the face of defeat – the epic was unfinished (Cowley), divisively constructed (Joseph Beaumont), or reconstituted (Milton), mocked (Butler, Dryden), and epic language, because it had no life as a structured whole, became dispersed into other forms (Marvell): the 'brief epic' was the order of the day and a mode of immediate response. 6) Royalist literature was condensed, flattened, stopped. Much of it was produced in covert manuscript form – the 'fugitive poetry' of Mildmay Fane, Second Earl of Westmorland, for instance – and some of it, like the plays of Thomas Killigrew, written on the run. Its main 'creative' drive was to plunder the resources of late Elizabethan and early Jacobean literature – Marlowe, Shakespeare, Jonson, Beaumont and Fletcher. Above all, royalist literature, in attempting to praise the royal martyr Charles, found itself a desacralised form despite itself. And yet it survived as the flag of a defeated party.[39] 7) Greater freedom of religious worship resulted in the rise of new literary forms as part of new practices of worship, from the conversion narrative, and the sung hymn as opposed to the metrical psalm, to the nearly unintelligible prophecy of the Ranters; Hebrew, such as it is understood, became the source language of this literature, as opposed to Latin and classical Greek.[40] Attempts were made at redeeming, in puritan terms, other kinds of secular literature. 8) Other genres were implicated in the national conflict. In particular, prose romance became very largely the possession of the Royalists, but with the regicide, Arcadian romance structure was understood demonstrably to have failed, and the new French forms of romance, incorporating the autobiographical device of *le récit* were imported. Equally significant, while republican historians reconstructed English history according to the formulae of Greek, Roman and Italianate historiography, Royalists, most notably Clarendon, were constructing from the experience of defeat an entirely new kind of history which located causation simply in the vicissitudes of personality, so that history was to be written through character. 9) The identities and allegiances created during the Civil War and its aftermath survived by being inscribed into a number of genres concerned with the land, landscape, cultivation and fishing. Thus, while one might expect to find cultural division persisting in the writing of national histories, the confrontation of royalism/anglicanism and puritanism/republicanism inside the genre of the fishing manual is more surprising. Indeed, the very broad co-ordinates of such writing (for everyone has to use the land in some sense) permits, as we shall see, the most conservative to confront the most radical on a number of topics ranging from political ideals to the structure of matter and habits of cooking.

The one major factor determining this generic agitation was the fragmentation of religious and political authorities, a process of which literary transformation was an active part. 'Dissent', religious and political, is refracted – both in the old sense of breaking open, and in the current sense of diversion or deflection through a medium – rather than merely reflected in literature. There is no piece of writing which escaped this effect, and many kinds owed their genesis to it. The royalist and episcopal position already had its own literary culture of praise and ridicule, and so long as genres which had their origins in England within this culture were used, it was always the force of the horrifying 'other' identity which did the invading. With new or 'recreated' genres (more often the possession of the 'good old cause'), the situation is different, but not unrelated.

The study that follows considers these patterns in a tripartite configuration. The first section explores conditions and contexts of literary production, and major constants or shifts within this area, such as the emergence of the newsbook. The second section is concerned with the uses made of literature in politics and religion: the rhetorical construction of public life, and the centre of the pamphlet wars. The third and final section deals with genre transformation in the period of upheaval, both in and of itself, and in the context of its social role.

Derek Hirst has recently argued that published 'literature' (in the conventional sense of the word) was used predominantly as a signal of civilisation and cultural superiority by Royalists.[41] While the sustained publishing activities of Humphrey Moseley, for instance, bear out Hirst's contention, there is evidence to the contrary, even for the most conservative definition of literature. The frequency with which parliamentarian apologists cited Shakespeare and Jonson is a famous piece of contrary evidence.[42] It does seems to be the case that royalism foregrounded 'literariness', yet parliamentarian and 'radical' cultures had their own forms of the literary; it developed in its ways the heritage it shared with the Royalists, just as they developed their share of the heritage. The disturbances of the 1640s gave literature new functions, troubling its ownership by different speech communities, and making it behave in unusual and exciting ways.

Most people, educated or not, had never known anything like the Civil War, and their uncertainty as to what would come next is understandable. The 'world turned upside down' syndrome is well known in the period.[43] Literature was turned upside down too. One example, taking its name from a play by Ben Jonson, is a tract entitled *The Case is Altered* (1649). It describes a post-regicide topsy-turvy England where altered times induce fantasies of perception and the country behaves paradoxically or impossibly – cheapness and plenty produce division and distraction, the House of Commons alleviates the lot of the poor and cleans up the whorehouses.

There was a recourse to the resources of literature to understand affairs. 'Readings' of literature into the contemporaneous were not merely the products of lively minds in the capital. The Yorkshire schoolmaster John Smelt, a man of strong royalist principles, taught his pupils in the 1650s that Agathocles in Justinian's *History* was Lord Protector Cromwell, and that:

> When we came to read *Homer*, he would take Occasion from the many Passages in that Poet, which the learned know are written for the Honour of Kings, to read us Lectures against Rebels and Regicides, whom he compared to the Gyants that fought against the Gods, and I do here offer all humble Thanks to God, that by this Means, I first received that Light which made me first discern the Iniquity of the Times, in which I was born, and hitherto bred.[44]

To impose such literary patterns upon real events is to risk mystifying and mythologising them. Even at its moment of defeat the Cavalier ethos gains some kind of aestheticised transcendence or immortalisation, although we are sure that what is behind the signifier is a much-deflated reality. By extension, the ultimate royalist symbol was the martyr prince, Charles I, celebrated in the very popular post-execution apology *Eikon Basilike* (1649). On the other 'side', mystification is achieved in the appropriate theological terms: Puritans and Parliamentarians are impelled towards some kind of millennium or perfect political state by divine power, either in the form of an externally felt Providence, or, more radically, through the internally dwelling and internally known Holy Spirit. The influence of a puritan writer, like Bunyan, today is rather greater than that of any Royalist, so it is hard to imagine how odd and threatening a Royalist would have found him. Bunyan was a soldier nonetheless, and it is the internal struggle to accede to the divine will which impels him: the Providence which sends a man in Bunyan's place to the siege of Leicester (and who is then shot dead in battle), and that internally bred fear which the young Bunyan feels will cause the church steeple, then the church tower, and then the whole church itself to fall on his head (*Grace Abounding* (1666), 31). The praise of monarchs is replaced by the internalised dynamic of godly selfhood, where the true king is Christ, not of this world. The transformation may be seen in *Paradise Lost*, where the place of the monarch in previous English epic (Spenser) is replaced by the individual moral agent – crystallised in the narrator's relationships with Adam, Satan and Eve (see below, 224–5).

These examples are extreme positions, whereas the condition of 1640s literature is more usually one of confusion or equivocation. One example that fills the middle ground, and that nicely demonstrates the linked significance of the personal and the political, is Henry Walker's *Ecce Homo: The Little Parliament unbowelled* (1644), in which the individual is presented as a microcosm of the Parliament itself, without forgetting the virtue of being a Parliamentarian: 'Look not without on Votes alone/But see whats hid in Flesh and Bone'. The woodcut on the front presents a figure which looks like Charles I in a pose of humility, and where the comparison passes the reader through the authority of Parliament (the Big Parliament) to man, the Little Parliament (see fig. 1). Who is this figure? Individual, parliament, king, the vaguely delineated prince of Marvell's poem 'The Unfortunate Lover' (c. 1648–9)? Similarly unexpected, the royalist apologist Henry Ferne presents the soldiers in the King's Army as ancient Israelites on their exodus from Egypt.[45] There could be no greater biblical image of elect nationhood, an image usually associated with Parliament and puritanism. The currency of images is common property.

In this context, genre and the manipulation of genre function as codes in which the *cognoscenti* discern possibilities of their presence, or that of their enemies. Whereas a genuine resurrection of the humanist utopian tradition was revived, by Milton in *Areopagitica* and elsewhere, as a mystical but disciplinarian commune by Gerrard Winstanley in *The Law of Freedom*, and as the republic of trade stabilised by the political 'balance' in the work of James Harrington, Royalists had recourse to the pastoral idealism of Sidney's *Arcadia* and its clones. Much to Milton's disgust, *Eikon Basilike* quotes Pamela's prayer in the *Arcadia*. But for Royalists, the anarchy which permeates Sidney's text was a threat against an ideal monarchical order. For these people the wreck of Arcadia/ England was too much to bear, and they consequently stopped using the Arcadian model.

The point around which these narratives and constructions of self and governance focus is the representation of the regicide itself. As Nancy Maguire has argued: 'Englishmen used the theatrical tradition to mask

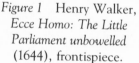

Figure 1 Henry Walker,
*Ecce Homo: The Little
Parliament unbowelled*
(1644), frontispiece.

(to disguise, to cover, to transform) the unprecedented act of judicial
regicide'.[46] In other words, the ultimate piece of enigmatic literature was
the representation of regicide or tyrannicide itself, which became the
dominant means by which different political versions of authority could
be asserted. The prevalent mode of perception was tragic; the dominant
mode of representation, tragedy. One Royalist put it this way:

This Bloody Stroke being struck upon the Royal Neck . . . it seemed
rather to fall upon the People than the King; for as soon as it fell upon his
Neck, the People cryed out with so grievous and doleful a cry, as I never
heard before: it raised a flood of teares, which sprung out of the Eyes of all
that had Ears to hear and Hearts to understand the Treason, from the
Noble to the Beggar.[47]

And better still, an anonymous elegy goes:

Kings are *Gods once remov'd*. It hence appears
No *Court* but *Heav'ns* can trie them by their *Peers*.
So that for *Charles the good* to have been try'd
And *cast* by *mortall* Votes, was *Deicide*.
No *Sinne*, except the *first*, hath ever past
So black as this.[48]

How are these images to be interpreted? In a way, they cannot be – it is precisely their doubleness (they refer to regicide but they do not disclose any clear answers) that impresses – and this is entirely debilitating, revealing perhaps a debilitated culture, a dead end. The same is true of so many elegiac and neo-elegiac lyrics of the period. Despite heavy contextual interpretation for a royalist or republican slant, the depiction of Charles I as royal actor on the scaffold in Marvell's *An Horatian Ode*, like so much of his poetry at this time, utterly resists interpretation.

But tragedy could be read in the opposite direction too. Regicides and republicans saw the deposition and killing of the tyrant as their great and positive tragic moment. Although the ancient sense of tyranny as gross and unnatural immorality (and which had survived in sixteenth-century drama) was effectively replaced in the politics of the mid-seventeenth century by the idea of tyranny as legal transgression, the two co-existed in attacks on royal prerogative and regicidal celebration.[49] To this extent, the great hope of the political radicals was for a political extinction, a moment of disappearance, an exit, the creation of a vacuum at the head of the state, just as a tragic hero in a Greek play disappears or is bloodily despatched in a revenge play.

Milton's defence of the regicide involved him in a redefinition of the contemporary understanding of tragedy. Milton's use of Shakespearean vocabulary from *Macbeth* to create a pejorative picture of the Presbyterian party in *The Tenure of Kings and Magistrates* (1649) has recently been discussed.[50] The Presbyterians (who resisted the trial and execution of the King) are described in vocabulary associated with the witches and Lady Macbeth in her guilty phase. Tragedy becomes the delay in not putting the King on trial, in not effecting 'revenge', thereby reversing the sense of the tragic in that most rapid moving of Shakespeare's plays, *Macbeth*.

The reason why Milton might well have entirely rewritten a royal play like *Macbeth* (and there is evidence that he planned his own version of the play) is because of his contempt for Charles I's own love of Shakespeare. *Eikonoklastes* makes much of the image of Charles as bad actor, hissed off the stage, and of the King's dangerously illusive immersion in Shakespeare.[51] Shakespeare's portrayal of tyrants is judged to be too indulgent:

I shall not instance an abstruse Author, wherein the King might be less conversant, but one whom wee well know was the Closet Companion of these his solitudes, *William Shakespeare*; who introduces the Person of *Richard* the third, speaking in as high a strain of pietie, and mortification, as is uttered in any passage of this Book; and sometimes to the same sense and purpose with some words in this place, *I intended*, saith he, *not onely to oblige my Freinds but mine enemies*. The like saith *Richard, Act 2, Scen. 1,*

> *I doe not know that Englishman alive.*
> *With whom my soule is any jott at odds,*
> *More then the Infant that is borne to night;*
> *I thank my God for my humilitie.*

Other stuff of this sort may be read throughout the whole tragedie, wherein the Poet us'd not much licence in departing from the truth of History, which delivers him a deep dissembler, not of his affections onely, but of Religion. (*CPW*, III. 301)

Milton's regicide tracts mark the beginning of his expulsion of Shakespeare from his dramatic inventiveness, and his attempt to create a new theatre for the republic. By contrast, classical drama becomes the site of civic liberation. *The Tenure of Kings and Magistrates* evokes the anti-tyrannical drama of Seneca, and specifically *Hercules Furens*:

> *Greeks* and *Romans*, as their prime Authors witness, held it not onely lawfull, but a glorious and Heroic deed, rewarded publicly with Statues and Garlands, to kill an infamous Tyrant at any time without tryal: and but reason, that he who trod down all Law, should not be voutsaf'd the benefit of Law. Insomuch that *Seneca* the Tragedian brings in *Hercules* the grand suppressor of Tyrants, thus speaking:

> > —— Victima haud ulla amplior
> > Poest, magisque opima mactari Jovi
> > Quam Rex iniquus ——
> > —— There can be slaine
> > No sacrifice to God more acceptable
> > Then an unjust and wicked King —— [52]

The same example is repeated in the *First Defence* (1651).[53] Earlier, on the title page of *Areopagitica*, lines from Euripides, *The Suppliants*, are quoted on how any person may come forward to speak on the public good. In *The Tenure of Kings and Magistrates*, Euripides (in his *Heraclidae*, ll. 423–4) also becomes an anti-tyrannical spokesman: 'How much more rationally spake the Heathen King *Demophoon* in a Tragedy of *Euripides* then these Interpreters would put upon King *David, I rule not my people by Tyranny, as if they were Barbarians, but am my self liable, if I doe unjustly, to suffer justly*.'[54] In the *First Defence*, Euripides' Theseus (from *The*

Suppliants, ll. 352–3) is quoted, recounting his greatest moment, when he made the people a monarch by giving them equal voting rights. Sophocles' characters (from *Oedipus Tyrannus* and *Antigone*) repeatedly proclaim that the state is popular.[55]

There are gender dimensions here too. Murdering a mother renders tyranny in symbolic dimensions. In *Eikonoklastes* (1649), to think of a parliament as female (not male) is to think of oneself as a god, above the people:

> And if it hath bin anciently interpreted the presaging signe of a future Tyrant but to dream of copulation with his Mother, what can it be less then actual Tyranny to affirme waking, that the Parlament, which is his Mother, can neither conceive or bring forth *any autoritative* Act without his Masculine coition: Nay that his reason is as Celestial and life-giving to the Parlament, as the Suns influence is to the Earth: What other notions but these, or such like, could swell up *Caligula* to think himself a God. (*CPW*, III. 467)

In *Paradise Lost*, Book 7, Mother Earth cannot bring forth creation until divine permission is given, thus pointing up the monarchism of Milton's God, but this quotation links more closely with the horrifying image of Death's rape of his mother Sin in Book 2: a further puzzle for the reader.[56]

Like-minded Puritans were also able to transform the meaning of tragedy for the purposes of Christian liberty. Peter Sterry, one of Cromwell's chaplains, knew Milton, but his use of tragedy is very different, even if dedicated to the same cause. In a Long Parliament sermon of 1647, Sterry developed the common 'theatre of life' metaphor to include the entire framework of Christian history. The Second Coming of Christ will contain events as dire as those in a tragedy, but also extreme joy at the apprehension of Christ's sweetness. In 1647, this looks like it was written under the influence of David Pareus's *Commentary upon the Divine Revelation* (Amsterdam, 1644), which analysed the Bible through the categories of classical rhetoric, and which Milton would use in the preface to *Samson Agonistes*. Later on, towards the end of his life, Sterry extended his discussion, using Aristotle's *Poetics* to develop a notion of tragedy as the 'tying' and 'untying' of Aristotelian plots in the life of Christ and all Christians: an application of truly Blakean proportions.[57]

Such writings are vitally part of 'real' history itself, urging their consideration alongside the mundanely polemical. They encourage us to link the order of literary language – style, syntax, and so on – with authorship and production because in that connection the action of political revolution was also imagined. A woodcut in a popular pamphlet from the early 1640s represents a pamphleteer as the barrel of a cannon, with his head at the breech.[58] The fuse is being lit by a Jesuit, but on close inspection, the Jesuit is really whispering sedition into his head and hence his pen. It is a very simple but faithful image of the sense of the involvement of writing in war and civil dissent, as well as the fear of divisive ideologies as the implantation of hostile outsiders. The images of firing words and of seditious whispering both occur in *Paradise Lost* (VI. pp. 584–94; IV. pp. 800–809).

In the very differences within and between types of literature is the crisis of authority that relates directly to the struggle at the centre of the state. In opposed but related texts (related by genre) are the fictions and traces of identity which were beginning to reshape the nature of political and religious public life. *Paradise Lost* might be the end of the 'big names' of epic discourse, but the period and the poem are the beginnings of the names of the liberal state. For most of the 1640s and 1650s, such genres remained in a state of ideological equivocation – internally confused or attempting to come to terms with new regimes. Since there was no effective or particularly violent censorship to deal with, these individually minor but collectively significant poetical breakings of the order of power could circulate largely unhindered.

In other words, the boundaries and contents of genres seem to be the focus for the way in which seventeenth-century people came to know themselves, and a means by which they tried to transform their predicament, just as they sought for new, reformed or revived institutions to solve their problems. As individuals they had by the early 1640s lost control over the wider processes by which genres were vitally involved in social relationships. That the most important political philosophy (and cultural production) of the period – *Leviathan* – should so intentionally and ingeniously make its points of greatest purchase through generic play (see below, 159–62), no less than Marvell's poetry does, is indicative of Hobbes's attempts to make genre reclaim the anarchy of events for the sake of order. By the summer of 1660 the revolution was lost but literature had triumphed.

PART I

Writing, Publishing
and Reading in the War

CHAPTER 1

Unstable Parameters

The Conditions of Writing

Production and Circulation

WHAT DID IT mean to write something, and for other people to read it in 1640? Did this mean something different in 1660? How did what was written come to be read in 1640? Was *that* different twenty years later?

At the centre of any attempt to understand the remarkable transformation of literary activity during the central years of the century must be the conditions of writing and the related issue of the nature of authorship. During the central decades of the seventeenth century, new kinds of author emerged in England, while some kinds of writing were doomed to extinction. Where were Gerrard Winstanley and John Bunyan during James I's reign? Where was the Cavalier court poet in the Restoration?

The capacity to put something into print grew in the 1640s. The precise relationship between the effect of the end of the royal censorship and the growth of the capacity of the presses (connected itself to decreased powers of printing monopolies) remains uncertainly known.[1] Yet the significance of putting something into print, where before it would have circulated only in manuscript, is highly visible in the period.[2] Putting something into print is closely associated with becoming an author. If religious publication prior to 1640 was largely in the hands of the clergy, so that even the most popular holy broadsheets were an attempt to make the alehouses in which they were posted holy, the 1640s and 1650s saw the emergence of lay religious authorship on an unprecedented scale.[3] Those who wrote political treatises, and those who published 'pure literature', also multiplied. Ultimately, many new kinds of authorship would appear, and the 'scene of writing' itself was generally and startlingly changed.

The first stage of the dispute between King and Parliament occurred on paper, and most at the centres of power must have hoped that matters would go no further. Yet before the first shot of the Civil War was fired, the phenomenon of increased print circulation had spread far beyond the immediate circles of political and religious privilege, and the political nation had surprised itself with the complexity and effects of a printed flux of information, as institutions and individuals jostled for supremacy.[4]

The often-claimed explosion of publications after the collapse of the censorship in the early 1640s – documented by Siebert, maintained by Hill and Annabel Patterson, challenged by Sheila Lambert – is most difficult to assess accurately, since our means of analysing published texts are thus far so primitive. A good piece of contra-censorship evidence is the fact that the Leveller William Walwyn had worked out most of his heterodox ideas from uncensored books widely available in the 1630s; what matters in his case is that a merchant had the buying power to obtain what was usually supposed to be socially exclusive reading matter.[5] The strongest element of the challenge made to the notion of the publication and ideas explosion is that since most of the books published in 1641–2 were very short, it may be that the total volume of published pages remained constant.[6] But if this is true, so also is it that the greater number of shorter individual items circulated more widely. To this extent there was a 'downwards dissemination' of print – a democratising of its availability. And there was still a sense – from all quarters – that the world had been destabilised by a printing surfeit. National perception had been changed for good by a media revolution.

We still need to know much more about the distribution of texts. Brief pamphlets and newsbooks were sold on the streets by hawkers, like the famous 'Parliament Joan', and bookshops became important meeting places for those attached to religious or political causes. As time progressed, different groups became more adept at subsidising publications, so that they could give tracts away for propaganda or proselytising purposes. The Levellers, and then later the Quakers, were masters of such strategies.

More information was available to all parties, and as a consequence, secrecy – withholding information, and displaying enemy information – was paradoxically a *public* obsession common to the nation, quite contrary to its pre-1640 association with the private deliberations of rulers.[7] Secrecy became a key element in the construction of different cultural identities: parliamentarian 'secrecy' looks different to royalist 'secrecy'. Lois Potter's emphasis on the obsession with secrecy in royalist literature is but half the story.[8] Both 'sides', for instance, published in newsbooks the intercepted letters of the enemy.

The pages which follow will give countless evidence of the power of pamphlets: they were read and responded to, and the printed matter generated during exchange was part of the wider process of division and fissiparation. One example in particular is worth mentioning here.

Francis Freeman, captain in the New Model Army, and later a Ranter, exchanged views with the royalist commander of Dunster Castle, Colonel Francis Windham.[9] The views and expression of each officer show the extent to which cultural stereotypes had grown by the late 1640s. As an example of royal treachery, Freeman cites *The King's Cabinet Opened* (1645), the influential pamphlet based on Charles I's captured correspondence. Freeman and Windham were at war with one another for the sake of two completely different (as they saw things) versions of life in England, and their exchange gives no better example in the period of the role of the printed book in fuelling that division.[10]

The effect of the expansion of the means of communication and the great variety of forms it took was a sense of living in a kind of public confusion. Those with a conservative view of society, those who saw the church and state as indissolubly linked, and the structure of authority stemming ultimately from the unitary power of the monarchy, were frightened and repulsed by the flood of publications which they saw about them, and the different, opposed claims for authority in those publications. The movement for the philosophical reform of the language in these years has been seen as a response to this sense that the confusion of tongues in the biblical Tower of Babel (Gen. 11:4–9) had returned: a sufficiently plausible suggestion, as long as we are also aware that there is a danger of being taken in by the writings generating the hostile image of Babel.[11] A faithful account of the 'Babel effect' would have to consider those who were glad of the advantages offered by the confusion of tongues. Different political and religious confessions effectively generated their own languages which were in many cases only partially interpretable by those beyond the immediate community of initiates. There was undoubtedly a public space in which all these languages could be debated – that was the enduring legacy of 1640 – but it was permeated by private languages, while the notion of a consensus of meaning in available public languages had disappeared for many. Viewed objectively, what was understood as enormity or anarchy was really the multiple capturing in words of the same events; many differing narratives being produced simultaneously to explain one single set of occurrences, and the repetition of these textual simultaneities over and over again for successive events. Familiar enough to us, but not to them. The witnesses to this inflated repetition seem to be telling us that it caused a social trauma.

Those who most disliked the information revolution wanted an abolition of all publications (and utterances) on public and private matters which did not emanate from an official source – royal authority. As the author of *Match me these two* (1647), an attack on both parliamentary journalism and the Levellers, put it, according to the statutes of fifteenth- and sixteenth-century monarchs: 'it is enacted and strictly defended upon grievous pain; that from henceforth none shall be so hardy as to contrive, speak, or set forth any false news, lies or tales of Prelates, Earls, Dukes, Barons, or great men of the Realme, whereby debates, discords, or slanders may arise.' Although few would have conceded this extreme position in practice, it does belie a deeply felt assumption concerning the relationship between the order of the state, and writing or print, the enablers of public opinion. Yet there was also the opposite response: within radical puritanism, for instance, the ecumenical minister or church member, who delighted in visiting different congregations, talking across jargons, was a new feature of English life. Ultimately, a new kind of attitude was produced whereby a latitude of views was possible, although such broad thinking, at first and in absolute terms, was very rare. For the most part, attentive minds registered the situation of divided, multifarious voices, and tried to grasp their predicament as best they could.

But public opinion had undoubtedly reached a new level of maturity, and the understanding grew that all words in the public sphere were attacking other words. There was a measurable social 'shock' which came with the new (relative) freedom to publish. The pamphlet exchanges of 1640–45, concerned mostly with church government and the debate on constitutional sovereignty, are riddled with an awareness of the effect of printed exchange on authorship, the author's social status, and authorial intention.[12] If attack had once been associated with satire, it was now absolutely everywhere: satire was but one category of a much bigger phenomenon which rightly deserves the name of pamphlet war.

Communication and Authority: The Public Sphere

The enhanced use of print made possible the exchange of views in a public forum – a readership largely in London, but also elsewhere in other cities (York and Bristol, for instance) and in the armies; a readership which could exert political pressure in certain circum-stances.[13] It may not have been large by modern standards, and it may have been concentrated in quite small groups of readers, but it did help to constitute a public opinion.

Objections to the new forum were commonplace, and often functioned as convenient polemical platforms. Instances of complaint are manifold. Bishop Joseph Hall, taking issue with 'Smectymnuus' (the pseudonym of a conglomerate of Presbyterian authors), is writing at a level above that of the publications he appears to be attacking: 'Lest the world should think that the Presse had of late forgot to speake any language other then Libellous, this honest paper hath broken through the throng.'[14] One did not need to be an imperilled bishop to feel press activity as a kind of virus. Henry Robinson was a leading tolerationist; he liked pamphlets, but even he was prepared to use the imagery of publication as contagion when it suited his polemical purposes – here when disputing William Prynne:

> I could much rather have bemoan'd in private that perverse and implacable spirit of yours, had not you of late so inconsiderately bespatter'd so many Pamphlets, which have infected the very aire, far worse than any most malignant epidemicall contagion, by having inherited the priviledge to be cryed up and downe the streets and publicke places, instead of Royall Proclamations, to the great scandall of your most conscientious Brethren.[15]

Moreover, royalist and anglican complaints of conditions in the 1650s are just as outraged at the hold which the Protectorate was able to achieve over presses. Richard Watson, made a bishop at the Restoration, recorded that 'it hath been as hard to find a Press for my Treatise that vindicated our Church, as for a Dedicatory Epistle to any Resident of our King.'[16] As comparatively late as 1648, the pamphlet itself was derided as a source of authority. Although not a Royalist, the anonymous author of one pamphlet objected generally to their use. The King's offers to Parliament for a settlement in pamphlet form offended the sense of credible authority: 'if you have no greater authority for it then printed Pamphlets, we will not so easily beleeve it; there is none will scripturize them no more than they will the ungodly Pamphlets of your Party.'[17] For his part, the King accused Parliament of breaking rhetorical decorum (see below, 38). The rules of the game may have changed, but no side or interest was prepared to sacrifice the use of older attitudes where it suited their purposes.

In this way, Richard Watson commented upon Milton's hypocrisy. Once Milton had argued for free speech; now he was servant of a tyrannous regime: 'More curious *Satyrists* had seen the light,/ If that poeticke *Areopagite*/ Had from your *Senate* gained the *Voting Word*.'[18] Instead, and in a direct redeployment of Milton's own images of truth, there is nothing but stifling and reductive pamphlet war:

> That all might be
> From *Viewes*, & *Censures*, or *suppressions*, free;
> That *Truth*, ris'n from the grave, might *London's street*
> Walke, uncontrolled, in her *winding-sheet*;
> Nor smother'd in the *baskets bottome* lie,
> Breathing *short whispers*, as forbid *the crie*;
> Or by *new Patent* mount th'*unsainted stall*
> In *Pauls Church-yard*, or *Peters Pallace Hall*.[19]

For a time, a certain kind of poetry became associated with protest and

satire, or, from the other point of view, of spreading untruth. Indeed, the
equation of satire and libel was widespread in the early and middle parts
of the century.[20] The schemes of popular verse were a symbolically and
mnemonically powerful mode of verbal attack, and the form constituted
a convention. John Bond's *The Poet's Knavery Discovered, in all their lying
Pamphlets* (?1641/?2) proclaims its function: 'Wittily and very Ingeniously
Composed, laying open the Names of every lying Lybel that was printed
last yeare, and the Authors who made them, being above three Hundred
Lyes.'[21] Bond adopts the form of a printed parliamentary order for
suppressing pamphlets, perhaps echoing the parliamentary declaration of
26 August 1642. His hyperbolic language recalls the prose of Nashe and
the coney-catchers of the 1590s (he is by no means alone in this); he
answers the poetical liars in fitting terms:

> The temporizing Poets have broached such impudent scurrility, and
> ementitious Pamphlets out of the inexhaust [*sic*] mintage of their roving
> fancies, that the whole City is embroydred with nothing but incredible
> lyes; that jars so much in the wearied eyes of the World, that the scarce-
> breathing mandrake could not digest the same. (Sig. A2r)

The tract reveals a considerable knowledge of the literary scene in the
early 1640s. He first identifies three 'lying' 'poets' – Henry Walker,
Thomas Bray and Phillip Harbert, and then proceeds to single out the
anti-Strafford pamphlets and Richard Overton's lampoons of Laud.[22]
These form single instances in a field of some three hundred published
since the execution of Strafford, says Bond. Richard Overton and others
are plainly identified as an '*Amsterdamian* pedant', an '*Antinomian*
Empyrick' and a 'company of fools', the latter being an identity
frequently imposed on radicals by Royalists. Most striking of all is the
physical sense of damage which Bond believes a printed libel will inflict.
If Laud is guilty or sinful, the law should punish him, 'but to see his grave
before his eys with lying libels: or to encounter with such extreams, as
the blasting tongue of infamy, is an act of higher suffering, then the just
censure of Law may permit'(4). Bond has words operating as weapons in
a way which Nashe would have approved, but the context demands a
more taxing engagement with the definition of truth. 'Lies', a seeming
shorthand for the whole subject matter of the tract, and especially those
which relate to the King, are dishonourable. At the same time, an
economic motive is not forgotten: the writer of anti-court and anti-
episcopal protest is reduced to the need to write for a living, a suspicion
which is not entirely without grounds:

> these temporizing Pamphlet-mongers, who for a little mercenary gaine,
> and profit, infused plenty of Gall, and Wormewood into their lying, and
> Satyricall lines. What a base humour is this in you, Poeticall Needy-

braines, who for a sordid gaine, or desire to have the Style of a witty Raylor, will thus impoyson your pen, and puzzle your sterile pages inventing such senceless, stigmatick, ballad Balderdash: as our very Street-Cantors, who would warble pleasantly through thr [*sic*] nose like an *Amsterdam* Zelot, at the insurrection of the flesh against the Spirit, for a Pot of Huffes Ale, and a huge subsidy toast: shrug to heare it, and with an honest scorne [s]hout at it. (Sig. A3v-4r)

Unfortunately Bond offended Parliament by aping its order form, and in April 1642 appeared *The Poet's Recantation, having suffered in the Pillory the 2. of Aprill. 1642* (1642), an account by Bond of how his muses had been the ruin of him (the records also show that he had offended by impersonating Henrietta Maria in a pamphlet addressed to the King).[23] He describes himself as a Perillus, outdone by his own invention, and a Cassandra, betrayed by his own 'bable crying', so that the distance between himself and those he attacked disappeared. He had stepped on the toes of the House of Lords, although it would seem that his punishment (to stand in the pillory) was not inflicted.[24] By the late 1650s, the association of most anonymous writing with libel or sedition was complete, as 'Adoniram Bansbottle' (a play on the real Adoniram Byfield, who first achieved fame as one of the clerks to the Assembly of Divines) admits in his analogy: '*I willingly confess, that a* Title Page *without the* Authors Name *prefixt in* Capitall Letters, *shews like a* Man *in the* Pillory *without a* Paper (*to specifie his* Crime) *on his* Forehead.'[25] The huge amount of unsigned or only initialled poetic libel (especially in broadsheet form) in the Thomason Tracts supports this perception.

At the opposite end of consideration from the professional writer's viewpoint, the dislike of the new pamphleteering was felt equally strongly. Edward Browne, who advertised himself as the Lord Mayor of London 'Sir James Cambell's clerk', bemoaned the recent fashion as 'lying and scandalous', as opposed to books of learning and religion. In a discourse which is typical of royalist works in 1642 – the madness of the times and the meanness of Roundheads are both mentioned – Browne complains, revealing how the crisis had lost him much capital:

no executioner I meane a Stationer or Printer had the heart to undertake the worke, and in excuse thereof told mee, That such a booke as that of thirty or forty sheets of paper is not like to sell in this age were the matter never so good, but if it had beene a lying and scandalous pamphlet of a sheete of paper that could produce a Scripture text, or some . . . tearmes against Monarchy and Hierarchy to up hold Anarchy, they would have embraced my profer, for it is like such would have provd vendable ware, if I could obtain an *Order* or *Vote* upon it. (*Sir James Cambells clerk* (1642), 7–8)

Notoriety sells a book, and zaniness was a good substitute for notoriety, as the newsbook writers demonstrated (see below, 57–62). After a fashion, the economics of the new situation were beginning to be understood. *The Downfall of Temporizing Poets* (1641) is a dialogue between a mercury (or newsbook) writer, a hawker of alcohol, and a drunken poet. Lightfoot the mercury fears the threat to his livelihood by the desire for drink: 'if it had not been for your tearing throat, my basket with papers would have filld my purse with crownes' (Sig. A2r-v). The worlds of popular consumption and of high politics were beginning to interact, making hacks like Bond into exposed political pawns, while Browne himself was attempting to boil down the teachings of puritan classics (Perkins, Greenham, du Bartas) for a popular audience, in a longer and older tradition of spiritually edifying literature.[26]

The fear of vastness was commonly expressed; vastness in the sense of an excess of printing which would exhaust the paper resources of the country. John Hall found it easy to vilify Prynne on account of the length of his publications. He used a common image which would soon be representing absolute political authority: 'I began to feare and tremble lest either you were in labour with some great voluminous work, which like a Leviathan would swallow up all the Paper, and be a means to raise Ballads and Pamphlets from three farthings to a penny a sheet.'[27] The print run for a pamphlet seems to have been one thousand.[28] Prynne's books were enormous, and there were many of them. Hall was probably referring to Prynne's *The Sovereigne Power of Parliaments* (1643), a huge collection of legal texts justifying parliamentary supremacy, and sponsored by Parliament.

Henry Parker may well have been trying to raise guilt among his own side when in 1642 he complained: 'Another advantage of the Kings party is by multitude of writings, invective and Satyricall.' And again, 'though too many papers are scattered of both sides, yet those of the Kings are most of them serious, and done by able men, whereas those of the Parliaments side for the most part are ridiculous done by Sots, or prevarications to the disadvantage of the party.'[29] Such comments are frequent, their particular narrative frameworks meriting consideration as different examples of the ways in which libel was constructed and imagined (positive and negative by turns):

> Among the many causes which have cherished and heightened our late and present distempers, there is none have been more powerfull then the audacious liberty, and carelesse permission of printed Pamphlets, which seeming inconsiderable, have better familiarity with the vulgar, and being fraught with reasons fit for their capacity, do not onely confirm those malignant whom they finde so; but by their tart aspersions laid on the best Persons, and their bold misinterpretations put upon the sincerest actions,

corrupt and poyson many times the best and purest integrities; while they of the adverse Party laugh in their sleeves to see so many good names sullied, and so little opposition to be made against them.[30]

This is very perceptive on the issue of readership, but it is rare for such statements to lack a certain naivety. The same pamphlet argues that libels should be suppressed at the source of the printing presses, and not simply prevented from circulating. But did anyone ever seriously think of any print control which did not involve the interruption of production? Or is the author imagining a restricted circulation, perhaps in manuscript only? Confusingly, the same tract (in a manner this time very similar to Milton's famous defence of press freeedom, *Areopagitica* (1644)) also objects very strongly to the imprimatur, despite its belief in the suppression of libels: 'that tyrannical passe-port of an *Imprimatur*; first spawned by the Inquisition, fostered by the Bishops and their Trencher-chaplains, and at last catcht by the turbulent Presbyterians.'[31] And again, the market never entirely disappeared from the awareness of contemporaries. Thus, the connection of controversial revenge with the book market was made by Milton who observed that in an animadversion, it was possible for the confuter to deprive the confutant of sales by quoting his entire tract in order to present disagreements with it (*CPW*, I.664).

In the transition from manuscript to print in the early 1640s, a good deal of revision of texts took place, in keeping with the requirements of the new market. The neo-dramas, dialogues and *argumenta* concerned with the Spanish match and James I's foreign policy were revised on top of the revisions which were made during the 'period of manuscript circulation', and then published again.[32] It is also noticeable that the return of a royal censorship in 1660 ushered in again a period of great inventiveness in manuscript circulation and scribal transmission.[33]

The interaction of manuscript and print during the Civil War should not be neglected. Throughout the later 1620s and 1630s, the gentry in the country were able to keep in touch with developments at Westminster by using a network which supplied them with a combination of printed works and manuscript materials concerned with politics.[34] Joseph Mede, the famous scholar of Revelation, compiled extensive newsletters in the 1620s. *Vox Borealis* (1641), attributed to Richard Overton, is a conversation between two Scottish 'scouts' (intelligence gatherers) who have been in London. The newsletters of one have been discovered by episcopal inquisitors and burned.[35] Commonplace books, of course, continued to be a dominant means of gathering information and of recording precisely the kind of literature which could only expect to have a limited public life. Commonplace books compiled during the 1640s are full of poetry connected with the

Civil War.[36] Mildmay Fane's 'Fugitive Verses' contains the kind of verse (mostly Horatian odes and satires) which could not be published, and the organisation of the volume follows the events from the regicide through to the proclaiming of Charles II King and beyond.[37] These lines from a piece called 'To King Charles' are typical of royalist Commonplace Book poetry:

> Circle with peacefull olive bowes
> And conquering Bayes, his regall browes
> Let his strong vertues overcome
> And bring him bloodlesse Trophyes home
> Strew all the pavement where hee treads
> With loyall hearts, or Rebels heads.[38]

A New Kind of Author

New politics, then, created new conditions for writing and new uses for that writing. The urban politics of the 1640s is the first widespread instance of an informed populace, with their opinion influenced by and influencing different political and religious stances and interests.[39] By 1659, partiality and truthfulness could be conceived of in sophisticated ways, a testimony to the growing up which had been done in the previous two decades:

> *most writers now adays appear in Publique, not crook-backed . . . but crook-sided, warped, and bowed to the right, or to the left.* For I have heartily studied to declare myself unbiassed, and to give an instance, That it is possible for an Ingeneous Man to be of a *Party*, and yet not *partial*.[40]

The acknowledged master of the new market was Marchamont Nedham, Gent., native of Burford, Oxon., sometime member of All Souls College, Oxford, classical republican, journalist. Nedham's notorious disloyalty (he swapped sides no less than three times in fifteen years) has brought him an unfortunate reputation which has obscured his remarkable powers as a journalist (see below, 67–8, 182–7), his comprehension of the nature of the publishing forum, and his originality as a political thinker. What Nedham (and for that matter, John Hall, and many other journalists) exemplified was the opposite of the 'loyalism' of so many staunch Royalists.[41] The last two of these qualities may be seen in *Certain Considerations Tendered in all humility, to an Honourable Member of the Councell of State, Aug. 1. 1649*, although his capacity to imitate popular forms of satire often masks this fact.[42] *Certain Considerations* is thoroughly Italianate, in a way which neither Parker nor Milton in their different ways had been (see below, 179–81), and presents a series of insights into the publishing situation and its politics without ever quite revealing the author's position. It is truly a piece of neo-Machiavellian *discorsi* writing, using the '*monuments of History and Policy*', and the '*best Opinions and Examples*', but compressed into a brief fourteen pages – that compression being so typical of Civil War literature. Nedham had been editing the Royalist newsbook *Mercurius Pragmaticus* almost since its inception in September 1647. *Certain Considerations* has been seen as a 'recantation' but, like his sometime crony of All Souls, the Ranter Abiezer Coppe, Nedham distances himself from commitment.[43]

What emerges is a digest of urban discontent, and the author is its master spokesman and analyst: the discontents of the people (a real worry to Parliament in the later 1640s), and their relationship with subversive political speech and writing, subversive sermons, satires ('Pasquils') and the 'Land-skip' of '*Eaves-droppers, Whisperers, or Informers*'. Ultimately, Nedham is suggesting a means for the government of the new free state to produce obedience and loyalty in the populace. His first advice is that there will probably be some resistance to a new government after a political revolution. The solution is to allow a wide toleration of different beliefs and opinions. Was Nedham seeking to have himself treated with leniency, or is there something more serious here? Or is it both? His vocabulary is clever, encompassing some keys words from the more extreme religious tolerationists: 'the cure of mutinous and dis-affected Spirits must . . . [not be] effected by Laws like Thunderbolts, but by the still small voice, the smooth oyle of gentle language, persuasive Admonitions and Declarations, hopes of mild government, pardon to offenders' (6–7).

Nedham's advice for governors who are subject to 'opprobrious Speeches against Government' is to ignore these voices, and do like the Romans: treat sedition as 'idle *Newesmongers*'. This advice is made by means of reference to Seneca, Suetonius and Livy, solid references enough, although it seems as if Nedham is confusing seditious speech with immorality – a concession to the general position of the kind of strict puritanical governance he seeks to attack. If we believe his claim that imprisonment gave him the leisure to explore classical sources, *Certain Considerations* sees the emergence of the republican theory which was later to emerge in *Mercurius Politicus*: 'the Governors in a *free City* or *State*, must bear with these things, and take heed in crossing the people in this licentious humor' (8). '*Pasquils* and *scandalous Pamphlets*' are equally to be ignored. The 'certain Itch of scribling' will always occur, and a ruler who punishes such authors will only magnify their importance, advice which is verified in the printer's conversations with Edward Browne (see above, 29). To allow press freedom for satires and pasquils is to make liberty present to the citizens. Yet while published writings, presumably of a secular nature, are to be permitted, seditious sermons are not since 'whatsoever is delivered under a religious pretence, strikes an impression upon the soul, and through the ear sinks deep into the minds of the vulgar'. The ancient equivalents were demagogues in Greece (who ruined many flourishing commonwealths) and the orators of Rome. Nedham singles out Savonarola's influence in Florence as an example of a sacred authority marred by megalomania. This prohibition introduces some degree of inconsistency into the argument, by which any careful reader is bound to feel troubled. Is a printed sermon or oration as seditious as a performed one? In the last section, this impression is enhanced on the one hand by Nedham's advice that there be no 'eaves-droppers and whisperers' who for hire make people incriminate themselves with seditious talk, and on the other, that there should be a few 'messengers' (Roman *lictores*) and 'scouts' or 'informers' (Roman *Speculatores*) who listen 'for the Princes private information in general' but who do not incriminate. Could there ever be such a fine distinction drawn between the two types? It seems doubtful. But then the whole pamphlet sets one's political sense on edge, with its rejection of the juridical terms which had dominated the arguments between King and Parliament, its exciting challenge to most orthodoxies, and its combination of possibility and impossibility. There is one clue early in the tract – Machiavelli (Nedham means the author of *Il Principe*) is decried as the '*Florentin devill*', possibly as a safeguard for Nedham himself, whose knowledge and use of Machiavelli in the republican cause was to become famous; the tract is really very Machiavellian. Is *Certain Considerations* a serious plea for toleration *with* social stability and civil calm, or is it the journalist's not entirely ingenuous apology for his work? The castigation of incendiary preachers would have found widespread support in 1649 from all kinds of people, but those same people would have found Nedham's apology for print unacceptable. Nedham may have been indulging in some special pleading, but he was also presenting a very new vision of public life in England.

One is equally troubled by the evidence we have of Nedham's social activity. His letters to his friend, the poet and clergyman, Henry Oxenden, refer repeatedly to the shared delights of drinking wine.[44] The new kind of author had a drinking problem. The tippling sessions which have gone down in history as part of the mythology of the Tribe of Ben (the young poets and playwrights who were tavern company for the elder Jonson), and which we can observe being disrupted by the Civil War in the early poetry of Henry Vaughan, are now part of the context for the generation of news and rumour. The first coffee houses opened their doors in the late 1650s, and were a further opportunity for public discussion and the exchange of information. In the early years of the Restoration, they were feared as sites of republican conspiracy.

The crisis of the 1640s introduced entirely new conditions of writing, of publication, and consequently, of authorship, and many experienced the expansion of public opinion as anarchy and disorder. But what was the effect of the new context upon the nature of the texts themselves?

Style Wars: Forms Confused

that my Translation may not appear too flat and *spungie*, having observ'd the most *depeditated* Authours of the times working in the same *vein*.

The Translator, George Bate, *A Compendious Narrative of the Late Troubles in England* (1652), Sig. A4r.

So hard a thing it is to speak without *tropes*.

George Lawson, 'Amica dissertatio'.

Rhetoric and the Pamphlet Wars

Seventeenth-century literature was in the grip of rhetoric: a technology of speech and writing inherited from classical antiquity, expanded, reformed and variously revived in the intervening periods. The two greatest Roman authorities on rhetoric were Cicero and, more extensively, Quintilian.[45] Their general precepts for organising the overall shapes of spoken or written discourses, and their more detailed or localised instructions for the fashioning of phrases and individual words, were widely followed and disseminated through the education system. Although there was an alternative way of organising words in logic, which increasingly had its adherents in the seventeenth century (see below, 163), it was assumed that the shaping of words in eloquent discourse would be effective or persuasive because it was a kind of verbal magic. By imbibing the wisdom of rhetorical tradition, and by obeying its precepts, it was possible for speakers to redeem language from mundanity and perhaps even from some of the taint of original sin (because the humanists tended to elide the classical and Christian senses of virtue). More in line with classical tradition, men could also use their redeemed words for the public good. In ancient Athens, the long-term consequence of rhetorical deliberation and decision-making in the public assembly was the formation of popular social and political consciousness.[46] Persuasion was of course the end of rhetoric, and if rhetoric did indeed carry redemptive powers, it was not always regarded in an unequivocally positive light: '*Eloquence*, whose end (as all the Masters of Rhetorick teach us) is not truth (except by chance) but victory, and whose property is not to inform, but to allure.'[47] The conditions of the times made one highly intelligent commentator talk of a '*Crisis of eloquence*'.[48]

In order to have the power of rhetoric, one needed education. Only those comparatively few men who had been to a grammar school would have encountered the study of rhetoric, and the chance to obtain a real knowledge was only available to the smaller numbers who went to the universities. Being empowered with rhetorical skills marked one's place in the social order, and anyone who came to be a published author without rhetoric was bound to stand out in the forum of public readership like a sore thumb. This, and the sheer weight of public outspokenness, in Parliament, from Parliament, in the pulpit, in the press and on the street, seemed to many to be unnatural and unhealthy. An anti-toleration pamphlet of 1644 complained of the '*Athenian* disease' of public speaking.[49]

For many, the rhetorical practices of the ancient Greeks were a reminder of how the arts of speaking could lead to social chaos. This was the fear of Thomas Hobbes. His earlier attempt at setting down a science of politics, *De Cive* (1642), identifies sedition with oratory.[50] For most of *De Cive*, the operation of rhetoric (as opposed to logic) is limited to explanatory similes set against the strong negative image of the seditious tendencies of orators in democracies. Occasionally, the power of images breaks out, as in the famous use of the fable of Medea and the daughters of Pelias, which illustrates the danger of faction:

> For *folly* and *eloquence* concurre in the subversion of government in the same manner (as the fable hath it) as heretofore the daughters of *Pelias* King of Thessaly, conspired with *Medea* against their father; They going to restore the decrepit old man to his youth again, by the counsell of *Medea*, they cut him into peeces, and set him in the fire to boyle, in vain expecting when he would live again; So the common people through their folly (like the daughters of *Pelias*) desiring to renew the ancient government, being drawne away by the *eloquence* of ambitious men, as it were by the witchcraft of *Medea*, divided into *faction*, they consume it rather by those flames, then they reforme it.[51]

As a rhetorical device demonstrating the danger of public rhetoric, this was an exception in *De Cive*. Another view is presented by Milton, who consistently showed a mastery of rhetoric, and conceived of it as fighting a battle in the cause of civic virtue.[52]

In England there were several different contexts for different rhetorics, and these were clearly connected with relationships of power and social difference. The operation of the different discourses which made up a large part of the content of religious life (liturgies, prayers, metrical psalms, sermons, homilies, and the innovations and evolutions of these forms during the 1640s and 1650s) would be an obvious example. Every institution had its rhetorics in this broader sense, since they needed words, and the other conventions which sustained verbal communication, to operate. Any speaker could be imagined as a classical orator, and it was speech, not print, which mattered:

> Neither am I ignorant or unexperienc'd, how much the less the mind is affected with reading, then with hearing; even by how much a *Preacher*, in the particular gift of utterance, is the more master of his tongue, then pen; and so can speak much more piercingly to the eye, as an *Orator*, then as a *Scribe*. But, what my Pulpit-conceptions do lose by the Press, as to their affecting heat; I hope they will have repair'd them by their informing light, the Judgement being more thorowly convinced by a frequent perusal, then a single discovery.[53]

Looking back to the 1620s Parliaments, Rushworth remembered men like Digges, Wentworth and Eliot as 'excellent Orators . . . not much inferiour to the chiefest of the Roman *Demagogues*'.[54] So also Joseph Caryll praised the members of the Long Parliament in 1646, and he went on to place rhetoric at the heart of the reformed religious attitudes which Parliament was supposed to represent:

> a *Rhetoricall declaration*: when besides a bare narrative of the facts, *&c.* (which is proper to history) we labour to finde out the severall circumstances and aggravations of every work, which may raise up our spirits, and warm our hearts in considering of, and looking over them. It is our dutie to make more then bare narratives and histories, we must clothe them with eloquence, and make oratory doe homage to the honour of God. The holy Pen-men have been admirable in this . . .[55]

Rhetoric was at the heart of political and other social theories and actions. Actors were frequently called 'orators' in this period. The Ranter Abiezer Coppe's knowledge of rhetoric (and classical literature) was essential to the development of his theology as well as his expression.[56]

Rhetoric was also frequently used in a negative sense. The Royalist Sir Kenelm Digby was likened by an enemy to a chapman, selling his 'small parcels of silken Rhetorick fine and course compliments, Scriptures woven at Oxford, Posies for Prerogative, Ribands for Vive le Roy'.[57] The kind of elegy which followed Laud's execution was a foretaste of what was to come in 1649, and its exaggerations irritated the parliamentary newsbooks, who complained of the 'loftiest *Hyperbolicall* commendation of this *Diabolicall Traitour*, as if they had plundered the *Parasites* at *Court*, or all *Bodley's* Library, for *Rhetoric* to furnish one swelling *Encomium*'.[58] Political writing, it was claimed by some, did not need rhetoric: 'accept it only as a plain peece of common talk, which I would have delivered, had I beene present with you: Such discourses need no dresse of

Rhetorique'.[59] Likewise, plain matter was especially appropriate for attacks on bishops: 'These few Leaves of Paper breake on through, after the humble remonstrance, with less noyse, because of lesse bulke; and not stuffed with the huskes of a bare pleasing speech, but presented to your view with more substance then Rhetorique'.[60] Of course, plainness was rhetorical too: writing in *Mercurius Britanicus*, Thomas Audley praised Sir Benjamin Rudyerd's sober *'blossomes* of Prudence and Rhetoricke'.[61]

When Charles I received the Grand Remonstrance, Thomas May reports that he was indignant at receiving a document which defied the categories of rhetoric: the King 'told them, that in all Aristotle's Rhetorics there was no such argument of persuasion'.[62] On the other hand, rhetoric was also associated with republicanism: it was more proper, historically speaking, to do so, and the connection was made increasingly during the later 1640s and 1650s. So, when the Elizabethan Jesuit Robert Parson's *Severall Speeches Delivered at a Conference concerning the Power of Parliaments* (1594) was republished in 1648, containing a discussion of the expulsion or removal of kings, it was entirely appropriate for the context that the tract was organised as a series of orations on forms of government delivered by Athenian orators.

In the political and religious works of the 1640s and 1650s, it was assumed that oratory could be transferred to the printed pamphlet, and that such printed oratory would play an active role in what was understood to be a war of words. The relevance of a number of different types of pamphlet should not be forgotten here. Published parliamentary speeches were dangerous objects. Sir Edward Dering's published speeches were burned (on account of their content) and he was imprisoned when it became apparent that he was veering towards supporting the King. The publication itself was an act whereby the ethos of virtuous speaking was literally extended into a wider forum of public exchange. Whether or not such publications declined in the later 1640s because Parliament had such confidence that it no longer felt the need to appeal to public opinion in this way remains to be seen. What is apparent is the expected effect of a published parliamentary speech; its special valorisation as a constitutionally condoned piece of speaking.

Such decorum was noted even during the Protectorate, when *Mr. Recorder's Speech to the Lord Protector* (1653) exercised classical oratory in the service of the Protector. By then, parliamentary rhetoric was firmly associated with anti-monarchical government, despite the passing of the republic itself. In this instance, civic loyalty is evoked while distancing the civic culture of ancient city-states. In this way *Mr. Recorder's Speech* acknowledges the behavioural sobriety that Cromwell approved:

> The solemnity of this day, wherein the Citizens of this great City appeare

in their severall companies, as so many Cities within the City, speakes
much to this; they leave it to other Nations to salute their Rulers and
victorious Commanders with the names of *Caesares*, and *Imperatores*; and
after triumphs to erect for them their *arcas Triumphales*; but if I mistake
not, their end, this day, is not any such outward Pomp . . . (4)

This City seldome goes alone in publique Actions: it was anciently called
by *Stepenides*, the heart of the nation; and if the heart be in a Politique
consideration, as it is in the naturall, it will communicate life and spirits
into the other members . . . (4–5)

Oratory belonged in printed form beyond assemblies too. Anthony
Norwood's *A Clear Optick Discovering To the Eye of Reason* (1654) is an
attempt to reconcile all religious positions with the needs of strong
government. It is a piece of rhetoric offered as advice to England's rulers
and the public no less than *Areopagitica* was, and Norwood is not afraid to
confess his position as a private citizen: 'The reasonable Caveat of a poor
obscure man may sometimes save a City'(1). While tyranny is to be ·
reviled, civil authority is made to seem natural or inevitable: 'It is as
possible to stop water from returning to its proper Center, as to dam up
authority from the Sea of the people'(15). This careful, prudent and
guarded public speech from a private man looks genuinely like the speech
of the 'middling sort' obeying the republican notion of public oratory
praised by the civic humanists. It reconciles public good and private
interests, against the other republican view that private interests must
sometimes be sacrificed to the public good. Indeed, Norwood's pamphlet
has been seen as important for its definition of liberty as the mutual
enhancement of private and public interests.[63] Its rhetorical origins and
posturing are implicitly connected with its political stance.

We know nothing of Norwood's background. Does his speech fit the
qualifications of education which Milton appears to impose on oratory in
the city in his translation from Euripides – that oratory should be left to
those who have the skill by education to speak?[64] Norwood's procedures
are echoed by the tracts and newsbooks of republican sympathisers in the
later 1650s whose social origins, even if they did claim to be 'gentlemen',
would hitherto have prevented such speech (see below, 196–200).

A contrast with the previous decade can be seen in Thomas
Warmstry's *Ramus Olivae; Or, An Humble Motion for Peace* (Oxford,
1642, 1644), an oration addressed to Charles I and Parliament from the
King's headquarters in the first Civil War. Warmstry postures as an
Athenian orator, and continually uses literary allusion and quotation to
point up royal majesty. Here, the graceful coalescence of forces in
allegiance under the prince looks like the Stuart image as presented in
masques. In the oration, such a vision is registered as a Senecan axiom:
'No Crowne more glorious on a Princes Brow,/As that which subjects safety

doth allow' (9). Learning is worn by this court orator as an ornament, dignifying the King, and underlining the refined resolution which monarchy should attain. Given the circumstances of 1644 in particular, *Ramus Olivae* could be accused of ignoring more pressing realities. Norwood's oration is more instrumental, and precisely the result of the conditions which *Areopagitica* eloquently defended in the year Warmstry was making his courtly oration.

There were however more serious orations published in Oxford in this year. Sir Robert Staplyton's translation, *Pliny's Panegyricke: A Speech in Senate: Wherein publicke thankes are presented to the Emperour Traian* (Oxford, 1644), was published with an epistle dedicatory to the young Prince Charles and the Thomason copy has a picture of the prince facing the title page. The speech survived the ruins of civil war in Rome, just as its translation (so Staplyton claims) will survive the English Civil War as advice for the prince (and future king). There is no explicit hint of an end for the Stuarts, but Staplyton's preface does ominously refer to the ruin of the Caesars (Sig. A2r).

We might imagine different kinds of rhetoric to be aligned with particular religious or political positions. It was once argued that the nature of a rhetoric and style was exactly commensurate with its ideas and its social location: Royalists like Sir Thomas Browne wrote in complicated, ornate ways, implying their belief in hierarchy and the mystery of monarchy; Levellers like Lilburne wrote in more plain, demotic prose, thereby revealing their innate democratic tendencies; Milton, caught in between, wrote in complex ways about democratic issues – elitist libertarian that he was.[65] This means that all ideas must be determined by their rhetoric, or that ideology and rhetoric are always coupled; the former seems absurd, and for the latter, while there is some measure of proof in some obvious cases, the idea of a shared educational culture at least initially does gives the lie to the thesis. That there are different contexts (for instance between Sir Thomas Browne's intended readership and Milton's) has also been neglected.

It has been more recently argued that there was a distribution of rhetorical usage during the Civil War and Interregnum: the Royalists used epideictic rhetoric, and the Parliamentarians deliberative and forensic rhetoric.[66] It is hard to find such a rigorous division in practice – the issue here seems to be one of usage: apologists for the regicide were following the charges made at the King's trial, *ergo*, forensic rhetoric would be used. Nonetheless, rhetorical construction – irrespective of the branch of rhetoric employed – did establish different identities. Yet if this became the case in the 1650s, and if it was noticeable to some degree in the 1640s, there was also a good deal of confusion. *England Know Thy Drivers, and their Driver* (1647) is Burtonian (usually a sign of royalist allegiance), but seemingly republican and utopian in its language.

Such examples point to the importance of common practices in rhetorical expression and exchange. Anyone comparing John Bramhall's royalist apology *The Serpent Salve, Or, A Remedie for the Biting of an Aspe* (1643) with John Milton's *Animadversions* (1641) would be struck by the rhetorical similarities of the two works. Both are animadversions (they both quote their opponents at length in order to confute them at greater length) written by university-educated men (one a cleric, one a cleric *manqué*) who knew the rules of the game extremely well. Milton's tract sets up the confutation as a lively dramatic dialogue by some clever extracted quoting of Joseph Hall's *Defence* (1640). By being quoted out of context, Hall is made to seem slightly nutty, and decidedly nervous at the bar of the law court where Milton has him placed:

> *Remonstr.* The *Areopagi?* who were those? truly my masters I had thought this beene the name of that place, not of the men.
> *Answ.* A soar-Eagle would not stoop at a flye, but sure some *Pedagogue* stood at your Elbow, and made it itch with this parlous Criticisme they urg'd you with a Degree of the sage and severe Judges of *Athens*, and you cite them to appeare for Certaine *Paragogicall* contempts, before a capricious *Poedentrie* of hot-liver'd Grammarians. (*CPW*, I.666)

Hall's fastidiousness is too harsh and will ruin the expectations of eloquence in Parliament. The opening preface to the reader (it is really a printed oration) in *The Serpent Salve* is just as rhetorical (and rebarbative) as anything Milton wrote. One is even surprised to find a man who was a bishop writing like this, but the analogy betrays the habit of rhetorical training in fashioning extravagant verbal devices (figures, tropes and schemes, properly speaking): 'Of all Hereticks in Policy, they are most dangerous, which make the Common-wealth an *Amphisbena*, a Serpent with two heads, who make two Supremes without subordination one to another, the King and the Parliament'(Sig. A2v). We should be less surprised when we learn that Bramhall is writing in the context of the controversy surrounding the publication of Henry Parker's *Observations* (1642). The dangerous doubleness of rebellion and schism is represented by the figures of Eros and Anteros in a sermon of 1642.[67] The web of fabular references in Bramhall's 'Epistle' is a way of preparing the reader for the suggestion that there is something in monarchical authority beyond mere rhetoric. Charles I's *Demonstrations* (1642) 'to a strong judgement seeme to be written with a beam of the Sun, and like the principles of Geometry doe rather compell then persuade'. By a reverse movement, the political order is made to appear more solid through the use of a metaphor often employed to describe the nature of rhetoric, that is, as if it were a building: 'Kings and Parliaments have the same ultimate and *Architectonicall* end, that is, the tranquillity of the whole Body Politicke: but not the same proper and next ends'(96). In effect, the orders of politics and of rhetoric have effectively merged; monarchy, says Bramhall, is the best oration.

Within this kind of polemic, mythic reference and mythic patterns are never far away. Henry Hammond, most respected defender of episcopacy, and father of the Restoration church, resorts to Virgil (and a scene from the *Aeneid* which Shakespeare famously used in *The Tempest*) to explain the explosion of politicised lay preaching:

> there are *evill Spirits* that come into the world, and which many times are by God permitted to seduce men, and that they may doe so the better, they constantly pretend to come from God, and assume divine Authority to recommend and authorize their delusions; (a thing so ordinary in all Ages, that the Poet that would express the Imbroyling of a Kingdome, thinks he cannot doe it better then by bringing in *Alecto*, a *Fury*, with a Message from Heaven, to avenge such or such an injury).[68]

The very nature of textual exchange undermined received notions of authorship by taking control of the text away from the author (even though animadversion had been producing similar effects since late-scholastic commentary and the More/Tyndale debates of the earlier sixteenth century). The location of the moment of authorship in a speech was diluted not only by printed publication in the sense that it is disembodied, but also by the possibility of one's own text being anatomised, split up and reused in an opponent's animadversion. Given that the copyright of the text, once sold to the publisher, was entirely the publisher's, there were in fact three stages of alienation of authorial control. Where much of this was happening, the effect was disturbing. But the response of individuals was ambiguous: Milton might have complained about the 'crabbed textuists', but he animadverted, as we have seen, with bravado. The response of controverters was rhetorically to put back the *body* – a sense of living human presence – into their texts to make up for their disembodiment by their enemies (hence the heroic figures in Milton's prose). What has been called Milton's 'vitalism' could be said of many other examples in the period.[69]

In the hands of the heresiographers, the sectarians began to take on the monstrous proportions which so many contemporary and later readers took or have taken as a truth.[70] It is a commonplace of seventeenth-century history that 1640s press freedom gave the religious radicals a chance to express themselves and thereby broaden their appeal: they were its beneficiaries. But they were also its first victims, for Thomas Edwards's *Gangraena* (3 parts, 1646), and other similar works, used reports (notably private newsletters) of sectarian gatherings and personalities to present a hostile image. The religious radicals were out-authored by words claiming to be their own. Publications like these strongly contributed to the republic's success in quelling the enthusiasm of 1649–51. By creating the impression of an anabaptistical threat to property, they also helped to create the climate which encouraged the Restoration of 1660.

The textual vitality of political discourse was such that it 'cooked' in the heat of controversial exchange, and as it cooked it had a rhetorical life which in fact constitutes what a literary critic would call a poetics. Milton, being a poet as well as a pamphleteer, understood this, and did not disguise the fact. He may be an outstanding and particularly sophisticated example, but he was by no means alone.

One feature which distinguishes Milton and other puritan writers is their transgressiveness. One of the most important features of puritan discourse is that it crossed boundaries from the religious to the political spheres. There was, after all, enough scriptural reference in royalist defences. But these largely magisterial pieces were not in the same mould as the blend of biblical and secular materials and approaches in, for instance, John Goodwin's *Anti-Cavalierism* (1642). The paragraph and period have an extremely fine-tuned dilation and cadence, the biblical phrases are in authoritative positions, and the dominant figure is of an apocalyptic order – it is a revelation of blood:

> And as all that saw that inhuman butchering and quartering out into pieces of the *Levites* wife by her own husband, cryed out, *There was no such thing done or seen since the Time that the Children of Israel came up out of the Land of Aegypt, untill that day*, Judg. 19.30. So doubtlesse whosoever shall consider what bloody and horrid intendments and attempts against this nation, have passed the hearts and hands of some of her own Children, may truly say, There hath no such thing been done or seen in the Land, since God first caused men to dwell on the face of it. (1)

Puritan ministers often achieved this effect of 'centredness' when they turned their hands to politics, and took with them the experience of sermon and devotional treatise writing. No less learned than John Goodwin was the Independent and educationalist Hezekiah Woodward. His directions for godly soldiers *A Good Souldier, Maintaining his Militia* (8 May, 1644) is as urgent as Goodwin's pamphlet in identifying an unholy enemy, entirely other to truth. The vocabulary of typology, alongside that of apocalyptic final confrontations (and martyrdom for the godly), is transferred to royal strategy:

> The Anti-Parliament have done all they could do, to promote Popery, to bring the land under an anti-Christian yoke and an Egyptian tyranny, according to the effectuall working of Satan in them, and with them all this while. From these premises it is concluded from the sacred Scripture, that to call this no Parliament, or that in Oxford a Parliament is a blaspheme against the Holy Ghost. (114)

In other words, the enemy is regarded as rhetorically powerful in a demonic way. The war of words was more powerful, in a way more deadly, more important, than the military war. Perhaps in a society which conferred a magical status upon words we can expect no less.

But it was precisely the events of war, and the phenomenon of lack of authorial control because of the predominance of readers over listeners, that ultimately resulted in a decline of confidence in rhetorical deployment. The naive usage of oratorical ethos disappeared, and a greater cynicism towards naming and persuasion emerged. For without a belief in ethos, language is reduced to a mere shell: it can manipulate, but it cannot embody virtue.

Representation and Interpretation

By the later 1640s, published political writing was displaying a remarkable ease and facility, not to say a confidence, in using different models to interpret or present events. Oratory was joined by a different kind of persuasive writing, as several modes of pre-1640 literature were employed in the new context, and became naturally changed in the process.[71] These discourses functioned as modes of simultaneous political commentary, explanation and satire.

By the later 1640s, even apologies and animadversions had succumbed in large part to the pressures of a new fashion. By permitting non-public modes of discourse to represent the public life, the public stage became represented in terms of other values and systems in English culture, and usually in a prejudiced way. As Parliament, and especially the Army, took an increasingly radical stance, supporters of the King took refuge in a melancholic rhetoric of inversion. Nathaniel Ward, author of *Discolliminium. Or, A most obedient Reply to a late Book, called, Bounds and Bonds* (1650), part of the Engagement controversy (the attempt by Commonwealth propagandists to encourage the swearing of oaths of allegiance to the new state, and the resistance to this attempt), uses neither melancholy nor inversion to vilify radicals by generating a hostile but inaccurate image of them. He speaks from his own position, and for the tract's duration we cannot easily tell his stance until he combines the confession of a desire for '*a mixt frame of Government*' with a sarcastic lament for the King: '*I believe the Revenues of this present Power, are at least* viis & modis, *5 millions per annum, whereas our late King's were but one; How happy then are we, that we are rid of such an oppressing Tyrant!*'(50). Fractured and obscure response can only be explained by the vile anatomy of the speaker: 'The constitution of my body was a cleare transparent Marmulate . . . till the derne, dreery, direfull dayes condunhill'd and uglified me into a darke dense lumpe, compounded of

Night-ravens gizards, Satyres Splens, Polcatts Lites, and Hedge hoggs Livers, Tortoises Garbages'(46). The literary father of this form of presentation is of course Thomas Nashe, whom John Taylor also imitated earlier in the decade. 'Self-eves dropping, Metamorphosing and Vizard-making' are the only activities for this creature who smokes (i.e. consumes) *salus populi* as tobacco. Unfortunately, the only available tobacco (welfare of the people) is 'Democraticall *Virginia*' which 'tasts like some Levellers old leathern linings, cut and dry'd over the Pan of a Close Stoole'(54). Clearly, what is in the atmosphere will not suffice. The speaker claims to be a gentleman of the Inns of Court, fearful of being in the dock rather than at the bar for his outspokenness which never quite hides itself in its clownish disguise. The Engagement Oath itself is thus subjected to obscure 'rustic' analysis – the best mode of advocacy:

> It must be a Nationall *Necessity*, and not a Partiall or Factionall: If my Mare hath the Scratches on her hinder Heeles, I must not cut off her four legs at her Body, and set her upon Tressels; or if she have a Gall'd Back, I must not flea off her whole Skin, and put on another of Poul-davis, or tarpaulling; if I doe, I shall wrong my Gyll, and my self too. (16)

John Cleveland's *The Idol of the Clownes, Or, Insurrection of Wat the Tyler* (1654) is equally typical of a kind of politicised literature related to the newsbooks, but with different aims and different achievements.[72] The Idol of the Clowns is of course Cromwell. Throughout the pamphlet, the story of Tyler masquerades as a foretelling of Cromwell's future demise. Tyler is compared with a contemporary rebel, Massaniello, who was also deliberately likened to Cromwell in a variety of iconographic representations.[73] Cleveland is concerned to create a narrative pattern of anarchy and disorder. Pieces of the armoury of parliamentary apology from the previous decade are thrown back at those who had once supported the Parliament – people who now find matters moving too fast and too far in the wrong direction. Thus, the Law of Nature becomes not an appeal in an argument but a mirror for the 1640s and 1650s. Henry Parker and Milton's favourite image from Ovid is returned to its association with rebellion, not liberty: 'They had risen like those Sons of the Dragons Teeth, in tempests, without policy or advice'(Sig. A4r; see below, 101). Leveller language reappears with ironic effect: the '*just rights and liberties of the people*', and is connected to its medieval counterpart: 'Wahan Adam dalf and Eve span/Who was than a Gentleman'(7).

Another strategy of attack was represented by Edmund Gayton's *Pleasant Notes Upon Don Quixot* (1654), which has been understood as a work typical of pro-theatrical texts of the Interregnum: the plea for plays is made on the grounds that the theatre would divert those who would otherwise engage in seditious activity.[74] Indirection is Gayton's procedure: he points up the function of romance as part of leisure and as an important component of the economics of authorship: 'Authors must sell *Romances*, or such *Books*,/Or else they will want money for the *Cook*.' This was a pressing truth for Gayton. He had been a bedell at Oxford, but was removed from his position in 1649, and was forced to eke out a living by writing in a variety of popular modes, including drolleries. The following commentary on the adventures of knight errant *manqué* and his zany becomes a commentary on the loyalist predicament in the 1650s. Annotation is achieved by way of contemporary observation, thereby forming a literary criticism (for it is no less) out of political and religious commentary. Gayton projects himself in his world into the wanderings of Quixote in his. He needs to dignify sordid London with the trappings of mock romance just as Quixote dignifies his. Cervantes's novel is a mock romance, Gayton is a mock writer.[75]

William Taylor's prefatory poem suggests that Gayton is bringing Cervantes's knight to such life that the reader sees him jumping out of the text with (mock-) heroic energy. In this way, Gayton's commentary rehearses allegorically civil war and revolution:

> If the Formalities were well compared, they would more resemble these new Orders of the *Tityrie-Tues*, the *Fellow Cues*, the confederates, the *Dead Boyes*, the *Tories*, the *John Dorians*, or the late Ranters, or the *Hectors*, whose rites and customes, were never fully executed (like these of the *Don*) without a *Tolosa*, or a *Molinera*, in plaine English, a whore or so, for creature-comfort, as they call it; or as the *Hectors* for *Carnelevation*. (11–12)[76]

If Quixote was a roaring boy or a Ranter (at least the pejorative image of one), Gyber the innkeeper is an Arminian, presumably for his generosity. Finding an analogy for Quixote's strength, Gayton recounts how a butcher once mounted the stage during the performance of a play called *The Greeks and the Romans*, and took the side of the Trojans, frightening the Greeks off the stage and preventing Hector from being killed. Hector had to throw the butcher back into the audience, so that Achilles could come on stage again and slay him. It is a comic interruption of legendary history (and, allegorically speaking, 1640s events), and one which does not escape contemporary echoes: the Greeks are called Myrmidons by Gayton, a common name among Royalists for New Model Army soldiers.[77] Gayton was presumably referring to a time before the theatres were closed, but his elision of three different times and places into one space is a good example of the way in which Civil War and Interregnum literature has textual moments which escape their own immediate location in a linear narrative to realise several other simultaneities. Imagination is expanded.

As *Pleasant Notes* continues, so it becomes less referential to the present and more involved in the exposition of Cervantes by way of simplifying the original narrative, some chapters being entirely in a verse version of the novel. The 1650s are taken up into the romance. Innuendo abounds: there are Shandyesque references to a 'cock and bull' story, while sexual exhaustion is rife: '*He saw a Mare tyed unto an Oake*] I believe *Rosinante* was a Gelding, or else a *stallion super-annuate*, otherwise this distressed Creature, at the Oake, might have mov'd him to some horse-errantry'(13). Into this less 'real' world are inserted the stereotypes which radicals and Royalists alike used to lambast Presbyterians, in particular Sir John Presbyter (see below, 303–4). In a similar way, John Hall made William Prynne into the Don Quixote of pamphleteering, a hack of no greater worth than Taylor the Water-Poet, and (more frighteningly) the personification of diabolical incivility: 'we must give you up as incurable, and say, the spirit of sedition, and *Jenkins* hath enterd this man, and the *Blatant-Beast* (in *Spencer* [sic]) is never like to be bound again so long as she survives in you.'[78]

Sectarians, Ranter, millenarians and occultists are merged into the narrative so that after a while the reader cannot tell the difference between English literature and the English Civil War. Religious piety is represented in extremes: 'annihilating himselfe with fastings, watchings and other afflictions', while the abhorrent is made most disgusting: 'O the *Basiliske*! what poysonous vapours would his eyes discharge, more dangerous then a menstrous Organ to our present mirrours!' Gayton is not just following Cervantes, not least of all because the commentary is replaced by Gayton's own poetry as the book proceeds. Rabelais and the language of the body are equally present as a new kind of expression is attempted, appropriate to the times.[79]

Henry Neville's series of coarse para-dramatic pamphlets, in which a parliament of (largely) royalist women (portrayed as men actors: '*Worthies*' in '*buskins*') ridicules men of their own side for their martial failures (and their consequent sexual shortcomings). The symbolic power of gender division is at issue. Their indifference towards different religions could be read as an early example of Neville's purported atheism, though there is little else to support this in the pamphlet. Neville, who was active as an army recruiter for Parliament, and who was friendly with the other parliamentarian republicans, Marten and Chaloner, sees the (?fictional) attraction of aristocratic women to powerful puritan evangelists as entirely sexual: 'Lady Kensington desired that Master *Saltmarsh* might be substituted in his roome, of whose great parts and able performances, shee had long experience, which presently was assented unto by all.'[80] The Countess of Carlisle, well known for her mediation between Henrietta Maria and important Royalists, is no less hungry for a particular type of intelligence:

And if he dare dispute the matter, wee will refer it to my Lady *Carlisle*. This is a Lady indeed, that seven years since took sayle with *Presbytery*, being charged in the *Fore-deck* by *Master Hollis*, in the *Poop* by Master *Pym*, whilst she clapt my Lord of *Holland* under the hatches. And this was a lucky *Supply* at that time because *Toby Matthewes* and *Wat. Mountague* were both *fled for Religion*. About 3 years since, being weary with that *faction*, she revived a correspondence upon the *Royall accompt*; among the rest with divers *foreine Ambassadors*; especially *Mons. Believerey*, till she was put in the *Tower*, where she now pines away for want of *fresh-Cod*; and knoweth not which way to lead her *Nags* to water, since the *State* hath cut off all her *Pipes* of Intelligence.[81]

The technique of using one index to talk about another (often as a kind of rhetorical disfigurement – *catachresis*) was by no means new to any form of ridicule in the 1640s.[82] What is interesting in Neville's writing is that sexual appetite provides him with a means of presenting motivations which cut across religious and political divisions within a national ruling elite. In Neville's *Newes from the New Exchange* (1650), the image of a lascivious Cromwell is reinforced by a picture of wife-swapping in the Council of State: 'Shee keeps mighty intelligence too with his Wife, and she with *Hugh Peters*, and *Peters*, with Mistris *Ireton*, she with *Bradshaw*, he with Madam *Castlehaven*, as *Cromwell* with Mris. *Lambert*'(6). In one sense this can be seen as an extension of the puritan castigation of women actresses in royalist circles, especially aristocratic women.[83]

But at the same time, this is also an identification of erotic superabundance with megalomania generally, perhaps the reaction of someone who holds the patrician values of classical republicanism.[84] Whether he favoured theatre closure or not, Neville the secular Parliamentarian and republican seizes a perception which blackens women. There is a mockery of any form of political action which appears to elevate the 'feminine' principle over and above a patrilinear, property-based order of society (and in Neville's view, that patrilineage was represented in the House of Commons). The feminine principle could be found in courtly politics, or, according to the satires, in the spiritual pretensions of grand puritanism. The satire provides the author with a mask – he says he means none of it seriously – but at the same time, the connection with an at least emergent republican view of society and politics is there. Later on, Neville would mock absolutist and divine right theory in a fantasy of sexual over-production.[85] We can find further related examples of this gender-specific discourse throughout republican publications. In what appears to be a Machiavellian formulation, Nedham writes: 'the *Interest of Freedom* is a Virgin that everyone seeks to deflower.'[86]

There is always a punishment at the end of the anarchic collision of indices, and the release of laughter in the articulation of ideas and events through the sexually alive body. In Neville's *An Exact Diurnall Of the Parliament of Ladyes* (1647), Prince Rupert is punished for his military failure by being tied to a post, and stung to death by porcupines (7).

The target of both royalist and republican attack was of course radical puritanism, and its reliance upon the inspiration of the Holy Spirit, be it in its Cromwellian (and therefore tyrannous) mode, or its rebellious, uncompromisingly sectarian voice. Puritan discourse and behaviour are usually thought to be entirely distinct from the travesties of Gayton and Neville, but in fact there is a connection. Prophecy may appear to be very unironic, but it lends itself to pathos and to allegory. Abiezer Coppe's holy fool is the most obvious example, not least of all because of his ironic literariness, but other examples come to mind.[87] Biblical models of selving (such as imitating Old Testament prophets) and of narrative structure lend themselves to the same functions as do those of Cervantism and more overt sexual travesty. What is being articulated is a form of textual heroism which cannot free itself from self-mockery, so that it begins to look like travesty itself. As we shall see in a later chapter, romance heroism was a cultural inheritance open to anyone's reconstruction. On the level of form, the meanings of heroism are the site not only of cultural battles, but also an uneasy and self-critical revelation of identity.

One corollary of this conjunction was a new use for crime fiction, instanced in the careers and published histories of Captain Hind, or indeed in Coppe's presentation of himself as a highwayman.[88] James Hind was eventually executed after a career of highway robbery, prompted, so he claimed on the scaffold, by his royalist principles. Some of the pamphlets also claim his active involvement in the royalist armies. In the texts, he usually appears as a Robin Hood figure, a patriot hero, whose exploits were a gesture of merry resistance to the Commonwealth. For their part, prophetic narratives were in a sense searching after a kind of glory, just as other narratives, such as Sir Thomas Urquhart's self-defences, searched after lost honour. Honour for Urquhart was rooted in his capacity to persuade his reader of the truth of his language theories, apprehended only after painful negotiation of the noble laird's syntax.[89] This was precisely the truth game played by prophets like Coppe and Thomas Tany.[90] And indeed by that self-effacing physician and Royalist, Sir Thomas Browne: at least that is how *Religio Medici* and the shorter works have been read in context. The effect of division is to induce offerings of dignified identity in obscure terms, as if ideological difference, or combat, forces disclosure only through timidity or capriciousness. Competing models of heroism frighten each other into shadows of what they should have been.

The final discursive possibility was utopia (see below, 172–6), the very map of perfection, trusted by scientific reformers and Diggers, but rejected by Puritans (Milton included) because it appeared to them as a freezing of the active life of the Holy Spirit.[91] But of course, these mock heroic travesties and the virtue narratives of status (Urquhart) and inspiration (Coppe) were attempts to avoid the utopia of self-restraint in puritanism, only to replace it by another utopia of bizarre imaginative fantasy or imagined grandiosity. As we have already seen, the references to Burtons account of melancholy are frequent, and they represent the hold which the dark side of utopian thought suggested in this period. It was not merely a royalist trait, but what we might expect as a more general response of disaffection at the predominance of war journalese and the continuing power of public rhetoric.

At the King's return, this interesting but confusing intermingling of forms was untangled, and a new form of public heroic triumph born. John Ogilby's description of the coronation entertainments of Charles II contain accounts of the painted imagery which greeted the King in his triumphal procession. A woman represented rebellion, and anti-rebellion mottoes from Virgil and Horace were inscribed under the paintings. In this way, the modes of attack upon Parliament (the 'wife' of the King and the state) by royalist and republican satirists were replicated, this time in the name of Restoration. Allegorical figures of Monarchy and Loyalty prevail over Rebellion, who identifies herself as Satan's daughter. But the most interesting image of all is that which directly allegorizes and bestializes Cromwell:

> The Painting over the Middle Arch represents the King, mounted in calm Motion, USURPATION flying before him, a Figure with many ill-favoured Heads, some bigger, some lesser, and one particularly shooting out of his Shoulder, like CROMWELL'S; Another Head upon his Rump, or Tayl; Two *Harpies* with a Crown chased by an Angel; Hell's Jaw opening. Under the said Representation of the King pursuing *Usurpation*, is this Motto,
> VOLVENDA DIES EN ATTULIT ULTRO[92]

War Writing

Nonetheless, the impulse to capture the events of war produced a new kind of realistic discourse. It lived inside, but was not identical to, the new journalism (see below, 54ff.), for reasons which will soon become apparent. Confusion was at its heart.

Accounts of the action in the Civil War reveal not only the 'facts' but also the eventfulness of human interaction in these desperate times. In this way, the manners of war are presented. The sense of difference from the past was frequently noticed: 'The Action of these times transcends the Barons Warres, and those tedious discords betweene the houses of *Yorke* and *Lancaster*, in as much as it is undertaken upon higher Principles, and carried on to a nobler end, and effects more universall.'[93] Accordingly, war writing has to capture the eventful: 'Generall Histories doe seldome approach the fountaine of action, and their glosse though beautifull, yet more dull cannot hold forth that native grace and lustre.'[94] Fragments are the order of the day:

> they that gather up so many divided Plots (as are now acted) into one modell, are wont to endeavour after a smoother path, a greater harmony, and more exact symmetry of parts; whereas the face of things is conscious of more disproportion, sometimes a confusion of business, and the severall scenes may easily swerve from the originall plot.[95]

Short pamphlet accounts of action turned the minor skirmish into vivid narrative cameos. More than fragmentary, these publications reveal the effects of fellow countrymen fighting each other in the description of strategies of attack and escape. The violence is arresting because it is not described with an overt emotive intensity; it never overrides the narrator's sense of partisan and local difference. Samuel Turner, a Londoner in command of a parliamentary unit, describes an attack by Cavaliers from Reading, in a letter to his brother:

> one *Thos. Hyat*, a fishmongers man, who lives in your division, was shot through the body with a pistoll shot, as hee was coming from his quarter to the Court of guard; hee was forced to make use of their language to save himselfe, and to cry out where are these Roundheaded rogues, but they pursuing of him, struck him through the hat with a Pole axe, but missed his head, I have great hope of his recovery.[96]

One of the most important war publications was Joshua Sprigge's *Anglia Rediviva* (1647), a celebration of the parliamentary Army's success in the First Civil War, between May 1645 and the end of 1646, under Fairfax's command. A good deal of heroic and epic allusion is built into the substantial text of 335 pages, alongside reports, letters, details of battle plans, numbers and names, killed and wounded, much of it culled from pamphlet and diurnal publications.[97] Each military encounter has its own distinct narrative shape, in which human vicissitudes become remarkable instances of how people behave under pressure, and how God deals with them. Thus, Colonel Rainborough's (later a Leveller leader) storming of Barkley Castle in September 1645 pits speedy parliamentary soldiers against blustering royalist officers. Equally speedy is the narrative itself, which runs detail and analysis together:

> The same day col. *Rainsborough* with his forces before *Barkley-castle*

EBEN EZER,

As a Thankefull Remembrance of Gods great good-

nesse unto the City of BRISTOLL, in preserving them
from the Forces of Prince *Rupert* without, and a Treacherous plot within,
to betray the City to them the seventh day of *March* 1642. T.P.dedicates this.

Exod. 12. 14. *And this day shall be unto you for a memoriall.*, ver.42. *It is a night to be much observed unto the Lord.*

Iudg. 5. 11. *They that are delivered from the noise of Archers in the places of drawing water, there shall they rehearse the righteous acts of the Lord, even the righteous acts toward the inhabitants of his Villages in* Israel.

O Thou who dost excell the highest praise,
Thou wonder-worker, life and length of dayes,
Thou never-failer in the mount to thine,
Onely wise, present, in each place and time,
What *Brazen* Colume, or what *Marble* stone,
Shall we *ingrave* thy noble Acts upon? ·
This *act*, thy strange *act*, counterplotting those
Blood-thirsting (*Foraine* and *Domesticke*) foes?
O native *City* how canst thou be still?
What would'st have more thy mouth with *praise* to fill?
Is *health*, or *wealth*, or *plenty* worth the having?
Or *feed immortall*, sent thee for *soule*-saving?
Or *Life*, that blessings make the rest to thee
Matters of *praise*? then sing a part with me.
Septembers seventh was thankfull for the *Scots*,
And we not for our *selves*, whose lives by *lots*
Like *Hamans* bloody prodigy was cast
This present *March* it might have beene our last,
The rising *Sunne* might warme our frozen brest,
More then a falling. *Scots* then, now we had rest.
Startle the *Muses*, rattle up the *Quires*,
Of *sweetest Musicke*, Citizens *Bonfires*,

Let *Bels*, and *Cannons* roare, your joyes *expressing*,
Young *Men* and *Virgins*, in your comely *dressing*,
Away to *Church* in *flockes*, the touling *Bell*
Toules now for *Heaven*, is not for death or *Hell*:
Each *streete* is echoing praise, the *sword* is staid,
The *horned Rammes* in *Isaaks* place are laid :
So let them *perish* and indure *disgrace*,
That Traytors prove unto their *native place*.
The *King* of heaven our gracious *King* preserv,
But those that doe his *Grace* pretend to serve,
I wish they may prove upright, faithfull, *good*,
But for to *plot* to shed their Neighbours *blood*,
As some have done, and in this *plot* would doe,
They prove no lesse then King and Kingdomes foe.
O *Prince* of *Peace*, let it not seeme too great,
That *Prince* and *Peeres*, and *Peoples* hearts may meet,
And all in *unity* and *peace* as one,
Build *Zions* walls, and downe with *Babylon*,
Till when, for mercies let us *thankfull* be,
And untill then, never unbend our knee.
So praise, and pray, and Fast and pray agen,
Vntill the God of *Peace* shall say *Amen.*

Printed at *London* for *Michael Sparke Junior*, 1643.

Figure 2   Eben Ezer (1643).

stormed the out-works and the Church, which were the main strength of
the castle, with Scaling-ladders, performing the service with so much
resolution & gallantry (both Officers and Souldiers) as quickly made them
masters of the place; wherein were taken 90 prisoners, besides 40 put to
the sword, amongst whom were a Major and a Captain. This was such a
terror and discouragement unto the Enemy within the Castle, to see the
resolution of our souldiers, and the execution done upon theirs in the
Church and out-works, that the Governour, Sir *Charles Lucas* (who
returned answer to the first Summons, that he would eat horse-flesh
before he would yield, and mans flesh when that was done: and upon
a second Summons sent as peremptory an answer;) yet now perceiving the
planting of our ordnance against him upon his own Works (which we had
newly gained) whereby we had a great advantage to play into the castle;
and sensible what he was to expect if he came not to present tearms, was
glad to sound a Parley, which was yielded to, and Commissioners sent out
to treat, and the Castle was surrendered upon these Articles. (125)

Sprigge's narrative is punctuated by several elegies and epitaphs on fallen
worthy soldiers, as well as thanksgiving poems. *Eben Ezer* (1643),

received by Thomason on 21 March of that year, is a similar work of thanksgiving (this time a poem) to God for preserving Bristol from Prince Rupert and his soldiers (see fig. 2). John Ward published verse that could have been sung for morale-boosting purposes in the parliamentary armies, although its readership would have been much wider.[98]

George Wither was not the only poet to compose on the field of battle. Some poems were regarded as a kind of martial trophy, to be displayed as a fruit of victory. Celebrating the capture of the Scilly Isles, John Haselock published a poem written in Pendennis Castle while it was besieged by parliamentary forces. The poem gives important evidence of the widespread habit of 'romancing' the Civil War: Pendennis Castle is imagined as Homer's heroine in the *Odyssey*, Penelope, resisting the advances of Fairfax the suitor, 'sonne of Mars, Bellonaes love'. The poem ends by hoping for the King ('Thine owne Ulysses') to rescue the besieged. Pendennis soon fell, however, and Haselock's purpose in publishing the poem is to point up the irresistible force of Parliament's advance. The poet did it for Haselock by appending a sentence from Ovid (*Ars Amatoria*, I. p.49) after the surrender: *Penelopem ipsum perses: modo temporis vinces.*[99] In this way, the immediacy of war writing is interrupted by other literary components that attempt to satisfy the needs created by the violence of war. Consolation, praise and generic overlay (such as romance and tragedy) supplement the unbearable rawness of reportage, and the dangerous power of rhetoric.

A broad and shared faith in the virtue and efficacy of public rhetoric had been replaced, under the pressure of political division, by a large number of different ways of fashioning a (sometimes oblique) political narrative. While, as we shall see, apologists for different positions sought to persuade by involving the reader in a debate structured by the tools of rhetoric, there were darker forces at work. Fictionalizing had supplemented or replaced controversializing. Persuasion for the moment was joined by critical narratives of the recent past, and war reportage was one of these. Of all the forms harbouring these kinds of discourse, one particular kind of publication stood out among all others: the news.

CHAPTER 2

Public Fora

What is the News?

> Since many Diurnals (for which we are griev'd,)
> Are come from both Houses, and are not believ'd;
> The better to help them for running and flying,
> We have put them in Verse, to Authorize their lying.
> > Alexander Brome, 'A new Diurnal of passages more
> > Exactly drawn up then heretofore. Printed and published,
> 'tis order'd to be By Henry Elsing the Clerk of the P.' 1. June. 1643

IN THE 1640s the newspaper, or newsbook, as it was then called, happened for the first time. There had been printed newsbooks in English, published sporadically and concerned mostly with foreign news (the printing of domestic news was illegal) in the 1620s and 1630s, as well as the advanced circulation of private newsletters.[1] In the war decade, they were published regularly (usually once a week), and they took hold of the nation with a momentous significance.[2] As we shall see, the newsbook was a highly important counter in politics, ultimately a channel of democracy, and had a literary impact which touched all other forms.

Newsbook circulation was broad and socially diverse. The capacity of the newsbook, 'mercury' or diurnal publication, to cross barriers of social difference was matched by the divergent backgrounds from which the newsbook writers came. Sir John Berkenhead and Marchamont Nedham were gentlemen, Henry Walker was an ironmonger turned Independent minister. John Dillingham was a tailor and an innkeeper, but one with more important connections in his family. In the case of Dillingham, occupation and writing formed two interconnected sides of a life, and what he heard from his customers informed the observations he made as a journalist.[3] Samuel Pecke, possibly a scrivener before he became a journalist, seems to have been the first newswriter with no other occupation.[4]

Figure 3 A Perfect Diurnall of the Passages in Parliament, 34 (30 Jan.– 6 Feb. 1642).

What was a newsbook like? By the mid-1640s, a reader might expect a conventional newsbook to be usually one quarto gathering, making eight pages of text. A title page would carry title and serial date (usually the week as well as the month and year), and some fairly clear signals of allegiance (or the absence of them might lead an alert reader to ask further questions). Royalist newsbooks made a feature of poetry as a prefatory device in this way. News narrative would take the form of a report from a particular place (London, Edinburgh, Paris), perhaps with the inclusion of whole letters carrying a report from an observer. Several reports would make up one issue. Until the later 1640s, statements of allegiance were for the most part confined to the viewpoints offered in the narrative, but separate commentary and political theory then emerged, and it was usually printed before the news items themselves. Committed pamphleteers knew they could exploit the demand for news in order to spread their views: *Chaos* (21 June 1659) was a pamphlet with various republican, utopian proposals and it looked like a newsbook. A much extended version followed on 18 July, by which time it had turned into a pamphlet proper (the title advertises a 'discourse').

Newsbook style was various. What enhanced its appeal was the potential for a variety of genres and styles to be deployed within a compressed textual space. One of the general arguments of this study is that generic interaction and disturbance were functions of civil unrest. In the mid-seventeenth-century newsbook, such mixture, compression and distortion were put to the use of first providing information, and then seeking the reader's sympathy through the process of narration.

The first serial newsbook, *The Heads of Severall Proceedings*, provides in its second issue a good example of the eventful and artful capturing of the news. It deserves to be quoted at length:

> Munday *November* the 29. there were letters Read in the Lords House, which came from *Ireland*, *importing* the necessity there was of a present ayde both by Sea and Land; for the security of that Kingdome, and quelling the Rebells before they were growne to too great a head, who daily increase there, and commit many outragious and Hostile Acts, wherewith the Lords acquainted the House of Commons, desiring their assistance for a timely reliefe, then was one Master *Shelden* a Recusant (who was suspected for a dangerous person) brought before them, but upon examination, giving a good account of himselfe, was discharged.
>
> There was likewise foure men brought before them for making a hubbub in the Hall, crying downe Antichrist and the Bishops, and saying if they could not be heard, they would have a farre greater number the next day to backe them; but they strongly denying the words, (with a sharp rebuke for their flocking thither) were discharged.[5]

The form is one of a historical narrative (yet not a chronicle) with inbuilt Protestant prejudices, but sufficiently opaque to render it on first glance an impartial account, which is what several newsbooks explicitly claimed to be. Its impact on the writing of history was immense (see below, 340, 344).

Proving itself such a useful tool in competition for the sympathy of a recently constituted public opinion, journalism rapidly became an intricate part of politics and of war. Parliament stole the lead in recognising the significance of appealing to, then even manufacturing and controlling, public opinion. One early pro-parliamentarian newsbook regularly featured a small woodcut of the House of Commons on the front page, thereby associating news with the authority of Parliament (see fig. 3).[6] The effect of newsbook propaganda was acknowledged by Charles I when he sanctioned the establishment of *Mercurius Aulicus* in an attempt to turn the allegiances of hard-pressed Londoners. *Mercurius Britanicus* was regarded as a weapon of war, and to be controlled accordingly. Other pro-parliamentary newsbooks were allowed to bypass the censorship regulations of 1643 in the cause of the printed assault upon the King.

The construction of newsbooks was often bizarre and gave a very unusual extra dimension to authorship. Dillingham, for instance, gathered intelligence from a Scottish knight lodging with him while mediating between the Scots and the English. Richard Overton created a literary figure out of the 'scout' or military intelligence gatherer.[7] It is no wonder that newsbook writers were regarded as literary pariahs. The writing of news existed in the margin between fact and fiction. Newswriters sought to create the illusion that the reader was himself witnessing the action. When news was scarce, as was the case in the winter of 1643, newswriters had to find ways of filling space with reading matter, but without taxing their readers with excessive non-news. Thus, false information was generated, concerning the Battle of Edgehill, for instance.[8] By contrast, there were no royalist accounts of the Battle of Marston Moor, such was the significance of the defeat for them. Journalists even debated the function of the newsbook itself, and the nature of recording events. In these circumstances, the roles of journalists changed as their skills accumulated. Captain Thomas Audley, the chief author of *The Kingdomes Weekly Intelligencer*, *The Parliament Scout*, and for its first fifty-one issues, *Mercurius Britanicus*, grew in confidence as an author, daring to foretell events, used good intelligence, and called for the reform of the parliamentary army at an early stage. It is important to remember that he was a soldier – a more sober but very real version of Nashe's author, Jack Wilton, page to the Earl of Surrey.

The language of journalism bears out these contradictions and connections in the arena of truth-telling and opinion manipulation. There are recognisable shared styles as well as recognisably individual styles. Even if the individual authors were not known by their own names, they tended to have a public identity in terms of the 'author' of the newsbook: Aulicus (Berkenhead), Pragmaticus (Nedham), Britanicus (Audley, Nedham, then Hall), Melancholicus (Crouch). It was a mask which permitted remarkable acts of authorship. Aulicus is fond of describing acts of individual heroism by royalist commanders, and likes to show the pole-axe at work. At the same time Aulicus and Britanicus often used each other's language to effect mutual ridicule, much like the trading of insults before a battle. The journalists were fascinated by the opportunity to 'swell', to expand from one to two sheets (or even more). They were in fact confessing the low status of newsbooks and expressing a hope for the greater esteem attached to learned folios. Thus, Aulicus's pride is seen by Britanicus as an expansion into a book of superstitious untruths, the *Golden Legend* of Jacopus de Voragine, but he claims for himself dignified chronicling of the kind to be found in Foxe's *Book of Martyrs*, so that his fat folio body will be chained in libraries and great halls, and will be quoted instead of his 'Cosen', *Mercurius Gallo-Belgicus*, the late sixteenth-century newsbook published in Cologne.[9] And Britanicus himself threatens to expand into a replacement of all the best learned authorities: 'I shall swell high, when the *Learned* begin to *land* upon me in a large Folio; *Tostatus* will be but a *Shrimp* in comparison, *Pineda* a Puny, and *Augustine* himself but like *Illiads in a Nut-shell*.'[10]

By the later 1640s, two kinds of journalism had emerged. On the one hand, there was a plainly expressed factual journalism, of the kind approved by Daniel Border, author of the *Perfect Weekly Account* and *The Kingdoms Faithful and Impartial Scout*, and on the other, a kind of banter and ridiculing writing, in which fact and the worlds of politics, religion and war are expressed in completely different terms. The former was more numerous than the latter, but not so much that the jocular newsbook was a negligible presence. No one should exclusively associate this kind of writing with cavalierism or royalism more generally, although it has been treated so many times:

> the Imparallel'd impudence of the Royall Pamphleteers hath so blowne up my sleepie Zeale to the Honourable Houses, (whom those pernicious Rascalls most villanously calumniate) that I can no longer containe my selfe; but being acted by a principle of love to those Noble *Heroes*.[11]

The frame of literary reference which is customarily associated with Royalists is common currency, and in this instance, is used by Hermes Stratjcus to beat the Royalists rhetorically on the pate:

> I would have quoted the Originall, but that I know the Greek is above the reach of M. *Elencticus* his noddle: He begins his Pamphlet with a storie out of *Lucian*, but who can think such a muddie-braine slave could have convers'd with the wittie *Lucian*, and remained so egregiously dull?[12]

In this connection, an interesting official document records the establishment of *Mercurius Politicus* in June 1650. Its contradictions seem all too abundant to a modern reader, but it is full of seventeenth-century good sense, and its author (very probably Nedham) is clearly experienced:

> The designe of this Pamphlett being to undeceive the People, it must be written in a Jocular way, or else it will never bee cryed up: for those truths wch the Multitude regard not in a serious dresse, being represented in pleasing popular Aires, make Musick to ye Common sense, and charm the Phantsie; wch ever savages the Scepter in Vulgar Judgmts; much more then Reason.[13]

Poetry accordingly became a device in the journalist's repertoire: 'Enter *Sisyphus* with his Stone, another trite-thread-bare-Fable, which the Foole *Elencticus* hath raked out of his Poeticall *Dictionarie*, who he sayes is the Emblem of this present Parliament.'[14] Neither are poems the preserve of Crouch, or Nedham in his royalist phase. *Stratjcus* finds verse an appropriate medium to reprove the fickle masses while praising Colonel Skippon:

> What matter? let the people matter still:
> Let them Petition till they have their fill;
> Yet thou art where thou wert, and wilt not cease
> To serve the state; 'cause 'twill not please:
> Tis farre below thy brave Heroick mind,
> To marke the whistling of the tumults wind;
> Beleev't, 'tis mutable, and will not last,
> He that applauds to day, will cry at fast
> To morrow, hang him up.[15]

These lines were painting an optimistic picture: in order to maintain public order in London in autumn 1648, and quell bands of Presbyterian-inspired rioting apprentices, Skippon put the city more or less under curfew, using hastily assembled groups of sectarians as auxiliaries.

It was not difficult to see through newsbooks, and for this reason, explicit statements concerning newsbooks nearly always devalued them. Second-class status was implicit in the journalist's label 'Mercurius'. Mercury was the messenger of the gods, and had a secondary status to Apollo, Jupiter, Mars and the others.[16] But such claims usually asserted the value of another kind of writing; they did not question standards of truth-telling. When the journalists made statements such as these, they often sound tongue-in-cheek: Nedham, Border and Pecke knew the value of their labour. James Howell's *Mercurius Hibernicus: Or, A Discourse of the Late Insurrection in Ireland* (Bristol, 1644) castigated the monstrous weekly births of newsbooks ('*those* Ephemeran *creatures, which* Pliny *speaks of, that are borne in the morning, grow up till noon, and perish the same night*') only to elevate his own slower gestation and Aulicus's superior style which, he claims, is the very 'shape' of Mercury himself. Whether contemporaries actually regarded newsbooks as secondary is doubtful.

Rivalry between newsbooks extended to imitation. There were counterfeit versions of the *Perfect Diurnall* and the *Continuation*, influential supporters of the Presbyterian cause.[17] At one point, two rival editions of *Perfect Occurrences* were produced by different printers, who thenceforth had to share publication.

Neither did allegiance determine readership. The royalist journal *Mercurius Aulicus*, produced secretly in London as well as in Oxford, and Charles I's concession to the importance of propaganda, has been regarded as largely accurate and for this reason was apparently popular with Royalists and Parliamentarians alike. *Aulicus* delighted in finishing each of its issues with a list of demonstrable falsehoods from parliamentary newsbooks. Berkenhead's only real gaffe was to give the wrong result for the Battle of Marston Moor. Yet between 24 November and 28 December 1644, *Aulicus* did not appear. This was Berkenhead's way of attempting to disguise royalist losses. *Mercurius Aulicus* may have been reliable, but it is difficult to believe that, for instance, the 'Yeoman Committee of Hertfordshire' in 1644 were all sectarian Brownists.[18] And yet some degree of fidelity to 'truth' was necessary: William Ingler's *Certaine Informations* relied almost wholly on rumour; it was regarded as dull and a laughing stock. *Mercurius Britanicus* was in no doubt that *Aulicus* told lies: 'Assuredly these men have an excellent faculty in the *deceivablenesse* of *untruths*, and if they had as great a power in working *lying wonders*, as in wondrous lying, might well passe for *Antichrist*.'[19] They also kept secrets: 'I shall then tell ye the next week there are some amongst ye, that communicate with *Oxford*, and exchanges intelligence, and write with Onions and in Tiffany, and in Characters.'[20] With regard to intelligence, strategies were developed which simulated truth-telling, such as the special section in *Mercurius Britanicus* on 'intelligence', as opposed to the introduction and ridicule or disproving of Aulicus; 'intelligence' was not always the transparent recounting of facts. *Britanicus* used the category called 'Quaeries', which existed between fact and rumour, building fictitious suppositions out of the known. Thus the presence of two foreign princes in the King's army leads to the suspicion '*Whether* Prince Rupert, *or* Prince Maurice *be most likely to winne the* Crowne?'[21] It is part of Nedham's purpose to make his readership appreciate *fear* in anticipation of the possible by referring to a truth which would have challenged the believable in 1645 when it was published: 'What *Rebels* still? As sure as can be King *Charls* is dead [the regicide was still four years away], and yet we never heard of it; I wonder we have not his *Funerall Sermon* in *Print* here, and the young *Prince* sent up to *London*.'[22] Nedham's sense of what was possible always appears as keener than any other journalist's, not least of all through his understanding of his opponents' strategies. Aulicus uses a 'rare device called a *Letter* to Prince *Rupert*, subscribed by a *Knight* that is an excellent Paper-engineere, they call him Sir *Gamaliel Dudley*'.[23] To tell a story is to weave a fiction. 'Once upon a time . . . ' begins one account which proceeds to include an explicit reference to the method of narration in Chaucer's *Canterbury Tales*.[24]

One of the lies recounted is the death of the author, which was told of *Mercurius Aulicus* in June 1644. The death of *Aulicus* was the death of the royalist cause, prophesied since the beginning of that year, and signalled by the lapse in standards of accuracy. *Mercurius Aulicus* replied that his ghost was just as much an author. The hard truth, of course, created a different kind of lie: misnaming. *Aulicus* tells of a heavy royalist defeat of some parliamentary troops 'which makes the *London* Pamphlets call this brave Garrison, *A nest of bloudy Papists* (for they ever have such expressions after a beating)'.[25]

The ridiculing banter which constituted the alternative to 'plain style' was largely concerned with naming. The possibility of public traduction and the rapidly generating public identities (in which the newsbooks played a major part) produced a showering of namings which grew out of single identities, be they people or groups. 'SAY'S Plots are vaine,' writes one commentator in 1648, playing on the names of two leading Independent politicians.[26] Read in any concentration, such discourse rapidly becomes boring and exhausting to the modern reader, and in part this was an effect of concentrated print forms and production.

This common currency of newsbook, mercury or diurnal writing is double-edged. On the one hand, it is a common language of political complaint, open to all comers. The effect is especially noticeable in verse which imitates sung ballads:

> Allmighty *Tom*, and Great King *Crom*
> *Well*, Arm'd with courage bold
> Determind are *Charles* shall not com
> From *Carisborowes* strong hold.[27]

> *Ramp up my* Genius, *be not retrograde,*
>   *But boldly nominate a spade, a spade;*
> *Let baser Varlets serve to paint the times,*
>   *And fairly varnish Kings, and great mens crimes:*
> *This (like* Joves *thunder) shall pride and vice controul,*
>   *The honest* Satyre *hath the happyest soul.*[28]

On the other hand, the common currency (a new kind of *loci communes*) is an arena for the style wars which grow out of the differences over verbal and rhetorical forms, and the differing models of authority associated with them. *Mercurius Insanus, Insanissimus*, 4 ([24 April] 1648) reports that the Puritan Richard Vines prayed for the King in the presence of loyalist nobility one morning, and then adopted 'STILO PARLIAMENTARIO' the following afternoon for a prayer in front of Fairfax: '*God turne the Heart of the King, and give him grace to repent of his grievous sins, and especially for all the Blood, that he hath shed in these crewell Civill uncivill Warres.*' The disturbance of the established order for this royalist journalist is a paradox in social conventions: withholding the sacrament from all but the 'godly' is 'curteous unchristianly' and 'Charitable Impiously'(29, mispaginated as 28). With no less vigour did a puritan journalist like Henry Walker in *Perfect Occurrences* stampede the image and ethos of the cavalier.[29]

Mercurius Insanus, Insanissimus, like *Mercurius Democritus, Mercurius Elencticus* and *Mercurius Melancholicus*, promotes an ethos of madness in retreat and defeat for the royalist cause: 'It is a shame, and quite well out of fashion for any man to be well in his witts these mad times, for he that is Maddest is esteemed wisest, And he that hath most discretion that can worke most destraction.'[30] True to its form, and its predictions, *Mercurius Insanus, Insanissimus* invents its own world of distraction. It is a world turned upside down yet not one of social inversion which it was feared the radicals would create, but one of exploitation which trickles down from an uncaring Parliament as published nonsense, finally returning to the place of its own origins:

> An order past in the House of Commons for the encrease of Beggars over all *England* and the Dominion of *Wales*, The Lords Concurrence was desired therein, which with all willingnesse was assented to. And further their Lordships of the upper House, Certified their Masters of the Lower House, That it were much in forwardnesse, for effecting of the business, to lay more Taxes and Impositions upon the People, and to stop their Mouthes with fearfull news of Letters intercepted full of dangerous Plots, Conspiracies, Feares, and Jealousies, from *Scotland*, *France*, *Spaine*, *Rome*, *Ireland*, *Wales*, *Holland*, *Dover* and *Dunbar*, *Utopia*, The *Devills Arse a Peake*, Written and Counterfeited by Rogues and Villanies, in *London* and *Westminster*, in private Chambers, and Base Bawdy Tipling Schools, full of nothing but lyes, *Walkerisme*, *Harruneyanisme*, *Atheisme*, *Rebellion*, *Blasphemy*, Nonsence, and Treason, Licens'd and Authorized, *Cum Privilegio*, G.M. Whilst C.R. is of no more estimation than a [inverted W] for God save the King. (No. 4; [26] paginated as 9)

Naming forms the basis of a series of registers and sub-narratives within the newsbook which ridicule and give shape to the objects of attack. The use of theatricality is properly part of a consideration of the transformation of drama during the period (see below, 70–92). Nedham's use of theatricality is crucial to his control of his readers' responses. For example, writing as *Mercurius Pragmaticus* in 1647, Cromwell becomes a mock king.[31] The first number of *Mercurius Candidus* (20 Nov. 1646) linked the prominent Independent Hugh Peter with Shakespeare (see below, 73–4, 81–3) but *Aulicus* was happy to describe him as simply the 'mad preacher' (2 March 1645).

Other journals were less distinguished, but more enduring and commercially successful. Daniel Border, who was also a physician of some kind, but who was not university educated, fronted a very successful collection of printers and publishers. Border's purple prose enhanced his own reputation and Grub Street's (from where he operated). It is easy to be attracted to the more stylistically extravagant (and usually much less long-lived newsbooks), but journalists like Border had an absorbing style which accounts for their success.

Like Audley, Border was a confident journalist, and in his case this reflected the public support he had. In a sense, Border's character as a writer was related to that of the extravagant Henry Walker. Although he was not particularly sympathetic to the King at first, after the regicide (to which he objected), he supported the young Charles II, the Levellers and the Diggers in *The Perfect Weekly Account, The Kingdomes Faithfull and Impartiall Scout* and *England's Moderate Messenger.* Border never gave wholehearted support to Lilburne, but he did concede that the Leveller manifesto was a good idea.

These 'middle-of-the-road' newsbooks were very powerful indeed (if the frequency of their survival and reference in other works is anything to go by), and their longevity suggests that they made considerable profits for their editors. Border, Pecke, George Smith (who ran the *Scottish Dove*) and several other 'mercuries' all became sympathetic to the Presbyterian cause in the later 1640s, a feature which aided the success of Presbyterian politics in London up to Pride's Purge. Smith and Pecke were examined before the House of Commons for their attitude towards the French, and these newsbooks were in Parliament's sights during the newsbook 'purge' of March 1646, when six newsbooks were suppressed.[32]

Border was dangerous as a paper enemy because he had discovered a tremendous formula. His army intelligence was never as good as Dillingham's or Walker's, but he balanced what he did have with historical parallels and anecdotes. Hard royalism avoided this. *Mercurius Aulicus* was master of (mock) romance structure. The parliamentary commander, Sir William Waller, is mockingly called at one point the 'Conqueror', and his wife a remora because she slows him down, preventing him from leaving Farnham.[33] Nedham's reply in *Mercurius Britanicus* is an intricate allegorical plot which engages intimately with Aulicus. The dimensions of popular romance often enter the action: 'Thus fell *Guy* (not of *Warwick*) whom this noble young knight exceeded in courage, more than the old Gyant did Captaine *Guy* in stature.'[34]

Other techniques were more blatant, less ridiculing and designed to induce fright. Bruno Ryves edited *Mercurius Rusticus* from Oxford during the six months it ran between June and December 1643. The purpose of the newsbook was stated on the cover – to give an account of the brutality and turmoil inflicted by parliamentary soldiers on the populace in the country. In mid-swing, Ryves was able to construct from the letters and other reports sent to him a chilling account of domestic violence. Where Jacobean sensation literature dwelt on the tragic dimensions of sexual jealousy, the Civil War newsbook has troopers as its evil agents, and in Ryves's narrative they do not function as vice figures (despite the survival of vice figures elsewhere – in Nedham's writing and in Leveller tracts, for instance).[35] *Mercurius Rusticus* was later published in a collected form twice in 1685. The last three numbers (perhaps because of the proximity of Christmas in number XVIII) contain an account of the iconoclastic destruction of cathedral ornamentation by soldiers, including shooting at a statue of the crucifixion in Rochester

Cathedral, a passage which carries the shocking impact of a re-enacted crucifixion.[36]

Iconoclastic anger leads to the destruction of the image, for the sake of respect for the truth beyond the image. But from the opposite point of view, the image comes to life and is reslaughtered or resacrificed; this time unnecessarily so: no atonement for mankind will come from this violence. This is coupled with references to the history of the English church from Saxon times, references to the French Wars of Religion, and stories of eminent senior divines being kidnapped by ruthless troopers. The composite result is a kind of 'disappearance' narrative as what for Ryves is a pillar of stability is literally dismantled.

On the other side, reference to popery and superstition is rife. The account of the taking of Holy Island in *Mercurius Britanicus*, 13 (16–22 Nov. 1643) is suffused with details of monks and miracles, the proximity of the dangerous Picts (that is, the forebears of the Scots) known by their habit of body-painting. The Reformation is replayed in miniature. The killing of Lord Brooke by a shot fired from Lichfield Cathedral was seen by Royalists as a divine judgement upon an aristocratic rebel. Audley turns the story around, so that the cathedral becomes a fearsome, demonic 'Monster', with '*bloody Anthems*' and '*murdering Organ-Pipes*'.[37] The objects of puritan complaint now become the agents of unjustified cruelty.

The information is not purely rustic (by which Ryves means provincial) in subject. The attraction of the famous Coleman Street Independent congregation is too great an urban horror to be ignored. Reference is made to it, as well as to the burgeoning sects in London generally, in the first number. By the fourteenth number, London becomes a permanent feature because, says Rusticus, the other royalist sympathiser, *Mercurius Civicus* (which was in fact more Presbyterian), is unable to publish news because of the power of the censorship.[38]

Possibly the most underestimated aspect of the Leveller movement is its involvement in journalism and, by such involvement, its consequent interrelationship with political views far to its right. The political differences between the Presbyterians and Independents (of whom the Levellers count, at least initially, as the radical wing) became a pamphlet war at the initiation of Henry Walker in late 1644.[39] Gilbert Mabbott, both newsbook editor and censor, produced *The Moderate*, which voiced Leveller proposals between the defeat of the Scottish army in August 1648 and the regicide, alongside a series of intriguing accounts of bizarre experiments.[40] The possibility of a royalist/Leveller alliance was seriously urged after the execution of Charles I by Daniel Border in the pages of *The Kingdomes Weekly Intelligencer*.

Elsewhere, however, the attitudes of newswriters, editors or licensers were various. Where Border seems to have taken sides, or pursued a line of interest, others, who condoned Leveller opinion, like Pecke or Gilbert Mabbott, were not Levellers but simply believed that *any* opinion should be published. In *Perfect Occurrences*, the editor Henry Walker tried to play down the differences between republican and Leveller extremists, although he put the Levellers in their place when there was no alternative.

But the Levellers had more enemies than friends among the newsbook fraternity. Royalists were at first fond of making fun of them. A number of these newsbooks provide the exciting evidence that some Levellers, notably John Harris, had been actors. Harris is seen by *Mercurius Impartialis* (12 Dec. 1648) as an actor (and therefore a vagabond or outlaw) as well as a rebel and writer of *Mercurius Militaris*: 'It is written by one *John Harries*, sometimes a Players Boy, a Rogue by the Statute; and since the suppression of the Play-houses, hath betaken himself to the Profession of a Printer'(2).[41] This description takes on larger narrative proportions as Harris commits greater crimes of misnaming. The strategy is of course one designed to diminish Harris, just as Cleveland would do with Cromwell:

> The Rebell in one of his Mercuries, professes he cannot conceive any case of his Majestie, other then of the great Idoll *Bell* in the *Apocrypha*: It was a very unfit Comparison, and might have bin better applyed to the great *Bell* and *Dragon* at *Westminster*. (2)

> In his last the Rebell moves like a Mad-man, and blenches not to call his Sacred Majestie the Grand Lye of the Kingdome, a Quack-salver, a Mountebancke. (3)

The habit of misnaming was common in loyalist newsbooks, using the kind of sexual traduction discussed above (47–50):

> when he [Harris] was a boy was caught in his Mistris *Mouse-trap*; and so turn'd out into the water at *Oldford*, is become a *Babe of Grace*, and for jerking of boyes, begins to jerk up the sisters of the *Seperation*, and to gaine favour with his fellow Actors at *Westminster*, writ a weekly play called *Mercurius Militaris*, hee removed from *Grubstreet* end, to *Colledge* hill.[42]

One did not have to be a Leveller to be a despised journalist. No one liked diurnal writers very much, or at least no one said very complimentary things in public about them. *A fresh Whip For all scandalous Lyers* (9 Feb. 1647) is subtitled 'A true decription of the two eminent Pamphleteers, or Squibtellers of this Kingdome'.[43] It is an attack on newsbook writers or editors in general and a personal attack on Henry Walker, the Independent minister, satirist and editor of *Perfect Occurrences*. Whether or not the author of this little pamphlet had read

Areopagitica, he scatologizes Milton's metaphor of books as living men. By extension, newsbook words are shit:

> I may not unfitly tearme him to be the chiefe Dirt-raker, or Scafinger of the City; for what every any other books lets fall, he will be sure, by his trotting horse, and ambling Booke-sellers have it convey'd to his wharfe of rubbish, and then he will as many petty fogging scrivenors do . . . put here and there to alter the sense of the Relation. (1–2)

This is a horrible image of the diurnal writer playing with other people's excrement in order to make his living. The extended comparison goes on to show how honest reporting is ruined by the newsbook writer's lapse into 'sports and pastimes', meaning both the jocular style which corrupts the plain events, and the fact that by enjoying himself on Saturdays, he has to break the sabbath in order to make the market by Monday morning. His printers are kept idle for a whole day, so that he continually risks economic ruin. The charge of sexual immorality is not restrained either: 'you should . . . find him abed, panting . . . as if he had over-rid himselfe, with riding too and agen from the Army, when God wot hee hath not been out of the Lynes of Communication; (but a little too much within the Lynes of M.M.)'(2–3). His whore is either the Leveller paper *Mercurius Militaris* or the royalist *Mercurius Melancholicus*.

The *ad hominem* attack on Walker comes at a time when he was becoming increasingly powerful as a minister and editor in London, but also in that period when anti-parliamentary, anti-Independent voices and demonstrations surfaced in London. There is thus a vague attempt to disguise the target's name, but the attempt is obviously and self-consciously farcical: he is still the 'Ironmonger'. Apart from being turned, by virtue of a grotesque blazon, into a man of nails, Walker is made into one extreme version of a metaphorical cluster frequently used in classical writing on oratory. As a news orator, he is a soldier. His publishing acts are weapons, and *A fresh Whip* claims he has done more damage than Essex and Fairfax's artillery. He has 'killed' Prince Rupert, Prince Maurice and Sir Ralph Hopton the royalist commander several times over, and his disrespect for learning is figured as a literal firing of ordinance at an Oxford college in order to damage its battlements, something which did actually happen during the siege of Oxford.[44]

Walker would have been chuffed by the comment. He had been a successful puritan pamphleteer and satirist, having begun as the 'ironmonger' tub-preacher: his skills are still not sufficiently recognised.[45] *Perfect Occurrences* blatantly took an Independent line in mid-1640s politics, and as a reward, Walker became a more or less official spokesman for this party in the Army and in Parliament (he relied on Hugh Peter for much information). Indeed, it is almost as if Walker helped to fashion political Independency when he presented Cromwell, in late November 1644, as an Independent before the rift with the Earl of Manchester. Walker was a great marketer of books and personalities. His (in)famous Hebrew word games – where the name of a prominent public figure was transliterated into Hebrew and then translated back into English in order to reveal a hidden and prophetic truth – intrigued the readership.[46] It has been suggested that army officers *paid* Walker for a mention in his newsbook; certainly, his advertising policy drew clients and readers. At the end of its life, in 1649, *Perfect Occurrences* had become an increasingly respectable official voice for the Army and the grandees.

Some scholars feel that the 1640s was the exciting decade of newsbook innovation, and that by contrast, 1650s newsbooks were dull and pedestrian, their opportunities stifled by Cromwellian censorship.[47] This is not the case. Rather, the newsbooks adapted resourcefully to very different conditions. *Mercurius Politicus* stands out as being the journal associated with the Commonwealth government, by being so long run, and by being so innovative in its presentation of political advice, notably the republican precepts delivered across several months (and which are discussed below, 182–7). Nedham set a trend here which was followed by *Perfect Passages*, and by John Streater in his *Observations Historical, Political and Philosophical* (1654) which ran for eleven numbers (see below, 198–9).[48] Streater was following Nedham in using serial publication to disseminate republican political thought, although *Observations*, unlike *Mercurius Politicus*, was more overtly critical of the Lord Protector. Accounts of the news are rendered with apparent objectivity, especially in the case of foreign news. But then prejudice enters as those who are writing against the free state have to be countered. Although books of various political viewpoints and associations were advertised in *Mercurius Politicus*, including many royalist ones, books are used in the text to underline policy. In a passage which seems to be speaking to the Dutch, and of the advantages for them of making peace with England, Nedham mentions a 'Pasquill' printed in Leiden 'called *Eutrapelus*, or the *Middelburgh* Tale'. It 'speaks in merry earnest some part of our disease'.[49] Whose disease? Is the journalist speaking in a deliberately obscure way to fox his readers into believing his impartiality? Or is everything meant to be perceived as not necessarily rosy at home? This would be in keeping with the advice given on conduct and constitution in a free state. It would also endow Nedham with a status above that of being a simple spokesman for the government.

The journalists of the 1650s had learned the lessons of the 1640s. They knew that survival meant the offering of information palatable to the government as well as interesting to the reading public. For its part, the republican government was happy to have a largely positive image of itself projected: apart from royalist newsbooks during the regicide period, there are comparatively very few cases of government censorship of newsbooks.[50] Conditions changed radically with the later Protectorate, when the government gave Nedham a monopoly, and thereby ended several hitherto friendly newsbooks. But opposition newsbooks, usually with rather short lives, continued to appear. If official newsbooks like the later *Mercurius Politicus* look enervated under the gaze of a tyrant, unofficial newsbooks continued to transmit the lively and democratic spirit of the 1640s.

Where programmatic use of the newsbook for the purposes of governmental propaganda was a feature of the 1650s, as juvenile animadversion was the rule of the 1640s, the newsbooks published during the year of regicide and revolution manifest both qualities, and they are at their most inventive in doing so. John Crouch's *The Man in the Moon* (1649–50) has been seen as a seventeenth-century tabloid in its attempts at sexual ridicule of the Council of State, and this method has been seen as being rooted in the gender dynamics of the time.[51] Possibly aiming at a more elevated readership, Nedham's *Mercurius Pragmaticus* (especially the second part 'For King Charles II', published from 17 April 1649) turns history into the chase beloved of the Leveller satirists: 'Now must the *Beagles* go a *hunting* again, and I must be the *Hare*.' Anyone who speaks out against the new regime is in danger. Leveller method is appropriate because Nedham offers support for the persecution of Lilburne and the rest. Sexual comedy enters, for the country's new masters are 'cuckolders' of the law. But in this instance, and unlike many others (see above, 47–9), gender reference is relevant to history, on account of the petitioning of Leveller women (however misogynist the viewpoint of the speaker):

> I marvell the *Levellers* durst venture their *wives* (as they did twice in one week) upon a voyage to *Westminster*; for the lusty *lasses* have had (as I told you they intended) a *Rendezvous* there to present a *Petition* in the behalfe of the *Free-born Champions* with *ten thousand* hands to it: At first it was reject- ed, but one *Wednesday* it was received and read; but no *answer* vouchsafed save that the *Serjeant at Arms* bad them goe home to their *housewiferie*, the *House* having no mind to deale with them in *publick* matters, whatever they mean in *private*. (No. 2 (24 April–1 May 1649), 10)

Nedham makes a nice reference to the exclusion of the domestic sphere from national political life, and then develops the confrontation into a mock-epic, the women firing '*hail-shot*' from their tongues, and Cromwell the mad bull coralled by the women into giving some verbal satisfaction for their demands. The narrative shape allows Nedham to cast his news, while also reflecting pointedly on the personal profiteering being made by the Cromwell family, especially Ireton, Cromwell's son-in-law. More- over, in this mocking frame, Cromwell's puritanism looks silly – such as the attention he gives to the prophet Elizabeth Poole.[52] The New Jerusalem is reduced to deluded visions, empty promises and unjustly harsh utilitarian schemes.

Nedham presents Cromwell, Ireton, Bradshaw and Peter exactly as Overton had treated the Presbyterian tithe-guzzlers in *The Araignement of Mr. Persecution* (1645; see below, 299–300). This enforces the connection with property, and between economic greed and denial of toleration. Taxation of citizens and the harsh treatment of beggars look like the different parts of a new policy of tyranny. But the tyranny is punitive in a deadly way, for the middle of the newsbook details the execution of uncompliant soldiers – first the Welsh insurgent Colonel Poyer, and then, at greater length, Cornet Robert Lockyer, who led an unsuccessful Leveller insurrection, and was subsequently executed. Nedham plays some interesting games with cultural symbolism here. Lockyer's famous funeral, with its display of Leveller colours, celebrates patriotic heroism, and is meant to frighten supporters of the government, but the sword laid naked on the hearse could equally symbolise (perhaps in other circumstances) the Machiavellian republicanism which Nedham later espoused (see below, 300–305). The Levellers are presented as the protectors of liberty (again, unlike Nedham's later criticisms of them), and this is aided by the satire on the new coin of the Commonwealth. The palms of virtue on the coin really signify knavery, and the laurel branch (standing for peace) is uninterpretable – it becomes an empty signifier.[53] Really, says, Nedham, etching his own devious imagination onto state apparatus, "'tis possible the world might be convinced, if in their *new Coin* they would represent *Cromwel* courting the *King* on the one side, and cutting off his head on the other.' (13)

Nedham has done his best to ensure that those who have already sworn allegiance to the Commonwealth will feel guilty, and those who as yet have not, will not. There is, he says, every chance that the Scots and the Irish will successfully rebel. He sounds ostensibly a Royalist, and also a Leveller fellow traveller, but the analysis already displays his later republicanism in its method. The masquerade is complete.

Dorothy Osborne reports that in an idle moment, 'for want of something else to do', she picked up a newsbook, and in it happened across some information which was of vital interest to her – the movements on the public stage of one of her suitors and the Commonwealth's marriage legislation.[54] This encounter did nothing, it would seem, to dissuade her of the scurrility and unreliability of the newsbook. Yet, as I am suggesting, and as her letter shows, they were at the heart of Civil War and Interregnum politics: the 'pulse' of the body politic, as Cleveland had claimed. After 1660, the serious-travesty newsbook, such as *Mercurius Pragmaticus*, was never so effective or centrally important, and its words and verse forms ended up in the world of popular pamphleteering. Even Ryves's *Mercurius Rusticus* was a second-hand popular swashbuckler, which, despite its relevance, never gained the stature of a Cavalier Redneck. The functions of the newsbook in the 1640s and 1650s were again split up and reorganised. The Civil War newsbook did sanction a genuine public discourse; thankfully it also cultivated as good a sense of humour. If the gathering and circulation of news prior to 1640 played an important part in the development of political awareness, the regularity and persistence of the Civil War newsbook meant that reportage and its mutations were firmly implanted at the heart of national literary culture. It had become the measure of truth in all senses of that word. While the instances of accurate intelligence, or the eloquent pleading for a particular cause, flourished in the London presses associated with Parliament and the Levellers, other voices from all quarters presented news through a scenario of dissimulation, disinformation and vilification. Confronting these newsbooks must have felt like a descent into hell.

Theatres Transprosed: The Career of Drama in the English Revolution

That newsbooks might steal the function of public broadcasting from the theatres was understood as early as the later 1620s. Yet the closure of the theatres did not mean the extinction of drama, so much as a migration of dramatic resources to the arena of the pamphlet, and the partisan role which they played. The history of this flight is one of the most intricately fascinating details of the Civil War.

In August 1647, the parliamentarian journal, *Perfect Occurrences*, reported that:

> A Complaynt was made of Players acting Playes publikely at the *Fortune* in *Golding-Lane* and in *Salisbury* Court, And the House [of Commons] wondred at the neglect of the Iustices of the Peace therein, to permit them, especially at this time. It was moved that the Commander in Chiefe of the Guard of the Houses might take care to suppresse them, but considering the dangerous season of the Plague, the House hoping that the Justices of Peace will observe their Orders, passed a vote that order be given to the Justices of Peace to take care speedily to suppresse them.[55]

Since 2 September 1642, one month after the outbreak of the English Civil War, the theatres and bear gardens in London had been closed by order of Parliament, partly for the sake of social control, partly out of a genuine sense of repentance and humiliation on the part of puritan M.P.s. During the following fifteen years, the London theatres were dismantled and destroyed. The Globe was demolished in April 1644 to make room for tenement buildings, and a similar fate befell the bear gardens in the mid-1650s (the bears were often shot). On 24 March 1649 soldiers, with the encouragement of sectaries, pulled down Salisbury Court in Fleet Street and the Phoenix Theatre. In the same year, the Fortune was also dismantled.[56] By the mid-1650s, the theatre was for most a memory, having been the attention of 'more severe correctors, who knowing not how to amend or repaire, have pluckt all downe, and left themselves the only spectacle of their times'.[57]

The theatre was by 1640 a well-ingrained, if economically precarious, institution in London. Its stages ranged from the popular fora of the Red Bull and the Fortune to the more exclusive, middle-class theatre at Blackfriars, and to the players and playwrights who found employment in court retinues. Many of the more vocal elements among the Puritans regarded the theatres as places where immoral and violent leisure activities could be indulged, and where the sin of idolatry could be committed by observing the stage spectacle, as opposed to the turning of the heart towards God in devotion and sober behaviour.

Despite the attempts of several scholars recently to show that at least some parliamentarian and puritan supporters, especially the more elevated and powerful ones, regarded the theatre as a favourable means of voicing criticism, if not of indulging entertainment,[58] the overall truth remains that the theatre became a victim of ideological division during the 1640s, and that the popular party was very largely antipathetic to it. There are some important exceptions, especially among the more secular Parliamentarians and republicans. In 1648, John Hall of Durham called for the opening of the theatres, and his journalism, like that of his associate, Marchamont Nedham, used theatrical language. Other republican theorists, James Harrington and John Streater, repeated the call in the 1650s. Nonetheless, the anti-theatrical prejudice, especially as it focused upon play performances during the sabbath, was sustained by parliamentary journalism:

I am perswaded in time they [the Royalists] will go neere to put downe all *preaching* and *praying*, and have some *Religious Masque* or play instead of Morning and Evening Prayer; it has been an old fashion at Court amongst the Protestants there, to shut up the *Sabbath* with some wholsome Piece of *Ben Johnson* or *Davenant*, a kind of *Comicall Divinity*.[59]

Three years later, Thomas Audley levelled the same charge at royalist journalists:

Malignants have stollen as much Holland of late from the Presbyterians, and the Independants, as hath made a thousand sheetes for the *Oxford* old Juglers to wrap their evill spirits in at *Aulicus* his *Maske* (who it is said hath contracted a Company for *Newcastle*, to shew Gamballs at Court this Christmasse)[.] The Mummers parts were drawne from a publike Conference betwixt six Presbyterian Ministers, and some Independants, held at Oxford on Thursday, *Novem.* 12.1646.[60]

The 'theatre' of state – by the mid-1640s the Parliament – was not to be regarded, said parliamentarian propaganda, as another kind of theatre: 'You say very true, it is the great Barne in W[h]itehall, since the State hath pulled downe the Globe, Blackfryres, the Fortune, and I make no question that wooden Babell shall be no eye-sore to you; there shall be no more playing or dancing there beleeve it.'[61]

Elements of the professional theatre took refuge with the King's supporters. Acting companies sought royal and royalist patronage during the Civil War, and actors enlisted in Charles I's army.[62] Some notable and elevated playwrights went into exile and wrote plays on the run: Thomas Killigrew claimed that he wrote *The Pilgrim* while in Paris in 1651. Yet in 1641 there were performances of playlets critical of Laud and Strafford in the popular theatres, and possibly also in the more courtly venues. Richard Brathwaite's *Mercurius Britanicus* (Latin and English editions, 1641), a pamphlet dialogue which may also have been performed, criticised the judges who found for the King in the ship money trials, and voiced support for Parliament (although it was also critical of religious radicals).[63] But by the mid and late 1640s, the voices of compromise – those who argued that the theatre could and should function as a moral and godly forum – sound singularly unconvincing.[64] As the quotation with which we began demonstrates, this hostility developed in the years after the closure of 1642, reaching a peak at the time of the execution of Charles I, and in the period immediately thereafter.

However, it is not simply this division and prejudice which should interest us. When an institution is suppressed, something must happen to its component parts. The material of the theatres might have been dismantled (as some were) plank by plank, but there were players and playwrights, and further supporting staff, in need of employment. Plays continued to be performed, especially during the urban turbulence of 1647–8, sometimes in makeshift venues such as tennis courts (but also at established theatres), even though the players risked violent interruption by soldiers, loss of costumes, and punishment.[65] The theatre popped up if given a chance. The ordinance against plays was renewed on 17 July 1647 until the end of the year, but in January 1648 plays were again being performed at the Fortune. On 3 February 1648, Beaumont and Fletcher's

Wit without Money was performed at the Red Bull. One week later, on the 9th, another ordinance was passed silencing the playhouses. Just over one year after the closure, in the summer and autumn of 1643, Sir Humphrey Mildmay went to see plays, including a 'playe of Warre', and 'a Playe where was a disaster', which possibly refers to the collapse of the stage or an audience stand, perhaps when it was interrupted by soldiers. He records seeing no plays between 1644 and 1647, but did witness performances in the autumn of 1648, including one at the Red Bull, which was still in business at the end of 1649.[66] In March 1648, actors petitioned the House of Lords to be permitted to play again, for the sake of their own livelihoods.[67]

Moreover, there was a language and culture of the theatre which would not simply disappear. Plays may not have been widely performed, but they were printed and widely read: the production of folio and quarto editions of the collected works of playwrights was particularly important. Despite fears that read, as opposed to performed, plays compromised their capacity for cryptic comment on contemporary events, some plays explicitly acknowledged the importance of pamphlet power.[68] Edmund Gayton refers with satisfaction to the 'works' as opposed to the 'plays' of Jonson, Beaumont and Fletcher, and William Cartwright. The books are the 'survivors of the stage'.[69] When he published it in 1652, Richard Brome referred to his play *A Jovial Crew: Or, The Merry Beggars* (which 'had the luck to tumble last of all [that is, performed last] in the epidemical ruin of the scene' in 1642), as a wounded soldier, a beggar because a casualty of war.[70] The longer anti-theatricality remained in the rhetoric of puritanism, of course, the longer theatricality was sustained, even if as a demonised myth. And by 1642, the public and court theatres were intricately linked to the other form of theatre or spectacle that articulated the structure and nature of authority in seventeenth-century English society, be it the theatre of a monarch's behaviour, or the theatre of public execution and martyrdom for faith: 'that Tragedy [the burning of Protestants in Queen Mary's reign], whose Epilogue was Flame and Fagot; or at least the *Fasces*, a bundle of rods, to younger men'.[71]

If the theatre was closed by those who found themselves in opposition to the King, then, as we have seen, the early 1640s also saw the rise of the printed pamphlet, that source of information and opinion which had been denied to the Puritans and the Parliamentarians under the censorship of the 1620s and 1630s. One obsession of the journalists was the banned theatre. The newsbooks tell of actors who became either preachers or soldiers. Some acting troupes went to Holland and France soon after the closure to play to English gentlemen in exile, and returned in 1647 in search of larger audiences.[72] Hugh Peter, Oliver Cromwell's chaplain, was supposedly an actor when an undergraduate, while John

Harris, once a boy actor, became a New Model Army officer and Leveller journalist, paralleling the careers of many French actors at the end of the following century who participated in the Revolution. Peter's name became inseparable in the royalist newsbooks from theatricality: 'he has a fine wit I can tell you *Sam. Rowley*, and he were a *Pylades*, and *Orestes*, when he played the womans part at the Curtaine Play-house, which is the reason his garbe is so emphaticall in the Pulpit.'[73]

Many playwrights found ready employment as pamphleteers, from writing characters and popular moralistic tracts to polemics, and as editors of (usually royalist) newsbooks. Those who would have been playwrights found no alternative but the news market. The theatrical language of the stage became a transprosed language of a disembodied and suppressed stage; of speeches and actions without the actors to give the characters living form. Thomas Hobbes tellingly saw in his friend Davenant's *Gondibert* (1651) a drama masquerading as a heroic poem.[74] On a national scale, this was nothing less than a major realignment of theatrical language in mid-seventeenth-century England.

News becomes the predominant motif in this pamphlet drama, continually arresting the attention of the reader: 'Some newes of more than ordinary consequence if it beare date from him,' says Cromwell as he opens Ireton's letter in *The Famous Tragedie of King Charles I, Basely Butchered* (1649; 40). Those political dialogues of the 1620s and 1630s which were first published in the early 1640s tended to lose their inherent dramatic, often neo-Marlovian, qualities, for the sake of registering the importance of the newsletter, the emblem and the anagram as readerly media.[75] The rebus had at least equal status with the dramatic, and the theatre was a necessary element in the formation of early mass communication. Cosmo Manuche's *The Loyal Lovers* (1652) constantly reminds its readers/audience of the significance of the 'news', the play beginning with the purchase of scurrilous books from a street vendor.

News and theatre interacted well before 1640. The emergence of news pamphleteering in the 1620s was satirised by Ben Jonson in *The Staple of News* (1626); it has been argued that this play represents an acknowledgement of the passing of news communication from the theatres to the printed page.[76] However, under the pressure of war, and the official removal of the institution, the new journalism became a site of theatre, and English people, deprived of their plays, looked around for somewhere to apply the language of performance, and found it in the events of war and revolution themselves. There is even some evidence which suggests traffic going in the opposite direction. Some newsbooks and journalists were traduced in bear garden capers.[77] The fusing of theatrical vocabulary with that of other institutions and sites of authority is demonstrated in a tract concerning allegiance to the fledgling republic:

But I perceive there is one thing stumbles many Barbatulous Ladds amongst you, enough, many think, to foment disaffection, and make any man a Malignant; And that is, a putting downe of Stage-Playes. Alter but the *Scene*, and many Pulpits will be as whimsically apish to your wild sence; and for sevearer Eares of Gentlemen, the *Tragick Comedy* of flacessent Tithes; supercilliously acted every seventh day by the Pulpits demised premises, terribly deploring the but necessary regulating of them, is super excellent.[78]

The dramatic forms which had seen life on the stage before 1642 were taken into the printed pamphlet. Again, this is not surprising given the ready popular readership which published quarto editions of individual plays had found before 1640. What is less expected is the disruption which the process of transprosing wrought upon dramatic form. As the end of the decade approached, so this process became more pronounced and bizarre.

Lois Potter's admirable survey of dramatic and theatrical developments during the war and Interregnum decades makes it clear that courtly and popular theatrical forms were truncated, compressed, or mixed around.[79] The dependence upon the past, witnessed in the continued publication in the 1640s of many plays which had been performed in the 1630s, was not merely the result of restrictions upon the conditions which would have made for a continuing and developing dramatic tradition. There is also a sense in which playwrights were able only to understand radical (and to them, horrific) changes and upheavals in the state and its running by recourse to explanations of action and character which had resided only or hitherto in the drama. In 1645, speculating rather scornfully on a rumour that Charles I was dead, Marchamont Nedham referred to a play by John Ford when he asked 'Can the *Cavaliers* be so impudent, as to play the second part of *Perkin Warbeck*, and carry one up & down in his likenesse?'[80]

As we have seen, journalism developed rapidly and in a complex pattern of cross-fertilising genres. Because royalism was identified with patronage of the theatres, parliamentarian anti-royalist reportage ridiculed Royalists in theatrical terms. *The Kingdomes Weekly Intelligencer*, 198 (23 Feb.–2 March 1647), 438, derided the commander of royalist forces in the north, the Duke of Newcastle, by then defeated and in exile, in theatrical terms. The effect is to vilify him and present him as powerless. The charges of effeminacy are consistent with Prynne's attacks on the stage (elsewhere Charles's privy council was described as a collection of hermaphrodites). Newcastle, who had been writing for the English players in Paris, has 'either an admirable temper and settlednes of mind, or else an infinite and vaine affection unto Poetry, that in the ruines of his Country and himselfe to[o] can be at the leisure to make Prologues and Epilogues for players'. On the other side, translation became a sign of royalist affiliation, as in Christopher Wase's 1649 monarchically slanted version of Sophocles' *Electra*. Theatricality was a means of belittlement: when the headquarters of the New Model Army were established in Whitehall, it was greeted as a recently erected playhouse.[81] In a more interesting way, reportage takes on well-known dramatic events as an explanatory device. The attempt of a (perhaps Jesuit) priest to convince a Cambridge undergraduate was represented as the temptations of the Devil in the guise of a priest, thereby replicating exactly the temptation of Faustus by Mephostophilis in Marlowe's play. The representation of events becomes a succession of fragments of dramatic memory, removing the event from any direct connection with its own unique eventfulness, but at the same time amplifying its meaningfulness. What has happened is that the recasting of the event in a well-known dramatic shape has turned religious division in the 1640s into a theatrically realised cosmic struggle. A godly Protestant writer might here have turned to the language of Job or of Revelation, but in journalism theatrical event becomes the medium of providential revelation. Thus, *The Kingdomes Faithful and Impartiall Scout*, 32 (31 Aug. – 7 Sept. 1649), 245, recounts a tragedy, played by some 'young Sparks' in Hampshire, of the trial and execution of Charles I in which the actor executioner really beheaded the actor playing the king. Had decapitation suddenly become irresistible? When interrogated, the actor-executioner said he was only playing his part: the stage and the real world had elided in a continuous tragedy of state.

Tragedy and tyranny had always been closely associated, and Milton's quotation of classical tragedians on the title pages of his regicide tracts is a strong witness to such a continuity of thought (see above, 17–18).[82] *Samson Agonistes*, especially if the earlier date of 1647–53 is entertained, becomes the archetypal puritan drama, interiorised in the minds of the prophet poet and the reader, who share inwardly the liberating action of the blind hero.[83] Pulling down the theatre of the Philistines is also an act of iconoclasm. The language of tyranny was, however, precisely that area which was most problematic for both sides. Who was the tyrant, King or Parliament? Only after the regicide did royalist journalists and dramatists choose to represent the Parliament or Cromwell as dangerously tyrannical. The dramatic representations of the Parliamentarians by the Royalists before 1649, and to some extent also thereafter, are often tragi-comic, because rebels are low characters who should succumb to comic justice. Aptly enough, *Mercurius Vapulans* (27 Nov. 1647, 7), linked Beaumont and Fletcher's *A King and No King* to the persecution of the King, while regarding differences between Parliament and Levellers as *The Comedy of Errors*. Despite the fact that the influential Italian tragi-comedian Guarini compared tragi-comedy to a republic (where government is mixed: tragi-comedy balances the humours of the body; tragedy purges pity and fear; comedy purges melancholy; hence the reversals of violence and of powerful oracles in *Il Pastor Fido*), tragi-comedy provided the generic means for Royalists to imagine the possibility of a happy ending for their plight.

In 1648, after serious discontent in London at the demands of the wars, and during the Second Civil War, royalist journalists returned to drama (in its printed form) as a means of belittling a character who was rapidly becoming one of the most powerful soldiers in Europe. The phenomenon is historically ironic, for it was the dramatic prose dialogue through which opposition to royal policy was voiced in the 1620s and 1630s. Thomas Scott's dialogue pamphlets and those he translated into English (his were also translated into European languages) are a famous example.[84]

John Crouch and Marchamont Nedham wrote respectively the first and second parts of *Craftie Cromwell* (1648), two play pamphlets which presented Oliver as a stage Machiavel, both Marlovian anti-hero and revenger. In terms of the earlier dialogues, to present Cromwell in these terms was undoubtedly to satirise him, but it was also to acknowledge his greatness. The dialogues committed satire on fearful enemies by bringing them onto the stage of the pamphlet, and to do so with a living monarch was illegal. Both plays are presented as part of a new ethos of melancholy and topsy-turvydom, a direct consequence of social disruption. This is a reflection of the sense of abeyance which prevailed as Parliament held the King, and some called for his trial, while the Leveller movement disrupted the parliamentary consensus from its own left wing. The prologue to *Craftie Cromwell* speaks this ethos of confusion, for which comedy becomes the appropriate genre:

> Smooth PLAUTUS, ARISTOPHANES his veine
> We now affect, not SOPHOCLES high streine:
> Yet thus we differ, they for mirth were fixt,
> But we have *Joy* and *Dolor*, both commixt. (Sig. A1v)

In this atmosphere, actors are devalued even as they are silenced:

> An Ordinance from our pretended State,
> Sowes up the Players mouths, they must not prate
> Like Parrats what they're taught upon the Stage,
> Yet we may Print the Errors of the Age. (Sig. A1v)

Cromwell is presented as ambitious for the throne, 'Oliver in his Glory as King', and he is impelled as a kind of perverse Hamlet. The anti-hero is presented as a classical hero (or indeed a frenzied lover):

> *One raves, as troubled with a boyling heart,*
> *He craves the favour of the blind gods Dart,*

Another lets his Oaths about to flye,
Which deafes mens eares like Joves *Artillery.* (5)

The anti-plebeian message is clear: 'The name of *Libertie* hath ever been the watch-word us'd before *Rebellion*, the idle eccho of uncertaintie'(3). Shortly after the start of the text, the ghost of John Pym, the great leader in the House of Commons who died in 1643, rises and reveals his puppet, the sleeping Oliver, in a replication of the opening scene in Ben Jonson's *Catiline*. Pym's ghost associates calls for liberty (the 'idle eccho of uncertaintie') with melancholy:

> From the black Lake that runs round *Erebus* I come, permitted by the *King of Flames*, to visit those that my Co-partners were, when I was cloath'd in flesh: I, whose projections grim and dangerous, brought a free people into slaverie, incensing them against their gracious Prince, and topsie-turvy turn'd all LAW and RIGHT. (6)

Set against the demonic conjuring in which two Jesuits are then seen to engage, is the ideal of citizenship which the play praises, and in which is located the functioning of the news itself. In a kind of echo backwards towards the urban patriarchalism of Plautus, as it was construed in Shakespeare's early comedies, and in Beaumont and Fletcher, *Mercurius Melancholicus* appeals to a London citizenship which has been put under hard financial and personal pressure by the Parliament's demands for war resources. A compressed form of mercantile exchange signifies the ideal (and the ideal status for news demanded by the journalists), before the melancholy underworld is entered:

> 1 *Citizen.*   Are you for the *Exchange*?
> 2 *Cit.*   Yes: I have appointed a *Venetian* merchant to meet him there.
> 1 *Cit.*   What Newes is stirring?
> 2 *Cit.*   None, but what *Fame* speakes i'th nose by the [D]yurnall, and the
>   rest o'the Gazets. (3)

The last two 'acts' of the play go to the Isle of Wight where the King is held prisoner by Colonel Hammond and other Roundhead soldiers, who have enough loyalty to disapprove of what they are doing but not enough to disobey a parliamentary order, as if Crouch were trying to appeal to many who were reluctant servants of an aggressive state. Prophecy was not beyond these plays. The 'headless trunk' may refer to Parliament or to a church without monarch or bishops, but the association of actor with King makes threatened regicide very apparent:

> *When the time comes that you shall see*
> *A headlesse Body Active be,*
> *And many horrid Deeds perform'd*
> *By a trunk, without an Head adorn'd.*(10)

Samuel Sheppard's *The Committee-Man Curri'd* (1647) is a satirical play pamphlet which responds both to the renewal of the ordinance against plays in July 1647, the unpopular excise legislation of that year, and to the widespread unpopularity of parliamentary committees. Lois Potter sees no serious content in the play, and her respect for its author is diminished by the large degree of plagiarism (from Stapylton, Suckling, and Webster), so that Sheppard is seen to rely not merely on the words but also the experiences of his predecessors.[85] This is somewhat unfair. Despite the poor quality of Sheppard's verse, he was already beginning to voice criticism of the Cavaliers (often drunkards in his writings), in part through the mouth of Loyalty, who has to accept exile in France, and becomes ill for want of money. Such a treatment was to be more developed and significant two years later in the post-regicide days, and Sheppard played a large role in expanding the scope of royalist self-perception. Moreover, however oblique his statements were, Sheppard was clearly trying to use the excise crisis in his play as a means of raising anti-parliamentarian (and hopefully pro-royalist) support, something which the Levellers never managed to exploit. An image of the excise man is actually burned in Sheppard's text, thereby going rather further than anything which really did happen.[86]

Such a move into the world of events is a strategy adopted by Nedham at the end of *Craftie Cromwell*, Part 2, where the trial and punishment of Captain John Burley, the royalist captain who attempted to rescue Charles from captivity in Carisbrooke Castle, is re-enacted. But Nedham works in much more specific detail than does Crouch: the opening dialogue is between Solon, a Royalist, and Ismeno, an Independent, and possibly a faintly disguised version of Nathaniel Ingelo, Independent minister and later ambassador of the Commonwealth to Sweden. The prologue invokes a string of previous dramatists to answer the dire situation of the King's imprisonment, from Sophocles, Euripides and Seneca through Shakespeare, Jonson and Webster to Suckling and Goffe: '*leave the Elisian Land./And hurrying hither, with their Delphick baies./ Blast their black soules, who do despise their laies*'(3). What will become a habit in royalist journalism starts here: the playwright is happy to let Ismeno reveal the evil advisers around the king ('how many Gavestons K. *Charles* once kept'(5)), while the claim to royal authority is presented in a pseudo-mystical language, continuous with the language of melancholy, but this time expected to provide unity and assent. In short, it is meant to cast an iconic spell on the reader:

Kings of their Kingdomes as the Centers are, to which each weightie thing it selfe exposes for as all mighty Rivers, flowing streames, the liquid powers what ere they be, do such in sundry parts by severall currents, great Neptunes bosome who as a Steward of the tumid deeps, doth send them back by many secret windings, and as fame tell[s] us, when the moisture needs, send forth her humed treasurs to refresh the Sun-burnt parched plains, so are Kings breasts, the depths where daily flow clear streams of knowledge. (4)

The origins of Nedham's treatment go back to an earlier play pamphlet of 1647, *The Levellers Levelled*, signed by *Mercurius Pragmaticus* (but Nedham disclaimed the authorship[87]), in which the characterisation is allegorical. The first scene involves a distracted character called England's Genius, who is rapidly overtaken by the presence of Apostasie, Treachery, Conspiracie, Democracie and Impiety, who are the 'five Adjutators or Levellers', in a scene of 'Confused Musick'.[88] The degree of specificity such as we might find in a pamphlet is avoided not because of ignorance of personalities or events – Nedham had been a journalist and gatherer of intelligence for too long not to know a great deal, as his voluminous parliamentarian and anti-parliamentarian writings show. He is also subtle and informed enough to show how frustrated the Levellers were after the quelling of the mutiny at Ware. Instead, and perhaps latching onto the habit of popular allegorisation in the toleration controversy of the early and mid-1640s, Nedham's purpose seems to be to create not only a new aesthetic of loyalism and martyrology, but also to restructure the tradition of tyranny and rebellion, as it was represented on stage. Presenting a real person (Fairfax, Cromwell) risked or entailed diminution, but an allegorical figure appears larger, is more undefined and hence more threatening. The Army grandees are menacingly referred to as 'Sophies of the State', as if they had been lifted from the oriental tyrannies in Fulke Greville's plays. Regicide and Parricide are two Independent ministers who manipulate the Levellers; the astrologer and popular pamphleteer William Lilly appears as Orioto, a magus and a pimp. John of London is of course an echo of John of Leiden, the sixteenth-century Anabaptist who believed in the community of goods and wives. John *Lilburne* came from Newcastle but his name is probably hidden in the play here. At one point (4), the figures kiss an effigy of the Roman conspirator, Catiline, who thus becomes an icon and a sacrament of disorder, in direct opposition to the (as yet) living icon, Charles. The demands of some Army radicals and Levellers to bring the King to trial (the threat of execution is already foreseen) is enough to make the Gunpowder Plot pale into insignificance: 'Let *Catesby*, *Piercy*, and that bloudy knot/Be Sainted now, or else at least forgot,/And let these vipers vindicate their crimes' (5–6).

Larger than life, or less than human, allegorical figures are used in the *Mistris Parliament* plays of 1647–8. In *Mistris. Parliament Brought to Bed of a Monstrous Childe of Reformation*, there might be verbal and scenic echoes of the heath scene in *King Lear*, but the play rapidly allegorizes religious policy. This time, the allegorical figures are more rather than less threatening on account of the unpleasant scene:

Mrs. *Synod.* . . . Will ye have a little Strong-waters, or a Cawdle to comfort ye?

Mrs. *Parl.* Oh sick, sicke, I must cast Nurse; Pray, reach me a Bowle: }hawe, }hawe. }. . .

Nurse. Well said Mistris, fetch it up; up with it; Heaven blesse me! What is't that lookes so red, Mistris?

Mrs. *Parls.* O, 'tis *Blood*, innocent blood. (4)

While in fear of death at childbirth, Mrs. Parliament confesses her own cruelty, before giving birth to a 'deformed shape, without a head, great goggle eyes, bloody hands growing out of both sides of its devouring panch, under the belly hung a large bagge, and the feet are like the feat of a Beare'(8). Through the veil of conventional monster description, the allegory conveys to us the birth of religious toleration.

The most telling merging of 'news' with drama comes with *The Famous Tragedie of King Charles I. Basely Butchered* (1649), most probably written by Samuel Sheppard. *The Famous Tragedie* has been neglected because it does not adopt the tragi-comic mode of most Civil War royalist drama. The play-pamphlet is based on major events in the Second Civil War, specifically the siege of Colchester. The reader witnesses a Machiavellian and sexually appetitive Cromwell scheming his removal of Charles in order to become king himself. Sir Charles Lucas and Sir George Lisle make a noble attempt to hold off the parliamentary forces of Fairfax and Ireton, but with starvation of the populace threatening, they surrender, having celebrated their own values of loyalism, civility and heroic bravery in a curious drinking scene which acknowledges but also criticises the ideal and culture of the Cavalier. Upon surrender, and despite Fairfax's objection, Lucas and Lisle are executed upon the orders of Colonel Thomas Rainborough. One of the soldiers is appalled by this breach of military code: he swops sides and hunts down Rainborough, assassinating him at the end of the fourth act as a kind of rapid revenge.[89] Meanwhile, Act 5 opens with the announcement of Charles I's execution, and the play closes abruptly with a chorus which presents the bodies of the King and his generals as unjust victims and sacrifices.

The play opens with the entrance of Cromwell and his most famous chaplain, Hugh Peter. The first sentence raises a parodic comparison, not for the first time in this kind of drama, between Cromwell and Peters, and Faustus and Mephostophilis, recalling from Marlowe's play the speech by Faustus at the beginning of scene viii, after the first chorus: 'My fine *facetious Devill*, who wear'st *the Liverie* of *the Stygian God*, as the white *Embleme* of thy *innocence*' (1). Cromwell's rhetoric reveals its own falsehood, presenting the siege of Colchester as like the siege of Troy.

The Greeks (Parliamentarians) are unfairly aided by the magic of Calchas, that is, false, persuasive rhetoric. But such rhetoric is seen to have worked, implying a sense of royalist acceptance yet disbelief of their defeat: 'I know that *Nectar* hangs upon thy lippes, and that the most absurd Syllogisme, or eare-deceiving paradox, maintain'd by thee, shall seem oraculous' (1).

In one sense, such portrayals are literally the effect of the lingering of court culture, and the values which it upheld in courtly behaviour and the modes of play or performance with which such modes were associated. For the Parliamentarians, the cult of loyalty and its associated values of sacrifice and heroism were ridiculous fantasies: writing in *Mercurius Censorius*, 2 (1–8 June 1648), 10, John Hall compared such behaviour among the Royalists to the romance figure of Fortunatus, and to the popular romance hero, Captain Jones. *The Famous Tragedie* presents Lucas and Lisle as Stoic warriors, ready if necessary to endure the harsh conditions of siege. This is a blatant exaggeration of the real situation in Colchester. The great length of the siege, the significance of famine, and the external events which made the maintenance of the defence pointless, are either rushed over or have even already taken place, so that the second act relies upon a sense of simultaneous struggle for victory and providentially inflicted defeat. Lisle expresses the hope that the Scottish army will succeed, and together with loyalist risings in Wales, the South and London, will cause the war to swing away from Parliament. But in the next speech, Lucas expresses his lack of faith in the perfidious Hamilton, the Scottish leader, and says that defeat is inevitable, that the best solution is to celebrate their loyalty in a drinking session: 'here let us frollick one halfe houre, *Mars* and *Thalia* sometimes doe accord, onely a Health or two unto our Royall Master' (15).

The author(s) of *The Famous Tragedie* could have exploited the severe justice of Ireton, if not the harsh conditions of surrender, on the very terms which the Parliamentarians themselves used. Instead a chivalrous and honourable Fairfax (who was in actuality unrelenting) argues against a bloodthirsty Rainborough (his Leveller history being the cause of this portrayal) that it is contrary to the 'Law of Armes' to execute their enemies. Once again, heroic honour is offered (and admitted as forceful by Ireton) against Machiavellian policy and Rainborough's not entirely unjustified call for revenge, after the sufferings of parliamentary troops. An appeal to natural law or natural justice (the dramatic precedent would have been *King Lear*) might have enabled a far harsher critique of the Parliamentarians. The execution itself is heroic, highly and self-consciously theatrical, and dependent in several places upon Webster. Lucas talks of making an 'exit', while a soldier recalls the madhouse scenes of *The Duchess of Malfi*: 'Your selfe must lead the dance of death'

(27). Masque and inflated *descriptio* are merged as Lucas heroically sees himself out by means of a ridiculous inversion of the apricot scene in Webster's play: 'Charge me then home, I love to chew those Winter-plums, they are those Cordiall comfits I accept, as sick men do great *Gallens* Antidotes; methinks the Earth goes round *Copernicus*' (28). Bullet ingestion is also how Lisle perceives his end: 'Oh! you have put Balls of wild-fire in my Bowels, I am all but one *AEtna*' (30).[90] At this point, the dying Cavalier becomes an absolutely literal rendering of the figure of civil distraction in *Craftie Cromwell* (ultimately inherited from the *furor* in Seneca's anti-Neronian tragedies *Hercules Furens* and *Octavia*): one who '*raves, as troubled with a boyling heart*'.

It is hard to take these heroic deaths without conceding an element of diminution and parody, which enhances our suspicion of an unstable cavalier ethos. A related effect is generated by the presentation of Cromwell as a character of levity, like Shakespeare's Richard III, as much as he is a Machiavel. Act IV opens with Hugh Peter acting as a pimp on Cromwell's behalf, attempting to persuade Mrs Lambert to put her body at Oliver's disposal. While Peter delivers a truncated Horatian Ode in praise of Cromwell's defeat of Hamilton's army in the north, Oliver looks on through a gap in the hangings, using Mrs Lambert's confession to Peter that she will submit to his master as a moment for his entry and triumphal capture of her. There is comedy and parody here, but also a largely undeveloped but nonetheless serious comment in the sheer sexual power of Cromwell. Mrs Lambert is genuinely traumatised by the jeopardy in which she puts her marriage vow. Cromwell, more used to the careful deployment of words, has to be reminded by Peter that it is physical contact which will make her submit to him.

What has happened is that the challenge to divine right kingship, and its concomitant patriarchal assumptions, has resulted in a perceived disruption in the sexually symbolic order. The significance of the *Mistris Parliament* play pamphlets of 1647 is that Parliament, commonly regarded as the 'wife' of the King, gives rapid and unnatural birth (since not engendered by the father-king) to a series of religious heresies, supposedly the final reformation of English religion.

In *The Famous Tragedie*, the sexual prodigy is treated differently. In Act V, Cromwell leaves the stage for the last time to govern through the Council of State. Having spent a night of 'Caligulan' pleasures with Mrs Lambert, during which time the King has been executed, Cromwell now appears as a corrupt version of a Machiavellian prince, a *Sforza*. The playwright is using the seduction scene of Mrs Lambert as a means of exploring the nature of Cromwell's success.[91] It is a work of art which is so well executed that it appears uncanny: 'Sir [says Mrs Lambert], you have robb'd me both of honour, and my heart at once; so strange a Fate doth sway me, that whatsoe're you judge to be convenient, I must not contradict' (41). The character of Cromwell has been transformed entirely from that which was implied by the many published letters and speeches concerning the military campaigns.

The element of sexual fantasy, perhaps connected with the notion of melancholy, seems to point towards a future theatre (albeit one that was never fully realised). Writers from various positions, royalist and republican, took up the earlier 'feminist' and 'mysogynistic' style of ridicule of the 1620s and 1630s, and used this to level satire at puritan or parliamentary magnates in the late 1640s. The divisions of sexual identity became a resource or memory which could be drawn upon to reshape the experience of the Civil War and 1640s politics. These pamphlets are highly scurrilous, their roots in Aretino seldom disguised, and their content is a mixture of what we might expect (with husbands away at war, sex-starved wives demand relief), and that which is more startling (see above, 47–8).

There were further dramatically expressed doubts concerning the free state. The view of the classical republic as the apogee of civic virtue had a negative counterpart in its image as a place of conspiracy, deceit and ruthless ambition. The young republic of England should not have been surprised to find its early propaganda matched by a fully fledged anti-republican play concerned with the murder of Cicero, *The Tragedy of that Famous Roman Oratour Marcus Tullius Cicero* (1651). The orgy of decapitation at the end of the play suggests a crude attempt to hint ominously at the regicide, but the speeches of Cicero impart a hope for the benefits of the republic (in language which English republicans used) which may in the end have been too good for this world:

> Two things I doe desire, and pray for; one,
> That I may leave the *Roman* people free,
> Th'immortal Gods cannot bestow upon mee
> A greater blessednesse: the other's this;
> That all may meet with a proportion'd fate,
> As their deserts have been unto the State. (Sig. B1v)

The 'Table richly furnished' of the earlier part of the play represents the corruption which Cicero's ideal of a society of eloquent, virtuous orators belies (and it certainly looks forwards to the feast with which the Son is tempted in *Paradise Regained* – another republican resonance). But cutting back the other way, the last lines are a warning to state criminals – the regicides themselves. The play has been seen as the work of a powerful aristocrat – perhaps someone like Wharton or Saye and Sele – who had been influential but found their own power appropriated by the mob, suggesting the wresting of control from the parliamentary grandees by the Independents in the Commons.[92] There has even been the suggestion that the play is a published version of an older play dealing with the dilemmas of aristocratic power in the nation. To this end, the play has been connected with the Greville circle, even (more contentiously) with Greville's anti-tyrant drama itself.[93]

T.B.'s *The Rebellion of Naples* (1649) is not so ambiguous but throughout its quaint (by the late 1640s) inventiveness (delivered with Marlovian extravagance) is a clear message from an absolutist state (Naples) which had tried unsuccessfully to be a popular republic to an oligarchic republic which should be a mixed monarchy:

> Let Kings beware how they provoke
> Their Subjects with too hard a Yoke,
> Let Subjects no rebellion move
> On such premises least it prove,
> As sad a thing . . . (76)

The plot is, so its author claims, based upon a first-hand witness of Massaniello's rebellion. Whether or not all of the events in the play have a basis in reality, an unfortunate Englishman is beheaded by the mob because he is thought to be French (and therefore loyal to the Bourbons) on account of affected dress. In short, he is punished because he appears to be courtly.

Within some communities performance of romance drama continued, thereby keeping alive one of the pre-closure traditions. Thomas Meriton's *The Wandering Lover*, published in 1658, is described as a 'Tragy-Comedie/Being/Acted severall times privately at sundrey places by the Author and his Friends with great applause'. The performance is acknowledged in the preliminaries as a remedy for the times: ''tis full season that our Comick play/Should be now acted in our solemn doom' (Sig. A4v).

Cosmo Manuche, who is styled 'Major' on the title pages of his printed works, produced a number of plays during the Interregnum, the association of some with the Castle Ashby collection implying that they were probably performed there (see below, 86–7). Manuche's work straddles performable drama, such as Meriton's plays, and the transprosed, satirical play pamphlet. *The Just General* and *The Loyal Lovers* were both published in 1652 as tragi-comedies, perhaps an indication of the marketability of this genre, or a signal of the plays' political affiliation. Either way, *The Just General* sophisticatedly buries Stuart hopes in a romance and pastoral setting. The play opens with a cessation of fighting in a war, permitting Arnesius, the young King of Sicily, to fall in love with the lowly but beautiful Aurelia. The King is clearly the young Charles II, whose 'Royal Father' has given him prudent political advice. Direct political parallels are avoided, but the 'melancholy' of late 1640s royalism is derided, while the people are presented as a dangerous mob, who make the general – Bellicosus – king, once Arnesius has left his court to search for the disappeared Aurelia. The pastoral disguises and reconciliation of Arnesius and Aurelia carry unmistakable Caroline echoes, although the urban sub-plot and the apparent references to civil war dramas of rebellion make it very much a product of the 1650s. Artisia and her associates are threatened with death for what is thought to be the abduction and murder of Aurelia, but the moment of execution (taking place on a 'Black Stage') is forestalled and prevented by the revelation of the king's true identity. Bellicosus is presented as a loyal retainer of the crown, a military ruler who is forced for the safety of the kingdom to accept the crown, but one who – like Euarchus in Sidney's *Arcadia* – relinquishes it as soon as the king reveals himself.

The *Loyal Lovers* is a shorter piece set in Amsterdam (a centre for Civil War exiles), and is concerned with the interaction of three 'Loyall Comrades' with some satirised puritan burghers. The play is a farcical pre-empting of *The Three Musketeers*, the Cavalier beaux making off with the daughters of Roundhead bores. We could be presented with three Royalists in exile, but we might equally be in London. The bringing together of a noble couple, Corianus and Apsia, in marriage, retains the romance motif, but it is generally relegated to the comic plot, together with the satirical treatment of Gripe-man, a Committee Man, and Sodome, 'One of the Synod', which Lois Potter sees as an attack on Hugh Peter.[94] There are certainly connections with Samuel Sheppard's dramatic attacks on Peter and other Puritans, but these scenes are less allegorical and grotesque than the anti-Parliament and anti-Cromwell dramas (see above, 80–81).

Some of Manuche's plays were performed in aristocratic households. The manuscripts which survive from the Castle Ashby library give rich evidence of the performances written or sanctioned by James Compton, Earl of Northampton.[95] The collection is a mishmash of dramatic interludes and fragments, famous, obscure and original, which function as a 'war literature' collection in much the same way as do Mildmay Fane's poems. As if to keep the old tradition alive, masque is frequently alluded to. Act 2 of Plautus' *The Captives* is juxtaposed with a tragedy of the Earl of Strafford set in the ancient world. There are translations of Seneca's *Agamemnon* and *Hercules Furens*.[96] The latter was presumably capable of radically different political interpretations, for it is the play consistently cited by republicans, most notably Milton and Nedham. There is a translation of Machiavelli's *Mandragola*, singularly appropriate for Compton because the play concerns in part the return of an exile from Paris. It is entirely adapted to an English context, the central scene being a 'piazza' in Covent Garden, Compton's version of Florence. One manuscript in the series contains a piece of prose called 'The Martird

Monarch',[97] which goes well with another Shakespearean play called 'The Cavaliers',[98] enforcing the link between Compton's interest in tyranny, ancient tragedy and royalist iconography. *Eikon Basilike* is ranked alongside the Bible, while the passage mediates the language of martyrdom: 'hee [Charles I] so continuously laid his scenes by which hee acted on this transitory stage, that he never omitted his publike or private devotions.'[99]

Royalist newsbooks not only used drama; they argued for its reintroduction. *The Parliament Porter* was short-lived, but in the space of its four issues, a reformation of the theatre was advanced. Comedies which mocked Puritans were to be abandoned, but 'it is the lustre and glory of our Nation to have vertue extolled and vice depredated even upon the publike Theater'.[100] The 'vulgar' should be instructed in these 'harmlesse recreations', so that the 'Comick Sock and Tragick Buskin be an adornment, & not a badge of contempt.'

This idea was taken further under the Commonwealth. *A Proposition for Advancement of Moralitie By a new way of Entertainment of the People* (1653, dated 1654) has been conclusively ascribed to Davenant.[101] The influence of Davenant's erstwhile companion in Paris, Hobbes, is evident in this brief proposal for the founding of a kind of masque drama, using masque-like machinery, which would keep the populus in order. Davenant had managed to ingratiate himself with the Protectorate, and it was probably the case that he had established the personnel and means for establishing his new kind of theatre by late 1653. The kind of drama described in *A Proposition* bears some resemblance to the opera which Davenant eventually did write and have performed in the later 1650s – a drama which was heavily censored by Secretary Thurloe and other government servants, and which abandoned all politically sensitive genres (especially tragedy).[102]

The tract itself, however, represents the most wholesale and undiluted influence of *Leviathan*, and incorporates in a compressed way the political and aesthetic ideals voiced in the *Preface* to *Gondibert* (see below, 213–14). Being guided by passions, people tend to be destructive and rebellious. While only encouraging military heroism (so Davenant reads the dominant ethos of Commonwealth England), the new theatre 'takes off that rudeness' by which people 'grow injurious to one another, and impudent towards authority'(2). The people must cease listening to seditious and divisive sermons, and be drugged by the visual and verbal rhetoric of the theatre: 'that Perswasion must be joyned to Force, it can be compar'd no other way then by surprisall of their Eyes and Ears' (11).

The hostility to oratory which moves and which uses reason is enforced by the idea of a heroic theatre that the audience simply receives in a passive manner:

their Eyes might be subdued with *Heroicall Pictures* and change of *Scenes*, their Eares civiliz'd with Musick and wholsom discourses, by some *Academie* where may be presented in a Theater severall ingenious *Mechanicks*, as *Motion* and *Transposition of Lights*, to make a more naturall resemblance of the great and vertuous actions of such as are eminent in Story.(14)

Paradoxes abound no less than in Hobbes. The text assumes that the theatrical representations simply create the desired response in the reader despite the power of moral choosing which classical literary theory assigned to audience members: the only examples of oratory identified are the famous pacifying speeches of Demosthenes and Menenius Agrippa (18). Heroic acts can be 'naturally' represented however exaggerated they are, and this is because in the end (as in *Leviathan*, see below, 160), experience *is* art as well as authority. Davenant seems to be placing his own position very carefully in the tract. On the one hand, he writes against a good deal of Commonwealth polity. On the other hand, he disparages some traditions of the pre-1642 theatre – such as men playing women's parts – as effeminate and 'soft'. This may be more to do with his own desire for a particular kind of theatre, than the simple motive to be cautious with the prevailing powers. In an appeal to the godly, the new theatre will provide dramatic 'parables' as a supplement to faith (23). *The Parliament Porter* (see above, 374 n4) refers to Queen Elizabeth's patronage of the theatres, and if the 'reformation' of the Commonwealth was regarded as a return to a kind of Elizabethan polity, then Davenant's project was to present a morally reformed drama, but one which was as heroic as the plays of the 1580s and 1590s had been.

When Davenant came to have *The First Days Entertainment at Rutland-House* (essentially a dialogue concerned with the moral status of theatrical performance) performed in 1656, his hope for a mass, popular audience was disappointed: the seats were so expensive that only the gentry could afford to attend. Much permitted drama in the 1650s was reserved for the entertainment of visiting foreign dignitaries. This was at odds with Davenant's apparent belief in the education of people – a reflection of Hobbes's own views, derived from his sense psychology, that a mass populace could be so instructed, and that indeed it was the sovereign's duty to do so, although not in any way recognisable by a humanist.[103] Indeed, Davenant had almost automatically slipped in the prefatory material for the *First Days Entertainment* into regarding his drama as a lure to bring the gentry into the city, thereby enhancing the wealth of the citizens.

But the hope for a new theatre was not Davenant's alone. In his prefatory poem to Richard Brome's *A Jovial Crew* (first performed 1642, published 1652), John Hall refers in Davenant-like fashion to plays as 'instructive recreations'. Was the publication of Brome's play part of a campaign – supported by a major republican apologist – to have the theatres open again? As a read text, *A Jovial Crew* – the last play to be performed before the closure of the theatres (see above, 73) – offers perspectives on how the many plays from before the closure, published for the first time or republished, might have been read in a war or Interregnum context. Brome's play presents a society of beggars who prevail for a time in an uneasy utopia of good-humoured deceit, until the resolution, when their threat to magistracy is resolved. The beggars' merry world, when seen in 1642, presents a nostalgic vision of refusal against the division of the state then taking place: 'No fear of war, or state disturbances./No alteration in a commonwealth,/Or innovation, shakes a thought of theirs' (IV.2.ll.91–3).[104] The utopia of 'exalted mirth' takes characters and audience beyond the preying emotional and economic bondage of the world, while the freedom which some of the characters pursue reflects the seeking of liberties in early 1640s London. In late 1650, Samuel Sheppard used Brome's model in his play-pamphlet *The Joviall Crew, Or, the Devill Turn'd Ranter* which traduces Ranter theology as Ovidian orgifying.[105] Enthusiastic utopia turns out to be a misguided and immoral fantasy of desire. Was Brome in 1652 attempting to intervene in the 'reformation of manners' debate at the point when the Commonwealth was attempting to reform its local as well as central practices of governance? Against the never-very-threatening Justice Clack, who wants to curtail the plays of the beggars, *A Jovial Crew* holds out a plea for a kind of social charity, coupled with associations of a lost society of rural pastimes and holidays, even though the harshness of life as a beggar is never forgotten. Rachel, one of squire Oldrent's daughters, offers to personate Utopia in the beggars' play, after which the Poet recommends a plot:

> I would have the country, the city, and the court, be at great variance for superiority. Then would I have Divinity and Law stretch their wide throats to appease and reconcile them; then I would have the soldier cudgel them all together and overtop them all. Stay, yet I want another person. (IV.2.ll.207–12)

That person is a beggar, who impossibly, in a utopian way, represents all of the things which other social roles are not and cannot be, because beggars are free from social responsibilities. Yet the play shows that beggars are also at the mercy of many deprivations. But at this point the play is interrupted by the watch, and 'utopia' is forestalled. Looking back to 1642, this moment uncannily represents theatre closure itself. From a 1652 perspective, the play equivocates between utopia and disciplinary provincial society, never quite making the connection between economy or property and the politics which the situation really demands. It has been argued that *A Jovial Crew* is a remarkable anticipation of the provincial response to civil war – lassitude and the deliberate attempt to avoid or frustrate armed division.[106] By 1652, and in a new age, Brome's play sends up utopianism, magistracy and tub preachers, but can offer no solution to the social dilemmas within or without the play. The role of the players who arrive at the start of Act V in the society of beggars points up the abjection and official 'absence' of players in the Commonwealth, while at the same time asserting them as the agents of political solution – it is they who present the masque of utopia. For John Hall, *A Jovial Crew* may have represented a literary interrogation of society which went beyond the mere travesties offered in royalist quixotic literature, and also beyond the imaginative capacity of the newsbooks which he wrote. Perhaps it would have been performed at the morally reformed, state and self-funded (indeed highly profitable) theatre of James Harrington's utopia, watched over by a benign censor, the 'prelate of the sock', 'Thalia'.[107]

And Harrington would have been amused to see the figure of the censor represented in the opening scene of a very obscure printed play entitled *Lady Alimony; or, The Alimony Lady* (1659), which has rightly been seen as registering the surviving talents of the popular theatres.[108] Davenant's monopoly of performances, his elitism and his rejection of improvised versions of 'representational' drama for the sake of instructive 'opera', are attacked in a play which investigates the relationship between censorship, theatre and social control.

Timon, a misogynistic playwright who laments the passing of public theatres, is permitted by the censor Trillo to have performed his relatively simple 'war of the sexes' play. Alimony – sexual satisfaction – is offered by a set of 'Platonic' ladies, who are out of sorts because their husbands are away at war. Their confidants are men allegorically associated with the urban life of the Commonwealth, such as 'Corranto' (the allegorical inflection of the *Mrs Parliament* play-pamphlets is firmly embedded here), as opposed to gulls like 'Sir Tristram Short-Tool'. The stage is periodically occupied with brutish soldiers and sailors, and there is frequent reference to Commonwealth military and naval exploits. If the confidants' judging of the ladies while sitting on 'Roman Exhedra' is a gentle sending-up of classical republicanism, an idealised Protectorate ruler is figured in the Duke of Seville (where the play is set). Not only does he reconcile apparently cuckolded husbands to mischievous wives, he also condones the kind of popular theatrical entertainment which has so unDavenantishly articulated and answered social and theatrical needs. Timon complains that theatre closure has turned plays into depraved and witless drolleries – a very narrow transprosing – but alimony is an alchemy which will heal the wounds of separation. In the Duke's 'free state', popular theatre responsive in detail to the pressures of life recreates the citizens of the republic.

When the public theatres were refounded under Killigrew and Davenant in the early years of the Restoration, did they reflect in their new drama any elements of the printed drama of the years of closure? If anything, the new drama was more highly, openly and crudely politicised than any previous example. This is exemplified in the metaphorical organisation of Dryden's Prefaces: Crites 'is a very Leveller in poetry'; Jonson 'invades authors like a monarch, and what would be theft in other poets is only victory in him'. The exclusive hyper-royalist 1660s theatre of Dryden, Killigrew and Roger Boyle, Earl of Orrery, did try to make a drama out of civil war forms, juxtaposing Cromwellian satire with a theatrically realised martyrology of the *Eikon Basilike* kind.[109] In this theatre, tragi-comedy, the mixed blessing of the 1640s, is the dominant mode: 'Beginning at the Death of King Charles the First, And Ending with the happy Restauration of King Charles the Second'.[110]

Shocked by the possibility that power need not be monarchical, and that *de facto* rule may prevail over *de jure* claims, early Restoration plays have capricious plots which reflect unpredictable contingency: 'Necessity makes actions Just./'Tis just because 'tis necessary' (*Irena*, (1664) Sig. H1v). So, while the Fletcherian plots of some tragedies, and the attempt to re-popularise the masque, referred back to the theatre of the martyr king, other plays emphasised the now limited nature of monarchical power. It is in this way, Nancy Maguire has argued, that post-1660 drama is inevitably 'split', according to the personalities and reflected presences of two different Stuart kings, an idealist and a pragmatist.[111]

But while the plays themselves were as dependent upon pre-1640 drama as Civil War drama was, the function of drama was in large part now to control. William Clerke suggested in 1662 that plays should 'hinder people from dreaming on rebellion which our late proceedings may at large instruct'.[112] Far from the embarrassment of *The Famous Tragedie*, where Charles I is executed off stage, *Cromwell's Conspiracy* contains the stage direction: 'Executioner cuts off his head'. Now the horror can be presented with full didactic intent.

It has been argued that Dryden's *Aureng-Zebe* (1675) signals the freeing of the drama from Civil War obsessions: 'The audience no longer needed to relive the events of the civil war years, and the domesticity glimpsed in Dryden's earlier plays takes over.'[113] Is this so for the drama as a whole? Possibly not. If anything, a strong and popular play like Otway's *Venice Preserv'd* (1684) merges the domestic and the political more closely for the sake of a condemnation of republics. Here, the split world is inverted: the republic is the low world (represented by the nonsense gurgling orator Antonio ['Nacky, Nacky, Nacky'] who mistakes Aquilina's attempt to murder him for a sexual advance). Honour, friendship and a dislike of corrupt tyranny mark the standards of the conspirators, especially Jaffeir and Pierre, who are themselves torn by fears of sexual treachery by so-called friends and by familial responsibilities. Pierre, who is about to be broken on the wheel for conspiracy, is stabbed mortally by Jaffeir, who also kills himself thus saving both of their honours in the face of a gibberingly awful government, although this leaves Jaffeir's wife, Belvidera, distracted to death.[114]

Such theatrical self-wipe-outs, once the admission of Cavalier defeat (as in *The Famous Tragedie*), are now a means of acknowledging resilience in a fallen world. For this reason, Otway's play is not so far removed from Milton's final triumph *Samson Agonistes* (1671). There is no space here to rehearse the arguments for *Samson* as an attack on the culture of the Restoration theatre.[115] Suffice it to say that its rigid neoclassicism, its *expulsion* of Shakespearean characterisation, its ignoring of Fletcher, and Milton's explicit denial of its performability, make it a textual gunpowder keg under the house of the playwrights. Milton might have claimed a moral role for drama in his Commonplace Book and the anti-episcopal prose, but his attitude changed by the late 1640s (see above, 76). The theatre in ancient Greece and Rome was a collective experience of the meaning of democracy in the republic, and its modern meaning was an internalised, read-only, version of that collective experience.[116] The hero's final destruction of the theatre (and his utter refusal to be hindered by his wife) is a revivification of the humanist anti-persecution drama of George Buchanan, which the English drama had been denying since the late 1580s. Dramas have no end to their obsessions and their politics; they continually reuse them, however the theatrical is permitted to exist.[117] For this reason, the transprosing of the theatres is not a gap in the history of English drama so much as a subject in itself, and an instance of the survival of one form temporarily inside the skin of another.

PART II

Rhetoric, Politics and Religion

CHAPTER 3

The Meaning of the Centre

When political theorists write on early modern political writing (but they call it 'thought' or 'ideas'), they focus, as is proper for their discipline, on the concepts which the language of political tracts can be said to articulate. But there is a great deal more to mid-seventeenth-century political writing. In chapter 1, we saw how the components of rhetorical tradition were embedded in early modern English society and letters. The language of the tracts, the variety of different means by which a position is made or defended, constitutes an extra realm of meaning which a concept-centred analysis might well miss.

This section is therefore concerned with textual elements like structure of argument, quotation and citation – particularly of works which do not necessarily belong within the realm of political discourse, such as poetry and plays. It is also concerned with the components of political tracts which have at first glance nothing to do with the conceptual content of the tracts. In this way, we can view the cultural history of Civil War political or religious ideas and expressions as they were mediated through words.

This is not to say that we should not be interested in the lives of the people who wrote these works, and how their immediate predicaments influenced their writings. It is of course the conjunction of life and action with writing and publication which enables us to understand the role of the written in important public events. Moreover, the significance of any part of a political tract depended upon its readership. It is the case that seventeenth-century readers did not (by and large) read pamphlets with the degree of conceptual subtlety which today's political philosophers can bring to bear on them, even the more narrow and elite readership of longer, sophisticated works.

The publication of pamphlets certainly infringed on the world of political action. Pamphlets were often designed to influence decision-making, and their presence often irritated one source of power or other – the King, the House of Lords, the House of Commons, the Protector. The printed pamphlet was one major way in which extra-parliamentary and extra-court politics could make an impact. Its use alongside that of the crowd still needs to be measured accurately in this period. When and how those with political authority chose to use printed media, and when they did not, is a question to which we shall return.

Political and religious tracts are nonetheless historically important in and of themselves, even if many of them were written very, very quickly and produced shoddily. The pamphlets from which the shifts in arguments between Parliament and King occurred themselves constitute, in most cases, much richer entities than the mere bones of argument. When the purpose of the pamphlet was to persuade or convince, every significant cultural resource which could signify in a pamphlet was used. These elements, which we can collectively call the 'rhetoric' (from the schemes and tropes of an argument, through metaphor and analogy, to quotation and citation), are inextricably part of the argument itself, and equally inextricably part of the pamphlet war. Conal Condren writes that political rhetoric was 'largely a matter of finding the right language *per se* through which to present a persuasive structure of political possibility'.[1] Rhetorics may or may not have been peculiar to the interest or faction they supported. The differentiation between these various ways of representing political life became more exaggerated as the 1640s and 1650s progressed; in effect, as republicanism and royalism emerged from what had once been a relatively homogeneous discourse. When read in context, the 'total' contents of the tracts add to our comprehension of the structure and structuring of early modern political awareness.

But homogeneity in earlier pamphlet literature was complemented by another kind of limit on the political imaginations of English people. It has recently been argued that political debate in English in the early seventeenth century was typified by exclusive languages, belonging to separate institutions – natural law for civilian lawyers; divine right theory in theology.[2] It was only when Charles I was unable to resolve significant differences with his subjects from the 1625 Parliament onwards that these different discourses began to jump out of their institutional boxes, and started to create new, unsettling ideas, arguments and perceptions. The continuation of this situation in the 1640s, with a greater emphasis upon controversial exchange (and the conducting of high politics through such exchange), meant that the power of mutating rhetorics literally began to re-fashion the means by which it was possible to imagine political life. The breaking of boundaries taking place in the late 1620s and 1630s was superseded by an exaggerated and sometimes desperate conflagration.

The interaction of the logic of controversial exchange and extensive debate with the unforeseeable outcome of events (such as battles) produced a new range of theories of state, the individual and their interaction. Theories of religion developed in a similar way. Moreover, the role of discourse and print in defining these entities meant that the book, little or large, was an inextricable part of the new awarenesses. The following four chapters explore that process.

To begin: if a particular debate is isolated, such as that between King and Parliament in the early 1640s, it is possible to show how ideas and their representation shift. Arguments and affective materials have expiry dates for different participants. The 1640s can be seen as a process in which the textual components of the controversy survived or not according to the degree of their utility. In the very early days, before fighting broke out, the difference between parliamentarian apologists and Royalists consisted in whether the monarchical constitution was seen to be 'mixed' or not, or how it was mixed.[3] The acceptance of a mixed constitution by the King coincided with the point at which the usefulness of the 'mixed' constitution idea for the Parliament ceased. At some point between 1644 and 1647, a notion of popular sovereignty emerged which no longer equated the people with their elected representatives in Parliament, but with the populace of the country, or at least all those who were not servants, vagrants or women. A little later, and certainly by the end of the decade, the plausibility of mixed constitution theory and hence the expectation that a settlement with the King might be reached, was replaced by the notion that Charles I himself was guilty for the sufferings of his people, and that he should therefore be punished. In this way, the nation would purge itself of 'blood-guilt'.[4] Later still, apologists for the new regime appeared to go back on their old resistance to ideas of passive obedience by urging people to be obedient to the new *de facto* rulers of the country. Absolutism – the notion that unlimited and indivisible sovereignty was the only possible political order – came slowly and never really completely for the English, despite the great appeal of patriarchal concepts of order.[5]

But how are such accounts to be extracted from the textual soup of the pamphlet page, without damaging the sense of multiple materials and perspectives meeting in one moment? How can we account for Prynne's introduction into the pamphlet arena of vast and complex agglomerations of textually represented legal precedent? These printed kaleidoscopes of juridical traces worked their way through the parliamentary consensus, enabling it finally to fragment.

The process of 'splitting' that concerns us here did not happen in a straightforward way, with one protagonist developing one idea or form of expression, to be controverted by an opponent. Instead, in several very important instances, authors suggested their enemy's future positions by giving voice to a fictional view of where they feared their opponents were in the present (or where they wished their readers to see their opponents). Far too much has been claimed for the import of the iconic nature of royalist literature, without appreciating the extent to which parliamentary apology stretched the shape of royalist discourse in very un-iconic ways. As we shall see, republicanism was explicitly suggested in pamphlets defending the prerogative of Charles long before a language of republicanism developed in the later 1640s. This is analogous to the time gap between the royalist accusation that the Parliamentarians believed in popular sovereignty and the wholehearted acceptance of these ideas in 1648 and 1649. Hobbes's nearly unwitting defence of the republic's *de facto* rule, in spite of his royalism, and the use made by some Royalists of John Lilburne as an example and victim of parliamentary tyranny, are, in this light, ironies left by history to posterity.[6]

Juggling Models: Parliamentary and Monarchical Apology

The King says; the Parliament denies; the King commands, the Parliament forbids: The King says the Parliament is seduced by a traitorous faction; the Parliament says the King is seduced by a Malignant Party: The King says the Parliament tramples upon his crown; the Parliament says the King intends War upon them: to whether now is the Subject bound to adhere?

Henry Parker, *Observations* (1642; RPECW, 50)

The King: In and Out of Parliament

When, by the summer of 1642, royal government had collapsed, Parliament attempted to control the King's power, and an exchange of views occurred as Charles defended his prerogative. In this exchange, positions and definitions mutated and blurred. *His Majesties Answer to the Nineteen Propositions of Both Houses of Parliament* (1642) was a 'voicing' of Charles by Lord Falkland and Sir John Culpepper: they turned the King into merely one of the three estates (while at the same time retaining major aspects of his absolute authority).[7] This middle ground was further exploited by the parliamentarian cleric Philip Hunton in *A Treatise of Monarchy* (1643). Hunton's strategy is to present all opinions as correct: 'Thus it appears that they which say there is *divinum quiddam* in sovereigns, and that they have their power from God, speak, in some sense, truth; as also they which say that originally power is in the people may in a sound sense be understood' (*DRD*, 177). The power of equivocation is enhanced by devoting extra space to those *non*-English political orders, so that we know the difference between black and white. Absolute monarchy is given a long section, 'though it does not concern us' (*DRD*, 182). In a 'mixed' monarchy, the crisis of the 'frame of government' comes with the question of who should judge a transgressing monarch. No part of the constitution can have the power to judge without compromising the very idea of a mixed monarchy. Hunton suggests that in extraordinary circumstances, there might be petitioning and ultimately even active resistance (of which he was very wary), but that this should be founded upon the laying open of the fundamental laws to the whole kingdom, so that every man may 'follow the evidence of truth in his own soul' (*DRD*, 188). And this power of judging should be moral. In other words, at the moment of resistance, and within the carefully equivocating description of Hunton's mixed monarchy, will is dissolved into an image of painful incertitude. Popular consent to a ruler is fundamental, but then in circumstances of conquest, people either give their moral consent to be governed by the conqueror (so that a new social contract is made), or they refuse consent, in which case they owe the conqueror no duty, but they may risk death. The synthesis again barely holds. If the three estates are at odds on any issue, allegiance is due to no one single estate without destroying mixed monarchy. So, 'non-decision' should be adhered to if tolerable (and this would encourage social cohesion), but if not, then again, there must be a collective soul-searching for allegiance in the light of that which 'stands for public good against the destructive' (*DRD*, 211).

Henry Parker was more direct and the most influential of the defenders of parliamentary authority. His *Observations Upon Some of His Majesties Late Answers and Expresses* (1642) roots popular sovereignty in natural law and an image of Edenic popular freedom. To this was added a notion that popular sovereignty, where the people originally conferred power on the king, was commensurate with the 'fundamental laws' of the kingdom, and for the parliamentarian apologists, this meant the constitution of the mixed monarchy.[8] As another important apologist, Charles Herle, put it: 'Their very stile *Comites* and *Peeres* imply in *Parliament* a *coordinative Society* with his *Majesty* in the *government*; they are in *Parliament* his *Comites*, his *Peeres.*'[9] The policies of the King and his ministers had, it was felt, violated the constitution. And by reference to scripture, the notion of mutual responsibilities could be reinforced, such as the covenant made between David and the Israelites when he became king (1 Chron. 11:2–3).[10] Moreover, despite the gaps in evidence for some of the Middle Ages, it was argued that the Norman Conquest had not abrogated the constitution as it had come to exist for the Anglo-Saxons. Within this constitution, it was the King's duty to protect his subjects, since *salus populi suprema lex*. This responsibility Charles I was not meeting.

Parliamentary apology was nonetheless cautious, for no one wanted to encourage popular insurrection or the abandonment of established privileges. 'I am as zealously addicted to Monarchy, as any man can, without dotage' said Parker (*RPECW*, 57). Yet in response, the royalist theorists generated a myth of kingship the richness of which had never been seen before. It laid the foundations for the contents of Charles's famous and extremely popular defence *Eikon Basilike* (1649), published just after his execution. Much of the contents of the royalist publications have been insufficiently explored.

For Royalists, the belief that the King corresponded on earth to God's power in heaven, thus discounting any claims to the original consent of the people in establishing monarchy, was as comprehensively substantiated as it was widespread, drawing on scriptural, rhetorical and logical resources to confirm itself. Often such writings were produced in response to Henry Parker's arguments for popular sovereignty, where the patriarchal analogy itself was derided as but rhetoric, 'some excellency in Princes by way of similitude' (*RPECW*, 49). Here is an example of logic from John Jones's *Christus Dei, Or, A Theological Discourse* (Oxford, 1642):

> Arg. 1 There is a rule in nature (to use the observers owne words) *Quod dat esse dat consequentia ad esse*. But the *esse* of a Republique cannot have a *simpliciter esse* without the *esse* of this power. Therefore he that is the Efficient cause of the Republique, is also the Efficient cause of this power. But (as I have prov'd before 2 n 5) God is the sole efficient cause of all Republiques, therfore he is also the sole efficient cause of this power. (9–10)[11]

Reason, a refraction of God's will, orders the structure of society as if it were mathematically proven. On earth, monarchical authority, like God's authority, is inescapable. Similar appeals to cosmological certainties were made by William Ball:

> Dominions are to Monarchs, as it were, material subjects, themselves (from whom their names result) as Formes. Now as the Form is more worthy then its matter, so is a free Monarch more worthy than this Empire, in respect of dignity politicall.[12]

A people are not bigger than a king, then, and this kind of reasoning drew equally ingenious responses from Parliamentarians. For instance, one author argued that kings cannot be divine institutions because they are not everywhere ubiquitous.[13]

Reason and more emotive appeals were used by Peter Heylyn in the less academically aimed *The Rebells Catechism* (Oxford, 1643), which quotes Elizabethan homilies against rebellion, portrayed as a version of Satan's original rebellion. Illogical absurdities which are the result of rebellions, such as the idea of a 'defensive' war by subjects against their monarch, are smaller parts of the total whole of human rebelliousness or sin – the 'rebellion of the tongue', the 'rebellion of the hand' (2–5). Parliamentarian political activity is presented as basic, profane disobedience. It leads to a frightening fragmentation.

In this more accessible discourse, a greater variety of tactics is employed. Gruesome rebels in English history are paraded, such as the Earl of Essex, father to Parliament's commander-in-chief. The sophistry of Parliamentarians and resistance theorists – Prynne and Buchanan – is ridiculed by dramatic reference. Buchanan's justification of resistance by stressing the distinction between office and person (fight the tyrant, not the institution of kingship itself) is seen as like the character Sosia in Plautus' comedy *Amphitrion*, at odds with himself and in two places at once (20). A more dangerous kind of literary doubleness is envisaged in another royalist apology:

> this [dispute] should expose us to so great an adventure, as not only to divest him of this suspected Arbitrary power, but to conferre an absolute Government to any whatsoever, renders no other axiom then the Poets, *Incidit in Scyllam capiens vitare Carybdim*.[14]

And poetry stays with Robert Mossom's reverence for kings: '*The People to their Soveraigns' Scepter brings/Their awfull reverence, and to* Jove, *their Kings*.'[15] The mythic is at the heart of this kind of apology: it is used liberally, and to the point of fantasy, to fashion and embellish an image of ineffable royal power. In disputing with Jeremiah Burroughs on the issue of allegiance, Henry Ferne's *Conscience Satisfied* (Oxford, 1643) uses the Cadmus myth, and the mythical figure of Orpheus, to suggest the primitive nature of parliamentarian theory – later, of course, Orpheus would be used as a name for Charles I in post-regicide laments (see below, 290):[16]

> the must suppose a multitude of people meeting together to contrive a Government, and these either to spring on a suddain out of the Earth, as *Cadmus* his race, but then in all likelyhood they would not so well agree; or to live dispersedly in Caves and woods, and so be brought together by some rude *Orpheus* his pipe, but then we cannot imagine such Rude men to be so Politique and Cautious as to make such a contrivement, for he tells us that the *Reason* which we see in this State is that same *Reason* that first contrived the Government when they made the first King. (9–10)

The prominent placing of these elements allows Ferne to expose the use by Parliamentarians (especially Parker) of both the analogy of the state as a building as well as their use of English history. Most bizarre of all, Ferne makes Burroughs's hard-hitting rhetoric appear as a theatrical decoration, precisely that which it is not. Burroughs has:

> set before his booke a Premonition (wherein he has painted out the

Resolver under severall shades of birds and beasts, as his flitting phansy led him a very piece of Pictured Tapestry, fitter to hang before the entrance of a Stage, then of a treatise concerning Conscience. ([Sig.]2v)

Royalist propaganda creates on the printed page a vision of royal authority like that which had been projected in the entertainments of the Caroline court.[17]

As we saw in chapter 2, a kind of reportage began to operate once the war was underway, and it is interesting that Heylyn cites the parliamentary newsbook *Mercurius Britanicus* more than once. Heylyn notes the ferocity of parliamentary fire against the King's person at the Battle of Edgehill, a particular instance of treachery, in much the same way that Bruno Ryves was to present parliamentary brutality in *Mercurius Rusticus* (see above, 63–4). *Passive* resistance should be the only response to tyranny, says Heylyn, significantly deploying the example of Roman citizens not rebelling against the tyrant Julian, but only using prayers and tears. In Heylyn's writing, apology (such as we see in Ferne) and journalism merged to find a bigger readership.

The writings of Dudley Digges (who died of disease in October 1642, while serving in the King's army) belong in one important sense to a separate tradition from most other Royalists (see below, 112–13). He was concerned to show that the subject's right of self-preservation could be renounced, and in this sense he and the other writers in the Tew Circle were involved in the same debate as the parliamentarian apologists.[18] However, while for Digges, representatives cannot be above kings, the fact that for him the opposite is being argued in parliamentary apology is an admission of the existence of an English republicanism, at the very least in the universe of discourse. There are long trawls through classical history because 'the same Artes which made *Rome* miserable, are visible in our calamities.'[19] When *Mercurius Aulicus* compares Charles I to a Greek or Roman leader, he could have had Caesar in mind, and equally, Pompey. Either way, it is the *virtus* which is usually associated with republican heroes which seems to matter:

That the King did not suffer His Souldiers to want anything, and therefore, that he had no need of the *Roundhead's* money; a gallant and magnanimous speech: and such, as it had been spoken in the times of the *Greeks* and *Romans*, would have beene honoured with a place in the most famous of their histories.[20]

A few pages before Digges has said that the conditions of Athens, Sparta and Rome do not apply to England. In terms of a consideration of different constitutional traditions and political languages, there is indeed no comparison to be made. In terms of a structural analysis which considers constitutions and power relationships, there clearly is a comparison. The Parliament, or a faction within it, is compared to an 'Appian decemvirate', which threatens not only to corrupt the minds of subjects with its propaganda, but also to control the army, thereby imposing an illegal absolute sovereignty or an unstable aristocracy or republic (which for Digges means a popular democracy).[21]

Echoes of ancient civil disorder rebound elsewhere throughout royalist apology: 'Not as *Caesars* Captaine Petitioned the Romane Senate (as *Plutarch* relates it) with his Hand on the Pummell of his Sword . . . '.[22] An anonymous royalist poet agreed with Hobbes in rooting such practice in the classical education of gentlemen at university: Cambridge undergraduates and Inns of Court students posture 'wth Scorpions taile/ Pretendinge Greekish liberty to raile'.[23] For Digges, republican thinking (so he has chosen to construe Parker's *Observations*) is a conceit, and to make Parliament the '*Assembly* of some mere popular *Republique*' is to take away from it that which makes it most English.[24] Thomas Morton agreed. Parliament had styled itself 'The perpetuall Senate, or Assessours of the kingdom, as some have endeavoured to derive their stile, as the Impresse of a Republick'.[25] In any case, ancient assemblies were originally elected as bodies to disseminate royal authority rather than to represent the people. Parliament in this frightened vision becomes the puppy of the *hoi polloi*:

> Now Division being almost inevitable, and power of dissenting necessary for ballancing the three differing parts of Parliament, to prevent this power of dissenting, were to destroy the ballance and being of Parliaments, and to make them Courts of popularity, where they that please the People should absolutely carry all things.[26]

Classicism also becomes a way of ridiculing parliamentarian apologists on the level of its very mythopoeic nature. In Henry Ferne's view, parliamentarian defence depends upon an unprovable fiction. And in establishing his own royalism, Ferne criticised the use of Plato and Aristotle as the foundation for political analysis, while identifying in classical sources (and at a very early stage as far as this belief was publicly acknowledged in the 1640s) arguments for the deposition of the King.[27] Foreseeing the 'killing' of monarchy, Digges sees the reduction of the order of state to a farce, where 'liberty and property must be sacrificed to a few ambitious mens *ragioni di stato*', and where government becomes comedy:

> if his [the King's] part in Parliament be the same with the flatterers in the comedy, *Aris, aio, negas, nego*; if he be but a *State eccho*, it is manifest he hath not so great a hand in the managing of his Kingdome.[28]

Far better the fidelity encouraged by feudal laws.

In reply to the basis of Parker's argument, that power is originally inherent in the people, Digges attempts to place the notion beyond the imaginable (unlike Ferne), and he does this not only with logic, but with images which come in part from Parker, and which were turned round by Milton in his defence of toleration:

> As for Power inherent in the People, how should we imagine such a thing? unlesse also he would imagine People to be *juvenes aquilone creati*; men like *grashoppers* and *locusts* bred of the winde, or like *Cadmus* his men sprung out of the earth; where none deriving from any pre-existent Parents, had all of them equall originall and power, and therefore subject to no civill Power but what by agreement they themselves ordained? But where man is borne of a Father, to whom by the Law of God and nature he is subject, he is so farr from having Power originally in him, as that he hath not his own originall being but only in subjection; either to his immediate Father, if his Father were absolute, or to him and his common Father, if his Father were a Subject.[29]

It is difficult to believe that, given the sophistication of his prose, Digges conceived of the people as anything more than the educated members of the political nation. Despite his castigation of over-fertile parliamentarian imaginations, Digges has had to have recourse to dense imagistic and generic reference to make his polemic work: it has broken boundaries for him. Moreover, Digges has a curious way of pre-empting radical arguments which would be made in the later 1640s while casting them in his own absolutist terms. For instance, the Leveller Richard Overton's definition of everyone as a king, priest and prophet in their 'own naturall circuit and circumference' is imagined as but part of the many kingdoms of a single king:

> If Princes be *Kings, Lords, Fathers, Heads,* &c.: to the single persons of the Subject only, and not to the universality of them, then is every single Subject by himselfe alone a body politique, whereof the King, as King, is Head, and so hath as many Kingdomes as Subjects. (4)

A more extreme divine right theorist was John Maxwell, a deposed Scottish bishop, whose *Sacro-Sancta Regum Majestas* appeared in 1644. All kings, says Maxwell, are Christ's vice-regents, and he attacks a number of populist political ideas. These are again rendered as myths in order to devalue them: the Cadmus myth, that men spring equally out of the earth, is noticed and rejected. Patriarchal authority is affirmed from Exodus (20), Aristotle's *Ethics* and *Politics*, and Book 1 of Homer's *Odyssey* (87). Like Digges, Maxwell imagines with contempt a republic, but not one based on ancient Rome so much as the utopias of Plato and More (106). A republic is a flat world with no authority and thus it is indeed a no place: how could it be a *respublica* at all (146)? (146) Throughout his book, Maxwell has stressed the unity of church and state, and he ends with the unifying visions in Augustine's *City of God* (5.5.24), which for him are 'golden expressions worthy to be set in letters of gold' (189). The figure of a unified, static harmony is complete.

Digges was also less uncompromising in his royalism than an ultra-hard *jure divino* apologist like John Doughty, sometime Fellow of Merton College. The learned literariness of the academy is seldom invisible in Doughty's unsigned *The Kings Cause* (1644).[30] Doughty uses Greek iconic concepts, some of them derived from Homer, to deify Charles: 'the truest and liveliest image of God upon earth' (3); 'we find in scripture the seat of royall judicature, as usually termed the *Throne* of God, as the Kings *Throne*, and themselves barely the Deputies or Ministers of Men, but Gods *Ministers*, his peculiar substitutes' (2). Such procedures were common to the divine right theorists publishing in Oxford during the first half of the Civil War. Edward Symmons, who is credited with innovating imagery in 1648 akin to *Eikon Basilike*, and with having a hand in that text, was propagating the image of royal martyr soon after the King announced his intention of defending himself in print in early 1642.[31] Symmons's language is remarkable, and possibly even a reflection of very early composition by the King of sections of what later became his full posthumous apology: 'a Christian *King* is also the *Image* of Christ as God'.[32] Here are visible the aesthetic terms upon which *Eikon Basilike* was to be written, and we cannot be surprised to find Milton constructing his iconoclastic aesthetic at the end of the 1640s (see above, 16–18) in terms which exactly correspond to those of Symmons and Doughty. There is even a sense of the iconography of the Stuart court masques invading this pamphlet as Doughty likens Charles's ancestry to the legendary King Agamemnon, 'fetching it downe from *Vulcan* to *Iupiter*, from *Iupiter* to *Mercury*, from *Mercury* to *Pelops*, and so onwards' (8).

But the image of anarchy is one somewhat altered from the always-controlled rabble of the Caroline anti-masque. Doughty brings together a series of stereotypes which were to become associated with and used by Royalists for the next fifteen years. The 'resistance' (it is his general word for the Parliament and the Puritans) reminds him of the *Bellum rusticum*, the Helots War or the Peasants War of early sixteenth-century Germany. Against the true pastorship of Charles are the 'pulpit barristers' who force 'by their powerfully delusive persuasions' the people like 'silly *Sheep* as they are (almost without the help of a Metaphor) into daily slaughter' (33). The supposed inspiration of the Holy Spirit among sectarians leads to linguistic anarchy:

ere long the written word must be thrown downe by as too straight, and concludent to the Spirit, and this moreover with a scoffe crying *Bibel, Babel, Bubel*; A Scheme much like to that in the old Poet, *Tite, Tuti, Tate, Tibi*, &c. ([Ennius, *Annals*, I. 1, p.104]; 35)

By 1647, the substance of royalist apology may not have changed very much from its profile early in the decade. But if we look at the publications of these later years, they are becoming if not nostalgic, then certainly devoid of a sense that the arguments have an urgent purchase on events. Robert Grosse's *Royalty and Loyalty* (1647) is a good example. The First Civil War had been won by Parliament, the King was in captivity, a settlement of some form was expected by most. Despite the unquiet in London, with Leveller activity and royalist and Presbyterian dissent, this work cannot square its calls for passivity with any form of royalist resistance or a diplomatic regard for the negotiations with the King, already under pressure from a dissatisfied Army. *Royalty and Loyalty* is in no sense a martyrological work, or an 'absolutist' one, but it seems very strange, quaint even, for royal prerogative to be stressed as a tax or 'custom', and for citizen-subjects (Grosse carefully elides the two categories) to love their prince. When Sophocles is cited on the great evil of anarchy, we are moving away from the earlier confident royalist use of dramatic allusion towards the tragic dimensions of post-regicide complaint. Ultimately, royalist and anti-royalist polemic interacted in a movement towards the generation of genuine republican theory and practice.

Absolutely the King

Where Digges's writing is distinguished by its echoes and allusions to a wide variety of sources, if only to reach the conclusion that the king is the whole of the law and the only representative of the people, Sir Robert Filmer's writing works by bluntly listing authorities, both those from which he draws support and those he attacks. *Patriarcha* is a difficult document to interpret because we do not know when precisely it was written, and therefore to which immediate controversial contexts it might belong.[33] Anti-Catholic and ultra-Protestant prejudice abounds, and any arguments that man is originally or innately free, or that the people have the right to punish or resist a prince, are rebutted. Filmer vehemently asserts that men are not originally free or equal. This does not mean that they cannot be free but that their greatest freedom is when they live under a monarchy. Indeed, Filmer is fond of taking classical texts popular with Parliamentarians and republicans and finding in them quotations that serve his turn: Lucan, *Pharsalia*: 'the liberty of a people which is subject to royal government is lost if they gain too great liberty' (3.II.145–6); Claudian, *De Consulatu Stilichonis*: 'Nor is there any more welcome liberty than to be subject to a good master' (3.II.114–15).[34]

Most of Filmer's works were written against parliamentarian apologists during the 1640s. When his cause failed, Filmer resorted to commentary on Aristotle and recent political writing, in a manner consistent with the greater openness of speculation that typifies Interregnum political theory. Throughout his works, Filmer argues (notably against Hunton) that a monarchy which is not absolute is a contradiction in terms. In *The Anarchy of a Limited or Mixed Monarchy* (1648), there is a rare expression, in near-mystical terms, of why it is that primitive equality cannot be:

> In assemblies that are by human politic constitution, the superior power that ordains such assemblies can regulate and confine them, both for time, place, persons, and other circumstances. But where there is an equality by nature, there can be no superior power. There every infant at the hour it is born in, hath a like interest with the greatest and wisest man in the world. Mankind is like the sea, ever ebbing or flowing, every minute one is born another dies. Those that are the people this minute, are not the people the next minute. In every instant and point of time there is a variation. No one time can be indifferent for all mankind to assemble.[35]

Changeability then becomes the basis of the argument for stability through authority. And although Filmer explicitly uses an image applicable to any period of time, the sense of uncertainty in these words suggests that the image is articulating Filmer's unease at the politics of 1647–8. Someone once must have summoned the people, and Adam being the first father was also the first king. All assemblies, and especially those in the Franco-British tradition, are summoned by the king in order to receive justice and commands. Such assemblies are always subordinate, especially assemblies of the commons: 'the president for the commons begins and ends his oration on his knees'; 'the Lords are to treat and to give counsel'; 'the Commons are to perform and consent to what is ordained.'[36] Even kings elected by a nobility must accept his absolute power after the election. In conceding that the legal precedents for parliamentary privilege are uncertain, Henry Parker is showing, says Filmer, that in actuality there is no parliamentary court which can bind the monarch.[37] Kings have the law in their breasts and cannot give up this power in any way to judges. The logic which makes populist arguments disappear is devastating, but we are never allowed to forget an anthropologically described sense of the abasing behaviour which monarchs require from their subjects. True majesty must be felt, and the vision is one of a seventeenth-century primitive monarchical community.

Filmer believes the concept of mixed monarchy to be an invention with no historical precedent. Mixed *government* Filmer finds first in Machiavelli, whose respect for the Roman republic in the *Discourses* had to concede an element of monarchy in the Roman Commonwealth. There is almost a sense of Machiavelli becoming a villain of political theory in Filmer's eyes, as he was in moral terms in the popular imagination. Filmer explicitly takes his lead from Jean Bodin's absolutist theories, which he claims expose the errors of Polybius, Machiavelli and Contarini – all apologists for popular government. Mixed monarchy, being self-contradictory, can only be 'fancy . . . a better piece of poetry than policy'.[38] Consultation and the balance of different voices from different constituencies in a nation are anarchy and sedition.

If *Patriarcha* was to be Filmer's most influential piece, the *Observations Upon Aristotle's Politiques* (1652) is the most interesting. It is an undeniably monarchical, anti-populist commentary on the *Politics*, in the context of the large body of republican theorising which went on after the execution of Charles I. With the exception of a few writers (Ascham for instance) and those referred to in the other post-regicide works (Grotius, Hobbes, Milton), there is little direct reference to contemporary theorists, despite the acknowledgment that 'original power by nature in the people . . . is the only theme now in fashion'.[39] Notable absences are Hall and Nedham (see below, 182–90), in the final postscript on obedience and usurpation, the reader is left to guess at which pro-Engagement writers are in Filmer's mind, if any.

Aristotle is treated as a kind of comic political theorist, rather than the majestic authority of the Middle Ages and backbone of some republican thinkers: an instance of Filmer's sense of his own modernity. His drive to classify, and, asserts Filmer, his reluctance not to offend any city or state by ranking one form of government above another, resulted in a confusion of parts and kinds of the Commonwealth, so confused, 'crabbed and broken', that modern politicians can make no use of him. His solution was to root political dynamics in wealth (as Harrington was later to do), rather than in roles. Despite Filmer's measure of respect for Aristotle, Greek political thought is, to a large extent, doomed to failure. It is the Bible which provides the account of the origins and descent of kingship, and without it the ancients were hamstrung, despite comments like Plato's 'the king is as a god amongst men'.[40] Those who attempt to recreate a politics based upon the 'independent multitude' (civil lawyers, Grotius, Selden, Hobbes, Ascham) are not only 'running after the opinions of philosophers and poets' in vain, they are also 'bringing in atheism'. The Law of Nature is really the moral law and consistent with patriarchal kingship.[41] 'Slave' and 'tyrant' did not exist as words in the original scripture, and neither did the names 'aristocracy', 'democracy', 'commonweal', 'state'. Furthermore, Aristotle's four types of government (a 'new conceit') came not from the *Politics* but, out of decorum, from the *Rhetoric*.[42] The accommodation of classical institutions to biblical politics which is found in civil lawyers, republicans, and Fifth Monarchists is quite simply denied.[43] In no sense was the political order of the Israelites ever popular, as far as Filmer was concerned.

What Filmer finds to admire in Plato and Aristotle is their acknowledgment that patriarchal authority was original, and from Aristotle, the statement that monarchy is the 'first and divinest' kind of government; nowhere is it represented as 'mixed' or deriving from popular permission. Filmer's Aristotle denies popular government and representation, and regards democracy as 'a corrupted sort of government'. By this interpretation of Aristotle, Filmer is able to detect the elitist in Milton.[44] The strength of the Romans depended upon the republic retaining monarchical principles in the consuls after the expulsion of the monarch (and not, as Machiavelli says, on the collective strength of free and armed citizens). For once, Filmer departs even from Bodin in denying the popular nature of Roman government. This is beginning to look like the kind of juggling with constitutional models one finds in Hobbes and Harrington, and there are Hobbesian passages on the necessity of curbing religious authority: *jussus populi* is really *jussus consulum*.[45]

But here, Filmer's patriarchalism sets him apart and also rather thwarts him. The banishment of the last Roman king, Tarquin, for his son's rape of Lucrece (the event which precipitated the Roman republic), is in a sense the most fitting punishment in a society favouring patriarchal and kinship values. Remarkably, Filmer errs here to side with the elder Tarquin. Surely, there should have been a petitioning of the father for the punishment of his offending son (possibly betraying Filmer's blindness to Roman customs).[46] And then Filmer proceeds to let the younger Tarquin off the hook by suggesting that Lucrece cared more about her reputation than her real chastity. Not that 'she was asking for it', but that by overvaluing her reputation, when the crucial moment came, she effectively became a whore:

> without wrong to the reputation of so chaste a lady as Lucrece is reputed to be, it may be said she had a greater desire to be thought chaste than to be chaste. She might have died untouched and unspotted in her body if she had not been afraid to be slandered for inchastity. Both Dionysius Halicarnasseus and Livy, who both are her friends, so tell the tale of her as if she had chosen rather to be a whore than to be thought a whore.[47]

And this, claims Filmer (rather flimsily), allows us to find no other reason for the expulsion of the Tarquins but that the Romans were wanton and licentious. The defender of patriarchal kingship smears the birth of a republic with the taint of female selfishness and vainglory. Rome was only great when it relied upon the monarchical power of fathers over children (even to the extent of killing their own children).[48]

Towards the end of the *Observations*, Filmer finds similar confusion in the free states in Europe. The Dutch are hampered because no one would accept their offer of a throne (Filmer makes no mention of the

Stadhouder), and they are consequently blighted by high taxes as well as divergence of religious practice. Venice is a republic only because it is a city, and has a very unusual natural disposition. The peculiarly complex system of representation there tends to a perversion of all forms of government. Everyone seems to represent everyone else, so that the Venetians 'are constrained to epitomise and sub-epitomise themselves so long till at last they crumble away into the atoms of monarchy, which is the next degree of anarchy'.[49]

These observations give a good sense of the forceful logic underlining Filmer's view of monarchical authority. Just as Digges was casting the English Parliament into the role of destructive republican senate, so Filmer was demolishing the sympathetic interpretation of the history of the Roman republic. In order to do this, he enhanced the patriarchal nature of his ideas with some startling anti-feminism.

Posthumously Iconic

As the negotiations between King and Parliament after the First Civil War faltered, and the hopes for a settlement between the parties became overshadowed by the emergence of sentiments, notably in the Army, for the punishment of the King, royalist polemic changed its direction and nature. The Royalists had lost their battle to maintain royal prerogative and divine right, and like royalist imaginative literature, royalist polemic lapsed into open anger and lament at the failure of its cause. The sophisticated and learned defences of the earlier parts of the decade, Ferne, Digges and the other respondents to Parker's *Observations*, gave way to a vituperative writing which owed more to the impulsive gesturing of newsbooks.

The author of *Independency Stript & Whipt* (1648) 'trembles' with rage, as if the orator were ready to punch his audience. This time it is the Parliamentarians and sectarians who are drowning the world in blood and eating tongues (censoring). The imagery of violence is rather less obviously biblically based, making more use of the classical idea of an underworld. Most noticeable is the pressure of the language of Independency, which was already beginning to bear republican overtones. 'Written by a lover of his *Country*, for the information of all such who hate *Slavery*, and love to live *Freemen*,' claims the sarcastic title page, while later on free states are labelled as tyrannies, and the speaker spits out disbelief at the phrase for the elect which circulated in the gathered churches: 'babes of grace'. Two works are singled out for vilification: *Ireton's Petition* and *The Royal Project*.[50] The sense of incipient tragedy is shared with republican discourse, but of course from the other side of the coin. The element of stoical humanism that

Figure 4 *Eikon Basilike* (1649), frontispiece by William Marshall.

Figure 5 Detail from *A List of all the Princes, Dukes, Lords, Knights, Generals* (1652).

was to be used by Commonwealth apologists is identified in the writings of Justus Lipsius who is attacked for his own criticism of James I and Charles I.[51]

So it was that Charles I came to be his own, or at least, his own co-authored, martyr in *Eikon Basilike* (1649), claimed as the most popular book of the century, and one in which Charles managed posthumously to outstrip Lilburne in the suffering stakes. So much has been written of *Eikon Basilike* that it may seem little more can usefully be added. From its first critical reader, the author of *Eikon Alethine* (1649), there have been a long line of distinguished commentaries on the iconic and imagistic nature of the text.[52] The iconoclastic responses of Milton and others in the early 1650s confirmed the iconic status of *Eikon Basilike*, while the strange mixture of tenses within it, and the last-minute change of title, point to the interrupted composition of the work, and the final assembly of its components by hands other than Charles's (see fig. 4).[53] What should be noticed too, however, is the constitutional nature of the work. The text may be unusually dense with metaphor, and it may be punctuated with prayers, but Charles and his co-author respond consistently to the charges made by parliamentarian apologists since the early 1640s.[54] To this extent, *Eikon Basilike* belongs with the line of royal apologies that had been constructing the icon of kingship. In every historical event focused upon, from the calling of the Long Parliament onwards, the voice of the King claims that he has acted quite legally, quite within the bounds of the constitution. The combination of political analysis of the 1640s with the carefully structured affective imagery is what makes *Eikon Basilike* so powerful. The section 'Upon the Insolency of the Tumults' uses the imagery of the ship of state to a degree hitherto unknown in controversial literature, and to the extent that the narrative of *Eikon Basilike* begins to resemble a romance (see below, 234–44). A long quotation is necessary to catch the effect:

> Some may interpret it as an effect of Pusillanimity for any man for popular terrours to desert his publique station. But I think it a hardinesse, beyond true valour, for a wise man to set him self against the breaking in of a Sea; which to resist, at present, threatens imminent danger; but to withdraw, gives it space to spend its fury, and gaines a fitter time to repaire the breach. Certainly a Gallant man had rather fight to great disadvantages for number and place in the field, in an orderly way, then skuffle with an undisciplined rabble.
>
> Some suspected and affirmed that I meditated a Warre, (when I went from *Whitehall* onely to redeem My Person, and Conscience from violence) God knowes I did not then think of a Warre. Nor will any prudent man conceive that I would by so many former, and some after Acts, have so much weakned My selfe, if I had purposed to engage in a

Warre, which to decline by all meanes, I denyed My self in so many particulars: 'Tis evident I had then no Army to flie unto, for protection, or vindication.[55]

In the following decade, where we can uncover royalist thinking from martyrological lament or attempts at compromise with the Commonwealth regimes, we find the concern with representation just as strong as it was for anti-Royalists. For Davenant, to make every subject a statesman (or we might say, a prophet) by endowing them with puritan sobriety is to place an excessive burden on the people. Only the representatives of the people should be sober.

Neither did the idea and presence of kingship ever disappear, as the attempt to make Cromwell king showed. Cromwell himself wanted a constitution with 'something of the monarchical' in it. The trappings of kingship look slightly out of shape, but nonetheless recognisable when lent to Cromwell, here in a manuscript poem collected by Thomason:

K. Cromwell (O)

It is I

Ascend three thrones, great Captaine Divine
By the Will of god (O Lion) for th'are thine
Come priest of god bring oyle, bring robes, & gold
Bring Crownes & Sceptres, itts now high time, unfold
your cloistred baggs [?]. you state cheats, Least ye rod
Of steele & Iron of ye King of god
Chastise you all wth wrath, then kneele and pray
To Oliver ye torch of Zion Starre of day
Then shout O Merchants, Citts, & Gentry sing.
Let all men bare heads cry. God save the King

Thomason noted 'written under his picture . . . and hung upon ye Exchange', on 19 May 1653. A longer heroic poem published later in the decade argues that Cromwell should have been made king, but it uses the language of the 'free state' with no sense of guilt or contradiction.[56] Less compromising publications maintained the picture of the Protector as a biblical, prophetic monarch, in line with the imagery of the poem, and openly Machiavellian.[57]

The lawyer Michael Hawke used the writings of the republic's apologist Anthony Ascham as well as Hobbes to argue that monarchy was ordained by God as the best kind of government; he also urged that the Protector was such a monarch. In his heroic genealogy, biblical and classical patriarchs, kings and tyrants, are lumped together in a truly post-regicidal defence of monarchy.[58] Cromwell was a monarch above all others because he did not inherit his throne, and, far from being a tyrant or usurper, because he was an exemplary hero and a saint: revenge was too effeminate for him. Moreover, his eloquence made him an outstanding courtier as well as a king.[59] Kings did not disappear from the arena of awareness, and of course it was in May 1657 that Cromwell actually rejected the offered title of king.

But while the kind of constitutional apology for monarchy, with which this chapter began, had its day again in the Restoration, many of the more respected monarchical defenders in the 1650s were compelled to take on the very different discourses of republicanism and the impact of a truly popular politics. Before we can consider these discourses themselves, we must confront the fact that all monarchical defence was a theology as much as it was a politics: religion mattered.

The Holy Commonwealth and the Breaking of Forms

When I shall see therefore all the Fables in the *Metamorphosis* [sic] acted and prove stories; when I shall see all the Democraties and Aristocraties in the World lye downe and sleepe, and awake into Monarchies then will I beginne to beleeve that Presbyteriall government, having continued in the Church during the Apostles times should presently after, against the Apostles doctrine and the will of Christ, be whirld about like a scene in a masque, and transformed into Episcopacy. In the mean time, while these things remaine thus incredible, and in humane reason impossible . . .
        William Chillingworth, *The Apostolicall Institution of Episcopacy*
                                                    (Oxford, 1644), 6

Cement in the Body

Religion is about ultimate destinies. It is concerned with how people think they should be in this life (or how they are told to be) in order to determine what will happen to them when they die. Or perhaps their destiny has already been decided by eternal decree, and life must be a response either to a wonderful or a horrific possibility. Belief is about conviction and the psychological and expressive dimensions of those convictions. Its imaginative scope is vast, and if political discourses make the connections between individuals and other individuals and institutions, then religion occupies the space of the individual's interiority and behaviour.

This might do as a modern description of faith, but it takes no account of the pervasive assumption in the seventeenth century that if society was not ordered by religion, and that order was unified, anarchy would ensue, and the souls of people would be endangered. It is hard for us to appreciate the grip of this assumption on English people. For one hundred years before 1640, England had had, with greater and lesser degrees of acceptance (and one five-year interruption), a nationally reformed church in which the monarch, as head of the church, sat at the head of a hierarchy of bishops, who administered a parochial system of worship that had its roots in the medieval past.

Everyone was bound up in the complicated system of representations which belonged to the church, from the symbolic significance attached to different parts of church architecture, to the knottiest problems of biblical interpretation. The Reformation of the sixteenth century had disturbed the previous ordering of symbols and practices.[60] The debate it started was still going on in the following century, and the tensions in the English church are widely acknowledged as one major cause of the Civil War, as the moving and rhetorically dense opening section of Milton's *Of Reformation Touching Church-Discipline* (1641) makes clear:

> Sad it is to thinke how that Doctrine of the *Gospel*, planted by teachers Divinely inspir'd, and by them winnow'd, and sifted, from the chaffe of overdated Ceremonies, and refin'd to such a Spirituall height, and temper of purity, and knowledge of the Creator, that the body, with all the circumstances of time and place, were purifi'd by the affections of the regenerate Soule, and nothing left impure, but sinne; *Faith* needing not the weak, and fallible office of the Senses, to be either the Ushers, or Interpreters, of heavenly Mysteries, save where our Lord himself in his Sacraments ordain'd; that such a Doctrine should through the grossenesse, and blindnesse, of her Professors, and the fraud of deceivable traditions, drag so downwards, as to backslide one way into the Jewish beggary, of old cast rudiments, and stumble forward another way into the new-vomited Paganisme of sensuall Idolatry. (*CPW*, I.519–20)

Having acknowledged this, we have then to consider the problems of the relationship between the languages or symbols of religion and their usage in the mid-seventeenth century. The 1640s can be seen as the triumph of a widespread reaction to the ceremonializing and hierarchizing of worship and church organisation in the 1620s and 1630s, itself a reaction to the plainness of an older Protestant generation.[61] The degree of innovation in the 1640s and 1650s was a rapid acceleration of ideas implicit in pre-1640 criticisms of the established church. Few of those who objected to the 'Popery' of Laudianism wanted reform to go as far as it did. Many supporters of episcopacy were definitely against Laud's 'innovations'. The speed of transformation meant that the languages by which ecclesiastical culture sustained itself were subject to an explosion of interpretations and meanings, the like of which had never been seen before in England. The force which became dominant in the early to mid-1640s (after the attempt to reform episcopacy itself failed in 1641), English Presbyterianism, found that it could not impose the rigid discipline it had hoped for, once the process of speculation and experimentation had started. At the same time, as we have recently been reminded, the unleashed religious forces of the 1640s met considerable resistance to change in parishes throughout the country.[62] The movement for self-governing congregations (Independency or Congregationalism) which had so troubled the Presbyterians was matched by the survival of Anglican practices in individual parishes. Nevertheless, Bishop Joseph Hall's sense of personal deprivation and distress was considerable and very real:

> By Vertue of an Ordinance of Parliament they must seize upon the Palace, and all the Estate I had . . . which they accordingly executed with all diligent severity, not leaving so much as a dozen of Trenchers, or my Childrens Pictures out of their curious Inventory. Yea, they would have appraised our very wearing Cloaths, had not Alderman *Tooly*, and Sherriff *Rawley* . . . declared their opinion to the contrary. These Goods, both Library and Household Stuff of all kinds, were appointed to be exposed to publick Sale.[63]

Hall describes the iconoclastic and sacrilegious damage done to Norwich Cathedral in the theatrical terms which were to typify some forms of (extreme) puritan satire:

> what a hideous triumph in the Market-Day before all the Country, when in a kind of Sacriligeous and profane Procession, all the Organ Pipes, Vestments, both Copes and Surplices, together with the Leaden-Cross, which had been newly sawn down from over the Green-Yard Pulpit, and the Service Books, and Saying Books that could be had, were carried to the Market-place; A lewd Wretch walking before the Train, in his Cope trailing in the Dirt, with a Service Book in his Hand, imitating in an impious scam the Tune, and usurping the words of the Litany used formerly in the Church.[64]

These were harsh times for the sometime purveyor of puritan satires himself. The country was, so to speak, in a religious abeyance, and with the overthrow of the bishops, all kinds of practices which had been hitherto restricted or forbidden suddenly sprouted, or developed in a relatively unimpeded way. Not without considerable difficulty, the Westminster Assembly had been able to agree on a form of worship (focused on lengthy preaching and praying), a catechism and a confession of faith, but the division of congregations into those considered to have, and those considered not to have, salvation, can only have increased divisions. When the church was refounded at the Restoration, practical morality and social cohesion were emphasised.[65] Gone were the apocalyptic statements of the previous decades, despite the genuine degree of piety which also prevailed. But by 1660, the church had of course divided: Dissenters and Catholics remained outside it in their own sub-cultures, with their own educational provisions and, to a lesser extent, employment systems.

What offended the Anglicans was that a unified whole could fragment into infinitesimal places of communal and individual authority:

> this Independant or Congregational way seemes to me the finest compendium of humouring and pleasing all those little fellowes that love not, that endure not to be subject to their betters; for by this meanes a little Kingdome and a Royall Priesthood is provided for every one of them; . . . and some had rather be chief but in a garden of Cucumers and govern but ten or twenty absolutely.[66]

According to the holders of this kind of opinion, the Catholic church was not the church of Rome but an ancient church from which the Church of England descended. Parliament, led by 'sectarian' interests had, not for the first time in history, betrayed the church.[67] George Hall appealed to the sons of ministers to sustain in history that which the Commonwealth so threatened:

> If with right Ordination (and the continued practice of the Church determines what that is) there be fruitfulness in their Ministry, if there be on their part laboriousness, watchfulness, desire to approve themselves to the consciences of men, endeavour to gaine soules unto God; if they be Doctrinall men (as Doctor *Donns* word was) . . . Living Lawes, their lives sound Commentaries upon their Doctrine, these be evidences enough, here be Almonds upon *Aarons* Rod.[68]

But the ideal sat in the midst of danger: 'Against us, in our whole Ecclesiastical Order, there hath been continued barking, *Martin* Marprelate, and Mar-Priest also, is still alive' (see below, 297–8).[69]

In part deliberately, but mostly by accident, a situation of great religious diversity had been manufactured. Many felt bewildered and depressed by the choices and the confusions. We have already seen the effect on preaching, and the impact on poetry was no less momentous. While prayer-book and liturgy competed with extended sermon and extempore prayers, the Bible was stretched to uses and interpretations with a density which had not occurred before in England.[70] The paradox was that most clergy (and M.P.s) were bound by an oath to establish national religious unity, but as time went by, so more diversity appeared. Hence the existence of different versions of architectural imagery (the common metaphor of building the church), and various kinds of metaphor of exodus or pilgrimage. It is no surprise that images of fragmented truth became equally popular.

In this situation, there were some surprising developments. For instance, a group of clergymen with anti-Calvinist views had been associated with Archbishop Laud before 1640. Some of them found livings under the patronage of the puritan and mystical Earl of Pembroke in the later 1640s, and they survived hard puritan investigation despite attacking the Assembly of Divines, and being associated with sectarians. They were associated with some enthusiasts, and some of their works survived in the Restoration as a kind of intellectual resource for the extreme Quaker perfectionism of the followers of James Nayler.[71]

There might have been cross-overs like this, made possible by a broad toleration, but the language of religious prejudice was never far away. Take Thomas Edwards's famous documentation of sectarian heresies, *Gangraena* (1646), or Richard Crashaw's terms of reversed Protestant iconography. Crashaw had become a Catholic by the time he wrote from Leiden in Protestant Holland, most probably to Joseph Beaumont.[72] The people there, he says, are given over to idolatry: 'they have set up in the great church of St Peter here the plaine Pagan Pallas, Cap a pee, with speare and Helmet & Owl & all, in the place of saints at least which heretofore it seemes usurped the window.'[73] For every sense of unity, there was an equal and opposite sense of profound antipathy. The symbols and codes of English Christianity were like a hall of opposed mutually reflecting mirrors, each surface containing its own set of symbols while offering a distorted and repellent image of its others.

Bishops, Presbyters and Puritans

The Elizabethan Presbyterians had argued that there was no basis in scripture for bishops. It was not a new argument, and some of the arguments against bishops in the 1640s came from surprising directions. Robert Greville, Lord Brooke's *A Discourse Opening the Nature of that Episcopacie* (1642) was an influential work by an important peer. His first objection is that bishops, being usually low-born, create a '*Chasm in Politiques*, as such *leapes* use to doe in *Naturals*' when they are elevated to sees. Indeed, Brooke's tract is so elegantly organised, with careful illustrative analogies and deftly placed sections, that it is unmistakably part of the educational nurture (humanism) which Brooke improbably claims bishops cannot possess. The attack grows in intensity: 'If you view their Civill Converse, they have practised little, but to wrangle down a Sophister, or to delude a Proctor, in the *University*; to say Grace to a Gentle-man, or acquaint themselves with a *Reading-Pue*, in the *Countrey*'(35). The actions and discourses of a simple minister are quite enough to exercise any single man to the full. On the other hand, bishops are only *jure humano* in their calling, and their true roles are hampered by the influence of the court's fickle, dehumanising influence and the intentions of princes. In this state, they are not free men, and so unfit to be Members of Parliament, unlike the landed aristocracy represented by Brooke and Essex.

It is not surprising to find Brooke extending the imagery used to vilify popery and popish '*media*' to bishops, for it was a standard device in Elizabethan puritan complaint. More exceptional are the perceived transferences of authority between political and religious spheres. These are offensive to Brooke, for bishops claim that a monarchical discipline is necessary in the church, and this itself has the unfortunate effect of improperly mystifying and dignifying monarchy (45). No bishop, no king.

In attempting to discover what a bishop might be, Brooke and Milton agreed that there seemed no justification in the Pauline Epistles for an ecclesial role superior to that of pastor. Furthermore, 'Any man might now in the conversion of the *Americans* or *Chinois*, give direction how to admit Members, elect Pastors, exercise the keyes, &c'(77). Taking his analogy from classical political divisions (monarchy, aristocracy, democracy), Brooke states that apostolic church government was and should be popular (in the hands of popularly elected officers (elders)), and that gifts (ministerial powers) should be communicated by presbyterial laying on of hands – so that the popularly elected officers confer evangelical power on the minister. Following a presbyterian model, Brooke regards sects as dangerous, but does not see the retention of bishops as the way to keep sectaries at bay, because it is the bishops who have caused separatism with their exclusive and persecuting policies. The question remains: how to establish a church *unity*?

In achieving a description of such a unity, body imagery was transferred from anti-Catholic Protestant polemic to anti-episcopal puritanism:

> It is writen of *Robertus Gallus* (who lived An. 1290.) that he saw in a vision, a goodly Bishop in a glorious cope, blessing the people; But he could see no head this Bishop had: he went nearer to see and espyed a head, but it was a wooden one, drye and without sense; when he desired to know the meaning of this vision, answer was made, That this was the Doctrine of the Church of *Rome*; as the head is to the body, such is the foundation to the building; far be it from us to build without a foundation.[74]

Milton does not initially reject bishops so much as denigrate the office because of its assumption of too authoritarian and 'Pontifical' a role. An apostolic bishop in Milton's view approximates to 'the gravest, and worthiest Minister'. The 'carnal appetite' of bishops is positively dangerous to monarchs, as is revealed in an extensive and dramatic account of how bishops have always ruined monarchs. It is a vision not without humour, as the descriptions of absurd prelatical vestments show. History, instanced in the testimony of Polycarpus and others, shows that bishops are presbyters (*CPW*, I.643–4).

The vision of those who objected to bishops, or to the Laudian view of episcopacy, was what is commonly known as puritanism, or, in its more accurate, pre-1640 term, 'godliness'.[75] While more extreme and extravagant forms of puritanism have occupied historians in the last three decades, it is important not to forget the centrality and power of more orthodox puritanism. It was a disciplined and disciplinarian form of worship, and assumed, in addition to great personal self-control, the rigorous enforcement of godly standards through magistracy. Throughout the 1640s and 1650s, Parliament and then the Commonwealth government remained faithful to this vision: a 'golden chain' linking reformed gentry magistrates, well-educated godly ministers and pious lay persons. The aim was not only the pursuit of true holiness but also the expunging of sin throughout society: 'If it be unlawfull for the Magistrate to hate his brother, it is unlawfull for him to suffer sinne upon him.'[76]

An exemplary Puritan in this sense, for his faith and ministry, and an excelling one for his publishing efforts, was Richard Baxter of Kidderminster. Baxter did not object to episcopacy *per se*, and never followed any particular form of church government beyond his function as a godly minister within the parish structure. His eclecticism has confounded commentators, but there is no mistaking his intentions in the vast amount of 'practical' literature he published, aimed largely at the 'middling sort', such as the enormously popular *The Saints Everlasting Rest* (1650), and his published skirmishes with those whose theologies and ecclesiologies he thought were dangerous. Baxter made sure that his practical works were cheaper than his controversial works, and he encouraged his readers not to bother with controversy because it detracted from central devotional matters.[77]

More zealous persecutors were irritated by Baxter's catholicity. Thomas Edwards, Presbyterian, and author of the infamous *Gangraena*, considered it a duty to root out errors; his writings are the best known among the puritan authors who made the printed book function as a kind of ministerial magistrate, obsessively documenting and condemning all forms of non-presbyterian worship. It was the pursuit of a particular unity of faith and practice of worship in the context of widespread disagreement of what that unity might be, and the inability of the government to impose a national religious settlement, that made documents like *Gangraena* as divisive as they were intended to be unifying. Bishops and the prayer book were to many Puritans instances of 'forms', and they compromised the working power of the Holy Spirit. The problem was that no agreement could be found with regard to what was the proper rejection of 'forms'.

Toleration: Cracks in the Mortar

that body-killing, soule-killing, and State-killing doctrine of not permitting

Roger Williams, *Mr. Cotton's Letter* (1644)

For Lord Brooke, the supreme principle in church affairs was right reason. Rather than separation of the godly from the ungodly, he recommends a commitment to '*Read*, pray, discourse, and conferre' with others until all doubts are satisfied.[78] Is this not hopelessly idealistic and politically naive? But, he says, in this state, no one must compel any believer.

As we have seen, Brooke's exposition is at odds with itself. He does not want bishops to compel individuals, yet neither does he want heretical sects breaking out of a fundamentally Presbyterian form of worship. This inability to imagine toleration was very widespread among nearly all religious groups at the time. Very few indeed were able to imagine a complete toleration. But for John Goodwin, to persecute an opinion or practice which might, upon further revelation, be found to be true, would be to risk angering God. Goodwin's method of persuasion is to elaborate on the meanings of being out of 'the way' of Christ in a narrative marked by crescendos of repetitive intensity. Persecution is imagined as an individual action which will be avenged by God.[79] A more durable and far-reaching method was developed by Roger Williams, whose *The Bloudy Tenent of Persecution* (1644) is one of the greatest and most original statements for religious toleration.[80] The essence of Williams's insights comes from a confluence of strict typological interpretation, which enabled him to think habitually in terms of simultaneously connected yet entirely distinct elements, and a clear grasp of the corporate entities by which Old and New Englanders associated with each other. In *The Bloudy Tenent*, the ancient city and the modern mercantile world are continuous. The church is like any professional or mercantile association within a state; if they cease to exist, or divide within themselves, 'the essence or being of the city' carries on undisturbed. It is imperative that the godly dissociate themselves from the ungodly in separate churches, but because church and state are entirely distinct (even if they do have similar shapes, and can only be comprehended by analogical comparison with each other), there is no threat in separation to the social order. Augustine's City of

God is thus redefined. Goodwin also uses the mercantile comparison, but he does not develop the sharply conceptual division between church and state sustained by Williams.

To tolerate or permit is to act for the sake of goodness, and is an imitation of God's own permission of the 'vessels of wrath' (Rom. 9:22). Williams also uses the parable of the wheat and the tares (Matt. 13:24–30) – Christ argues that the weeds (tares) must be left in the ground for fear of uprooting the wheat (the true believers). The elect are there, as yet undiscovered, in every nation. This is not as knowing or elegant as Milton's solution in *Areopagitica* (1644), but its imagistic energy is more than sufficient, especially as Williams turns the image of the field to represent the battlefield of the Civil War in England. Christ is thus the 'great politician for the peace of the field which is this world', and by His example, toleration should extend even to Catholics. Not only bishops, but also Presbyterians and Independents, allow the authority of the civil magistrate to trespass on the ground of individual conscience, and thereby assume improperly the 'crown of the Lord Jesus'.

Williams does not return to classical Greek for his definition of heresy (choice) as Milton does. He turns to the Greek of the New Testament:

> this *Greek* word *Hereticke* is no more in the *English* and in Truth, then an *obstinate* and *wilfull* person in the *Church* of *Creet*, striving and contending about those unprofitable *Questions* and *Genealogies*, &c. and is not such a *monster* intended in this phrase, as most *Interpreters* run upon, to wit One *doctrine* in *Fundamentalls*, and as the *Answer* [of John Cotton] makes the *Apostle* to write in such *Fundamentalls* and *principall points* wherein the Word of God is so cleare that a man cannot but be convinced in *conscience*, and therefore is not persuaded for matter of *conscience*, but for sinning against his *conscience*.[81]

Conscience is the faculty which should be allowed to maintain an unhindered communication with God, the difference here between Williams and Cotton being the degree to which the conscience of any one individual needed protection from temptation.

But by the same token, Williams also makes it clear, as Keith Stavely has recently shown, that being a true Christian – being most receptive to the Gospel – is to disqualify oneself from participating in government.[82] Stavely points up the consequence of Williams's disbelief in extant forms of human polity: 'the same reasoning that discountenanced medieval Christiandom and the Elect Nation also frowned upon the imagining and building of alternative forms of human collectivity.'[83] Cotton's assumption that an individual could be persecuted for sinning against his conscience was evidence of a presumption on John Cotton's part that he knew what was the truth, and this for Williams was idolatry – characteristically explained by Williams in terms of misplaced imagery.

And once liberated, conscience (in a conscientious magistrate) always risked becoming a persecuting agent itself – hence the need for Christians not to be governors. In his way, Williams had created a system which was as paradoxical with regard to the nature of authority and action as that of Hobbes (see below, 156–7).

Another great tolerationist, John Saltmarsh, avoided Williams's impasse by merging the terms of parliamentarian apology with those of radical puritanism. Thus, *Dawnings of Light* (1646) explores the supernatural 'interests' of God, nation, Parliament and people, while enhancing the sense of liberty of conscience by putting all matters of toleration and separation as questions. God works through the providences of history: this is how we see his 'effluxes', and in order for further truth to be revealed, there must be no 'fixation' of any practices of worship (98), only a willing openness towards divinely sanctioned revelation. The influence of Milton is detectable: 'for this *unity*, it hath such cold principles as freeze and congeal *multitudes heterogenially* together in the *worship of God*, and then puts the name of *Schisme* upon all the *Reformed Churches* that will not come into the dark with them' (57). Parliament is the voice of God, and the supplement to the monarchy's reforming duty (while the monarch is unavailable), so that Saltmarsh's godly representative is an active hero, as opposed to Williams's private man, debarred from taking any action.

However imperfectly understood, liberty of conscience justified the possibility of an escape from the restrictive forms of the established episcopal church (or indeed, the presbyterian alternative which replaced it) into worship which emphasised the personal experience of the Holy Spirit. Hence the great outpouring of puritan forms dedicated to this end, which have been the subject of so much attention in recent years: extempore preaching, prayer and song; the confessional narrative; inspired prophecy.[84] They were all contributing towards a version of selfhood which ultimately put the individual believer above the claims of state religious compulsion.

The Grand Puritan Sublime

We tend to forget the richness of expression which this triumph of puritanism conferred upon literary production, and the further opportunities it afforded in the relating of public to private worlds. At the risk of recycling a commonplace, the simple fact was that the dominant unifying image used by puritan writers, especially ministers, during the Civil War, was of the English as the Israelites on their journey out of Egypt into Israel.[85] Such patterns of using biblical texts, imagery and phraseology were spread across English religious discourse, and they worked, in various ways, into the most magnificent and visionary expression of the puritan ideal.

Sir Henry Vane stands as an exemplary radical Puritan who was influential in government for twenty years. His views on toleration are well known, and his associations with Milton and Roger Williams in an attempt to sway Cromwell towards a policy of greater toleration are now coming to light.[86] Vane's writings on both public and private matters are examples of an ethical discourse which assumed the division of church and state, but which also demonstrated how the two spheres were nonetheless connected. Vane's republic is a meritocracy of believers. We should note how the vocabulary of freeborn Englishmen and militant republicanism is merged with that language of the spirit:

> none be admitted to the exercise of the right and privilege of a free Citizen, for a Season, but either such as are free born, in respect of their holy and righteous principles, flowing from the birth of the spirit of God in them, (restoring man in measure and degree, as at the first by Creation) unto the right of Rule and Division, or else who, by their tryed affection and faithfulness to common right and publick prudence, have deserved to be trusted with the keeping or bearing their owne Armes in the publick defence.[87]

In the 'private' writings, notably the inscrutable *Retired Mans Meditations* (1655), the centrality of scriptural interpretation is evident:

> in the opening of mystical and dark prophecies, that which principally is aimed at and applied throughout, in this Discourse, be the inward and spiritual meaning of them: know, that it is not to exclude thereby their literal and historical sense, but to shew how well both may stand together. (Sig. a4r-v)

The imagery characteristic of radical puritan usage – the seed, light, and so on – and the 'mystical' interpretation of scriptural texts, are all present in Vane.[88] Such language serves to connect man with God, and man and God with society. Vane's view of the potential perfection in man is beautiful:

> man than hath a perfect, compleat, intellectuall and rationall life springing up in him, which is so far from being lessened or interrupted by death, and the laying down of the use of his bodily life for a time, that it never comes to its full and mature perfection until then, and as a consequence hereof, the body be re-assumed incorruptible. In this property and operation of humane life, man bears the figure and image of the witness of the Holy Ghost. (53)

Such discourse represents the high point of puritan optimism concerning the nature of mankind and mankind's relationship with God. Similar examples are to be found throughout Milton's prose and in the writings of Cromwell's Chaplain, Peter Sterry. Both men of letters used a variety of literary devices to fashion the public as well as private 'grand Puritan sublime'. The view that the Independents had no imaginative heyday until the Restoration is quite erroneous.[89]

Prophetic discourse, especially by lay people breaking quite clear from conventional forms of religious discourse and publication, has attracted much comment, especially that of religious sectarians and of women prophets.[90] Within this ferment, more orthodox godly women should also not be forgotten. Elizabeth Warren reworked a number of patristic and Reformation authorities into an authoritative prose. Her attraction to economic metaphors (*Spiritual Thrift* being the title of one tract) is of course consistent with a long tradition in Christian theology, although some have claimed that she makes an especially domestic use of her materials, transforming the language of theology with tropes produced in and through female experience.[91] Although her capacity to express herself was much less competent, Mary Pope, a member of the Erastian Thomas Coleman's congregation, certainly can claim a rhetorical and interpretative originality. Against the political Independents, she theorized natural law with the King very much still at the head of the church and the state. Charles is a 'bishop elder' as well as a magistrate. For Mary Pope (as for other godly women authors such as Mary Pocock) the country was the wife of the king, and this was what constituted the body.[92] The state is a big family which has become overdetermined by liberty: usually there should be the glue of obedience holding the whole together. Too much freedom of conscience, too much 'opinion', she said, has a levelling effect. Familial forms of obedience are the natural laws necessary for stability.

The terms usually associated (then and since) with the sentiments to which Mary Pope objected are 'freedom' and 'liberty', and there has been one notable recent attempt to show that innovations in religious thought during the 1640s and 1650s were not at all in the cause of freedom, since all religious thought in the seventeenth century was predicated upon a predominant notion of obedience to God.[93] While concurring with many points that make up this argument – and in particular that religious differences occurred within a more or less shared religious national culture – we should not assume that religious obedience is wholly synonymous with civil obedience. That liberty went hand in hand with an ordering structure which made that liberty possible (such as law and personal discipline) was, as we have seen, a widely held assumption. That human sinfulness was at the heart of nearly every theology also goes without saying. Thus, 'liberty of conscience meant submission to God, therefore, and not to self', since to locate liberty purely in the self is to make it sinful.[94] But this should not discount the possibility of sympathetically imagining different orders of godliness (on both collective and individual levels), and it is the very possibility of imagining and acknowledging difference as a religious truth (within the self) which is in danger of being forgotten. The puritan sublime is the expression of differences in church discipline and personal regulation within a culture of shared assumptions and shared words. From the dynamic of competing differences (differing interpretations of biblical signs) comes one of the sources of the flurry of naming in the period. Imagination is an anachronistic word, for it comes too close to the human 'invention' which the godly so feared. Nonetheless, imagination in the sense of the capacity to generate autonomous and rapidly changing interpretations of the Bible is an accurate description of the phenomenon.

In this way, the conviction that God's will could be fulfilled through Ranterish swearing or multiple sexual couplings is an instance of 'perfect freedom' – and the barrier between discipline and liberty has disappeared. Richard Coppin's following in Oxfordshire and Kent was a group of 'Seekers' in which any form of worship was acceptable because no 'forms' mattered in the face of the imminent arrival of the higher dispensation. There seems to be no other authority in Coppin than that of an indwelling God; once a person realises this, they are freed from sin. Accordingly, Coppin's writing is usually allegorical, employing scriptural language which applies willy-nilly to Parliament and King alike. It acknowledges no boundaries whatsoever, and has the traces of the rhetorical and theatrical shaping which we find in Coppe, or the 'centred self' of most early Quaker discourse. Thus George Foster could see himself – the site of his prophetic dream-visions – as the centre of a unity, in which was enfolded a communist message:

> A company of men and women standing upon *Sion*, having harpes, and made Musicke; and then came some others and they danced; and there was one more glorious then the rest in the midst of them. And then I beheld till he that was in the midst of them did go into them all and they became as one.

> I saw in a vision a man giving away his money to another, and also giving away food to feed him, and cloth to cloath him. And I heard a voice say, this man lends unto the Lord, that man feeds the hungry and cloaths the naked, lends unto the Lord.[95]

This mode of expression and declamation must have seemed truly anarchic to the orthodox, and frighteningly so. No less disturbing was the appearance, speech and writing of the early Quakers, who, more consistently than any other sect, inverted orders of social hierarchy and propriety as a witness to the truth of their sense of Christ within, or 'inner light'. Throughout the 1650s, disputations between puritan ministers, Presbyterians, Independents and Baptists on the one hand, and Seekers, Quakers and other enthusiasts on the other, made for a dialogue often of mutual incomprehension.[96] Going naked as a sign of inner perfection was coupled with a no less startling style of verbal delivery, making scriptural phraseology equivalent to human speech, a 'zero degree' of illuminated prophecy:

> Dwell in the light, which is the condemnation of the ungodly, for all they that are contrary to the light, are without the cloathing of God, among such doth the Lord send some of his Children, to go naked and put off their cloaths; a figure and a signe of their nakednesse, who are, naked from god, and cloathed with the filthy garments, so ye all dwelling in the light, which never changeth, ye stumble not but are led out of darknesse, and from among the unbelievers, where the signes are sent, and such as are from God, which light leads up to God, in which is the unity, so in the light all dwell.[97]

All Alone

The Puritans, however, did not have a monopoly on the expression of private versions of selfhood. After the defeat of the King, and of the episcopal ideal, Anglicans were left with literally no externals. Sometimes they were allowed to worship together by the Commonwealth authorities (as was the case in parts of London, in Oxford and elsewhere), but even then, they were limited to single, autonomous, surreptitious congregations. The ejection and even violent persecution of bishops and loyalist clergymen makes, as we have seen, for sad and sometimes harrowing reading. Yet in these circumstances, Anglican divines did address the individual believer in sermons and devotional treatises made for private reading. Devotional works by contentious men such as Duppa and Hammond were the easiest books to have published. Onto these works rubbed, to a greater or lesser extent, a usually bitter response to public affairs. Jeremy Taylor's *Holy Living* (1652) is the best known example of this kind of writing. Brian Duppa's published sermons of this period sound puritan, or nothing in particular:

> For doe but consider with thy self o sinner, think of it seriously, the Angels that were by, when God stampt his Image on thee, when he wash'd thee in Baptisme as clean as the untouch'd snow, when he married thee to his son Christ Jesus, made thee a temple of his holy Spirit, how can they either *know* or *joy* in thee, when that image is rased out [,] that innocence polluted, that constraint violated, that temple turn'd into a sink of filth, into a den of Serpents.[98]

But the Anglican edge is never hard to find:

> Let the *Separatist* boast of his *private Spirit* that hath *revealed it*, or the
> Bishop of *Rome* cite his *infallible Chaire*; every one is not wax enough to
> take impression at this : But if *our Saviour* set his *divine Seale* on; if once
> find his . . . *ipse dico, I say to you*, then let him that hath eares hear.[99]

This world of privatised public devotion is evidence of an episcopal and
ceremonial church in existence but without its external structure of
governance. In the same way, Henry Vaughan's poetry mixes royalist
militancy with treatment of the inner self, and his prose works and
translations belong exactly to this milieu (see below, 269–73). Sir Thomas
Browne's intricately patterned prose writings also search for the shapes of
divinity in the natural world: another set of Anglican gestures.[100]

Taylor's most famous single work, his *Liberty of Prophesying* (1647), is a
plea for persuasion rather than persecution – and this from a man who at
other times vigorously asserted the episcopal order. Taylor (who was able
to function as a bishop in 1650s Ireland) was voicing a central pacifist
strand in Christian thinking, no less so than Walwyn the Leveller did,
although we could say more cynically that anyone subjected to the New
Model Army at the height of its power would be likely to turn to gentle
persuasion as a solution. Taylor was sure that there was heresy, but he
uses arguments which are similar to those of high tolerationists, like
Williams:

> he who would not have men put to death, or punished corporally, for such
> things for which no human authority is sufficient either for cognizance or
> determination, or competent for infliction, that he persuades to an
> indifferency when he refers to another judicatory which is competent,
> sufficient, infallible, just, and highly severe. (347)

Doubt is crucial: 'I am not sure that such an opinion is heresy; neither
would other men be so sure as they think . . . if they did consider it
aright'(359). Neither was this, claimed Taylor, a statement in favour of
indifferency, except in so far as indifferency was taught in Christianity
before the church erred into popish tyranny. *Liberty of Prophesying* can
almost sound like a well-informed radical puritan document, with its
emphasis upon the union of all believers as the 'communion of saints'. If
this had been the case, Taylor would have had to dispense with the
primacy of ceremony in worship, to elevate the church invisible to such a
position; and it would have been too far for him to go. Nonetheless, his
defence of toleration is a true piece of Anglican ecumenicism in the
aftermath of the Church of England's dismantling.

The displaced episcopalians placed the greatest emphasis upon the
personal devotional treatise. Taylor's *Holy Living* (1652) stresses
ceremonies, and set forms of prayer and hymn. In doing so, and in

providing extensive advice on practical behaviour, it constitutes an interiorizing document (albeit with an emphasis upon externals) which sits beside the Calvinist manuals of experimental religion. And if the hold of predestination doctrine was being dispelled in various corners of the puritan consensus, Taylor's emphasis upon behaviour had a similar effect. The integration of stoical thought within the section entitled 'Instruments or Exercises to procure Contentedness' contains the seeds of the argument for the advantageousness of religion and the friendship of God in the Restoration Church of England which was to irritate Bunyan.[101] Of course, Taylor makes it quite plain that regicides and dismantlers of the church deserve damnation: what keeps *Holy Living* firmly in the frame of the mid-century are its oblique (and less oblique) references to the national calamity, which retain the sense of divine justice being acted out, as much as they try to see beyond the horizon of regicide:

> For it is a sin that turns an ague into a fever, and a fever into a plague, fear into despair, anger into rage, and loss into madness, and sorrow to amazement and confusion. But if either we were innocent, or else by the sadness are made penitent, we are put to school, or into the theatre, either to learn how, or else actually to combat for a crown. The accident may serve an end of mercy, but is not a messenger of wrath. (80)

The 'Puritan moment' may, in its most extreme form, have effected very few people. Its discourse may have been extremely limited. Godliness was not only much more widespread, but also far more rigidly disciplinarian and limiting in subjective potential. Yet it seems to have touched everyone who thought and wrote religious discourse. Even (or rather especially) as a demonised other, the fear of inspired puritanism disrupted the discourse as well as the material of the church. The garment was indeed rent, and it could not be repaired. The matter of expressing oneself as a religious subject had undergone a massive transformation. As events progressed in the 1640s, popular radical puritanism found itself embattled with its sometime co-religionists, and in order to survive, it needed a politics. The next chapter is the history of that politics, and the crucial role played in that history by the printed book.

CHAPTER 4

Discourse from Below:
The Levellers, the City and the Army

that liberty of discourse by which Corruption & tyranny would be soon discovred[1]

go purge, goe purge; one penniworth of the *Agreement of the people*, with a little good resolution taken morning and evening, will work out this corruption[2]

> *Divine verse, and Sacred Theologie,*
> *the Mistresse of the Arts Philosophie:*
> *With faire Historia, wee and they do mourn,*
> *for that a* Lilburne *on the earth was born*[3]

Urban Drama

EVERYONE LIKES THE Levellers, or at least that image of the Levellers projected by left-wing politicians today and celebrated by the annual rally at Burford, once a scene of the Levellers' sad nemesis. The attractiveness of mid-seventeenth-century populist radicals who appear to be demanding the fundamentals of modern democracy, and demanding it in a simple yet exciting way (quite unlike other discourses in the period), is easy to understand. But the Levellers remain a victim of their own success. Despite the relatively large number of modern editions of their works, and the greater number of books devoted to them, they remain misunderstood and badly served by the majority of their commentators.

The Levellers should be seen as standing for a particular kind of social action – in behaviour and in the texts – and this is true from Lilburne's first publication A *Worke of the Beast* (1638; before there was a Leveller party) onwards. Focusing upon their ideas or their politics alone has tended to make them appear less interesting than they really are.[4] Equally misleading have been other claims for the long-term influence of Leveller thought, claims which have obscured the specificity of Leveller discourse and action.[5]

It is possible to extract a Leveller political theory, but it is inconsistent and variable because it changed rapidly in a very short space of time, and different Levellers or groups of Levellers had different, sometimes contradictory ideas (for instance on the nature of the franchise).[6] That the Levellers are not democrats in the modern sense of the word used to be employed as an argument to dismiss their significance. Fortunately, this kind of philistinism has recently been decisively trounced, but it still leaves us with a rather incoherent picture of Leveller views and activities.[7] Anyone who has looked at a Leveller tract will be struck by its colourfulness. Yet such has been the effort to contextualize the Levellers and to categorise their ideas, that they have begun to appear in secondary literature as rather grey, lifeless shadows.[8]

Leveller activity cannot be accounted for in the same way that we would examine a radical religious sect. The Levellers did not meet or sustain themselves in the same way as the conventicles, and their writings have in consequence a very different character, despite the fact that many Levellers were also religious radicals (and some very interesting and unusual ones at that). The Levellers are best understood as clever manipulators of the media opportunities available in the 1640s. The major personalities in the Leveller movement each had a pre-Leveller career in which they used print to make extreme cases for toleration and religious liberty. Their appearance in print was the act of freedom for which they campaigned. The growth of their movement was made possible by the developed possibilities for communication in London and in the Army. Leveller organisation was focused on the presentation of petitions, and pamphlets, the very currency of their protest, were frequently displayed in their demonstrations.[9] Newsbooks as well as pamphlets played a crucial role in this process (see above, 64–5). When their exploitation of communications (and the consequent advance of their ideas) became too much of a threat to their immediate opponents (but sometime friends), who were the generals of the New Model Army and the 'other half' of a broad radical puritan coalition, their communication lines were broken, and they ceased to exist, except in the sense of more sporadic printed protests in the 1650s; nothing on the scale of 1647 and 1649. Their accumulation of ideas is rapid but in many instances also naive. Only relatively late in the day did they become openly anti-monarchical, and that was really by imbibing an echo of classical republicanism. They were not hard and fast republicans. But they were recommending annual elections to Parliament (and other controls on possible abuses and corruption of parliamentary privilege) as early as October 1645. Like a newsbook, their political make-up was accretive, and like a newsbook, Levellerism was easy to tear up when used by its dominant consumers.

To 'level' in the sense of removing inequalities between men first appears in the early seventeenth century; it was associated with local rioters in these years.[10] The earliest public evidence of one of the 1640s Levellers at work is John Lilburne's punishment in 1638 for allegedly helping to print, in Holland, works critical of the bishops, and for aiding their distribution in England. Other figures who would become Leveller activists were also associated with Lilburne, or supported his cause in these years.[11] Lilburne was sentenced to be whipped through the streets of London to the pillory, and to be imprisoned before and afterwards. His actions were part of the general protest of puritanism during the 1630s. Lilburne was pardoned by the Long Parliament in 1641, along with the other victims of Laudian policy – Burton, Bastwick, Prynne and Leighton – and he remained in broad alliance with puritanism, and sided with the Independents until 1646 (Oliver Cromwell was for some time, in so many words, his patron).

As has often been noticed, Lilburne's behaviour and his representation of it are martyrological, reminiscent of Foxe's *Book of Martyrs*, and linked with the similar sufferings of Burton, Bastwick and Prynne and earlier Elizabethan and Jacobean Puritans.[12] Initially, his style had nothing to do with the Levellers, and its appeal to those who wanted to see victims of governmental tyranny was such that royalist apologists enlisted his works in their cause.[13] It is an obvious way of using a well-known tradition to enhance one's appeal, and *A Worke of the Beast* is entirely concerned with depicting its subject as a victim of tyranny:

> . . . at the last my mouth was gagd, and by them baselie staide;
> And threatened there once againe, that my backe should be wipt,
> If that my tongue but one word more, against Romes Preists let slipt,
> Thus with a straight Gagg in my mouth, about an houre stood I. (34)

Gagging is of course the most literal and visual image of censorship. The whole machinery of state persecution – such as making defendants swear incriminating oaths – is exposed in a narrative of heroic resistance, and surrounded by a rhetoric of anti-popish apocalypticism.

The world of the apprentice is also revealed in these tracts. Lilburne himself was an apprentice with the printer and prominent Particular Baptist William Kiffin. Behind the surface of religious rhetoric, we can glimpse the world of artisan existence, and the interpenetration of religion, economics and politics for these urban toilers. This is evident in the way authorities are answered and rebutted. 'Freeborn men' are those who have passed from apprenticeship to being their own masters. Such glimpses are also available in the churchbooks and devotional publications of the separatists (and later on, the Dissenters), or indeed in the writings of many articulate artisans, whatever their allegiances (royalist prophets like Arise Evans and Walter Gostelow would have to be included).[14] But with the Levellers, or those who were to become so, the representation relates lived reality to political demands. The world of the shop or the merchant's office becomes thrown into political representation through polemical effort:

> They doe not rest here neither, but are yet further authorized with a generall Ordinance of this very Parliament, contrary to all law, justice, equity and reason, under pretence of searching for scandalous Books, to call numbers of deboyst men with Smiths and Constables, yea and trained Bands also (when they please) to assist them, and in most bold and tumultuous manner to break open and rifle, even the Parliaments owne (in all their greatest dangers, troubles & distresses) most faithfull friends Houses, Chests, Truncks and Drawers; and from thence to rob, steale, and felloniously to carry away such of the Possessors proper goods, choice Linnens, and best things, as they please, as well as Books new and old, after they have put the owners themselves out of doores, and commanded Constables to carry them before a Committee, and from thence to prison.
>
> Where they may without any consideration rott, if they will not either betray both a good Cause, and some other of the Parliaments best friends, when they had few others, or else submit to their unjust lawes; besides, it is a common thing for such lawlesse men to breake in, and search honest mens shops, when neither the owners nor any of theirs are present to see what businesse they have there.[15]

But it is doubtful that the Levellers ever successfully exploited to the full the interests of the urban guilds and companies.[16] Their own ideals in religion and politics had already taken them beyond this immediate world, while their political ideas and stratagems were projections from this world of urban production and commerce. Their themes were to be taken up again by London radicals later in the century.[17]

The Levellers were prominent in campaigns against instances of legal tyranny, and often the impulse for political and juridical renovation came from religious principles. Equally, religious zeal and economic motives were closely bound up. Having been economically disadvantaged in the 1630s on account of their religion in their native Shrewsbury, the separatist Chidley family profited in 1640s London as drapers (stockingsellers). Despite being a Leveller activist, Samuel Chidley continued to prosper in the late 1640s and 1650s, as did other more elevated Levellers, such as John Wildman. In the Restoration a combination of persecution, plague and the Great Fire conspired to ruin Chidley.[18] At the height of the Commonwealth, he was a prominent separatist, practically a gentleman and a worthy Leveller, and his intransigent zeal was nearly as prepossessing as Lilburne's.

Figure 6 John Lilburne, *The Triall of Lieut. Collonel John Lilburne* (1649), frontispiece.

Lilburne's *Christian Man's Triall* (1641) is notable for its use of legal language, and ultimately a dependence upon Coke and Prynne's works (see fig. 6).[19] Lilburne's obsessive detailing of his trials and interrogations, his personalisation of issues, and his symbolic gestures, have been much remarked. But it would be wrong to suggest that this element represents a diffuseness and lack of focus representative of the Levellers' fundamental weakness – the lack of a clear programme and strategy.[20] Rather, the writings should be seen as a complex part of the interactions and negotiations by which religious radicals, discontented citizens, soldiers and women discovered political action. Viewed in this light, every tract represents one stage further on in a process of political education.

Enforced imprisonment was used (perhaps deliberately in some instances) as a way of making a point. Usually incarceration led to a flurry of pamphleteering and petitioning. We should also not forget that the very site of print production and the dissemination of information is often the reason for imprisonment and persecution. A petition from William Larner's wife, Helen (appended to a tract by Larner; petitions from wives were a famous Leveller strategy), claims that Larner was arrested on the 'false suggestion' of Joseph Hunscot, Beadle of the Stationers' Company.[21] Like Larner's tract, Richard Overton's *An Arrow Against All Tyrants* (1646) is a letter addressed to the republican M.P. Henry Marten, who appears to have collaborated with the Levellers at this time. The last four pages present Overton's petition for his release to Parliament, the text of the order for Overton's original arrest, and a postscript by Overton which actually accuses Marten of not being true to his representative responsibilities. Again, the focus is upon the treatment of information and speech acts. Marten had not been present in the House of Commons when Elizabeth Lilburne's petition was read out, and so missed the protest. At the very end of the tract, somewhat uncannily, and Marten having been reminded that artisans are as free-born as the most eminent men, Overton produces a Nedhamesque comment upon those he regarded as career politicians:

> have a care of the *temporary Sagacity* of the *new Sect of OPPORTUNITY POLITITIANS*, whereof we have got at least two or three too many; for delayes & demurres of Justice are of more deceitfull & dangerous consequence, then the flat & open deniall of its execution, for the one keeps in suspence, makes negligent & remisse, the other provokes to speedy defence, makes active and resolute. (20)

There is a 'cartoon'-like quality to much of Overton and Lilburne's self-presentation, and to much else in Leveller pamphlets, but it would be wrong to see this as a simplification. Some of this style must have grown out of the earliest forms of neo-dramatic pamphleteering, particularly in respect of Overton and Lilburne.[22] Yet this does not tell the whole story by any means. The origins of civic Levelling lay in calls for religious toleration against an intolerant presbyterian majority in Parliament and the Assembly of Divines. In urban centres, and in the parliamentary Army too, there had been a broad alliance of what would have been called the 'godly' party before 1640. Many of those who were to become Levellers, like Lilburne, shared a cultural experience with those from whom they would eventually become alienated. In the 1630s, Lilburne knew the Presbyterians Bastwick and Prynne, and was punished in their cause. Like Cromwell, who befriended him in the 1640s, he liked the poetry of George Wither, extracts of which were to occupy space in some Leveller tracts.[23] In Leveller tracts can be found a particular puritan hybrid.

When the split really widened, and a true Leveller party emerged, this mode of representing culture and using it stayed with the Levellers, as much as it remained the possession of their opponents. But in the new and (to them) unusual way in which they had to seek support, and motivate resistance, the cultural materials of the Levellers embedded in their language began to behave in unforeseen ways. Their rhetoric acknowledges the power of commerce, as it had been discovered by the pamphleteers of the 1590s, but unlike Nashe, Greene and the coney-catchers, they did not allow the festive to contain protest. Rather, the festive became the motor of subversion. Appealing to many different kinds of religious radical, and signalling sympathy for those suffering economic hardship, the Levellers developed a montage of forms which emulsified the Leveller cause on the page of the pamphlet. There is no greater representation of this feature than the often collectively authored Leveller and Army petitions, in which proposed Leveller constitutions and state reformations bind together different interests.[24] It is not a language in which an essential 'truth' would have been felt to reside (unlike say a sermon or a confession of experience), but in so far as it was concerned with the self-representation of persecuted heroes, character became 'dilated' in a manner similar to the way we have already seen with Lilburne. In becoming on the printed page 'bigger' than one really is, one becomes more than oneself, more than the subject position prescribed in the social order permits. And in this sense the Leveller pamphlet commits an act of textual revolt, one that is entirely consistent with the real revolts of which Levellers were sometimes capable. Lilburne's metaphors for his activity (often specifically pamphleteering) are taken from remarkably crude conceptions of popular heroism. Even late in his career, writing from Bruges in February 1653, he says he wants to box Cromwell on the ear. He thinks of his writing as 'little Rhetorique', the product of a 'dull pen', as opposed to the 'gallant Ennobled and Heroick minde', which he would rather not subject to the terms of submission required by the English government.[25] He recalls his trial, with the prosecutors expecting him to 'rant' in a high-flown manner, whereas he outmanoeuvred them with tact: 'such a cuffe under their other eare'.[26]

The dilated or transformed character of the textual Leveller (Overton, for instance, was keen on using animal identities both for himself and his opponents) functions as a kind of mask for the other dimensions of personality which we might expect to find represented. In doing the work of Leveller propaganda, the subject for whose rights the printed word spoke became reinvented. Overton was incensed by the capricious behaviour of the supposedly 'saintly' Lieutenant-Colonel who arrested him in 1649, but his description of this man is not so removed from how a Presbyterian would have viewed a Leveller: 'an Hocas Spocas, or a Fiend in a Juglers Box, they are not flesh and bloud, as are the wicked, they are all spirituall, all heavenly, the pure Camelions of the time.'[27] Having spoken in his earlier tracts as an abject separatist, Overton speaks as a true-born Englishman through the voice of an anti-puritan satirist.

All of this is related to recent accounts of popular politics during the mid-seventeenth century which have stressed the use made by 'conservative' or royalist journalists of popular, carnivalesque cultural forms, over and against the serious and biblical language of radical movements.[28] But it is clear that the Levellers were using these popular cultural forms in their own language. The textual results might have been slightly different from the popular royalists, but the sources and the context were the same.

While the genesis and development of Richard Overton's satires is so complete a *satirical* subject that it is best considered in conjunction with other forms of satire in these years (see below, 298–304), there are further aspects of his writing relevant to the concerns of this chapter. *An Appeale from the degenerate Representative Body* (17 July 1647) is a masquerade – a supposed appeal from Parliament to the people (assumed in this case to be the Army) – and it was unprecedented.[29] Levellers used masquerade where courtiers would use dissimulation. This imitation of Parliament, consistent with Overton's satirical strategies, and the unusual tenor of his entire outlook (here described as degenerate), is of course a *representation*, a perverse form of what Parliament is actually meant to be.[30] The representation is as original as Overton's radical definition of Reason: '*Reason hath no president, For Reason is the fountaine of all just presidents.*'[31] Not as textually cluttered as Lilburne's works, there is nonetheless some very direct glossing on the title page, matching biblical references to the contemporary situation in London. In fact, the tract exemplifies Leveller formation, crossing from religious to secular demands, and still deeply responsive to the threat of persecution: 'by such as preferre presidents and formalities, formes and figures, before the substance, life and spirit of all just presidents and Lawes, I may probably be censured and condemned for this present enterprize'.[32] Overton's version of natural law – that it is irrational to endanger oneself and one's family – a form of suicide – also creeps into the tract, and no opportunity is lost in exploiting the ruin of private concerns through public events. The masquerade at this point involves the lifting of parliamentary terms, such as necessity, which are given their 'true' context of meaning. Power and people are the forms by which abstract concepts live in the world,

and it is this rather metaphysical framework which Overton adds to the
kind of persecution narrative made famous by Lilburne. Juxtaposing his
own persecution with the army to such an extent, he really says 'come
and rescue me'. Marten is shown trying to save him, but fails to keep
Overton out of Newgate.[33] To tie his own claims to those made by
Fairfax and the Army is to make a very large and authoritative claim – a
good example of the mutability of 'Leveller' allegiances, and within a
page, the entire authority of both Houses of Parliament has been
challenged.[34] The hyperbole of Overton's Marpriest tracts remains; the
decision to use it must be because of its effect on readers – talk of M.P.s
stopping the mouths of the oppressed and crushing their petitions is the
most immediate way to voice an appeal. Upper-case letters and
extravagant word-play proclaim significant items, typically indicating the
issue of authorship as in a tract like *Plain Truth without Feare, or Flattery*
(By 'AMON WILBEE' (1647)):

> such is the equity, honesty and truth thereof that had I ten thousand
> lives, I would engage them all for the justification and maintenance
> thereof, and this I will say concerning that AUTHOR, that He deserves
> to *weare the* LAURELL from all that have writ (in that observant natture)
> since the Parliament began.[35]

It is here that the figure of inversion becomes decidedly pronounced:
Parliament having relinquished its role of protecting its constituents, the
real Parliament is now the people, so that the purpose of the masquerade
on the title page is finally revealed. But the people are not just political
representative: they are the 'body naturall', and in this greater corporal
collectivity have the authority to cut off the 'body representative'. The
circle of the carnivalesque is complete too. The voice this time is of an
artful dodger: 'what have they done I pray you as hitherto, but fob'd,
befool'd, and deluded you; say and unsay, backward and forward, hither
and thither, no man knowes whither, and all but to circumvent, delude,
and delay you, that they might gather time and ground.'[36]

Vox Plebis (1646; see below, 150) shows in enormous detail Lilburne's
examination in the House of Lords, together with a reprint of the charges
against him. This includes an attack on his goalers (47–8), and an
account of the very close captivity of Lilburne, all for the purpose of
showing how extensive prison surveillance and brutalisation was – a
feature of Wildman's writing as much as of Lilburne's. The massive
egotism involved in Leveller writing and rights claims was much noticed
by contemporaries – Cromwell said that there was too much 'will' in
Sexby's speeches.[37] Most hostile witnesses regarded writing as at the
heart of the Leveller intransigence, and assumed that authorial
intransigence was interchangeable with intransigence in court.[38] From
whoever's viewpoint, the trial portrayal becomes effectively a

dramatising of the common law as it affects people, in which anti- and pro-Leveller writers try to seize the initiative for representing what is legally correct. Even in the case of possibly fake petitions, it is hard to imagine how they could have failed to move or to appear genuine (even if naive) to a reader.[39] It is also hard to see how they could not but have raised fears among the propertied for their own livelihoods and well-being, even when Lilburne is framed to make his rhetoric look exaggerated.

On the other hand, the civic fun of the Leveller pamphlet attempts to appeal to different civic bodies (for instance, the apprentices), thereby creating on the page a kind of crowd politics – perhaps a more successful demonstration on the page than ever any real demonstration was. But by 1649, the Foxean figures of tyranny and persecution had been replaced by a representation of the more insinuating and politic tyranny of the Rump and its subtle control of opinion (including the invention of the pejorative name 'Leveller'):

> And though the better to insinuate themselves, and get repute with the People, as also to conquer their necessities, they have bin fane to make use of those very principles and productions, the men they have so much traduced, have brought to light: yet the producers themselves they have and doe still more eagerly maligne than ever, as such whom they know to bee acquainted to their deceipts, and deviations and best able to discover the same.[40]

The writing is somewhat clumsy, perhaps a deliberate adoption by Lilburne of a demotic mask. It is nonetheless a mask which stays in place for the sequel tract, *The Second Part of Englands New-Chaines Discovered* (1649), where the Leveller view of failed negotiations between themselves, Army and Parliament is viewed as an account of texts (remonstrances, petitions, letters) not achieving their goals in politics.[41] As we have seen, such an awareness of the necessities and possibilities of communication was fundamental to 1640s politics. But where those in the political nation got on with the business of negotiation – so that we only come to have a commentary on its significance in a work of history, such as Clarendon's *History* – communication is very much at the heart of Leveller writing consciousness. Knowing and using these sinews of communication and power suggests the 'newness' which the Levellers felt about their situation, the freshness of newly formed public opinion. What is on the page is again an extension of that which was at the heart of Leveller activity; the petition was both chosen and forced upon the Levellers by their predicament. Its centrality is attested by the use of petitions by Leveller women.[42] The page becomes a critical display of the sinews of influence and power across the political spectrum, including the politics of gender. Lilburne is acutely aware of status difference in his complaint that the grandees treated the King, held at Hampton Court, in a stately

and courtly manner which helped Charles in his last attempts to make
himself popular. Lilburne's sinuous sentences fuse to make a narrative of
the republican coup which is relentlessly angry, punctuated by the
leitmotif of lamentation, and which is remarkably sophisticated as a
historical analysis despite its stylistic simplicity.

The oral qualities of Lilburne's writing have frequently been noted,
and the significance of speech within his tracts is no less important. After
the politics of the text comes the politics of speech. One can almost hear
the urgent voices, as much as one can in the transcription of the Putney
Debates:

> It was insisted upon . . . that a motion should be made to this House for
> the procurement of a Law enabling them to put to death all such as they
> should judge by Petitions or otherwise to disturbe the present proceedings;
> and upon urging that the Civil Magistrate should do it, It was answered,
> that they could hang twenty ere the Magistrate one.[43]

Under interrogation, Overton steams with righteous anger:

> *Presid.*   Mr. Overton . . . We are not upon any Triall of you; we are
> onely upon the discharge of our dutie, and that trust committed unto us
> by the Parliament, to make enquiry after the authors, contrivers and
> framers of the Book; . . . we sent for you, and are to return your Answer
> to the House, howsoever you dispute their Authority.
> *R.Overt.*   Dispute their Authoritie, Sir! That's but your supposition, and
> supposition is no proof. And Sir, as you say you are to discharge your
> dutie, so must I discharge mine. And as for matter of triall, I am sure you
> taxe me in a criminall way, and proceed to question me thereupon.[44]

As much as there is an all too vivid awareness of power relations through
the reporting of crucial moments of communication, so also there is a
distrust of and disgust at these fora of persecution. Compared with
Lilburne, Wildman was an eloquent man, but he treats eloquence as a
sign of deceit, in preference for the 'experimentall truth'[45] of the
gathered churches, a quality which chimes with the 'woefull experience'
of Overton's satires against presbyterianism.

Looking at modes of representation in Leveller tracts is one way of
proceeding. Another approach is to explore the circulation of different
kinds of tracts, and the other texts which resided inside Leveller
publications. Lilburne is famously portrayed at his trial defending himself
with a copy of Coke's *Institutes* in his hand (see fig. 6).[46] Magna Carta
was another favourite, and there is a particularly urban image of Lilburne
scrabbling around in London trying to find a copy of that work. So other
books never leave the Leveller text, re-emphasising the significance of
print as the medium of ideology for the Leveller propagandists. In one
sense, this is a repetition of the strategy of quoting law used by Prynne in

The Sovereigne Power of Parliaments (1643). Moreover, the immediate context of Leveller tracts is, in part, the context of the newsbook: their arguments are modified and determined by this context. The role of Gilbert Mabbott's *The Moderate* and John Harris's *Mercurius Militaris* in effecting the transmission of Leveller ideas is substantial.[47] In a way, the Levellers were ahead of Parliament in their use of print, and saw themselves as descendants of earlier transgressive exploiters of print, especially Martin Marprelate. Parliament was not really prepared to use the presses in this open way, and neither was the Council of State. Once parliamentary predominance in the capital had been established printed material issued by Parliament returned to its function of controlling opinion, and the investigation and silencing of newsbooks carried on apace. By contrast, Leveller and proto-Leveller use of printed pamphlets was often noticed by hostile witnesses. A good example is the spoof Leveller pamphlet attributed to William Prynne, *The Total and Finall Demands already made by, and to be expected from, the Agitators and Army* (1647), which mocks the Levellers by assuming their voice. The tract refers in its margins to the effect of tracts in the ranks of the Army, among others Overton's Marpriest tracts and Lilburne's *Regall Tyranny Discovered*; all these tracts are seen to induce a desire to put the King on trial. No other radical group was ever so associated with the presses. Later on the Quakers made use of print in an innovative way, an achievement we are only just beginning to understand and acknowledge.[48] The extent of the Leveller reputation with print is a witness to the size of Lilburne's textual ego.

Before the differences of Putney, the Army collectively authored texts. A *Declaration, or, Representation* (1647) calls itself a 'Narrative of the Officers' (it was written by Rushworth), and was acknowledged as the binding expression of the democratic principles of the Army.[49] The ship of state image is unexpected, but reassuringly commonplace:

> we shall for our parts freely and cheerefully commit our stock or share of interest in this Kingdome, into this common bottome of Parliaments, and though it may (for our particulars) goe ill with us in one Voyage, yet we shall thus hope (if right be with us) to fare better in another.[50]

The Case of the Armie truly Stated (October 1647) was probably written by Wildman and signed by agents from five regiments. It brings to Fairfax's notice the fears of the soldiers that their officers were about to betray them. Again, textual vehicles are stressed: 'Narratives, Representations, Ingagement'. An actual narrative takes shape, with a particular focus upon representation.[51] It was at this juncture in the Army that the influence of the urban Levellers – especially Lilburne – was at its highest, and *The Case of the Armie* looks as though the effect of Lilburne and Overton's writing strategies had taken hold. The tract propounds a very crudely expressed 'ascending' theory of power, but it works entirely within its own framework. Political analysis in narrative form is an important part of the argument, and the (textual) war part of the perceptive frame of the piece:

> his Excellency slighted their Command, at Colebrooke, professing he knew no Parliament, to which he should send, are by this made guilty of the highest treason, and so a snare is layd for his Excellency and the Army, that when the enemies shall have the advantage, they may be declared traytors.[52]

A *Declaration of some Proceedings* (February 1648) was produced in order to attack Lilburne and Wildman by George Masterson, who had spied on a Leveller meeting. The tract is very open in allowing both sides of the debate a voice. Where, in *The Araignment of Mr. Persecution*, Overton put '*Gangraena*' Edwards's words into the mouth of Mr. Persecution in order to frighten and to ridicule, and succeeded, Masterson's recounting of Lilburne's words creates a 'Lilburnian narrative', the texture and tenor of which convincingly commands our attention and sympathy. Masterson's report of the circulation of *The Mournfull Cryes of many thousand poor Tradesmen* and *The Earnest Petition of many Free-born People of this Nation* at the meeting writes Leveller history in ways acceptable to Lilburne and Wildman, even as the tract was trying to cut the other way. Neither can Masterson stop Lilburne from appearing as a martyr. Yet the resort to propaganda as a way of demonstrating victimisation, even in this indirect way, is, as we shall see, no final or successful response to the Leveller dilemma.

The Uses of Books

Behind or within this textual pot-pourri, was there a consistently expressed political philosophy? Was there a set of principles which typify a Leveller way of thinking, or a procedure of analysis, anterior to the *Agreement of the People* and the other petitions?

Whereas Lilburne seems to have functioned as a performing 'text' for the movement, a figurehead and centre of attention, rather like George Fox was to become for the early Quakers, there is evidence of a more serious, heretical and humanist philosophy finding its way through to the other leaders and organisers.[53] Overton also had his moments as a persecuted figurehead (not nearly as many as Lilburne), but it is possible to find in his writings the clearest philosophical expression of the Leveller idea of natural law. Overton's interpretation of this emphasises the limits of self or being, and is somewhat at odds with the impression of 'dilation' or *amplificatio* that we have seen at work in other kinds of Leveller tract:

> Now as no man by nature may abuse, beat, torment or afflict himself, so by nature no man may give that power to another, seeing that he may not doe it himselfe, for no more can be communicated to the generall, then is included in the particulars whereof the generall is compounded; for that were to goe beyond it selfe, for *Being* to goe beyond the *power of being*, which is impossible.[54]

This is the view accepted as authentic by commentators on the history of the idea of natural law and natural rights.[55] In Overton, there is clearly a rational view of nature based in part on the heretical notion of the soul as reason.[56] And in Walwyn, as I have argued elsewhere, the exposure to humanist texts in translation (Plutarch, Montaigne, Charron) produces what would appear to orthodox Calvinists as a dangerous cocktail of dissembling reasoning – that kind of *paradiastole* which Hobbes so feared.[57]

William Bray, famous for his Leveller activity in the Army in the 1640s, was still active in Levellerish ways just before the Restoration. His internalisation of Charron seems even more developed than Walwyn's. On Cromwell's closure of the Barebones Parliament, he wrote (perhaps echoing Walwyn's pacifism): 'And so I shall conclude this my Answer with the saying of *Charron* in his Book of Wisdom; *Male cunst a minstrat impetus*. Violence doth nothing well.'[58] The world which produces this kind of thinking is a world of books, in which different members of the 'middling sort' educate themselves with various works from which can be derived insights and techniques necessary for a Leveller project and a Leveller version of society. Some literate merchants, tradesmen and artisans became sufficiently skilled in these verbal techniques to speak out, and, in a way, to become leaders of their communities. William Walwyn's activities in democratising the parish of St James, Garlickhithe, which preceded and then ran parallel with his political career, are a ready example. We should remember here the domestic world of the godly in the 1620s and 1630s. The later Ranter Jacob Bauthumley was punished (as was his father) for permitting the repetition of sermons by Jeremiah Burroughes in his house – he was punished by having his business ostracised within the local community. As far as we know at present, Burroughes was the first person to suggest in print (in 1643) that England did not necessarily need a monarchy.[59] The potential for the transmission of radical political ideas in godly circles is only too evident.

This culture was a world of lay knowledge of various sciences, but a knowledge which again was not unbookish. Richard Overton found support for his doctrine of the mortality of the soul in the writings of the French Paracelsan, Ambrose Paré. Paracelsans were the more usual medical authorities for those not members of the medical profession, and Paré is best known for his publications on monsters. As Christopher Hill has so magnificently demonstrated, Winstanley's religious ideas grow from the same context even if it is difficult to tell precisely which books he used.[60] The recent picture which has emerged of Winstanley as the failed merchant and bankrupt of early 1640s London supports this view: a man who lived in a world of books, but one who through bitter experience turned what these told him into a far more radical proposal and practice for re-organising the world.[61] The educational reformer Samuel Hartlib busied himself collecting information on educational projects among such people.[62]

So we are not dealing with a world of spontaneous, autochthonous proto-socialists and proto-communists. We are dealing precisely with a literate and skilled urban group, the most socially mobile part of the early modern population. They were fashioned by puritanism, but also by the ideals of sixteenth-century educational theory. They were the people for whom reading was commodified in the 1580s and 1590s, and with the new freedoms for publication in the 1640s, we could say that they had grown up. So, if not 'gentlemen Levellers', certainly they were burgher Levellers. This was the world of the 'middling sort', which bridged the gentry and the labouring poor, the readership of the poetry of John Taylor and George Wither. By associating Wither with Lilburne, Taylor was acknowledging the politicisation of this world.[63] Overton's incessant bookishness is attested in his own narrative of his arrest in the spring of 1649, *The Proceedings of the Councel of State* (1649):

> Well, he having ransack'd the house, found many books in the beds, and taken away all such writings, papers, and books, of what sort or kind soever, that he could finde, and given them to the souldiers, (amongst which he took away certain papers which were my former Meditations upon the works of the Creation, intituled, *Gods Word confirmed by his Works*; wherein I endeavoured the probation of a God, a Creation, a State of Innocencie, a Fall, a Resurrection, a Restorer, a Day of Judgment, &c. barely from the consideration of things visible and created: and these papers I reserved to perfect and publish as soon as I could have any rest from the turmoils of this troubled Common-wealth).[64]

Overton was a General Baptist, and, quite consistently with their habits, he says he has been working at a kind of deist treatise. With the kind of confidence and contempt for worldly authority which only someone who had been a hardened separatist for many years could have, Overton sees the state apparatus of the republic as yet another superstructure of religious superstition. He had out-Hobbesed Hobbes (see below, 155–63).

We should be under no illusion that the Levellers could not think for themselves, and that they had a rich context and means for doing so. Their ideas certainly had the capacity to shock their natural allies, although at the same time they also had much in common with some of them.

Going forwards from the earlier tracts, Lilburne's *Regall Tyranny Discovered* (1646–7) is a good example of a more mature Leveller tract at work. Lilburne's earlier habit of presenting himself as a martyr never diminished in his writings, but by 1646 the Leveller version of natural law theory had emerged. Lilburne effectively parodies the kind of pamphlet or publication which his opponents would have published, but he does this without sacrificing any persuasive purchase. The kind of relentless numbering of positions and animadversions which one would find in a Prynne tract appears here, but the extent of Prynne's juridical enumerations is curtailed. Likewise, many of Lilburne's references are to historical works which men like Prynne made much use of. In Lilburne's case, the various references to Speed, Daniel, Coke, Polydore Virgil and Prynne himself are turned against the body (Parliament) whose apologists had originally used them in its defence.[65] The pamphlet itself becomes a celebration of the politics to which it belongs by foregrounding how it is constituted and how it is the very special property of the Levellers. Lilburne writes from prison and he refers to those tracts which have incriminated him (Samuel Sheppard's journalism and Edward Bowles's *Plaine English*), while also citing other significant Leveller and related documents – his wife, Elizabeth's, petition for his release (although he claims he wrote it), his own *Liberty Vindicated Against Slavery*, one of Richard Overton's Marpriest tracts and John Cook's *Vindication of Professors*. The attack then is concerned with the law of *habeas corpus*, which Parliament has suppressed in the same way that it has gone back on its commitment (according to Lilburne) to remove the Norman Yoke. At the very centre of all this presented power relationship is (and it passes the modern reader almost without notice) a clear desacralising of the notion of kingship. Lilburne the subject and the status of the King are the two opposite ideological nodes of the pamphlet; it is the reader's task to determine their correct relationship, and they are left, as it were, trembling in the air, in an uncertain relationship to each other.

The Levellers were once thought to have rejected the idea of a common law. Theirs was the most extreme example of the notion that the Norman Yoke had to be thrown off; they did not, so the view goes, believe that there was a recoverable, pre-Norman constitution which was not corrupt. But it has been shown that not the common law but the form of its dispensing was what gave them offence. Thus the common law should exist in an ideal state – a body of law textually represented, but which should be properly interpreted and executed in practice. In this way, the common law begins to look like the rather nebulous fundamental law, or the natural law which Overton so praised. In other words, the Levellers tended to merge positive and divine or natural laws.[66] To idealise, allegorise and analogise in this way would be to link legal complaint with the cosmological reorganising which many Levellers professed. It would also connect with the idealising presentations in the Army of the troops as God's agents, and it was also a version of theological reasoning, such as one might find in a work on church government. These modes of representation are at the heart of the possibility for the mass raising of consciousness, as occurred in the New Model Army and the sects.

The Putney Debates effectively represent the end point of the first and most successful phase of Leveller discourse in action.[67] In the manuscript account of this meeting between the Army commanders and Army Levellers and agitators, it is not difficult to see many views being held in common, and why Cromwell was so attractive to officers and soldiers alike. In the debates, Cromwell appears keen to introduce an honest countenance among soldiers based upon internalised self-discipline – a genuinely and publicly expressed puritan heroism. This includes being able to confess absolute convictions to God when speaking publicly, with no dissimulation. Yet he had problems with imagining a Leveller England, thinking it would be like dissipated, impoverished and cantonal Switzerland. These comments are illustrative of the affective nature of Cromwell's perceptions and utterances.

Engagements were seen as a form of contract (*PL*, 10). Engagement relates directly to responsibility and the extent of 'unbounded' liberty expressed in the major Leveller tracts; this was the hub of the difference between the two sides. Yet the sense of the presence of God here seems important – God is what is with one in one's loneliness (in rebellion or resistance) as a political agent; hence the significance here of the collective prayers (*PL*, 101). Prayer creates a sense of collective identity, and makes individuals aware of the power which takes people beyond that which they can rationally conceive. Sexby, later a staunch republican, puts it like this: 'The Lord hath put you into a state, or at least [suffered you] to run you[rselves] into such a one, that you know not where you are. You are in a wilderness condition' (*PL*, 102). Curiously, there is a lot of loneliness, a sense of singular and collective uncertainty as to whether the Army is fulfilling God's purpose, and this transposes readily onto spiritual autobiography, connecting the characteristically Leveller to the characteristically puritan. The bringing together of different religious wills is evident in Rainborough's famous speech on equality of consent, and the response is with Ireton who says suffrage must be rooted in property qualifications. He stresses having a permanent interest in the kingdom, and sees the radical position as avoiding all civil law and reverting dangerously to the law of nature, where liberty is reduced by the collision of so many individual rights of nature. Indeed, Ireton maintains that the propertyless have no birthright to the franchise (but only the most basic rights, like that to breathe the air). Speaking in Rainborough's support, Nathaniel Rich used the example of the Roman senates setting 'interests' in property.

Rainborough himself did not regard the authority of civil superiors (including the propertied and magistrates) as in any sense binding – he says he may know who are his civil father and mother, but this does not bind him (*PL*, 61). With property so discounted, Maximilian Petty wanted to see the franchise broadened (*ibid.*). For Ireton, the soldiers' rights (as Rainborough would say) are 'coming up' out of nothing, appearing from nowhere, which itself is a good illustration of the originality of what is being suggested. It is also a version of the figure of the dragon's teeth which had so occupied political apologists in the early 1640s.

As one reads further through the Debates, so the power of interests becomes more apparent. Ireton assumes that there is a constitution for the purposes of maintaining liberty through the protection of property (*PL*, 82). On the contrary, Wildman thinks in terms of the vulnerability of the people and their need for indemnity and further protection from King and Parliament (*PL*, 91). Cromwell has an acute sense of needing to subordinate the Army to the Parliament (*PL*, 97). The form of the government did not seem to matter to him either, as he demonstrated from the history of the Jews, who lived happily under a variety of different forms. What matters is the liberty sustained by a form, and to that extent the deliberation should be left to Parliament.

These matters were not resolved at Putney. The *Heads of Proposals* (Sept. 1647) had stated that there should be biennial parliaments, an extended franchise, a ten-year government by a Council of State, and a severely limited (and very vaguely defined) monarchy. Putney did not resolve the question of franchise: as we have seen, the more important issue in the debate was religious toleration, focused upon the experience of martial sainthood. The Army Council's *Remonstrance* of November 1648 proposed an elective monarchy, an extended franchise, rule by a Council of State, and the trial of King Charles I. The Levellers objected to none of this, but they did object to the Army and Independent (or republican) desire to purge the Commons of the M.P.s still willing to negotiate with the King. This the Levellers readily identified as a further alienation of the representative, opening the way for tyrannical rule by a Council of State. The Levellers became highly vocal critics of the two central institutions (the Rump Parliament and the Council of State) of the new free state, proclaimed a week after the execution of the King, and its tyranny was confirmed by the suppression of Leveller-associated mutinies in the Army in April to May 1649. One set of godly republicans trounced another set in the name of maintaining stability in the early days of the new state.

Levellers Republicanised

One major problem in Leveller writing needs to be resolved. How was it that a movement which had its origins in radical puritan experience and which founded its politics in the urban sphere could come to entertain serious regicidal and then republican ideas? Most accounts of republicanism in the 1640s see it as an elite interest. The reasons are complex. The dominant framework must be the same one that applies to the Leveller theory of rights – that ideas dripped out of the political nation to the literate 'middling sort'. Those Levellers who, like John Harris, had had experience of the theatres knew about resistance from its representation on the stage. Captain William Thompson's tiny pamphlet *England's Standard Advanced* (20 Aug. 1649) sees a worse tyranny than monarchy 'under the Notion of a *Free State*', and he cites John Cook's *King Charls his Case* (1649) in support of this view.[68] At the same time, some prominent Levellers were from families connected closely to the gentry, so that the kinship nexus, as it were, was the avenue down which the classical idea passed.[69] This is true for Walwyn, Lilburne, Wildman and Sexby. The experience of the last two in the Army democratised their consciousnesses.

Englands Miserie, and Remedie (1645) is thought to be the first Leveller tract to voice classical republican ideas and sources. It has been attributed to Sexby.[70] The tract alleges judicial abuse of Lilburne and falls back upon Buchanan's *De jure regni*, Livy's *History* (Decade 5 and Book 8), and Pliny's *Panegyric* to prove that supreme power is in the people (4, 6). A concern with institutions begins to join the usual concern with tyranny. Bacon is also invoked on unjust sentences being worse than a crime (5), although perhaps more interesting is the quotation at the end of lines from Wither's poem *Vox Pacifica*. Wither is the popular poet who had confronted directly in his verse the relationship between kings, representatives and people.[71]

It is also clear that the experience of political campaigning effected a political education of the chief Levellers, so that they ended their careers sharing a knowledge of the art of politics with those against whom they were pitted. William Bray answers Harrington's *CXX Political Aphorisms*

(Aug.–Sept. 1659) on republican and Harringtonian terms, but with a nice carnivalesque personification:

> our Common Lawes as to the generality flowed first out of *Normandy* . . .
> As *Cicero* was bold to derive the Pedigree of his Roman Law from the
> great God *Jupiter*, so (saith he) I hope without offence, I may be
> imboldened in the person of our Common Law, to say, That when the
> *Lawes* of God and Reason came first into England, then came I in.[72]

Lilburne's political education in exile in the early 1650s is strikingly represented in *L. Colonel John Lilburne revived* (1653), three letters written from exile in Amsterdam and Flanders, 'Shewing the cause of his late long silence, and cessation from Hostility against alchemy St. Oliver, and his rotten Secretary'. Exile gave time for reflection, for reading, time to convert partial into fully-fledged republicanism. Polybius is 'wise and wel-pend', and his works provide parallels between Leveller politics and Greek or Roman experience. The portraits of virtue and valour in Plutarch and Polybius perform a similar function, inducing in Lilburne the kind of cultural relativism which we have seen in Walwyn, and again stressing thoughtful, diligent reading:

> Having red so much of famous Plutarchs Lives lately, with so much
> delight and seriousnes as I have done (reading for many daies together
> fiftie of his large Folios in a Day, and also largely takeing notes as I reade
> (my common practise in reading any book that pleaseth me) I hope
> shortly in a few lines, which I intend to present him with, to let him know
> I now fully understand his meaning. (23)[73]

Predictably, it is the classical treatment of tyranny which is the great bogey (Lilburne reveals himself to be a belated Tacitean and stoic in this respect), so that, altogether, 1650s Levellerism has a very unusual classical element, made distinctive by the use of popular modes:

> *The cleare unspotted Faith*
> > *Of Romans, we adore:*
> *And vow to be their faithfull friends,*
> > *Both now and evermore.*
>
> *Sing out ye Muses nine,*
> > *To Ioves eternall fame:*
> *Sing out the Honour due to Rome,*
> > *And Titus worthy name.*
>
> *Sing out, I say, the praise*
> > *Of Titus, and his faith:*
> *By whom ye have preserved bin*
> > *From Ruine, Doole and Death.* (22)

An anonymous controverter of Lilburne pointed out that he had the wrong Titus, and suggested that, patriot as he was, Lilburne's intemperate nature had led him into textual and legal snares.[74] Like Milton's Satan, Lilburne had erred, and his redactions from Plutarch are often rather blundering, uncontrolled repeatings of the translated texts. But Lilburne was unrepentant, not least because he had seen beyond a virtue-centred view of political behaviour with the help of Machiavelli. He understands that states which begin in violence will produce further violence from those who will take revenge on them; the example is Tarquin.[75] Further Machiavellian analyses are offered in the exile and post-exile tracts, in addition to praise of another embattled, patriotic Machiavellian, John Milton.[76] For the controverter, this was only more evidence of Lilburne's corruption: from Machiavelli he would only learn to be a Borgia, or a fomenter of destructive popular sedition against the (English) senate.[77]

Other clearly republican Levellerish tracts, appearing before 1649 include *Vox Plebis* (19 Nov. 1646; see above, 138). In this connection, it is important to regard the Levellers as a broad coalition of different individuals with similar but not always identical or closely aligned views. *Vox Plebis* is sometimes attributed to Marten (and now also Nedham), and it defends Lilburne when he was prosecuted by the House of Lords for allegedly insulting the Earl of Manchester.[78] Republics are referred to ('a Republique that is well-ordered, ought to give easie accesse to those that seek Justice by publique meanes' [1, 59]; bad citizens are always punished in a republic [61–2, 66]). There are more Roman references – the Tarquins (3), Cicero (23), Livy (64), and then, calling on more recent writers, Machiavelli (60), Guicciardini (65) and masses of other *discorsi* style examples; Ralegh is also used in a republican way to comment upon free states in Greece (63, 65, 68). In addition free grace, natural law and divine right are clearly identified (4), and Magna Carta is regarded as but a confirmation of these earlier inheritances.

But to what extent Leveller thought was able to dwell on the significance of particular constitutional features, as opposed to the desirability of good (if not also godly) leaders, remains to be seen. If anyone was able to generate a truly militant rhetoric, which incited people to violent uprising, it was Wildman, especially in *Putney Projects* (1647). Cromwell and Ireton are 'valiant Champions', 'gallant Patriots; and those most noble *Heroes* of our Age' (2, 8), but they have betrayed the Army and the people after the Army Engagement on Newmarket Heath of 5 June 1647. The usual Leveller complaint of oppression is made, but this time it is combined with a register of popular chivalry. Within this framework, Cromwell's interest in reaching a settlement with the King – deeply duplicitous from Wildman's point of view – is presented as intoxication by deadly courtliness. Character is as dilated as ever in Leveller tracts, and allegorically Spenserian:

> suddenly the Kings flatteries proved an intoxicating cup, which polluted their judgements, and poysoned their hearts, and from that bottomlesse fountaine of wickednesse, tyranny, and cruelty, the Kings heart, was infused such venemous notions into their braines, as converted all their speeches, actions, and councells into a courtly forme. (11)

Towards the end of the tract, heroic names and chivalric codes are being used with bitterly ironic sarcasm. Against the idea of a council to advise the King, Wildman doubts that it could effectively arbitrate between the King's and the people's interests, even if its members were 'such chaste virgins, as to loath the defilements by Court embraces, but also such Noble Heroick Champions, as would make their integrity their shield' (24–5).

One year later, however, Wildman was confidently citing what would become in the following decade the major classical sources for republican government – Aristotle and Polybius, as well as Diodorus Siculus, Xenophon and Cicero. In fact, the frame of textual reference in *The Lawes Subversion* (1648) is very sophisticated, and indeed looking towards Harrington:

> Every Nation is but a rude indigested *Chaos* a deformed lump untill Lawes or rules of Government be established, Lawes are the *vis plistica* [sic] or formatrix that formes the principall vitalls, the heart, the braine, the liver of the Commonwealth. (2)

Yet this is not divorced from the heavy populist tones of the slightly earlier works. Rather, Wildman has evolved, and his ideas were echoed by other republicans in the 1650s (see below, 196–9).

By the mid-1650s, these 'politique' Levelling tendencies had also incorporated a fully-fledged theory of republican assassination, so that in the writings of Sexby and the actions of the unfortunate Miles Sindercombe are replicated the representation of republican conspiracy as shown on the Renaissance stage. Yet Sexby's famous *Killing Noe Murder* (1657) is no work of mere revenge: 'It is not my Ambition to be in Print, when so few spare Paper and the Press, nor any instigations of private revenge or malice' (3). This has gone a stage further than, for example, Lilburne's reading of Machiavelli during his exile, so that he could learn what went wrong with the Leveller movement of the late 1640s. *Killing Noe Murder* (1657), written under the pseudonym of William Allen, is a highly wrought piece of tyrannicidal classical republicanism, the work of serious bookishness and meditation.[79] It was deliberately designed to immortalise through print Sindercombe, who was condemned to die for his attempt on the Protector's life, and who died in mysterious circumstances in his cell the night before his execution (he may have poisoned himself).

Killing Noe Murder (1657) is an invitation to Oliver Cromwell to allow himself to be executed for the sake of the English people. He has done great things, but he has become a tyrant in doing so. In a strange and direct reversal of patronage relations (an indication of the refined nature of Sexby's thought), Cromwell is urged to submit to the 'honour of dying for the people'. While Cromwell lives, citizenship is denied, and Sexby shows how much more he had read in the decade since the Putney Debates by listing classical and Renaissance anti-tyranny sources (at least 17 different authors are named). In Sexby's vision, tyrants become monsters who tear the bodies of their victims. *Killing Noe Murder* is printed densely on thin paper – it looks like a Quaker tract – and through this fugitive, desperate appearance, looks the part of its recommendations. When Sexby speaks, we are no longer listening to the officer of the New Model Army, but Catiline, a Catiline who has been freed of anti-republican aspersions and has adopted Milton's recommendation that a private person may 'resist':

> Some I find of a strange opinion, that it were a generous and a noble action to kill his Highness in the field; but to doe it privately they think it unlawfull, but know not why. As if it were not generous to apprehend a thief till his sword were drawn and he in a posture to defend himself and kill me. But these people do not consider that whosoever is possest of power any time, wilbe sure to ingage so many either in guilt or profit, or both, that to goe about to throw him out by open force, will very much hazard the totall ruine of the Common-Wealth. A Tyrant is a Devill that teares the body in the exorcizing, & they are all of Caligula's temper [margin: *Sueton. in vit. Calig.*], that if they could, they would have the whole frame of Nature fall with them. Tis an opinion deserves no other refutation then the manifest absurdity of it self; that it should be lawfull for me to destroy a Tirant with hazard, blood, and conclusion, but not without. (13)

Yet Sexby published *Killing Noe Murder* with the help of the Royalist, Silius Titus. The fortunes of royalist conspiracy were bound up with those of republican conspiracy, and the sense of a collective cause, such as is signalled in the civic fun of the 1640s Leveller tract, is gone. The tyranny of state is presented as an imposition of the will of Whitehall upon a reborn Hebrew state – a formulation which sounds either Harringtonian or Fifth Monarchist, but not Levellerish. After Burford, Sexby served in the Army for the Commonwealth, negotiated on its behalf with the *Frondeurs* in France, but managed still to convert some of the French rebels to Leveller principles. Like a Restoration republican (indeed, like Algernon Sidney), his behaviour and opinions were ambiguous, and this was part of the meaning of his republicanism, as it was for Sidney. Milton's principles were more apparently consistent, but Sexby's sensitive and empathic response to the poet's treatment of tyrants is a measure of the assimilation of 'high' republican views by someone who came from the lesser ranks. In the posthumously published 1659 edition of the tract (Sexby had died in the Tower of London in January 1658), the 'learned Milton' of *The Tenure of Kings and Magistrates* is cited, and in particular his use of the examples of resistance in Samson and Samuel. As we have seen, in 1653, Lilburne had already translated from Latin a long passage from the *First Defence* on resistance, and he had hailed Milton as a great 'patriot' (see above, 150). The stress on the right to resist by 'private hands' means either that Sexby had seen a copy of the first edition of the *Tenure*, or that he had some knowledge of *Samson Agonistes* – which perhaps was already in existence.[80] Nonetheless, *Killing Noe Murder* does represent a real decline from the writings of 1645–9: when Clarendon acquired a copy in exile, he chuckled at its 'wit', finding no difficulty in adopting it as part of the royalist resistance. His own close relations with Titus may suggest that *Killing Noe Murder* was more of a royalist instrument than Sexby or previous historians realised.[81]

The more radical Leveller ideas, especially the religious and philosophical ones which lay behind the political ideals, remain more compelling and extreme than the politics of 1647–8 – hence the abiding interest in Richard Overton and William Walwyn. But what place was there for such idealism after 1649? The discovery of secular republican theory was, for the godly Levellers, like experiencing a fall in the very moment of their defeat. The Leveller movement and its culture is best understood as a moment in the politicisation of the 'middling sort' in the very special circumstances of the later 1640s. When that moment had passed, new allegiances and ideas were entertained in an evolving process. 'Levelling' was the negotiating of rights; in the 1650s, the Levellers had become very largely either republicans, millenarians or Quakers.

CHAPTER 5

Political Theory as Aesthetics:
Hobbes, Harrington, Winstanley

To what Disease in the Naturall Body of man, I may exactly compare this irregularity of a Common-wealth, I know not. But I have seen a man, that had another man growing out of his side, with an head, armes, breast, and stomach, of his own: If he had had another man growing out of his other side, the comparison might then have been made.

'Mixt Government', *Leviathan*
II.29, ed. C.B. Macpherson (1968), 372–3

MOST POLITICAL DISCOURSE during the 1640s is brief and employs the bricolage of techniques and arguments which we have seen in the preceding two chapters. Longer works, such as Hunton's *Treatise on Monarchy*, are more consistently integrated and unified but they too make the tools of rhetoric and logic answer the needs of argument, never giving these tools privilege above the matter at hand. Yet it so happens that the two most significant and memorable contributions to political theory produced in the Interregnum do just that. They involve breathtaking feats of imaginative daring, using art to restructure politics and religion, breaking down the barriers between different kinds of writing, and different areas of life. They produce conclusions which seem to live outside history. This is not to say that Hobbes's *Leviathan* (1651) and Harrington's *Oceana* (1656) do not belong to long traditions of social philosophy; they do.[1] But they also reconstruct a social vision of human life in a way which none of the works immediately preceding them had done. That *Leviathan* was conceived and written in exile in France, away from the controversial exchanges of the Civil War, and *Oceana* in the internal exile of retirement during the early and mid-1650s, has not a little to do with this detached originality. Yet both understand acutely the issues which underlay practically every debate in the 1640s (and which so many tracts had struggled to grasp), the nature of the self or individual, and its relationship with that which governs it. Winstanley's utopian writings are in some ways very different kinds of texts, yet they employ methods and reach conclusions related to both *Leviathan* and *Oceana*, and this is to do with their emergence from a common moment.

Both *Leviathan* and *Oceana* are ironic works, telling 'truths' which do not fully accord with their authors' intentions, and they are prismatic texts, yielding different and diverse conclusions, depending on how they are viewed. Their opposite is Gerrard Winstanley's writing on behalf of the mystical communist utopia, although all three authors share several qualities precisely because they are being so daring. Winstanley's writings do not use *inventio* in the same way as Hobbes and Harrington, but they reject all received traditions in order to structure a social vision out of their own resources.

Hobbes's Body

What is a state? Hobbes says in the 'Introduction' to *Leviathan* that it is an 'Artificiall Man', created in imitation of man, 'that Rationall and most excellent worke of *Nature*'.[2] This vast figure has a spiritual and physical constitution which corresponds to the dimensions of the natural human body:

> though of greater stature and strength than the Naturall, for whose protection and defence it was intended; and in which, the *Soveraignty* is an Artificiall *Soul*, as giving life and motion to the whole body; The *Magistrates*, and other *Officers* of Judicature and Execution, artificiall *Joynts*; *Reward and Punishment* (by which fastned to the seate of Soveraignty, every joynt and member is moved to do his duty) are the *Nerves*, that do the same in the Body Naturall; The *Wealth* and *Riches* of all the particular members, are the *Strength*; *Salus Populi* (the *peoples safety*) its *Businesse*; *Counsellors*, by whom all things needfull for it to know, are suggested unto it, are the *Memory*, *Equity* and *Lawes*, an artificiall *Reason* and *Will*; *Concord*, *Health*; *Sedition*, *Sicknesse*; and *Civill war*, *Death*. Lastly, the *Pacts* and *Covenants*, by which parts of this Body Politique were at first made, set together, and united, resemble that *Fiat*, or the *Let us make man*, pronounced by God in the Creation. (81)[3]

Few Europeans would have been able to imagine such an integrated picture at this time, for 'the term "constitutionalism" had no currency in the political thought of the late fifteenth and sixteenth centuries . . . a constitution was an explicit declaration of law by the prime political authority . . . constitutions were sets of historically established, even fundamental, laws'.[4] However, bodies *were* constitutions.[5] Thus, Milton used the virtuous Christian individual as a metaphor for a redeemed Christian Commonwealth:

> To be plainer Sir, how to soder, how to stop a leak, how to keep up the floting carcas of a crazie, and diseased Monarchy, or State betwixt wind,

and water, swimming still upon her own dead lees, that now is the deepe designe of a politician. Alas Sir! a Commonwelth ought to be but as one huge Christian personage, one mighty growth, and stature of an honest man, as big, and compact in vertue as in body.[6]

Leviathan's political body is a direct reflection of the rational and sensationalist psychology written against any claim that the divine could operate by inspiration in man. All is produced by sense, and when not controlled by reason, consciousness degenerates to the operation of the passions:

> All which qualities called *Sensible*, are in the object that causeth them, but so many several motions of the matter, by which it presseth our organs diversely. . . . And as pressing, rubbing, or striking the Eye, makes us fancy a light; and pressing the Eare, produceth a dinne; so do the bodies also we see, or hear, produce the same by their strong, though unobserved action. (86)

Fantasies, dreams, visions, imaginations are all 'fictions of the mind' (89), produced by this sense psychology system. *Leviathan* contains the most important articulation of this belief, but Hobbes had constructed an earlier version of this system in *Human Nature* and *De Corpore*, both of which were written in 1640.

Together with his denial of Aristotle's metaphysics, and following from his belief that the soul cannot exist without the body, Hobbes argues that the universe is entirely corporeal:

> the *Universe*, that is, the whole masse of all things that are . . . is Corporeall, that is to say, Body; and hath the like dimensions of Magnitude, namely, Length, Bredth, and Depth: also every part of Body, is likewise Body, and hath the like dimensions; and consequently every part of the Universe, is Body, and that which is not Body, is no part of the Universe: And because the Universe is All, that which is no part of it, is *Nothing*; and consequently *no where*. (689)

Bodies, however, can become disordered internally, and hence prone to disharmonious behaviour externally. In natural men, productions of the will, like passions (and other unruly emotions), must be mastered or regulated. In the social body, the 'artificiall man', passions are rebellious or revolutionary discordances which must be cured by proper political order.

The regulator of the body politic, the suppressor of the passions, is the covenant, by which individuals agree to give up their natural rights of self-protection in order to be protected by the sovereign. The covenant in the body politic occupies the same place as reason in the human body.

Hobbes's state appears to operate (his exact term is 'resemblance') just like a human being;[7] it has an internal physiology which, for all its

Figure 7 Thomas Hobbes, *Leviathan* (1651), engraved title-page.

theatrical dimensions, works rationally and mechanistically. Its soul is its sovereignty, that which makes the machine operate, that which gives it life. Society is 'anthropomorphised' as an 'artificial' man whose 'selfhood' predominates over the selfhoods of the people because they are but 'bodies' subject to 'motions'.[8]

In other words, Hobbes's definition of a person is turned inside out, amplified, and spread across society. Its definition comes from the operating parameters of civil society 'inwards' and moves towards the regulation of the subjects (the literal persons). Such an interpretation is supported by the engraved frontispiece (see fig. 7). Here, the sovereign is the 'head' of the body politic, the body and limbs of which are constituted by the subjects, all of whom are shown looking up to the head of the sovereign. The massive figure shown here is not the sovereign, as is often supposed, but the body politic itself. Yet it also seems as if subjectivity (the people) and political representation (the sovereign authority) are elided in the very constitution of the body by the people. Hence the incidental sketching, in particular copies which have survived, of the heads of Charles I, Charles II or Cromwell onto the face of the figure: the picture makes Hobbes's description of political power satisfy a number of different political sympathies.[9] We cannot tell who is ruled and who is ruling – a problem which, as we shall see, was blatantly apparent to Hobbes's first readers.

Elsewhere in *Leviathan*, it is not difficult to mistake the commonwealth for a very powerful sovereign prince, by virtue of the force of the metaphor: 'the Multitude so united in one Person, is called a COMMON-WEALTH, in latine CIVITAS. This is the Generation of that great LEVIATHAN, or rather (to speake more reverently) of that *Mortall God*, to which we owe under the *Immortall God*, our peace and defence'(227). This is so extreme as to be almost satirical of earthly authority – perhaps especially so in the context of the state formation taking place in 1650–51.[10] Is not the commonwealth becoming the sovereign, and the sovereign the commonwealth? Is it possible to personify the state without simultaneously evoking the figure of the person usually associated in European history with its governance – the prince? Such a collapsing of distinctions, by the force of rhetorical prowess, is a common feature of *Leviathan*, a fulfilment of the effect of this beast. Moreover, in this description, the sovereign acts *and* has authority – which constitutes a doubling of the division of the civil functions of covenant-making introduced at the end of *Leviathan* Part 1, and which thereby provides the mighty person of the sovereign with a legitimate personality absent from the motion-driven subjects. We have arrived at a self – the commonwealth – with an originating centre that is a total expression of all the subjects, and which neatly dispels all the problems of inner dissent which arise in states, since only the sovereign is allowed to do anything.

Most people, and especially Parliamentarians and republicans, thought otherwise. In 1645, George Wither provided precisely the opposite version of the body politic to Hobbes. Whereas a natural body, says Wither, cannot do without a head, the 'vitals' of the body politic lie in the body:

> A *King*, is but a *substituted-head*,
> Made for *conveniencie*: And, if thereby
> The *bodie* seem to be indangered,
> (If *Power* it hath) it hath *Authoritie*.[11]

If Hobbes's body is entirely different from this tradition of representation, it has nonetheless has been seen as the perpetrator of secular superstition: his view of the power of the sovereign through the fear which the subject experiences has been regarded as occupying the same place as the phantasms which operate in superstitious societies –

especially pagan ones.[12] This cannot be so. Hobbes is attempting to redescribe the human psyche and the collective political psyche so that the nebulous delusions of the past may be forgotten. The history of people who believe in dreams, visions and fairies is a history of certain idols of the mind that should be dispelled exactly as Hobbes's old master Bacon (in the *Novum Organon*) said they should. It can only be the case that dissension and civil war come from those whose fancies tell them erroneously that simple egotistical oration or rebellion will achieve liberty. True 'liberty' for Hobbes is defined precisely by the covenant in the state of society.

What is unusual in Hobbes's description of the operation of people, society and sovereign as a body politic is that no body has an 'essence' because 'essences' for Hobbes are metaphorical descriptions of transcendental entities which he believes are simply *not*. Individuals, be they subjects or sovereigns, may take on roles – they may be actors or authors, for instance – but they do not have inner selves defined as 'souls' or approximate psychological figurations like 'the heart' around which a central explanation of character and agency may be focused, and which is a feature of just about every other contemporary description of people and societies. They simply have functions.[13]

In several passages throughout his writings, Hobbes redefines vocabulary usually associated with heroic and transcendentalised conceptions of human beings (a language of inward essences) in terms of his materialised human. This vocabulary is then mapped onto the description of the body politic. Sometimes the 'artificial' appears to be driving the natural, so that the sovereign as 'soul' of the state provides a defining picture of 'reason' in the natural body of each individual.

Despite his elevation of his materialist and geometrical vision over authorities, the political passions (the passions in the body politic) are registered for Hobbes through and in classical literature and rhetoric. As we have seen, in Hobbes's view, the English Civil War was caused by too many English gentlemen imbibing republican ideas in their reading at school and university of Greek and Latin texts (*Leviathan*, 267). Words and books are the corruptors of the material human – quite the contrary view to Milton's. While in fact most educated English people did not think of a political order beyond monarchy (at least before 1650), Hobbes was fixing upon the exposure of men to ideals of rhetoric and eloquence. The Ciceronian ethos of virtuous speech is a discordant anarchy within the body politic.[14]

In fact, bodily imbalance in Hobbes is registered by means of genres (and vocabulary associated with them) whose constructions of agency are dangerous to the integration of a whole self (as it was viewed by Hobbes). Once again, genre plays a crucial role in the articulation of a political critique. 'Glory' is identified in *Human Nature* as a kind of pride – 'the passion which proceedeth from the imagination or conception of our *own power* above the power of him that contendeth with us'.[15] It is not an innate quality but an illusion in the human machine created by a deluded interpretation of the power relationships which prevail in the greater 'artificiall man' of society. One of its origins is the reading of romances:

> the *fiction*, which is also imagination, of actions done by ourselves, which never were done, is *glorying*; but because it begetteth no appetite nor endeavour to any further attempt, it is merely *vain* and unprofitable; as when a man imagineth himself to do the actions whereof he readeth in some *romance*, or to be like some man whose acts he admireth.[16]

The same figure occurs in *Leviathan*. The compound imagination deludes the individual into the belief that he is heroic:

> when a man compoundeth the image of his own person, with the image of the actions of an other man; as when a man imagins himself a *Hercules*, or an *Alexander*, (which happeneth often to them that are much taken with reading of Romants) it is a compound imagination, and properly but a Fiction of the mind. (89)[17]

Literary genre functions in Hobbes as a means of articulating the kind of human activity which runs away from the hold of natural law. The distance between life and art (as between nature and culture, once civil society has been formed) disappears:

> as in raising an opinion from passion, any premises are good enough to enforce the desired conclusion; so, in raising passion from opinion, it is no matter whether the opinion be true or false, or the narration historical or fabulous; for, *not* the *truth*, but the *image*, maketh passion: and a tragedy, well acted, affecteth no less than a murder.[18]

Sometimes, passions are excited at plays whose causes are incidental to the performance itself. Their interpretation nonetheless involves the effect of drama, even if it is delusive: at a performance of *Andromeda* at Abdera, the audience fell into a fever and pronounced iambics 'with the names of *Persius* and *Andromeda*' on account, says Hobbes, of the extreme heat, although it was thought at the time that the affliction was the effect of the 'Passion imprinted by the Tragedy' (*Leviathan*, 142).

And Hobbes's understanding of authority is closely related to the notion of acting, in both theatrical and juridical senses. Going back to Greek and Roman etymology, 'person' is shown by Hobbes to come from the words for 'face' and 'disguise' or 'outward appearance'. In this sense, when someone participates in any form of human exchange, they are acting, and they are acting by authority. It may be that they are speaking for themselves, in which case they are a '*Naturall Person*', and their authority, their 'Right of doing any action', is their own:

The word Person is latine: insteed whereof the Greeks have πρόσωπου, which signifies the *Face*, as *Persona* in latine signifies the *disguise*, or *outward appearance* of a man, counterfeited on the Stage; and sometimes more particularly that part of it, which disguiseth the face, as a Mask or Visard: And from the Stage, hath been translated to any Representer of speech and action, as well in Tribunalls, as Theaters. So that a *Person*, is the same that an *Actor* is, both on the Stage and in common Conversation; and so *Personate*, is to *Act*, or *Represent* himselfe, or an other; and he that acteth another, is said to beare his Person, or act in his name; (in which sence *Cicero* useth it where he saies, *Unus sustineo tres Personas; Mei, Adversarii, & Judicis*, I beare three Persons; my own, my Adversaries, and the Judges;) and is called in diverse occasions, diversly; as a *Representer*, or *Representative*, a *Lieutenant*, a *Vicar*, an *Attorney*, a *Deputy*, a *Procurator*, an *Actor*, and the like. (217–18)

But if they are personating someone (by which Hobbes means if they are representing someone as a lawyer would), then they are acting 'by authority', conferred by the person whom they represent (Hobbes does not entertain the other possibility of an actor acting by the authority of the author who wrote a particular play).[19] Hobbes seems pointedly concerned with those who make a covenant with an actor, without knowing what authority he has. When a group of many authors give their authority to one, each person is an author and 'owns' the action of the one 'actor'. Their authorship is precisely that of the vast Leviathan itself.

But these relations become inconsistent precisely at the point where the divine and human interact, and where personal and public cross. Idols cannot be authors because they are 'nothing' (*pace* Pye; see above, 158–9). Hobbes regards them as a kind of state religion, their authority coming from the state, so that they could not have existed before civil society. Superstitious fictions are erroneously personified to create such idols – a form of fantasy as opposed to real authorship or representation. On the other hand, Moses, Christ and the Holy Ghost can 'personate' God: they become actors for his authority. But how this representation is achieved is not broached: presumably Hobbes accepts the relevant biblical accounts. Yet still, these relationships of personation or representation are described as 'fiction' (219). The argument that *Leviathan* is governed by two logics – one of epistemology, the other of Protestant teleology – can be used to resolve this apparent discrepancy.[20] Books I and II are founded upon Hobbes's materialist epistemology, while Books III and IV present Hobbes's rational Protestant interpretation of Scripture, and the Protestant, anti-'priestcraft' framework should govern any reading of these parts of the treatise. But a more faithful account of the experience of this aspect of *Leviathan* would be like looking through a lens with a rapidly changing focus, each of the two foci revealing different truths, at odds with each other, yet simultaneously represented. The doubleness is suited to *Leviathan* at its moment of publication: Hobbes's other writings present a vision much more acceptable to most Protestants, if not to every anglican apologist.

Although he does no more than allude in passing to theatricality, Hobbes is interested in these 'artificial' representations of power that were included in *Leviathan* as a means of explaining precisely how it is that sovereigns come to have power – a machinery absent in the explanation of the earlier *Elements of Law* and *De Cive*. As long as there are laws and covenants, authority and acting will operate in such differentially related terms. Authority is power in a society where laws are obeyed, and where, indeed, there is the possibility that an author or an actor can break the Law of Nature.[21]

Sir Robert Filmer identified these problems in his disagreement with Hobbes of 1652, *Observations Concerning the Originall of Government*: 'if every man covenant with every man, who shall be left to be the representative? If all must be representatives, who will remain to covenant?'[22] For Filmer, as for many others, people are defined primarily through their social role. There is also an inconsistency in Hobbes's depiction of a sovereign, which might be a single person or an assembly (the latter possibility is never extensively discussed). But an elected king can only be the representative or 'minister' of the sovereign power (246), thereby bringing forward the covenant into the functioning of civil society in time, rather than at the moment of its founding. Elsewhere, the making of the covenant, and by implication, the state of nature, have a kind of mythic status, a 'noplace' which exists textually but not historically, as an account of the origins of civil society.[23] In this explanation, Hobbes has succeeded in reducing the category of a person to a phantasmal spectre, whose 'essence' is in no individual self but in the body of the state as a whole, strung between the image of the natural man and that of the artificial man. Just as Leviathan is the commonwealth and the sovereign, just as the covenant is made in and out of history, so Hobbes's image of the person is dotted in different proportions and distributions across the system of his politics. Once civil society is established, just as the natural is subsumed into the civil, so the selves of natural men become small parts of the greater self of the commonwealth.

That much of what Hobbes has said was not new has been noticed before. Much of the effect of originality is generated by the fact that Hobbes was deriving his entire theory from his psychology of self-preservation, and he expected his readers to accept this derivation from experience, although his ideas are nonetheless closely interrelated to those of contemporary authors and pamphleteers.[24] It is to some extent the case that Hobbes achieves newness by offering extreme versions of accepted positions (for instance, all human actions stem from fear), but none of his originality in *Leviathan* would have persuaded were it not for the extraordinary rhetorical *fiat* of the work. It is not merely that *Leviathan* is 'the most stylishly written work of political theory in any language'.[25] The *Elements of Law* and *De Cive* contain many examples of Hobbesean inventiveness but they do not offer the totalised vision of *Leviathan*, and they do not induce in the reader the impression of simultaneous magnificence and confusion. *Leviathan* even puts logic (in the form of the syllogism) to work as a rhetorical device, effecting an inward persuasion where interior categories of thought are nonetheless emptied out into the concept of representation by the 'actor'.[26]

Leviathan is truly a text of revolution and watershed: the subject becomes interchangeable with the sovereign at the moment of covenanting, so that the possibility of accession to power is theoretically a possibility for everyone. Any author can be an actor, if not a player king. The making of the covenant is a forever present political unconscious – since nowhere in *Leviathan* is the making of a covenant actually described as a historical or institutional event. In his imagining of society as a 'person', Hobbes was producing a paradoxical, artificially natural view of political life, one that through its purported roots in experience linked him with the radicals rather than anglican rationalists and Royalists. No wonder the text of *Leviathan* intermeshes so closely with *Paradise Lost*.[27] And in the very colossus of thought it set up, *Leviathan* was the enigma of its time: it still is.

Harrington's Commonwealth

The self as a citizen whose speech and actions constitute political life has disappeared from Hobbes's ideal state. The 'free-born Englishman', and the virtuous citizen of classical republicanism, political anthropologies against which Hobbes wrote, have been abolished. Or if we can see the republican tradition in Hobbes's assemblies, liberty is confined therein by the covenants between authors and actors which are described as 'chains', 'which they themselves, have fastned at one end, to the lips of that Man, or Assembly, to whom they have given the Soveraigne Power; and at the other end to their own Ears' (*Leviathan*, 264).[28]

Where the definition of life for Hobbes is pure motion, for his republican disputant, James Harrington (1611–77), an older, Platonic, definition stands. Government is the soul of a city; reason being used in a debate in the commonwealth is virtue, and virtue results in good laws:

Now government is no other than the soul of a nation or city; wherefore that which was reason in the debate of a commonwealth, being brought forth by the result, must be virtue; and for as much as the soul of a city or nation is the sovereign power, her virtue must be law. But the government whose law is virtue, and whose virtue is law, is the same whose empire is authority, and whose authority is empire. (*The Commonwealth of Oceana* (1656), in *Political Works*, ed. J.G.A. Pocock (Cambridge, 1977), 170)

In other words, although he uses analogies, Harrington does not have recourse back to the human anatomy, or to the skein of artificial tissues and sinews (covenants, contracts, authors and actors) which make it cohere.

Yet this is not to say that Harrington discounts the human body and its figurative uses. In *The Prerogative of Popular Government* (1658) he twice refers to Harvey's discovery of the circulation of the blood. Just as Harvey had discovered something which God had originally made in nature, so Harrington is bringing to light something already there (412). In this respect, the difference between Hobbes and Harrington is between two differing conceptions of nature and the material world. Although Harrington was a firm believer in the pre-eminence of nature, he also believes in an extra material reality (God). Man is the mediator between God and nature, and the formation of government is the fulfilment of man's duty.

Where Hobbes elides categories, partly through his materialist epistemology, Harrington's degree of abstract thinking maintains broad analogies within and across the tripartite system of government, commonwealth and immortal commonwealth.[29] Harrington accordingly believed that just as the natural world was permeated by vital spirits (ultimately emanations from the divine), so the political world was permeated by related sets of spirits. It has been argued that Harrington's adherence to the Paracelsan system in this respect led to a view of the world redeemed by a divine pantheism rather than by Christ, although the texts themselves seem unclear on this issue.[30] The difficult prose style of *Oceana* is partly caused by this analogical habit, and although Harrington lacks elegance, the best comparison that can be made with him in this respect should be the writings of Sir Thomas Browne, with a large dash of Aristotle's *Politics*.

Abstracted thinking through figures, such as we see in Hobbes, is either avoided or localised, and instead principles are derived from discrete bodies of writing all of which contain discernible facts concerning the relationship between people, property and representation. But Harrington is nonetheless prone to mythologise his political vision, a feature which partly reflects his immersion in

Machiavelli (and possibly also his interest in occult systems of thought).[31] The Commonwealth is female (and perhaps government is male), so that the collective political 'she' acts: the 'commonwealth . . . performed her duty towards God as a rational creature' (218). A commonwealth is also a 'national conscience', so that it belongs to an abstract realm, yet there is a form of embodiment – personification – which functions at the very least as a mnemonic device. On the one hand, the female commonwealth is a romance heroine ('the most obstinate assertress of her liberty', 158) and on the other a mother: 'What ever was in the womb imperfect as to her proper work, comes very rarely or not at all to perfection; and the formation of a citizen in the womb of the commonwealth is his education' (303–4).

But is this method of personification any more than a vivid means of explanation? Does Harrington overdetermine his system of representation? Where Hobbes is consistently inconsistent, Harrington is not, for while his Commonwealth is conscience and a woman, the people are the 'materials' which make up the building of the woman. Government is a superstructure raised by the 'art' of prudence. Ideally, it should be 'natural to the known foundations'.[32] It should also aim to be 'immortal': 'the people never die nor, as a political body, are subject unto any other corruption than that which deriveth from their government' (320). And in describing that which was 'immortal' or 'transcendental', Harrington needed that mode which Hobbes regarded as vainglory – romance (see below, 246–9).

The legitimacy of such personification was one of a number of fundamental differences from Hobbes. The human form itself is limited to descriptions of men who should ideally be virtuous in their industry and their speech, although Harrington did use an illustrative analogy in his later writings: 'Formation of government is the creation of a political creature after the image of a philosophical creature, or it is an infusion of the soul or faculties of man into the body of a multitude' (*A System of Politics*, 838).[33] Political perfection is represented in the voting habits of the Venetian senate, an institutional capturing of Venice's unique 'balance' and 'libration'. For Harrington, towns are welcome parts of the infrastructure of wealth, whereas for Hobbes they are 'little Wormes' gnawing inside the stomach of the body politic with their propensity to tamper with laws, just as aggrandisement is 'insatiable appetite, or *Bulimia*' (*Leviathan*, 375). Theatricality for Harrington is also classical and political, associated with the exercise of virtue in collective debate, oratory and decision-making, rather than the emphasis upon social unity, representation, and the possibility for deceit in Hobbes:

> himself, in the great hall of the Pantheon or Palace of Justice situated in
> Emporium the capital city, created, by the universall suffrage of the army,

Lord Archon, or sole legislator of Oceana; upon which theatre you have, to conclude this piece, a person introduced whose Fame shall never draw his curtain. (*Oceana*, 207)

The theatre is the crucible of politics, bringing together the power of the one and the many: 'Invention is a solitary thing' – only one can legislate, but 'the people have the ultimate result' in judging. Charles I may have made a fatal mistake in choosing to rule without Parliament, yet for Harrington when a commonwealth 'is at a loss', or at its point of origin, it needs a solitary inventor to establish laws – Moses in Israel, Olphaus Megalator in Oceana, Oliver Cromwell in England (*The Prerogative of Popular Government*, 391).

Oceana posits an entirely different attitude to the texts upon which it is constructed than is to be found in *Leviathan*. Indeed, one senses that Hobbes did not care too greatly for the textual integrity of the books he used because his perceptions, derived so he claimed from 'experience', were finally superior. Harrington tends to let the texts have their own sense, even though he does see his own categories in them. There is a sense that he is listening to them, and enjoying their specificity. A 'balance', after all, may be seen in pastoral verse, which Hobbes would have been more inclined to regard as fantasy (see below, 247). To Harrington, Hobbes's 'authorities' look invented because the natural is abstracted into the rhetorical shape of the body politic. Hobbes replaces *auctoritas* with 'experience' derived from sense perceptions. In fact, Hobbes believed that *auctoritas* was in no sense consonant with experience, whereas Harrington thinks that within the body of past knowledge, the truth of nature – experience – is to be discovered; or at least in part. Harvey's writings are a text, an authority, but they identify a phenomenon already instituted in nature by God (*The Prerogative of Popular Government*, 412). Elsewhere, Harrington becomes irritated by a disputant who accuses him of inventing only names, rather than proposing a new political order. Harrington's point is that the names of *Oceana* reclarify the relationship between political discourse and the realm of experience: 'what oft was thought, but ne'er so well expressed', and, we might add, perceived. To this extent, it is hard to see Harrington's text as a utopia.[34]

The sense of the vastness of the body of the state in *Leviathan* is conveyed by Harrington in his disagreement with Hobbes. In the easily decipherable name list of *Oceana*, Harrington figures Hobbes as Leviathan, so that the reader has the impression of the gigantic sea monster bobbing up and down through Harrington's text – not an unapt description for an author whom Harrington disagreed with, but was dependent upon.[35] Just as Hobbes, in his letter to Davenant, permits the vastly disproportionate representation of whales on maps as cartographers' conventions (see below, 227), so Harrington in turn sees 'Leviathan''s writing as a huge geographical construction, not suited to the real language of ancient prudence. Harrington's assessment of Hobbes is equally paradoxical. *Leviathan* is anathema to Harrington because it is 'artificiall', because it is built upon paradoxical reasoning. Harrington parodies Hobbes: 'An whole army, though they can neither write not read, are not afraid of a platform, which they know is but earth or stone, nor of a cannon which, without a hand to give fire unto it, is but cold iron; therefore a whole army is afraid of one man'(*Oceana*, 162). This is a sound parody, and Harrington proceeds:

> he [Hobbes] saith of Aristotle and of Cicero, of the Greeks and of the Romans, who lived under popular states, that they 'derived those rights not from the principles of nature, but transcribed them into their books out of the practice of their own commonwealths, as grammarians describe the rules of language out of poets.' Which is as if a man should tell famous Harvey that he transcribed his circulation of the blood not out of the principles of nature, but out of the anatomy of this or that body. (162)

Where Machiavelli builds out of *auctoritas*, Hobbes destroys. Harrington believes that no explanation of the affairs of men will be true unless it acknowledges society as an extension of nature. Since Harrington also believes that society is not artificial, it cannot be explained as a unified Hobbesean body. Yet what he does say is no less an abstraction than is to be found in *Leviathan*. *Oceana* defines the principles of government as twofold: internal, and related to the goods of the mind; external, pertaining to the goods of fortune. Authority belongs to the category of goods of the mind, while power and empire belong to the goods of fortune. Government is a 'creation' and a 'superstructure', the offshoot of the mind that makes best use of the goods of fortune, and that which, in its proper interpretation of nature, mediates between man and God. In *Leviathan*, the equivalent of 'creation' is the actor representing the author; in Harrington, the creation of the state is represented as a sexual and cosmological alchemy with a redemptive purpose. A *System of Politics* dwells on the analogy of the egg for state formation:

> Those naturalists that have best written of generation do observe that all things proceed from an egg, and that there is in every egg a *punctum saliens*, or a part first moved, as the purple speck observed in those of hens; from the working whereof the other organs or fit members are delineated, distinguished and wrought into one organical body.(839)

The *punctum saliens* becomes the first mover of the state – the sole legislator or a council.

Hobbes is mistaken, says Harrington, when he says that prudence, or the reputation of prudence, is power, because it confuses the two categories of internal and external goods. Prudence for Harrington is a kind of learning:

> the learning or prudence of a man is no more power than the learning or prudence of a book or author, which is properly authority. A learned writer may have authority, though he have no power, and a foolish magistrate may have power, though he have otherwise no esteem or authority. (*Oceana*, 163)

Likewise, both Olphaus Megalator (Cromwell idealised) and the Council of State read books, 'labouring in the Mines of *Ancient Prudence*, and bringing her hidden *Treasures* unto new Light' (201). Hobbes and Harrington appear to each other, from the viewpoints of their respective systems, as artificial thinkers.

Thus, while Hobbes was able to stop an entire tradition of political thought in its tracks by inferring that liberty can only be negatively defined as freedom from constraint, Harrington has no trouble in dismissing Hobbes's famous statement because it pays no attention to the specific combination of different 'goods' in a particular balance. In other words, Harrington has the means to see liberty simultaneously in both positive and negative lights.

While Hobbes was trying to limit and redefine the language of philosophy, in a work which was deliberately preferring the vernacular to Latin, Harrington's makes capital of a lexical free-for-all. Harrington 'aestheticisation' of the state is linguistically typified in the use of adjectival nouns (an 'Agrarian', a 'Gothic' describe different kinds of property-based power relationships), and is based upon the notion of the 'balance', the possession of which determines power in a community. Land is the 'balance' in the country, money the 'balance' in a city. The 'balance' is meant in the sense of an equilibrium of opposed or contending forces – such as those represented by the tripartite division of ancient political theory: monarchy, aristocracy, democracy. The 'balance' fulfils God's intentions for any one human society:

> Kings, no question, where the balance is monarchical, are of divine right, and if they be good the greatest blessings that the government so standing can be capable of; but the balance being popular, as in Israel, in the Grecian, in the Sicilian tyrannies, they are the direst curse that can befall a nation.[36]

And Harrington says with increasing frequency that most balances require popular government, so that monarchs become rareties among nations. 'Modern prudence', the 'Gothick balance', began in Rome when the dictator Sulla (nearly as frequently cited a tyrant figure in the mid-seventeenth century as Catiline) alienated popular government by establishing military colonies. Harrington's avowed aim is to revive the traditions of 'ancient prudence', including classical republicanism, but to do so he has in effect to extend its vocabulary in English. A successful balance achieves a 'libration', the oscillation of the components of a society to achieve a fixed and stable position, rather like the motion of a galaxy in space; Harrington takes his word from astronomical discourse. The state is a *stasis*, and successful governments must also involve some degree of 'rotation' of office. The 'motions' of the commonwealth – its laws and government – are 'spherical': 'the centre of this commonwealth, are the agrarian [a tax on property to regulate wealth] and ballot: the agrarian by the ballance of dominion preserving equality in the root, and the ballot by an equal rotation conveying it into the branch, or exercise of sovereign power' (*Oceana*, 230–31). Harrington describes the members of Oceana's senate and house of representatives as 'galaxies' (knights for the senate, deputies for the representatives' chamber; three galaxies are elected respectively for one, two and three years), and Olphaus Megalator's choosing of parties resembles accounts of God's creation of the world: 'which lists successively falling (like the signs or constellations of one hemisphere, that setting cause those of the other to rise) cast the great orbs of this commonwealth into an annual, triennial and perpetual revolution' (228). The 'orbs' of the commonwealth are the civil, military and provincial spheres. Representatives in the different chambers should 'rotate' through regular elections, a term which caught Milton's rebuke as it suggested the capricious wheel of fortune (*CPW*, VII.435), and part of a vocabulary which irritates one of the characters of *Oceana* itself.[37] Harrington has gone far beyond Hobbes's attribution of the cause of English republicanism to the reading of classical texts. He has used invention, in the sense of an adumbration upon the basis of previous wisdom, bringing it back to life through a rediscovery and reinvention of the commonwealth as stellar artifice. Harrington's rhetoric makes the commonwealth vitally alive in the interrelationships of its parts.

For Harrington, a state is not an artificial body (*pace* Hobbes) but an artificial universe, separate from the created universe, but like it in its oscillating stability. As God breathes life into the universe, so political life is infused into the state by its first mover. In so far as a universe is a 'body', so is Harrington's commonwealth, but because several words will suffice to explain the state (since different analogies may represent the same 'nature' and 'reason'), Harrington departs from the strict analogy of *Leviathan*, and thus from what he regarded as Hobbes's mere rhetoric. In a more Platonic (and some would say even Cartesian) fashion, words exist as a mediator between the mind of God and the mind of man, just as the commonwealth is a conceptual foreconceit which performs a redemptive function when it is properly realised among men.

A historically apt term like 'imitation', and an anachronistic one, like 'originality', both make little sense when applied to *Oceana*. As we have already seen, Harrington's own sense of invention includes the discovery of what is already there.[38] He also makes analogy with New World discovery, claiming that Columbus made a map before he sailed which helped him find the Americas, although of course he had never crossed the Atlantic before.[39] Milton derided this doubleness in Harrington: 'new or obsolete forms, or terms, or exotic models' (*CPW*, VII.445). But Harrington himself was loth to take any credit for the invention of the term 'balance', and blames it variously on Aristotle, Machiavelli and Bacon (*Essays*, 29), and this returns us to Harrington's sense that he is 'discovering' rather than inventing, although, in fact, his writings reveal (in our terms) a true originality.

Harrington's method throughout his works is to demonstrate by reference to historical example the operation of different balances in the past, and the importance of popular 'prerogative' in governments. To some of his disputants, such investigation and hypothesising was too experimental, fictional and insufficiently concerned with the foundations of government: 'It is not difficult to invent variety of Formes the parts of each which taken separately, may maintain a faire Correspondence and Agreement among themselves, and yet the whole be far enough from attaining to Perfection.'[40] In *The Prerogative of Popular Government*, the method is defended in the wake of the attack on *Oceana*. The focus of governmental decision is nearly always the representative chamber, in which decisions are made, be it the Sanhedrin, the Greek *ecclesia* or the Senate. Of all chambers, it was in the Hebrew Sanhedrin that God was most present. Hobbes (and the later refuters of *Oceana*) are rebutted through a series of historical counter-examples.[41] At the same time, the identities of English institutions and offices change, as they take on very different natures: Harrington's knowledge of English titles testifies to his historical knowledge (and his reliance upon scholars like Selden) as much as it enables a projection into the future (*Oceana*, 192).[42] In the renaming of England as *Oceana*, the reader is meant to see the old identity in the new, so as to appreciate better the meaning of the change. This notwithstanding, the author of the *Considerations* claimed that the only 'agrarians' Harrington could find were in Israel and Lacedaemon.

Property and production, agricultural or 'industrial', are seen as the root of the way in which a society's political order should be determined: 'tillage, bringing up a good soldiery, bringeth up a good commonwealth' (*Oceana*, 158). Imbalance in a society need not just be political. True, Harrington sees the downfall of Rome as the result of an imbalance between nobility and plebeians, but in some societies too, there can only be one mode of production: '*Your* Agrarian . . . *must indeed destroy Industry*' (*Oceana*, 232).

To suggest, however, that Harrington explores closely the relationship between class or order and mode of production would be an exaggeration. Indeed, economic and political determinism are often in an uneasy and unrevealed relationship. Property is named and land is assumed to be productive. The political superstructure is there to satisfy the different kinds of social elevation which these property relations produce. Government should be rational, thereby quelling lusts in the populace. Modesty should dictate a just division of property, and this should be replicated in the political sphere: dividing and choosing in property is debating and resolving in politics (174).

Much of *Oceana* is delivered as an oration: deliberative and forensic rhetoric are frequently in use. Although the voice of the people is the voice of God, government, which Harrington fits into the category of 'invention', requires a single will: hence the crucial role of Olphaus Megalator in the foundation and running of Oceana. Hence also the charge that Harrington's people are not the free-speaking and virtuous citizens of the classical republic (as Pocock would have), but Hobbesian subjects bound by their place in the body politic to obey the sovereign, with no freedom beyond that which the sovereign supplies.[43] Harrington does not construct people as Hobbesian subjects, but through his terminology he does make people into parts of a system, and seems not to focus on individual powers or rights. In *The Prerogative of Popular Government*, popular government does not mean that the people have oratory – the power to debate or deliberate – for that would lead to anarchy (479; see above, 35–40). The people have the 'result', that is the power to vote and judge upon the deliberations of the aristocracy, and this is their will. Harrington admires Hobbes's location of freedom (in debate and deliberation) as anterior to will (422); in the republic, these functions are split between aristocracy and people, and the anarchy of unbounded oratory is avoided, but not in Hobbes's authoritarian terms. And of course, Harrington does allow great latitude of private speculation: commentators too often forget that Harrington's verbal superstructures are directed towards the specific end of discussing government. This does not mean that the closed motion of the system discounts other and different modes of thought and action. The citizens do not spend all of their time voting.

It seems sufficient for Harrington to have popular government assessed in terms of election and ordination, taking the terms *chirotonia* (a hand gesture interpreted as popular suffrage) and *chirothesia* (ordination).[44] The analysis of these functions in the Greek city states parallels the debates on church government in the 1650s. The Greek (and Hebrew) roots shared between much ecclesiology and Harrington's analysis could be read as a secularising of the issues exercising the puritan consensus during the Commonwealth years.[45]

History and literature in Harrington are the means to the proper understanding of how it is that people become empowered (see below, 246–9). The response to Hobbes is often to reassert the claims of a historical and narrative analysis of society as a whole in which totalities are described as systems or constitutions (Harrington and Filmer), not as bodies. The political system of Harrington, by giving the citizen less clarity of definition than Hobbes's subject, could be said to let human activity have a greater sphere of action. But then whoever said that Hobbes was describing people and society in a 'realistic' mode? The deeper we go into *Leviathan*, the more we feel that we are reading satire, or a vision which abuts life obliquely and ironically, implying much more than is literally on the page.

By contrast, the style of Harrington's post-*Oceana* works displays increasing clarification, an indication of their author's desire to make his works have an impact upon the political life of the Commonwealth. They are easier to understand, although they also involve significant shifts of opinion. In the context of the need to communicate with a reading public in the fragile days before the Restoration, Harrington's predicament was no different from Milton's. But the obscurity of *Oceana* deserves further pondering: it could be seen as an attempt to veil the extent of Harrington's critical republicanism in 1656, given the clampdown on Fifth Monarchists and anti-Cromwellian republicans. There is contemporary corroboration of this view.[46] *Oceana* could also be like it is precisely because in its obscurity it was finding its own identity. Textual difficulty functions like a near-impenetrable mist from which emerges something very original. Harrington knew this too, so we do not need to worry that we are viewing *Oceana* anachronistically from a late twentieth-century viewpoint. What would a post-Restoration Harringtonian text have looked like? Would he have produced a startlingly new version of his republican theory? The possibilities of what might have been are intriguing.

'Action is the life of all'

When a society is fundamentally disrupted, we might expect to find in political writing a retreat from expected constitutional parameters to new foundations for the social order, and such is the case with Hobbes and Harrington. The former has recourse to his mechanistic individual, the latter to his own notion of the balance. So strong is the concern with explaining the roots of their respective political visions that the questions of origins and generation are important themes, under the category of the author in Hobbes, and the imagery of creation in Harrington. Many commentators have claimed to find utopia – the discourse on an imagined ideal society – at the point of the break in the continuity of political and religious theory and practice. And anyone who explores the ideal societies in *Oceana* and Winstanley's *The Law of Freedom* would be forced to agree. Hobbes has been claimed as a utopian writer of sorts, and many writings produced between 1640 and 1660 have been classified as utopian.[47]

But the moment of revolution is too much even for the genre of utopia to answer, and the texts that are conventionally regarded as utopian have least in common with that tradition, although they do have, in some ways, vital similarities with the utopian tradition's greatest *exemplum*, Sir Thomas More's *Utopia* (1516).

In the 1640s, More's masterpiece is usually alluded to as pie-in-the-sky invention by people accustomed to the grim realities of civil conflict. More was remembered by the Levellers as an anti-courtly hero, a martyr to the tyranny of Henry VIII. Milton derided *Utopia* as a flat and lifeless map of an ideal state, of no relevance to the vibrant *negotium* recommended in *Areopagitica* (CPW, II.526). But Milton was accepting a commonplace view of *Utopia* as an ideal 'grid' of the world, a social blueprint which could supposedly be imposed on a real society.

More's text never yields this reading. Rather, *Utopia* was the victim of a literalising habit which had taken hold long before in the decades following More's death. The two-part structure of *Utopia* (the critique of the way things are in Europe followed by the account of the ideal society) is meant to produce in the reader's mind a sense of surprise and shock at the juxtaposition of the unacceptable present with the way things might ideally be, but never could be. The shock produces a revelation in the reader, even a renewed apprehension of divine grace, as the text urges the reader to a third position: to strive harder for the ideals in this world, away from worldly corruption, towards, but never reaching, the ideal (because it never could be reached).[48] This interpretation fits readily with the activism of *Areopagitica* and the emphasis upon civic virtue in the writings of the Commonwealth republicans.

Equally important is what Hobbes, Harrington and Winstanley share with More: precisely that capacity to reflect upon creativity and origins themselves, a quality that none of the other utopian and millennial schemes of the 1650s display.[49] Our triumvirate of seventeenth-century authors have very different parameters. Winstanley (and other Diggers) began an ideal society out of radical religious and extreme Leveller convictions, and Winstanley theorised it to its fullest extent after its collapse. Hobbes constructs an ideal of rational obedience out of the ruins of royalist defence; Harrington's republic arrives from the comparative analysis of histories and legal codes. Yet, like More, all have at their heart an encodement of what a person is, what creativity is, and how these two categories relate to how persons should co-exist. In doing so, and going now a long way beyond More's *Utopia*, they take the ultimate category of creativity, godhood, so to speak, inside their definitions either of society or of individuals. To this extent they are worthy of consideration outside the immediate context of controversial exchange, and as discrete but related theoretical productions of the revolution.

As I have shown elsewhere, Winstanley makes God (Reason), man and nature continuous, busting the logical consistency of his language in the process.[50] Harrington, as we have seen, resists interpretation in his description of political participation as creation. Hobbes's social body articulates his social contract and gives it consistency.

Winstanley's now justly famous vision is inextricably linked to the attempt by himself and others to implement it. Not only does he write without the educated enrichment of Hobbes and Harrington: his discourse, like most products of the radical religious ferment, disregards the distinction between words and the world. Winstanley's understanding that God lived inside all created objects and that God was Reason is elaborated in his earlier pamphlets of 1648, but his 'writing' was incomplete until he started digging:

> I was made to write in a little book called *The New Law of Righteousness* . . . yet my mind was not at rest, because nothing was acted, and thought run in me that words and writings were all nothing and must die, for action is the life of all, and if thou dost not act, thou dost nothing. Within a little time I was made obedient to the word, in that particular likewise; for I took my spade and went and broke the ground upon George Hill in Surrey, thereby declaring freedom to the creation. (*The Law of Freedom and Other Writings*, ed. Christopher Hill (1973), 127–8)

For Winstanley, the true church is this mystical agriculture. The complications of organising his communist Eden, and the sufferings of the Digger community itself (see below, 334), were ahead of Winstanley when he wrote these words. At this point of origin, which Winstanley describes as a dream vision (anathema to Hobbes), the utopian tradition is fulfilled by the abolition of private property, since the earth is re-imagined as a common treasury, the cultivation of which is the meeting of God, man and reason. Harrington, of course, bases his theory upon private property (which is not a primary concern for Hobbes), but Harrington and Winstanley share a need to demonstrate the interaction of divine and human. And this puts both authors into the frame of action, because political participation in the eternal commonwealth of Oceana and digging the common land are both fulfilments of ancient and divine wisdom as action: they are, literally, alchemies of the state and the spirit rolled into one. Just as the ancient Israelites exemplify popular government for Harrington, so those who dig are the Israelites in the age of the spirit for Winstanley, who offers a very special definition of the commonplace description of the godly as Israelites:

> No man shall have any more land, then he can labour himself, or have others to labour with him in love, working together, and eating bread together, as one of the Tribes or families of Israel, neither giving hire, nor taking hire. (*The New Law of Righteousness* (1649) in *Works*, ed. E.H. Sabine (New York, 1941, 1965), 191)

On the contrary, Hobbes's analysis of the Bible in Book III of *Leviathan* is a critical review of scriptural contents that denies republican or Levellerish parallels with Israelite or New Testament people. And yet Hobbes claims that the meaning of the 'kingdom of God' is a civil society, operating by a covenant with God, in this world and with a sovereign.[51]

Selfishness and imagination in Winstanley are the dark forces which lead to exploitation, poverty and starvation. The redeemed, perfect individual who has cast aside these qualities is part of the godhead, occupying an equivalent space in his system to mechanistic man in Hobbes's system (where mechanistic man is all that God has allowed us to see). And just as the proper functioning of the balance leads to social harmony in *Oceana*, so Winstanley looks towards a restitution when natural as well as political turbulence will disappear:

> When mankind shall be restored, and delivered from the curse, and all spirited with this one power, then other creatures shall be restored likewise, and freed from their burdens: as the Earth, from thorns, and briars, and barrenesse; the Air and winds from bitternesse and rage one against another. (*Works*, 169)

In all Digger writings before the collapse of the Surrey community, institutions do not seem to exist, beyond the strong image of digging as the restitution of a primitive Christian community. Any such superstructure was merely part of the edifice of tyranny, and it had to go.

But can the immanence of the spirit be made into a robust and lasting social practice? Although the appeals to Fairfax, Cromwell and Parliament show Winstanley and other Digger authors trying hard to reconcile their belief with the realities of economic deprivation, the gap between theory and practice was too great. Even before the Cobham Diggers were evicted, their ideals were being compromised by the laws of supply and demand, and of pure survival (see also below, 334). Just as the Ranters' sexual theory was too feeble to withstand official interrogation, so digging was found out by uncomfortable economic realities. And *The Law of Freedom* turns to the importance of laws, and a revamped guild structure,[52] seemingly over and above the claims of inner freedom: it is assumed that the enlightened citizens will simply do their duties because they will come to understand that this is the true fulfilment of God's will. Or, looking at *The Law of Freedom* another way, Winstanley's ideal citizen contains an internal knowledge that is perfectly commensurate with those laws and forms of authority which occupy an external space in Hobbes and Harrington. Winstanley's desire to make all structures of authority come out of inward inspiration bears comparison with Seeker and Ranter thought, but very few in his day would have agreed with him, or even began to see like him. Most Puritans would have found the Augustinian inflection of Baxter's *Holy Commonwealth* (government is there for Christian ends) or the millennial republicanism of John Eliot or John Rogers (with a scripturally derived theocracy of government by the elect) both more acceptable and more comprehensible.

What did the life of action amount to for these three thinkers? Hobbes certainly had an influence, but not in any way that can have pleased him, for his enemies made best use of his philosophy. On his return to England, he was kept silent and out of active life: his greatest public impact was upon attempts to revive the theatre and to redefine the uses of poetry (see above, 87–8 and below, 214). Winstanley began a remarkable if short-lived experiment, and his influence was felt not only in the Digger communities in Surrey, Buckinghamshire, Northamptonshire and Middlesex, but also at the centre of power and, more widely still, through his books. Harrington's career is one of a retreat from the obscurities of *Oceana* into clarity as he sought to make his ideas work. By 1659, the Rota Club was an impressive gathering of radicals, republicans and ex-Levellers, and its influence was considerable.[53]

Winstanley would have to wait a very long time before he gained a wide currency. Hobbes and Harrington synthesised new versions of the state, and their respective visions were internally self-consistent, if frequently paradoxical in the means by which they sought to communicate. From the acts of creation and maintenance that their texts imagine, the map of political theory was to be rewritten in the following century.

CHAPTER 6

The Free State in Letters:
Republicanism Comes Out

Who . . . defile the English tongue with their Republick words, which are
scarce significant to a Monarchicall understanding,
    Jasper Mayne, preface to translation of *Lucian* (1664), Sig. Aiv.

ROYALIST APOLOGY AND propaganda developed a largely unified set of
arguments and images, both for what it defended and what it attacked.
The Levellers discovered their identity through the politics of their own
petitioning. Both groups were taking issue with an authority which won
the war, and then, in a drastically changed fashion, was at the centre of a
republican government. How did parliamentary apology become
Commonwealth apology? When did it cease to acknowledge that
England was a kingdom? And were the defenders of Parliament,
Commonwealth, and ultimately the Protectorate, touched by events so
profoundly that they too wrote with the startling originality of Hobbes,
Harrington and Winstanley?

Parliament felt justified in taking arms against the King, and royalist
apology and propaganda was unified in the view that Parliament's course
was unlawful and rebellious. Parliamentary defence began, and a large
part of it remained, monarchical in nature until the late 1640s. But as
time passed, as victory in the Civil War was accompanied by failure to
reach a settlement with the King, so Parliament was forced to set terms
in ways which it, as a body, was extremely reluctant to do. It found itself
in situations which most of its members did not like. After the First Civil
War, Parliament was ruling the country without the King, although the
institution of the monarchy had not been abolished. How did
parliamentary defences differ between 1642, 1645, 1647, 1649?

Constitutional inexactitude and unease generated a series of un-,
extra- or anti-monarchical discourses all of which may be related to the
phenomenon of republicanism in mid-seventeenth-century England. It is
because of these conditions that republicanism was a highly literary
affair: it flourished as a mode of speculation and propaganda, even
though the political reality it claimed to support was in many ways very

unrepublican. Moreover, republicanism was deeply literary by nature.[1] Yet these facts do not mean that republicanism did not exist before 1650 (contrary to a view common among historians), or that its literariness made it of secondary importance.[2] Its emergence was a consequence of the conjunction of events with the classical inheritance of humanism, and its popularity a result of the imaginative opportunities that parliamentary supremacy in the 1640s, and then a genuine republic in the 1650s, presented to educated people. But because it was the product of a victorious interest, and because it was a mode for the privileged and the government, republicanism was never forced to use literature (unlike the Royalists and Levellers) to fight a cause (as opposed to apologise for it) until the late 1650s – when it was too late.

Approximate Discourses

Pamphlets making use of the classical republican notion of tyranny, such as *A Discourse of Tyrants and Tyranny* (1642), with its references to Lucan, the pro-republican poet-historian of the fall of the Roman republic, circulated in the early 1640s.[3] George Wither's translation of Nemesius (1636) carried a reference to a 'free state', prefiguring his claim nine years later that most Lords ignored their duty to the 'Re-publike'.[4] Ancient republican perspectives frequently fuelled the accusation of tyranny against increasingly powerful monarchs in Renaissance Europe. The association of tragedy with republicanism formed part of the theatrical experience of the 1610s and 1620s and was reasserted throughout the 1640s and 1650s in republican literature: Marchamont Nedham cites Seneca's *Hercules Furens*, in his defence of the republic; Milton was soon defending his opinions by reference to ancient notions of free speech and oratory in this play and others.[5] And as far as we are able to tell, those Englishmen who were genuine republicans before 1649 – like Henry Marten – did practise a literary classical republicanism (see below, 283–5).

   Republicanism as a set of practised political principles grew out of a body of literary texts being available to interpret predicaments which began in disputes between powerful aristocrats, gentlemen commoners and the monarchy. The aristocrats and gentry felt that their property (and hence their liberty) was under threat. The matter of property (as opposed to tyranny) grows steadily in importance in republican discourse, but this does not mean that it was unimportant until Harrington made so much of it in *Oceana* (1656). The rise of the Sidneys in the sixteenth century was based on property rewards – accumulations which they saw as reconfirmations of the baronial power of their ancestors, the Percys.[6] Marten's republicanism was rooted in his property rights. His ideal constitution was one where propertied men elected representatives to a single chamber.[7] Although George Wither was swayed between supporting some kind of limited monarchy or not, the paradigms of his political philosophy are taken from property disputes, around which he was able to theorise his version of liberty.[8] Another country gentleman was Sir Cheney Culpepper, who, like Marten, looked forward in 1644–5 to a single chamber, no nobility and the monarch as a mere figure-head.[9]

Beyond this we can go little further in identifying hard republicanism before the 1650s, for the identifiable republicans wrote and published very little which relates to the subject. But a more recent view in political theory argues that while some parliamentarian apologists worked within the constitutional model of mixed monarchy, others, like Henry Parker and Nathaniel Bacon, were producing in the 1640s a model of aristocratic republicanism rooted in a notion that politics in Britain was essentially and originally democratic.[10] At most, the monarch was *primus inter pares*.

With such a bricolage of institutional and discursive matchings and mismatchings during the 1640s, it is not surprising to find other writings in defence of Parliament entertaining republicanism, and later on becoming part of the official language in defence of the Commonwealth. The case of the parliamentarian apologist Henry Parker, author of the *Observations Upon Some of His Majesties Late Answers and Expresses* (1642), the single most influential tract of the period, is an important example.

In 1642, Parker also published *Accommodation Cordially-Desired*, which, as its title implies, and like the *Observations* (see above, 99–100), is not an anti-monarchical tract.[11] Indeed, the distinction within the pamphlet is made between Holland the exact republic and England the exact monarchy. While Parker's argument fits broadly with the general parliamentarian attack not on the King but his evil advisers, Tacitus' perceptions of the weakness and corruption of tyranny are present:

> Some Princes (to use the words of *Tacitus*) are so informe and credulous, that they remaine *jussis alienis obnoxii*, and *non modo Imperii sed libertatis etiam indigent*, they are so enslaved to their best flatterers that their very Diadems are as it were aliend and made prostitute to seducers, and those their flatterers and seducers (in the expression of *Tacitus*). (14)

How are we to take Parker's words? 'Manly Logick' preferred to 'effeminate Rhetorick', certainly bears republican hints, although this is coupled with an anti-Ciceronian phrase, 'the chiefest fraud of the Orator is to passe over that part of businesse which requires most proof', so that there is also a seemingly anti-republican set of associations at work here. Parker has been seen as an original thinker within a democratic tradition which has been called an 'Aristotelian populism'.[12] According to this view, people, for their own well-being, are indissolubly incorporated into Parliament; every one has a natural and rational impulse to incorporate into a body politic, or a state, and this is a 'reason of state'.[13] Parker also assumes that Parliament represents the people, so that the popular will can only be expressed in that body. In fact Parliament (not the people) has a sovereignty almost as absolute as Hobbes's sovereign power, just as Sir Cheney Culpepper's 'democratical interest' in Parliament could not be resisted.[14] Yet Pocock maintains that Parker was no 'classical republican', and he supports this with Parker's own denunciation of Machiavelli.[15]

Any careful reading of the *Observations* would confirm this view. Yet, two years later, Parker produced in *Jus Populi* (1644) another defence of parliamentary supremacy which is markedly more classical in its mode of reference than the work of 1642. A host of authors, including Plato, Aristotle, Cicero and Suetonius, enable Parker to manufacture a picture of the English monarch as if he were responsible to the Roman people (19–29). We see Roman emperors as well as senates, but the aspect is one of empire as extension of republic, where the ruler is dependent upon the people, who are the life-blood of the state. Scripture as well as the ancient Greeks and Romans say that princes must sacrifice all to the public good: Cicero's noble but humble magistrates become the ideal monarchs, ever vigilant and labouring for their people (29). It is an image quite contrary to the icon-king of the 'State-Theologues' (royalist apologists) and Parker knows it (21). Queen Elizabeth (here Parker anticipates Harrington: see below, 246–8) understood this wisdom, a law both of God and Nature, just as Charles I apparently does not. Parker did not argue republicanism, but he did influentially instil classical republican visions into the rhetorical reservoir of 1640s politics.

The most important apologist later in the decade was Anthony Ascham, assassinated in 1650 by Royalists just after his arrival in Spain as ambassador for the republic.[16] His most famous work, *Of the Confusions and Revolutions of Government* (1649), recommends obedience to the new government on grounds of self-preservation (in the second edition, he used Hobbes to bolster his argument). Another tract, Γενεσις καὶ τελος εξουσιας, *The Originall and End of Civil Power* (1649), signed by 'Eutactus Philodemius' (the 'well-ordered democrat'), was attributed by a knowledgeable contemporary to Ascham. The tract recommends annual parliaments for the encouragement of virtue and prevention of tyranny. The author also admits to an interruption in constitutional government, as well as an end of monarchy: but although the army have pulled down

Charles they have not had a hand in the establishment of the post-monarchic state, which, according to many (so he said), had reverted to an aristocratic government. Shortly after this, 'Eutactus Philodemius' claims that the King's words in the coronation oath are those of election, so he claims that England is an elective monarchy. None of this appears republican *per se*, but it does again display the unconnected components of the constitution of a free state.

Commentators have hitherto concentrated on *Of the Confusions and Revolutions of Governments* as the representative Ascham piece, and hence do not see Ascham as a republican. But if Ascham was 'Eutactus Philodemius', he was playing a major role in a very firm emergence of republican thought.[17] Another work signed by 'Eutactus Philodemius', *An Answer to the Vindication of Dr. Hamond* (1650), is full of Italianate references, and the force of populism comes at the point where the popular origins of power are affirmed from an unlikely source. 'Eutactus' draws on the work of the Jesuit rights theorist and utopian writer Adam Contzen who writes in the language not of classical republicanism but in one where republicanism survived in a theological guise:

> There is no power but of God (saith he) '*Cum Respublica constituta est, in ejus* (i.e. dei) *potestate est. regimen Monarchicum, vel Aristocraticum, vel populi politiam instituere, atque ita respub. a Deo primo et immediate est: Magistratus ad ea* (i.e. Rep.) *designati a Deo mediate a populo immediate potestate habent, quae ex natura rei, est* TOTA *in Communitate primo & immediate*. Contzen, 5.8.5. (15)[18]

Such arguments came from a tradition where Jesuit intellectuals would incite Catholic populations to rebel and murder Protestant princes with natural as well as popular right – hardly a sensible source to use in 1650.[19] The 'Consent and vote of the people' is also derived from Hobbes's *De Corpore Politico* (1640), Part 2, chapter 1, although 'Eutactus' cautions against this writer's 'dangerous, and unsound principles in other respects'. 'Eutactus' is introducing, or prolonging, as an Italianate 'statist', a vision that is not entirely republican in the sense that Pocock would require but that, like sections of mid-1640s Milton, displays a sinewy sense of secular power relationships in defiance of royalist apology. It is a new mixture in the stew of English political pamphlet language, and a feature which would become common in republican discourse in the following decade. Part of this is communicated through playful but pointed Italian proverbs: '*Buon dritto & buona lingua in [?]lite vincono* (He must have a good cause as well as a good tongue, that will overcome)' (2); '*La moscha che ponge la Jartaruca rompie il becco* (the Fly that bites the Tortois breaketh her beak)' (14).

Ascham's account of history aligns him more closely with open republicanism. Heroical time, 'when *Nimrod* prov'd the stoutest hunter, and *Hercules* travelled to tame Monsters or usurpers, the world was in this subjection', still exists as at least a trace in most empires. The unlawful exertion of power (tyranny) was and is to be resisted, and this was the occasion in the heroical period of many songs celebrating the valour and virtue of Hercules. When Ascham says that the heroic period is still alive, he is justifying the resurrection of heroic songs.[20] For, in extraordinary times, 'the ancient right of using of things, as though they had still remain'd in common, is revived'.[21] Primitive reversion in the context of the end of monarchy is a necessity; heroism returns, and Ascham's (and 'Eutactus'') writings seem in this respect like part of an attempt to revive republican culture by looking first to a vision of man in the state of nature.

The Free State Speaks

With the establishment of a non-monarchical state, republicanism suddenly became fashionable, and was actively promoted by those who were employed by the government to run the propaganda machine. To this extent, the fact that the most prominent literary republican of the early 1650s apart from Milton, Marchamont Nedham, had already changed sides twice previously, is a testimony to the 'manufactured' nature of republicanism, which had to be literally 'constructed' in the 1650s as an official ideology. Political conditions had changed, and the previous and deeply rooted assumption that England was a mixed monarchy was now no longer applicable in the way it had been.

The attempt to construct a new state ideology came soon after the birth of the republic. Nedham's *The Case of the Commonwealth of England Stated* (1650) was published in order to encourage the taking of the Engagement Oath. The immediate context is signalled by separate sections addressed to those parties opposed to the Commonwealth, a strategy similar to one Nedham had used before.[22] But the tract is showered with quotations in the text, in the margins, and on the title-page which bear impeccable republican and stoical credentials. An entirely new conception of the state is offered in the conjunction of quotations from Aristotle and Tacitus which use, in the negative sense, two words soon to have a more positive rendering:

> And this he proveth, as did the wisest of philosophers, by the perpetual rotation of all things in a circle from 'generation to corruption'. . . . 'There is,' saith Tacitus, 'as it were a wheeling of all things and a

revolution of manners as well as times.' (ed. Philip A. Knachel
(Charlottesville, Va., 1969), 7)[23]

Providence allots to every government its period of time, and the
implication of Nedham's first chapter is that Providence will give the free
state a long run. Reasons of security – the sword is the foundation of all
governments, those who do not submit to the conquering power lose all
right to its protection, and so on – are offered as the standard defence of
the new government, but finally a free state, it is argued, always excels a
monarchy. The prevention of corruption in a free state is again a
dominant theme: 'when Rome was in its pure estate, virtue begat a desire
of liberty, and this desire begat in them an extraordinary courage and
resolution to defend it'(113). The final section on the free state ends with
a tremendous flourish from Virgil and Seneca's *Hercules Furens* on the
merits of martial strength for the sake of defending a flourishing peace.
Ancient drama is the site of crucial debates on the meaning of liberty in
the city state.[24] Civic virtue and martial prowess become overwhelming
images in the tract – serried ranks of senators and soldiers, 'every way
qualified like those Roman spirits of old' (114–15). And liberty at home
breeds wealth and power abroad. Dante, Machiavelli and the medieval
German poet Gunther of Pairis are summoned as authorities against
hereditary succession; at best a monarchy should be elective, while only
in extreme circumstances should single rulers, like the Roman dictators,
be appointed. The best heroes are virtuous generals, and these are best
appreciated by senates, as opposed to kings and tyrants, who are often
jealous of such success. Nedham is not looking back to the heroic age, as
Ascham does, but he does regard the culture of the free state as
quintessentially heroic.

Neither is a king the best guarantor of religion: Nedham manoeuvres
around the powerful traditions of Christian kingship not by offering an
alternative model but by shrewdly alluding to the current
Commonwealth clamp-down on religious enthusiasm, especially the
Ranters (123), without forgetting the degree of relative toleration which
comes with a free state. Taxes and the exemplary punishment of
Levellers are a fair price for the greater public good of liberty.

If Nedham had once collaborated with the Levellers, it was now
necessary for him to put them down in print. He wished to prevent the
growth of Leveller support (or to win hitherto Levellers over to the
republic), and like May before him, he constructed New Model Army
soldiers and artisans as small property owners who, like the Roman
soldiers, had taken arms to defend their own liberty. That some Levellers
did see themselves in this light is due not to Nedham's influence, but
their own reading (see above, 148–53).[25] The Levellers and Leveller
principles are identified with rule by the multitude and Aristotle's

'*Isonomia* – equality of right, the very political equality of democracy – a 'levelling down' which restricts personal growth and freedom; it is Tacitus' 'Parthian looseness' and Sallust's aboriginal rudeness (99–100).[26] Moreover, the 'language of our Levellers in their late petition' must be returned to them: it is their dissension which encourages foreign opponents of the republic. The free state must in response arm itself, and this in turn causes even higher taxes.[27] The image of the Leveller mob as the Athenian populace electing monstrous tyrants and demagogues (did Nedham have Lilburne in mind?) to positions of high office is clearly meant to frighten. Ancient 'levelling' always resulted in the banishment of worthy officers on the meanest of charges, but neither Greek nor Roman 'levellers' were so mad as to propose Digger communes (109). Councils of wise men are always necessary in truly free states: 'we read in what a flourishing condition the commonwealth of Athens continued as long as affairs were ordered by that famous council, the Areopagites; and no sooner did the power come into the hands of the people but afterward all turned to confusion' (105).

In the government newsbook, *Mercurius Politicus*, Nedham, with the help of Milton, perhaps, and John Hall, continued to sustain a literary ideology of republicanism, blending together English traditions of anti-courtliness and Machiavellian injunctions under the umbrella of the 'free state', a label which infuriated Royalists and radicals alike. *Mercurius Politicus* is often squashed into too narrow a space in general histories of republicanism. What is remarkable about this newsbook is that it resurrects or recovers a tradition of Renaissance republicanism and utopianism, and accommodates that to the natural law defences of parliamentary and popular right. Surprisingly, given the esteem in which the maritime empire was held by other republicans, Venice was regarded by Nedham not as a free state since a 'standing senate' prevailed there. *Mercurius Politicus* had more thoroughgoing plans for the English republic, and he registered a distinct hostility towards the English aristocracy.[28]

Reading through successive issues it is possible to see an assembly of fragments of a purportedly lost or suppressed republican identity. More's *Utopia* is one element, but much earlier than that is the idea that Julius Caesar organised an ancient British republic when he invaded the country. Here, the ancient constitution, a concept which had dominated parliamentarian apology in the 1640s, is seen as having had a republican form. Various authorities are also introduced, not least of which are Plutarch, who is shown to have praised free states, and Guicciardini, who is cited saying that free states are more pleasing to God than any other form of government.[29] Such *sententiae* are repeated or developed through successive editions, with a 'file of examples'. Numbered maxims of state from Machiavelli take up much space, while the apologists for the new government were forced to reverse the terms of parliamentarian apology. Where in the 1640s, resistance to royal authority was based on the notion of a recovery of a constitutional balance which the King had alienated, and had thereby endangered the safety of the people, it was now necessary to make the *de facto* rule of the sword (power by conquest) commensurate with that which was natural. Having in the 1640s argued from a conservative position, Parliament had now to justify something which was distinctly new and 'revolutionary'. Machiavelli was the best tool, although Hobbes's pre-*Leviathan* works were also useful. Examples are frequently repeated in *Mercurius Politicus*, with a seemingly limitless range of sources from Roman history: perhaps a testimony to a desire to educate and influence in a basic and unambiguous way. Poetry is frequently used, and is a way of maintaining a connection with an older English republican tradition: Thomas May's translation of Lucan's *Pharsalia* is quoted, in one instance focusing upon Cato as an example of republican austerity (see below, 203–7).[30] In another place, Cato's funeral oration in praise of the republic's fallen hero, Pompey, is also deployed.[31] Yet Nedham is well known for advertising literary works by Royalists in *Mercurius Politicus*, perhaps as a way of signalling accommodation.

The programme of 'republicanising' in *Mercurius Politicus* presents reasons for and against a free state. The reader was given weekly lessons in Machiavellian political theory, which was based upon what may appropriately be termed a Roman anthropology (76 (13–20 Nov. 1651)). Roman customs of proclaiming freedom (77 (20–27 Nov. 1651)) precede a discussion of the way in which republican succession prevents corruption (78 (27 Nov.–4 Dec. 1651)), and defeats faction and self-interest (79–80 (4–18 Dec. 1651)). Importantly, a large degree of social function is given to the private sphere (81 (18–25 Dec. 1651)): people are likely to be the best means of their own remedies, but the creeping in of 'self' in purely private terms, either in the public or the private sphere, is rejected. Families must also be prepared to make sacrifices for the sake of common liberty (83 (1–8 Jan. 1652), 1320). It is here that *Mercurius Politicus*'s resolutely secular republicanism chimed most obviously with godliness.

Nedham's republic is as meritocratic as Milton's. In free states, people are less luxurious than in monarchies (84 (8–15 Jan. 1652)), and are imbued with a more magnanimous spirit (85 (15–22 Jan. 1652)). As long as the people always give their consent, there can be no tyranny (86 (22–29 Jan. 1652)). The form of a free state is of course consistent with Nature and Reason – Nedham uses Cicero's *De Officiis* to demonstrate this, as Milton did in his *Defences* – whereas tyrannies veer from one form to another (87 (29 Jan–5 Feb. 1652)): the co-existence of several elements in a republic, even if mutually opposed, is a guarantee of balance, continuity and accountability (91 (26 Feb.–4 March 1652)).

Such an optimistic front sounds far too good to be true, and was entirely unconvincing to many, as those newsbooks that managed to publish against *Mercurius Politicus* attest. But Nedham was too good a manipulator of public opinion, too good an 'undeceiver' of the people, to let the republic stand without its virtue tried. So in one series of *Mercurius Politicus* (92–7, 4 March–15 April), objections to the free state are refuted. The Royalists fear a levelling – to which Nedham replies that the free state does not introduce a community of goods but preserves propriety. He amusingly provides examples of monarchs who behaved as Levellers, like Louis XI of France (92 (4–11 March), 1458–9). Too much popular power at Florence led to the 'levelling' politics of Savonarola – clearly a dig at radical puritanism. A free state does not cause confusion in government, because latitude of choice is not levelling: already the idea of an 'elective' state where liberty is defined by the choices available to the propertied is being mooted (93 (11–18 March, 1652)).

These 'editorials' were brought together, sometimes by a simple sequential printing, in Nedham's *The Excellencie of a Free State* (1656). In this one-volume version, Nedham emphasises the Areopagus, which, he says, avoids a 'kingly' tyranny (8; he was probably thinking of the Protector), and, as if it were the English Council of State, is told secrets of state during intervals between sittings of the Assembly in Athens, to whom the Areopagus was finally accountable. By contrast, monarchy is again regarded as Levellerish, although very shortly after the publication of this work, Nedham was to defend a return to monarchy in connection with the proposal to make Cromwell king.[32] Yet Athens is still a place to be wary of, and Nedham's emphasis here is quite unlike the open entertainment of both Athens and Rome in the mid-1640s as models of liberty. The people are by nature tumultuous, and elsewhere we are told how Greece was often a victim of its own volatile populaces. Nedham was also fearful of the threat to liberty which could come with military success abroad, the establishment of a standing army, and the transformation of generals into dictators. Nedham's allegiances appear to shift between Athens and Rome. In the autumn of 1651 he was clearly impressed by the popular control invested in the Athenian assembly. But just a few months later, Athenian instability was emphasised. Once the Roman people had their own assembly, they prevented the tyranny of the senate. The threat came from the corruptions of *imperium*.

Two important points need to be made in conclusion to this consideration of Nedham as republican thinker. First, in summarising so much political wisdom and historical writing, even to the extent of lists of political maxims, Nedham had taken the art of policy-making to a truly modern conclusion: his lists do not contain general aspects of the prudence of the governing power, but are a programme for the flourishing of a state throughout time.[33] Second, Nedham's obsession with the power of rumour, and the need for the 'whisperers' of dissent to be controlled, is a strong indication of the overwhelming truth that his theory of republican government was one made entirely within the framework of a society experiencing the intense circulation of information – in the news and elsewhere. He wrote and published that which he believed he was required to do, and he knew that his republican synthesis was no more than a currency seeking to gain the highest credit with the 'political nation'. He knew that he risked being interpreted in ways contrary to his intentions – hence the careful anticipations of Levellerish 'misreading'; an exercise on Nedham's part in journalistic damage limitation. Knowing that he was in such a cleft stick underlines Nedham's significance in his time (see above, 32–5): he was manufacturing republican and sometimes even populist ideology in ways which he or his masters might not have wished, and he was innovating in the area of the popular circulation of powerful political ideas. In this latter sense, he had seemingly given 'reason of state' thinking to the 'people', and this was of enormous significance. No wonder so many governments feared him; no wonder he was subject to such vilification – just like the thinker behind so much of what he wrote – Niccolò Machiavelli.

Nedham's acquaintances and associates used literary reservoirs to enrich the image of republicanism. With John Hall, the republic of the mind – the ideal of educational reform – imposes itself on the citizens, and this in itself is a hitherto under-recognised achievement. Addressing the Rump Parliament in his unremittingly Baconian and 'modernist' *The Advancement of Learning* (1649), Hall warns that the new republic will come to nothing unless the propagation of learning is reformed.[34] The constitutions of 'literrary Republicks' are crucial to the well-being of political ones. For his biographer John Davies, he was insufficiently rewarded for his talents at university, the 'Ectype' of monarchy, while another source reports that it was the rigidly hierarchical order in his own college, St John's, which impelled him towards popular government.[35] Hall agrees with Ascham that the age is pregnant with 'Heroick designs' to reconstitute the scattered body of learning, fragmented into as many parts as Medea 'cut her little Brother into'; civil society is to be judged by the degree of its education.[36] The image is a positive use of Medea; Hobbes's use is more pessimistic (see above, 36). Heroic similes abound: every major point is illustrated by one – scientists are saved from the fate of Ulysses, 'who wandring through Hel, met all the ghosts, yet could not see the Queen'.[37] Knowledge it was which made almost every worthwhile achievement of the ancient Greeks and Romans – the examples given are copious. More significantly perhaps, it is knowledge which has ensured the survival of ancient civilisation to the present day, in order that its republican excellencies may be imitated in the new free state of England.

Early in *The Grounds and Reasons of Monarchy* (Edinburgh, 1651), Hall associates royalist political theory with discursive obfuscation: 'Phylologicall and Rhetoricall Arguments, have not a little hindered the severer disquisition of reason, and prepossessed the more easy mindes with notions so much harder to be layd aside, as they are more erroneous'(10). This is an instance of Hall's Baconian modernity, and it seems to be at odds with his republicanism. Indeed, Hall understands that the needs of modern politics and knowledge are very different from those of the ancients, despite the still relevant guide that ancient texts supply. The result is, in Hall's writing, a very unusual deployment of vocabulary, some classical, some not, that conveys his sense of chronological doubleness. Thus, in the modern world '*the* Crisis *of Eloquence is not a little altered*', and he appears to mean this in the sense of the needs of modern politics: in the ancient world one had to speak to large as well as small audiences, but in modern times only a few are addressed, and this is connected with shortening of speeches *and* the creation of monarchies.[38] There is no sense of 'crisis' as such: Hall is using the medical sense of the word (a critical point in a disease) as a metaphor for the critically effective design of eloquence. Modern politicians should be '*forming all our thoughts in a* Cone, *and smiting with the point*'.[39] His emphasis on brevity is similar to Nedham's preference for the maxim: both are modern in stressing the design of distinct policies, and both are separating such designs from absolutist ideals. Hall seems to see the process as still continuous with the ancient art of eloquence, but smiting now with the point in the pamphlet and the newsbook.

Hall's heroes, including Milton (who was a republican) and Bacon (who was not), are pressed into defending the new order. Ralegh is another favourite: 'too generous and English for the times' (*Grounds and Reasons of Monarchy*, 45). The intellectual energy is impressive, as monarchy is shown to be inconsistent with the Old Testament and the law of nature, while all aspects of monarchy are associated with fantasy – things, in Hobbes's words, which are not. The model of the body politic with the king as its head is 'onely Metaphorical and proves nothing' (17). Hall has in fact imbibed Hobbes's empirical method, but without returning to the body metaphor (see above, 155–8), so that in a sense he is the truest disciple of the Hobbes of *De Cive*.[40] Like Milton, Hall engages in deliberate reversals of monarchical givens, including turning around his sources: 'whether they be Founders of Empires, or great Captains (as *Boccalini* distinguisheth them) ought rather to be remembered with horror and detestation, then that undue reverence which they commonly meet with'(15). Monarchs grow from the weakness of popular government – instanced by Romulus at Rome (a very novel historical view) and Theseus at Athens; Augustus was a usurper, and people are most enamoured of monarchs when their manners are most corrupt. Scottish history proves Hall's case (the immediate context is the Republic's recent defeat of Scotland in the summer of 1650; Hall was in Scotland with the occupying forces), where evidential *lacunae*, a kind of superstitious mist for scholars, obscures the exercise of analytical reason: Macbeth's 'death is hid in such a mist of *Fables*, that it is not certainly known'(35). Hall equates Scottish (and hence Stuart) knowledge with the frequent use of fables by royalist apologists.[41]

In opposition to superstitious monarchy, Hall presents images of 'rational vastness' for the achievements of the new state, a hugeness of proportion which is part of his sense of the sublime as a fitting response for the 'new mould'. The state becomes aware of imperial ambition (which the typically republican Hall never discounts) 'and like a wakened Gyant begins to rowse it selfe up' (19). Learning was traditionally associated with the patronage of the court. Hall puts it with his printed oration at the centre of the republican agenda.

Hall might have deeply admired Milton, and he might also have been involved in an attempt to propound a republican aesthetics of the sublime (in his translation of Longinus), yet he expressed himself in a rational discourse which went against the traditional association of republicanism with virtuous oratory. In the preface to his translation of Longinus, Hall writes that oratory is fitting for tumultuous times, although generally it has been outdated, and large-scale oratory, such as was practised in Athens, has gone forever. Eloquence was necessary to help reason (although contradictorily, and again like Hobbes, Hall is true to classical rhetorical theory in describing how it was meant to *prevail* over listeners). Such was the measure of Hall's modernity, despite his connections with deeply neoclassical *literati* like Thomas Stanley and John Davies. And it is because of this dividedness that, despite Hall's own influence in the 1650s, commentators have found him so secondary.[42] I think rather that they have simply failed to listen properly, for Hall is, as we will see in several other respects, as acute as Nedham (see below, 214–15).

With Milton's (the third of the republic's hired defenders) republican writings, there is no clash between ancient politics and the pressures of modernity. In the first instance, and as we have seen, Milton was offering versions of republican liberty in free speech at the latest by 1644, and his doubts concerning the monarchy are evident even earlier in the private notes he made in his Commonplace Book.[43] In fact, although there is no explicit rejection of monarchy in anything Milton published before 1649, one could argue that the civic optimism of *Areopagitica* marks the high tide of his republicanism, and that the rest of his writings on civic life represent first defensive, then repressive and finally defeatist responses to the republican ideal.[44] Certainly, when looking back on his activities in the early 1640s from the vantage point of 1654, Milton saw himself as living to 'advance the cause of true and substantial liberty' (*CPW*, IV.624).

In the *First Defence*, Milton poses as that great defender of republican virtue, Cicero, and says that Salmasius is no orator:

> as with that famous Roman consul who, when retiring from his magistracy, swore in a public meeting that the Commonwealth and that city was safe because of his exertion alone; so I, as I now put the finishing touches to this work, would dare to say, calling God and men to witness, that in this book I have shown and brought to the surface from the greatest authors of wisdom, . . . matters in which I trust . . . the English people has been satisfactorily defended. (*PW*, 253)

There is a classical republican parallel of Cicero's cautioning of the senate's negotiation with Antony and the Vote of No Addresses.[45] '*Respublica*' literally means not subject to individual ownership: 'Learn, slave, learn, scoundrel, that unless you remove the master, you remove the commonwealth: it is private things, not those of the public, that have a master' (*PW*, 73). Cicero, as voiced by Milton, becomes Salmasius' corrector (*PW*, 86–7), and Cicero the dominant authority in the *First Defence*, but Milton additionally throws the book of republican and anti-tyrannical statements and sentiments from classical literature at Salmasius. Thus, even in that most classical of monarchies, Sparta, the people are above the king (*PW*, 180).

The *Second Defence* is equally cast as a republican oration, in which is embedded the account of polemical controversy as heroic action (see below, 212–13). Cicero is quoted yet again (*CPW*, IV.643): Milton's impersonation has more in common with the radical religious voicing of Old Testament prophets than with the modernity of Nedham and Hall. The texture of the *Second Defence* is never less than deeply readerly, so that the speaker is precisely the kind of inventive and learned citizen envisaged in *Areopagitica*. The address to Queen Christina is a deliberately Ciceronian piece of panegyric designed to vilify Salmasius all the more (*CPW*, IV.602). The virtue of the citizen defender of the republic is conveyed by a series of *partitios* concerned with different aspects of the orator's good character and life. Anti-republican conspirators – Catiline and Antony – are aligned with Milton's opponent, Pierre Du Moulin, further enforcing the image of Milton as Cicero. Milton saw his role as reliving the ethos of the golden age of republican liberty and oratory, bringing it back to life in the better circumstances of a Christian dispensation.

The appeal of republicanism was even greater in the private sphere where the household was usually thought of as a little monarchy. Francis Osborne was one of those gentlemen who saw fit to tarnish the Stuart reputation by publishing scurrilous accounts of the court.[46] Like many republicans, Osborne had had a courtly career, in his case as Master of Horse for Sir Henry Herbert, Master of the Revels. In the early 1650s he resided in Oxford to supervise his son's education, and his writings at this time, especially his popular *Advice to a Son* (1st edn, 1656), are the private element of a republican ethos. It may well be that his own education was more than generously supplied by an immersion in Cicero.[47] Osborne's contribution to the Engagement controversy is offered as a piece of state-building after Cromwell, figured as Roman hero, has shut the gates of war.[48] The exclusion of kings from the political nations – and specifically, the three estates – was familiar enough in 1651, but Osborne has some interesting and unusual aspects to his republican defence. First of all, and apart from his religious scepticism, he is very generous to the Levellers, admiring their ideas, but concedes that they were motivated by evil consciences and counsel.[49] Second, the analysis of tyranny has some nicely mythical formulations. Idolatry in kings or tyrants is described as a Promethean transgression, robbing God of His divinity. Examples of Hebrew kings and ancient monarchs dazzling their subjects are given, and again, one of the prime illustrations is rape.[50] Court poets are regaled for sustaining royal myths, and Osborne makes his most unusual move in criticising Queen Elizabeth (who was not necessarily a true Protestant for him) for encroaching on English liberty by not naming her successor, and thereby letting in the unnatural and tyrannical Scottish line.[51] By contrast, senates at worst only cause division 'which if pure from *popular ambition*, may possibly occasion *more good then hurt*', and in this way Osborne turns around the frequently made allegation in monarchical apology that division is bad.

The many burdens (including children and court favourites) and moral impropriety of monarchies are juxtaposed with the proper employment of men of ability in republics. Moreover, public language will be saved, if not enhanced, in the encouragement of many orators, as opposed to one orator king: '*oratory* will still keep in repute, as having more affections to worke upon in a *Republicke*, then a *Monarchy*: one judgement being easier forestall'd then many.'[52]

Republicanism also infected those modes of political discourse that sought to root explanations in cosmology and the natural world. While George Wither was constructing a republican prophetic poetry (see below, 230–32), he was also thinking through a serious republican polity albeit one which was in favour of a Protector, and one in which the claim of divine inspiration held sway. *The Moderne Statesman* (1653) was the result, so he claimed, of meditation during an illness ('an arrest from heaven'). Assembling Hermes Trismegistus beside Plutarch and Livy on his title-page, Wither offers a reconciliation of providentialist cosmology and classical politics. The images by now are familiar: the English nation is seen waking up and roaring like an angry lion (45–6); their revival is like Samson's final triumph (66), and such an event can be seen in the wider context of the universe: 'a *Commonwealth* in its growth is uncertain, and the means whereby it shall acquire strength lie hid in the eternal decree, until by the working of Providence they are presented to public view' (21). Providence and man's desire for knowledge of the future are embedded in Wither's 'naturalism', a kind of early deism which accounts for his mortalism, his belief that religion is naturally implanted in man, and his confidence in revelation through nature. Hence the frequent natural analogies: states grow like vegetables (22; 35). Such a view also allows Wither to assimilate Roman stoicism (which he regards as a kind of piety), producing a version of public virtue which looks as confident or naive as Leveller republicanism, but which is staunchly anti-Machiavellian.[53] His attitude towards astrology is ambivalent, but he takes issue with the attack on university learning, and in particular the works of John Webster.[54] Wither appears to miss the point of Webster's call for a revision, rather than an abolition, of learning, and is more concerned to stress the compatibility of learning with claims for reliance upon the inspiration of the Holy Spirit.

Limited monarchy eventually worked its way back into a republican framework. *A Plea for a limited Monarchy* (1659), sometimes attributed to Sir Roger L'Estrange, Charles II's censor and a keen Tory propagandist, goes beyond the models of limited monarchy proposed in the later 1640s because it views the political order through the lens of 1650s republicanism. Thus, the bricolage of political language reaches its most refined: 'I come now to assert, that our former Government, eminently, included all the perfections of a Free-State, and was the Kernel, as it were, of a Common-wealth, in the shell of Monarchy' (5). The pre-Civil War monarchy was a good thing; Cromwell should have been proclaimed king; England is a monarchy and a republic; the nation has said goodbye to its tyrannous past, and it cannot learn that which is inappropriate: 'they have (God be thanked) forgot their *Norman*, yet they will hardly learn *Greek*, much lesse, *Utopian*: That, in the late Protectours times, our Lawyers, with one voice, importuned him, rather to assume the stile and power of a King'(3). This was directly contrary to the 'high republican' view expressed by Sir Henry Vane in *A Healing Question propounded and Resolved* (1656), where the Protectorate was portrayed as a reversion to a state of nature, from which the 'honest party' of the 'good old cause' should extract the nation by forming a new representative body (20–21). *A Plea for a limited Monarchy* has an interesting relationship with a tract written ten years earlier, and received by Thomason just one week before the execution of the King. *A Vindication of the Army* (22 Jan. 1649), written by a 'well-affected Christian Souldier', fears the establishment of an aristocratic republic, perhaps on the Venetian model, something which would not suit the English body politic. The author supports the

Army and Leveller claims for legal reform and other abuses (the Army has 'twelve Herculean labours' to perform), but regards any harm done to the King as a crime against God. Rule by a single person is regarded as inevitable. The tract contains an account of the emergence of republican discourse in the public sphere during the war decade, very possibly pointing to a preference for Greek rather than Roman republicanism, and therefore quite against the preferences of the Commonwealth apologists:

> *England*, within these 8. last yeares past, hath payed deare for the learning her Latine tongue, as Delinquent, Malignant, Sequester, Secure, Compound; and I dare say, two or three Greek words shalbe more worth to it then all those, and the like, if they will understand and follow these, which is no more then *Homer* read long ago. (4)

Milton's last defences of an English republic, the two versions of *The Readie and Easie Way to Establish a Free Commonwealth* (February and April 1660), are commonly seen as a sad bewailing – a jeremiad even – for the free state in the face of the Restoration. This has been seen as especially true of the second edition.[55] Given the gloomy final sentence of *The Readie and Easie Way*, and Milton's bright portrayal of productive creativity in an uncensored society in *Areopagitica*, compared with the perpetual Council of *The Readie and Easie Way* (which seems to 'freeze' society in the opposite manner to the form of public exchange and political life suggested in *Areopagitica*), these claims must be taken seriously. But a second look at both versions of *The Readie and Easie Way* reveals another view – one which is in fact a development consistent with Milton's own republicanism. It is possible to regard the two *Readie and Easie Ways* as equivocating pamphlets, yet still as republican as the earlier works: less democratic but equally republican.

The parallel with the classical republics is still there:

> Nor were our actions less both at home and abroad then might become the hopes of a glorious rising Commonwealth; nor were the expressions both of the Army and of the People, whether in thir publick declarations or several writings, other then such as testifi'd a spirit in this nation no less noble and well fitted to the liberty of a Comonwealth, then in the ancient Greek or Romans. (*CPW*, VII.356)

The Army and the People have become authors and they have made their point in their rhetoric and their heroic actions (see below, 212–14).[56] Neither is this divorced from a Machiavellian perspective, for Milton's citizens must continue to depend upon their 'own active vertue and industrie' (*CPW*, VII.362).

How does Milton do it? In the first instance, the return of monarchy threatens because some of the people have been 'nourished from bad principles' (*CPW*, VII.355). The eating figure takes us back to the centrality of education in Milton's thought, since eating is the Miltonic figure for reading and edification. Education is crucially connected with liberty of conscience towards the end of the tract (*CPW*, VII.384), and arbitrarily offered as the solution to the preference for successive parliaments (*CPW*, VII.372–3; 437). Second, the Army is seen as a considerable power – the arm of Providence and Machiavelli's armed citizens. To rely on it is not to compromise the freedom in the free state, even if democracy is compromised. And of course, Milton offers a highly decentralised view of political power, in which political skills are acquired in local congregations before any role in a central representative is assumed, and in which the categories of the English gentry and nobility are redefined to take account of the godly elite who will in future rule.[57] Freedom is a state of being, to submit oneself to courtly flattery is to put oneself in a state of bondage. No less in *The Readie and Easy Way* than in the previous tracts, this state of republican being is offered in a rhetoric of liberty in which the ethos of the commonwealth and of public virtue is carried as the seed of liberty within the rhetorical patterns of the printed oration.

Milton's denial of earthly kingship is matched with an idealising faith in an abstracted 'minde and approbation of the Armie'. Dissension among the people or by individuals in the Army is unimportant and separated from this abstract will which identifies with the ethos implied by the rhetoric. The idea of a perpetual Parliament is not proved so much as exhorted (although in the first edition, some compromises are offered): successive Parliaments (and Venetian-style dukes) are derided as a 'conceit' and the ship of state metaphor hauled in (the perpetual politicians are perfect oarsmen) to do its work (*CPW*, VII.369; 374–5). Continuity in 'immortality' is the goal of the commonwealth, certainly a Machiavellian notion, but also one which outkings kingship. The Grand Council is full of patriots supercharged with virtue; individual mortality does not dent the collective reservoir of virtue which always survives. The downplaying of the millennial element in *The Readie and Easie Way* by some commentators may be a mistake, for the reservoir of virtue in Milton's argument only has meaning in the context of an awaited Second Coming. And this biblical idealising – another form of unifying cement – is matched by Milton's description of the English republic as unlike the Dutch 'many sovranties in one Commonwealth . . . many Commonwealths under one sovrantie' (*CPW*, VII.385). Trade is relegated to a brief final consideration, despite the prominence of commerce and property in Harrington's republican theories. Milton's textual ambiguity here goes against the unity he urges for the state. On the one hand, trade flourishes more in republics than in monarchies, yet luxuriousness should not be allowed to endanger religion and liberty, so that Milton does not finally integrate trade into his system of virtue. As in the earlier pamphlets, the problem of the place of commerce remains unresolved.

The second edition of *The Readie and Easy Way* is less obviously republican. Among the expansions made by Milton is an account of the course of parliamentary resistance since the calling of the Long Parliament, which necessarily plays down the classical parallels, and the presence of pure oratory in the first edition: too much liberty in some ancient senates led to ruin (*CPW*, VII.438–9). Clearly, the discomfort which Milton felt about the Protectorate, and which surfaced in the first edition of *The Readie and Easie Way*, and earlier, has had to be dropped.[58] Yet the history of compromises made in the treatment of Charles I and the bishops is presented in order to enhance the sense of betrayal that the readmission of monarchy would be. In this sense, the expansions support the account in the first edition of the location of the essence of republican virtue in the army – the real force of change. The verbal resonances between *The Tenure of Kings and Magistrates* and some of the late 1640s Army tracts suggest that this was a view of some standing.[59] The presentation of monarchical preference and rejection of the 'good old cause' as a 'strange degenerate contagion' is a reintroduction of the terms of the divorce tracts – Milton's most intimate dissection of public and private liberty; arguably his most original and radically religious contribution.

Milton seems to adopt Harrington's notion of the 'balance' for his own purposes (see below, 248) – the perfectly stable relationship between senate and people without rotation. Harrington's republic is imagined by Milton as a jarring inversion of *Areopagitica*'s vibrantly productive city state and nation: the activity should be in the city, with harmony in the senate or council. Several layers of election from the local level upwards achieve this refinement, which begins to look like the degrees of refinement in creation, as represented in *Paradise Lost*, Book VIII: 'for it may be referrd to time, so we be still going on by degrees to perfection' (*CPW*, VII.444). More extreme still, but in a sense most republican too, those who are convinced of monarchy have forfeited their right to vote.

Looking back to the middle of the 1650s from 1660, Milton may well have felt anguish for the lost opportunities of republicanism. Although he had continued to serve as Secretary for Foreign Tongues, like many republicans, he was dismayed by some aspects of the Protectorate, and regarded Cromwell as the kind of military dictator who, according to ancient prudence, brought about the decline of commonwealths.[60] Indeed, the second edition of *The Readie and Easie Way* carries an adaptation of two lines from Juvenal's first satire ('I too have given Sulla the advice to sleep deeply as a private citizen'), which has been seen as addressed to Monck, but has now been seen also as a reference to

Cromwell. Dominion as well as autocracy was Milton's fear – another Machiavellian idea. Looking back from 1660 to the attempts to structure a republican culture in the early 1650s, it must have seemed as if all had come to nothing.

The Republican Advance

If republicanism appeared completely out of fashion, even totally irrelevant, at the Restoration, its achievement was far greater in contemporary terms than is usually recognised. Quite apart from those religious radicals who saw their futures protected by a free state, the republican moment created a set of allegiances among the middling sort (significantly not the gentry) which was resoundingly republican and resoundingly secular. Foremost among these was the publisher John Streater, famous for his contentious publication of Harrington's *Oceana*.[61] Streater was certainly influenced by Harrington, but his own tracts, which date back to 1653, two years before the publication of *Oceana*, are an example of an indigenous classical republicanism. Harrington (whose own works are discussed in detail above, 163–72) may have had a greater influence long term upon the history of republican ideas, but his impact upon the republicans of the 1650s, however considerable, should not be allowed to silence the presence of other voices.[62] Some of Streater's writings are little different from republican late Leveller works. Indeed, Streater's defence of himself when prosecuted for publishing seditious pamphlets in 1654 is similar to Lilburne's defence of himself. Like Lilburne, Streater uses Horn's *Mirror of Justice*, and Habeas Corpus, and even refers to Lilburne's trial of 1653.[63] Streater's pamphlets on the eve of the Restoration are concerned to limit Army power: he fears the untrustworthiness of military councils. His support for the recalled Rump is based upon the continuity of original 'Good Old Cause' aims ('Security of *Life*, *Liberty*, and *Estate*') with classical republican ideals of virtue:

> *Trajan* the Emperour, of whom *Dio* writeth, That when he created a Captain by girding on his Sword, offered him the Sword first naked, and said to him, *Here, take this Sword: If I command well, use this for me; and if I do amiss, use it against me.*[64]

There is purely Harringtonian regret for the failure of an English empire, which would have made 'Trading abound, and money as plentifull as dust', and Cromwell is compared to Nero: good for the first five years (on the authority of Suetonius and Tacitus), bad after that. The moment of making Cromwell a monarch risked the creation of dynastic struggles on the York/Lancaster scale, precisely the kind of arrangement which aristocrats like Algernon Sidney saw at the centre of their own republicanism. Monarchs are tyrants; and the retention of power can only remain with those who are untyrannical.[65]

Streater's *A Seasonable Advertisement to the People of England* (1659) is constructed as a piece of oratory from the chief citizen of the city of Mitylene on whether to choose a prince or a free state after a line of princes have become extinct. Mitylene is meant to stand as an ironic example against England, for, after copious reference to Machiavelli, and the states of liberty in Venice and Florence, the Mitylenans profess dislike for the Venetian laws and prefer monarchy. The fear of what might well happen in England is apparent, and intimated with bitterness: 'And that if any one would set up liberty in Mitylene, let them burn all Laws and Statutes; for such understood that to be perfect Liberty, where none obeyed, all commanded, and every one did what he list'(8). This is incredulous anarchy or utopianism, as well as having some parallel with Milton's desperate pleadings in 1660. Earlier, Streater's republicanism was far more optimistic. In *A Glympse of that Jewel, Judicial, Just, Preserving Libertie* (1653), written while he was serving with the Army in Ireland, he looked admiringly to the example of the Spartan King, Lycurgus, who encouraged his citizens to discuss liberty. The dutiful citizen who has regard for his neighbour's liberty is made a hero by comparison with Hercules, who was 'deified for imploying his strength in delivering the oppressed out of the hands of the oppressors' (Sig. A3v). The conditions for citizenship are nonetheless harsh, for everyone must study the 'laws of the commonwealth' and the mysteries (7–8), and the public good must always come before private interests. The political education of all means that private interests will always harmonise with public requirements, just as the laws must meet the inward rationality of every citizen. Fascinatingly, the spectre of the rape of Lucrece as a political *topos* appears yet again (see above, 109):

> Though Rome had no Politicall Laws to check the tyrannicall pride of *Tarquin*, yet they had a virgin-Law of Nature which beamed out of an eternall Law, which was of strength and force to revenge a modest *Lucretia*, and expel so licentious a Prince from his dominions. (9)

Again, the example of the virtuous man returns: Caius addressed the people of Rome, not the Senate, in his orations and he restored to them their authority (14). Republics must allow greatness to grow in great men, and one of Streater's unRoman and unnoble examples in this respect is the 'contemptible [i.e. low-born] *Marsionella*' of the Neopolitan Revolt of 1647, who resisted a tyrannous ruling power: Streater's attraction to Massaniello is an instance of a turning round of a notable anti-Cromwellian *topos* (9). Later on, Major-General Fleetwood is regarded as equally virtuous in ending the Protectorate of Richard Cromwell.[66]

Streater's republicanism lives best and most extensively in his newsbook, *Observations, Historical, Political and Philosophical* (1654), which ran for eleven numbers between 4 April and 4 July, and which, according to Streater, 'grated' the Protector.[67] It is an extensive serialised commentary upon Aristotle's *Politics*, and had reached the third chapter of the first book by its last issue. Streater is first and foremost an Aristotelian, then a Ciceronian, and finally a Machiavellian republican. Just prior to this, he published, in four stages, an English translation of Suetonius' life of Julius Caesar, prefixed to a newsbook entitled *Perfect and Impartial Intelligence* (23 May–2 June 1654). Caesar's failings as an orator, his blatant ambition and his ruthless use of the people for his own ascent to power are meant to be read as a veiled parallel with Cromwell's rise. In the first number, the newsbook provides a brief commentary on Suetonius, which is really an incitement to revolt: for a flatterer to compare any ruler to Caesar (as much Cromwellian panegyric did) is to suggest that they should also be killed by a Brutus ([6]).

The new ways of reading in the Commonwealth are measured by the comments on censorship in *Observations*, No. 1 (4–11 April 1654): if the *Observations* themselves are to be banned, then why not the Bible, and then Machiavelli, Suetonius, Tacitus, Polybius, Plutarch and Bodin (1–2). In later issues, free speech and the right to public meeting is ranked almost above every other liberty (7:52; 8:57–8). Patriarchal divine right theory is next defeated by patriarchal republican theory, as Streater appeals to Aristotle to show how fathers in different spheres do not have the same authority (2:9). The domestic unit is important for Streater: matrimony is preferred to whoredom and sodomy (unregulated sexual desire leads to all kinds of tyranny), while breeding is to be controlled for the sake of strong children (3:18–20). The vision in *Observations* is certainly artisanal: republican freedom is to be accommodated to the apprenticeship system, just as domestic peace is to be regulated for the sake of public well-being. All (men) should be free and all should govern (although wives are to be elevated above servants). Heroism is to be a nationally shared public quality: 'some may say that the begetting and increasing of heroickness in the brest of a people may administer cause of fear in those that govern', but Streater wishes all soldiers to be Caesars. Public and private fuse: all members of the commonwealth should be productive for public causes, just as Augustus wore a cloak woven by his daughter. Wealth is absolutely positive in value: the voluntary poverty of religious houses is regarded as unnatural (6:44), and elsewhere Streater encourages the growth of manufactures and commerce.[68] He also proposes public theatres, especially if anti-tyrannical heroic drama is performed (4:30). The similarity with parts of Nedham's *Mercurius Politicus* is marked, but Streater's newsbook lacks the complicated conflicting loyalties and cultural symbols that Nedham yoked together so remarkably. *Observations* is the voice of a simple and genuinely popular classical republicanism.

We should therefore note an interesting element of cultural anthropology in Streater. It was not unusual for republicans and Commonwealthsmen to celebrate the advancement of learning and industry (see above, 187–9). But such is Streater's enthusiasm for the ancient economy, that *Observations* No. 6 attempts to portray ancient culture as almost Christian, even puritanised. In what is clearly an attack on priestcraft, the 'magic' or superstition of kings and the Roman Church – a magic which corrupts the earth and the human body – is seen as a corruption of pagan religion in the city states where an approximately true apprehension of God as a series of causes was shared by the people (6:44).

Several other republican works of the mid- and late-1650s reconfigure national life in ways similar to Streater. *Sullogologia; Or, An Historical Discourse of Parliaments* (1656) has been associated with Streater, and is a compendium of historical sources offered in octavo form.[69] A mythical past for society is given in biblical giants and tyrants – Cain and Nimrod – which connects directly with Milton's use of giants in *Paradise Lost*, Book VI. From this past, laws emerged to establish and nourish liberty: 'the people, as from so many Conduit-Pipes, the *aquam vitae* the Law, that fountaine wherein the life and liberty of the people is conserved, might receive'(3). The uses of different chambers in ancient free states repeats the interests of other English republicans: 'afterwards in *Curia & Foro* the Athenians also in their temple called (by reason of a speciall judgement) *Areopagus*, and in the place called *Palladium et Pritaneum*'(3). The author's intention is to make the English Parliament a historical site of free speech (Coke's opinion that it is, is preferred to Valla's judgement that it is not), and, to this extent, Parliament is described as a kind of natural law, given to the English after the second Fall of the Norman Conquest as a palliative (7–8).

By forcing an initial focus upon the 1640s, we have observed the fragmentary coming together of the 'language of republicanism', apart from the pressing issues of kingship, resistance and obedience. What is most remarkable is the sheer variety of inventiveness throughout the period, however slight any single pamphlet might be. Within, without or against a Harringtonian frame, by the late 1650s, republicanism of one kind or other was known to a large proportion of the literate public. Republican apologists thought they were advertising a heroic present. But that very inventive and expansive interest was also a function of a national uncertainty with regard to what should replace the monarchy and why. The noble ideals of republicanism, as they related to the world of political action, were the sources of its greatest weakness. If it had proved difficult to establish a republic, republicanism had flourished as a literary gesture, for or against the Commonwealth. In the third and final section of this study, we shall see how the dividing of national culture was articulated in different but central kinds of literature.

PART III

Mythologising Calamity:
Genres in Revolution

CHAPTER 7

Heroic Work

Epic Divides; Heroic Diatribes

To frame a Discourse, concerning the supremacy of Kings, the Allegiance of Subjects, and the unlawfulnesse of Rebellion . . . is to make *Iliads* after *Homer*.

Robert Mossom, *The King on his Throne* (1643), 1

IN THE SIXTEENTH and seventeenth centuries, epic poetry was regarded as the most important verse genre, the apogee of civilisation. Anyone with serious poetic aspirations had eventually to write an epic, so that writing epics should be seen as a seventeenth-century career goal. Epics were also meant to provide a grand, transcendentalised expression for their time.

The Civil War 'internalised' the epic, be it as royalist retreat or as fallen Miltonic individualism. By this is meant a process of transformation in which epic and heroic language was made to refer to inward states of human constitution and consciousness. Classical epic characters and narrators have at times an inward cast of mind: Virgil's are the most memorable. But the language of Civil War epic was forced to confront the dividedness of its own war-torn, factional culture, and in doing so, replaced the battle scene with a novel inscription of the political and religious subject, just as the the events of the 1640s and 1650s put nails in the coffin of feudal aristocratic values. Classical and biblical epic language was redeployed to answer inner needs, so that for the first time, the language of the sublime signified kinds of individualism. Against this tradition, which at one stage represented the militant triumph of puritanism and the Parliament, Davenant and Hobbes's important writings on epic were pitched.

Epics for Civil Wars

If we were to look at the sum total of translation and imitation of the classical epic in Elizabethan and Jacobean England, we would find the *Aeneid* of Virgil the most popular subject. The *Aeneid* tells of the founding of Rome out of the ruins of Troy: it is a poem of national regeneration, which echoes even in Shakespeare's *The Tempest*, in the return from Prospero's enchanted island to a reformed Milanese court (perhaps a version of the Jacobean court).

But in a civil war, the epic poem which rapidly gained popularity and relevance was Lucan's *Pharsalia*, a pro-republican account of the rise of Julius Caesar, the defeat of Pompey, and the end of the Roman republic. The *Pharsalia* (as it was called in the seventeenth century) is an ironic anti-epic, deliberately written as a formal parody of the *Aeneid*, in order to demonstrate that civil conflict cannot be represented in Homer and Virgil's language of international wars.[1] The parallels between Rome and England were often noticed at the time. Lucan actually lived during the reign of Nero, and finally committed suicide to avoid persecution by his emperor. The violence as well as the difficulty of Lucan's language are remarkable, even when set beside the battle scenes in Homer's *Iliad*. Scattered throughout pamphlet literature are allusions to and quotations from Lucan's poem.[2] Even commentary on mock romance acknowledges Lucan as the courageous, significant and better other: 'our Country man [it is Don Quixote who speaks; Lucan was born in Roman Spain] *Lucan* . . . when all the stock of wit was vented in flattering the victorious side . . . [was] for the weaker party.'[3] Yet even then, Mildmay Fane thought that the descriptive achievement of Lucan's epic was outdone by the reality of war:

> If Lucan were againe to write
> The Art & Stratagem of fight
> Now with a swifter stile t'enforce
> The onsett by th'Courageous horse . . .
> His ould straine I should give way & yield
> To blaze this new Pharsalian field.[4]

Conversely, other poets felt unable to live up to Lucan when describing battle scenes (here, at sea, against the French in 1654): 'were I Lucaniz'd,/My Pen this Victory had highly priz'd,/And made as famous by inauspicious stars.'[5] After the Civil War, Harrington turned to Lucan to illustrate the breakdown of communication between Charles I and Parliament.[6]

While it is evident from imitations of Lucan that he was read widely in Latin (remember Marlowe's translation of the first part of the *Pharsalia*), he could also be read in Thomas May's important and popular translation, published in 1626–7, with an added *Continuation* by May of some seven books, first published in 1631.[7] As we shall see, the career of May and his poem have a curious interrelationship with the process of the Civil War itself, just as Gorges's translation of 1614, and the Lucanic poetry of Michael Drayton and Samuel Daniel, offered oblique criticism of Jacobean arbitrary preferment and corruption.[8] Indeed, May's *Continuation* was dedicated to Charles I, partly in an attempt to be named poet laureate in succession to Ben Jonson. The *Continuation* was supposed to direct readers' perceptions of Lucan's original poem so that they would be aware of the necessarily different states of late republican Rome and Caroline England, between the divided, strife-torn city-state and the triumphant achievement of Charles's personal rule without Parliament. Yet, as David Norbrook has recently shown, the dedications in the first full edition of May's translation (dedications which were rapidly cancelled and cut out after publication) were to aristocrats and gentlemen critical of royal foreign policy.[9] There seems then to have been a connection between May and courtly opposition at this early juncture. Whether or not May's eventual secession to the Parliament as its historiographer in the early 1640s had anything to do with the fact that Davenant rather than May became Charles's laureate, the historical irony from the vantage point of the mid- or late 1640s must have been glaringly obvious. May's other influential publication, *The History of the Parliament* (1647), was an exact reversal of the aims of his *Continuation* of Lucan – to show the parallels between Rome and England on the road to civil war, including a fair quantity of quotation from Lucan. In May's Latin translation of his *Continuation*, *Supplementum Lucani* (1640), genuine hostility to the monarchy is registered in the suppression of passages recording imperial clemency.[10]

All this information does little justice to the experience of reading Lucan, in the original Latin or in May's translation. Images of slaughter and carnage are the *leitmotifs* of the poem:

> The souldiers throng'd could scarcely wield at all
> Their killing hands, the slaine could hardly fall
> Supported so; but number did oppresse
> The dying people, and dead carcasses
> Encreasde the slaughter, falling heavily
> On living bodies. (2nd edn, 1631, 2.ll.201–6, Sig. C1r)

It was precisely this kind of language which attracted observers of the English Civil War and its aftermath. For instance, *Concordia rara sonorum, Or A Poem Upon the late Fight at Sea* (1653), by 'I.D.', celebrated a Commonwealth naval victory against the Dutch in the Three Days' Battle of 18–20 Feb. 1653, the occasion also of Marvell's satire, *The Character of Holland*. Lucan's description of the battle between Pompey and Caesar's fleets (*Pharsalia*, 3) becomes the means by which the Dutch war is articulated:

> Men now, with men contend, and Ships with Ships,
> One body 'gainst another; here one skips
> Into his enemies Deck; but beaten back,
> He leaps to's owne. (10)

So, in poetry which was published alongside, and interpenetrated, the language of early journalism, Lucan's collage impressions of mass destruction dominate perceptions.

Lucan's epic is governed by a prophetic structure in which the fall of Pompey and the death of the republic are foreseen. But this prophecy is known through the invasion of corpses, raised from the dead as oracles, which also suggest the mass deaths of soldiers in battle *and* the symbolic rendering of the body politic. In Book 6, just after the half-way point, Sextus Pompey visits the witch Erictho, who sends messages to the underworld by what seems to be sexual foreplay with dead male bodies. Finding a recently killed soldier from a battle, she brings him back to life 'with warme blood, opening fresh wounds, she fills/His breast: and gore to th'inward parts distill' (Sig. L1v), and with other liquids and invocations eventually 'the clotted blood grows warme againe . . . [he] at one bound/Stands bolt upright' (Sig. L3r) and tells of the horror to come. After his prophecy, the resurrected soldier 'with a sad looke . . . begg'd for death againe' (Sig. L4r), and has to be incinerated by the witch. This figure of yearning for death becomes a highly directed unifying principle in Lucan's epic, as if the author were constructing a fate-driven suicide or self-destruction ethos for himself or his civilisation. The similar function of the fury Alecto in the *Aeneid* should be noted: for contemporaries, witches in epics were an obvious way of allegorising mistaken claims to divine inspiration or justification, in the figure of a demonised female (see above, 81).

Or they provided opportunities to explore the boundaries of knowledge. An unpublished alchemical heroic poem entitled 'Lithochymicus or A Discourse of a chymic stone praesented to the University of Oxford by Basset Jhones Now paraphrastically Englished by the sayd Author', uses May's version of Lucan's witch in a long poem to explore the place of necromancy in the alchemical process: 'Heere he wishd theyre bodies/unconsumd, for them, with Caliope/in Lucan's Supplement, he could have/drensh'd with blood, to cause their speake.'[11]

Most moving and horrifying in the *Pharsalia* is the extinction and literal evaporation of Cato's army in the Libyan desert. As epic writing goes, it is also generic extinction. Lucan, whose sympathies were certainly republican and with Pompey, makes final attrition take on cathartic proportions, as the republic's citizen-soldiers disappear in a plague of snakes and corrosive desert winds:

> A little snake, but none more full then she
> Of horrid death, the flesh falls off, that nigh
> The wound did grow, the bones were bared round,
> Without the body naked shewes the wound.
> His shankes fall off, matter each member fills,

His knees are bar'd, his groine blacke filth distills,
And every muscle of his thighes dissolues:
The skin, that all his naturall parts involues,
Breaking lets fall his bowels . . .
This is but small I speake; burnt bodyes run
Melted by fire in filth, but what fire ere
Dissolv'd the bones? no bones of his appeare
Following their putrid iuice, they leaue no signe
Of this swift death. (9.ll.766–74, 783–6, Sig. R1v.)

May's *Continuation* of Lucan brings the history of Rome forward to the assassination of Julius Caesar, as retribution for the alienation of the republic. This is interesting and unexpected – it might have made more sense to reach the establishment of the empire under Augustus, celebrated by Horace as the 'rebirth of the republic', thereby bringing together the histories of Rome and England in an awareness of two parallel 'imperial' paxes.

For whatever reason, Lucan and May's translation remained a powerful influence, instanced in Abraham Cowley's unfinished epic of 1643 (unfinished because the royalist victory upon which the final books of the epic were to be based simply did not arrive), entitled *The Civil War*, which borrows from the proper title of Lucan's epic, *De Bello Civili*.[12] The transpositions and inversions of genre and subject matter so typical of this period, and which are usually associated with Parliamentarians like Milton, are characteristic of Royalists too, although the results are different. As one commentator has written: 'it seems to me that the poem had begun to fail, had moved into conflict with itself, before history started to provide the wrong plot.'[13] Cowley identifies King Charles with Pompey, the monarchy with the republic. This is curious because it flies in the face of Cowley's intentions – in Lucan the republicans are destined, prophesied, to defeat, although the royalists are supposed to be the final winners. Another interesting parallel (or mismatch) is that Lucan's republican defenders are the Roman patriciate, with noble status, whereas the Caesarian army is plebeian in construction. So, Lucan's status division provides Cowley with a means of organising class or order at least somewhat against English actuality.

Lucan's tone of lament keeps surfacing throughout Cowley's three books, and the dismemberment conventions of the *Pharsalia* remain, here describing the royalist siege of Lichfield (2.ll.107–12) through Pompey's siege of Dyrrachium (6.ll.169–79):

Some whilst the walls (bold men!) they'attempt to scale,
Drop downe by'a leaden storme of deadly haile.
Some with huge stones are crusht to dust beneath,
And from their hasty *Tombes* receive their *Death*.

> Some leave their parted hands on th'highest wall,
> The joynts hold fast a while, then quake, and fall.

Charles then is the true protector of liberty, and by means of the patrician/
plebs parallel, Cowley is able to cast the Parliamentarians and Puritans as
generically 'low' rebels. But as soon as he does this, his treatment of them
becomes somewhat comic, so that the epic mocks itself despite itself, as it
cannot take something which is overwhelmingly true in a serious manner.
The description of Sir William Waller certainly frightens ('this fertill
Monster thriv'd,/This *Serpent* cut in Parts rejoyn'd and lived' (1.ll.463–4)),
and pre-empts Dryden's figure of the First Earl of Shaftesbury's son in
Absolom and Achitophel (1681) ('a shapeless Lump like Anarchy'). But surely,
even the staunchest Royalist could not take this seriously:

> Three thowsand hot-brained Calvinists there came;
> Wild men, that blot their great Reformers Name; (3.ll.59–60)

> The dismall Haer'esy of wild Muncers crew,
> Hether twelve hundred stout Mechanicks drew.
> Those Christian Monsters! Wretches that begit
> Confusion here, and must inherit it.
> All things (they hold) to all must Common bee;
> Are theise they who defend our Propertie. (3.ll.87–92)

The mixture of satire (on the Puritans) and elegy (notably on the
death of Falkland at the end of Book 3) has been seen as an indication of
the poem's failure: 'a deeply flawed undertaking, its rhetorics even more
intractable than its subject matter'.[14] But Cowley's design can be
defended. Epics, after all, being the highest genre, were supposed to
contain elements of all other genres within themselves. In fact, Cowley
has established a very clearly demarcated generic dynamic which
corresponds to the power divisions of the Civil War itself. The epic
structure of *The Civil War* is a conflict between masque and elegy
(royalism) and satire/scatology (parliamentarianism, puritanism) with
epic narrative as the negotiating middle ground between the two. It is an
example of genre dynamic as a refraction of real power relations and
differences in exactly the terms upon which this whole study is founded.
We find ourselves wondering how Cowley would have continued this
process had he been able to complete his epic. What remains unstable in
the poem is the relationship between Cowley's royalist apology and
panegyric and the circumstances of history of which we have a more
impartial knowledge. The embarrassment that Cowley's narrator begins
to feel in Book 3 at the unwritability of his task is the strongest witness to
such incertitude, despite the earlier statements of certain royalist victory.
There is nothing inherently wrong with *The Civil War* as we have it. It is

an original, inventive and exciting project upon which history literally foreclosed. Its doubleness is in fact of two sorts – on the one hand the dividing dynamics of its own components, and on the other, our sense that it is broken by history. As such it is typically of the Civil War.

The rapidly changing fortunes of the early stages of the Civil War have their effect too. Naturally, Cowley celebrates the royalist victory of Roundway Down (13 July 1643), which coincided with the reunion of Charles I with his Queen, Henrietta Maria, at Kineton. The latter is represented as an Ovidian chase, in parallel with the real battle some distance away: 'Through the glad vale ten thousand *Cupids* fled,/ And chac'ed the wandring *Spirits* of *Rebells* dead' (1.ll.497–8). Kineton was actually part of the field for the indecisive Battle of Edgehill (23 October 1642), described by Cowley as an 'almost-*Victory*' (2.1.42), so that the hunting scene becomes a fictitious rewinning of a previous battle. The passage is also written in the language of the court masque, used by Charles as a vehicle to suggest his pre-eminent power. Such language is a clear signal of the heroic status which Charles was to have achieved, had the epic been completed.[15]

Instead of turning to Lucan's witch Erictho, Cowley takes from the *Aeneid* Alecto who protects the parliamentary Army. Her quelling of 'Great *Brittaines* aged *Genius*' and the ploughman just before she starts the Battle of Hopton Heath is not only a comment on the destruction of agricultural fertility by fighting, but also the suppression of an older poetic that had celebrated a national spirit. While villainous and inadequate parliamentary commanders have to be hidden by Alecto in a cloud from the heroic onslaught of the Royalists (imitating Homer and Lucan), the death of the Earl of Northampton on the battlefield is an astonishing merging of contemporary battle accounts, Lucanic motifs and possibly also elegies on Northampton.[16] The pace is arrested as a superhero is fashioned in the moment of death:

> At last hee groanes and reeles with many'a stroake;
> The *Brambles* round all dread the tottering *Oake*.
> They proffer *Life*, but hee to them disdaines
> To owe one drop in all his generous veines.
> Hee scornes to'accept the safety of his *Head*
> From *Villaines*, who their owne had forfeited.
> The fetterd Soules below of those hee slew,
> Curst his free *Spirit*, whilst up through aire it flew.
> Looke back, great *Spirit*, as thow doest mounting goe;
> And see *thyselfe* againe i'the field below. (2.ll.51–60)

Yet this sits ill with the following passage that describes the burning of Birmingham by Prince Rupert in early April 1643. Cowley ignores the claims made by some royalist apologists that the burning was done after

Rupert had left and against his orders, and seems happy to see the burning as a punishment for the death of the Earl of Denbigh in the siege of the city a few days beforehand. It is also a fitting punishment, for Birmingham, supplier of arms to Essex's army, and strongly puritan in its allegiances, is imaged as the forge of Vulcan, its inhabitants the Cyclops, destined to be defeated by the Olympian gods.

Although Book 2 of *The Civil War* was not meant to be its centre, it does occupy such a position in the poem's unfinished state. As such, its internal development is highly significant for the rest of the poem and provides an important point of comparison with other epics written in the period. Just above one half of Book 2 celebrates the royalist victories in the west in 1643. The rest of the book transports the reader to the underworld or hell, where we learn that devils are Puritans and Parliamentarians, and that Lucifer is controlling the rebellion. There is even a parliament in Hell (ll. 506–605), which contains parliamentary slogans and procedural vocabulary. It is unlikely that Milton saw a manuscript copy of the poem, but the parallel with *Paradise Lost* is obvious. The possibility that Milton might be answering Cowley in his own version of the parliament in Hell is an issue which will have to be entertained.[17]

This section of the poem also features a number of abstract qualities (good and evil) which have the effect of psychologising the poem in a neo-Spenserian way. We are in a classical epic world of battlefields, but the imagery of division, the metaphors of disease in the state, and the terminology of psycho-religious disorder (borrowed from contemporary heresiography), make the links between inner and outer states which certainly would have attracted both Milton and Pope:[18]

> Through all the *excrements* of state they pry,
> Like *Emprickes* to find out a *Malady*.
> And then with desperate Boldnesse they endeavour,
> Th'*Ague* to cure by bringing in a *Feaver*:
> This way is sure to'expell some ills; noe doubt;
> The *Plague* will drive all lesse *Diseases* out: (1.ll.111–16)

Sexual decrepitude is a means of representing the deformity of puritan doctrine and its hostility to the ceremonies and rituals of the English church:

> There *Schisme*, old *Hag*, but seeming young appeares,
> As *snakes* by casting skin renew their yeares.
> Undecent rags of severall dies she wore
> And in her hands torne *Liturgies* she bore. . . .
> *Sedition* there her crimson *Banner* spreads,
> Shakes all her Hands, and roares with all her Heads.

Her knotty haires were with dire *Serpents* twist,
And all her *Serpents* at each other hist. (1.ll.215–18;221–4)

This is of course an allegorical account which links doctrine with forms and with states of mind. As such, there is more to Cowley's verse than the simple location of it somewhere between Tasso, Spenser and Milton.[19] 'Ingrate' (1.1.80) is a word which looks forward to *Paradise Lost*, and Cowley refers here not, as Milton does, to Satan, but to the English, who have not appreciated how fortunate they were during the years of Charles's personal rule in the 1630s. But to go further down this road of exploring interiorised self-division would place Cowley at odds with his own loyalties and cultural traditions. He would have to come out of the other side of the process which the first three books of *The Civil War* only begin. In his own way, Milton was able to go through the imaginative process of inward division and reconstruction, and that he was able to do so has not a little to do with the side he chose, and the opportunities and habits of perception which belonged to that side.

It is difficult for Cowley to escape historical ironies in his poem, which any informed contemporary reader would have noticed. Prosperous cities – not only Birmingham, but also Bristol, Exeter and Gloucester – are the places where puritan and parliamentarian support flourished. Cowley's narrator deals with this problem by having the royalist armies rescue the glorious, loyal pasts of these cities (especially Exeter) from their present disloyal and indeed infernal inhabitants, thereby restoring their true identities. Like Birmingham, the landscape of Bristol is tainted with demonic traces; in this case, the defences of Bristol are likened to the hills thrown up by the hundred-handed giants in their rebellion against the gods.[20] Less defensible is the telling of lies: the Bishops' War is made much less of the royal farce it was (1.ll.97–106), and the King's withdrawal to Oxford is concealed (1.1.345).

Cowley's *Civil War* is not a great poem, but it is nonetheless remarkable for its attempt to address a contemporary reality in epic terms. While its 'politics' are sophisticated enough to analyse the Civil War and its outbreak in religious and economic terms, most striking of all is the change of tone between Book 2 and Book 3, from the use of Lucanic horror to suggest an unwanted but surmountable interruption in English history (liberally mythologised throughout the early parts of the poem) to the sense of being completely overwhelmed at the end of Book 3, where the epic stops. In fact Cowley ends with the much-lamented death of Lucius Cary, Viscount Falkland (influential intellectual and patron), apparently caused by exposing himself knowingly to enemy fire. Whether or not this was an intended sacrifice on Falkland's part, there is a clear sense of matters having gone too far. In this way, the lament seems to pre-empt the sentiments of many elegies written for Charles I later in the decade.[21] Even if the King and his supporters were being punished for their sins, says Cowley, Falkland's death seems to outstrip the claims of divine justice: 'Our Sinnes are great, but Falkland too is slaine'(3.1.648).

The Heroic Republic

Despite the military victories of Parliament in 1644 and 1645, royalist pamphlets continued to exploit epic language right up to the execution of Charles, even if they turned to the Troy legend as a more fitting source than the Roman civil wars, with royalist commanders appearing as Agamemnons, Parliamentarians as traitorous Thersites, and the New Model Army as destructive 'bloody Myrmidons'. But while the epic fittingly framed royalist degeneration, other epic theorists and practitioners were led to redesign the genre in very different terms. The parliamentarian and puritan appropriation of epic theory and intentions is one of the most exciting literary events of the century, largely because it seems so very daring.

Where Cowley subsumes a military command into epic status, Milton's prose works, published between 1640 and 1660, repeatedly include all those in the nation on the side of reformation in an epic venture. The interruption caused by national division in the development of the poet turns the relationship between art and life the other way round: in such times of stress, action becomes the epic; the instruction which heroic literature performs becomes relocated in singular acts of heroic virtue, be it defeating tyrants, the 'vigorous production of books', or oratory which dignifies the puritan republic.[22] The distance between epic incarnations and contemporary signifieds in Cowley, which, as I have just said, tends to irony in spite of itself, disappears as Milton's men become books, and books become men – 'the precious life-blood of a master spirit'. Note that epic intention is implicitly linked with reading and religious tolerance, a humanism which makes Milton's contemporary aims continuous with the direction of his classical and Italianate sources, as opposed to the disjunctions which echo throughout Cowley's text.

In the *Second Defence of the English People*, the English become a collection of Spenserian heroes 'accomplishing the most heroic and exemplary achievements, since the foundation of the world', being of 'pre-eminent virtue and a nobility and steadfastness surpassing all the glory of their ancestors' (*CPW*, IV.548–9). Within this reformed nation, and at its centre, is the prophet poet who becomes the pre-eminent epic hero and a poem himself: 'a composition and pattern of all the best and honourablest things' (*CPW*, I.890). In order to achieve this, he must internalise the experience of all that is praiseworthy – the *Geist*, so to speak, of the Commonwealth. The extent of fusion of poetic selfhood with national destiny is striking, and indicated at one point by a dilation which is more typical of a Gothic novel than a late piece of Renaissance humanism:

> Now, surrounded by such great throngs, from the Pillars of Hercules all the way to the farthest boundaries of Father Liber, I seem to be leading home again everywhere in the world, after a vast space of Time, Liberty herself, so long expelled and exiled. (*CPW*, IV.555).

The description and praise of his countrymen is explicitly framed within the rules of epic decorum:

> just as the epic poet, if he is scrupulous and disinclined to break the rules, undertakes to extol, not the whole life of the hero whom he proposes to celebrate in his verse, but usually one event of his life (the exploits of Achilles at Troy, let us say, or the return of Ulysses, or the arrival of Aeneas in Italy) and passes over the rest, so let it suffice me too, as my duty or my excuse, to have celebrated at least one heroic achievement of my countrymen. (*CPW*, IV.685)

Calumny has turned the poet-orator into a hero – 'I did not realize that I was a hero' (*CPW*, IV.607), and Milton revels in Alexander More's accusation that he is a monster, for he takes this as meaning he is the Cyclops Polyphemus (*CPW*, IV.582; see Virgil, *Aeneid*, 3). To have one's books burnt is to be cremated heroically in the Herculean way, given that books for Milton are living men (*CPW*, IV.653). Heroic writing is imagined as no less violent than fighting: 'I met him in single combat and plunged into his reviling throat this pen, the weapon of his own choice' (*CPW*, IV.556; see also 630). While Milton's puritanism remained elitist, one of the achievements of the prose is to marry by means of discursive process the Reformation ideal of directly felt divine inspiration with the ethos of epic poetry.[23] Where the medieval and sixteenth-century tradition of poetic prophecy as political complaint was acknowledged by prominent Puritans (such as John Cotton) as valid and continuous with the present, in a line which included Virgil, Dante, Petrarch, Chaucer and Langland, Milton's regicide tracts, *The Tenure of Kings and Magistrates* (1649) and *Eikonoklastes* (1649–50), become epic acts in which tyrannicide is textually committed, continuous with the real beheading. In Milton's republic of the imagination, the reader has to apprehend anti-monarchical epic action, to be refashioned as one of the republican heroes. The sentiment is similar, if not quite so optimistic or complex in Milton's republican admirer, the educational reformer John Hall: 'this Heroick learned Age, not merely rising to thoughts of Liberty, but instead thereof foolishly turning their wits and swords against themselves in the maintenance of *Them*, whose slaves they are.'[24] Yet even as Milton was seeing his early versions of liberty in the anti-episcopal tracts and *Areopagitica* coming to fruition in the early days of the new state, Davenant was attempting to pick up the pieces left by Cowley by publishing an epic (and romance) of defeat, *Gondibert*, which looked forward to better times. The preface was published in Paris twice in 1650, together with the important response from Hobbes to Davenant, before the poem itself was published in London in 1651. The exchange of letters between the two is nothing less than an attempt to do precisely the opposite of what Milton's pamphlets had achieved – to take epic back from national identity, and locate it in the education of princes:

> The common Crowd (of whom wee are hopelesse) wee desert; being rather to be corrected by lawes . . . then to be taught by Poesy . . . Nor is it needfull that Heroique Poesy should be levell'd to the reach of Common men; for if the examples it presents prevaile upon their Chiefs, the delight of Imitation . . . will rectify by the Rules. (13)[25]

The notion of *furor poeticus* is rejected specifically through its association with religious enthusiasm: '*inspiration*; a dangerous word'. Such poets (Spenser and Milton must be in his mind) 'should not assume such saucy familiarity with a true God', and Hobbes delivers a rational blow to prophetic dilation by his empirical definition of poetic activity: 'Time and education begets experience; Experience begets memory; Memory begets Judgement, and Fancy; Judgement begets strength and structure; and Fancy begets the ornaments of a Poeme.'[26] In Hobbes's account, the epic poem becomes a workmanlike manipulation of pawns, the components of the poem, while Davenant's poet is 'like' a general, looking down on his troops, rather than actually being a general or martial hero, as Milton would have it. It is not the case that there is no dilation of heroic intention in Hobbes, like some huge imagining of the human form that seems to be a feature of revolutionary times.[27] Hobbes's dilated body is of course the picture of the commonwealth on the front cover of the first edition of *Leviathan* (1651), variously held to be Charles I, Charles II or Cromwell, depending on which version or copy one looks at (see above, 157). This is not to say that the ideal values associated with epic are discarded. But, as Hobbes admits, since epics traditionally reflect on the glory of the ruler in whose reign they are written, it is only fitting in the circumstances that *Gondibert* uses fictional characters, taking the scene of heroism away from the historical stage. In this sense, the royalist epic imagination retreats or internalises, in a somewhat similar way.

However, the entire foundation of republican poetics is to make politics poetic, demonstrated by the heroic verse which was written to praise Oliver Cromwell in the early and mid-1650s. Milton's enthusiasm for liberty was eagerly greeted by John Hall, who was responsible for the first English translation of Longinus' Περι Υψους; *On the Sublime* in 1652. Translation of Longinus from Greek into Latin occupied some Oxford academics in the 1630s, but the context for the interpretation of the text was different by the early 1650s.[28] Longinus is famous for associating the writing of the best poetry with conditions of political freedom, and the English of Hall's translation bears special consideration. For instance, sublime poets '*burn* up all before them', and their poetry 'wheresoever it *seasonably* breaks forth, bears down all before it like a whirlwind'. In just such a manner Marvell's Cromwell (in 'An Horatian Ode') goes 'burning through the air', 'And palaces and temples rent'. At an apocalyptic moment in history, a sublime response is required of the heroic poet. Moreover, this brief moment of sublime theorising in the early 1650s is a cogent reconfiguring of the sublime as a response to a civil war and revolution nearly one hundred years before the beginning of the great period of sublime theorising in the eighteenth century (see above, 182–8). A very inferior kind of sublime praise poetry to Marvell's also circulated at the time, but the intention is the same as Hall's intention – to identify state formation and Protestant imperialism with sublime poetic achievement. So, in the little-known poetry of the Presbyterian minister John Ravenshaw, Cromwell's aims are seen in international terms:

> Goe on Brave Heroe with thy fatall steele
> And Clash that Man of Inde untill he reele
> With dreadfull horror let th'usurper know
> Babels Confusion In his Overthrow.

And, as with Milton, to imagine a hero is to turn him into a poet ('In thee A Subject bore A poets [part]'), as much as the poet in part becomes a warrior:

> Wee nor Could manage speare nor Pike advance
> But wee can trayle A fancy shall enhance
> Thy highborne spirit who art growne to bee
> Protector to the muses pedigree.[29]

Cromwellian energy transfers through the medium of epideictic verse, engendering sublimity and the heroic poet.

Ravenshaw's lines allude to Cowley's *The Civil War*. At the end of Book 1, the narrator, pouring scorn on sectaries, invokes God to confound the King's enemies if He cannot move their hearts: 'Goe on, great *God*, and fight as thou hast fought./Teach them, or let the *world* by them be taught'(1.ll.575–6). Quite apart from the complications which this raises in respect of Ravenshaw's poem (for Ravenshaw makes Cowley's God Cromwell), there is a clear indication here of a limit in Cowley's epic strategy, and one evident in relation to *Paradise Lost*.

Nowhere in his poem does Cowley's narrator ever assume the voice of
God. The creator is in several places called upon but never speaks:
'*Father* of *Peace*, mild *Lamb*, and gaullesse *Dove*,/Gently allay, restore to
us our sight,/And then, say once more, *Let there bee Light*' (1.ll.568–70).
Without such an engagement, the interconnected issues of creation,
creativity, authorship and authority, and the psychological dimensions
which come with them, are avoided as they were not to be in *Paradise
Lost*. Cowley's mental-martial malaise remains at but one level of epic
interrogation, and it stays unresolved. In effect, Cowley finds no solution
and no revelation in his poetic treatment of division and civil war.

But some years before Milton began the initial dictating of his epic,
Cowley refashioned the epic again in his *Davideis*, published in 1656, and
probably written between 1650 and 1654. This time, Cowley managed
one more book than *The Civil War*, so that he completed one third of a
projected neo-Virgilian twelve-book epic ('I have had neither *Leisure*
hitherto, nor have *Appetite* at present to finish the work, or so much as to
revise that part which is done').[30] The number of extended passages
which Cowley took from *The Civil War* and reused unaltered in *Davideis*
(especially the description of Hell) might lead one to suspect that
Cowley was attempting to go down a similar road.[31] This is not the case,
and the hints of a revolution in the epic – such as invoking the Holy
Spirit as Muse to inhabit the temple of the verse, and claiming to speak a
real, literal truth, as opposed to an allegorical one – are forestalled by a
narrative which again withholds revelation. *Davideis* offers instead a
mannered account of the undulating fortunes of private and public virtue
and jealousy in Davidic Israel, and this is offered in a spirit of moral
reformation:

> It is not without grief and indignation that I behold that *Divine Science*
> employing all her inexhaustible riches of *Wit* and *Eloquence*, either in the
> wicked and beggarly *Flattery* of great persons, or the unmanly *Idolizing* of
> *Foolish Women*, or the wretched affectation of scurril *Laughter*, or at best
> on the confused antiquated *Dreams* of senseless *Fables* and *Metamorphoses*.
> ('The Preface of the Author', *Collected Works* (5th edn, 1678), Sig. C3v)

And in the context of royalist defeat, using the language of the
Engagement controversy, Cowley offers poetry which tries to forget
divisions in the past:

> that we have submitted to the condition of the *Conqueror*, we must lay
> down our *Pens* as well as *Arms*, we must *march* out of our *Cause* itself, and
> *dismantle* that as well as our *Towns* and *Castles*, of all the *Works* and
> *Fortifications* of *Wit* and *Reason* by which we defended it. (*Poems* (1656),
> Sigs a4r-v)

In some remarkably intelligent commentary, Cowley voices his fear that to remain a royalist epic writer is to condemn oneself to poetic extinction: 'The truth is, neither *We* nor *They*, ought by the *Representation* of *Places* and *Images* to make a kind of *Artificial Memory* of those things wherein we are all bound to desire like *Thermistocles*, the *Art of Oblivion*.' 'The names of *Party*', he says, are sometimes all that there is to difference (*ibid.*). Perhaps it is because Cowley did not acknowledge the magnitude and irreversibility of division that his epic endeavours were so limited.

The potential for allegory, or extra-literal exploration, ends after the cosmological section in the first half of the poem. Satan is confined to Book I. The tyranny of God is raised here, but then also dropped. The last two books are more a history of David's exploits. The displeasure of Saul for Jonathan, which had resulted in conflict in ancient Israel, is resolved after a battle with the Philistines, by promises of loyalty which bind the passions causing conflict in the first place:

> Not *Sauls* proud heart could master his sworn Ey;
> The *Prince* alone stood mild and patient by,
> So bright his sufferings, so triumphant show'd;
> Less to the *best* than *worst* of fates he ow'd.
> A victory now he o're *himself* might boast;
> He *Conquer'd* now that *Conqueror* of an *Host*.
> It charmed *through tears* the sad Spectators sight,
> Did reverence, love, and gratitude excite,
> And pious rage, with which inspir'd they now
> Oppose to *Sauls* a better publick *Vow*.
> They all consent all *Israel* ought to be
> Accurst and kill'd themselves rather than *He*.
> Thus with kind force they the glad King withstood,
> And sav'd their *wonderous Saviours* sacred blood. (*Collected Works*, 145)

Cowley has abandoned in this poem his rule (almost faithfully kept elsewhere in the poem) of one sentence per rhyming couplet which signified the respect for hierarchy in *The Civil War*. Nonetheless, the kind of control which the prosody achieves is of the order which Dryden had available to him when he turned epic to mock-epic during the Exclusion Crisis. *Davideis* has been seen as a political allegory of the Interregnum, and more convincingly, but not conclusively, as a statement of political despair which pays homage both to monarchy and republicanism. Tyranny in the character of Saul is abhorred but mixed or limited monarchy is emphasised in Book IV, and prosodically pointed up in the limit of a half-line:

> Obey him gladly, and let him too know
> *You* were not made for him but he for *You*,

And both for *God*.
Whose gentlest yoke if once you cast away,
In vain shall *he* command, and *you* obey.
To foreign *Tyrants* both shall *slaves* become,
Instead of *King*, and *Subjects* here at home. (*Collected Works*, 136–7)

There are obvious connections with contemporary politics, but also a great deal of distance from them. The allusiveness which Marvell, for instance, or Milton, could deploy, so that the informed reader is convinced of the pertinence of allusion, is absent. The early 1650s was the period when the state of ancient Israel was used as the focus for debate and expectation over what a finally reformed and even millennial state of England might look like.[32] On this context, *Davideis* remains silent.

Davideis initially suggests a parallel between Saul and David and Cromwell and Charles II. Cowley's David endures a period of exile at the court of the pagan King Moab (?Louis XIV). But there the parallels end: as Corns has shown, Cromwell was notoriously unhandsome, Cowley's Saul the opposite.[33] Perhaps the poem offers a fantasy of Restoration, similar to some of the verse in Fane's 'Fugitive Poems'. Or perhaps it is a celebration of the triumph of the 'royalist underground' in the early 1650s.[34]

Cowley's language seems to move away from these contexts to a realm of removedness. In the Preface of 1656, the realm of retirement or retreat is seen as a place where poetry would be redundant. Thus, the volume in which *Davideis* appears effectively cancels the poem's epic function as public commentary.

Creating Interiority

Interiority was the mode towards which civil war epic tended; not the interiority afforded to the characters of the classical epic, but the kinds of interiority generated by the Civil War and the Interregnum. How did the capacity of epic poetry to talk about inwardness come about?

One solution was allegory, with heroic action figuring the inner life. Both Milton and Cowley rejected the chance to allegorise interiority in the chivalric and romance terms made popular by Spenser, and as we have already seen, Cowley was unable to exploit the opportunities which would later exercise Milton. But others did attempt the allegorical. Henry More produced in *Psychozoia* (1642; 1647) an allegory of the soul's life in Spenserian stanzas, using Plotinian categories of transcendental life. The composition of *Psychozoia* in the early 1640s is not as old-fashioned as it might at first appear. In the previous decade, neo-

Spenserian verse allegory had remained popular in the universities, instanced in the success of Giles and Phineas Fletcher, and More was a Cambridge academic. In the first half of the 1640s, Milton had not lost faith in the efficacy of allegorical verse. In fact, *Psychozoia* is offered by More as itself a revision of Spenserian poetry: 'Nor Ladies loves, nor Knights brave martiall deeds,/Ywrapt in rolls of hid Antiquitie;/But th'inward Fountain, and the unseen Seeds,/ . . . I'll sing' (1.1.ll.1–6).[35] Moreover, More's sources and his general reading, although located in a rather refined academic context, do show the effects of an invasion into England and English of a variety of continental mystical writings, all of which greatly expanded the potential for English people (including the most extreme Puritans) to talk of an inner life.[36] Despite More's attempts to explain his allegory in his prefaces, it is not difficult for the reader to become lost. By his own confession, More often lived in a world where words became forgotten:

> I was so immerse in the inward sense and representation of things, that it was even necessary to forget the oeconomie of words, and leave them behind me aloft, to float and run together at randome like chaff and straws on the surface of the water.[37]

The language of *Psychozoia* is always trying to break forms and boundaries. Transcendental concepts are not merely named, usually with a derivation from Neoplatonic terminology, but also given a pattern of circulation. Ovidian mythology and the epic device (2.5) of the voyaging narrator are two devices used as explanatory analogies, but the poetry moves from the allegorical vehicle of the name towards the description of that which is beyond forms:

> And this I wot is the Souls excellence
> That from the hint of every painted glance
> Of shadows sensible, she doth from hence
> Her radiant life, and lovely hue advance
> To higher pitch, and by good governance
> May wained be from love of fading light
> In outward forms, having true Cognizance,
> That those vain shows are not the beauty bright
> That takes men so, but what they cause in humane spright. (1.12)

The crossing of thresholds from the ideal to the real is achieved by reflective perception; a Plato's cave in reverse for the ethereal forces – 'In this clear shining mirour *Psyche* see/All that falls under sense.' The sensible world is marked by physical suffering, and no less palpable is the promise of Christ's Second Coming (1.53), but the allegory remains general rather than specific in its reference, and increasingly, more inwardly focused. Accounts of creation and its forces are important for epics: they are at the centre of *The Faerie Queene* and *Paradise Lost*, but their significance extends beyond their boundaries. In *Psychozoia*, however, 'the inmost Center of Creation' (2.2.l.1) draws all elements into itself.

'Inside' the poem is a debate on church politics. Later in Canto 2, in the section added between 1642 and 1647 (stanzas 57–125), there is a debate on the relationship between revealed religion and toleration which returns to the political dilemma we find in More's prose writings from the late 1640s onwards, but which his poetry often seems to ignore. More was clearly responding to the Civil War:

> I would be very loth to be so farre mistaken as to be thought a Censurer or Contemner of other mens Religions or Opinions, if they serve God in them in the simplicity and sincerity of their hearts, and have some more precious *substratum* within, then inveterate custome or naturall complexion. All that I mean is this: That neither eager promoting of Opinion or Ceremony, nor the earnest opposing of the same, no not the acutenesse of Reason, nor yet a strong, if naked conceit, that we have the Spirit of God, can excuse a man from being in any better condition then in the Land of Brutes.[38]

In the characters of Pico (woodpecker) and Don Psittaco (parrot), More juxtaposes a Laudian ceremonialist (even Laud himself) with a Presbyterian Calvinist.[39] With echoes of the Bower of Blisse (*The Faerie Queene*, 2.12) always present ('it was to weet, a trimly decked Close/ . . . The Eastern End by certain steps they climbe/To do their holy things, (O sight divine!)' (2.58.ll.1–5)), ceremonial high church worship, which had taken hold in some Cambridge colleges during the 1630s, is gently sent up. The sensuous appeal of the objects of ceremony is ambiguous in More's moderate view. On the one hand, it risks idolatrous superstition, on the other, it may have its uses. More's major character Mnemon is suitably taken in by the appearance of piety, only to be reprimanded by the stern Psittaco, in whom is revealed an intolerant and inflexible Presbyterian discipline: 'O had we once the power in our hands/How carefully the youth wee'd catechise,/But bind Gods enemies in iron bands' (2.72.ll.1–3).

Despite his own mild episcopal allegiance, More's Platonic rationalism did put him in a close relationship with the more tolerant Independents, some of whose more eminent members enjoyed the patronage of the Commonwealth and were made heads of Cambridge houses. How often More was prepared to acknowledge this is another matter. In *Psychozoia*, puritanism is Presbyterianism, and Psittaco's bigoted intolerance is compounded by his reliance upon two (somewhat unlikely) friends: Graculo (jackdaw), a scholastic divine, and Corvino (crow), tradition. The positions of each speaker are unnaturally skewed together, Corvino's aversion to dissent serving to support Psittaco's desire for (Presbyterian) uniformity. Historically, this could only be viewed as a great irony, although it is not out of keeping with the way in which arguments were purloined by different sides throughout the 1640s. The detail continues to be satirically amusing as well as astute: Psittaco's caressing of the cord around Corvino's robe amply signifies the Presbyterians' desire for clerical castes and élites: 'and held by holy belt/*Corvino* grave, ne did his hands abhor't/When he the black silk rope soft fimbling felt/And with his fingers milked evermore/The hanging frienge'(2.83.ll.1–5). Mnemon defends the Platonic and mystical piety of which More and the other Cambridge Platonists (Whichcote, Cudworth and John Smith) were contemporary exponents:

> Gods Spirit is no private empty shade
> But that great Ghost that fills both earth and sky,
> And through the boundlesse Universe doth ly,
> Shining through purged hearts and simple minds. (2.91.ll.2–5)

Graculo's accusation that such worship is an 'idle Circle round' delights Mnemon as an accurate description of meditation and devotion. It is not the simple reliance on Psittaco's Holy Spirit, and later in the canto, More distinguishes Mnemon's position from what he calls enthusiasm, who is represented in the female character Glaucis, the pejorative image of an over-emotional woman prophet or sectary. The perversion of enthusiasm leads (and this is described in a passage of remarkable power) to democracy and anarchy, a self-consuming force as opposed to the crushing torrent of absolutism: 'So to an inward sucking whirlpools close/ They change this swelling torrents surquedry,/Much treasure it draws in, and doth inclose/In'ts winding mouth, but whither then, there's no man knows'(2.130.ll.6–9). Such a society has become brutish, and the following few stanzas are concerned with predatory animals. More's conclusion was that his country had been torn apart by the unbounded outward expression of interior powers.

The other long allegorical and theological poem produced in these years was Joseph Beaumont's *Psyche* (1648; 2nd edn, 1702). Like More, Beaumont was a Cambridge academic (Fellow and Master of Peterhouse, close friend of Richard Crashaw), but his open royalism was of a much more urgent character than More's. A 'news' letter he wrote to his father from Cambridge recounting the visit of Prince Charles and the King to the University in March 1641 reports Charles's assurance to the Vice-Chancellor: 'Whatsoever becomes of me, I will charge my sonne upon my blessing to respect ye university.'[40] The sense of an imminent storm bluntly interrupts the colourful accounts of oratory and worship in the rest of the letter.

Beaumont was forced to leave Cambridge and his books in the 1640s.

Psyche was written for the 'avoiding of meer Idleness', and tells the story of a:

> Soul led by divine Grace, and her Guardian Angel, (in fervent Devotion,) through the difficult Temptations and Assaults of Lust, of Pride, of Heresy, of Persecution, and of Spiritual Dereliction, to a holy and Happy Departure from temporal Life, to heavenly Felicity.

Beaumont stresses the exclusive qualities of the poem: poetic genius and appreciation are not common capacities. He also intends *Psyche* to stand for the unity of 'Christ's Catholick Church', a sentiment which would have found little support if *Psyche* had ever been read by a broad, non-loyalist readership.

Within a few stanzas of the opening, the reader is pitched into an internalised world of emotional despair, dominated by the threatening figure of Satan:

> The Hall was roof'd with everlasting Pride,
> Deep paved with Despair, checker'd with Spight,
> And hanged round with Torments far and wide:
> The front display'd a goodly-dreadful sight,
>   Great Satan's Arms stamp'd on an iron shield,
>   A Crowned Dragon Gules in sable field. (1.12)

Psyche takes More's anti-enthusiastic allegory and adds to it a sense of internalized emotional stress. Canto 1 does in fact contain a parliament in Hell and a Satanic rebellion, as in *Paradise Lost*. During Satan's speech, which is the incitement to demonic rebellion, 'Heresy' is introduced as his 'Secretary'. During Psyche's victories, such as the defeat of lust, conventions are reversed (*Aphrodisius* is a charming hero with improper allure), and attention is focused upon flight, this representing the escape of Psyche from that which threatens her. It is also a recurrent figure of escape for the author:

> To *Heav'n* to *Charis*, to *Syneidesis*
> Her winged thanks she speeds; but all aray'd
> In scarlet with her cheeks, whose graceful Dress
> The beauty of her Penitence display'd.
>   Blushes, though Blames own Colours, are not blam'd:
>   The greatest shame is not to be asham'd. (2.155)

If the natural world became for Henry Vaughan a place where the sacred could be experienced in the absence of the national church (see below, 267ff), for Beaumont, Psyche's transports are a poetic journey equivalent to that elevation which the decorations in Peterhouse chapel were meant to induce in beholders.

Psyche's life is interrupted by rebellions against her integrity which are dispelled in the allegory by royalist means. A king offers to take revenge on 'Rebellion's fiery Boils' (even though earlier it is an interiorised excess of desire which causes Psyche's 'belking Tumour' to split). In Canto 4, actually entitled 'The Rebellion', a praise of poetry comes precisely in the middle. Oratory and poetry are elevated as a superior form of existence. 'Encomiastic suavity' is coupled with George Herbert's 'oure and precious Metal cast/In holier moulds'.[41] Above all other poetic genres is ranked epic, and all shorter verse aspires to reach 'the *Thunder* of an *Iliad*' in bite-sized doses 'which chirp'd, pip'd, crackled, squeak'd, and buzz'd about;/ *Mushrooms of Verse*'. The rebels are the passions, and, while inviting the reader to look beyond the immediate frame of the narrative, Beaumont makes the description of the self's struggle for pious interiority merge with the struggle between King and Parliament:

> And here I challenge any heart to read
> This stories riddles, and forbear to sigh;
> Seeing servile feet tread down the noble Head,
> And common *Slaves* with tyrannous Licence fly
> > Upon their *Lord*: O who secure can be,
> > When *Reason* must be bound, and *Passion* free! (4.211)

Psyche is addressed in Canto 5 as a queen, indeed very like Henrietta Maria in the courtly literature which idealised her union with Charles. What touches Beaumont most closely and what the poem articulates most strongly (inverting the usual relationship between signifier and signified in the allegory) is Civil War and ejection ('jostled out our Liberty').

Prophetic Resolutions

More and Beaumont had created a heroic discourse of inwardness which Milton and other puritan poets could exploit in different ways.[42] Milton's departure point is different from Cowley's, who leaves a greater distance between human and supernatural worlds. The digression on '*Gods Poem, this Worlds* new *Essay*' in *Davideis* is in the mouth of the narrator, not an angel, and we lose this perspective by the end of the poem. The account of the creation at the end of Book I is not linked by imagery or any other means to any other aspect of the poem, and Cowley's creation is *ex nihilo*, not *ex deo*, as it was with Milton, thereby losing the opportunity to engage with the question of authorship.

Paradise Lost is usually thought of as the great epic achievement of the age. Although it is largely a Restoration poem, it was probably begun as early as 1655. It is therefore odd that little attention has been given to its relationship with Civil War epic theory, either Milton's, or anyone else's. How does it relate to Cowley's unfinished epic or Hobbes's theory? The answer lies in a new kind of internalising, and in the assumed link which we have already seen between heroic action and heroic writing. In the first instance, *Paradise Lost* is neither wholly Homeric nor Virgilian, and certainly not entirely Lucanic. It also involves romance.[43] Moreover, it is hexameral, finding the immediate pattern of its language in Renaissance creation epic, like Tasso's, but also much more closely, Josuah Sylvester's translation of du Bartas' *The Divine Weekes and Workes* (1606), and Phineas Fletcher's *The Apollyonists* (1627).[44] The plate tectonics of *Paradise Lost* are to be found in the Book of Psalms, as Mary Ann Radzinowicz has recently argued, and in *Paradise Regained*, the Son voices Milton's defiance of Davenant's absolute, asserting the supremacy of Hebrew poetry over the Greek (4.ll.334–42).[45] While Milton's epic is a history which tends towards the Fall of Man, starting just after the Fall of the rebel angels, it is also the history of the prophet-poet, figured as the narrator, as he prophesies to the 'fit audience . . . though few'. It is through the narrator's sympathy or lack of it with the other characters, especially Satan and Adam, that the reader is able to apprehend the state of loss and the memory of a lost perfection which is so central to the poem. We could be witnessing a kind of internal history of the individual, in which the major protagonists are internal aspects of a central self. In this sense, we could say that the poem was truly puritanised, even more so in the light of the near-Quakerish metaphors of light and illumination which predominate in both of Milton's epics.[46]

Raphael's account of the war in heaven likens 'spiritual to corporal forms', so that he can be understood by Adam and Eve. In this way, Milton's war represents a reversal of Lucan in the reconstitution of bodies (albeit bodies which are simultaneously material and immaterial, real and allegorical; external and interiorised). Satan is pierced by Michael's sword, and actually dismembered, but he knits together almost immediately and heals soon afterwards (6.ll.320–53). The conceptual battleground matters most: the 'cubic phalanx' (6.l.399) of the angelic army, signifying virtue, is juxtaposed with the 'hollow cube' (6.l.552) of the deceitful infernal host. Satan confuses parleying with actual combat, which seems to evoke the pamphlet wars as much as Civil War battles. By the same token, the rebel angels' artillery 'levels' so that the angels tumble on each other, and hierarchy is removed (6.l.591). Satan's carping at this confusion has been seen as a Miltonic reference to royalist satire, but it could also be seen as Levelling satire (see below, 298–304), which Milton might equally have abhorred. Or is the angels' response – hurling mountains at the Satanic army – another image of levelling? Perhaps it is more appropriate, visually echoing the biblical phrase of 'levelling the hills' in man, and fitting also in that the uprooted mountains suitably match Satanic transgression, and cast the rebel angels into a subterranean darkness. Milton did not want a Leveller republic, but he was at one with them and the Army in desiring a rapid overthrow of a transgressing tyrant. Others have seen the representation of the Satanic army as a putting down by a disillusioned Milton of the classical republican ideal itself.[47] But then again, God's elevation of the Son through 'merit' is a fulfilment of the republican ideal. Satan's failure to understand this (the cause of his rebellion) marks the failure of sympathy in him, a sympathy which Adam and Eve share in their fall, and which they carry with them out of the poem towards mankind's promised 'Paradise within thee, happier far', the real escape from epic degeneration and failed revolution.

Milton was not the only poet to interiorise the epic. In 1661, in the very early years of the Restoration, a strange long poem appeared entitled *A Sea of the Seed's Sufferings* (prosodically and lexically dependent, like *Paradise Lost*, upon Sylvester's du Bartas), written by the itinerant Irish Quaker John Perrot.[48] It might not have appeared so strange if one had had one's eyes on the most extreme end of the Quaker press for the previous three to four years. Perrot had led a group of men and women Quakers on a proselytising mission to the Mediterranean in the summer of 1657. The ultimate aim was to convert the Ottoman Emperor to Quakerism, making him see the inner light. This first aim not succeeding, Perrot and one other Friend set off for Italy across Greece, to attempt the conversion of the Pope. After many adventures, Perrot was arrested by the Inquisition in 1658 in Rome, having been betrayed by an Irish priest in St Peter's Basilica (Perrot had apparently asked him how to obtain an audience with his Holiness). Perrot spent the next three years being tortured (beaten with a bull's dried penis) in the madhouse prison in Rome before his eventual release.

During this time he produced a plethora of writings, most of it in prose, but also *A Sea of the Seed's Sufferings*, and all of these pieces (notably the latter) sublimate the experience of being tortured or beaten into sanity (Perrot's Quakerism was defined as a mental illness in Rome) into a spiritual allegory built out of natural imagery. In *A Sea of the Seed's Sufferings*, self is split into several allegorical presences, most notably the worm and the seed. These are threatened by a series of hostile elements, until the true nature and location of God is discovered. It is a truly sectarian piece of writing, accepting the dispersal of the self into a series of natural symbols, unlike the fear of fragmentation expressed in the royalist epics of Beaumont and Cowley, and the aetiolation which comes with self-consciousness in *Paradise Lost*. Where Milton 'likens spiritual to corporal' things when necessary, while claiming generally to speak a literal and substantial divine truth, Perrot uses his allegory in the first sense to place the spiritual *within* the corporeal (Spenser's *The Faerie Queene*, 2, only gives a map of the internal). This is the literary correlative of the 'inner light' theology, one which Milton approached, but was not able finally to reach. The depiction of moving bowels, which were associated with pity or tender feelings, becomes the most striking way of communicating the pressure on the conscience in response to suffering. It is both a literal and a figurative disembowelling:

> Thou Drop, Thy Channel's more than many Brooks,
> On Thy Grief's Streams my mourning spirit looks;
> Yea, for thy sake my Bowels are a River,
> Pour'd on the ground's, my Reins, my Heart and Liver. (22)

By contrast, the focus on bowels and the womb in *Paradise Lost* (2.778ff.) becomes a literal expression of revulsion from birth given by the female as it is an allegory of the birth of Death from Sin: 'this odious offspring whom thou seest/ Thine own begotten, breaking violent way/ Tore through mine entrails, that with fear and pain/ Distorted, all my nether shape thus grew/ Transformed' (2.ll.781–5). So, we come full circle to the images of dismemberment so effectively placed in Lucan and May's translation, but in Milton locating sin in a terrible moment of sexual difference, and in Perrot allegorically expressing the rebirth of conscience while never forgetting literal persecution – the central internal and external experiences of nonconformity.

Perrot's poem is also a journey: that of the seed in search of its own regeneration. In consequence, blood rises around the worm threatening to drown him. Sea and blood begin to take on an equivalent status, as, in keeping with Perrot's belief of the revealed truth of God in nature, accidence is assimilated to substance. *Paradise Lost* begins and ends with journeys. In fact, royalist and puritan epic forms meet in the figure of journey, even if in different ways. In this respect, all are connected by different forms of defeat. In *Gondibert*, the ideal of Baconian scientific discovery, which signifies virtue in the epic, is regarded as needing the New World to fulfil itself: a flight into exile across the rocky waves of the Interregnum: 'Heav'n's reserv'd World they in the West shall see;/To which this stone's hid vertue will direct'(2.6.32).[49] No less a serious Baconian, Perrot, who cites liberally the writings of the German mystic Jacob Boehme and Sir Thomas Browne, allegorises magnetism: flesh becomes the '*Adamant*', the hard loadstone or diamond, which the sweating blood of the worm fails to move or melt. Davenant was actually arrested at sea while sailing to become Governor of Maryland, while Perrot's voyages are as reflected in his allegory as are his experiences in Rome, natural philosophy being as important as persecution.[50] At the centre of this is the question of the claim to control (an epic poet is like a God) and to have received inspiration. Out of Milton's account of God's creation, of which his own authorship is a repetition, eventually come Adam and Eve, likened after the Fall by the narrator to native

Americans (9.ll.1115–18). Milton looks back to a state of prelapsarian perfection in Eden, Davenant and Perrot see different versions of resurrecting it in different kinds of worldly perfection. But Hobbes seems to differ from Davenant here. There is no possibility of revival in exiled retreat, and he expresses this in the vocabulary of epic invention: 'fancy' and 'philosophy' are effects of European civility, and there is no possibility of resurrection among the 'Barbarity of the *American* sauvages'. Invention of a Miltonic or Perrotian kind is a dangerous colonial adventure which can only incur risk:

> Beyond the actuall workes of nature a Poet may now go; but beyond the conceaved possibility of nature never. I can allow a Geographer to make, in the Sea, a fish or a ship, which by the scale of his mappe would be two or three hundred mile long, and thinke it done for ornament, because it is done without the precincts of his undertaking; but when he paynts an Elephant so I presently apprehend it as ignorance, and a playne confession of *Terra incognita*.[51]

Metaphors of dangerous exploration and uncharted dimensions were used to articulate the perils of sectarian experiment:

> the *Roundhead* is faln himself into a subdivision of *Presbytery* and *Independency*; the latter in its full latitude is like a *Megallanica* a vast unknown tract, no man can tell how far it reaches, only coasting upon it such discovery is made as finds it a place of priviledg for all Sectaries in the world, and how many those are or may be no man can say for certain, until the devil hath done brooding.[52]

So in the end, the Hobbesian epic poet is a slave to nature, to a repetition of what is naturally probable, not what is allegorised or personalised fantasy. Epic and epic poetic activity really were about 'flight', and in its republican or puritan modes offered vertiginous odysseys of subjectivity, the transgressive liberty of regenerate citizens. Satan's flight is to do with corruption, and it is presented to a large extent in terms of the vocabulary of colonisation – a feature which has been seen as a critical glance by Milton at the colonial policies of the Protectorate in the Caribbean in the mid-1650s.[53] Satan's journey in *Paradise Lost* has been compared to the great Portuguese epic, the *Lusiads*, of Camoens (like the first edition of *Paradise Lost*, in ten books), translated by Sir Richard Fanshawe in 1655.[54] The text of *Paradise Lost* makes a number of specific allusions to *The Lusiads*.[55] The ending of the *Lusiads* in the Ovidian episode on the island, like the retreat to the colonies in Davenant's *Gondibert*, could be seen as a departure point for a response from Milton. So could Camoens's celebration of da Gama's voyages: Satan's voyages are, after all, demonic affairs, doomed to failure. In putting down Satan, Milton was putting down the romance, and any claim for voyages of discovery to be represented in heroic terms. More pertinently, Fanshawe prefaces his translation with a translation of Petronius' 'Rapture', a short commentary on epic language, which is critical of Lucan's historical epic. Petronius offers his own version of a more obviously Virgilian epic style. Fanshawe sees this as a forerunner of the Virgilian epic of empire which is the *Lusiads*, '*a mixt nature* between *Fable* and *History*'.[56] Fanshawe's preference for Petronius' dicta begins to look like a turning away of the sublime from the association with free spirit and liberty (or republican Longinus), and a linking of it with a more obviously royalist aesthetic, '*amidst a world of pleasant extravagancies, from a breast inflamed with fury, than a deposition as of sworn witnesses to* tell the truth'.[57] Through its negative presentation of imperial and colonial endeavour, *Paradise Lost* is a response in kind to Fanshawe's Camoens, while the retention of Lucanic versions of the martial inside *Paradise Lost* signals Milton's republicanism, this time very obviously in defeat.

Fanshawe's translation could also be seen as an act of idealising wish-fulfilment, unlike the escape in *Gondibert*.[58] Da Gama's loyalty to the Portuguese King and the sincerity of the sailors, translated by Fanshawe as 'noble *Cavaleers*' (2.76), stand as exemplary qualities of nationhood. Throughout the epic, the Moorish King functions as a Satan figure – the 'other' who must be overcome. During the voyage, stories of the Portuguese struggle for nationhood are related: in a feudal system, kings express and embody the liberty of their people (4.19–21). Rebels and traitors are derided in the same language as that of royalist propagandists like Samuel Sheppard. Allusion to Lucan only suggests infernal rebellion, as opposed to civil war (4.32–3).

The middle of Canto 6 praises the English aristocracy and court through a medieval Anglo-Portuguese marriage alliance. At the centre of this passage is a joust, so that pageant and knighthood are celebrated. The Portuguese win the contest but they are feasted in good humour by the Duke of Lancaster. Before another story (this time in Germany) can begin, a storm interrupts, so that regal and chivalric civilisation appears always prone to disruption by tempests – well known for their association with fortune. The lot of land-bound feudal knights is considered fortunate compared with the merchant knights of the sea. This tension in Camoens has been noted frequently by scholars, and it is difficult to see how Fanshawe could exploit the guilt concerning economic gain so prominent in *The Lusiads* for a 1650s English context. But just as controversial discourse, as we have seen, figures exploration as religious transgression, so Fanshawe maps religious and political experimentation in the Interregnum onto the epic's mythopoeia. Thus, after the storm in Canto 6 (which suggests civil war), the sea is tamed by nymphs, and the wind-deity Notus (who desires Galatea) is presented as a libertarian Ranter:

Fayre *Galatea* likewise lays the case
To blustring Notus, who, full well she knows,
Hath many a *long* sigh fecht for that sweet Face,
And is at her *devotion* doth suppose.
The *Raunter* (scarce believing such a grace),
His heart too ample for his bosome grows.
    The pleasure of his *Mistresse* to fulfill,
    He thinks it a cheap bargain to sit still. (6.90)

Again, the portrayal fits with some hostile portrayals of the Ranters themselves.[59] The tenth and final canto is presented as an attack on tyranny, and the victory here (in the final establishment of the Portuguese empire) is followed by recommendations that the ambitions of churchmen be curbed, that taxes be eased, and the assertion that royal service is a duty (10.149–51) – all clearly directed at the shortcomings of the Commonwealth government.

Satan's discussion with Chaos in *Paradise Lost* (2.ll.980–1010) has been seen as an ironic parody of the discussion in *The Lusiads* between da Gama and the Zamorin of Calicut, when the former tries to secure a trading agreement for Portugal's glory, rather than her profit.[60] Milton is suggesting that da Gama and Camoens have disingenuous intentions, and this moment would take its place alongside the other criticisms of worldly republicanism and imperialism in *Paradise Lost*. There would be a connection here with the criticism of merchants in *Areopagitica*, but *Paradise Lost* offers no resolution itself because, unlike *The Lusiads*, it is not concerned with money. The real context of Milton's epic in this respect is the contest with Royalists over the uses of the heroic and other epic motifs.

In the royalist epic, flight ambiguously figures exile or retreat – a concern for which Cowley at least (whose fantasy in 1656 was to retreat 'to some of our *American Plantations*') was reproved. Indeed, for Hobbes, there can only ever be the state of civilisation (in Europe or America) and behind it, nature. In this sense, Dryden's *Annus Mirabilis* and *Absolom and Achitophel* both represent a Restoration denial of epic flight in heroic terms. Another Restoration commentator associated Lucan and Milton pejoratively with republicanism, and recommended that 'every potent Inspiration' be redirected to the service of the Royal Society.[61]

It was a new age. Mock-heroic subject matter (the ironic parallel of Davidic politics with Whig conspiracy and the Protestant succession) regulated Miltonic energies in a way which would have been pleasing to Davenant. At the same time, Dryden happily inhabits the vehicle of Miltonic syntax and prosody, taming it with the couplet, directing its energies (which Milton saw as a literary component of liberty) to the service of an authoritarian aesthetics.

Translations of Virgil in fact greeted the return of Charles II.[62] When

Dryden came to translate the *Aeneid* (1697), he retained from Sir John Denham's translation, *The Destruction of Troy* (1655), the final lines depicting the murdered Priam: 'On the cold earth lies th'unregarded King,/ A headless Carkass, and a nameless Thing'(549). More than this, Dryden signalled his indebtedness to Denham in his marginal notes, thereby reusing one of the most famous figurations of the regicide. Denham's translation was made first in the late 1630s, and then revised for publication in the 1650s with a distinct royalist, post-regicide slant. Recent commentary has shown how Denham's English vocabulary exaggerates the architectural words in the Latin, as if to shore up the ruins of the foundation destroyed in the poem (so that Trojans/future Romans are Royalists, and Greeks are Parliamentarians).[63] The sections of the *Aeneid* translated are from Book 2, the stealthy invasion and destruction of Troy by the Greeks, recounted by Aeneas during his sojourn with Queen Dido in Carthage. The translation necessarily becomes a figuration of the English Civil War and the regicide, although with no direct parallels between the poem and English events. Justifying his 'loose' translation, Denham makes explicit his intention: 'if *Virgil* must needs speak English, it were fit he should speak not only as a man of this Nation, but as a man of this age.'[64] Harrington's republican translation of *Aeneid*, Books 1 and 2 (1658), preoccupied with matters of land, and the ascent to power and lineage, makes an instructive comparison with Denham's mannered commemoration of regicide. Where Denham has Pyrrhus stab Priam in the heart (repeated by Dryden), partly because decapitation is too painful and indecorous for a Royalist to depict, Harrington literally represents regicide: 'Which words by unrelenting *Pyrrhus* said, The other hand strikes off old *Priam*'s head.'[65] Denham's final couplet stresses the king's tragic royalty: he is headless. Harrington's dead Priam by contrast becomes one of the common people: 'His mighty trunck upon the shore is thrown/A common carkass, and a corse unknown.' That Aeneas is already on his way to Rome seems to mean that Denham intended the poem to prophesy Stuart restoration, but the sheer violence of the later parts of the translation, and that most memorable description of Priam's corpse, evoke an almost unbearable sense of defeat and loss. When royalist fortunes were at their lowest ebb, all epics failed them – Virgilian as well as Lucanic. Dryden's translation has been noted for its sense of fatigue and tiredness at Trojan as well as Greek civilisation; his use of Denham's line is an instance of a Restoration man of letters disillusioned with the restored monarchy seeing a resonance in the experiences of a poet in the previous generation.[66]

Perrot and Milton had a fellow traveller in heroic agency and poetic innovation, and that was the celebrated poet and soldier George Wither. Little read now, Wither's early courtly career, his alienation from the

Stuarts and his career as parliamentarian soldier and self-appointed poet of the Commonwealth are equally little known.[67] Prophetic invocation is a major feature of the confessional verse in which he debates with himself the political, religious and military predicaments of the nation. In *Vox Pacifica* (1645), inspiration comes to him through the 'VOICE' which his poetic competence cannot always catch:

> The VOICE there mentioned, was but a *Sound*,
> Not then, articulated into words;
> The perfect forme thereof I had not found,
> Not what interpretation it affords. (2)

After this delineation of inwardness, key parliamentarian issues are discussed: the fact that itinerant preachers can make more money than parish ministers, that the soldiers of the parliamentary army have a stake in the affairs of the nation and should therefore be heard, that the division of the clergy threatens to lead to an endless atomisation of the churches into infinitesimally small sects. Just as the voice is difficult to interpret, so the 'form' of the truth which will redeem England cannot yet be apprehended – so in a sense Wither is a Seeker in religion, as much as some of his statements make him appear a Leveller in politics. Wither uses an epic simile of discovery to give the quest for the form, and the dangers of that quest, a shape:

> It is indeed a *Thing*, which neither had,
> Nor shall, no man have any certain shape;
> A thing, in making still, but never made,
> A card drawne out of some *Utopian-Map*
> To make your Pilots steere they know not whither
> Till they arrive at the *Antipodes*
> To saving Truth, or, else be carried thither
> By many clinging winds, on many Seas,
> Where they shall split upon the rockie shores
> Of Heresie, or suffer shipwrack there,
> Where melancholy Desparation roves;
> Or else, into those Creeks be driven, where
> > They moored lye in dull *Securitie*,
> > Or, laid upon a Carnall *Libertie*. (123–4)

Wither's indecision is characteristic. He wants liberty but he does not want heresy – yet he was already in a position of heresy in the eyes of many. He wants liberty but he wants to make a reconciliation (he sacrally calls it an 'atonement') with the King – yet already in 1645 he can glimpse the possible execution of Charles (148–9).

Campo-Musae, Or The Field-Musings of Captain George Wither (1643) is a stirring call to arms in the form of a prophecy. The space created for meditation by the disabling of Wither's troop results in an internalising of the war as the debate between opposed issues and loyalties. As ever, Wither is painfully honest (or so it seems) with the scene of his writing. His muse is Pallas Minerva, goddess of war; interruption and disturbance dominate the poet's space. The craggy repetitions feel like poetry written between cannon-fire:

> My *Pen* I re-assumed, in hope, to shew
> My *practice* never prov'd my words untrue.
> My *Pen* I re-assumed; and (full of matter)
> Sate down to write: but, ere I ought exprest,
> The Trumpet sounding, all my thoughts did scatter,
> And gave me, since that houre, but little rest.
> Destructive times, destructive muzings yeeld,
> Expect not therefore method now of me. (3)

Speculum Speculativum (1660) was inspired by the Restoration of Charles II, but despite the open welcome offered to the returning King, Wither remains hostile to bishops and chary of the role of kings: 'We have a *King* (GOD prosper him:) but, hark!/He, hath a *people* too will find him work./He may perceive before this year wheels round,/That, with a *wreath of thorns*, they him have crown'd' (6).[68] Wither even explains the regicide: 'Once when sick to death the *Body* lay,/ 'Twas cur'd by taking of the Head away' (17), a phrase which a contemporary annotator explicitly associates with Charles I.[69] But more pressingly in this poem, the prophecy of the imminent sufferings of the godly under the new regime is divulged in terms very similar to those of Perrot's sufferings and Milton's visions. The violent terms of Army and Leveller pamphlets reappear in a ghastly new context:

> Where *Sin* and *Death* are Twins conceiv'd together,
> Though born a little while before each other;
> And, will in very ugly shapes be found
> In many places, ere this year goes round;
> Portended and attended in strange wise,
> With *Ominous Events*, and *Prodigies*:
> We shall see *Gown-men* tread on *Men of War*,
> High *Courts of Justice* called to the *Bar*;
> Those, of whom no man lately stood in dread,
> Arraign the Living, and condemn the Dead. (14)

Wither in fact sues for reconciliation.

The history of the epic during the English Revolution is a process, from May's Lucan, through Cowley's *Civil War*, Davenant's *Gondibert* (and Hobbes's Letter), Cowley's *Davideis*, to *Paradise Lost*, in which kinds of subjectivity are 'discovered' – as epic and heroic patterns are worked upon by divided perceptions and divided ideological requirements. The Civil War ended the popularity in England of the greatest civil war epic, Lucan's *Pharsalia*; indeed, the Civil War had proved the decadence of aristocratic, martial, honour culture, and after 1660 traditional epic was no longer possible. But it also enabled religious difference to be voiced as a state of mind, as an internal history of the Puritan and Quaker individual: an odyssey of subjectivity. Where this might involve an inward turn for the defeated and withdrawn Royalist, puritan republicanism was most heroically engaged in its inwardness. The triumph of puritanism in the 1650s was concerned with the matching of inner and outer frames of awareness. Colonising inner space was what mattered, although the public sublime continued in the poetry of later republicans.[70] So, where Cowley in defeat demonised the other of sectarian dissent, Milton had no choice in defeat but to acknowledge that the other (Satan) was part of himself as much as it should be reviled: 'this thing of darkness I acknowledge mine'.

Mr Hobbes in Love: The Quest for Real Romance

If you have done with the first part of *Cyrus* . . . I have a third tome here against you have done with the second; and to encourage you, let me assure you that the more you read of them you will like them the better.
Dorothy Osborne to Sir William Temple, 25 June 1653

They *made sport* with the Relations of Burnings and Massacres, and heard them as some *Romance*, when themselves sate voting securely at *Westminster*, snorting upon their downe beds.
George Bate, *The Regall Apology* (1647) 68

Romance was seen as an opposite of epic, and while some epics had turned to romance sometimes to resolve themselves, the behaviour of romance in the Civil War cannot be seen in such easy terms. In many ways, romance was a more historically responsive genre than many others, in particular epic and satire, in that the changes it suffered during the 1640s and 1650s as a consequence of civil war and revolution were part of a larger process already taking place before 1640, and which continued after 1660. This makes mid-century prose romance both less and more interesting than other forms of literature. Defined in the broadest sense, prose romance also worked at all levels of the book market, from the most elegant folio to the skimpiest duodecimo. The structures of plotting in romance, simple or complex, thus reached the widest possible range of readership.

Like play texts, the prose romance benefited from the greater possibility of publication after 1640. The effect was not immediate, and this was because of two factors. First, the productive capacity of the printing industry would have to grow in size in order to accommodate the massive texts of the romances. Second, both romances composed in English and English translations of foreign romances (there were more of the latter) took a long time to produce. Only after periods of (enforced) inactivity were gentlemen and aristocrats able to produce such works. Such was the time required to fashion a romance that few translators were able to make a living from their work. In the 1650s, romance translation was the last refuge of aristocratic literary patronage.

The End of Arcadia

Studies of romance seem obsessively concerned by their readerships, as if the texts themselves were insufficiently interesting. That romances, especially Sidney's *Arcadia*, were read by courtly women is a commonplace. The following observation would have to be that most early and mid-seventeenth-century English romances were written by men, despite the opposite case in France. What saves these truths from becoming platitudes is the fact that in no other genre is the matter of identification between characters and readers so prominent in the intention of the author and in the assumptions of the readership. We are dealing with something which approaches, in its concern with reader response, the modern mass market for romance in cheap novels and in films. And this is why prose romance should not be confused with dramatic romance in the period, for while the two forms are related, their production and reception are not. And in no other genre was the form so shared between those with differing allegiances. As we shall see, romance articulated the modulating experiences and desires of the governing elite: it was the vehicle of aristocratic and gentry republicanism as much as it was a tool of royalism.

Prose romance was not 'stopped' by the Civil War and forced to reconstitute, as was the case with epic. This is not to say that some romances from the 1640s were unfinished: some were. The important factor was the dual function of romance which had developed earlier in the century. Romance was perennially concerned with the presentation of virtuous ideals and vicious opposites. For this reason, it, and its parody, the anti-romance, could always be denigrated as an object of pure pleasure. Thus, a parliamentary newsbook of 1645 derisively reported that a letter from the King entertained like 'a Love-sick *Novice* the famous Histories of *Don Quixote*, and *Amadis de Gaule*'.[71] But romance had also gained serious status as a form of *roman à clef*, offering hidden comment on political, religious and philosophical matters. The potential for the romance to articulate hidden agendas at a time when the country was saturated with them was evident to many in the 1640s.[72] The concern with mapping public events in romance structure led to an overdetermination of the form, depriving it of any intrinsic life. The largely Sidneyesque romances of the 1640s were drained of life by the very politics they sought to address. New forms of romance had to be found or invented to satisfy changed readerships, so that the 1650s witnessed an interesting period of experimentation in romance design.[73]

Romance was habitually derided as a form that induced vainglory and illusion in the reader through an over-indulgence in the imaginary and the fantastic. Hobbes's insights are very sharp but not untypical (see above, 159–60). But politics *is* concerned with the imaginary and the fantastic. 'Lived' romance (for instance, Prince Charles's adventure with Buckingham to woo the Spanish Infanta) was a feature of 1620s and 1630s court politics. Imagining ourselves as more than we are – amplified into the glory of a romance character – may have been the only means of resolving those greater issues of power, authority and allegiance which confronted individuals. The extraordinary events of the 1640s seemed to many commentators as if life had in any case become a romance. As we shall see, the fictive forms provided by romance enabled many political imaginations to comprehend, analyse and think their way out of the dilemmas of the 1640s and 1650s.

Paul Salzman has written with extreme clarity on early modern fiction, and his insights into Civil War romance would be entirely acceptable were it not for the fact that he claims that 'romance was able to deal with the Civil War, by absorbing it into fiction', rather than being broken like epic.[74] The prejudice against epic is misjudged, and there is substance in the notion that, like the epic, the looser structures of romance were divided and developed by different needs.

John Barclay's *Argenis* (1621) used romance to discuss the use and abuse of power, with a heavy reliance upon Machiavellian concepts. It was written and published initially in Latin (followed by the first English translation in 1625), and it rapidly gained the respect of important people, like James I. By matching the characters to significant figures (specifically Henri II and Henri IV of France, the Duke of Guise, Philip II of Spain), the romance plot articulates an allegorical account of (west) European politics in the later sixteenth and early seventeenth centuries. At the same time, analytical statements made by the characters function as political commentary and advice.

Argenis was popular with James because of its unqualified support for absolute monarchies, and the ignoring of parliaments. Like Sidney's

Arcadia, *Argenis* explores the consequences in states of weak monarchs who make poor decisions. Poetry provides a frequent running commentary on events, the intention being that the veiled romance discourse of *Argenis* should become a new kind of entertaining and educative literature, mixing reality or fact with imagination and fantasy. The result was a refined, highly aestheticised component in courtliness, something which became as important an element in the construction of 1630s court life as romance and pastoral fiction itself.[75] This reading habit was not just limited to courtiers: the Presbyterian schoolmaster from Warwick, Thomas Dugard, read the *Arcadia* in 1642 alongside theology, logic and classical literature.[76] There could also be a critical, even anti-courtly, current running in this literature. Thomas May's translations of the poetry for Sir Robert Le Grys's translation of *Argenis* (1628) played up tyranny and land disturbance (12–13).

It was still possible to read Sidney in a non-politicised way in the mid-seventeenth century, as William Bosworth's *The Chast and Lost Lovers* (1651) shows in its long chain of imitations of Ovid, Marlowe's *Hero and Leander*, Sidney, Spenser, Ralegh, Virgil, Pindar and Horace. Or indeed as Anna Weamys's *A Continuation of Sir Philip Sydney's Arcadia* (1651) demonstrates in its entirely unpoliticised wrapping-up of Sidney's more richly suggestive original. Prefatory material praises Bosworth's capacity to write like an Elizabethan, and Weamys is described as the female organ of Sidney's spirit. As if it were to be misinterpreted, commendatory verse in the *Continuation* by the royalist James Howell, and other references to Howell's *Dendrologia, Dodona's Grove* (1640/50), hide Weamys's romance in an unpolitical copse, like a babe to be concealed in 1651 from rapacious enemies. If there is any public reference in Bosworth, it is in a suffixed poem 'To his dear Friend Mr. *John Emely* upon his Travells' (123), possibly a reference to an exile abroad.

The Chast and Lost Lovers and the *Continuation* of *Arcadia* were exceptions. Romance was seen to be a political form by members of both sides in the political conflict. The royalist plotter and poet Edmund Waller, and the parliamentary leader Lord Saye and Sele, were both reported to have written romances in periods of retirement immediately following action in the war. Sadly for posterity, neither survives.[77]

Sir William Sales's *Theophania* (1655) 'Or Severall Modern Histories Represented by way of Romance: and Politickly Discours'd upon; By An English Person of Quality' is a much underrated and understudied political romance, written some ten years before its publication. The unfinished *Theophania* concerns itself with a royal romance between Charles I's daughter Mary and William II of Orange, and with the Earl of Essex's involvement in the Civil War. *Theophania* resists the influence of any continental model. Its publisher Thomas Heath claimed it had 'nothing of the *Spanish* Designe, the *French* fluency and Courtship, the

Italian gravity . . . his Designes are naturall, correspondent, and effective; his Scenes probable, and suitable; . . . his discourses and reflections solid and mature' (Sig. A4r). The debt to Sidney is more apparent: '*Nec divinam* SYDNEIDA *tenta/*Sed longe sequere, & Vestigia semper adora' (t.p.). It is an extremely penetrating account, and this is attested by the annotation left in surviving copies.[78] One contains marginal identification of the allegorical names, while another provides a key to characters and places. The publisher's preface invites the reader to make such a web of connections: 'you will find Man, and the Passions of Man (the great Engines of our Conversation) and (it may be) Traverses of State, set down as in a Mapp or Chart before you' (Sig. A3v).

Sales's treatment of heroic characters could be seen as a way of allowing readers to empathise with his fictional versions of important political figures. Thus Demetrius, the young Prince of Orange (who marries a Stuart princess), is allowed an inner life:

> If then I love with such an ardent flame; if I am in my imagination already a King; and if my ambition be much greater then thy self didst ordain; in what do I contradict thy will? Is it an infringement of thy commands, to anticipate thy desires? Or am I less a Lover, or less ambitious, because my Love hath raised my Ambition to a heigth [sic] so far above thy pretences? Is it against the laws of piety to be directed by that supreme law of laws, that ought to be the guide of all our actions, Reason? which assures me, that in complying with thy desires I submit myself to a perpetual slavery; but in the fruition of *Mariana's* love shall at the same instant become possessed of a vast Empire. (75)

This of course is precisely the use of romance which Hobbes depicted as a dangerous illusion, and a cause of political conflict (see above, 159–60). The appearance of the Earl of Essex in *Theophania* also signals the sympathy in this romance for aristocratic prowess in the parliamentarian cause.

That the allegorical romance was essentially a magisterial form was made clear by Sir Percy Herbert's *The Princess Cloria* (parts 1–2, 1653; complete 1661). Like Barclay, Herbert was a Roman Catholic, and his estates were sold in 1651. His writings were a result of enforced leisure. The romance allegorises a wide range of events in seventeenth-century Europe, displaying a detailed knowledge of secret diplomacy. In *The Princess Cloria*, romance fiction is 'added' to history in order to sharpen the opportunity for moral education. This does not prevent romance versions of Civil War battles, which interestingly correlate with newsbook accounts. The romance versions are disarmingly familiar and unfamiliar – precisely as we might expect from a marriage of fiction and history – but the essential grittiness of the detail and the plain style keep us firmly on the battlefield. Here is the Battle of Edgehill:

Figure 8   Detail from *New Articles for Peace, Delivered by the Kings Majesty*
(1648), title-page.

they both met upon a large plain in an open Countrey, that afforded room
enough for an equal contention, if the Fates had at all proved indifferent
in the encounter: The first charge was given with fury sufficient by both
sides, however the Kings Horse without any known cause whatsoever, of a
sudden gave back, and not long after most shamefully turned their backs,
though the Foot with incredible gallantry, still continued the Fight with
honour and safety; *Euarchus* upon this (however not being so much
amazed as displeased) presently rid amongst the flying Troops; as it were
calling both Gods and men to witness, concerning the justness of his
Cause. (167)

The picture of the King (Euarchus/Charles I) imprisoned on the Isle of
Wight looks more like an emblem or the simple, cartoon-like woodcuts
which were used to represent his imprisonment (see fig. 8). And this fits
with romance to produce a curious dual vision of the present. Thus,
Princess Mary (Cloria) is secretly visited while her father is captive, and
during the Army debates:

as she was further proceeding in her discourse, the Dwarf informed them,
that there was newly arrived in the Castle Hall a young maid of excellent
beauty, who deserved with much earnestness to be brought presently into

the Princesses presence, as privately she had some secret to discover. (217)

As in *Theophania* the romance concern itself is with the marriage of Princess Mary (Cloria) to William II (Narcissus). History is changed considerably but not entirely. Cloria and Narcissus marry after the death of Euarchus (Charles I), whereas in fact William and Mary married in 1641. The correct date of William's death (1650) is observed, as are those for his son's struggle for power, but Cloria's activities in England are invented. Only with the Restoration could it be finished, with a happy reassertion of the Platonic glory of the 1630s: 'Beauty overcoming War, it self becomes most famous.' Princess Cloria's allegorical significance, 'national honour', is finally affirmed. The romance is a supplement to history with the effect of making the reader apprehend the higher truth in the phenomenal. This has been connected with the apparent lack of agency in the characters (they are all part of a divine plan), and the desire on Herbert's part to make his reader experience a stoical expulsion of emotions. History fulfils itself in the Restoration, but even if it did not, the reader would be spared the effort of worrying about the state of things.[79]

A manuscript continuation of Sidney's *Arcadia*, possibly by a member of the Digby family, and written in the 1650s, presents the Civil War and execution of Charles I initially as a prophecy. Then, when these events occur in this continuation, a comment is made: 'they turned the fabricke of Monarchiale goverment, into a confused chaos of Democracie and fulfilled the tenour of what the oracle to Basileus delivered in Delphos, by the end both of the King and Kingdom of Arcadia, wherewith this my history also, of Arcadia shall have an ende.'[80] England is Arcadia, Arcadia is England. As Lois Potter says, 'not only the kingdom but the genre itself is thus destroyed by the king's execution.'[81] *The Princess Cloria* provides reactions rather than answers, and its arguable insufficiency in this respect points to one reason why post-Arcadian romance faded away. Not only was it associated with royalism, and its fictionality drained by allegorical pressure, it had no answers within itself for the predicament in which many of its readers found themselves.

Interlude and Exile

By comparison with *The Faerie Queene* or *The Princess Cloria*, or Samuel Sheppard's Spenserian attempt at a war romance in verse, *The Faerie King* (c.1650–55), Davenant's *Gondibert* is an even more arcane romance, and its relevance to the 1650s harder to see, for the poem is set in a kind of early medieval Lombardy, as opposed to Spenser's indeterminately gothic sometime.[82] This could be seen as an attempt to avoid any reference to the present (Davenant wrote the first two books in exile in Paris, well away from the traumatic events of the late 1640s), but the poem certainly attempts one of the goals specified for poems in Davenant's preface – the educating of princes and courtiers (see above, 214). In this way and interwoven into the chivalric narrative are a series of knowledges for princes, courtiers and men of learning. Just how exclusive Davenant imagined his readership should be is difficult to tell. *Gondibert* would have been an expensive book when published, but no more so than a good-sized collection of sermons. To some extent, this cuts across Davenant's ideas for mass indoctrination as opposed to elite education: the paintings in Astragon's Palace in Book 2 look not unlike the images recommended in the entertainments designed for mass consumption (see above, 87–8).

But all of this points to Davenant's modernity, his avoidance of a supernatural machinery (much noted in 1651) and his association with Hobbes. One function of the distant setting was to suggest that the superior knowledge of this time would become forgotten, but would then be rediscovered (in Davenant's not too distant future). It is just as legitimate to see *Gondibert* as an attempt to use romance to project a gloriously achieved edifice of public and private stateship; to re-endow that which Arcadian romance had forfeited – 'To overcome the world, till but one Crown/And universal Neighbourhood he saw' (2.8.36). This is partly achieved by the reassertion of the chivalric. Gondibert fights and kills his evil adversary Oswald early in the poem. This leaves him open for the hand of Rhodalind, daughter of King Aribert, who represents public life: Gondibert is intended for the throne. However, the large middle section of Book 2 is concerned with the consolidation and education of the hero until, swayed by the charms of Astragon's daughter Birtha, a marriage is proposed and a vision of universal monarchy and peace offered.[83] Davenant's preface is dense with references to classical epic, and hardly any to chivalric or gothic tradition, but the unfinished poem complicates itself in a romance fashion, as when in Book 3 Rhodalind reappears to unsettle Gondibert's heart and the world's peace. Book 3 was written in prison, and finished abruptly after Canto 7, when Davenant thought he was about to die. The poem ends with no conclusion, apart from pointing to the need for good, virtuous, improving courts to be distinguished from bad, fickle, power-hungry ones (3.7.106), a constant theme of the poem. Self-control by the triumph of art over nature can regulate destructive passions, but even then Gondibert's smoothness becomes shaky:

> Yet something he at parting seem'd to say,
> In pretty Flowe'rs of Love's wild Rhetorick;

Which mov'd not her, though Orators thus sway
Assemblies, which since wilde, wilde Musick like.

'Mariage is too oft but civil warre' (3.1.42) hints at allegory, but in a more literal manner, the way in which the female characters hide their feelings is seen as indicative of the dangerous closeness of the court 'who daily are/In Prides invasions, private faction, vers'd;/The small, but fruitful seed of publick warre.' Where in Davenant's earlier works, such as *Salmacida Spolia*, a whole people appears to rebel, dissension in *Gondibert* first comes from powerful aristocrats. Yet King Aribert is old and without heir: the possibility of a revived line is not offered in the unfinished poem, so the reader's view of monarchy is left enfeebled. And the means to power lies in secret devices – disguises or prophetic emeralds in cabinets – representations of the secret cabinets of letters, so crucial to civil war leaders. Keeping secrets to oneself is a heroic action; historians are rather feeble chroniclers because they do not have access to genuine motives or causes. The claims of an aristocratic internal virtue, cultivated through right education, are plainly stated in *Gondibert*, but how they are to be exercised in the fickle and treacherous world of courts and monarchies – a world of exterior display – is left unexplained.

French Confessions

When Arcadian prose romance failed, a solution had to be found. Davenant began an interesting experiment in *Gondibert*, but he was unable to complete it. Those who had spent time in France, and many of those who stayed behind, would be satisfied by different forms of prose fiction, forms which ignored the political for the personal, and which demanded much more time and concentration of the reader. Such romances were to be found in France, those of Gauthier de Costes de la Calprenède and Madeleine de Scudéry being the most famous. They were enormously long (which did not seem to put readers off) and adopted complex structures quite unlike the Arcadian patterns. These new structures offered readers new forms of identification. The romance-reading public was not disappointed.

La Calprenède and Scudéry broke with the episodic and chivalric forms in their own tradition to produce romance with epic structure. These romances grew in the literary salons of Paris and the characters in the romances were meant to exemplify the *préciosité* studied in the salons themselves. *Préciosité* was imported into England by Henrietta Maria when she came to be Charles I's wife, and the fashion always reeked of popery and the most effete courtliness. Nonetheless, the romances enjoyed a wide circulation in French and English translation during the

1650s. The evidence suggests that the longer they were the better. Also, the interest primarily in love and not war was attractive to readers – perhaps as a form of escape. Indeed, in some of Dorothy Osborne's letters, it almost seems as if her consciousness is dominated by romance, into which the world (sometimes represented by the reading of a newsbook) rudely interrupts. The opportunity to read these works as political *roman à clef* is consequently drastically reduced or transformed, if not eliminated.[84]

Scudéry made cross-generic claims for her romances, immunising them from the reputation for fantasy which plagued romance tradition. Like epics, they began *in medias res*, and like histories, they dealt, so she claimed, with the manners and customs of people as they really were. To a large degree, exotic dress and settings (Turkey, Granada) defamiliarised French modes of etiquette and civility.[85] Or the same result was achieved by amazing landscapes:

> he was more surprised when he heard all places resoun'd both with Celestiall and Subterranean Thunders, which by terrible convulsions of the Earth seem'd to shake the Center of the World, and to remit nature to its first Chaos; a thousand burning stones flung from this flaming Gulph were shot into the Ayre with fearefull hissings . . . [86]

In other words a genuine realism of behaviour is inserted into romance narrative, as opposed to the hyperbole and exaggerated descriptions of desire in Arcadian romance.[87] Thus, there are still romance motifs – such as the sea, that 'Theater of Inconstancie' – but extravagant shipwreck is expelled in favour of action and contemplation allowing the reader to judge the hero 'by the motions of his soul'.[88] In this way, the possibility for a landscape to become familiar and hence emblematic, and for characters to become easily allegorical, is avoided.

The *romanciers* offered stories concerning different characters, and invited their readers to ponder the merits of the decisions taken by different lovers. Dorothy Osborne was a perfectly pliant reader in this respect: 'there is a Story of Artemise [in La Calprenède's *Cleopatra*] that I will recomende to you; her disposition I like extreamly, it has a great deal of Gratitude int; and if you meet with one Brittomart pray send mee word how you like him.'[89] Initial stories related to the eponymous character spin out into many secondary stories. Narrative closure in these romances is a non-concept. More significantly, much space is given over to individual characters (not just the main ones) to narrate their own stories. A first-person narration is offered in terms of a direct identification with the reader on the subject of love and morality. And the present situation is only knowable through an understanding of the conditioning events of the past. Since the *vraisemblance* of the narrative was meant to reflect lived conventions and experiences, the French heroic romance offered to its readers a fictionalised form of selfhood which, we might say, is equivalent within its readership to the 'selving' of the confessions of experience (early spiritual autobiographies) produced in some puritan churches.[90] There is indeed an emphasis upon 'experience' in Roger Boyle's *Parthenissa* (1651–69), the only native romance to follow the French model. Roger's more famous brother, the scientist Robert, wrote an autobiographical romance as a young man, which contains a conversion experience.[91] In other words, readers of romances – notably Royalists and especially women – could escape from the disappointments of Arcadian romance into the fuller personalising world of the French import. Dorothy Osborne's letters show that her reading of romances is not to do with political preference (it might have more to do with religious *mores*), but is essentially a matter of status. With the French heroic romance, English readers, aristocracy, gentry and the upper middle classes, began to fuse into a common readership and to share a common conception of selfhood, of passion, desire and necessary restraint.[92] The level of rumination by the first-person narrator on the events recounted parallels the discussion in the spiritual autobiography of the external forces working on an individual.

Like the confession of experience or spiritual autobiography, action is described retrospectively, and is that which leads up to the moments of stasis when debate and decision-making take place. Character – the whole of the self – is what finally matters, and the effect of first-person narration (self-accounting) is compounded by the tendency for characters to become versions of each other, mirror images reflecting ultimately back on one moral and passionate agent – the reader. Extended character portraits – dealing with all kinds of incidental details – are also important: some of Dorothy Osborne's comments are related to the contents of the portrait rather than the narrative.[93] What evidence we have suggests that where romances were read, they could become the dominant way in which an individual understood him or herself – at least as far as the private or domestic sphere was concerned. The preference for romance in royalist propaganda supports this view, and is strangely unlike the subsumption into romance structure of moral and pious books in eighteenth-century novels, such as Richardson's. Indeed, there is a tension in domestic space here. Milton asserts that his domestically concerned *The Doctrine and Discipline of Divorce* (1643) is 'no meer amatorious novel', but it does deal precisely with what the new romance (as opposed to old, chivalric romance) handled.[94]

A further cohesive effect is achieved by the interweaving of the *récits* into one large, interconnected pattern, so that major characters from one subsidiary narrative appear as minor characters in another, and settings are also repeated. The effect is something like reading the *Old* and *New Arcadias* consecutively, or, indeed, like reading a Civil War battle narrative with a different subject matter. At the same time, there are breaks in narrative continuity, with both backward- and forward-looking scans. Unlike Arcadian romance, there is no small set of characters or events, but a multifarious baggage.

Yet the use of the *récit* in this way privileges the speech – the 'I' of the narrator – over action, again in contra-distinction to the tradition, and with the effect of encouraging speculation rather than closure. It has been suggested that the narrative direction becomes circular because so expected after so much speculation during the *récit*, just as a confession of experience usually reaches the one conclusion of the sense of achieved grace.

However, not even Scudéry freed herself from political connotations. Towards the end of book one of *Clelia*, the rape of Lucrece by Tarquin is used, in which the narrator appears to encounter Tarquin personally, and brings down, in a veiled way, all of the public associations which the story had accrued by the seventeenth century. The point is not, as has been argued, that Scudéry makes political comment, or that 'secret' decisions are at the heart of the turn of events, but that the subjects who narrate the action are as important moral beings as are princes.[95]

No native heroic romance was possible for English people before 1660, apparently, without also returning to a politicised form of narrative. Thus, Roger Boyle's (Lord Broghill and later Earl of Orrery) unfinished *Parthenissa*, six books (1651–69), is a hybrid of two forms. Boyle was an adviser to Cromwell, but later an architect of the Restoration. *Parthenissa* follows Scudéry's principles of unity, and there are the complex interconnections between sets of characters and the positioning of stories, but politics and the arts of war sit alongside the concern with love. *Parthenissa* was already well underway in December 1649, when his brother noted that despite Roger being forced by military responsibilities to 'leave' his 'Parthenissa', he was as good a general in Munster as his fictional ones were in Assyria, and that he was as eloquent 'with masters of garrisons, as mistresses of hearts'.[96] There is a discussion of the history of Rome after the assassination of Julius Caesar, which asserts that power must be located in a single individual, despite the nuisance of always agreeing to abide by monarchical authority. Ventidius, a Roman general, is clearly a Parliamentarian (possibly a classical republican), and argues for representation by ballot, and kingship, if it has to be, should be elective. Artavasdes remains a staunch loyal monarchist, but the views of both are balanced by means of the distribution of *récits*. The two commanders fight on different sides, but find friendship while lying wounded in adjoining beds. The rape of Lucrece and the consequent expulsion of the Roman kings is regarded by Artavasdes as a bad event, after which Rome lost its way. Why did the Romans believe the testimony of a woman?[97] The example and argument is the same as that used by Filmer to justify absolute monarchy (see above, 109). Artabanes is a Spartacus figure who leads a noble revolt: does this make him Cromwell? Robert Boyle thought that Artabanes was Orrery himself, Parthenissa's lover.[98] One-to-one mapping does not easily stick, but the respect for the compelling figure of Hannibal (for we are placed at one point in the Carthaginian Wars) surely invites the parallel with Cromwell. One character is dissuaded from assassinating Hannibal:

> shalt thou Kill a Conqueror whome the Gods have free'd from their own immediate punishment (Thunder) by covering him with Lawrell: shalt thou make away an Enemy who in thus giveing thee the Power to destroy him, makes it a Crime to doe it? besides he is one who owes his Conquests only to his Courage and conduct.[99]

Other stories seem to represent the split loyalties frequently suffered within families during the conflict. But there is no direct mapping of English events onto the narrative, as there is in Herbert's *The Princess Cloria*; Boyle's preference for the older romance motif of revolt by a son against his father precludes such a close parallel. Rather than a 'magical' resolution (as in Sidney's *Arcadia*, when Basilius wakes up from his supposed death), resolution lies in the hands, or rather, heads, of the characters, and it requires of them demonstrations of honour and loyalty, and high friendship: 'whilst my Love was kindling, my Friendship transcended it, but now it burnes, it has consum'd my Friendship, & I feare will consume me, unless you afford me as much Love, as you inspire.'[100]

Patriarchal power, largely within the domestic sphere, is debated in *Parthenissa*. Are fathers (or kings) all powerful, or should their judgements be consistent with 'Reason'? The situation is similar with regard to the discussion of male and female authority in Milton's divorce tracts. Reason is a measure of fit companionship between the sexes, but patriarchal power finally prevails. At the same time, most of the dilemmas in *Parthenissa* are consequences of power vacuums created by weak kings, and yet the enemies of Boyle's heroes are often virtuous men. In this way, the equivocating circumstances of civil war are inscribed into the romance, as much as Boyle carries measured respect in his pamphlets for the Irish nobility he fought against. One of the anachronistically juxtaposed historical periods is that of ancient Rome, and the cycle of usurpations recounted here significantly reflects on classicism in 1650s English politics, although it is no more than an echo and one part of the balance of perspectives and views rendered by a full reading of *Parthenissa*. The entertainment of different political theories identifies *Parthenissa* as a document of the parliamentary nobility disaffected by the events of 1648–9. Boyle's inability to finish *Parthenissa*

is an instance of his inability to resolve the issues of allegiance, honour
and love. The glory of winning a kingdom for a woman is imaginatively
sustaining, even if angry patriarchs finally take revenge.

Boyle's romance was a prelude to his plays, in which the theme of
balance was replaced by a more openly expressed guilt for the regicide.[101]
But the complications of French romance, the personalising power of the
récit, and the intrigues of strong women characters had freed English
prose fiction from its Arcadian inheritance. Arcadia was over.

As much as *Gondibert* and its critical apparatus, *Parthenissa* was a
watershed. It was the last stand of Renaissance heroic romance, truly
Sidneyesque in its mirroring of its aristocratic hero/author. But in its
interiorising transformations of the genre (as we have seen in the case of
epic), it also enabled something very new in a changed age, just as the
Civil War itself expunged gothic England. In it, we can begin to see the
eighteenth-century novel.

Republican Romance

One author interested in the removal of the gothic was James
Harrington. As we have seen, in *Oceana*, politics and economics are
yoked together through plainly literary perspectives. One important
example of these perspectives was romance. Indeed, it is precisely at the
places where Harrington does not pursue economic and monetary
analyses (which would become familiar by the end of the seventeenth
century) that he uses generic frameworks as a means of providing a
unified account of particular polities. The rise of the yeomanry is seen as
a feature of the reign of Elizabeth (Queen Parthenia). Once they have
their freedom, the yeomanry make excellent infantry (here Harrington
imposes upon an English situation the Roman and Machiavellian idea
that the best soldiers are those who are free, propertied citizens of
the commonwealth (see above, 183)). During Elizabeth's reign, the
yeomanry were preferred by the Queen, says Harrington in terms which
we might expect of a late-1640s royalist propagandist: 'Queen Parthenia
who, converting her reign through the perpetual love tricks that passed
between her and her people into a kind of romance, wholly neglected the
nobility.'[102]

Where romance is an illusion for Hobbes, romance narration – or at
least a highly idiosyncratic version of narration – frequently interrupts
Harrington's political analysis. By using it as a mode of representation,
Harrington makes romance part of political life, a kind of dissimulation
used by Elizabeth for the maintenance of her power. In fact, the opening
of *Oceana* moves from a pastoral, idyllic vision into romance modes. The
beginning almost reads like a romance history, Harrington's suggestive

naming being very typical of 1640s and 1650s romance, especially with the instance of James I as Morpheus going to sleep, taking the well-being of his kingdom into soporific realms with him. These apparently inconsequential details are rather central in Harrington.

As we would expect from the translator of Virgil's *Eclogues*, pastoral provides the opportunity for the articulation of what makes a nation strong, although it contains a surprising departure from pastoral representation. 'If the people be the sheep of their own pastures, they are not only a flock of sheep, but an army of lions,' yet if someone else's sheep feed on their land (and here Harrington means a foreign or princely army), they are in peril.[103] Romance is at odds with the unselfish world of *Oceana*, for romance implies an enriching of women beyond the boundaries of the agrarian balance, and as such it equates with covetous courtliness:

> There is in this agrarian an homage unto pure and spotless love, the consequence whereof I will not give for all the romances. An alderman maketh not his daughter a countess till he have given her twenty thousand pounds, nor a romance a considerable mistress till she be a princess; these are characters of bastard love. But if our agrarian exclude ambition and covetousness, we shall at length have the care of our own breed, in which we have been curious as to that of our dogs and our horses. (240)

Yet Harrington literally says that a reign has become a genre, so that we might imagine civil life and government in Elizabethan England – all of the institutions and interstices of power which made being alive in Elizabethan England what it was – infected with the structures of narrative and identity which we associate with romance. Parthenia is a romance name. Elizabeth's relationship with her subjects is imagined as a long mutual wooing of love games, of desire deferred through intricately engineered feints and turnabouts. The longevity of her reign was achieved by this deferral: by refusing to close the romance with her people by marrying a foreign prince, or by preferring a high aristocratic family or faction, she sustained her popularity at the risk of creating the huge anxiety surrounding the succession – a factor which looks through the lens of romance like the ultimate lover's tease.

And it was this 'romance', according to Harrington, which was the cause of the Civil War forty years later:

> By these degrees came the house of commons to raise that head, which since hath been so high and formidable unto their princes that they have looked pale upon those assemblies. Nor was there anything now wanting unto the destruction of the throne but that the people, not apt to see their own strength, should be put to feel it, when a prince, as stiff in disputes as

the nerve of monarchy was grown slack, received that unhappy encouragement from his clergy which became his utter ruin. (198)

By contrast, Harrington regards Charles I as a politick lover of no stature.[104] It is as if Sidney's *Arcadia*, and *The Faerie Queene*, have been backed like a veneer onto the surface of English history (see above, 170).

In the classical republican frame, the genre of romance, as political behaviour, becomes the superstructure of the Elizabethan state, enabling Elizabeth to retain her regal status while acknowledging that the 'balance' (Harrington's famous term for the property relations which determine the nature of power in a state) of the monarchy was popular: 'the exercise of principality in a commonwealth, than of sovereign power in a monarchy'.[105] Romance as 'politick strategy' is compounded with Harrington's characteristically Machiavellian analysis of government:

> Certain it is that she courted not her nobility, nor gave her mind, as monarchs seated upon the like order, to balance her great men, or reflect upon their power now inconsiderable, but ruled wholly (with an art she had unto high perfection) humouring and blessing her people.[106]

From the point of view of 1656, and compared with great empires in history, the Elizabethan state was but a 'shadow' of a commonwealth, but Elizabeth's politics had in Harrington's opinion attained the 'full perfection of the orders requisite unto popular government', while soundly securing the status and means of the monarchy, and giving to the English a key to future political peace. Sadly for the English, neither their two next kings, nor they, understood this prudence. Quite against the masculinist prejudices of republican discourse (was Harrington remembering his time at court?), Elizabeth's 'romance' was ensuring that late sixteenth-century England was a popular state. Elizabethan government was the interplay of romance and pastoral, and it was a republic lost.[107]

And if a commonwealth by Harrington's definition is a replicated universe (see above, 169), genre is that component which gives it continuity in time, and therefore is its narrative. This is especially fitting given the conceptual status of genre. Elizabeth perpetrated her 'romance' as if she were giving it as soul ('government') to her commonwealth.

Harrington's use of romance is a strong signal of its usefulness and significance to republicans, and echoes of this usage can be found later in the century (see below, 331–2). Platonic idealism was also eminently suited to romance representation: both Samuel Gott's utopia *Novae Solymae. Libri Sex* (1648) and Nathaniel Ingelo's *Bentivolio and Urania* (1660) are defences of puritan theocracy and God's Providence. The former uses love entanglements or 'some unhappy marriage' to point up their ultimate frivolity (in art as well as life) in a pious society of the self-controlled, highly educated and virtuous elect, while the latter includes a history of the victory of oligarchical puritan republicanism over the Levellers.[108] Yet if the importation of French prose romance and the innovations of Davenant, Boyle and Harrington exemplify the maturing of a genre in the context of a civil crisis, the text as *roman à clef* returned with the Restoration in the form of Richard Brathwaite's *Panthalia; Or, The Royal Romance* (1659), prepared in the press just after the abdication of Richard Cromwell and the recall of the Rump Parliament. By the time it appeared for sale, it was able to celebrate the return of Charles II. It is a confident text, using romance motifs to signal royalist triumph (unlike the troubled first version of *The Princess Cloria*). Brathwaite reinserts Arcadia into the English romance map (James I appears now as the negligent Basilius). But Brathwaite is wiser than his royalist predecessors because he appears to adopt Harrington's romantic explanation of Stuart failure (and praise of the Elizabethan polity). Yet *Panthalia* forecloses on this perceptiveness to let romance enact the (tragi-) comic closure of Charles II's arrival.

Brathwaite had nonetheless been touched by the general shift in the genre, and he had profited from the textual predicaments of Boyle and Harrington. In the Restoration, romance was faced with different problems. If Aphra Behn's prose fictions are about the possibility of the end of civilised values, in that the villain of the *Love Letters* (1684–7) is supposedly an adulterous seducer representing the supporter of Monmouth, Lord Grey (immoral libertinism equals Whig politics) who threatens to destroy all social bonds based on honour and dignity with his libido, Boyle's are a search for a meaning, in the same way that Harrington's use the romance motif.[109] To that extent, Boyle is truly of the 1650s – searching classical history in romance terms. In Aphra Behn, romance inscribes honour back into social relations, whereas in Boyle, romance searches for the meaning of honour between love and war. Harrington had made romance show where Hobbes was wrong.

CHAPTER 8

The Instrumentality of Lyrics

The Lyric in the Republic

Lyrics kept the gentry and the nobility together during the Civil War and the Interregnum. The verbal forms which the 'political nation' used to praise each other in their public lives and to adore each other in their private lives had a greater resilience to the pressure of change than did almost any other form. As the work of Arthur Marotti and Gerald Hammond shows, collections of lyrics, in manuscript and when published, are extensions and agents of the conventions and expressions of communication, in an honour-bound society which stressed the importance of roles, and the sustenance of families by prudent and successful marriages.[1]

Often the published collections of lyric verse represent provincial records of local resilience during the periods of upheaval – the neutralism and indifference which pervaded most districts.[2] The Civil War enters the poetry, but the form ensures the continuity of civilisation inside the order of words. Robert Herrick's *Hesperides* (1648) is an obvious example of this phenomenon. The solidity of a lost world of Christian paganism, of rural Catullanism, of maypoles and churching ceremonies, is projected into the reader's mind, in the face of its own destruction. Herrick's pastoral world seems secure until a gaping hole appears in the text:

> I write of *Groves*, of *Twilights*, and I sing
> The Court of *Mab*, and of the *Fairie-King*.
> I write of *Hell*; I sing (and ever shall)
> Of *Heaven*, and hope to have it after all.[3]

The opposition between traditional, festive culture versus reformed, usually urban puritan culture was how the conflict was experienced.[4] In this model, the Civil War was the culmination of longer-term cultural tensions, just as Herrick's *Hesperides*, published in 1648, contains many poems composed as early as 1618.

A comparable example to Herrick's volume is Clement Barksdale's

Nympha Libethris (1651), subtitled 'The Cotswold Muse', 'presenting some extempore Verses to the Imitation of yong Scholars'. Extempore relates to the imperatives of radical puritan worship (extempore prayers and preaching), but the poems are nothing of the sort. Barksdale wishes to imply that his poems are hasty compositions for the schoolroom, in line with habits among the gentry in the early seventeenth century, but of course he is also mocking his cultural opposite. The volume is situated in a pastoral mode, although none of the poems are truly pastoral in terms of generic tradition. Picking up on the royalist associations of pastoral, Barksdale's poems are offered to the reader as the survival of a culture: they document the safe escape of Prince Charles, the future Charles II, over the frozen Wye after the taking of Hereford in 1645. Barksdale's capacity to talk about simultaneously realised contrary experiences deserves high praise. It is the poet's attraction to the old poetic ethos of Jonson, Fletcher and (early) Davenant which has kept him from engaging in serious civil debate (he refers specifically to a deferred project to translate Grotius), yet the poems document with real acuity the effect of the conflict on letters:

> As the *Armies* did against each other fight;
>   Even so doe our moderne *Historians* write:
> Each for his *side*. The *Stationer* says, *Buy both*:
>   Compare them, and you may *pick* out the Truth.[5]

The most popular kind of collection of lyric poetry in the earlier seventeenth century had been that of love sonnets and love poetry more generally. Sonnets were *rites de passage* for young men. The Civil War played funny tricks here too. Nicholas Hookes's *Amanda* (1653) was addressed to an 'Unknown Goddess'. Usually there was a genuine mistress behind the poetic fictions of love poetry, even if her name was disguised, as it usually was. The unknown goddess is an absent centre of Hookes's volume, a person yet to be known, and as such the collection seems strangely apt for a time when lovers' liaisons might be threatened by all kinds of disruption. Yet *Amanda* was also written against the grain of the times, so that it is a new form of 'dissent':

> Though wit th'unsavoury thing be out of date,
> And judgement triumph in the fancies fate,
> *Poetry's* heresie, and schisme pure,
> As is *Free-will* or humane literature. (Sig. A8r)

There is an echo here of Henry More's association of poetry with enthusiasm (see above, 221), but the spiritual eroticism of *Amanda* is more forthrightly and less playfully offered as literature which will redeem public life from the quagmire of newsbooks and pamphlets: 'The Presse grows honest, and in spite of fate,/Now teems a Wit, that is legitimate' (Sig. a1r). The volume bears the imprint of Humphrey Moseley, but far from the blatant royalist iconography of many of Moseley's 1640s works, *Amanda* is poetry for a new age. It is not loyal or 'engaged' poetry, but it takes into its almost deliberate old-fashionedness the language of enthusiasm as its means of reforming love poetry. Thus, there is a poem entitled '*An Enthusiasm* to Amanda *feasting*', and reversals of well-known myths: in 'A melancholly Fit', a woman rescues a man from hell, thereby turning about the Orpheus and Eurydice story (22–3). It is only near the end of the collection that the veil of highly sensual but spiritualised verse for a person who does not exist is dropped. In 'To his most Noble Friend Sir T.L.B. of Shingle-hall', the old iconography returns in a lament on royalist military failure: 'Had they such *Martial Souls*, such *fighting hands*,/Redemption of their *Rights*, three [printed crowns] and *lands*/ Were easie work' (54). The first part of the volume contains the verse to Amanda, passing through castigations of 'Ranters' (not sectaries but whoring young gentlemen) to an apotheosis of desire in 'To Amanda supposing and wishing shee were with childe': 'The maine thing that I wish implicitly/Is this, would I were *brought to bed* with thee'(88). What the speaker has actually said is that his desire ought to culminate not in Amanda's insemination, but in his own pregnancy, giving birth to *Amanda* the volume of poems. But the rest of the volume concerns itself with poems on public affairs. On the one hand, Hookes's *Amanda* seems to be saying that enthusiasm should be reserved for private life: passion is not for the public stage. On the other hand, the collection identifies a mode of human experience – desire – which has to be regulated if not also expunged. Amanda herself does not exist, and after the Restoration, the poetry addressed to her would sink into demise too.

As much as *Amanda* is an example of an unusual kind of love poetry, so also the 1640s produced some interesting variations on the standard forms of politically engaged verse. In 'The King's Verses', a manuscript poem which is difficult to date, but which is probably either late 1630s or very early 1640s, certainly pre-execution, the King himself speaks to the people.[6] In this poem, the king is not just the vicar of Christ, but the companion of God: 'God and Kings doe pace together/But vulgars wander light as feather.' The people are depicted as immature, shallow children, crying needlessly when their father the king will put all to rights. The limiting of royal options by publications ('rayling rhimes and vaunting verse') is acknowledged: the poem attempts to spirit away dissent by its assertion of deified royal parenthood. But the King's actions in this poem are not passive. In a traditional way, he must be served by his subjects. But he is only a king 'in a play' if he does not also exercise a rigour over his subjects in order to keep them obedient and away from rebellion for the sake of 'ancient rights': 'you keepe your antient face/ Your feare would soone outface his might/If soe you would oblige his right.' The language of politics becomes interestingly confounded as proper roles under a monarchy are confused. In hindsight, the most naive statement of kingly power comes with the assertion that when he is ready, the king will call the parliament that will satisfy the complaints in the kingdom: 'The Parliament I will appoynt/When I see thinges more out of ioynt/Then will I sett every thinge streight.' So much for the Long Parliament. The king (whom we assume to be Charles) even threatens the fatal punishment of rebellious subjects – 'make mee not still/Whome I woulde save unwillinge kill.' Not being a player king, this monarch is slow to take 'revenge' on his subjects, although when he does it will be with certain deliberation. If that 'revenge' became the attempt to arrest the five members of the House of Commons, it is clear how out of touch this poem was.

While on the one hand Hookes's *Amanda* was poetry for a new age, and on the other volumes like Herrick's *Hesperides* sustained a memory of pre-Civil War culture in published form, the lyrical verse produced at or around the time of the regicide and the emergence of the republic is often strangely suspended between two worlds, and between different imaginative realities.

Marvell, John Hall and other forthcoming young men provided commendatory verse for Richard Lovelace's *Lucasta* (1649), one of the greatest lyric achievements of the century. Lovelace's royalist career, from his involvement in the Kentish Rebellion (1642–3) to being a colonel in the King's Army (1645), writing poetry in prison, and dying in extreme poverty, is well known. *Lucasta* and the posthumously published volume also entitled *Lucasta* (1659) document Lovelace's engagement, so that it is hard to credit some of the claims for Lovelace's disengagement. Being forcefully imprisoned and writing from confinement is no resignation.

More significant is the sheer brilliant surface of Lovelace's verse, and how this brilliance had a cultural function.[7] In the first instance, it is not simply a Cavalier sign. Francis Lenton's commendatory poem proclaims Lovelace as the new Sir Philip Sidney:

> Thus if thy careles draughts are cal'd the best,
> What would thy lines have beene, had'st thou profest
> That faculty (infus'd) of Poetry,
> Which adds such honour unto thy Chivalry?
> Doubtles thy verse had all as far transcended
> As Sydneyes Prose, who Poets once defended. (ll.15–20)

> Where thy seraphique Sydneyan fire is raised high,
> In Valour, Vertue, Love, and Loyalty. (ll.25–6)

Into the last couplet creeps an inference of royalism, but for the most part the lines praise aristocratic *sprezzatura*. The Sidney family were decidedly unroyalist during the Civil War; Sir Philip's descendant, Algernon, was an officer in the parliamentary forces, and later a famous republican.[8] The interpretation of the Civil War as the last baronial conflict in England makes *sprezzatura* a common property of the leading aristocrats on both sides.[9] And a brilliant performance, on the page and the battlefield, would not exclude godliness: Sir Philip Sidney's translation of Mornay's Neoplatonic treatise on the soul was published in 1646 as part of a phalanx of puritan idealising texts.[10]

Lucasta begins with two songs of separation, the second on 'Going to the Warres'. These are followed by 'A Paradox' where Lovelace confesses his Sidneyan allegiance: 'And Heav'nly *Sydney* you/Twice read, had rather view/Some odde *Romance*, so new'(ll. 20–22). Further emplacements of poems written before 1640 come after war poems. This sustains yet mutates Lovelace's Sidneyisms. *Clitophon and Lucippe translated*, for instance, originally published in 1638 with Anthony Hodges's translation of Achilles Tatius's romance, makes the brilliant surface a subject as well as an effect:

> Pray Ladies breath, while lay by
> Caelestial *Sydney's Arcady*;
> Heere's a Story that doth Claime
> A little respite from his Flame:
> Then with a quick dissolving looke
> Unfold the smoothnes of this book. (ll. 1–6)

Occasionally the 'surface' is broken by poems which reverse the smoothness and simplicity of the songs, as with 'Being treated to Ellinda', a Jonsonian celebration of gastronomic plenitude and human fecundity: 'For glasses, heads, hands, bellies full/Of Wine, and Loyne right-worshipfull'(ll. 11–12). But the collection fixes in the justly acclaimed 'To Lucasta. From Prison' where the interpenetration of media is achieved by elaboration on the motif of being both inside and outside the prison. For imprisoned, the speaker is 'free' from Lucasta, and regretfully so. This leads on to a series of imagined objects of desire – peace, war, religion, Parliament, liberty, property, reformation, public faith. The sixth stanza addressed to Parliament is representative of the devaluation which is found is every object:

> I would love a *Parliament*
>   As a maine Prop from Heav'n sent;
> But ah! Who's he that would be wedded
>   To th'fairest body that's beheaded? (st. VI)

The only object that can dignify the speaker and his lover is the king. But who is the king? The post-regicide publication, and the sense of stanza VI, rule out Charles I, and stanza XII implies that the King is God as creator ('He who being the whole Ball/Of Day on Earth, lends to it all'). But stanza XIII suggests that day is now obscured by 'an universall mist/Or Error'. Surely God could not be obscured? So perhaps the king is Charles I (the poem being written before the regicide)? Or is the very body of the Godhead (Lovelace employs a mystical cosmology) harmed by the 'Error' – presumably of regicide?

> And now an universall mist
>   Of Error is spread or'e each breast,
> With such a fury edg'd, as is
>   Not found in th'inwards of th'Abysse.

In the final stanza, the speaker calls for a 'sacred Beame' from the king to guide him, but the disturbance in the last four stanzas of the poem elides the figures of King Charles, God, and Lucasta herself, who is of course usually the addressee of the lyrics.

Lovelace's poetry has been the occasion recently of a critical difference. Do both *Lucasta* volumes reveal the complicatedness of Lovelace's politics, or are they openly royalist and cavalier? Does love jostle with war, or are both unified in an arcane vision of the romance knight-lover?[11] In fact, both views are true. Lovelace's private world is necessary to his predicament: it both agitates and supports his heroic self-presentation. Desire also undercuts the martial, for in the course of the two volumes, the comparisons with Sidney manifestly fail to be realised. The satisfaction of the drinking song is too easy compared with the self-restraint and frustrated desire of the Elizabethan poet-hero. Lovelace's final volume is an account of cavalier destitution *and* a confirmation of the demise of a literary mode, even as it poetically excels itself.

Lovelace's poetry is a very clear example of the damage done to the lyric tradition by the Civil War. By contrast, Thomas Stanley's poetry represents a successful attempt to maintain a continued expansion of English lyrical capability by appropriating classical models. If anything, Stanley's experimentation and translations amount to a professionalising of letters, beyond the boundaries of the traditional claims of patronage. His three-volume *History of Philosophy* (1659–60), a series of lives and brief summaries of the views of ancient philosophers based on a translation of Diogenes Laertius, attests to this kind of activity. Before Stanley, no one had translated quite so much anacreontic verse, and so much from the *Basia* of Johannes Secundus. Along with John Hall, he is perhaps closest to that other translator and man of letters, John Davies of Kidwelly. Stanley was yet another ardent Royalist, but like Lovelace, his circle of friends included Hall and Marvell.

The *Poems* of 1651 relentlessly pursue the aim of collecting a series of lyric verse. The 'Anacreon' cycle, based on Henri Estienne's Latin

translations from the Greek (1554), are typical of the volume. Here is
'The Dream VIII':

> As on Purple carpets I
> Charm'd by wine in slumber ly,
> With a troop of Maids (resorted
> There to play) me thought I sported:
> Whose companions, lovely Boies,
> Interrupt me with rude noise:
> Yet I offer made to kisse them,
> But o'th'sudden wake and misse them:
> Vext to see them thus forsake me,
> I to sleep again betake me. (ll.1–10)

Stanley's project represents an attempt to shore up the ruins of
civilisation, avoiding the personal engagement (and hence complications) of Lovelace. But it was not the survival of passionate and
erotic lyricism which the 1650s witnessed, so much as a new life for the
epigram. Authorities on earlier seventeenth-century lyric collections
note a coalescence of sonnet and epigram, and a mixture of the two in
the 'sweet epigram'.[12] The phenomenon is present in Ben Jonson's
published verse, and still visible in Herrick; it may reflect the continuing
influence of the Greek anthology. If the sonnet itself absorbed the Civil
War, fragmentation and despair were most evident in the preference for
epigram. Some of it was satirical (for which, see below, 308–17), but
much of it was not. Thomas Pecke's *Parnassi Puerperium* (1659) is
exemplary – the volume presents translations of earlier Latin epigrams
(those of Sir Thomas More and Sir John Owen), as well as several
original series by Pecke, notably 'Heroick Epigrams Upon Some choice
Passages in the Lives of the Twelve Caesars', which timeservingly praises
Richard Cromwell, but offers increasingly underhanded criticism of
tyrannical emperors. More significantly, a general sense of irritated
fragmentation is produced – nothing seems to connect very well, or very
easily, with anything else, as the subject matter ranges from the rape of
Lucrece (*again*) to wise magistrates who keep Ranters in awe, and poets.
'J.D.'s' preface to Joshua Poole's *The English Parnassus* (1657), 'Being a
short Institution of English Poesie', puts epigram in a generic category all
of its own, while satire, pastoral and georgic are each regarded as sub-
categories of the dramatic (Sig. a4v). Although J.D. regards poetic
language as in a process of continual alchemical purification (but not
with poets who make chemistry itself their subject matter), perfection
appears to be declining from the acknowledged heights of the
Elizabethans to little pieces of rhymed virtue: 'public favour so increased
their pride/They overwhelmed Parnassus with their tide.'
     An explanation of why this should have been felt is a rather difficult

undertaking. By analogy with the sonnet's absorption of the vocabulary and master tropes of civil war, political revolution and religious radicalism, the epigram's sudden emergence in this singular way is a direct reflection of the fragmentation of meaning seen first in the partisan growth of public signs, and ultimately in the competing claims for truth made by so many near incomprehensible sectarian languages.[13] Poetic skill is retained but in a way that is an intelligent complement to the half-understood two-line prophecy of radical puritanism.

And yet formal innovation only tells part of the story, for the lyric in the 1650s also became the possession of women. Of course women had written lyrics, even sonnet sequences, before – Aemelia Lanyer being a prominent example.[14] But where (mostly aristocratic) women had appropriated the male voice of the love lyricist in order to perform a critique of Petrarchan love conventions, the female lyric in the Interregnum possesses exactly the same voice as the male lover and poet, although often for different ends. The honour for most of this innovation goes to Katherine Philips, friend of Henry Vaughan and Abraham Cowley. Such was Philips's capacity to transcend voices that men used her poems as models for their own verse.[15] Donne's ability to effect male-female reciprocity, and to voice lesbian desire, is directly and effectively appropriated by a woman.

Philips was not published until the late 1660s, but many of her poems were written before 1660 and they circulated quite widely in manuscript. 'Upon the double Murther of King Charles I, in Answer to a Libellous Copy of Rymes by Vavasor Powell' is a classic piece of royalist antiphonal satire – it could have been written by Cleveland or a host of other men. 'On the 3rd of September, 1651' is a poem of royalist lament, which has affinities with Vaughan (imagery of light) and Donne (concepts of negation). Majesty has died like the setting sun, and is seen to pull all down with it. Here, Philips inverts the heroic associations surrounding Lucan's Pompey and Milton's Samson:

> Unhappy Kings, who cannot keep a throne,
> Nor be so fortunate to fall alone!
> Their weight sinks others: Pompey could not fly,
> But half the World must bear him company;
> And captiv'd Samson could not life conclude,
> Unless attended with a multitude.
> Who'd trust to greatness now, whose food is air,
> Whose ruin sudden, and whose end despair? (ll.21–8)

A recourse to a stoical virtue, inward reliance and private friendships is Philips's response. Of course, this is not unusual for royalists, although like Vaughan, her verse escapes from the blatant signalling in much royalist verse, and this may explain why she was read by Puritans. But in her verse addressed to female friends, she finds an entirely unique voice in the male world of the sea voyage, 'from Tenby to Bristol, begun Sept. 5 1652, sent from Bristol to Lucasia, Sept. 8, 1652'. The poem is not so much romance as realistic, dispelling the tight concision and mannered intimacy of the verse epistle, and finding female friendship, surprisingly, in the very middle of the storm:

> The amorous wave that shar'd in such dispense
> Exprest at once delight and reverence.
> Such trepidation we in lovers spy
> Under th'oppression of a mistress' eye.
> But then the wind so high did rise and roar,
> Some vow'd they'd never trust the traitor more. (ll. 21–6)

Part of this expression must be rooted in that quintessential war experience of the woman being left behind at home to run affairs while the men are away fighting (and Philips's husband was a staunch Parliamentarian and Cromwellian). Such was the inspiration behind Lucy Hutchinson's stunning biography of her husband. But Katherine Philips steps out of all female conventions when she adopts the voice of the male lover in 'To the truly Noble Mrs. Anne Owen, on my first Approaches':

> Madam,
> As in a triumph conquerors admit
> Their meanest captives to attend on it,
> Who, though unworthy, have the power confest,
> And justifi'd the yielding of the rest:
> So when the busy World (in hope t'excuse
> Their own surprise) your Conquests do peruse,
> And find my name, they will be apt to say,
> Your charms were blinded, or else thrown away. (ll. 1–8)

Manifestations of female authorial power, such as this is, were taken to their extreme in the writings of Margaret Cavendish, Duchess of Newcastle. Her confidence was of course aided by her aristocratic status, but she wrote not romances but utopias, not psalms but highly unusual secular verse which dared to discuss philosophy and ethics. Her discussions of the predicament of the female author, rightly celebrated in recent criticism, lead on to a blazing demonstration of the female imagination.[16] One of her 'Claspe' (book opening, hence 'clue') poems in *Poems and Fancies* (1653) invokes an expressive freedom which none of her male contemporaries pursued (with the possible exception of Wither, and the Pindaric Ode, as practised by Cowley (see below, 285–6) was also regarded as a 'free' form):

Give *Mee* the *Free*, and *Noble Stile*,
Which seems *uncurb'd*, though it be *wild*;
Though It runs wild about, It cares not where;
It shewes more *Courage*, then It doth of Feare. (110)

The poem which follows is entitled 'The Hunting of the Hare': the hare has the free style and he is the victim of a hunt. The inference we are to draw is that free authorship courts rebuke. The poem also represents the plight of a woman as an author:

Betwixt two *Ridges* of *Ploud-Land*, lay *Wat*,
Pressing his *Body* close to *Earth* lay squat
His *Nose* upon his two *Fore-feet* close lies,
Glaring obliquely with his *great gray Eyes*. . . .
    The *Dogs* so neere his sharp *Heeles* did get,
That they their sharp *Teeth* in his *Breech* did set.
Then tumbling downe, did fall with *weeping Eyes*,
Gives up his *Ghost*, and thus poore *Wat he* dies. (112)

It is a very unremittingly sad and painful poem, and the modern reader must wonder how a seventeenth-century person, used to hunting as part of everyday life, would have responded. Cavendish does not stop here either, for she rails against mankind's tyranny, while still implying sentient pity:

Yet *Man* doth think himself so gentle, mild,
When he of *Creatures* is most cruell wild.
And is so *Proud*, thinks only he shall live,
That *God* or *God*-like Nature did him give.
And that all *Creatures* for his sake alone,
Was made for him, to *Tyrannize* upon. (112–13)

What we are witnessing in the history of the lyric is the finishing of a 'great tradition' (the Renaissance love lyric) by the impact of the civil conflict. Fissiparation of the sonnet and the ode into smaller verse units like the epigram – as the assumed dominant genre – comes as no surprise; neither does a revived neoclassicism, in an attempt to keep the lyric uncontaminated. That women, freed temporarily from traditional roles by civil disruption, should seize such an initiative, has been neglected for too long, and we still need to understand more about this kind of poetry before our view of the literary canon is properly renewed. Nothing has been said in this section of sacred verse, and the puritan love of psalm translation. In fact, the history of the love lyric in the 1640s and 1650s is matched by a politics and transformation of holy poetry which was of even greater importance.

Battle Hymns of the Republic

As we saw in chapter 1, the Civil War and Interregnum gave rise to new kinds of authorship as a result of radical puritan worship and politics.[17] These were specifically centred on the spread of experimental theology and the practice of prophecy. They were also an extreme.

The Civil War was fought in large part over religious difference, and the difference was known in the dividedness of religious ritual and experience, from the most ceremonial, externalised, and witty example of Laudian worship to the most anti-ceremonial, internalised and spontaneous gathering of sectarians.[18] The subject of this section is the politics of different sound patterns in the English Revolution, specifically in poetry, as poetry was used in religious practice. It assumes the dominance of the prayer book and, after 1611, the King James Bible, in the established church, and that the revolt against these works as 'set forms' (and therefore as examples of 'carnal' worship) resulted in an inventiveness with sound and sense which ultimately produced autonomous sound forms. In other words, the English Revolution produced the English hymn as we know it, many decades before it is usually assumed to have emerged.[19] Also, the battleground for such auto-nomy was focused not merely in the collective performance of religious sounds (services of worship) but in all other forms of devotional discourse, including the religious lyric, which, despite its general direction towards private acts of reading, played out within itself the symbolic and phonic battles of the broader sphere. Indeed, the lyric in its well-known royalist mode (for instance, the poems of Robert Herrick and Henry Vaughan) achieved its autonomy by retreat in defeat, although its materials were inextricably involved in its religious opposites, as we shall see.

In Thomas Edwards's famous attack on the sects, *Gangraena* (1646), an Antinomian hymn is quoted (Antinomians believed that grace removes the need for believers to obey the ten commandments):

> The blood of Christ our great High-Priest,
>   which once for us was shed,
> Hath purg'd the blot, and cleans'd the spot
>   wherewith we were besmear'd
>
> A glorious thing, a wonder strong
>   that sinne should not defile,
> And those are all to Christ more dear
>   that once did seem so vile. (2.15)

Hymns were not supposed to be sung in English churches: only the singing of metrical psalms, in strict accordance with scriptural originals, was allowed. In the *Directory for Public Worship* (1646), the Assembly of Divines' attempt to establish a new non-episcopal order of worship, collective psalm singing is described as an internal and external witness of godliness ('the voice is to be tunably and gravely ordered, but the chief care must be, to sing with understanding, and with Grace in the heart, making melody unto the Lord'), where the literate should guide the illiterate with their psalm-books. Set forms dominated the sound patterns of English worship in the seventeenth century, be they the liturgies of the established church or the psalms sung in the national church of the Commonwealth and by nonconformists. The venerable New England Independent, John Cotton, maintained that 'every spiritual Song fit for private solace, is not fit to be sung in the solemne Assemblies of the Church for publique edification.' He went on:

> The translating of the *Psalms* into verse, in number, measure, and meeter, and suiting the Ditty with apt Tunes, are help[s] to stirre up the affection: And the singing of *Psalmes* being appointed of God, they tend to make a gracious melody to the Praise of God and edification of his People.[20]

The Antinomians' hymn breaks up even this mild formalism, and adds to the escape from scripturalism.

Edwards's fear was of the free spirits of inspired sectarians breaking the prohibition on singing anything but psalms. In fact, the conversion of hymns from private and unsung compositions to songs of collective performance had already begun by 1640.[21] George Wither had published books of hymns for congregational singing in the 1620s, even though his 'hymns' were for the most part versions of psalms. William Barton published hymns for use in worship constructed entirely from scriptural phrases, claiming that they were 'plainer then *Psalms* and more suitable to our condition', until a better translation of the psalms appeared.[22] In 1651, while offering three hymns to the government on the occasion of the first anniversary of the regicide, Wither judged that hymns were public prayers. He wrote them for a duty: 'I owe it, to prepare proper Hymnes of that daies Celebration, with some other brief Commemoration, to keep in mind Gods late mercies to this Republique.'[23] Wither's *Britain's Second Remembrancer* (1641) intended its users to sing the 'poenitentiall hymns, spirituall songs, and morall odes' in family groups. Hymns in this context are the fullest means of conveying councils and consideration, even when the messenger was the Holy Spirit. Wither's preferred worship is the small group or conventicle – precisely that kind of puritan private religion which had so many in trouble with Charles's bishops. Wither sees his hymns as gestures of reformation against centuries of profane abuse, and his vision is of a renovation of public as well as private worship. He imagines the public sphere as a puritanised ancient city state:

so innumerable are the foolish and prophane *Songs* now delighted in (to the dishonour of our language, and Religion) that HALELUIAHS, and pious Meditations are almost out of use and fashion: yea, not in private only; but at our *publick feasts*, and *civil worship*, also, Scurrilous and obscoene *Songs*, without respecting the reverend presence of *Matrons, Virgins, Magistrates,* or *Divines*. Nay, somewhere in their despight, they are *called for, Sung,* and *Acted*, with such abominable gesticulations, as are very offensive to all modest heavens, and beholders; and fitting only to be exhibited, at the Diabolicall Solemnities of *Bacchus [,] Venus,* or *Priapus*. (11–12)[24]

How would Wither have responded to the 'Anglican' poetry of Robert Herrick, merging church ritual with pagan rites and imagery, and the ideals of the Book of Sports? There is a rumour that some of the lyrics in Herrick's collection of sacred verse, *His Noble Numbers*, were sung in his congregation. That this collection of verse replicates a Laudian and Arminian conception of ceremony and salvation doctrine, in addition to its royalism, has been very well demonstrated in recent work.[25] The collection alternates between private, epigrammatic verse, and examples of courtly religious performance, such as 'To God: an Anthem, sung in the Chappell at White-Hall, before the King'. None of this is markedly conceited (indeed, the verse strives for Jonsonian plainness), but it does confess courtly sacramentalism. The theatricality of 'Good Friday: Rex Tragicus, or Christ Going to His Crosse' pre-empts regicide imagery, and gives added significance to earlier poems in the collection which figure coronation and crucifixion:

To God

> Do with me, God! as Thou didst deal with *John*,
> (Who writ that heavenly *Revelation*)
> Let me (like him) first cracks of thunder heare;
> Then let the Harps inchantments strike mine eare;
> Here give me thornes; there, in thy Kingdome, set
> Upon my head the golden coronet;
> There give me day; but here my dreadfull night:
> My sackcloth here; but there my *Stole* of white.

The occurrence of religious themes in the secular verse is equally revealing. Although some of Herrick's poetry was written before 1620, it was not published until 1648, and recent opinion regards many poems in *Hesperides* as late 1640s compositions. As Gerald Hammond has recently argued, Herrick's 'Ceremonies for Candlemass Eve' celebrates seasonal change (and with it the staidness of ritual) in the very terms which parliamentary soldiers used when removing icons and ornaments from churches:

> Down with the Rosemary and Bayes,
> Down with the Mistleto;
>   In stead of Holly, now up-raise
> The greener Box (for show). (ll.1–4)[26]

There is no better example of the split in religious sensibility in the 1640s and 1650s than Herrick's poem on the ceremony of churching and Milton's sonnet 'Methought I saw my late espoused saint' (?1658). For Herrick, the ceremony of churching in the Anglican church becomes a (frankly, hideous) retrieval of a besmirched-in-childbirth woman as a virgin. The scene is quite literal (although chastity is metaphorically equated with virginity):

> Put on thy *Holy Filletings*, and so
> To th'Temple with the sober *Midwife* go.
> Attended thus (in a most solemn wise)
> By those who serve the Child-bed misteries.
>
> *She who keeps chastly to her husbands side*
> *Is not for one, but every night his Bride:*
> *And stealing still with love, and feare to Bed,*
> *Brings him not one, but many a Maiden-head.*
>   ('Julia's *Churching, or Purification*', ll.1–4, 13–6)

In Milton, however, purification ritual (specifically Hebraic for the fundamentalist) is rendered as a figure for a spiritual purity, presented as an ideal state of companionship in the world beyond. The poem is radically internalised, and seems all the more purely Petrarchan (for it is a Petrarchan sonnet) for being so.

Within the national church, the fetishising of psalm singing was eroded under Laudian influences on habits of worship. Hymns, including Richard Crashaw's, were sung at Peterhouse Chapel in the 1630s and the early 1640s, as part of a highly ceremonial and ritualised form of worship. The hymns were seen, along with the other innovations in the service, as the resurrection of a tradition of worship which pre-dated the Reformation.[27] If the 'worshipper's own ceremonial actions bec[a]me the ritual memorial of Biblical events', then the hymn singing was analogous to this formalised worship, and was therefore less individualising than has been suggested, and than was to be the case in the gathered churches.[28] After the regicide, this tradition lived on in the published literature of martyrology. *Psalterium Carolinum* (1657) is the 'Devotions of His Sacred Majestie in his Solitudes and Sufferings', rendered into verse by Thomas Stanley and set to music for three voices, organ or theorbo (double-necked lute), by John Wilson, one of Charles I's court musicians. There is also a commendatory poem by Henry Lawes, stressing the avant-garde nature of Wilson's music. The performed effect (*Psalterium Carolinum* was published

Figure 9 Richard Crashaw, *Steps to the Temple* (2nd edn, 1646), frontispiece.

in different versions for each part) must have been astounding, for Charles's comments on the Civil War are rendered as a highly up-market version of sung metrical psalms. Even more appropriate for current purposes are the telling manuscript insertions in the bass line part in the Bodleian Library copy, which identify each 'psalm' with a different stage of the conflict: 'Uppon his Ma[jesties] calling this Lo[ng] Parliament' (Sig. X1r); 'Uppon the Ear[l of] Straffords Deat[h]' (Sig. X2r); 'Uppon the various events of war; Victoryes & Defeats' (Sig. Ff1v).[29] Thomason had a manuscript copy of 'Prayers/Used at Paris September. 1648',[30] testifying to their unprintability and the fact that they circulated in manuscript:

> O Lord guard the Person of thy Servant Our King
> Who putteth his Trust in Thee.
> Send yet to Him and to those that are
> for Him helpe from thine Holy Place.
> And do thou ever more and att this

an informer

non for a work

A Protestants Meeting.

Figure 10 John Bunyan, *The Life and Death of Mr. Badman* (1680).

time especially most mightily defend him.
Confound the designes of all those that rise up against Him.

Neither should such poetic divisions be dissociated from the sense of visual space which they communicate. The woodcuts accompanying Richard Crashaw's *Steps to the Temple* (1648) show a variety of people entering a building which looks suspiciously like a Counter-Reformation church (see fig. 9). Opposed to this we could set the woodcut in Bunyan's *The Life and Death of Mr. Badman* (1680) of a group of Dissenters (described as 'Protestants') meeting in a field, entirely without the material presence of a building (and its sacramental associations), although presumably so to avoid persecution (see fig. 10). In the middle is Herbert's *The Temple* (1633), which is relevant to the Civil War because of its continuing wide circulation in the decade following its publication, and because of its role in the religious politics of the Interregnum.

Herbert avoids the obvious externalisation (as well as the Romish

traits) of Crashaw by troping the fabric of the church – the 'externals' of
the temple – as the words of poetry (just as the Communion sacrament
was regarded as a 'speaking' image). So, the lyric poetry which famously
makes sacred the courtly tradition familiar to Herbert's family is also most
Protestant in its 'middle way', making words do the work of, and actually
become, ceremonies and externals. Such a move explains the popularity
of Herbert with all denominations far into the eighteenth century: the
troping of the church as sacred poetry allows for a variety of different
interpretations, according to different versions of reformed religion.[31] On
the one hand, the hieroglyphic habit in some of the most well-known
lyrics ('Easter Wings'; 'The Altar') takes the reader from the word into
the picture – the iconic, the fixed object. On the other, the sheer
inventiveness of rhythmic variety creates a sense of spontaneity, with its
breaking out of set forms in the joy of enthusiastic rapture:

> My love, my sweetnesse, heare!
> By these thy feet, at which my heart
> Lies all the yeare,
> Pluck out thy dart,
> And heal my troubled breast which cryes,
> Which dyes. ('Longing', ll. 79–84)

And such enthusiasm exists as a reading effect of Herbert while still
maintaining the sense of fidelity to biblical literalism.

For these reasons, *The Temple* came to have an impeccable authority as
a kind of manual or handbook on the godly parish, which was, of course,
the most immediate and vital context for the religious politics of the
Interregnum – the first image of the religious community which people
had. Parish worship was where older forms of religious practice survived
and where all innovations were put to the severest test.[32] So, while a
Herbert lyric was adapted as royalist propaganda in the 1640s, another
interesting instance of Herbert's text at work was a controversy over an
appointment to a living at Brinkworth in Wiltshire in 1654, between a
protectorate imposee and the Antinomian, occultist and sometime army
chaplain, Henry Pinnell.[33] Brinkworth had been the home and living of
the influential Antinomian, Tobias Crisp, and Herbert's poetry is made
to defend the claims of an Antinomian.

The picture of common people wandering around the country north of
Salisbury Plain with Herbert and occult philosophy in their heads, as
Pinnell claimed they did, should be taken seriously, as much as we should
note that one of Herbert's earliest editors and imitators, Christopher
Harvie, was also the author of a treatise against rebellion, while a
Herbert lyric was adapted as a way of identifying sympathetically with
Charles I's predicament.[34] And this intermixing of traditions which we
have thought hitherto to be entirely separate occurs 'on the ground' in

other areas of the country during the revolution. In Interregnum Wales, the absence of a national church had the effect of destabilising the genres and signifying power of literary forms associated with the sacred, thereby producing a genuinely original poetry. At the same time, there is a battle for the allegiance of readers fought between different types of church polity, but using the same textual materials as the site of meaning – the continental occult, exactly as we have seen it used in Wiltshire.

The poetry of Henry Vaughan needs no more introduction than Herbert's *The Temple*, especially the lyrics in *Silex Scintillans* (1650, 2nd edn 1655), which, in a clear imitation of Herbert's holy transformation, move away from the earlier secular translations and poems of retirement. That Henry's brother, the hermetical philosopher Thomas, was accused of immorality and ejected from his living at Llansantffraed by the parliamentary investigation of the church in Wales, is well known; the Vaughans' allegiances are in no doubt. What is not often considered is the unusual definitions into which the lyrics of *Silex Scintillans* are thrown by the context of withdrawal and defeat. Vaughan follows Herbert in describing his poems on the title-page as 'sacred poems and private ejaculations', but the author's preface changes the description of the poems to 'hymns'. Strictly speaking, the only singing permitted in pre-1660 churches was of metrical psalms. 'Hymn' referred here to songs of praise which did not originate in the Scripture. Vaughan's use of 'hymn' is of a distinctly private kind:

> he that desires to excel in this kinde of *Hagiography*, or holy writing, must strive (by all means) for *perfection* and true *holyness*, that *a door may be opened to him in heaven*, Rev. 4.1. and then he will be able to write (with *Hierotheus* and holy *Herbert*) A *true Hymn*.[35]

'Hymn' seems to equate with a prayer, and set within the devotional traditions which inform *Silex Scintillans*, it is clearly a private prayer. Drawing on hermetic and occult language as a source of symbols for the presence of the divine in creation, Vaughan moves from ceremonial, ritual and orthodox theological subjects to a location of the sacramental in the natural. Take, for example, the first stanza of 'Cock-crowing':

> Father of lights! what Sunnie seed,
> What glance of day hast thou confin'd
> Into this bird? To all the breed
> This busie Ray thou hast assign'd;
> > Their magnetisme works all night,
> > And dreams of Paradise and light. (ll.1–6)

If these lyrics are regarded as hymns, sung prayers to God, then we can argue that there is a freeing of the speaker from forms. Although some dispossessed Anglicans developed sung hymns in the 1650s, 'The World' claims a private status, enforced by the speaker's 'I'.[36] The simplicity of diction, the rhythmic patterns, and the figure of a lutanist in the second half of the first stanza implies a kind of inward apocalyptic song:

> I saw Eternity the other night
> Like a great *Ring* of pure and endless light,
>   All calm, as it was bright,
> And round beneath it, Time in hours, days, years
>   Driv'n by the spheres
> Like a vast shadow mov'd, In which the world
> And all her train were hurl'd. (ll.1–7)

It comes as some surprise to find someone who should be Vaughan's opposite, the Independent minister and Fifth Monarchist, Morgan Llwyd, sounding not unlike him. Llwyd came from Wrexham, where his gathered church was unusually ecumenical, entertaining Presbyterians and Quakers. He was a major figure in the Committee for the Propagation of the Gospel in Wales, the body which ejected Thomas Vaughan.[37] Today, Llwyd is regarded as the finest Welsh-language prose stylist of the seventeenth century. His poems, written during the 1640s and 1650s in Welsh and English, were clearly designed for congregational performance, and they address the conflict centrally: one is entitled 'The Desolation, Lamentation and Resolution of the Welsh Saints, in the Late Wars. Sung in 1643'. 'Sung' is important: there is no sense of any utterance which is not public, in the congregation, and put into musical form. The millenarian expectations of Llwyd's congregation seldom disappear in his poetry, even at Communion:

> By breaking bread we show thy death and mind
>   thy wondrous love
> Untill thou come to us againe in glory from
>   above
>
> Then shall the sun moone stars & aire, and earth
>   even changed bee
> & wicked men and devills shall roare but then
>   secure are wee.[38]

The apocalypticism of Vaughan and Llwyd is sometimes strikingly similar. Civil disruption dissolves the barriers between cults, just as apocalypse dissolves objects, and promotes the interchangeability of physical media:

> When through the North a fire shall rush
>   And rowle into the East
> And like a firie torrent brush
>   And sweepe up *South*, and *West*,

When all shall streame, and lighten round
   And with surprizing flames
Both stars, and Elements confound
   And quite blot out their names.
                       (Vaughan, 'Day of Judgement', ll.1–8)

Before one houre before day is darke
that great Ecclypse is neare
one fierce and farewell storme & then
the evening will be cleare. . . .

. . . Sing on a brittle sea of glasse
Sing in a furne of fire
In flames wee leap for joy and find
a cave a singing quire.[39]

Where Vaughan translated hermetical works by Henry Nollius and Oswald Crollius in 1655 and 1657 (the latter was also translated by Henry Pinnell), Llwyd was busy translating parts of Jacob Boehme from English into Welsh, Boehme appearing already from 1644 onwards in English translation.[40] In the Renaissance, alchemical, hermetical and occult writings, both practical and contemplative, shared common elements. The most central of these was the belief that man could, by means of acquiring the correct names of the objects in creation, return to the state of pristine knowledge and spiritual perfection known by Adam.[41] These aims were almost naturally consonant with the millenarian expectations of radical Puritans, as Ben Jonson had foreseen four decades previously in *The Alchemist*.

In which case, why was it that ecclesial and political opposites should have been interested in incorporating and using the same material? First of all, in Henry Vaughan, the apocalypse is the Day of Judgement, not the Second Coming of Christ. The millennium is subjugated to the always present, gradual slowing down of the world; the apocalypse becomes the poetic mode of apprehending final purification and resurrection, even, as Alan Rudrum has reminded us, the resurrection of the animals, vegetables and minerals.[42] By contrast, Llwyd explicitly states the distinction between Second Coming and Day of Judgement/ end of the world. But then again, Llwyd's sense of the Second Coming was not simply the bodily return of Christ, as it was for the Fifth Monarchists, or just the return of Christ 'within' of the Ranters and the Quakers, but a middle version in which both returns took place simultaneously. Llwyd died in 1657, just as the Protectorate had more or less controlled the Fifth Monarchist revolt, and it seems as if he became more of an 'internalist' in his later years. In this case, his mystical spirituality is functioning in the same way as that of the Vaughans (and

possibly also reinforced by a shared rejection of predestinarian theology).
Here is Llwyd from a Boehme-inspired prose work entitled 'Where is
Christ':

> He [Christ] is stiled the brightness of the fathers glory, because in the
> eternal still liberty he maketh a glance, which taketh its original out of
> the sharpness of the eternal nature. He is called the love of the Father,
> because the Fathers first will to the genetrix [female parent] of nature,
> desireth only this his most beloved heart, and this is the best beloved
> above nature, and yet is the Fathers own essence.[43]

The effect in Thomas Vaughan is not so very different:

> According to that speech of Hermes Trismegistus: 'Each thing whatsoever
> bears within it the seed of its own regeneration.' Proceed then patiently,
> but not manually. The work is performed by an invisible artist, for there is
> a secret incubation of the Spirit of God upon Nature. You must only see
> that the outward heat fails not, but with the subject itself you have no
> more to do than the mother hath with the child that is in her womb.[44]

It is difficult to say how far either of the Vaughans believed in a popular
dissemination of such knowledge or ideas; whether they felt, for
instance, as Giordano Bruno did and as Pinnell did not, that the occult
was for the elite only. Certainly, Llwyd was attempting in his poetry at
least a dissemination to the social whole of the congregation, just as
there is evidence of Boehme being used as cosmological underpinning in
handbooks for some of the London Independent congregations.[45] If the
Vaughans spoke to disaffected royalist gentry, Llwyd and his fellow
evangelists spoke to the empowered pro-parliamentary gentry who were
governing Wales. In this instance, the hymn gives a finely nuanced
further insight into the politics of alchemy and the occult during the
Interregnum.[46]

Vaughan scholars tend to regard him as inevitably correct, by virtue of
status and education.[47] In this simulation of Vaughan's views, Llwyd,
Vavasor Powell (another poet) and Walter Cradock, the key figures in
the itinerant ministry of the 1650s, were 'presumptuous, often poorly
educated, and indifferent or hostile to Anglican traditions'. The last
claim is true, but the first and second cannot be sustained. Cradock's
copy of Sir Francis Bacon's *Advancement of Learning* (1625 edition) still
survives.[48] The value of Jonathan Post's reading is that he is able to show
how Vaughan reviled the radicals, both in the frequent anti-puritanical
references, but also in poetry like 'The Men of War' which offers a
contextual reading of the phrases from Revelation which Fifth
Monarchists like Powell used to justify militancy. So the first four lines
imitate the evangelical appeal:

> If any have an ear
> Saith holy John, then let him hear.
> He that into Captivity
> Lead others, shall a Captive be.

But then the reversal of the sense comes in the second four lines:

> Who with the sword doth others kill,
> A sword shall have his blood likewise spill.
> Here is the patience of the Saints,
> And the true faith, which never faints.

For Post, there is only one reading: that of the patience which Vaughan adduces.

To claim that Vaughan is simply letting the Bible speak its 'true' meaning as if it were not always subject to interpretation for any viewpoint is a surprising claim to make. And as we have seen, Vaughan and Llwyd's apocalypticisms coincide as well as differ. Another problem is the attempt to see Henry Vaughan's association of himself with the myth of an ancient British church, by calling himself the 'Silurist', as a historical vision of Anglicanism which supplanted the puritan claim for the direct and immediate inspiration of the Gospel.[49] In fact, Llwyd and Powell had their own ancient British myths, working in the same direction as Vaughan's. They could even be said to be more authentically ancient British in being faithful to the Welsh language. Some of Powell's poetry kept Welsh bardic forms in existence, while Llwyd's national myth is of the earlier Elizabethan order which merged British Protestantism with imperial expansion:

> our british climate was so cold, soules frozen
> were to death
> we were for want of light & zeale a barren
> tedious heath
>
> Our northwest cutt to Indies mines, I meane to
> heavenly gold
> we mist it, summer was so short and winter
> was so cold.[50]

Vaughan's 'armies' become representative of purely heavenly incarnations, thereby assuming a gap between heaven and earth, signifier and signified, which belies puritanical or Fifth Monarchist literalism:

> Armies thou hast in Heaven, which fight,
> And follow thee all cloath'd in white,
> But here on earth (though thou hast need)
> Thou wouldst no legions, but wouldst bleed.

> The sword wherewith thou dost command
> Is in thy mouth, not in thy hand,
> And all thy Saints do overcome
> By thy blood, and their Martyrdom. (ll. 21–8)

This, of course, is no indication that Vaughan was a pacifist, or that he did not condone the policies of those who sought to punish resisters of the established church before 1640 or after 1660. It does, however, enable us to see a poetry in which the function of vision is directed to things not of this world, and where the state of rapture and ejaculation is linked very much to an established church: 'I'le not stuff my story/With your Commonwealth and glory.'

By contrast, the itineracy of the propagators of the Gospel is borne out in what is a superb poetic cycle by Llwyd, called *1648*. With the power of the Holy Spirit very much on earth in godly men, a seasonal division of winter, spring, summer and harvest is introduced to intimate the growth of excitement for the Second Coming. Divorced from the context of set forms in worship, and from the privacy of meditation (one always has the sense that this poem should be sung too), final struggle between good and evil is grotesquely rendered:

> A thousand dayes great Beelzebub and Pope
>   his son and foole
> made christendome their slaughterhouse, the
>   church their dancing schoole
>
> And Hell breaks loose, the smoke comes up,
>   the hounds gods people trace
> The sons of God whom Jesus bought, they
>   hang before his face.[51]

This kind of poetry is seemingly not without humour: Jesus outwits the Jesuits, the instruments of Satan who is 'tyring' his 'titts' as the great day approaches, and Italy's 'gouted' leg will be cured or cut away.[52] The answer to Vaughan, as it were, comes with the assertion that out of the midst of sectarian division in England, which Llwyd himself resisted, will come a truly godly 'army':

> Out of all these will Christ compound
> An army for himselfe
> so satan getts of all these sects
> the parings and the pelfe.[53]

It will indeed be a transcendental army, a genuine elect, formed out of the trial of all truths in a tolerant society, and one which was possibly beyond Vaughan's political imagination, although not beyond his poetry. The final 'Harvest' section changes tack again, employing pastoral and georgic imagery, except that this time apocalypse is introduced, to produce an interesting variation on Marvell's Mower poems:

> The field is large, the barne at hand
> the reapers quicke and wise
> The stubble flames, and sinfull soules
> lye downe and never rise.[54]

The reapers are massive, terrifying figures and not always framed by another set of realities, thereby achieving the mollifying effects in Marvell's 'Upon Appleton House'. Singing becomes the symbol of agreement, even if it contains difference: 'Agree Agree, You sing one song/but differ in the tone.' Finally, the figure of the hourglass, used frequently elsewhere, sustains the image of eternity:

> In summer Christ is all in all
> as Pope in winter was
> But after harvest God is all
> Then, never turn our glasse.

For Vaughan, the 'glass' (as mirror) is certainly far above man – 'To leave those skies,/That glass of souls and spirits, where well drest/They shine in white (like stars) and rest' ('The Proffer', ll.22–4)

Some of the models used by Llwyd (and Vavasor Powell) were from the bardic tradition, and are alliterative (*cynhanedd*), including *englynion* (alliterative verses in four lines, with each line structured on 10–6–7–7 syllables) and *cywyddau*, poems with alliterative rhyming couplets of seven syllables each. Welsh literary culture worked to fill a gap created by the English repression of non-scriptural forms, although metrical psalm form continued to provide a model for the hymn.

The printing in parallel of hymns by Vavasor Powell with antiphons by his opponents creates quite literally a sound battle on the page, so that printed medium embodies iteratively a country at war (with the Dutch) and at war with itself. In republican London, the victories of the army over the Scots and the Royalists at the Battle of Worcester were celebrated in some of the more famous Independent congregations with hymns similar to Llwyd's, if not so prosodically rich. In these works, victory (and glorification) becomes the possession and the experience of the congregation, as battles (in this case, against the Scots at Mussleburgh) are fictionally re-enacted within the metre of praise:

> Fifteen select Troops of the Church
> All Covenanters sure,
> Came trooping forth, and some did swear
> That *Cromwells* Honour to prove.

> Dead or alive their prisoner
> Some cry'd they would him bring,
> And offer him a sacrifice
> Unto their new-made King.[55]

Hymns were also sung in Thomas Tillam's Seventh Day Baptist congregation.[56] In *The Temple of Lively Stones* (1660), Tillam prints several hymns and justifies them as a kind of collective prophecy (274–9, 285–8). Objections to hymn singing are rebutted by reference to practice in the primitive churches, according to the histories of Eusebius and Socrates. Singing for Tillam may be '*jointly, singly,* or *inter-changeably*' (288–9). Sectarian literature provides many further examples of extempore, 'gifted' singing, in and out of congregational worship.[57]

It comes as no surprise to find hymn singing being reviled by the more orthodox. 'So when instead of *singing of Psalms,* they shall introduce into their Assemblies the *singing of Silly* HYMNES, of vulgar Composure', said Thomas Willes in 1659, 'which whether for *Rime* or *Reason,* are not much to be prefer'd before those which the common Ballad-mongers sing in the streets under the name of *Godly Ballads*', he saw the desecration of 'Gods holy *Ordinances*'.[58] Militant hymns were also parodied in popular verse form, which suggests a continuity of some hymn forms with verse libels, satires and ballads. Thus, *A Hymn to Cromwell* (1659) hints at an interchangeability of forms, just as some ballads had both parliamentarian and royalist versions:

> *Tredagh* he took by Storm, and there he got much
>   Riches;
> But *Ards* and *Inchiquins,* has made him wrong his
>   Breeches.
> *Let* Cromwels *Nose still Reign, let* Cromwels *nose
>   still reign,*
> *Tis no disgrace to his Copper-face, to Brew strong
>   Ale again.*

The argument of this section is that the so-called 'metaphysical' religious lyric was the product of a particular space in English history when the relative absence of invented forms from church services, or the withering effect of liturgy and set prayers themselves, forced the emergence in established religion of the mannered and mystical poem in which the Church of England could be metaphorically represented. Herbert was the master, Vaughan his more than worthy successor. The emergence of dissent, and the context therein for the deprivatising of the hymn by its use in the freer and more spontaneous, but still regulated, acts of nonconformist worship, ended that space. The similarities in sources and strategies shared by Henry Vaughan and Morgan Llwyd are witness to what could happen in that very process of change which was the Interregnum. Their differences mark a cultural schism, and they prophesy for one a kind of poetical extinction.

After 1650, the religious lyric as such seems to have declined, despite Herbert's enduring popularity. The hymn grew. During the Restoration the 'regularisation' of Dissent in the face of persecution, the conversion from sects to churches, was paralleled by the incorporation of hymns into services where only psalms and prophesying had been permitted previously.[59] This was so in the baptist churches, Bunyan contributing to the trend, though it was his associate Benjamin Keach, first author of a Dissenting rhetoric (*Tropologia* (1680)), who produced the first baptist hymnal.

If inventiveness in religious discourse was once the province of aristocrats (the Sidneys, for instance) for very private acts of worship, and the rest laboured under the drudgery of the Elizabethan or Jacobean 'forms' of authorised translations and settings (Sternhold and Hopkins), the emergence of separatism or nonconformity created not only new private authorships, but brought inventiveness into the collective space of the gathered church. While this process in its militant and millennial form can be seen at work in the poetry of Morgan Llwyd, by the end of the century, the result could be said to have been a new poetic. The hymn was a site of negotiation, on the one hand permitting the merging of individual with congregational identities, and on the other, holding in tension the relationship between ministerial and lay interpretative powers (ministers usually wrote the hymns, but in their performance, they became the private *and* collective prayers of the congregation).

Isaac Watts (1674–1748), Independent minister, is usually accepted as one of the great hymn writers of the eighteenth century. His arrangement of repeated consonants and mutating vowels, with the stark imagery, is a strategy directly in line with Morgan Llwyd's:

> His dying crimson like a robe
> Spreads o'er his body on the tree;
> Then am I dead to all the globe,
> And all the globe is dead to me.

But Watts also takes into his non-congregational verse the same attitudes, so that the biblicism which one finds in Llwyd and Powell, for instance, is reorganised into a realistic sublime in classical prosody (here sapphics), without the troping characteristic of Vaughan:

> When the firce north wind with his airy forces
> Rears up the Baltic to a foaming fury,
> And the red lightning with a storm of hail comes
>   Rushing amain down,

How the poor sailors stand amazed and tremble!
While the hoarse thunder like a bloody trumpet
Roars a loud onset to the gaping waters
    Quick to devour them.

In fact, Watts revives the prophetic tradition within the hymnodic: setting the crucified Christ beside the anguished poet figure in a replication of Milton's early poem 'The Passion'. And if the site of worship is the ground of Watts's diction, invention for him means the inhabitation of Milton's muse, so that *Paradise Lost* reappears inside the lyric:

Give me the Muse whose generous force
    Impatient of the reins
Pursues an unattempted course,
Breaks all the critic's iron chains,
And bears to paradise the raptured mind.

There Milton dwells: the mortal sung
Themes not presumed by mortal tongue;
New terrors and new glories shine
In every page, and flying scenes divine
Surprise the wond'ring sense, and draw our souls along. . . .

The noble hater of degenerate rhyme
Shook off the chains, and built his verse sublime,
A monument too high for coupled sounds to climb.[60]

In a far more direct way than any other literary form, the lyric really was an instrument of religious policy in the mid-seventeenth century, a testimony to the importance it had achieved by 1640. Its divisions in the Interregnum represent the dividedness of inter-denominational strife, and the differing potentials for human expression and self-definition contained therein. There is no sense of etiolation in Vaughan's poetry, as there was say in the cavalier lyric, rather a politicised saintly retreat. On the other hand, another kind of potential for verse – the congregational hymn – grew elsewhere which, never wholly devoid of millenarian hopes, found itself truly visionary when claimed by a Miltonic poetics in the work of Watts.

Two War Genres

The two most public kinds of verse in the 1640s and 1650s – panegyric and elegy – were curiously least subject to change. Certainly panegyric and elegy were subject to changing political pressures on their form, but these were more direct and as nothing compared with the transformations suffered by other genres. And yet the two genres were crucial elements in the culture of civil conflict, and the survival of their forms became bound up with the fortunes of the parties and groups they served.

Panegyric

Edmund Waller was a great writer of panegyrics, as the widespread acclaim for his poem 'Upon His Majesty's Repairing of Pauls' (?1635) attests. But pre-war panegyric (even if literally *just* pre-war) has the glozing texture of a world without cannon, musket-shot and maiming. Waller's 'To my Lord of Falkland' casts its subject as Apollo, the artist-warrior who suppresses the rebellious giants. This is most ironic, for the poem was occasioned by Charles's expedition against the Scots in 1639, a notorious military failure for the English. It is not dismissive of the 'horror' of 'the blind events of war', but the subject of Falkland is subsumed into a praise of the island kingdom, where civil war is but a rewarming of warlike spirits for future scourging of foreign foes (again, odd, since England and Scotland were still two separate kingdoms). The poem is prophetic, linking national genius to an alternative destiny for the nation than the one seen by the swain in Milton's *Lycidas*:

> In a late dream, the Genius of this land,
> Amazed, I saw, like the fair Hebrew stand,
> When first she felt the twins begin to jar,
> And found her womb the seat of civil war.
> Inclined to whose relief, and with presage
> Of better fortune for the present age,
> Heaven sends, quoth I, this discord for our good,
> To warm, perhaps, but not to waste our blood. (ll.25–32)

The poem is in line with Waller's earlier panegyrics to Charles (portrayed as Aeneas when pursuing his Spanish match), and deeply influenced by the interest in painterly form at the Caroline court. It is in many respects little different from the young Abraham Cowley's panegyrics of 1633, celebrating the return of Charles from his coronation in Scotland, to initiate what Cowley imagines is the golden age.

We are now able to understand very clearly the way in which poets during the Interregnum responded to the new age by reconstructing the relationship between English poetry and classical antecedents.[61] Marvell in particular has been seen as no longer a political fence sitter in 'An Horatian Ode Upon Cromwell's Return from Ireland'. Instead, he is seen

to be creating a specifically republican version of both ode and
prosphonetikon or *epibaterion* (a poem on the return of a hero). The
ambiguities of the poem are in fact replications of the tensions which are
necessary to the life of republics. And this is in distinct contrast to the
unitary praise of Charles, the bringer of peace and the arts, in 1630s
panegyric, best instanced in Sir Richard Fanshawe's 'An Ode Upon
occasion of His Majesties Proclamation in the yeare 1630. Commanding
the Gentry to reside upon their Estates in the Country'.[62]

Indeed, as soon as Fanshawe himself is confronted by the scene of war
and civil dissension, a very different kind of poetry emerges. 'On the
Earle of *Straffords* Tryall' compares the trial to the assassination of Julius
Caesar, and it does so in a complicated way. Strafford is presented as a
supreme artist-deity (he is compared to Jove and Juno in line 7) weaving
eloquently his own tragic plot, bowing out through his own execution in
order to bring the country to peace – for Strafford told Charles to give
assent for his execution. The Roman comparison is deliberately
disjunctive; it seems as if Parliament is being compared with the
conspirators in Rome. If the Senate had tried Caesar, says Fanshawe,
they would have found the love and pity to reprieve him; so in a sense by
trying Strafford and *not* finding pity, the English Parliament are less than
their classical forebears. The final couplet carries the unmistakable
warning, despite the poem's assurance of Strafford's nobility: 'So fell
great *Rome* her selfe, opprest at length/By the united *Worlds*, and her
owne strength' (ll.41–2). The disjunctions are poetic intimations of civil
disruptions, while the poem's mode is actually a resurrection of the
conspiracy poetry surrounding the assassination of the Duke of
Buckingham by John Felton in 1628, some of which praised Felton as a
noble classical conspirator.[63] Strafford had been a supporter in the 1620s
of parliamentary resistance to royal impropriation, with which
Buckingham was associated, but the latter's assassination made Strafford
a firm supporter of the idea of arbitrary government. Perhaps unwittingly,
Fanshawe's poem makes history catch up with Strafford, so that he
becomes a victim of that which he had been trying to escape.

Panegyric is confused by the Civil War. Not in the first instance: the
simple praise of parliamentary commanders makes stirring reading: 'Great
MASSEY'S Heart;/That was the Fort no Engine could beat down,/Nor
Mine blow up, more strong then was the town.'[64] Such verse is not
generically unknowing either:

> 'Tis said, the Satyr fled from man aghast,
> When he perceiv'd his breath at the same blast
> To cool and heat; sad had that Satyr been,
> He might from flames the like effects have seen.[65]

But the case is different with royalist panegyric. Unlike parliamentary panegyric, which was often published separately and appeared in the newsbooks, royalist panegyric is characterised by its desire for privacy, and thus is in a sense paradoxical in relation to its form. Although much royal panegyric was not published pre-1640, the tendency to keep royalist panegyric secret by the late 1640s was high indeed. And when the King was executed, elegy and panegyric were fused: a bringing together of genres which was just as confused as the poems which praised Cromwell. A good example of private and dissenting panegyrics are the 'Fugitive Poems' of Mildmay Fane, Earl of Westmoreland. Fane published his poems of retreat and devotion, *Otia Sacra*, in 1648, but his political poetry was reserved for a private manuscript.[66] A mixture of apparently inconsequential travel poems (the consequence of an exile) and satires are mixed with versions of twenty Horatian odes and two epodes, all of them addressing pointedly but privately public issues. Christopher Wase's private Latin poem on Cromwell hysterically inverts panegyrical expectations:

Cromwelli apparatus

Arma parat, Ferrum, Ferroque potentius Aurum
      Plus . . . cum horrenda Relligione minax
Est etiam occultam secto sub corde flagellum
      Caetera sunt Phalerae.[67]

Cleveland's 'The King's Disguise' could equally be seen as a royal elegy. There is a curious sense of power contained: 'Oh the accurst Stenographie of fate!' (47). The poem is the beginning of royalist lament – although it is *sui generis* – the first indications in the disguise of the King's game being truly up. There are dating problems with 'The King's Disguise' – was it a prophecy of the king's death?[68] The distance from this kind of elegy to mock elegy is not so great:

Am I awake or dreame? can it be sed,
Englands Arch Traytor thus to hell is fled?
With Strange Dilemmas, is my soule perplext;
On this side murther, Treason on the next: . . .

Who now shall rob the Church, pull windows down,
Who now shall dare to trample on a Crowne?
Who now shall lead the Saints by springs and fountains.[69]

By contrast, Milton's panegyrical sonnets are consistent documents of first parliamentarian, then openly republican liberty. Even Sonnet X, 'To the Lady Margaret Ley', perhaps written in 1642, looks back to the adjournment and dissolution of the 1629 Parliament as the beginning of the downfall of Margaret Ley's father, James Ley, Earl of Marlborough, so

that the republican *language* of parliamentary resistance in the late 1620s
again becomes the focus of the call for real liberty now that Parliament
has been recalled. Ley himself is compared to Isocrates, the orator whom
Milton would imitate in *Areopagitica*, while Charles I is implicitly likened
to Philip of Macedon, who defeated Athens and Thebes at the Battle of
Chaeronea. Writing from the vantage point of 1642, the fate of civil
liberty was still threatened by Charles. As Marvell would do in his 'An
Horatian Ode', Milton rediscovers Horace's republican intentions inside
sonnet form.[70] Sonnet X echoes the praise of a man's official life in
Horace's *Odes*, 2.1.

The three sonnets on the heroes of parliamentary victory and the
republic, Fairfax, Cromwell and Vane, similarly resurrect Horatian
procedures. The sonnet to Fairfax, written in August 1648, repeats the
topos of the citizen republican general victorious over foreign rulers of
Odes, 1.35 and 2.20. The poem celebrates Fairfax's success in the Second
Civil War, and looks forward to an imminent peace when Fairfax will
become a leading guardian of virtue in a state once more reconciled unto
itself. Although it is unusually unknowing for Milton, this sonnet nonetheless contains the prophetic hint of Fairfax's retirement rather than his
redeployment as a senator. The 'false North displays/Her broken league'
is a reference to Scotland, and it was the need to defeat the Scots in the
summer of 1650 which led Fairfax to resign his command of the army.

As Milton gained political influence and insight through his
government post, so the sonnets became more directly engaged in real
politics. The sonnets addressed to Cromwell and Vane were
interventions penned in the summer of 1652 in the attempt of the more
extreme Independents – Milton, Vane and Roger Williams among them
– to win a greater degree of religious disestablishment and toleration than
the Committee for the Propagation of the Gospel considered appropriate
(see above, 267). Milton's closing lines in the Cromwell sonnet reiterate
in already well-known Miltonic language the need to escape from all
forms of bondage and custom:

> new foes arise
> Threatening to bind our souls with secular chains:
> Help us to save free conscience from the paw
> Of hireling wolves whose gospel is their maw. (ll.11–14)[71]

Vane is imaged as a senator, sagely determining courses for peace and
war, making the free state the time when panegyric is at its most effective
– not a piece of grovelling courtly flattery but a true piece of virtuous and
politically effective oratory.

Waller had compared Charles to Amphion in his 'Upon his Majesty's
Repairing of Paul's:

> He, like Amphion, makes those quarries leap
> Into fair figures from a confused heap;
> For in his art of regiment is found
> A power like that of harmony in sound. (ll.11–14)

The renovation of the west end with a classical portico ('Those state-obscuring sheds, that like a chain/Seemed to confine and fetter him [St. Paul] again;/Which the glad saint shakes off at his command', ll.20–22) is set within a framework where Charles as artist-king rebuilds the ship of the church. Such a poem was unwritable in the 1640s, but in the Commonwealth, the state itself becomes music fashioned from chaos. Marvell, who had already used some of Waller's imagery from this poem in 'An Horatian Ode', goes on to present Cromwell as a Commonwealth Amphion in the 'First Anniversary':

> Such was that wondrous order and consent,
> When Cromwell tuned the ruling Instrument,
> While tedious statesmen many years did hack,
> Framing a liberty that still went back,
> Whose numerous gorge could swallow in an hour
> That island, which the sea cannot devour:
> Then our Amphion issues out and sings,
> And once he struck, and twice, the powerful strings. (ll.67–74)

Marvell happily forgets until later in the poem the resentment which many supporters of the republic had towards the Protectorate, and carefully shows how Cromwell welds a republic (but it *is* now the Protectorate) together from separate elements, so that it is in line with the panegyrical strategy of 'An Horatian Ode'. Waller's 'A Panegyric to my Lord Protector' follows Marvell in its length – perhaps an instance of the need to apologise for the Protector, who emerges in both poems in the place usually occupied by the king. In Marvell, the Amphion comparison puts Cromwell beyond mere kingship, while Waller reuses images from his panegyrics for Charles I, this time incorporating war as the achievement, rather than war's deferral:

> So when a lion shakes his dreadful mane,
> And angry grows, if he that first took pain
> To tame his youth approach the haughty beast,
> He bends to him, but frights away the rest.
>
> As the vexed world, to find repose, at last
> Itself into Augustus' arms did cast;
> So England now does, with like toil oppressed,
> Her weary head upon your bosom rest. (ll.165–72)

On the other hand, Waller seems incapable of praising Cromwell as a

Thus Englished.

WHenas the *Belgick Lyoness* began
To roar, within the *British* Ocean,
She and her whelps then gaping after Game,
Themselves a Prey unto the Sea became.
She threatned MARE CLAUSUM out of date
To make, and sacred Rights to violate.
A horrid Dinn out of her thundring Jawes
She sent; the Beast was known too by her Pawes,
Fierce *Neptune* laid about him in the Sea,
Swinging his Mace; what Flesh and Blood, said hee,
Can this endure? Cease, *Belgian*, to provoke;
Cease to insult, and learn to bear the yoke.
Then th' *English Mastiff*, arm'd with rage and Right,
The *Belgian* Brute nobly assail'd by fight.
Both Parties close ingage, Cannons display
Horror and tempest; Both would win the day;
The quaking Shores in trembling fits did lie,
The azure Flood became a Purple-Die;
Here fearful Thunders crack, here Lightnings flie;
Fire makes the Sea to foam, Smoke cloud's the Skie.
Alas! What woful wreck must needs be there!
What horrible amazement! grief and fear
Where death, arm'd with a thousand shot, did sink
Men, and gave them a thousand draughts to drink.
The world seem'd topsie-turvie, and it's frame
Dissolv'd, hell broke loose, *Ætna* like belch't flame,
And made the Deep to boile. Fierce *Æolus*
And *Neptune* both gaz'd in a silent muse,
And stood amaz'd, with all the Nymphs divine;
The Fish seem'd pickled in their native Brine.
At length, the *Lyon* erest-faln, rent, and torn
By *English* Arms, hie's to her Den forlorn.
She grinn'd, and roar'd; but pray what hath she done
Worth all her noise? She's strip't, and whip't, and gone.

All haile fair *Britain*, Lady of the Sea,
Weilding it's Scepter by an ancient Plea.
Courage, make sail apace now, scour the Main,
And take the Sea's dominion once again.
And you ye brave * *Triumvirs*, let's reherse
Your rare renowned Acts in lofty verse.   * *The three English Generals.*
But thou poor piteous Town-talk MARTIN, go,
Goe prethee TROMP, let th' *Orange* Faction know
Their hopes are shatter'd like thy Ship and Saile;
Tell thine thy Fortunes in a woful Tale.
Tell th' *Hogens* all their Fortunes; Help's too late
For broken STUART from their broken State.   *From*

Figure 11 'Anglia Victrix' from *Mercurius Politicus*, 144 (17–24 March 1653).

king. To this extent, and unlike Marvell, his poetry has been seen as to some degree unresponsive to the Commonwealth, and still locked into the perceptions and preoccupations of an earlier age.[72] But Waller's parallel might have been meant deftly: just as Augustus' Principate succeeded a republic and claimed to embody its best virtues, so the Protectorate follows the republic. Charles II's famous comment that he wished Waller had written him as good a poem as he had for Cromwell could have been a jibe at a turncoat. It could also have been a genuine piece of judgement, but if it was, Charles might equally well have complained that Waller had written him the same kind of poem as he did his father. Waller's panegyric on Cromwell is a true commonwealth poem, while 'To the King, Upon His Majesty's Happy Return' reworks elements from the panegyrics to Charles and to Cromwell. In this sense, it was indeed no compliment, unlike Dryden's Restoration poem *Astraea Redux*.

Whether all defences of the Commonwealth government were republican or not (and many of them were not), there was still something which grew into a recognisable poetic language of the English 'free state'. During the first Anglo-Dutch War, Nedham (most probably) translated from Latin and published in *Mercurius Politicus*, 144 (17–24 March, 1653) a poem entitled 'Anglia Victrix' which becomes distinctly republicanised in its transition from Latin to English (see fig. 11). The painterly appeal of this poem, its elision of maps, allegory, realistic seascapes (a speciality in Dutch art) and classical marine *topoi*, is unmissable. The poem is in fact making claims to be part of a republican iconography, and this fits with other details which emerge from the past, such as the retention of Mantegna's 'Triumphs of Caesar' frieze from the royal collection (perhaps intended to reflect the Free State or Cromwell's glory) and Lely's solicitation of the Council of State for work in the early 1650s.[73]

Earlier versions of a republican poetic came from 'R. Fletcher' in *Mercurius Heliconicus* (Feb. 1651)[74] and *Radius Heliconicus: Or, The Resolution of a Free State* (1651; 28 Feb. 1651). Fletcher is possibly the poet who translated and published Martial's Epigrams in 1656, although the poetry appended in this volume would disqualify 'R.F.' from being a straightforwardly committed republican.[75] Nonetheless, the poetry is less troubled about the new order than is Wither's:

> Crownes were but gallant robberies at first.
> And Conquerors heroick theeves that durst
> Attempt the worlds inslaving, why should we
> Repine then to behold a Monarchy
> Rak'd up in dust? (*Mercurius Heliconicus*, 1, Sig. A2r)

There is a definite Machiavellian quality to this view of historical process. Fletcher's purpose is to show that equality is in the order of nature, for this is part of his argument to encourage people to take the Engagement Oath:

> All further why's ought in coelestial ways
> Will sinke your souls, and prove the Remoraes
> Of hop'd salvation. He which took our head
> From off our shoulders, has not banished
> Our Lawes with his departure. (*Ibid.*, 5)

Radius Heliconicus (a single sheet) focuses upon public life in the republic: 'Fame is the life of action'. The poem recommends, in a Miltonic way, a retrieval of ancient liberties from present blindnesses:

> Man hath a free
> Tenure and birthright of his libertie.
> Custome enslaves us all: Our fathers were
> Blinded, and we born heires of their feare.

The bondage of custom is described as a process of devious namings – original conquest is still domination, but it is called prerogative. The reasoning is neat, the syntax skilfully disposed within the couplet. Again, flight is figured as republican liberty ('we soar above/Such Sphears, own no Superior lesse then *Jove*') and nature has become a common property – rather more Diggerish than republican or Leveller. Fletcher tells his readers that their instincts should lead them to sense liberty internally, through their own exercise of reason and civility 'an inbred Justicer', and this points towards a civil religion. The vagueness of the poem would not make this incompatible with puritanism, but it does appear to point both to deism and stoicism.[76]

When the Rump Parliament was restored in 1659, republican praise poetry reasserted itself:

> What makes our Muses silent now to be
> In this great change? Were all for Monarchie
> Inspir'd and tun'd? *Athens* I'me sure free State
> Brought forth great Captains, as well men of pate.
> Your Fountain's dry, or else your great *Pan's* dead,
> Are all come life-lesse souls ha'ing lost your head?[77]

But in a tract of 1659 which mocked the Commonwealth government, and which was signed falsely by 'officers' in Chester under Major-General Lambert's command, the chief panegyrist of the Commonwealth, Payne Fisher, was ridiculed, exemplifying the low esteem of Protectorate hacks. The disjunction between epic fury and domestic diminishment is readily apparent:

That he do first exactly describe the Situation of the whole Country and it's Commodities, as Cheese &c. Then the temper and constitution of the inhabitants: Next, that he take fit similarities out of *Virgil*, *Homer*, *&C.* whereby to express the numerous Armies, their Courage, and Manhood in the onset; the number of blows given, and received; the Neighing and foaming of the Horses, the glittering of the Armour; how the sky look'd all the while the Conflict lasted; the nimbleness of the vanquisht, and the confidence they reposed in their feet. Also that he rouse up his Muse in a thundring *Panegyrick* to the prowess of the victorious Lord *Lambert*; and a woful *Elegy* on those his Enemies, whose hard fate it was to be kill'd alive: But in the last place, and that more especially, that he present the *Parliament* with a Thanksgiving Coppy of Verses on their multiplied successes?[78]

It is not hard to see why Fisher was so ridiculed. In Latin or in translation, his verse grates on the ear. The celebration of Cromwell's martial success does share many elements with Marvell's poetic language, but it was transparent even to contemporary tastes: 'Which you do seek *Charybdis* sad to fly,/And would put off the Rub of Monarchy'.[79] The verse can be blunt in its politicising too:

> Applauded by the righteous while he fights
> For the Republicks private rights
> And common too
> A Deadly scourge of Tyranny? And superstitious Vanity.[80]

It was probably just as well it was so blunt: Fisher's Latin poem *Marston Moor* (1650) was composed as royalist panegyric, yet was published, little altered, as parliamentarian. But the picture of Cromwell as mower is good, linking georgic virtue with apocalyptic power:

> Not much unlike a Husbandman, who goes
> Through all the fields, and with his Sickle mowes
> The riper Corne, and the first Grass for hay, . . .
> Where e're he comes making an open way,
> Alaies those Plants which did so glorious stand,
> Like to dead stubble, on the mowed land . . .
> So do those towring lightnings sadly cleere
> The place from Troopes, and make a *Vacuum* there.[81]

There was another way in which panegyric was also transformed in the Interregnum.[82] Cowley's *Pindarique Odes*, published in the 1656 collection, do not address any particular English figure – in fact the relationships upon which Pindaric models could be used are no longer there. With such an absence, the odes (especially the direct translations from Pindar) evoke figures of strength from the ancient world – Theron, Prince of Agrigentum, Chromius, son of Agesidamus. The energy of these poems lies resoundingly in the poetry itself, rather than in any relationship between Greek matter and English politics:

> To *Theron, Muse*, bring back thy wandring Song
> Whom those bright Troops expect impatiently;
>   And may they do so long.
> How, noble *Archer* do thy Wanton *Arrows* fly
> At all the *Game* that does but cross thine Eye?
>   Shoot, and spare not, for I see
> Thy sounding *Quiver* can ne're emptied be;
> Let *Art* use *Method* and good *Husbandry*,
> *Art* lives on *Natures Alms*, is weak and poor;
> *Nature* her self has unexhausted store,
> Wallows in *Wealth*, and runs a turning *Maze*,
>   That no *vulgar Eye* can trace.
>   *Art* instead of mounting high,
> About her *Humble Food* does hov'ering fly,
> Like the ignoble *Crow, rapine* and *noise* does love,
> Whilst *Nature*, like the sacred *Bird* of *Jove*,
> Now bears loud *Thunder*, and anon with *silent joy*
>   The beauteous *Phyrgian Boy*.
> Defeats the *Strong*, or'etakes the *Flying* prey;
> And sometimes basks in th'open *Flames* of *Day*,
>   And sometimes too he shrowds
>   His soaring *wings* among the *Clouds*.
>
> ('The Second Olympian Ode', st. 9)

These poems have been seen as engaging in covert praise, and by reference to the 'Old *Fraternal* quarrel of thy *Race*' calling up powers to sustain the Stuart line in future. But the commentary in the notes pulls the other way into more purely poetic considerations, and the poet repeatedly refers back to the fashioning power of his muse. The last line quoted above echoes the soaring Cromwell in Marvell's 'Horatian Ode' and the figure of the poet in Longinus' *On the Sublime*, but the political resonances of these texts do not appear in Cowley's poem. The non-panegyrical poems in the sequence have been seen as offering a cryptographical account of the possibilities of future redemption, the issue of accommodation with the Commonwealth, and the values of present friendship.[83] But even the least obscure poetry here shares with the panegyrics an interest in creativity and transcendency – the source and the end of this poetic energy. In this way, the *Pindarique Odes* represent Cowley at his most Marvellian, and the originality of his verse is enhanced by its freedom from the obligations of panegyric; obligations which so hindered Waller and Payne Fisher.

Elegy

On the face of things, elegy did not look to have survived the Civil War intact any more than panegyric did. The comparison between Henry King's touching, intimate, moving elegies written before 1640 (notably the famous *Exequy* on his wife [c. 1624]; also the elegies on Donne and Gustavus Adolphus) and the so-called elegies on Essex (really a satire), and the martyred royalist officers, Lucas and Lisle (really an unusual, rasping war poem) is startling.[84] But it would be wrong to suggest that elegy ended with the regicide, or shortly thereafter.[85] Rather, the death of the King sucked all elegiac energy into its own subject. Elegies on Charles went beyond the rules of the form and disbelief was a dominant theme. Elegies on others, especially those with royalist sympathies, tended to become infected with the huge grief required for the royal martyr. *Lachrymae Musarum* (1649), the collection of elegies for Lord Hastings, is the most famous example. And of course grieving for a king unjustly killed also becomes mourning for the passing of an era and a civilisation. The 1640s are littered with elegies on real and abstract subjects which ominously prophesy a cultural deluge. For Royalists, elegy attaches itself to everything, whereas even in death, an elegy on Cromwell tended to be panegyric (if it was not satire).

King's 'A Deep Groan at the Funeral of Charles I' written in March 1649, is, like its accompanying elegies an angry record of the desecration of the Church by Parliament and Puritans. But the opening lines are a real elegy. The sense of the unbelievable having happened, that there need be no withholding of emotional outpouring, is superbly communicated in a series of rising crescendos:

> Call for amazed thoughts, a wounded sense
> And bleeding Hearts at, our Intelligence.
> Call for that Trump of Death the Mandrakes Groan
> Which kills the Hearers: This befits alone
> Our Story which through times vast Calendar,
> Must stand without Example or Repair.
> What spouts of melting Clouds, what endless Springs
> Powr'd in the Oceans lap for Offerings,
> Shall feed the hungry Torrent of our grief
> Too mighty for expression or belief?
> Though all those moistures which the brain attracts
> Ran from eyes like gushing *Cataracts*,
> Or our sad accents could out-tongue the Cryes
> Which from mournful *Hadadrimmon* rise,
> Since that remembrance of *Josiah* slain
> In our *King's* murther is reviv'd again. (ll.1–16)

Hyperbole is understatement in this poem, but it bears conviction. Within two months of the regicide, successive editions of *Eikon Basilike* began to carry prefatory verse elegies.

Royalists were practised in producing elegies which, given the circumstances, could not sustain their traditional generic boundaries. In Oxford, 1643, William Web published *The Satyrick Elegie Upon the Execution of Master Nathaniel Tomkins*.[86] When such criminal activities, as Royalists claimed, occurred, there could be no true grieving. The greatest crime was of course the execution of Charles I. In 1649, an anonymous author published *A Flattering Elegie Upon the death of King Charles*. The subtitle reveals the true intent of the poem: 'the cleane contrary way'. 'Flattery', usually associated with courtly corruption, becomes the key word. The author cannot flatter the martyred monarch, but he will flatter those responsible for Charles's death. By the twelfth line, we realise that flattery really means damnation. The regicide is so momentous, it forces words into new definitions in order to meet the situation: 'I flatter none but such, and still I pray/ They may be blest the clean contrary way.' (ll.11–12) The elegy becomes a complaint against Parliament and puritanism, and the object of the King's dignity is temporarily lost in a scatological account of sectarianism and political sedition, before the poem returns to an extended analogy between Christ and the Jews and Charles and the English. The Devil has visited England and, unwell, has taken a purge:

> And from his gut beneath he vented out
> An ill look't vermine with a fiery snowt,
> Who as he squirted from's infernall Breech,
> It scalded him and made his Divelship screech.
> A mighty blackfac'd worme he eke did void,
> And those two have our happinesse destroy'd.
> And thus the Divels excrements did vent
> A cursed Army; and a Parliament.

A Salt Teare: Or, The Weeping Onion, At the Lamentable Funerall of Dr. Dorislaus (18 June 1649) takes the occasion of Isaac Dorislaus's funeral as an opportunity to expose the hypocrisy and cruelty of the regicides.[87] The poem presents a curious mixture of political caricature and animal satire:

> O how damn'd BRADSHAW quivers as he comes!
> And FAIRFAX groanes! And CRUMWELL bites his thumbs! . . .
> Here, went *Lieutenant-Generall* Crocodile,
> And's *Cubbs*, bred of the Slime of our Rich *Nile*.

The greater crime of Charles's execution hangs over the poem, and, in a version of Menippean metamorphosis, Dorislaus in hell suggests that his murder has been orchestrated by the Council of State in order to breed loyalty to the free state.

Elegies could be most indirect, but even here Fane preferred to write some of his most contentious verse in Latin. Some are even more removed but yet still apparently in the context. One of the most private examples here would be Richard Washington's manuscript elegy on Massinger which he wrote in 1650 on his copy of Massinger's *The Picture* (1630). Literature and literary hero-worship become (but it is not quite certain) the replacement for the lamenting of Charles:

> To the Memory of that all
> greate architect of Poetry
> Mr. Philip Massinger
> Most honourd friend thy picture as wee goe
> by th'age to some shall never patternd bee
> Apelles in his arte did all surpas
> but Massinger to thee he nothing was
> sterne Johnson [sic] and our smooth-tongued Shakespeare's Layes
> May crye them up but thou shalt weare the Bayse.[88]

In an elegaic publication on the regicide, *The Princely Pellican* (2 June 1649), one of the poems is claimed to have been written on the morning of the execution, 30 January 1649. In this poem the executed King becomes 'Albions Niobe', a weeping statue made in the poem, and shoring up a ruin for the future. Niobe is also the basis for the metamorphosis at the end of Marvell's 'Nymph Complaining', where the nymph imagines herself turning into a statue weeping for the death of the faun. The poem has been seen as a lamentation for the desecration of the church in the Civil War. *The Princely Rebellion* makes further royalist capital from Niobe. The most common biblical figure associated with Charles at his execution was Josias, instanced in *Jeremias Redivivus, Or, An Elegiacal Lamentation on the Death of our English Josias* (30 May 1649), attributed by Thomason to Walter Montague. Although Marvell's 'Unfortunate Lover' is now thought to refer to the newly unfathered princes, Charles and James, there is an embedded use of Josias in it.[89] Both classical and biblical *topoi* in the elegies were performing a function which the art of the Caroline court was achieving when Charles was alive. The masques, for instance, famous for amplifying the reputation of Charles as peacemaker and absolute power in the kingdom, *froze* the image of the King in order to glorify his earthly power. Now dead, not unrelated art forms turn the really frozen King (in *rigor mortis*) into pieces of literary memory for the future. So it might have seemed in 1649 to loyalists, the court and all it stood for was packed like ice into the elegy forever.

Perhaps the most startling form of elegy was the pastoral, yet at the same time very expected given the popularity of pastoral drama in the Caroline court. *Orpheus his descerpsion* is a manuscript poem copied by Thomason (E 541(8)), and placed in his tract collection in February 1649, in the month following the execution of the King. It laments the disappearance of Apollion (Charles I), and is notable for its studied poise, as opposed to the histrionics of other royal elegies. Regicide is written into the pastoral mode. Note how the action, the moment, of decollation is suspended into slow motion:

> See see wild Satyrs how they runne
> All smeard with Blood, what have they done?
> The Muses all in a rout do stray
> Phaebus hath flung his harpe away,
>   And heer's a Crowne
>   Comes tumbling downe
> The head rould after which it did weare,
> Whose Blood and plaints yet sad the aire.

The green world is burned, for the laurel tree of poetry has turned yellow, and in a time when day and night are reversed, divine alchemy performs the final transformation:

> And his fine beames to dust do turne
> According to that Art, whereby
> Nights may be day, by Chimistry;
>   So that calcind
>   Tho here hees shrin'd
> Hee may spring out in purer light
> And bee disvellupt from this Night.

Like the Niobe figure, the swain who speaks the poem imagines himself and his lover, Corinna, petrifying as they look at the royal monument, gaining an impression from it just as the sea makes the sand on the sea bed wavy. Such is the new poetry, without a court to patronise it.

Many elegies were not published in 1649 for obvious reasons of discretion, and many never found their way into print. The fact that so many elegies for Charles were published is remarkable in itself. In the world of manuscript poetry, in commonplace books and poetry collections, a flurry of elegiac writing is to be found. Some writers dated their compositions, or dated the poetry of others they copied into their commonplace books. A firmer loyalist man of letters than Christopher Wase (see above, 279) one could not find. In the manuscript book of his poems and letters, fears for the safety of Charles are expressed as early as

June 1648. A poem commemorating the coronation of the King is immediately followed by two extracts from Lamentations.[90]

The gamut of Caroline elegies did nearly as much as *Eikon Basilike* to establish the tradition of the Royal Martyr. Milton, who had been an excellent and innovative elegist, wrote none after 1640s, unless Sonnet XV 'On the late Massacre in Piedmont' is counted. His response to the regicide was to argue for the dignity of encorpsing Charles I.[91] Elegies, like panegyrics, were not voguish with republicans; the famous elegies to Cromwell are really panegyrical and they had to be so.[92] This was so even in the aftermath of the Restoration when Milton's sonnet on Vane was published in a volume commemorating his life in the face of his execution. But republican poets were sometimes touched by royal elegy, more subtly than *Eikonoklastes* was by *Eikon Basilike*. The anonymous *Somnium Cantabrigiense, Or a Poem Upon the death of the late King brought to London* (1649) attacked the royalist poet John Quarles's *Regale Lectum Miseriae: Or A Kingly Bed of Miserie* (1649), a volume featuring a dream poem, in which the dead king appears and speaks, and a classic regicidal elegy with a black block of ink printed on every verso against the text of the poem on the recto. *Somnium Cantabrigiense* satirises Quarles with a character poem, and then voices a dream poem through Quarles's persona, so that it is in a sense a republican elegy on the dead king. In this mock dream vision, which is related to Lucianic satire and Marvell's 'Tom May's Death', Quarles the dreamer is made to praise the free state and the New Model Army, while a sibyll prophesies England's freedom:

> This Troop besmear'd, with blood & dust thus cri'd
> *England* is free, great *Jove* be magnifi'd,
> And our just cause exaulted, thus they went,
> Untill they came, where sate the Parliament,
> And *England's Genius* in the midst enthron'd
> Whose Temples were with Verdant Laurell crown'd. (6)

The shouting soldiers wake up the poet whose elegy on Chalres that was supposedly interrupted by the dream is then disclosed. It is truly *awful* and, from the satirist's point of view, deliberately so. Royalist mock-elegy can be convincingly angry, but it never danced on a grave so irreverently: 'Could *Charles* expire, and yet not comet burne?/ . . . To tell the wandring world his fall drew nigh:/. . . expire,/Old loyall flames, which Subjects hearts should fire./O ye – O ye'. And the royalist elegist yawns into slumber to meet the extinction of his cause and his form.[93]

George Wither's *Westrow Revived. A Funeral Poem without Fiction* (1653) is equally unusual, and goes further than Milton in inventing a form. Thomas Westrow, fellow soldier, is mourned by Wither in four long verse cantos which are typically prophetic. In a sense, the poem

provides the resolution to the problem of 'what to do with grief' posed by
Milton in *Lycidas*. If that poem overcomes its anxieties concerning the
ultimate destiny of Lycidas through the prophecy of Peter against the
bishops, Westrow's death (and exemplary life) provides the inspiration
for Wither to establish an ideal of behaviour and state of mind from the
physical absence of the subject:

> I think, it may be inferred be, from hence,
> Things may be known, beyond the reach of *sence*,
> Without *corporall presence*; and that we
> Of *some things*, though but part of them we see,
> May know the rest: (7)

There is some relationship here with biographies of puritan ministers, but
Wither is effectively trying something very new. Indeed, the exemplary
characterisation bears some comparison with the exemplary presentation
of the Son in Milton's *Paradise Regained*.

Hostile propaganda suggested that the radicals had no time for the
civilisation of poetry, but the truth is very different. There are a number
of Leveller elegies, most of them lamenting the assassination of Thomas
Rainborough. Unlike the prophetic motif which works inside Wither's
elegies, Leveller elegy finds the genre a fit vehicle for the model of simple
patriotic virtue upon which so much Leveller propaganda relied. This
does not stop a playing upon the names of party as a means of expressing
Leveller values in W.G.'s elegy of 1649 on Susanna Harris, wife of
the Leveller soldier and journalist John Harris. Note also the joke on
Leveller publishing in small book formats:

> Within this scared Dust SUSANNA lies
> Obscur'd from *false-accusing-Elders* eies:
> Once *Independent*, as are they that be
> The *Servants* of *One-God*, and none but He.
> A *Leveller* in *Folio*, such an one
> As Lov'd to *Levell* an *Usurped-Throne*.
> A *Royallist* besides, (and here is all
> The *Sable* that attends her *Funerall*.)
> For, She her *Crown*, her *Country*, and her *Mate*,
> Preferr'd and *Fancy'd* more then *Earthly State*.[94]

So the propaganda function is never surrendered even in an elegy. The
reference to 'Usurped-Throne' is anti-republican, and the elegy concedes
in its coding the Leveller-royalist negotiations which took place in this
year. Indeed, it would seem that this elegy is making capital for the
Levellers from the popularity and political vitality of the regicide elegies,
quite unlike most of the Rainborough elegies, which argue that the

assassination (in October 1648) is a strong argument not to make a treaty with the King.

Most who had written elegies before the Civil War and the regicide wrote them differently afterwards. Marvell's mannered elegies on Villiers and Hastings become the Machiavellian panegyric on Cromwell. Henry Vaughan's two excellent war elegies (on R. W. and R. Hall) work within standard conventions of the praise of virtues untimely terminated, but his one Interregnum elegy, 'To the pious memorie of C. W. Esquire' of 1653, bears all the marks of his 'internal apocalypse' (see above 267–71), his response to the downfall of church and monarchy. The first poem (1645–6) shows this only towards its close, while the last (1653) is transformed throughout. In the middle comes a poem, written in 1648, which appears already to be under the emotional sway of the regicide, and balances imagining heroic martial feats with a transcendentalising vision. Wither ploughs the transcendental awareness of perfections and virtues back into practice, whereas Vaughan makes them the point of resolution, or rather, disappearance, complete with Virgilian suffix (*Aenerd*, 11.97–8):

> That we can only reach thee with the mind,
>   will not in this *dark* and *narrow glasse*
> Let thy scant *shadow* for *Perfections* passe,
> But leave thee to be read more high, more queint,
> In thy own bloud a *Souldier* and a *Saint*.
>
> —— *Salve aeternum mihi maxime Palla!*
> *Aeternumque vale!* ——
> (An Elegie on the death of Mr. R. *Hall*, slain at Pontefract, 1648
>   (ll. 70–77))

Royalist elegy versus republican panegyric: this seems to be the frame of poetic identity and dynamic in the 1640s and 1650s. Draper's study of the funeral elegy established continuities between Caroline elegy and the Romantic lyric. If he had considered panegyric too, he would have found republican and Whiggish migrations into elegy, as that tradition sustained itself during the eighteenth century – in imaginative hibernation, so to speak. But who can say what forms there would have been if the King had not returned? If the republicans in the Rump had prevailed in 1660, would there have been a return to the short-lived iconography of the early 1650s? Would heroic panegyric have returned, or would the compromise with inherited forms have continued? Would it have become progressively easier to praise the 'free state', or would patronised creativity have continued to be so disabling in these circumstances? The effect of the Restoration on poetry is so great that it is very difficult to imagine how things might have been.[95] I suspect that further innovations by Marvell, Wither and Milton in the arena of public poetry would have produced an entirely and excitingly different trajectory in English verse, as prophetic and visionary as anything Shelley would have admired or penned. History not being so obliging, Civil War and Interregnum occasional poetry leaves us with a genre dynamic in which imagined histories, identities and destinies are tested, revised and often extinguished.

CHAPTER 9

Satire: Whose Property?

Difficile est Satyram non scribere.
Juvenal, *Satire* 1, quoted in Marchamont Nedham,
The Great Accuser Cast Down (1657), title-page.

TRADITION HAS IT that the high age of satire began sometime shortly after 1660, and tradition is strong in the consideration of satire because comparatively few now read the genre, preferring to rely upon an assumption. Verse satire is supposed to have grown in achievement and capability (these assessments are usually concerned with matters of style) until the high days of Pope and the Scriblerians, when the powers of denigration were matched by the appropriate subject matter of a corrupt and materialistic national administration. This is, of course, not the only view, but even if we were to praise the civilised languor of Pope's *Imitations of Horace*, we would be committing ourselves to a view of satirical literature as a technical achievement, and to a social angle inherent in nearly all of this poetry of looking down from the pinnacle of lofty poetic musehood onto the ignorant, filthy and repulsive *hoi polloi* below us.

This version of literary history is wrong, and a result of the confusion of royalist sentiment with neoclassical taste. And yet it is still widely accepted. Restoration satire certainly had its origins in the satirical strategies developed by royalist pamphleteers in the 1640s.[1] The most enlightened recent study of the origins of eighteenth-century satire, ties Dryden, Oldham and Pope to Cleveland and Cavalier wits.[2] At its more impressive, high Restoration satire *is* a product of a revived royalist culture, but not only that.

There was a history before this familiar history of satire, a history which produced a satirical literature, and meanings of the word 'satire', which have been largely obscured by the Restoration itself. This is the history of some almost forgotten voices by which means puritanism and Dissent made itself felt. We can find this alternative view of satire in Dryden's preface to his poem *Religio Laici* (1682) as follows:

295

They who will consult the Works of our venerable *Hooker* . . . may see by
what gradations they [the Elizabethan Puritans] proceeded; from the
dislike of Cap and Surplice, the very next step was Admonitions to the
Parliament against the whole Government Ecclesiastical: then came out
Volumes in English and Latin in defence of their Tenets: and
immediately, practices were set on foot to erect their Discipline without
Authority. Those not succeeding, Satyre and Rayling was the next: And
Martin Mar-Prelate (the *Marvel* of those times) was the first Presbyterian
Scribbler, who sanctify'd Libels and Scurrility to the use of the Good Old
Cause. Which was done . . . (their serious Treatises having been fully
answered and refuted) [that] they might compass by rayling what they had
lost by reasoning.[3]

Dryden assumes that verbal abuse, notably the attacks on Bishops Bridges
and Cooper by Marprelate in the late 1580s, was a last ditch attempt by
the Puritans to fight dishonestly a battle which they could not win. So in
this history of satire, unlike the one of received literary criticism, satire
does not come from 'above', but from 'below', or 'those in opposition',
rather than from members of an establishment or an elite. Indeed, it was
the access of all parties to the representation of English 'popular culture'
– the world of syncretic folk beliefs, magic, simple astrology, carnival and
charivari – which made the circulation of satire on equal terms possible
(see also above, 26–32).[4]

Satire 'from below' was the most socially active (and dangerous) form
of discursive attack before 1640. Its combination of speech from a
position of abjection and its irreverence give it a quality which we have
largely forgotten how to read. This literary loss of memory was no doubt
aided by the prominence of views like Dryden's, and paralleled by the
prosodic veneer of post-1660 satire. Yet the Marprelate 'tradition', as it
should be called, played a crucial role in the establishment of religious
toleration during the 1640s, a feature which is fictionalised in its
literature. Moreover, as royalism failed, and its satirical voice changed
from bumptious ridicule to unconfident, spiteful bumbling, and as
puritan satire found that its own voice was becoming redundant, or
unacceptable in its own camp, so distinct satirical identities changed
hands through the medium of the printing press. Courtly and university
satire emerged from the privacy of manuscripts to become one of the
marks of royalist identity, while Royalists, including the influential
Cleveland, used the voices of radical Protestant tradition to strike at the
orthodoxy – by then the Parliament.

Marprelate Revived

'Martin Marprelate' was an Elizabethan Puritan (but not a separatist) who used humanist devices of jest to ridicule the Elizabethan church settlement in a series of printed personal attacks on bishops. The mode was salacious and popular, offending the Queen by becoming the reading matter of courtiers. Two men, John Penry and Job Throckmorton (the latter most probably the real author of the tracts), were executed for their involvement in the production of the tracts.[5] Authorship was indeed directly punishable in a society where one church and one church only belonged to a single state. The Marprelate tracts were and are great fun to read. Their jesting humour (related to that of the stage) is an offensive irreverence and a blasphemy to the language of the sacred, and the majestic language of the state. By the early 1640s, Marprelate had become a literary tradition and a legend of transgressive resistance, transforming the writing even of his enemies.

Just as the transprosed drama of the 1640s tended to ignore its immediate predecessors of the 1620s and 1630s in preference for allusion to and imitation of the famous plays of the 1590s and 1600s, so the controversial satire of the earlier 1640s played out the divisions of the Marprelate years. While some of the Marprelate tracts were republished in the 1640s, Thomas Nashe, who had risen to prominence by being hired to controvert Marprelate, reappeared not only as a style of abuse but as a *persona* in John Taylor's *Crop-Eare Curried, Or, Tom Nash His Ghost* (1644), an attack on Prynne. This is a clear example of the significance of *performance* in satire: the attack came from one person directed to another person, not to a set of ideas, in precisely the way that Dryden records. Indeed, 1580s puritan satirists, using the mixture of humanist and popular modes characteristic of Marprelate, generated a recognised mode of invectives and flytings.[6] The sense given in the printed puritan satire of a heavily dramatic function in the *persona* tells us much about attitudes which early modern people had towards controversial writing: it was really an extension of an orally delivered performance. And in its deeply irreverent jesting voice it was at its most transgressive. Satire was a form of cursing, a verbal utterance which was assumed to have magical properties. The laughter that satire released was a way for political and religious communities or community values to be sustained.[7]

In the late sixteenth century, Marprelate caused nearly as much offence to his own party, as he did to the bishops, and many Puritans were quick to dissociate themselves from his methods. Such reactions were still prominent even among radicals in the 1640s. The Independent Sidrach Simpson said in 1644 that the godly should be in the way of

Figure 12   Richard Overton, *A New Play Called Canterburie his Change of Diot*
(1641), title-page.

persuasion and exhortation to achieve their ends, not the malicious and
subversive 'calumny' of Martin. Marprelatish calumny is expressed by
Simpson as a many-headed monster as dangerous as the error-excreting
Papal dragon of *The Faerie Queene*:

> There are two too usuall errours in handling Controversies. One to make
> the difference voluminous and many-headed, that so it may appeare more
> horrid, monstrous and irreconcileable: the other to make the Opposites
> odious, by charging their reall or supposed faults upon their Tenents; for
> every man is glad to heare something against those they hate, and ready to
> believe it without any, or on very slight examination.[8]

But there was some consolation for the godly in laughter. When Lilburne
was interrogated for helping to distribute books by Leighton and Burton
in 1637, he was warned that they contained only railing (and were
therefore libellous) and no 'solid' matter. Satire, libel and pamphlet were
interchangeable words at the time.[9] Lilburne replied that Leighton so
feared for his personal safety at the hands of the bishops, that 'he made
that Booke to make himselfe merrie'.[10] When you are the object of
persecution, satire can lighten the burden of danger, and strengthen
personal resolve.

The person responsible for the resurrection of Marprelatean satire was
the General Baptist and later Leveller Richard Overton. Overton had
been responsible for many of the short pamphlet satires of Laud published
in the early 1640s, often with woodcuts which Laud himself noticed:
'base pictures of me, putting me into a cage, and fastening me to a post by

a chain at my shoulder.'[11] (see fig. 12). Fellow Levellers remembered
Overton's distinctive style:

> for the complexion of my Friend Mr Overtons pen, truly it commonly
> carries so much truth and reason in it, though somtimes in a Comick, and
> otherwhiles in a Satyrick stile, that I do not wonder you shun its
> acquaintance, and you did wisely by this touch and glance think to passe
> him by without provoking of him. (*WWW*, 406)

In the mid-1640s, the main force for religious persecution was not the
bishops but the Presbyterians, especially those in the Assembly of
Divines. It would therefore have been inappropriate to reinvent
Marprelate's *persona* in the 1640s since he had supported Presbyterianism
in the 1580s. Instead, Overton created 'Martin Marpriest', the 'son' of
Marprelate, in a series of brilliantly funny pamphlets between 1645 and
1647, the most famous of which is *The Araignement of Mr. Persecution*
(1645), and which satirically argued for a toleration of the sects.

Overton's Martin Marpriest is a more distinct figure of *Christian* folly
than his father, the title-page of one tract referring directly to the
relevant passage in Corinthians (Cor. 1.20).[12] The appropriation of the
folly motif links Marpriest more overtly with the Erasmian tradition of
reform by holy satire (*Moriae Encomium*), and Overton is equally
Erasmian in his use of rhetoric as a trope for religious deceit and
dishonesty. Persecution becomes an allegorically expressed force which
navigates its way by metempsychosis through different forms of post-
Reformation religion:

> Mr. Sound-judgement . . . found him [Mr. Persecution] at length
> amongst the Papists, under the name of Mr. Spanish-Inquisition; but the
> subtile Fox no sooner perceived their Authority, but shrunke out of his
> Roman Papall robe, and presently turned Protestant, clad with an English
> episcopal habit, under the name of Mr. High-Commission, but Constable
> Reward-of-Tyranny, with old Woefull-Experience, and honest Sound-
> Iudgement being acquainted with his trikes, made after him whereat he
> cast of[f] his Laune sleeves, Hoode, Typpit, &c. and forthwith, least of all
> trades should faile, became a zealous Covenanter, in the godly shape of a
> Presbyter, changing his name into Classical Presbyterie (a new cheat to
> cozen the world) and then Scholer like, as if it had been for a goodly fat
> benefice, in the twinkling of an eye jumpt out of Scotland into England,
> and turn'd a reverend Synodian, disguised with a Sylogistical pair of
> Britches (saving your presence) in Bocardo, and snatching a Rhetoricall
> cassock he girt up his loynes with a Sophisticall Girdle, and ran into the
> wildernesse of Tropes, and Figures, and there they had lost him, had it
> not been for the Spirits Teaching. (1)

In this highly spirited and much underrated writing, it is noteworthy that the closer we come away from superstitious and ritualised religion, the more words matter, so that the Holy Spirit, almost represented as the exclusive property of the sects here, is opposed to the vacuous wilderness of Presbyterian rhetoric. The method continues in Overton's Leveller tracts, such as *The Complaint* (1646). The proximity of Overton's *topoi* to John Taylor's in his attack on a particular Presbyterian, William Prynne, should also be remembered:

> I leave to *Prinnes* Logick to resolve, and reduce the Contradictory by *Impossibility*, which if he doe not in *Calerent*, he cannot escape doing it in *Bocardo*, where I leave him to read over his *Fleta*, it may teach him more Law and Conscience then to excuse the Rebellion in *England*, by a Rebellion in *Ireland* of their own making, as that is the best colour which yet this Brazen face can cast upon it.[13]

We are in fact in a world of carnival, charivari and barley break, which itself is related to medieval complaint. The allegorisation of different theological positions enables the evocation of a world of appetitive and bulbous comic buffoons that simultaneously reduces and makes more frightening (because so simple and impersonal) the threat of persecution. Mr Persecution has a gigantic hunger for tithes, greedily consuming all that is given to him, and while he ingests and consumes without restraint, censorship is hideously described as a plugging of all orifices, so that the sectarian is punished with massive constipation: 'to bloke up all passages, stop all mouthes, and fortifie himselfe round, he turn'd reverend Imprimatur'.[14]

The crowning success of Overton's strategy is his creation of a trial scene in which persecution is arraigned and punished in exactly the same way that a religious nonconformist would have been treated. By the same token, the voices of persecution are quoted from works of the heresiographers, especially Thomas Edwards and his *Gangraena*. But within this general framework is this carnivalesque world in which cosmic forces meet as comic yet potent forces. The technique goes beyond Marpriest in that it extends to the visual. Martin Marpriest is depicted as a Bull of Bashan (Ps. 22:12) tossing over his head as he writes a tract a Presbyterian divine (see fig. 13), while on the other side, Presbyterians and radicals are derided by presenting the former as a fool (this time a jester) riding the latter (as a donkey) in a use of the skimmington ride. The details are interesting: Marpriest has books on his shelves, stressing the learned respectability of the radical cause (and pointing to a central aspect of Leveller activity). The Presbyterian and the donkey-Marpriest both wear spurs, possibly because they are both being presented as idiot knights and braggart warriors, Quixotes of the tub.[15] The flux of identities made possible in printed satire also achieves more than the dramatic roots of these characterisations permit. Overton

Figure 13   Richard Overton, *A Sacred Decretall* (1645), Sig. *2r.

creates the figure of Sir John Presbyter as the major *miles gloriosus* to attack (and the source of very many imitations in the Civil War decade). But in successive pamphlets, Sir John is metamorphosed into a baby with one of the chief Presbyterians, John Bastwick, and the Scot, Jockey, as his godfathers, and the Whore of Babylon as his godmother, an inverse parallel to Marpriest's own genealogy. He is given a 'corall' or teething ring, to stifle his miserable wailings, the 'corall' representing the Ordinance of Tithes passed by a Parliament in which the Presbyterians had considerable influence. In an arbitrary and destabilising way, characters rename each other with little warning and no apparent reason. Overton is in fact representing the calumniation process going on in front of us within the pamphlets, turning his own sectarian abjection into sceptical derision.

Overton's Marpriest tracts were partly motivated by the hostile response accorded to his defence of the mortalist heresy, *Man's Mortallitie* (1643). Another man of letters with radical religious ideas, whose treatment by the heresiographers encouraged him to resort to satire, was John Milton. The negative reception of *The Doctrine and Discipline of Divorce* (1643) famously brought forth Milton's poems in favour of religious toleration, and against the Presbyters, as well as *Areopagitica*. Earlier, in the anti-episcopal tracts, Milton used Marprelate's techniques against the Bishops as Overton was to use them against the Presbyterians.

The final divorce tract, *Colasterion* (1645), is distanced from the other tracts, coming, unlike them, after the publication of *Of Education* and *Areopagitica*. *Colasterion's* roughness and spite struck contemporaries. Writing to Richard Baxter in September 1659, William Mewe recalls how, although requested by the Assembly of Divines to answer *The Doctrine and Discipline of Divorce*, he was scared into silence by Milton's 'Scurrilous Fiercenes' in *Colasterion*.[16]

Colasterion is many kinds of satire: anatomy, Marprelatish jesting, and 'rough *Sotadic*'. In fact, at the end of the tract, after a sustained, contemptuous dismissal of an opponent, Milton threatens: 'to curle up this gliding prose into a rough *Sotadic*, that shall rime him into such a condition, as instead of judging good Books to bee burnt by the executioner, hee shall bee readier to be his own hangman' (*CPW*, II.757). Milton threatens scurrilous verse (perhaps of the Cleveland-Walker-Taylor variety), so as to induce suicide in his opponent. But in fact, the 'gliding prose' has contained just as much Sotadic, and as we know, if *Colasterion* did not induce real suicide, or even textual suicide, it did cause one instance of textual infertility – William Mewe *was* frightened into silence.

In the earlier *Animadversions*, Milton addresses the same context as Overton does, although perhaps also with an eye on the court as well as Lambeth Palace. He approvingly cites Bacon's remark that satire against the bishops by Puritans was suppressed, but not vice versa, so that there is already for Milton a sense of an unbalanced satirical tradition created by episcopal and royal censorship. Satirical anatomising is introduced as the discourse which reveals corruption, once liberty of the press is permitted. Milton is being polemically wise in this tract, for he sees satire as a democratic replacement for the kind of moral surveillance conducted by disguised princes on their people.[17] In a nascent way, Milton is showing how the free circulation of books becomes the morally honest force in a free state, and for this reason, satires must be sharp and not toothless:

Who could be angry therefore but those that are guilty, with these free-spoken, and plaine harted men that are the eyes of their Country, and the prospective glasses of their Prince? But these are the nettlers, these are the blabbing Bookes that tell, though not halfe your fellows feats. You love toothlesse Satyrs; let me informe you, a toothlesse Satyr is as improper as a toothed sleekstone, and as bullish. (*CPW*, I.670)[18]

This strategy reaches its imaginative zenith in *An Apology against a Pamphlet* (1642) (*CPW*, I.914–17), where Milton replies to the reply to the attack on Joseph Hall in *Animadversions*. Section 6 is structured as a jesting anatomisation and mocking textual charivari in Marprelate's manner. Milton returns to Hall's claim to be the first English satirist, and argues that the 'toothless satyrs' were inferior to Latin, Italian and English medieval satires. He clinches his argument with a typical piece of genre-bending, emphasising the heroic nature of satire – its risk-taking nature – as opposed to 'toothless' ineffectiveness or the smug sneer of early Cleveland:

> a Satyr as it was borne out of a *Tragedy*, so ought to resemble his parentage, to strike high, and adventure dangerously at the most eminent vices among the greatest persons, and not to creepe into every blinde Taphouse that fears a Constable more then a Satyr. (*CPW*, I.916)

The author of the *Modest Confutation*, Hall's defender, is represented as a hopeless Polonius crying out from behind an arras, while Hall himself is pictured as senile. Milton says that he first found Hall young and then, because of the poor quality of his satires, 'desperate', the subject matter indecorously low: 'the ordinary subject of freshmens tales, and in a straine as pittifull' (*CPW*, I.915).[19] Neither does Milton stop to use bawdry in his attack. Innuendo and bawdy references are all Hall and his ally are worth, but Milton appears to be implying that real satire is above that. Indeed, where Overton returned to Marprelate in 1645, in the same year Milton had reverted to ressurrecting older forms of satire (the threatened 'rough *Sotadic*'), just as his entire literary enterprise became uncompromisingly classical in its republicanism. The habit would be seen in an extended form in the satire on Charles I in *Eikonoklastes* (see above, 16–18).

Overton's allegorical vilification was soon imitated by those hostile to Independency and the sects:

> My body I give to the earth, which I ordained to be wrapped or shrouded in twelve sheets of paper, sewed together, taken out of the books heretofore written by my dear sonnes, to wit, *The Arraignment of Persecution*, *Bloudie Tenent*, and *Comfort for Believers*. My coffin to be framed by my dear son and long-breathed preacher, Ives the box-seller, whose christian name I shall not nominate, for that I conceive he never had any. Then, my obsequies to solemnize with all lustre, thus: my body to be borne, from Guildhall to Paull, by six of my deare sonnes, the

expounders of God's word, to wit, *Wiet*, the cobbler; *Sammon*, the shoe-maker; *Tue*, the girdler; *Lambe*, the soape-boiler; *Hawes*, the broker; and *Hobson*, the taylor. Mr. Burton, Mr. Knowles and Mr. Simpson I ordain as chief mourners, to follow the hearse. *Mr. Goodwin* and *Mr. Saltmarsh* before the corpse, and then the whole rabble of my deare children to follow howling like wolves, chattering like pies, and houting like owles.[20]

Also influential was Overton's travesty of Cromwell as a bull – a representation which signalled Leveller writing to contemporaries, and which was imitated by Nedham in *Mercurius Pragmaticus* (see above, 68–9). The image also had astrological connotations (Cromwell was a Taurus), as well as invoking the winged bull in theatres, and bear-baiting: an image sufficiently widespread to enter the dream-worlds of Fifth Monarchists.[21]

Satire and 'Popular Culture'

In his eclectic exploration of popular culture and its socio-economic roots in seventeenth-century England, David Underdown fixes upon these kinds of sparring figures as representations of 'real' popular culture.[22] But of course they are nothing of the kind since they belong already to the culture of print. The burgeoning culture of the news becomes the context of, and the concern within, the Marpriest satires and others like them. There seems to have been an initial outburst of news interest and publication during Charles I's disastrous war against the Scots in 1639. In Overton's earliest attempt to revive Marprelate, a tract called *Vox Borealis* (1641), signed by a persona called Margery Marpriest, the figure of the 'spy' (agent of military intelligence) is adopted as the voice of mediation. The 'spy', of course, often had to maintain a false identity, in order to pass between lines, and so becomes a manifestation of the way in which the communication of news is almost implicitly connected with disguise. Can you trust what you read? To a degree that is still not appreciated, there is no clear division between satirical stance and news authority. This, coupled with no previous experience of a free press, provides the conditions of flux in which Civil War satire flourished.

One element turned to satirical use was character writing, imagined by *Mercurius Britanicus* as a continental infection. Associating such news with the Dutch made it seem inherently to do with republics, free speech, confused systems of authority and religious toleration: 'The first *originall sin* in this kind was derived from the *Dutch*, and from thence this received (though not its first being) its maine *subsistence*, when the suckling *Mercurie* was scarce able to stand *high-lone* without their help.'[23] *The Character of a Cavaliere* (1647) is an example of the mode operating for the Parliament.

In this context, the elements of popular culture central to Underdown's account become so many appropriations by the culture of the printed pamphlet. Royalists are equally capable of deploying the 'carnivalesque' body:

> Within this House is to be seen
> Such a Monster as hath not been
> At any time in England, nay
> In Europe, Affrick, Asia:
> 'Tis a round body without a head
> Almost these three yeares, yet not dead.
> 'Tis like that beast I once did see
> Whose tail stood where the head should be:
> And (which was never knowne before)
> Though't want a head, it has horns good store . . . [24]

What is crucial here is our definition of 'popular'. As soon as a purportedly popular image became part of print culture it leaves behind the oral, perhaps preliterate, and behavioural reality which is the context for the customary sense of 'popular'. But it is never entirely unpopular: the modes of inversion function to give controversial writing the status of the clash of bodies so typical of what we know as the textual representation of the popular (instanced in the famous work of Bakhtin on Rabelais).[25] So, ecclesiastical debate is portrayed as a kind of Punch and Judy show (puppet theatres actually survived the closure of the theatres), with Sir John as a ridiculous Hercules with his club, or like a version of the tyrant Nero.[26] Some of the Digger pamphlets used scatological carnivalesque to ridicule political and judicial ceremony: lords and judges, all fools, compete to be blessed by the king's fart.[27] But at the same time, there is a socially downwards dissemination of satirical forms which have their origins in classical literature, and many which would have been unknown were it not for their discovery by the humanist enterprise. Thus, one very appropriate and popular form was the Lucianic journey to the underworld, the Menippean satire which becomes through Sir Thomas More's translations an adjunct to the folly tradition. As Ben Faber has shown in his interesting work on popular satire, Homeric and Lucianic patterns were used by Royalists and Parliamentarians to form a visual and verbal universe of popular satirical significations.[28] So, both the fervent Royalists John Taylor and Martin Parker, and the Parliamentarian and Independent Henry Walker, happily denigrated each other in these Menippean terms, making Homeric and

Lucianic imagery part of the universe of 'popular' representation, almost imperceptibly merged with traditional memories like the mouth of Hell.

This kind of satire, of which Marprelate was undoubtedly the most famous exemplar, defamed the target of its attack. Marprelate's crime was that he had insulted not just the Bishops, but also the Queen, in her role as head of the church. To that extent, satire was widely regarded as libel, and associated with affronts to the dignity of the monarchy. This was the case in the 1580s and 1590s, but the attitude prevailed in the 1640s and 1650s, and was sustained by that republication of documents from the Marprelate controversy. Libel as offence or as generic tag could be applied to many different kinds of controversial publication, but it seems to have had a special association with satire. While the authority and dignity of Queen Elizabeth was more than enough to make satires appear fragile and imperilled (but less so towards the close of her reign), satire as libel was obviously more powerful in a context of political turmoil. Satire was encouraged by, and played a significant role in, the defamation of *all* kinds of authority. It is notable that the monarch was not the object of satirical attack by Parliamentarians, not perhaps until the defence of the republic in the early 1650s.

The development of a recognisably royalist mode comes with the verse of John Cleveland, and Cowley's anti-puritan satires. Yet Cleveland's 'The Hue and Cry after Sir John Presbyter' (written ?1646–7; published 1649) borrows very directly from Overton's portrayal in words and in woodcut.[29] Here, the details become almost too sharply defined:

> With Hair in Characters, and Lugs in text;
> With a splay mouth, & a nose circumflext;
> With a set Ruff of Musket bore, that wears
> Like Cartrages or linen Bandileers,
> Exhausted of their sulpherous contents
> In Pulpit fire-works, which that Bomball vents;
> The *Negative* and *Covenanting* Oath,
> Like two Mustachoes issuing from his mouth. (ll.1–7)[30]

This is not really popular verse; it's too mannered and curt, a feature which almost resists its satirical purpose. But it occupied the public space in which the definition of 'popular' consists. Davenant had published his satirical mock-epic 'Jeffereidos' (written in 1630) in the *Madagascar* volume (1638), thereby freeing that satire from its courtly and diplomatic context.[31] Cleveland's poems circulated first in London in manuscript. They were then published originally in pamphlets made up of a composite of satirical forms: verse, prose and woodcuts. In this way, refined wit moves 'down' into the popular space. There is a *sprezzatura* at work as the catalogue of ridiculous and stupid drooling pictures of the Presbyter moves surely towards the final reality of puritanism: a senseless

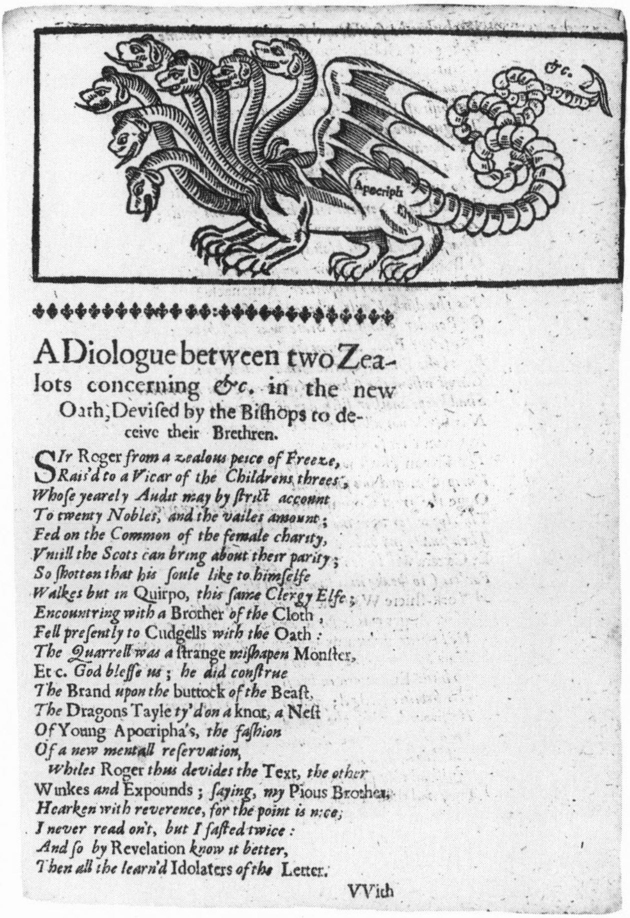

A Diologue between two Zealots concerning &c. in the new
Oath, Devised by the Bishops to de-
ceive their Brethren.

SIr Roger from a zealous peice of Freeze,
Rais'd to a Vicar of the Childrens threes,
Whose yearely Audit may by strict account
To twenty Nobles, and the vailes amount,
Fed on the Common of the female charity,
Vntill the Scots can bring about their parity;
So shotten that his soule like to himselfe
Walkes but in Quirpo, this same Clergy Elfe;
Encountring with a Brother of the Cloth,
Fell presently to Cudgells with the Oath:
The Quarrell was a strange misshapen Monster,
Et c. God blesse us; he did construe
The Brand upon the buttock of the Beast,
The Dragons Tayle ty'd on a knot, a Nest
Of Young Apocripha's, the fashion
Of a new mentall reservation,
  whiles Roger thus devides the Text, the other
Winkes and Expounds; saying, my Pious Brother,
Hearken with reverence, for the point is nice;
I never read on't, but I fasted twice:
And so by Revelation know it better,
Then all the learn'd Idolaters of the Letter.

                      VVich

Figure 14   The Decoy
Duck (1642), Sig. A4r.

belching sound. Indeed, in the quotation which follows, it may well be that Cleveland is both using and abusing Overton's *Martin's Eccho* (1645) in that the sectarian is as bad as the Presbyterian, however good his satire:

> Then what Imperious in the Bishop sounds,
> The same the *Scotch* Executor rebounds;
> This stating *Prelacy*, the *Classick* Rout,
> That spake it often, ere it spake it out.
>   So by an Abbyes Scheleton of late,
> I heard an echo supererogate
> Through imperfection, and the voice restore
> As if she had the hicop or'e and or'e. (ll. 39–46)[32]

Money, hunger and sexual innuendo are standard devices in anti-clerical satire, but Cleveland's verse seems cleverly and programmatically royalist. There is no sense of defeat or impotence (as we shall see in other late Cavaliers), but rather a reserve which emphasises rage through restraint: 'How could successe such villanies applaud?/The state in *Strafford* fell, the Church in *Laud:*/ The twins of publicke rage adjudg'd to dye.'[33] Most readers of Cleveland do not realise that his poetry was published as part of the very politically directed and enormously popular prose satire, including *The Character of a London Diurnall* (1647) and the anti-rebellion tracts on Wat Tyler.

But whatever Cleveland's intentions, there is also an uncertainty in his verse which hints at its own unoriginality. This is because 'there is no style or form which will not be capable of being used by the enemy.'[34] No genre or form is stable in its usage; all statements one might make could be mimicked or ventriloquised by the other side. So the popular jesting or ballad-singing voice adopted by Nedham whether writing for Parliament in *Mercurius Britanicus*, King in *Mercurius Pragmaticus*, or republic in *Mercurius Politicus*, becomes a frighteningly unstable and slightly insane presence evoking the power of the public presses, in addition to the menace of the enemy.

Instabilities of meaning like this were more likely when there was ideological confusion – such as in the mid-1640s, when the puritan and parliamentary consensus had started to fissure. Early 1640s satire was different. 'A Dialogue between Two Zealots', first published in *The Decoy Duck* (1642), might employ apocalyptic imagery in words and pictures (see fig. 14), but its depiction of a puritan minister is unmistakable:

> While *Roger* thus divides the Text, the other
> Winks and expounds, saying, My pious Brother,
> Hearken with reverence; for the point is nice,
> I never read on't, but I fasted twice,
> And so by Revelation know it better
> Then all the learn'd Idolaters o'th'Letter. (ll.17–22)[35]

Similarly stable in their meaning were Abraham Cowley's two verse satires *The Puritans Lecture* (1641–2) and *The Puritan and the Papist* (1642–3), the former using a singular Juvenalian voice of denunciation, the latter a Horatian dialogue of mutual recrimination.[36] Typography is the focus of derision, since Cleveland satirises here the 'Et Cetera' Oath, taken in the Convocation of 1640. Many objected to the hollowness implied by the avoidance of naming which occurred when the '&c.' was used as a contraction of the printed oath. Cleveland associates this reductive knavery with puritanism. The first published version printed 'et cetera', thereby ruining the effect of the precise '&c.' which had been used in the earlier manuscript versions. The final verse paragraph has the zealots performing a drinking song, which makes them sound like Cavaliers, thereby reiterating the potential for confused identities, although here the drinking song appeals exactly to Cleveland's most sympathetic readership. The final couplet has the '&c.' implying the final disappearance of sense into alcoholic oblivion: 'While all that saw and heard them joyntly pray,/They and their Tribe were all &c.' (ll.61–2).[37]

The tradition of *Epistolae obscurorum vivorum* is relevant here in Cleveland's zany naming games, to the extent that we do question whether 'The King's Disguise' (written in 1646, published in 1647) is really a satire. It is equally a panegyric or an elegy (see above, 276–94). It seems at first as though the speaker resents the King for alienating his sovereignty in a disguise, but then we learn that the disguise itself – outwardness with no inner truth – is a capitulation to the discursive trappings of Parliament, the 'self-denying Ordinance'. Thus, the King's sad predicament is an occasion for a characteristic satire of appearances. The King has been disguised by the constraints of parliamentary words (for the London diurnals are in Cleveland's sights) and New Model Army power. His disguise is verbal indecency, so that the unfortunate and unjust predicament becomes the ridiculous parody of regality in the satire itself:

> A Libell is his dresse, a garb uncouth,
> Such as the *Hue* and *Cry* once purg'd at mouth.
> Scribling Assasinate, thy lines attest
> An eare-mark due. (ll. 71–4)[38]

But in achieving this manoeuvre, Cleveland denies satire or 'wit' to the enemy.

'Smectymnuus, or the Club Divines' (? *c.*1642) repeats the devices of 'The Two Zealots', but this time emphasising the monstrosity of the Puritans. Cleveland uses the elements of represented 'popular culture', relocated in the garish belittling world of religious and political faction. He had achieved a complete language in fact for describing Presbyterian activity, as 'The Mixt Assembly' shows:

> A Jig; a Jig: And in this Antick dance
> *Fielding* and doxy *Marshall* first advance.
> *Twiss* blowes the Scotch pipes, and the loving brase
> Puts on the traces, and treads Cinqu-a-pace.
> Then *Say and Seale* must his old Hamstrings supple,
> And he and rumpl'd *Palmer* make a couple.
> *Palmer's* a fruitfull girle, if hee'l unfold her,
> The Midwife may finde worke about her shoulder.
> *Kimbolton*, that rebellious *Boanerges*,
> Must be content to saddle Doctor *Burges*. (ll.67–76)[39]

The lesson would be carried into the 1650s, where Cleveland's influence, as after 1660, was considerable.[40]

But where the Marpriest writers, and in his own way, Cleveland, seem purposefully and singularly directed towards the denigration of the enemy, satirical verse became self-satirical and self-destructive within royalist culture. The cause of this may have to do with military defeat itself. If the product of the cavalier poets was continuous with their behaviour itself, Suckling's cowardice in the Bishops' War became a celebrated mishap among royalist sympathisers. What should have been clear satire very nearly becomes panegyric as Cromwell's boldness (in this instance, Pride's Purge) cannot but be admired. In any case, for many loyalists, it was difficult to tell whether Parliament or Cromwell and the Rump was the worse evil:

> Let Faux his Powder-Plot amaze no more;
> Since one Breath blew the Howse out of the Doore.
> I need not bid you wonder (Times to come!)
> A souldier spake, A Parliament was Dumbe.
> Silenc'd It was Brave Generall by Thee:
> Well may'st Thou boast of Christian Libertye,
> For free Christ's Power did never more Increase,
> Then when He made the Devils hold their Pe[ace].[41]

Wit became a sign of royalist affection and distraction, and perhaps the most famous circulating verse in this respect was that of Sir John Mennes and Dr James Smith, collected in *Witt's Recreation* (1641) and *Musarum Deliciae* (1655). Court poetry, perhaps as polished and mannered as Ben Jonson's, did the work of street ballads, or alehouse entertainment. Mennes and Smith met regularly in a kind of drinking club to compose these songs and lyrics, the activity of which is figured in *Witt's Recreation* as hordes of dancing satyrs.[42] The epigram is claimed as quintessential for such revelry: 'Epigrams are like Satyrs, rough without,/ Like Chesse-nuts Sweet, take thou the kernall out.' The kernel in Samuel Sheppard's case is to make Leveller arguments for popular government work for Royalists in a witty reconsideration of the body politic metaphor. The compression of the epigram is particularly effective in disguising commitment:

> You are the braine, the Liver and the Heart,
>   Wee are the Hands
> Of this great Body, and the Vitall part,
>   The Feet whereon it stands,
> The Bones, and Bulke, which must the Burthen beare,
>   Therefore without offence
> With you wee (some) may claime an equall share,
>   'Specially in the Common Sence.[43]

By the mid-1650s, the demands of the market for 'drollery' verse were irresistible: 'Plain Poetry is now disesteem'd, it must be Drollery or it will not please'(Sig. A3r). As late as the mid-1650s (although it had probably been composed beforehand), Suckling as braggart warrior still seemed a cause for railing celebration:

> when the Scots Army came within sight
> And all men prepar'd to fight a
> He ran to his tent, they ask'd what he meant,
> He swore he must needs go shite a . . .
>
> To cure his fear he was sent to the Rere,
> Some ten miles back, and more a,
> Where he did play at Tre trip for Hay
> And nere saw the enemy more a.[44]

The habit of turning to the involvement of literary figures in the fighting sets up a negative critical perspective which looks forward to Rochester's attacks on Dryden, if not to Dryden's attacks on Shadwell and Pope's on Grub Street. In this respect Mennes is merciless, eliding Davenant's venereal disease (by which he lost most of his nose) with the events of his capture by the Parliament:

> Soon as in *Kent* they saw the Bard,
> (As to say truth, it is not hard,
> For *Will* has in his face, the flawes
> Of wounds receiv'd in Countreys cause)
> They flew on him, like Lions passant,
> And tore his Nose, as much as was on't.[45]

Sir John Denham also revealed his versatility by writing a series of ballad-drolleries. 'News from Colchester Or, A Proper New Ballad of Certain Carnal Passages betwixt a Quaker and a Colt, at Horsly near Colchester in Essex' is typical of its kind in taking as its subject the sectaries (in this instance the Quakers), and associating religious enthusiasm with unnatural or exaggerated libido.[46] The associations of madness are enhanced by using 'Tom of Bedlam' as its tune, while the jauntiness of the verse and the references to Christmas point up festive cavalier and royalist culture. The joke at the Quakers' expense becomes theological: we are made to realise that the Essex Quaker who wanted to marry a mare (so the ballad proclaims) literally makes a new Sodom (a derogatory Quaker name for Rome) in Colchester.[47]

Denham's more obviously 1650s poems and his satires of the previous decade are also documents of exile, and their satirical energies are directed towards a voicing of that exclusion. Exiles are depicted in conversation (Sir John Pooley and Thomas Killigrew), in anti-puritanical, body-affirming antics ('To Sir John Mennis being invited from Calice to Bologne to Eat a Pig'), and on the disgrace of royalist emissaries in the early 1650s ('On Mr. Tho. Killigrew's Return from his Embassie from Venice, and Mr. William Murray's from Scotland'). Hilarious railing at one's comrades seems to function as a celebration of the cavalier ethos:

> But who says he [Killigrew] was not
> A man of much Plot,
> May repent that false Accusation;
> Having plotted and penn'd
> Six plays to attend
> The Farce of his Negotiation.[48]

Denham knew how to achieve similar effects back in the early 1640s. 'A Speech against Peace at the Close Committee' (1643) is the voice of John Hampden threatening to destroy monarchy and church for the sake of personal gain. That in itself is unremarkable, but the tune used is 'I went from England', so that the author behind the mask signals his own departure from the scene. Satire and exile become delicately inter-involved, a surprising feature given the crudeness of the satirical surface.

This kind of bantering verse, irritating to read in any number above five, and sub-libertine in flavour, unhealthily inspects its own melancholy in myriad forms and sub-genres, Mennes's epigrams representing in their closure a forerunner of the mock-heroic couplet. This is in contrast to the triumphant mock-elegies, characters and litanies of the imprisoned Sir Francis Wortley.[49] Mennes is often politically indirect, which is not surprising: he had little to be cheerful about. On the other hand a drinking song put into the hands of a Parliamentarian or Puritan is a more sinister instrument. 'Keep thy head on thy shoulders' was written by John Lookes to celebrate the execution of the Earl of Strafford (1641):

> Though Wentworth's beheaded,
> Should any Repyne,
> Thers others may come
> To the Blocke beside he:
> Keepe thy head on thy Shoulders
> I will keep mine;
> For what is all this to thee or to mee?[50]

When mimicry enters the repertoire of techniques in this verse, its potential changes. Impersonation is used in *Rump Songs* (1662) to ridicule Parliamentarians: 'Next, for the State, we think it fit/That Mr. Pym should govern it,/He's very poor.'[51] The self-ridiculing speakers are the result of aggressive treatments which appear to us as less morally comfortable than the seemingly righteous violence of Marprelate and

Overton. These imitated voices become the royalist version of the many-voiced monster of democracy in Thomas Jordan's 'The Rebellion':

> Come Clowns, and come Boys, come Hoberdehoys,
> Come females of each degree,
> Stretch out your throats, bring in your Votes,
> And make good the anarchy.[52]

Alexander Brome, no relation of the playwright Richard, produced a series of songs and verse satires which set the cavalier ethos firmly on edge, without any recourse to a puritan mode. Definition of viewpoint here is achieved often by pairs of songs addressed to each other, and by unusual identifications. 'The Leveller', for instance, is sung by a cavalier persona who does not reveal directly any known Leveller opinions. He tries to make friends with the Leveller, supposing that the Leveller wants everyone to have titles and wealth, as opposed to virtue being proven by merit. Is this a real Leveller, or the use of the name as a tag for something else? And having disabused his companion, who is unfittingly 'mellow', the speaker dissociates himself from his position of apparent civic virtue in order to praise a pleasure orgy of drinking and tobacco. All viewpoints are suspended, and the ethos of retreat from thought and public affairs complete. Then in the next poem, entitled 'The Royalist's Answer', a royalist voice distinct from the speaker expresses the anti-rebel sentiments which we might expect in Cleveland's verse. This voice puts sectarians and radicals back into hierarchised categories:

> There's a necessitie
> That there should be degree.
> Where 'tis due we'l afford
> A Sir John, and my Lord,
> Though Dick, Tom and Jack,
> Will serve you and your pack,
> Honest Dick's name enough for a Digger. (ll. 20–26)[53]

Those rich enough to rule (here Brome makes reference to the sale of titles, and seemingly welcomes this invasion of the nobility by new money) ought to be given the reins of power; rulers are 'fools' in that they would take on such responsibility. So this Royalist is very much an 'I'm all right Jack' person, who seems to merge in the last stanza with the drinking speaker of the first poem. Brome is not trying to point up a common humanity by fusing what have been hitherto carefully maintained distinctions, but he is trying to make the song see through social divisions and reorganise society in the alcoholic terms demanded by one aspect of his culture. More recognisable is 'A Satyre on the Rebellion' which presents a world turned upside down; an innocent monarch usurped by power-hungry incompetents; and retribution waiting for the rebels. Brome's capability with classical satire (elsewhere he translates Persius) is brought out in his deadpan, deliberately bad line. Here, Sidney's claim that poets do not lie because they do not affirm anything is inverted because the 'truth' of the times and the potential of poetry do not match. Poetry is not the same as weeping: 'I'll only weep our misery and ruth,/I am no poet, for I speak the truth'(ll.7–8). The poem seems to deny its own virility, as if it had reached its own end:

> Urge me no more to sing, I am not able
> To raise a note, songs are abominable.
> Yea Davids psalmes do now begin to be
> Turn'd out of church, by hymnes extempore.
> No accents are so pleasant now as those
> That are Caesura'd through the Pastors nose. (ll.1–6)[54]

What could be the function of a satirical verse for Royalists once their cause had been seemingly irrevocably lost? The poetry of the 1640s had a cause to fight for, but in defeat, satire had no function of providing an overcoming of powerlessness because for most Royalists the culture of loyalism had drifted away. Absence typifies this verse, instanced in 'The World is Turned Upside Down', a poem on the banning of Christmas:

> The serving men doe sit and whine,
> And thinke it long ere dinner time:
> The Butler's still out of the way,
> Or else my Lady keeps the key,
> The poor old cook,
> In the larder doth look,
> Where in so goodnesse to be found.[55]

The poetry articulates dearth and famine as a figure of exhaustion, as much as drinking was a figure of oblivion.[56]

This was not the only response. Exposure to the court in France during the years of exile produced a more civilised and less despairing response to powerlessness. The writer of *Mercurius Curiosus* (12 Sept. 1654) gives the sense of the non-participating part of the political nation looking with amused disdain at the participating Commonwealth nobility: 'the ridiculous attempts of those who would govern this new-moulded Commonwealth by Antient principals, just as if they should bring the old memories of K. *Henries* days to our Accoutrements now a dayes.' The intrigues of the city and the gossip of women require a 'Gentile and Picquante *Raillery*', while Oliver's court is in need of a critical mirror in the form of court entertainment: 'I'm sure *Benserade* in his *Grand Ballet* (represented publiquely in the *Louvre*) could *raile* at all the Noblemen of the Court, and take no exception.'

In *A Satyr Against Hypocrites* (1655), Milton's nephew John Phillips seems to accept the new order (by then the Protectorate), and locates it at the centre of the social order before proceeding to satirise this puritanised society for general vices which are never wholly puritanical. It is almost as if (but never quite) the divisiveness of the previous fifteen years had been forgotten, and satire of the Joseph Hall variety could be written again. *A Satyr against Hypocrites* uses the kind of appearance-based, surface-obsessed modes of observation which Marvell had used when satirising the Dutch in 'The Character of Holland' (1653). Marvell had used pamphlet representations of English sectarians as well as of the Dutch to construct his satire, and Phillips returns the satire to one of its sources, although he also avoids the *ad hominem* attack which Marvell had engineered in 'Flecknoe' (?1645–6) and 'Tom May's Death' (1650).

If Phillips generalised the targets of satire, the republic itself, or those who wished to profit by it, used the satirical achievements of the previous decade to attack foreign enemies. Marvell's 'The Character of Holland', written in the hope of attaining office, and possibly at Milton's suggestion, uses the imagery developed to attack the sects and applies it to the Dutch in a dazzling and devastating surface of gross associations.[57] The commercial prowess of the Dutch is inverted, so that they are revolting in their consumerism. Marvell deftly uses precise pictorial scenes, as well as monstrous or scatological imagery; the combination of the two harks back to Cleveland's 'The Mixt Assembly', where he confesses the pictorial source of his disfiguring traduction: 'A strange *Grottesco* this, the Church and States/(Most divine tick-tack) in a pye-bald crew' (ll.6–7).[58]

John Collop claims to make poetry reborn in the collection of verse he published in 1655, *Poesis Rediviva*, directly alongside his essay *Medici Catholicon*. The reference to Browne in the latter title is a hint that, while poetry might be in need of new life for a new age, its author wore the literary colours of the previous twenty years. The heroes of the poet are Sidney, Donne, Scaliger (an authority on satire) and Grotius. *Poesis Rediviva* is a product of retirement, its mode is as melancholic as the other distracted royalist imitators of Burton, and its language as brittle and atomistic as Cleveland's: '*Democritus-like I laugh at the shittlecock world, and exquire the causes of the spleen in the beast, the Rabble.*'[59] Unlike Cleveland, Collop is moderately in favour of toleration, deriding the extremes of Roman Catholicism and sectarianism. Like Phillips and unlike Cleveland, Collop does not make his stand on behalf of embattled royalism, but writes in a state of conscious, never-ending, and therefore habituated, despair, as if the extinction of virtue in the Civil War is internalised in each individual as a parasite. This state of being is not mundane at all. The lurid colours and relocated infernal imagery serve to make the journey of Menippean satire part of an interior landscape:

the love of this Euridice *stung by the old Serpent, teaches me a descent into this home-bred hell we carry within us; where foul tormenting passions reside like furies; Lust is tied unto a Wheel, Care and Envy, Vultur-like, feed on the Heart and Liver, while Incontinence pours water into Sieves.*[60]

Poesis Rediviva is a carefully arranged series of poems, with a variety of subjects and genres included. The personality of the speaker-poet, so crucial to the articulation of satirical verse, is aware that he lives in an age of lesser poetic inspiration, but it is nonetheless an age of (at least pretended) inspiration. God's poetry is creation, and poetry is a divine gift, but unlike Milton's narrator, who has confidence enough to imitate God, Collop's speaker can only invoke a double awareness: 'Poets are Prophets, and the Priests of Heav'n:/ Though to Hels mimicks Idol Priests th'names giv'n.' The satirical poems in the collection are concerned with the politics of religion. Their master is Donne, and they resort to criticism through generalized roles and characters, as opposed to the very personalized kind of satire which Marvell had been able to supply. In 'A Defence of Curiosity: an unsettled mind in unsettled times; to weak Calumnie and proud ignorance', Collop suggests that it is precisely the times which produce such generalised treatments. It is not, however, the more obvious, most Cleveland-like poems, such as 'On the Masters of the Science of defence in Controversie', 'The Polemick Protestant D.', 'The Presbyter', 'Prophanum vulgus. The People', 'Sectaries', which are most arresting. Collop has a very unusual form of indirect and highly imagistic meditational verse, akin in some ways to Lovelace's 'grasshopper' lyrics. In 'The Jesuite', the speaker could have a pretentiousness of the kind we associate with Browning's *personae*. The dramatic irony is not forcefully sustained and in this indecision lies the melancholic desperation which frighteningly undercuts the speaker's certainty:

> See, see the subtile texture of each line!
> The Spider spins her curious web lesse fine.
> Th'Spider infusing poison, thus takes th'Fly,
> While in her web she weaves her destiny.
> Beware of th'Net which from a Spider came;
> Nor for the light of heav'n mistake hells flame:
> Like sacred bellows they the soul may blow,
> Whether to make it to Contrition glow,
> And zealous fervor, or to subtilize,
> And make't to flames of Contemplation rise.
> But ah! with soul on Contemplations wing,
> Most deal as boyes with birds do in a string;
> Draw down on seeds of errour for to feed,
> Or by officious handling make to bleed.

> A spark of heav'n devotion may inspire;
> Contentions flames are kindled at hells fire.[61]

The difference between this demanding, thoughtful poetry, and 'Itur Satyricum', written on Charles II's return, and not a satire but a fusion of masque, pastoral, revel and panegyric – in fact, a dance of the satyrs whose retirement had been so grim – could not be more marked.

The satyrs did come out of the woods in the early 1660s with the publication of *Rump Songs* (1662), the first part of which was an anthology of royalist, anti-puritan verse written and circulated since 1639, while the second part mostly contained a scatological medley of verse celebrating the Restoration, a complement to the roasting of any poor animal's behind during the bonfire parties which greeted the return of Charles II.[62] Far from the spiky discrimination and anger of the earlier satires, *Rump Songs* Part II legislates a festive shitting by witty gentlemen upon the heads of the godly, as well as cannibalism and cuckolding: '*Bum-Fodder*: or, *Waste-Paper, proper to wipe the Nations RUMP with, or your Own*'.

A Great Forgetting

With the Restoration came rules. Dryden's prefaces to his major satires and his essay on satire extract the genre from the uncertain state in which it had existed between 1640 and 1660, and ultimately claim it for High Tory neo-Catholicism. The preface to *Absolom and Achitophel* (1681) seems equivocal: 'The Commendation of Adversaries is the greatest Triumph of a Writer; because it never comes unless Extorted. . . . If I happen to please the more Moderate sort, I shall be sure of an honest party.' But the longer preface to *Religio Laici* (1682), mentioned at the beginning of this chapter, associates reason and true faith with majesterial religion, low and irreverent satire with dissent and heresy. This distinction between good satire and bad satire is accompanied by a forgetting of the nature and roots of the Protestant tradition. 'A Man is to be cheated into Passion, but to be reason'd into Truth' is a position which enables Dryden to shift the blame for abusive writing and, more surprisingly, for the demented wit associated with satire, onto the sectaries:

> when their cause was sunk in Court and Parliament, they might at least hedge in a stake amongst the Rabble: for to their ignorance all things are Wit which are abusive . . . even the most Saintlike of the Party, though they durst not excuse this contempt and vilifying of the Government, yet

were pleas'd, and grin'd at it with a pious smile; and call'd it a judgement
of God against the Hierarchy.[63]

In the *Essay on Satire*, Cleveland appears as an original genius whose
powers of gritty invention are to be harnessed and refined in a less
divided age.

Such refinement is a further forgetting of origins. As Dryden grew
older in the Restoration, so he became more involved in that
characteristic literary activity of the Royalist in defeat, translation, so
that *The Hind and the Panther* (1687), the last major satire, stresses its
heroic prosody and turns to Boccaccian and Chaucerian fable as a vehicle.
At the same time, the language of Civil War satire itself was refined.
Spotting lines of 1640s and 1650s verse which appear to have been lifted
and reused by Dryden, Butler, Oldham, Rochester and ultimately Pope,
is a favourite pastime of several scholars, and need not be dwelt upon
here. It is worth noting, however, how a ballad called 'The States New
Coyne' is refined in its harshness for Dryden's *The Medall* (1682):

> Saw you the States mony new come from the Mint?
> Some People do say it is wondrous fine;
> And that you may read a great mystery in't,
> Of mighty King *Nol*, the Lord of the Coyn.
> They have quite omitted his Politick head,
> His worshipfull Face, and his excellent Nose;
> But the better to tempt the sisters to bed,
> They have fixed upon it the print of his Hose.[64]

> Of all the Antick Sights, and Pageantry
> Which English Ideots run in crowds to see,
> The Polish Medall bears the prize alone:
> A monster, more the favourite of the town
> Than either Fayrs or Theatres have shown.
> Never did Art so well with Nature strive;
> Nor ever Idol seem'd so much alive:
> So like the Man; so golden to the sight,
> So base within, so counterfeit and light.

Where Marprelate did survive was in Marvell's *Rehearsal Transpros'd*
(1672), which returns to absolute ridicule in order to attack Restoration
bishops, particularly Samuel Parker. The second part acknowledges that
Parker saw Marprelate in Marvell, while Marvell saw the 1640s royalist
ballader Martin Parker in Samuel Parker. But this play of names should
not disguise the fact that ex-republican opposition M.P.s like Marvell,
and plotters like John Ayloffe, turned to verse forms no less involved in
controlled vilification than Dryden was (for instance, in the 'Advice to a
Painter' poems). The potential for wildly destabilising imitated lunacy or

folly in Erasmus, Marprelate, Marpriest, and Marvell (and not pictorially frozen in the Cleveland/Dryden manner) was inherited by Swift, especially in *The Tale of a Tub* (1704), so that the dissociation of persecution and ridicule became complete, and the satire of the book, the vehicle of the word, dominated the satire of religion.

CHAPTER 10

Calamity as Narrative

On the Land: Landscape, Pastoral, Piscatorial

The View from Up Here

TRANSFORMATIONS OF THE countryside, of property relations, of attitudes towards nature, take place over much longer periods of time than a mere two decades. Or at least they do in England. Thus, although shifts in land ownership have been seen as a long-term cause of the Civil War, and although property was a central issue in the dispute between King and Parliament, property, especially the land, does not figure in the representation of war and revolution. To take another example, the enclosure movement had been depriving the poor and enriching the wealthy for centuries before the 1640s. It was only as a consequence of the economic disruption caused by the Civil War itself that enclosure became part of the popular politics of the later 1640s, even though enclosure had been a concern in earlier utopian writing. And yet representations of the land and attitudes towards the natural world were as subject to ideological division as historical writing, and were as much a site for the inscription of the revolution as anything else.

It is generally assumed that the pastoral was somehow superseded or displaced in the seventeenth century by the georgic.[1] In the pastoral eclogue, the shepherd speakers do very little except sing, but in the georgic, work (ploughing the land) is the dominant activity. This has been explained by Anthony Low, and by James Turner, as an effect of the class struggle in its historical process: the bourgeois world of work replaces the aristocratic one of leisure.[2] In this transformation, royalist poets tried not to use the georgic mode, or when they did, to pretend it was really pastoral; Puritans believed in labour and wrote an honest georgic, one which was interinvolved with the agricultural reforms of the natural philosophers. According to this view, George Wither was a georgic hero.[3]

As we shall see, culture and genre did not interact in this straight-

forward fashion. It seems that the poetry of landscape and of place which
so often deployed pastoral and georgic took within itself not so much
class struggle as the very immediate fact of regicide, recast as royal
sacrifice, as a means of registering a new age. Sir John Denham's poem
Coopers Hill is one such example, first written just before the outbreak of
hostilities, but then republished in a revised form as royalist propaganda
in 1655 (but even in its earliest unpublished version of 1641 it was already
a royalist poem). Where the chorography of pre-Civil War country house
poems is stable and assured (for instance in Ben Jonson's 'To Penshurst'),
perceivable reality in Denham (and of course also in Marvell) is not. The
city in Denham's poem (which includes a reference to Waller's poem on
St Paul's Cathedral) seems menacingly close to the estate (the country),
despite the speaker's assurance that it is 'but a darker Cloud', 'like a Mist
beneath a Hill':

> While Luxurie, and wealth, like Warre and Peace,
> Are each the others ruine, and increase;
> As Rivers lost in Seas some secret veine
> Thence reconveies, there to be lost againe.
>
> ('A' text, Draft III (1642), ll.37–40)[4]

Certainties dissolve, losing their clear definition. The Thames is rightly
acknowledged as a sinew of trade and wealth, almost bringing the
pollution and corruption of commerce with it, as much as its benefits: 'to
us no thing, no place is strange,/While thy faire bosome is the worlds
Exchange.' (ll.217–18) The river disappearing because engulfed by the
sea (used also by Marvell in 'Upon Appleton House') was also an image
for the alternating appearance and disappearance in history of religious
heresy, as used by Sir Thomas Browne. There is also something
unsettling about the landscape which takes it beyond the control of
metaphysical conceits: '*Windsor* the next (where *Mars* and *Venus* dwels,/
Beauty with strength) above the valley swels/Into my eie' (ll.49–51).
Something like an early eighteenth-century couplet effect is intimated
by the placing of such threatening but deferred dilation within the
couplet itself. Then, after the habitual praise of monarchs and their
beneficent effects upon the landscape, Henry VIII and his Reformation are described centrally as a kind of violence: 'What Crime
could any Christian King incense/To such a rage?'(ll.152–3). This
perplexing paradox reverses roles: 'Their [Princes'] charity destroyes,
their faith defends' (l.168), to such an extent that the Henrican
Reformation undoubtedly becomes a representation of a ravaging
parliament (later Cromwell), and Charles I can be glimpsed as the
church in exactly the same sacrificial terms which characterise Royalist
panegyric:

> Then did Religion in a lazy Cell,
> In emptie, ayrie contemplations dwell;
> And like the blocke, unmoved lay, but ours
> As much too active like the Stork devours. (ll.169–72)[5]

Royalty and religion are hermits in exile, but in the case of the 1642 edition, before the course of the war had taken hold.

So, no less than in Marvell's more famous 'Upon Appleton House', the world enters the landscape in the poem, but here, rather than confident praise, a landscape sublime is created by this indirect expression of violence done to a king and culture. The poem was celebrated in the following century as a paragon of *concors discordia*, where the emphasis is on a final harmony. Read in its context, however, in 1642 or 1655, Denham's poem reverses the coupling to *discors concordia*. Not only that, mental activity (Denham means the Reformation, but the words he uses associate with the kind of Baconian-puritan ferment beloved of Milton) encroaches on the landscape as a further blow to tranquillity: 'Can knowledge have no bound, but must advance/So farre, to make us wish for ignorance?'(ll.179–80). The poem resolves in a stag-hunt where the king (Charles I) hunts, but where the stag is a monarch, producing a proleptic image of divided kingship akin to the dividedness which appeared in the drama as soon as Charles I was executed. It is of course part of poetic tradition to compare stags to monarchs, but the stag here is also other things. He tries to hide in the herd (of cattle) whom he had formerly ruled, but they chase him away: 'Like a declining Statesman, left forlorne/To his friends pitty, and pursuers scorn' (ll.275–6). A reference to Strafford perhaps? Where Marvell uses water to resolve his poem in an imagined apocalypse of eternal correspondence, Denham turns to blood but retains the image of a sea battle:

> But fearless they pursue, nor can the floud
> Quench their dire thirst; alas, they thirst for bloud.
> So towards a Ship the oarefin'd Gallies ply,
> Which wanting Sea to ride, or wind to fly,
> Stands but to fall reveng'd on those that dare
> Tempt the last fury of extream despair.
>   ('B' text (1655; 1668), ll.305–10)

The suppression of these lines in the first edition may have been caused by an inhibition (they are present in the first draft): at the point of publication, Denham could not face such an heroic description of the recently executed Strafford, and one which appears to sanction the hunters. In 1655, the simile was a useful way of generalising (Denham's protective strategy) and the memory was by then less painful.[6]

A king is chasing a king, and only a king should kill a king, so that a kind of political forgetfulness is taking place (true history is being ignored). The stag was like a statesman; this could be taken as an anti-parliamentarian image, so that Denham's poem could be said to enact a political revenge. But this identity does not hold, and a more curious reversal ensues. At the very point of the stag's death, the hunters (presumably including the king) become imaged as the subjects of the realm (medieval knights) pursuing the king (King John) to sign Magna Carta at Runnymede, although the stag is also described 'like a bold knight errant' before the hunt, wandering unchallenged across the land. In this shift of time, the conflict between king and parliament is forgotten, the language of tyranny (the very stuff of 1640s polemic) replaced by an older fiction:

> Here was that Charter seal'd, wherein the Crowne
> All markes of Arbitrary power layes downe:
> Tyrant and Slave, those names of hate and feare,
> The happier stile of King and Subject beare. (ll. 313–16)

Subjects should give love, and kings liberty – the feudal past without Magna Carta failed because of an armed system of mutually destructive desires:

> Kings by grasping more than they can hold,
> First made their Subjects by oppressions bold,
> And popular sway by forcing Kings to give
> More, than was fit for Subjects to receive,
> Ranne to the same extreame. (ll. 343–7)

But if this were a resolution which we might expect, the ending is far less happy. Denham returns to the imagery of deluge, arguing metaphorically that laws, as banks raised by the husbandman, save the land from disastrous flooding, whereas if a river (figuring the king) is diverted, with the similar intention of saving land, it may well flood anyway: 'Stronger, and fiercer by restraint, he roares,/And knowes no bound, but makes his powers his shores'(ll. 341–2). The people are imaged as plains (that is, flat, level), who have hopes of being fulfilled by a crop not devastated by the flood, as if kings have a tendency to become tyrants if not restrained by law. But then, Denham implies, so do the people, almost naturally demanding satisfaction, unless forced by law into 'love'. In 1641–2, the dialectical interaction of royal and popular demands is left tantalisingly or perhaps more accurately, worryingly, open.

In the 1655 (and 1668) version, all references to Charles by name are changed to 'the King', and the use of the past tense is played up, for the king is dead. 'King' itself is omitted at line 118 (the reference to Henry VIII's dissolution of the monasteries), no doubt in a protest against the anti-monarchical language of the Commonwealth. The poem is deftly rewritten with several omissions and insertions, in addition to countless local revisions. Certainties and solidities are further diminished: Edward III's 'institution' becomes but his 'design' (ll.86; 104). Charles is figured in *Edward III* as 'the Souldier and the Saint' (l.110), echoing the martyrological associations of the earlier version (now brought to historical truth), but also offering an alternative image of martial saintliness to its most popular subject in the mid-1650s: Oliver Cromwell. In 1655, the zeal of the Reformation, prefiguring puritanism, is amplified: the land now looks as though it had been barbarously invaded (l.150), as it had been for Denham by the New Model Army. In the closing passages, Denham swaps sets of lines so that the poem ends with the Thames bursting its banks. The mutually controlling pressures of monarch and people of the 1642 version (however unusually unsettling it may seem) is replaced by one of chaos and anarchy in a deluge. Indeed, what has happened is worse than any regal tyranny. Charles (now obviously represented in the stag, rather than Strafford) is hunted by a lawless mob. The couplets of the later version seem more highly regulated, but the energy they release in their *discors concordia* is more devastating.

How different was the task of representation half a century later, and it is well worth pondering the differences in order to point up Denham's singular achievement. By 1704, when Pope began to write 'Windsor Forest', a poem which directly commemorates the achievement of *Coopers Hill*, the process of control, of the forgetting of the problems raised by Denham, was complete. Pope pays tribute to the previous poetic praisers of Windsor – Denham in *Coopers Hill* and Cowley. The forgetfulness is such that no mention is made of Denham's involvement in the war, the confiscation of his house by Parliament, or the fact that he changed *Coopers Hill* when the war started, to make it fit a specifically propagandist purpose. More important, there is no embarrassment at all concerning the presence of industry (hard agricultural labour): all is confidently appropriated for a greater harmony: 'Rich Industry sits smiling on the Plains,/And Peace and Plenty tell, a STUART reigns.' Such a harmony replaces that bitter anarchy which prevailed before the enclosure of the forests, the Norman kings representing a kind of tyranny which is paid for by the death in hunting of William Rufus. The Norman kings are presented as Nimrods, mighty hunters and Old Testament tyrants – exactly the same terms used to describe Cromwell in the 1650s. And these Nimrods 'level towns': by 1704 it is posssible to insert some curious mixtures of perspective. By one reading, the political vocabulary of the 1640s which remains in 'Windsor Forest' is associated with violence: the huntsman 'lifts the Tube, and levels with his eye'. Natural production is perfectly consonant with violent disruption and consumption. Tyrants are sublimated below water: the pikes become the

'Tyrants of the watry plain'. In the light of Pope's later attack on sublime poetry and its theories, *Peri Bathous, or The Art of Sinking in Poetry* (1713), tyranny is already being associated with the realm of darkness, turned into an imaginative phantasm. At the same time, there are two (not one) martyr-kings in the poem (l.313): Charles I does not receive as much attention as Henry VI. Yet again, the syntax reverses, as Henry VI and Charles I are brought together in the meditation on St George's Chapel in Windsor Castle. Pope cannot answer the regicide effectively here: the poetry becomes inadequate: 'Oh Fact accurst! What Tears has Albion shed,/Heav'ns! what new wounds, and how her old have bled?' Moreover, the verse paragraph reaches the height of unconvincingness in the again suspiciously self-parodic divine command of Anna: 'At length great ANNA said – Let Discord cease!/She said, the World obey'd, and all was Peace!' Pope is embarrassed. In the context of 1640s polemic, especially divine right assumptions, Denham could justifiably project a martyrological event inside a landscape poem. In 1704 and 1713, one could hardly proclaim the ineffability of a Stuart without evoking memories of a civil war, two serious rebellions and a bloodless coup. The royal presence is also desacralised and performs the function more of a poetic machinery.

Denham's poetry has recently been placed in a different context; not in a historical line, but by direct and involved comparison. *Coopers Hill* has been juxtaposed with George Wither's poetry (see above, 230–33). Both poets were involved in a property dispute with each other, and where Denham was re-presenting old forms in an external landscape, in royalistically tight couplets, Wither created an internal landscape, appropriate to his own religion and in his own experimental form of 'open' verse. In chapter 7 I argued that these internalised landscapes, especially as they were constructed in epic form, correlated with a revolutionary or radically puritan imagination and subjectivity.

But both categories, external royalist landscape and internal puritan one, are processes, involving narratives, or parts of narratives, in their elaboration. A truly liberated subjectivity, perhaps imaginable in the more immediate aftermath of the demolition of monarchy, would result in the renunciation of all forms of formalistic restraint, in a freeing of narratives, of prosody, and the political valency of one's material.

Such a poem is Marvell's 'Upon Appleton House'. In its praise of Fairfax, it is of course a history of the Reformation, and a far more optimistic one than Denham's. Yet at its most arresting moments, 'Upon Appleton House' manages to suspend a directed political meaning (or it forecloses on a singular reading) but also, arguably, makes us forget that we are under the bondage of verse.[7]

While there is a compressed tree fable in the poem, stanza 56 punctuates a previous section where the Mowers have appeared as

'Israelites', Nature's New Model Army soldiers, with the dominant impression that we are looking at a representation – it is always somebody's point of view, not an absolute truth. So, the 'scene again withdrawing' is accompanied by the realisation that to imagine the grounds of Nun Appleton as Levellerishly flat is simply the viewpoint of a painter: 'A levelled space, as smooth and plain/As cloths for Lely stretched to stain.' The Levellers in stanza 57 take their origins from the 'naked equal flat', and all activity on the plain seems to enhance this egalitarianism: the villagers chase their cattle, which makes the land even flatter, after the scythe has been over it. Quite apart from the obscurity of the image, the reader is then surprised by the last two lines: 'Such, in the painted world, appeared/Davenant with the universal herd.' The reference to a painting of the creation in Davenant's *Gondibert* emphasises the fact that the poet is looking at a scene and making something else of it, to the extent that it is freed from the associations and histories which bind Denham. The plain is also a *tabula rasa* (ll.445–6), linking with the imagery of creativity in stanza 6 of 'The Garden', so that the possibility of endless representation becomes the feature of this liberating meditation, while Davenant, in Marvell's view, is lumped together with the 'universal herd' of his own making. Is this Davenant as the stag of *Coopers Hill*, trying to hide to avoid death (and thereby an allusion to his Interregnum career), or is it a way of putting down the Royalist (and his absolutist literary theory) by linking him with the vulgar he sought to control?

In this setting, while the world becomes but a set of representations, attention focuses very definitely upon the liberated self of the speaker. He is not terrified by a monarchical river, but wonders in a boat upon it, simply as a different means of achieving a perspective. He becomes a fisherman in stanza 81, but not long enough for it to gather the royalist associations which it would have in Walton's *Compleat Angler* (1653). Indeed the line and tackle are cast away as 'idle utensils', the important point being that perspectives are constantly modified, so that being is constantly changed and seemingly extended beyond the boundaries of the self, but without engaging with the transcendentally numinous.

Marvell's poetry is often seen as imitating and anglicising the French *libertin* tradition, usually as a consequence of coming into contact with the literary tastes of Sir Thomas Fairfax himself. But the *libertin* poetry of St Amant and Viau does not have that much to do with what is at the centre of this English libertine moment. Freed from traditions, the focus of the speaker seems to be on smaller and smaller elements, almost in a search for the causes of things, or the individual political subject:

> They seem within the polished grass
> A landskip drawn in looking-glass,

> And shrunk in the huge pasture show
> As spots, so shaped, on faces do -
> Such fleas, ere they approach the eye,
> In multiplying glasses lie. (ll.457–62)

Helped a good deal by Lucretius' description of the universe in *De Rerum Natura*, an atomistic view of the universe becomes the means whereby the libertine can even transcend nature, and the constraints which it places upon the self. Although Margaret Cavendish, Duchess of Newcastle, does not usually rebound images off each other in a Marvellian manner, in *Poems and Fancies* (1653), her speculation on forms is similarly rooted in a sense of human boundaries:

> To give us sense, great paines to feele,
> To make our lives to be *Deaths wheele*;
> To give us *Sense*, and *Reason* too,
> Yet know not what we're made to do.
> Whether to *Atomes* turne, or *Heaven* up flye,
> Or into new *Formes* change, and never dye.
> Or else to *Matter Prime* to fall againe,
> From thence to take new *Formes*, and so remaine.
> *Nature* gives no such *Knowledge* to *Man-kind*.
> > 'A Dialogue *betwixt* Man *and* Nature'

In this kind of discourse, any form of political or religious doctrine (divine right, paternalist monarchy), supported by any system of metaphysics, where the end is to produce an account of how man is connected somehow with divinity, is bound to be reduced and indeed made superfluous, as a kind of phantasm. The remarkable feature is that the seed of the demolition begins in considerations which are individual and unit-sized.

In the Field, By the Stream

People take consolation in the land for different reasons in times of strife. Gerrard Winstanley and the Diggers are now, as we have seen, justly famous for their brave attempt to create a communist utopia by cultivating common land in Surrey (not so far from Coopers Hill) and Buckinghamshire, and Winstanley's powerful visionary writings are properly revered.[8] If Marvell and Margaret Cavendish imagine a merging with their landscapes by virtue of altered perspectives, Winstanley's writings claim that cultivation of the land in common *is* a merging of the individual with the godhead in nature.

Winstanley's writings have only received a wide readership in this century. A work which has never been out of print since its first publication is Isaak Walton's *The Compleat Angler* (2nd edn, 1655), subtitled 'the contemplative man's recreation'. It has survived as a popular book because it is a fishing manual. But of course, it is much more than this. Walton was an unrepentant Royalist, and a man of letters whose *Lives*, when published in the Restoration, did much to claim Donne and Herbert for an Anglican literary culture – a view which is at odds with the realities of the church between 1610 and 1633. 'Angler' plays on 'Anglican', and between the advice on who lives where under the surface of the water, how to catch him, and how best to cook and eat him, is a record of several Anglican ideals in abeyance. Angling is analogous to ministry – fishing is preaching to convert, alluding to the gospel parable (Matt. 4:19). The references to particular characters (Ouldsworth, Featley, Morley, Nowell, Sir Henry Wotton) and the unusual oscillation of genres (especially pastoral and liberally quoted chunks from du Bartas and Drayton's *Polyolbion*) relocate the national crisis in a natural landscape, no less than does Winstanley, or Denham, or Marvell. For Walton, sitting patiently by the river bank is a form of invoking security. Disappearing into the landscape is a means of escape from the dangerous 'landscape' in which man places himself.

The prefatory poems tend to jar in their learnedness with the simplicity of Walton's text – at least as it first strikes the reader. The libertinism that survives in these poems – Thomas Weaver's 'pleasures sweet and high/Prostrate to our embraces lye', for instance – is at odds with the contents of the text, and with living in that lyrical never-never-land which we have already seen (see above, 325–7).

Chapter 1, Part 1 begins with a conversation between an angler, a falconer and a hunter. They apparently meet on commonland, and seem intent on using the countryside, or rather its 'natural tenants', for their own ends. There is no hint of poaching, of infringing on someone else's property, although admittedly, ownership is a concern later in the work. Yet this is at odds with the castigation of money-getting men who do not have the time or will for leisure, and Piscator the speaker invokes Lucian and Montaigne to make his point here. Alluding directly to Virgilian pastoral, Piscator explains that angling combines leisure and labour (160). The poor are praised for their meekness and lack of courtly corruption – for they shall inherit the earth. But then the allegory is political rather than economic: the falconer likes 'high-soaring birds', seeing a reflection of nobility in his art. Cromwell is compared by Marvell to a falcon: is this a fable of ambition and overreaching, and is poverty in Walton a synonym for the ejection of Episcopalians in the 1640s? Mr Venator the Hunter admires the capacity of what lives on land to supply the considerable hunger of the people. Is this an allegory of greed or appetite? Fishing is to be recommended because it requires calm and quiet, and is consonant with worship and proximity to God. Water – the sea as well as rivers – is praised because it facilitates travel; to the civilisation of Italy, and away from internally divided Britain. Angling becomes an art, derived from pre-deluvian times, as if it were almost part of the *prisca theologia*, the hermetic *nous*, or Pythagorean philosophy (35–6). Angling reconciles contemplation and active, experimental life. Catalogues of famous rivers and fishes are merged with Herbert's devotional language. We learn of some fish from du Bartas's *Divine Weeks*, which anthropomorphises as well as praises God's creation. The fishy world becomes a natural sacrament in a similar way to the function of nature for Vaughan in *Silex Scintillans*. In this context, the quotation of pre-Civil War pastoral verse is nostalgic, and interestingly so, given the function of *The Compleat Angler* in fashioning a history of Anglicanism *avant la lettre* from the lives of Elizabethan and Jacobean churchmen. And of course, it is a world of maypoles and barley break – the world celebrated in Herrick's *Hesperides* – with 'an honest Ale-house where we shall find a cleanly room, *Lavender* in the Windows, and twenty *Ballads* stuck about the wall' (77). Alehouse fishing anthems are later performed (185). The pastoral interludes which interrupt the piscatorial gastronomy are an instance of Walton not being able to see beyond the idealised landscape of timeless English sociey he has evoked. That he quotes Marlowe and Ralegh's famous pastoral exchange (and later Donne's piscatorial parody of Marlowe) from his recollected position of actually sitting in the countryside associates poetry with the everyday experience of living.

Going fishing feels like a remarkably naive retreat given the national politics of 1653 – the dissolution of first the Rump, then Barebone's Parliaments, the proclaiming of the Protectorate, and the emergence of militant Fifth Monarchism. Sir Richard Baker's *Chronicle* (1643) of English monarchs – already outdated historiographically, but still very popular – is cited because it contains a couplet on the simultaneous introduction of beer and the carp to England. But just when the reader begins to feel that the world of politics has been banished, Piscator surprises us with the tale of the gypsies, who, having obtained money by deceit and 'secret' means, fight over who should have the spare shilling. And there are also the beggars, who dispute in 'beggarly Logick' over whether it is easier to rip or unrip a cloak, or whether they amounted to the same thing (161–6). The interpretation demanded is complex. There is a nearly explicit comparison of the gypsies with the dispute between King and Parliament over ship money, while the beggars are likened to religious sectarians. It is the gypsies and the beggars – the outcast vagabonds – who are by contrast the heroes of the Ranter Abiezer Coppe's *A Fiery Flying Roll* (1649). Yet the gypsies are certainly inside the pastoral/piscatorial landscape, while the beggars identify themselves with the stage beggars of Jonson and Fletcher (and Brome). As in 'Upon Appleton House', the perspective of art – the frame of perception – defines the parameters of the real.

Walton's pastoral and piscatorial had its ideological opposite in the 1650s in the *Northern Memoirs* of Richard Franck, written mostly in 1658 although not published until 1694. Franck, born and educated in Cambridge, was a captain in the New Model Army and served in Scotland in the 1650s; much of the information contained in *Northern Memoirs* is concerned with Scottish fishing. He then resided at Nottingham and was forced to flee to America during the Restoration, but returned and was living in the Barbican when his book was finally published. His one editor, Sir Walter Scott, was respectful of his angling knowledge, but unjustly harsh on his literary merits: 'superior to the excellent patriarch Isaac Walton, in the mystery of fly-fishing, as inferior to him in taste, feeling, and common sense'.[9] It is not difficult to see how Scott reached this position, for by the time he wrote Franck was immersed in the culture of enthusiasm prevailing in London and the Army. He was familiar with Boehme, Van Helmont, Sendivogius, astrology and other occult writings, and his style reflects this: 'the Vernon Ingress smil'd a Blessing, when she sent the melodious Harmony of Birds to melt the Air. . . . We read in the *Sanhedrim*, that the Seed of *Hagar* stood in opposition to the Seed of *Sarah*' (1; 19).

Different knowledges, cosmologies, pieties, and political visions, produce in Franck a deep resistance to Walton, despite his own respect for the literary achievement of *The Compleat Angler* and his humility: 'I can raise my Scenes no higher, to elevate this admirable Piscatorian Science, beyond the *Elizium* of the Angler's *Arcadia*' (xiii). Yet he has a boast:

> I can in these Northern Tracts, to bring you a Discovery of some of her Rarities, whose solitary Shades strike a Damp to my Pen, because to behold there such unexpected Landskips, Meanders and Labyrinths (which I frequently met with) as exposed my Resolution to a farther Progress, whereby to discover all her Northern Gaities that shin'd so splendidly every Fir-wood, as also in her lofty domineering Hills. (vii)

Franck considered Walton's knowledge to be inferior to his own, and derived from books rather than angling experience. Of fly-fishing, Franck wrote '*Isaac Walton* . . . has imposed on the World this monthly Novelty, which he understood not himself; but stuffs his book with Morals from *Dubravius* and others' (148).[10] Thus, Walton is a 'formal Opinionist', rather than a 'reform'd and practical Artist' (150). This opinion was based not only on a reading of *The Compleat Angler*, but also, as we have seen, upon an encounter between the two men, so that *Northern Memoirs* resembles the kind of journey with encounters recorded by John Taylor earlier in the century, and the friendship literature which was to grow during the Restoration.

The literary is acknowledged by Franck – 'had I rob'd *Virgil* to adorn my Muse, peradventure my Fancy had been more fruitful' – but held at bay in order for the experience of nature to lead on to deeper forms of contemplation: 'pray excuse me if I wander too far from the Water-side, to gaze and admire these glorious Metaphors, the Divine Oracles of him that made them' (xii). The identification of natural objects as metaphors of the godhead clearly signals occultism, and a transcendentalising habit of looking beyond appearances.[11] Students of angling, says Franck, should 'omit the thoughts of Elements, to mingle sometimes their Contemplations with things more sublime' (xv).

But the 'literary' is not entirely displaced by the 'occult'. The Scottish landscape repeatedly appears to Franck as that of Arcadian romance: '*Ar. . . .* here we assume a Poetick Liberty, in some sort to call *Scotland, Arcadia. Th.* This is a pretty Romantick Notion'(115). It is also quite surprising, given the habit of reading England as the disrupted Arcadia of the later sections of Sir Philip Sidney's popular work.[12] One of the most concrete events recounted in *Northern Memoirs* – the overland transportation of a sailing vessel by the New Model Army (under Dean's command) from Inverness to patrol Loch Ness – suspends belief sufficiently to seem like an episode in a romance: 'Do you Romance, or not, to tell me that an Island swims in the midst of the Ocean, and a Ship fluctuates in the midst of the Highlands; where every Rock represents a *Charibdis*, and every wave threatens an Inundation?'(167).[13] As we have seen, where Royalists tended to give up on *Arcadia* at about the time of the regicide (since Basilius [read as Charles I] was not in actuality resurrected), and where some literary supporters of Parliament and the Commonwealth attempted highly ethereal, Platonised romance allegories, Franck's use of *Arcadia* represents another way of carrying over the politicised literary inheritance of a previous age.[14] The piscatorial pastoral becomes the contemplative space of regenerate militant puritanism. Even the arch-royalist James Howell's romance *Dendrologia: Dodona's Grove* is referred to at one point, precisely to point up its opposite in Franck's world (36). The speaker called Theophilus marvels 'Is it a Romance, or a real Story?' (163), when Arnoldus (the voice of Franck) recounts the tale of Billie Pringle, a popular Scottish story concerning a cow which drank some liquor. Rustic philosophy such as this, derived from folk-tales, is part of the 'experience' which Arnoldus elevates above book-learning. In the sphere of literary politics, Franck's true arcadia also works against the kind of cavalier mock romance written to satirise puritan and republican grandees and ministers (see above, 285). Nottingham is Franck's exemplary commercial entrepôt, and Nottinghamshire countryside a genuine arcadia, 'England's Elizium'

(231), if there is to be such a place in the world. The city is even described in terms more fitting for French heroic romance than the English model: 'a beautiful and imbellish'd Seraglio, where every Street, nay every Port, represents as it were the new Face of a Court' (240). And yet despite Franck's apparent countenancing of romance constructions, he also says that plagiarising from other authors (such as angling authorities) is to engage in 'Romantick Fictions' (241).

Like Walton, Franck weaves contemporary politics into his narrative, although this is complicated by the late Restoration additions to *Northern Memoirs*, so that two sets of historical predicament are woven into the narrative. There is no doubting his New Model credentials, as his description of the Civil War takes Charles's blood-guilt as its central focus: 'Nor stop'd it here neither, for the cultivated Fields stained all over with English Blood (beyond all precedent till the Life of that non-Such *Charles* expired).' Three of his 'four great Harries' are well-known Commonwealth men – Ireton, Vane, Neville – but the fourth, '*marvelous Andrew*, or *Andrew Marvel*', did not have such a grand reputation until the Restoration, so that at the very least we must suppose some later revisions.[15] Restoration republicans and Whigs who are also praised are Algernon Sidney, William, Earl Russell, and Alderman Henry Cornish, all of them executed in the first half of the 1680s, thereby enforcing the suspicion that Franck was involved in opposition politics.[16] The late 1650s was a repetition of an earlier predicament: 'Forty one all over', and Franck wonders whether the solution is action or contemplation for anyone: 'Rocks and Rivers with Hermetick Groves, shadowed with purling Streams, will for ought I know better answer our present Occasion, than a Foreign Hope can insure us Accomodation' (41). The occasion to publish is made by 'a valourous Prince (whose Heroick Vertues like a *Corona* surround him) [which] presents me with an opportunity to step into Scotland'. Presumably Franck does mean William, and his own personal safety after the Glorious Revolution. Or was this sentence written before or in 1658, and the object of admiration Oliver Cromwell, or even Richard Cromwell?

Franck is undoubtedly a staunch Cromwellian. Medals of the Protector are objects of his admiration as much as the models he says he saw of Elgin Cathedral. Cromwell is the sixth 'harry' and the greatest object of Franck's praise.[17] 'You will find him at *Dunbar* swadling the Scots.'[18] The picture is as brutal as contemporary reportage: 'the Conqueror's Army sprinkled the Earth with bloody Sacrifices, converting the green Meadows into purple Planes'(215). Towards the end of *Northern Memoirs*, Arnoldus is asked why he wrote his work in 1658 but then 'spread his net' to 1685, and the answer given seems to be one concerned with providing the reader with a sense of historical perspective: 'I lived in the Reign of five Kings, and in the Time of four great Worthies' (242).

Was O.P. (Oliver Protector) one of these worthies, as well as the greatest 'harry'?

> I leave that Bone for you to pick. But this I assert, that great English *Hero* was exemplary in Piety, eminent in Policy, prudent in Conduct, magnanimous in Courage, indefatigable in Vigilancy, industriously laborious in Watchings, Heroick in Enterprize, constant in Resolution, successful in War; one that never wanted a Presence of Mind in the greatest Difficulties; all the world owns him for a great General, that influenced all *Europe*, gave Laws to all neighbouring Nations, and disciplined *France* with English Arms. (242)

But his puritanism and his military experience are not in doubt, as he distances himself from the rich cooking instructions built into Walton's book. In Franck's eyes, Walton's book is cloyingly civilised, assuming plenty, and locating fishing at the heart of a domestic festiveness:

> to furnish every Angler with a new Bait, was the studious Invention of *Isaac Walton* Author (as you may read) of the *Compleat Angler*, who industriously has taken care to provide a good Cook, (supposing his Wife had a finger in the Py) which will necessarily be wanting in our Northern Expedition. (49)

Not that Franck is an anti-feminist: his experience grows from an austere code of greater deprivations in the service of the Commonwealth. Cooking for Franck is to be kept simple and plain: 'Nonno, let a dish of Sewins [bull-trouts] serve for Supper, rather than dream of delicious *Regalia*; and instead of an *Olio*, a broil'd Haddock; or it may be a Scots Collop, if we can get it' (189). Food has its own politics, which reflect larger issues: 'What matters it then for Cooks, where every Man may dress his own Commons.'

Franck's narrative and dialogue accounts of evening fishing at Ingleston and Castleton parallel the 'real pastoral' passages in Walton, but they fix in an entirely different political sensibility and tradition to Walton's. Franck's doubts are those of a serious republican:

> *Th.* Come then let us break the heart of these Hills, and bless our Eyes with a Landskip of the lowlands, that serve as a Sanctuary to shelter us against Storms, and Protection against impetuous Rains. But what *Eutopia's* this that dwells below us?
>
> *Ar.* It's neither Sir *Thomas Moor's*, nor *Bacon's Atlantas*; here we have already made a fair Discovery. (165)

Food provides a departure point for the consideration of the uses of nature. What are the boundaries of man's legitimate use of nature, and where can he be said to do violence to it? In Franck's view, Walton's festiveness is transgressive and proud, Walton himself out of the true way of experienced knowledge. To this extent, Franck really regarded himself as a piscatorial hermetic magus.

Gerrard Winstanley has also been regarded as a hermetic magus, seeking to return to an Adamic knowledge of, and communion with, the natural world. The Digger tracts – especially those of Winstanley – reconcile the language of radical religious inward illumination with that of Levellerish complaint against the wealthy. I have argued elsewhere that the contradictions in Winstanley's utopian description created an ambiguity as to where 'God's garden' actually was: was it man, was it nature, or was it both?[19] Such irresolution indicates the degree to which Winstanley's praxis was unformulated – at least until it was too late. Winstanley's open-ended cosmology is perplexing until one realises that it is a silence which relates directly to vegetarianism. If Winstanley had been a vegetarian with a theory, he would not have left his description of God, man and nature so loosely defined. If man and nature were so continuous, each with God immanent, then killing fellow creatures, and harming living flesh, would have been unacceptable, and Winstanley would have had to think again about the implications of his metaphors.

The Diggers at Cobham sowed corn, parsnips, carrots and beans, and the emphasis in their tracts is always upon cereal production. It would seem that they were functioning as a vegetarian community, but not in direct response to the carniverous preferences of the propertied, and, indeed, of the New Model Army, where provisions of fruit were distinctly frowned upon. At least at the beginning of his community, it is difficult to see how the Diggers were not *forced* to resort to cereal and vegetable production and consumption. They were vegetarians because they were poor. If Digger attitudes became ideological vegetarianism, in a way which has become hidden to us, it soon broke down. Seed and animals had to be sold by the Diggers to remain solvent, and animals were probably consumed.

By the time the fully-fledged utopian vision of *The Law of Freedom* (1652) was published, the Digger colony had been destroyed by violence and economic duress. Winstanley was nothing more than a neo-Hartlibian projector, and the place of flesh-eating in his utopia plainly visible:

> If any want food or victuals, they may either go to the butchers' shops, and receive what they want without money; or else go to the flocks of sheep and cattle, and take and kill what meat is needful for their families, without buying or selling.[20]

Before his public demise, Winstanley's understanding of Genesis was controverted by William Rabisha, who claimed to have been a royal cook, and was the author of a popular cookery manual.[21] Rabisha's equally heterodox interpretation of the Book of Genesis makes Adam an entirely earthly creature, with no immanent godhead such as is to be found in Winstanley.[22] Thus, all natural objects are prone to consumption, with or without respect for bodily integrity: 'Break that Deer; Leach that Brawn, Rear that Goose; Lift that Swan; Sauce that Chicken; Unbrace that Mallard; Unlace that Cony; Dismember that Heron; Display that Crane; Disfigure that Peacock; Unjoint that Bittern.'[23]

Despite his radical religious sentiments in some of his writings, Rabisha appears to be offering a world of plenty, a vision from the land of cockayne, something which would have been deeply offensive to a real vegetarian like Roger Crab. Christopher Hill has written a fine essay on Crab, the hatter from Chesham whose career in the service of the parliamentary army led him to radical religion and thence to vegetarianism and the renunciation of alcohol, in the cause of purity.[24] The publisher's preface to Crab's *The English Heremite* (1655) lists the miserable fates of several tyrant-gluttons in history, and living gluttons like Wood, the 'great Eater' of Kent, who could consume a whole sheep in one sitting. Crab's discourse takes the form of an inverted fleshly festiveness, in which a surfeit of roots and cereals replaces meat. The Gospel of John forces Crab to change his ways: 'and instead of strong drinks and wines, I give the old man a cup of water; and instead of roast Mutton, and Rabbets, and other dainty dishes, I give him broth thickned with bran, and pudding made with bran, and Turnep leaves chop't together (1–2). Crab's influence has been underrated. A poem by 'J.B.', apparently the publisher of *Gentle Correction of the High-Flown Backslider* (1659), implies that Crab leads a sect of vegetarians:

> Illustrious souls more brighter then the morn,
> Oh! how dark mortals greet you still with scorn,
> Admiring us your homely sack-clothe dress,
> Heaths, roots, and every vegetable Mess
> On which you live; and are more healthy far
> Then Cannibals, that feed on luscious fare;
> But how will you be their Aeternal wonder,
> When you appear (Bonarges) sons of thunder. (4)

Between Rabisha and Crab comes Richard Franck, whose immersion in natural detail is also in places reminiscent of Gerrard Winstanley's visions of a return to Eden through the communal cultivation of the land. The Scottish landscape makes Franck imagine he is in the state of nature. It is as if a landscape has been provided for the republican stance. And this itself takes Franck into a series of speculations on man in nature: precisely the kind of discourse which has made Winstanley's tracts seem so remarkable, but which is also present in other radical books of the 1650s:

Thus we may read the State of the World; but that which I always approved of as the best State, was to seek the Blessings of Content in every Condition. Then welcome Woods, Rocks, Rivers, Groves, Rivulets; nay its possible the very Shades of a Forest, in some measure answer to the Comforts of Life. (241–2)

No less than Rabisha, however, Franck was no Digger. Natural felicity suggests to him a state of spiritual regeneration. It is the kind of discourse which we find in the description of nature by the General Baptist and Leveller Robert Everard. Before the Fall, said Everard, man lived in a state of uncorrupted nature (rather than relying upon a supernatural 'light').[25] Franck wants to return to a state of paradisal nature, a state obscured not so much by mankind's original sin as by a national reprobation: 'This was once the blessed State of *Adam*, and a regenerate state (to be born again in Spirit) is the same with us now: for Primitive Purity can never be blotted out by National Impiety'(244). Being born again in the Spirit equates regenerate behaviour with Edenic happiness, and it permits the eating of meat and the drinking of alcohol (207), but does not suggest a complete Digger-like reversion to the state of nature and agricultural communism. It was a position involving that kind of puritan sobriety which Winstanley regarded as but the beginning of his renovation, and which the Ranters labelled hypocrisy.

So who owned the country? Who had the right to use it? If the dominant voices of the eighteenth century are to be believed, it was the confident voices of civilised landowners, praised in happy versions of Denham's originally uneasy poem. And the ideal of bountiful countryside supporting church and state was sustained in the perennially popular *Compleat Angler*. Yet just as true republican history was recast or dimmed in the light of succeeding ages, so the other voices of the land have been forgotten or where known (as in the case of Marvell) unrecognised. By putting neglected material back together with its more famous relatives, we can see how the Civil War and the revolution vitally affected the perception of nature and the land. When the affairs of men became unbearably chaotic, it was the resort of all, and the site of tremendously powerful metamorphoses – reimaginings of people, power, history and the very meaning of respect itself.

'*I was there*': *History as Imagined Present*

And next (as if their bus'ness rul'd Mankinde)
Historians stand, bigg as their living looks;

Who thought, swift Time they could in fetters binde;
Till his Confessions they had ta'en in Books:

But Time oft scap'd them in the shades of Night;
And was in Princes Closets oft conceal'd,
And hid in Batails smoke; so what they write
Of Courts and Camps, is oft by guess reveal'd.
(Sir William Davenant, *Gondibert* (1651), 2.v.61–2)

The writing of true history was generally regarded by the early Stuarts as one of the great cultural triumphs of their age, a consolidation of more than one hundred years of humanist endeavour against mere chronicle and obvious monarchical propaganda.[26] For John Hall, writing in 1645, chronicle was the simplest mode of historical writing, and therefore the place for the reader to familiarise himself with the form before progressing to the more complex and useful Plutarch.[27] History was the opposite of romance, and its true duty was to record the contingencies of events as they happened without idealisation or the embellishments of poetry, those 'Bratts of Invention & Spawne of Idle Houres'.[28] Henry Carey, Earl of Monmouth, wrote that people ought not to celebrate their national past in a mindless way but should use history to understand what at present they are.[29] It was also a convenient way of understanding human otherness: 'history afforded the reader travel to foreign lands.'[30]

Historiographical Revolutions

At the centre of the historiographical revolution of the early sixteenth century was the recovery of the texts of Cornelius Tacitus, whose influence was to extend for centuries from this point. What Aristotle was to political theorists, Tacitus was to historians. Tacitus' ironic and austere style, and his dislike of the excesses of rulers, made him popular with anti-courtly and republican writers, most famously instanced in the Tacitean echoes of Thomas More's *History of Richard III* (1513). However, Tacitus' tight reserve could easily work as a model of pro-monarchical writing.[31] It is no coincidence that Clarendon's *History of the Rebellion* displays an admiration for Tacitus, whose cool appraisals of men in power were the inspiration for the European-wide interest in 'reason of state', and whose models of perception could be used to construct discourses which argued both for and against any kind of constitution.

Such a multi-valent potential for interpretation was not limited to Tacitus. Livy might have been unequivocally identified as the pro-republican historian of the fall of the Roman republic, but Polybius, the sixth book of whose *Histories* is usually assumed to be a starting point for classical republican theory, was published in English translation in 1648 with a large crown printed on the title-page.[32] No one could mistake the affiliation signalled here. Indeed the classical republican image of civil discord could easily be put to anti-republican uses, instanced in Clement Walker's quotations of Livy's correspondence, Cicero and Tacitus when castigating the political Independents in 1649.[33] Within the anti-monarchical consensus, the grandees preferred Tacitus to the Livy of the gentlemen republicans and Levellers.

History is no easier to disentangle from other forms and genres in the period, and here Tacitus seems to have suffered guilt by association. Along with the Tacitean plays of Jonson and Thomas May, Tacitus was often linked with the kind of analysis found in Machiavelli's writings, which were themselves a special kind of analytical historical writing. For this reason, Tacitus received a certain amount of moral disapproval. He was also distorted in the 'reason of state' manuals which reduced his perceptions to a list of useful points of advice. In some special cases, this advice took satirical form, as with Venetian Traiano Boccalini's defence of free states, *Ragguagli da Parnasso* (*News from Parnassus*; 1612–13), first published in English translation in 1656.

The uncertain or ambiguous applications of the historiographical tradition in the mid seventeenth century, and the comparatively exaggerated mutability of the genre, made seventeenth-century historical writing a highly complex affair, a body of materials most demanding to analyse. It is possible to chart a process of increasing competence in the early seventeenth century, as pageant and antiquarianism were further discarded.[34] It used to be thought that early seventeenth-century historical writing was backward: 'Seventeenth-century English historians in general either lacked imaginative referents entirely or evolved ones that were not suitable for literary embodiment.'[35] Hobbes thought that most readers of histories were interested only in violent battle scenes.[36] And it is true that Sir Richard Baker's feudal and heroic *Chronicle* (1643; nine editions by 1696) remained popular throughout the century. But whatever the predelictions of readers, we now know that this severe judgement is unjustified. Where pre-1640 English historical writing attempted to use the histories of other nations to improve itself, the effect of the Civil War was to encourage English historians to match the achievements of their classical forebears. And they did this through a direct engagement with the affairs of the time. As Martine Brownley says: 'The civil wars abruptly ended this historiographical retreat into the more distant past. With this subject a weapon, historians entered the political arena.'[37]

Historical writing can be analysed in two ways. First, it has, in the old-fashioned sense, a 'contents', the linguistic representation of the objects and events which constitute human interaction, from statutes to limbs and artillery. Second, that representation forms a significant pattern in its own right – stylistic, lexical, rhetorical. Guicciardini was commended by John Hall not only because he wrote lively history about his own times but also because his mixed style was both 'grave' and ornate.[38] The master tropes which have been seen to govern the nineteenth century had their counterparts in the seventeenth century and the Civil War disrupted them.[39] The combination of both produce what we might call the 'rhetoric of history', the total textual effect of a work of history. Such a focus can lead to reductive accounts of historical writing, but careful characterisations are not without usefulness. Cornford took Thucydides to be working out tragic patterns of self-destruction in the Greek city states.[40] In the Machiavellian tradition, such patterns were developed into a consideration of which route to decline a state would adopt.

It was precisely this kind of meditation on the course of events to which Hobbes objected. Thucydides was especially worthy of translation into English because he neither 'inserted discourses' into the 'contexture of the narration' nor speculated on the aims of men which evidence would not reveal.[41] Hobbes admires Thucydides because he concealed his intelligence in a silent but perspicacious ordering of events and materials which convinces the reader that he is actually watching 'live' the events being described.[42]

The great length of history books was a good sign of their fidelity to the complexity of events. John Hall regarded the epitome as the enemy of history, and suggests that the habit of producing brief extracts from larger works acts as a kind of censorial index on the reading of longer works of history. He even suggests that epitomes are responsible for the destruction of many works of history.[43] Nonetheless, Hall falters when he tries to decide which is the more effective educational device:

> you should extract Politick Observacions, without which the reading of History is little worth and Fables were as good as Historyes, & yet under the veyle of Fables lay hidd all the Divinity and Philosophy of the wise Ancients, but because History represents things really done, therfore they sink into the mind with more weight, & fill the braine with more substantiall Ideas, though I must say that I find my selfe somewhat benefitted by tales were told mee when I was a child, & truly I think they sharpened somewhat my imaginacion; & this I conceave the reason why the polite Scot bids put Historyes into the hands of sleeping children.[44]

Hall was writing in Durham at the end of the first Civil War, just before he went to Cambridge and London, where he would discover his republican principles. Already in this work we can see the preference for analytical history with associated moral and strategic comment (as in

Machiavelli's *Discorsi*) which would become a hallmark of English republican thought, and he would redeploy parts of his *A Method of History* in his republican proposals for educational reform in 1649 (see above, 187–8). Would republican Hall have been so ready in 1651 to condone fable, that method of secret conveyance which had rapidly become associated with royalist propaganda?

The outbreak of the Civil War produced a considerable disruption in the imaginative effort which went into the creation of historical writing. The sources which had been found in surviving documents of the past were suddenly being made in momentous events of the present. The sense of the present as emergent past was everywhere. The documented evidence of this nearly present past was constituted by the newsbooks, whose materials rapidly found their way into the 'histories' which began to record the English Civil Wars even before they had ended. It was such a reliance upon newsbooks and pamphlets which famously troubled the chronicler of the times, John Rushworth:

> the impossibility for any man in After-ages to ground a true History, by relying on the Printed Pamphlets in our days, which passed the Press whilst it was without control, obliged me to all the pains and charge I have been at for many years together, to make a great *Collection*.[45]

Where Greek and Roman historians oscillated between rapidly moving battle scenes and oratory, the latter is replaced in England by printed matter. Publication replaces oratory as the *topos* of represented war.

By 1644, a historical perspective on the Civil War and its causes was possible. Parliament seems to have encouraged several publications, such as *An Orderly and Plaine Narration of the Beginnings and Causes of this Warre* (1644). *A True & perfect Journall of the Civill Warres in England*, No. 2 (30 April 1644) was published 'To prevent Erroneous Information'. Here, the newsbook itself was functioning as history, and the text includes references to Tacitus and Sallust, together with hefty *sententiae*: '[To seek to protect one's portion is not the smallest virtue]' (10).

The Presbyterian schoolmaster John Vicars's series of long chronicle pamphlets are effectively a series of amalgamated newsbooks written in the sermon rhetoric of popular puritanism. Vicars was in his sixties in the 1640s, and his language of heroic righteousness conveys the 'old Puritanism' of which we see a close relation in the writings of George Wither.[46] Indeed, there are instances of the publication by puritan ministers of biblical histories which were clearly intended to be typologically transposed by readers onto the events of their own times. Hezekiah Woodward's *The King's Chronicle* (1643) consists of a history of bad Hebrew kings, who did not defend their nations, and counter-examples of good Hebrew kings who did. The text is inviting a response which would encourage the publication of the allegorical histories by nonconformists in the Restoration.[47] But non-puritan divines published the same kinds of histories too, and allegorical history was not the only resort of puritan preachers.[48] The influential Independent minister William Bridge used historical writing to provide considerable evidence of the popular origins of sovereignty.[49]

Not surprisingly, English history itself was seen as a way to understand present troubles. Edward Chamberlayne's *The Present Warre Parallel'd* (1647) concisely recounted the rebellions during the reign of Henry III. The vocabulary is that of 1640s pamphleteering (but drawing extensively on medieval historians) representing Henry's rebellious Parliament and the Earl of Leicester, the English Catiline. Henry is initially politically unskilled, but he has learned at the end to court favour by forgiving many of his subjects. Before the reader reaches the more than plainly stated pragmatic advice to kings and subjects at the end of the tract, he has become bound up in the familiar language of contemporary division. Chamberlayne's work was re-published in 1660 as *The Late Warre Parallel'd*. Remarkably, the only change in addition to the title was the section on advice 'For the People' (22). There is no mistaking Chamberlayne's monarchism when this became '*To the Subject*' at the Restoration.

Momentous events provoked grand responses, courtesy of Tacitus. Abraham Wright produced an account of the trial and execution of Strafford in Tacitean Latin, citing Tacitus, Machiavelli, Guicciardini, 'Comineus' (de Commines) and 'ye [unidentified] English history' in the process.[50] Tacitus was no stranger to the stage of politics: in 1626 Sir John Eliot had suggested in a parliamentary speech a parallel between Sejanus and Buckingham by quoting Tacitus. He was promptly imprisoned. In Wright's text, the interaction of text and event becomes part of the world of observation as well as the world of action.

In fact, historical writing developed under the pressure of controversial needs and inside pamphlet discourse which was generically non-specific. James Howell's repetitive and regrettably shallow (if colourful) propaganda on the King's behalf is an example of the royalist use of historiography. *The Preheminence and Pedigree of Parlement* (1644), written while Howell was imprisoned in the Fleet Prison, and featuring the famous woodcut of Howell under an oak tree (associating royalism and Druidic myth), puts forward the image of a mixed monarchy, in which the parliament is the harmonious 'organ' where the three parts of '*Monarchy, Optimacy* and *Democracy*' co-exist. In this idealistically represented constitution, Charles is Caesar, and Howell offers himself as an English Tacitus to the French Tacitus, Philippe de Commines. Howell was in fact royal historiographer, and this tract makes ironic reading in the light of his more pessimistic comments in 1648 that royalist defeat was the result of a defective political system.

Print, Oratory and the Classics

Thomas May's *History of the Parliament* (1647), and his *Breviary* (1650), are very original in their classicising of English history, the latter focused centrally on the image of the people as English versions of the Roman ideal of armed freeholders. For Royalists, like Howell and Cleveland, these men, such as Cades, Tylers, Straws and Ketts, were rebels. But until the late 1640s, both sides were agreed that the English constitution was essentially sound, if in need of renovation.

The role of May's *History* in disseminating a republican view of the national predicament has been discussed in a previous chapter (see above, 205). Parallels between ancient Rome and England are made where in May's translation of Lucan's *Pharsalia*, and his *Continuation* of that poem, Rome was presented as being fundamentally unlike England.[51] Where Clarendon would, as we shall see, find causation in personality, May assumes the existence of a force controlling human destinies. It is presented as an inscrutable Christian God, but the level of classical allusion makes us intuit the force also as fate.[52] The Duke of Buckingham does not need to be analysed in any depth because other forces are at work, not least of all a 'people' continually outwitted by a supernatural force:

> At the death of that duke, the people were possessed with an unusual joy, which they so openly testified by such expressions as indeed were not thought fit nor decent by wise men upon so tragical and sad an accident, which in a Christian consideration might move compassion, whatsoever the offences of the man were.
>
> To such people that distich of Seneca might give answer:
>
>> *Res est sacra miser. Noli mea tangere fata.*
>> *Sacrilegae bustis abstinuere manus.* (Epigramm. IV.9)
>
>> Sacred is woe; touch not my death with scorn:
>> Even sacrilegious hands have tombs forborne.
>
> And it may be that God was offended at the excess of their joy, in that he quickly let them see the benefit was not so great to them as they expected by it. (12–13)

We are not told precisely who the people are. In the passage above, they could be the *hoi polloi*, although elsewhere, May clearly intends 'people' to signify a propertied and politically represented citizenship, loose enough not to discount the aristocracy. Such flexible definitions are enabled precisely by classical parallels. Sir John Eliot's use of his freedom to speak in the 1628 Parliament is seen as the kind of freedom which Tacitus defended in censuring Thraseus Poetus, and the dissolution of that Parliament is compared to the Battle of Philippi, after which the people 'never looked back to their ancient liberty'. The 'liberty of the subject' becomes in May's discourse the language of ancient liberty, defended by right-thinking gentry and freeholders against selfish courtiers (19; see above, 183–4, 196–200).

Once the major events of the Civil War and those leading up to it become the focus of May's attention, there is less opportunity and less need to enforce the Roman parallels. Since the Romans lost their ancient liberty in the Empire (however much Augustus might have 'refounded' the republic as empire), it was clearly prudent not to draw the comparison too closely. What takes over is a rapidly moving account of the operation of a tyranny and the resistance to it. Sir Benjamin Rudyerd's famous speech in the House of Commons, interpreted by Clarendon as a warning of the horrors of civil conflict, becomes for May a great oration by a virtuous man in the cause of liberty (72–7). Unfortified London is like ancient Sparta: defended only by the 'hearts of courageous citizens' (330). But so as to make his parallels the more convincing, May invites his readers to consider how fitting they are, as in the comparison between the attractiveness of the king to those who pursue private interests (according to May) and the followers of Caesar and Antony (*ex Romanis nobilibus et fortibus*, not *ex subditis Romanorum*) at Philippi, who, according to Dio Cassius, were promised '*imperium in omnes gentiles suos*' (271).

Predictable forms of human behaviour come in responses to the false show of tyranny, instanced in the flocking of some Parliamentarians to the King. Vain orator-M.P.s whose speeches have not been well-received are tempted, like Coriolanus and Julian the Spanish General to defect, while others are 'bewitched' by the 'rhetoric' of monarchical appearance:

> There is a difference between wisdom and good parts, such as we count eloquence, wit, polite learning, and the like: and that wisdom which is least adorned with such dresses as these is usually at such times most safe in itself, and freest from being corrupted; as that beauty is, which is set off from the least witchery of attire: for that beauty which is curiously decked, as it is most subject to be tempted by others, so it is most apt to be proud of itself, and by consequences to betray itself to such a temptation as is great enough. (179)

May's posturing in his speaking voice as an informed but removed observer has been underestimated. 'How far the earl of Strafford did in his lifetime divide the king's affections from his people and parliament . . . I cannot surely tell' (95), says May almost coyly, before continuing to emphasise the divisiveness of Strafford's trial itself, and after comparing his portrait of Strafford with Appian's of the notorious Roman dictator Sulla. The speaker's stance enables May to investigate with apparent impartiality the way in which public opinion, manipulated by the media, became alienated even from the representatives of the people:

> The fears and jealousies that now reigned were of a sadder nature than the fears of any former times had been. Two years before, the people feared that whilst this king lived they should never see a Parliament, but now they began to fear that no parliament could do them good. (136)

Although other histories, particularly Clarendon's, acknowledge the significance and power of opinion, May is singular in showing opinion at work through his largely 'tragic' republican narrative.[53]

In fact, the three books of May's *History* document the author's response to the change which the 1640s brought to English politics and to the nature of writing on public issues. The first part, which goes from Elizabeth's reign up to just before the Irish Rebellion, is written within the 'closet republican' frame of the 1620s and 1630s. It is Lucanic and mythologises tyrants. The second book, which is chiefly concerned with the negotiations and bluffing which led to the outbreak of hostilities, is most notable for its use of printed publications (including newsbooks). The third book represents a synthesis of the former two in that there is a return to the classicising habit, but this time the printed sources are less visible in the narrative, and the narrator appears not as a committed Lucan or Tacitus, but as Dio Cassius, known for his impartiality. In this way, May achieves a kind of majesty, definitely still a republican one, and a mode which was sustained in the *Breviary*. Parliament's historiographer knew exactly how history had favoured his cause, and he made it part of official parliamentarian discourse.

Lucan continued to be the guide of Commonwealth and Protectorate historiographers in the decade after May's death, although May's writing itself had a more direct influence on the pro-Cromwellian *Britannia Triumphalis* (1654), a history of the Commonwealth between the execution of the King and the beginning of the Protectorate. Richard Hawkins's celebration of national heroism quotes lines from *Pharsalia* fourteen times in some two hundred pages. The connection between the adventuring prowess of Ralegh and the courageous men of the Civil War makes Lucan an apt presence.[54] Moreover, Hawkins's description of the Civil War as part of this illustrious history is, though brief, made through an especially violent Lucanic lens:

> The *Caesarians* and *Pompeians*, when they contended for the whole World, fought not more Battels, in the several Provinces thereof, then these two parties did in the narrow Lists . . . They scorned to owe their lives to Armor, and sometimes would charge in their shirts with bravery

and undauntedness. They ran on the mouth of the Cannon; nor did their great Souls fear to have their Carkasses torn in little pieces.[55]

In his comments on the 'life and history of Thucydides', Hobbes praised the Greek historian's representation of speech, which he regarded as the only permissible deviation from narrative: 'the grounds and motives of every action he setteth down before the action itself, either narratively, or else contriveth them into the form of *deliberative orations* in the persons of such as from time to time bare sway in the commonwealth'.[56] Hobbes's opinion of orators is ambiguous: he does not like anarchy caused by many effective orators in Athens, but admires a strong orator like Pericles, who was able to govern Athens as a monarchy. Oratory is however an unambiguously important part of historical representation, not least of all because it helped the reader apprehend 'the same passions that they were in that were beholders'.[57] We should therefore not be surprised to find oratory figuring largely in the history of another admirer of Thucydides, and sometime friend of Hobbes, Edward Hyde, Earl of Clarendon. By contrast, although Thomas May frequently quotes printed documents, his Tacitean history does not generally use oratory. Where both are similar is in their incorporation of the printed materials which played such a crucial role in the conflict. In Clarendon, printed declarations are often transformed into oratory, while in May, they tend to stay exactly as they are – printed ammunition (as was also the case with Rushworth). Both historians are expanding the dimensions of historical writing by acknowledging the communications revolution which had taken place during the course of the 1640s. When Clarendon explicitly discusses communication (and its complication, censorship), he is not unbiased:

Notwithstanding these sharp Declarations (infallible Symptoms of sharper Actions) which were with equal Diligence dispersed by either side among the People, save that the Agents for the Parliament took as much care to Suppress the King's, as to publish their own; whereas the King's desire was that they might be both impartially read and examin'd, and to that purpose always caused those from the Parliament to be printed with his own, They had the power and skill to persuade Men, who, but by that perswasion, could not have been Seduced. (V.132)

The first six books of Clarendon's *History of the Rebellion* were begun in 1646 on the Scilly Isles, where Clarendon had sought refuge. Clarendon wrote until the late 1640s, and then did not complete the *History* until his fall from office in the later 1660s. The grandiose scheme of publishing the *History* for the first time in the early eighteenth century (complete with its own political intentions), and the tradition of Clarendon publication thereafter, has obscured the discontinuities within the text of the *History*. The first six books were revised after their first drafting, but the manuscript gives access to a text which was written in the immediate aftermath of the events it describes.[58]

We might imagine then a history accurately disposed, and brought to convincing life with reported oratory, the qualities which Hobbes praised in Thucydides. Indeed, Clarendon was anxious when the King fled from Hampton Court because he feared he would cease to have access to materials he was using to write his work.[59] Yet nothing could be further from the truth in this anxious text which surrounds a disinterested majesty with a fearful apprehension of what had ruined England. By 15 November 1646, Clarendon had completed sixty sheets of his *History*, and he was thinking of it already as a combination of *discorsi* history and persecution narrative: it would exceed that which Davila wrote of twelve kings, and would be like Foxe's *Book of Martyrs*.[60] Where May vilifies Royalist deceit and 'Papist' superstition in a language of increasingly republican dimensions, Clarendon implies the fear of the uncontrollable in the effect generated by the juxtaposition of narrative with the discontinuous and unrooted presences of oratory and of 'characters'. Although the 'characters' were to be much expanded in the final version, their impact in the earlier manuscript is still considerable. May controls and directs spite as if he were Juvenal; Clarendon pretends to be Thucydides, taking the reader into a world of passions which only simulate disinterestedness.

The *History* begins by acknowledging the power of a wrathful Providence punishing England for the pride and folly of Englishmen (I.2). Clarendon chooses not to root the causes of the 'rebellion' in Elizabeth's reign. In what appears to be a semi-critical reference to May or to Harrington, Clarendon seeks instead to look at a phenomenal now:

> by viewing the Temper, Disposition, and Habit, of that time, of the Court and of the Country, we may discern the minds of Men prepared, of some to do, and of others to Suffer all that hath since happened; the Pride of this Man, and the popularity of that. (I.4)

By avoiding causes, the sense of being in the middle of the action is enhanced, but of course silent prejudices creep into the narrative by virtue of the absence of interpretative signals, signals that are beyond the level of simple human motivation. We know for whom May writes and why he does so. We know his history is propaganda. Clarendon's *History* is not, in its original incarnation, published propaganda (its first readers were royalist exiles), but it is the work of a sophisticatedly committed man, and the text confesses prejudice indirectly and in a way which has yet to be properly understood.

Clarendon's constitutional royalism, and his attempts to reconcile King and Parliament in the early 1640s, are well known. He acknowledges early on in the *History* that the dissolution of parliaments was a major cause of dissent in the kingdom, as were the 'evil advisers' in Charles's court, a clear indication of his dislike for royal favourites and the influence of Henrietta Maria. It is in the description of the ending of the 1628 Parliament that Clarendon gives the clue to his rhetoric away. Despite the voting of five subsidies for the King, the Parliament was prorogued 'with strange Circumstances of Passion'. Note how the phrasing avoids causation: we do not know whether the passion was a cause or a consequence; it was simply there, and being irrational, is immediately identified as a sign of trouble.

Clarendon's response to Buckingham's decision to end the Parliament is one of no surprise – given that Buckingham knew nothing of 'popular councils' – but for Richard Weston Earl of Portland's support for this, there is complete wonder. By their advice, it is as if the King temporarily lost his mind. The reader feels amazed too, and the beginning of a certain degree of hopelessness at the situation. While we experience this, our attention is taken up with the description of Buckingham, so that such explanation as there is is rooted in the vicissitudes of character:

> I wonder less at the Errors of this nature in the Duke of Buckingham; who, having had a most generous Education in Courts, was utterly ignorant of the Ebbs and Floods of Popular Councils, and of the Winds that move those Waters; and could not, without the spirit of Indignation, find himself, in the space of a few weeks, without any visible cause intervening, from the greatest height of popular Estimation that any person hath ascended to (insomuch as Sr *Edward Coke* blasphemously call'd him our Saviour) by the same breath thrown down to the depth of Calumny and Reproach. I say, it is no marvel (besides that he was naturally [inclined] to follow such Counsels as were given him) that he could think of no better way, to be freed of these inconveniences, and troubles, the Passions of those Meetings gave him, than to dissolve them, and prevent their coming together: and that when they seemed to neglect the publick Peace, out of Animosity to him, that he intended his own Ease and Security in the first place, and easily believ'd, the Publick might be otherwise provided for, by more Intent and Dispassionate Councils. (I.10)[61]

The 'wonder' for us is in the magnetic attraction of the picture of Buckingham, and the way in which personality is merged with action. Later, the Duke's character determines a long digression on the political events of the 1620s. The rooting of causation in character is rhetorically compounded by the sea imagery, itself both biblical, epic and romantic in origin. Buckingham does not by any means escape from history in this description of him, but he does sufficiently stand out so that he begins to look like a character in a prose romance (see above, 237). Indeed, there is a clear link between character formations that are eventually dehistoricised (as in the English versions of French heroic romance) and character formations which 'step out' of their history, and absorb the contingencies of historical cause and effect into.

Put this inside a discourse which in fact breaks Thucydides' rules (but not excessively) by patterning events and actions as neat parallels, and dialectical contradictions, and the authority of Clarendon's *History* is complete. It keeps a kind of classical cohesion by giving powers of prolepsis to characters: James I prophesies that the King of England will only prevail if he satisfies the Parliament, and his son finds that this is true. It is also worth pointing out here another force operating on Clarendon while he composed the *History*. As well as reading Machiavelli and Davila – the latter a disengaged Tacitean historian – Clarendon admired Guido Bentivoglio's *The History of the Warrs of Flanders* (1635–40), translated by Henry Carey, Earl of Monmouth and published in 1654. Bentivoglio was a Ciceronian, pro-Spanish historian, who repeatedly prefers moral statement to dispassionate analysis. His reportage of diplomatic speeches (as opposed to printed information) appealed to Clarendon, and was clearly a model for character. It is also difficult to see how Clarendon can have failed to read Bentivoglio's history as Carey did: a parallel account of the English Civil War, with the Spanish as the Royalists, and the Parliamentarians as the Dutch rebels. Humphrey Moseley's publisher's preface implies the parallel between Bentivoglio's contempt for Dutch Protestants and the attitude the loyal reader should take with Puritans. In an earlier translation of another work by Bentivoglio, *Historicall Relations of the United Provinces* (1652), Carey inflects his translation towards his cause, as Bentivoglio says 'that this new Commonwealth [the United Provinces] is not likely to continue in its present condition, but that it will rather fail therein shortly, and be again reduced at last to the Government of one only'(48). Bentivoglio was wrong, but his translator was right. Carey's translation also strains or bends definitions: he calls the Elizabethan Calvinists 'Parlementarians' because he says they wanted a national religion controlled by Parliament (77–8). There was no such usage of the word in the later sixteenth century. Carey has invented the definition in order to evoke the Erastian parliamentarians of the 1640s. Identity is rewritten and projected backwards onto English history.

When Clarendon leaves simple human agency, he is often to be found endorsing the fears of those many who saw the country disrupted by an alliance of print, puritan preaching and discontented gentlemen. Buckingham's assassin, Felton, is described as being motivated by 'some Transcripts of such Expressions (for the late License of Printing all mutinous and seditious Discourses was not yet in fashion) and some general Invectives he met with amongst the People' (I.53). Clarendon was no lover of Buckingham but in this scene he is fashioning the myths of later royalist and Stuart ideology. There is even an introduction of a courtly language, recognisable as such, and even if ironic, nonetheless signals a particular kind of value. Portland's intrigues are exposed in particularly French terms: 'he frequently expos'd himself, and left his condition worse than it was before; and the Eclairecisment commonly ended in the discovery of the persons from whom he had receiv'd his most secret intelligence'(I.110). These kinds of locutions may be related to Clarendon's own preference for French rather than English translations of the classics. The English, he maintained, did not understand their own language sufficiently well for it to be a fit vehicle for ancient wisdom.

In later books, the irrational power of the mob, a force which cannot be explained so much as imagistically described, is attributed to the familiar cause of puritan preaching: 'I must not forget, though it cannot be remembered without much horror, that this strange Wild-fire among the people, was not so much and so furiously kindled by the breath of the Parliament, as of the Clergy'(VI.39). When Charles's words themselves condemn the religious separatists (among others) as a chief cause for discontent in the City and the nation, the effect of blame is complete (VI.204). By putting these words into the mouth of the King (because they *are* his words) Clarendon keeps his distance, but his *History* becomes, in consequence, more committed and less discriminating. In these sections, the *History* moves towards the kind of representation of sectarians which is to be found in the heresiographers Featley, Edwards and Pagitt, and more significantly, in contemporary histories such as Clement Walker's *The History of Independency* (1648). In this work, the popular parliamentary history of Joshua Sprigge, *Anglia Rediviva* (1647), the most influential account of parliamentary military success, is denied generic status as a history in order to be reviled as a 'Legend or Romance of the Army'(6).

In the opening sections of the *History*, Clarendon was writing about the more distant past. We would have to concede that the shaping powers which are manifested here have a greater chance to work on material recessed further back in memory, and which has not left such a degree of printed evidence. We might expect Clarendon to lose some of the effect of the earlier sections in the later books which were composed in the 1640s. If there is a different reading experience, when the reader is actually placed in the events of war, character and oratory still function as dominant controlling devices. Charles I's speech at York in 1641, placed at the beginning of Book IV, is not only very long but a very powerful means of voicing sympathetically royalist views and strategy. Elsewhere, snippets of conversation enter the text, such as the urgent but uncertain discussion over strategy at Edgehill (VI.83). By contrast, May depicts Charles listening to petitions at York which he is seen to treat suspiciously and to disregard.[62] Clarendon's *History* displays none of the sacramentalism which is to be found in *Eikon Basilike*, but Charles does appear as a sacred king when he is depicted renewing his coronation oath in 1642 (V.293–305). Clarendon's writings are rightly judged to display, in general, none of the features of royalist discourse from the 1640s, but there are important places where these elements show through.

Clarendon's most significant achievement, and a feature which has gone largely unrecognised, is his capacity to render battle scenes in a tight, spare, wholly unornate style, which nonetheless contains within its paragraphed movements, the ebb and flow of battle:

> The Earl of *Essex* continued still at *Warwick*, repairing his broken Regiments and Troops, which every day lessen'd and impair'd; for the number of his slain Men was greater than it was reported to be, there being very many kill'd in the Chase, and many who died of their wounds after they were carried off, and, of those, who run away in the beginning, more staid away than return'd; and, which was more, they who ran farthest and fullest told such lamentable Stories of the defeat, and many of them shew'd such hurts, that the terror thereof was even ready to make the People revolt to their Allegiance in all places. (VI.100)

Some Clarendon authorities have claimed that the section completed after the Restoration and Clarendon's final retirement from politics is not significantly different from the earlier part.[63] Such a judgement depends upon how the evidence is viewed. In fact, as we move away from the first six books, and the very well-remembered and documented early stages of the conflict, so a more rapidly moving narrative sets in. Books become shorter. The 1650s are compressed into the last four books. Battles are less extensively described, and characterisation leaves behind the actual character, to become integrated into the narrative.

Inside the particular stylistic models chosen by each historian, there lay a structure of explanation. Initially, all of these early histories of the Civil War accepted the declarations issued by the King and the Parliament (especially the Grand Remonstrance) as the starting point and parameter-defining circumstances of the conflict. This consensus significantly ended in 1649, and new parameters of explanation filled their place.

If Tacitus was May's model as historian, Sallust was Milton's. Indeed, Milton believed that Sallust's method was a methodological embodiment of republican virtue, and one which was inherited by Tacitus. Milton's *History of Britain* is an application of Roman historiography to ancient British, Roman-British and Saxon sources, up to the time of the Norman Conquest. Where May's historical writing documents his successive drift towards the parliamentary Independents in the later 1640s, Milton's

History is a document of his own eventual conviction that the Independents and the Army should reshape the kingdom, and his frustration with the Long Parliament in the 1640s and Cromwell in the 1650s in delaying reform. Milton's *History* has not generally been well-served by its editors and interpreters, but now painstaking work enables us to see the first part being written (perhaps) in early 1649, and the later part in 1655.[64] This account regards the text of the *History* as a truly republican endeavour, but one whose significance was obscured not only by the difficulty of seeing the real political context of the composition, but also by the later appropriations of the text and its accompanying materials by Whigs and Tories with different preoccupations. Milton's pessimistic implied parallels between early and current national history were a reversal of the picture painted by the influential member of the Long Parliament, Nathaniel Bacon, in *A Historicall Discourse of the Uniformity of the Government of England* (1647). Bacon argued that the pre-Roman government of Britain had been republican (and also Christian), and he used the accounts of May's favourites, Tacitus and Dio Cassius, to prove this. Since much of this system had survived the Norman Conquest, it was for the Long Parliament to make a restitution of ancient rights against the encroachments of monarchs and their henchmen, the clergy. Bacon was excluded from the Long Parliament in Pride's Purge, but returned to the Rump Parliament, and published a *Continuation* of his history to the death of Elizabeth, this time (appropriately) stressing the superfluity of aristocrats, for, of course, the House of Lords had been abolished in 1649.[65]

Myth-Making

Despite the innovations of the 1640s, George Lawson could still claim in 1657 that the English did not write good histories, and that foreign historians who used English sources should be wary of misleading accounts of the English constitution. In particular, Lawson was scornful of descriptions of absolute monarchs.[66] He was in fact acknowledging the amount of myth-making which had taken place; myths which obscured a faithful account of government. When Lawson wrote this, he could not have seen the as yet uncomplete *History* of Clarendon, but even if he had done, his impressions would probably have been the same.

Hobbes's 'history' *Behemoth* (c.1668) is just such a piece of myth-making. Hardly surprising, we might say, from someone with such a powerful original mind, to whom the writing of a history like Clarendon's would have seemed too tedious to contemplate. *Behemoth* is in any case a dialogue rather than a narrative, and its sources, so Hobbes claims, are not contemporary documentation but James Heath's decidedly royalist and often unreliable *Chronicle*. Hobbes was away from England for longer than Clarendon, so his need to use contemporary documentation was greater, but his practice apparently hardly reliant at all on these forms. Yet Hobbes did translate Thucydides earlier in his career, and, as we have seen, he was committed to the principles of impartial history writing. 'There be divers men that have written the history, out of whom I might have learned what they did, and somewhat also of the contrivance; but I find in them little of what I would ask' (45), says Speaker B, who denies that Speaker A has digressed from the narrative precisely because he is providing an account of causes as well as actions.

Behemoth begins not *in* the action but from a removed perspective, 'as from the Devil's Mountain', and as such opinion and events are powerfully shaped throughout the dialogue. In this way, Hobbes adopts not a Thucydidean or even Tacitean posture but that of Machiavelli in the *Discorsi*, commenting on historical events through his own interpretative framework. The parallel does not quite work: Machiavelli comments on Livy's *History*; Hobbes comments on the events of history, and that we know he is using Heath as a crutch for his defective memory merely decreases the value of *Behemoth* as history. But the dialogue is as historical as Hobbes ever becomes. He admits that Charles I had financial problems, and turns this immediately to the reason why Charles could not keep his 'corrupted' people in line by force. This is a Machiavellian rather than a Hobbesean suggestion, but as we move into Hobbes's attribution of blame, the framework of *Leviathan* begins to exert its hold on the text.

Speaker A blames seven groups in the kingdom – Puritans, Papists, sectarians, republican gentlemen, merchants, self-interested adventurers and the plain ignorant. There is probably no connection between the seven groups and the seven churches in the Book of Revelation (it would be a very Hobbesean joke were that the case), and in the first three categories come those who are the target of Hobbes's satire in Book IV of *Leviathan*. Rebellion is bred from the exploitation by illusory authorities of irrational qualities in human beings. The power of the Roman Catholic church lies in convincing some people that they will be damned if they do not refrain from sex (7). The sources of these illusions of the temporal power of religious authorities, especially the Pope, lie far back in Christian history. Throughout this time, it is precisely the power of unchecked oratory which enables illusions to spread, first in unlicensed conventicles, and then through the universities of medieval Europe. Indeed, one of the most potent illusions is that of 'separated essences', sustained by the wide acceptance of Aristotelian teaching, whereby the false myths of priestcraft are intellectually sustained.

It could justifiably be objected that *Behemoth* is no history but more of Hobbes's political theory. Yet just at the point where we feel this, the

late 1630s comes sharply into focus and we are in the beginning of the
Civil War. At the same time, Hobbes employs a form of character
writing which does not reduce all causation to the uncertainties of
clashing personalities, but which vividly puts people as actors in his
broad scheme of grand delusion. Along with extempore prayer and
private inspiration, preaching persuades while concealing its own
seditiousness:

> they so framed their countenance and gesture at their entrance into the
> pulpit, and their pronunciation both in their prayer and sermon, and used
> the Scripture phrase (whether understood by the people or not), as that
> no tragedian in the world could have acted the part of a right godly man
> better than these did; insomuch as a man unacquainted with such art,
> could never suspect any ambitious plot in them to raise sedition against
> the state, as they then had designed; or doubt that the vehemence of their
> voice (for the same words with the usual pronunciation had been of little
> force) and forcedness of their gesture and looks, could arise from anything
> else but zeal to the service of God. And by this art they came into such
> credit, that numbers of men used to go forth of their own parishes and
> towns on working-days, leaving their calling, and on Sundays leaving
> their own churches, to hear them preach in other places. (24)

But shortly after this, the reader of the dialogue is taken again into a
consideration of centuries-old causes of the Civil War, so that there is a
simultaneous apprehension of present and deeply recessed past. Such
oscillations in the pattern of focus – we cannot call them digressions – are
repeated throughout the text. Unlike the parallels of classical republican
history and the typology of biblical history, Hobbes's history explains
causes and events by synthesising history as process. Harrington's desire
to rectify the failures of history means that Hobbes's particular
achievement in this respect is not open to him (see above, 168). By the
time we are finally given a more or less continuous historical narrative –
over one quarter of the way through the text – our capacity to judge is
entirely governed by the force of Hobbes's historicised sociology.

Given the weight of centuries of illusion, it is not surprising to find
men acting, in Hobbes's view, through the power of illusions, during the
dispute between King and Parliament. The latter can only put
accusations in vague and empty terms to the King, most of which were
functions of the deceptions of puritan religion. But in the narrative
sections inconsistencies and gaps in Hobbes's explanation creep in. The
only element which Speaker A believes the parliamentary army to have
over the King's is 'spite', a remarkably reductive and insufficient
statement, while Hobbes has no apparent way of dealing with the
question of finance. The reader is duped by seeing only one side of the
coin: that Charles needed money and it was simply for the Parliament to

vote it to him. It is in these moments that the reliance on Heath emerges, and we question the quality of Hobbes's text. Indeed, at one point propaganda and Hobbesian analysis merge. Hobbes identifies the lack of resistance in London to the Army as the decisive event in the eventual raising of a republic and a tyrannous Protectorate afterwards, and at the same time he sees Cromwell's only intention being to make himself king, a point made frequently in royalist newsbooks from 1647 onwards.

The fourth and last dialogue in *Behemoth* could be said to be a reverse version of May's *History*. Starting with the rise of the republic and its governance through the Rump Parliament and the Council of State, aspersions are cast on those who would follow the anti-monarchical writers of Greece and Rome, as opposed to the true science of politics which Hobbes had discovered and which took many years of careful study.

It was possible for those away from the action, and without reliable information, to write informed and relatively impartial history. One example which casts a shadow over *Behemoth* as a work of history is Sir Hamon L'Estrange's *The Reign of King Charls: An History Faithfull and Impartially delivered and disposed into Annals* (1655). There is no doubting L'Estrange's sympathies: the preface defends Charles against his Commonwealth detractors and chides the Presbyterians for supporting a cause which led (to their own great regret) to regicide (Sigs A3v). L'Estrange says he relied for his information from verbal reports (after the examples of Thucydides, Xenophon and Herodian), and that he relied upon one person above all others (Sigs. A4r-v). The result was a relatively 'impartial' history, not unlike Clarendon's, and one which angered die-hard royalist men of letters like Peter Heylyn.[67] Clarendon's unbiased bias would probably have met a similar reception had it been published in 1655, and *The Reign of King Charls* serves a very useful function in indicating that climate of opinion. L'Estrange was a Calvinist Anglican and monarchist of the old school, looking back to an ideal of the Stuart monarchy which had disappeared by the late 1630s. His history ends with the execution of Strafford: one wonders if L'Estrange would have been able to continue into the 1640s. His final words – '*Cetera desiderantur*' – seem to indicate not (266). Like Cowley with his poetry, L'Estrange found himself disabled by history, although his achievement is greater than he thought: '*Times* better for the *History* than for the *Historian*; for while they render *Truth* more *resplendent*, they usually bring the *Relator* under a *cloud*. Whence the bane of all faithfull *Tradition*, that an *Historian* is rarely *found*, untill the *Truth* be *lost*' (Sig. A2r).

It should be apparent by now that the writing of histories *in* the Civil War was a heavily disrupted business. The history of men was more mutable, more open to differing interpretations and alternative political uses, than would have been the case without a social crisis. The examples chosen of May, Clarendon and Hobbes reveal the different pressures and contradictions, internal and external, to which historical writing was subject. We should notice in conclusion that the 1650s were not a time when, so far as surviving evidence permits us to know, histories of the Civil War were begun (although some slowly growing works were progressing then). The 1650s was a decade marked by the publication of utopias and related kinds of theoretical discourse – *Leviathan*, *The Law of Freedom*, *Oceana* – which were the result, it goes without saying, of the break in the tradition of government experienced in that decade. *Oceana*, as we have seen, attempts to synthesise all historical accounts of the past in order to escape from history into a timeless world of complete and hermetically sealed representation. During the intense political speculation of 1659–60, not history, but many different competing notions of *now*, *now as the past*, and *now as the way forwards* were offered.

It is no surprise to find the Restoration as the time when histories were published, especially those written during the Civil War. The reputation of Clarendon was established in a post-rebellion publishing project, albeit one ultimately on the verge of a new century. The great puritan memoirs, recounting in a variety of ways the rise, decline and fall of a cause, belong to these years. The disappointment of millennial hopes, and the resumption of the identity of the persecuted in history was widely adopted and enforced by the deep resonance of biblical echoes.[68] This is part of another story. What we should acknowledge is the ability of the present in its sheer unaccountable disruptiveness, and in its own new ways of talking to itself, to transform the making of historical knowledge. The emergence of an accurate and complete national history, so hotly pursued by the early Stuarts, was interrupted, but the Civil War made that history, when it finally emerged, a much more capable form of writing. In fact, despite the powerful claims which providentialist patterns of history made on English imaginations, both Clarendon and the republican historiographers had disrupted these large-scale deterministic narrative shapes to produce something much more problematic. The Civil War made modern English history writing what it is: we should no longer recognise Clarendon as the sole actor in this achievement.

Conclusion

In Nigel Williams's transhistorical novel *Witchcraft* (1987) is the following typical paragraph:

> on the road behind me the red estate car had reappeared suggesting that we were once again poised on some razor-thin temporal line between 1650 and 1986. This effect was further confirmed by a fat man who galloped past me on a small and not very efficient looking pony. He was wearing the jerkin, the sash and the helmet, but he had also a pair of horn rimmed glasses and as he passed me he winked coarsely, bouncing up and down in the saddle and said, 'Kills yer bum this does.' Roundheads and Cavaliers were hacking and slashing at each other wildly, although for the most part the conflict seemed shadow play. I could see no sign of blood. The bare headed man, who had a thin, posh voice, was screeching to the scattered figures. 'For God's sake can we have some order! The Royalists are in the wrong place. This is not Edge Hill. We cannot fight the battle of Edge Hill under these circumstances.' Another foot soldier of the Parliamentary forces panted past me. 'You should have seen fucking Naseby,' he said, 'Naseby was a total cock up.' (212)

The narrator, who thinks he has merged his time with the seventeenth century, is confused by a mock Civil War battle conducted by the Sealed Knot (he is not disabused of his half-illusion for several pages). Nigel Williams's hectically funny Scene is in fact very faithful to Civil War narrative: merging different time frames, but with the reportage being faithful to the immediacy of the moment.[1]

In his *Memoirs of a Cavalier* (1720), Daniel Defoe constructed an 'autobiography' from a series of news pamphlets and newsbooks, documenting the Thirty Years' War in Europe and the Civil War in England:

> I had no Occasion to follow them, not being in a Condition to attack their whole Body: but the Dragoons coming out into the Common, gave them another Volley at a Distance, which reached them effectually; for it

357

killed about 20 of them, and wounded more; but they drew off, and never fired a Shot at us, fearing to be enclosed between two Parties and so marched away to their General's Quarters . . . Our Men, after the Country Fashion, gave them a Shout at parting, to let them see we knew they were afraid of us. (186)

Like Williams, but closer to the moment, and the requirements of his own time, Defoe is simulating Civil War writing, and if one does not recognise it as Defoe, one cannot tell that it is not a pamphlet from the 1640s. Quite apart from Defoe's choice of a gallant royalist officer for sensationalist purposes, the narrative constitutes a cultural memory of the chief events of seventeenth-century English history. It is also a homage to the subject of this book – the great literary transformation of the mid-century – and in particular the rise of journalism and the rapid circulation of news pamphlets and other kinds of printed information. There are countless other witnesses to the literary impact of the Civil War and Revolution: most satirical poetry, elegy (especially Gray's *Elegy Written in a Country Churchyard* with its awesome invocation of Cromwell), the hymn, John Locke and his remarkable impact, the eighteenth-century Milton industry and so on – all the subject of further study. That the later chapters of this book have run to a few considerations of Restoration and early eighteenth-century aftermaths is a testimony to the unsegmentable continuity of history.

The march of history can, however, function as a kind of amnesic drug: all these later manifestations of literary Civil Warism tell us little of their origins, of the conditions which made them possible. For this reason, some summary statement of the discoveries made in the previous pages is in order. First of all comes the large-scale, politicised use of print in the Civil War decade. This was a capitalisation of existing practices and resources, but one which accelerated the public uses and common awareness of print far beyond all previous conceptions, even as it slowed down the publication rate of didactic literature, like sermons. The new conditions radically destabilised conceptions of truth, trustworthiness and authority, and challenged existing notions of authorship. The uneasy juncture of patronage and the marketplace was a well-known fact of the professional writer's life by 1640. The politicising of that area caused, as we have seen, much stress, and the emergence of a new kind of author: a hack who would write for hire (and who would therefore adopt any ideological position), but someone who nonetheless had their own political agenda, perhaps in a very sophisticated and advanced form. The author who wrote for hire was an inherently divided being, just as other traditionally strong identities in print (such as that of the gentlemen) were shattered by the onset of the war. And the sense of print expansion, with its multiple untruthful truths, was enhanced by other changes which concentrated literary activity into the world of the pamphlet and the newsbook: notably the closure of the theatres. This does not mean that manuscript circulation of literature, and the function of the pulpit and the tub, in their respective communities, were unimportant. Yet time and time again, the evidence suggests that the world of print was an increasingly powerful point of reference for other modes of communication. 'Scribal publication' did not stop, but the role of print did sharpen the distinction between the two kinds of publication, and the different associations attached to them.[2]

The new conditions of writing opened a new chapter in the history of rhetoric. The classical theories for organising public speech were at first enthusiastically adopted by both sides in the national conflict, more often than not as a sign of intrinsic virtue, as much as a mode of persuasion. But the experience of debate in print, in such an extended and complex process, taught new lessons. Rhetorical efficacy was not always to be found in oratorical formulae, or in logic, but in a variety of indirect and insinuating modes of address. Replaying the events of the 1640s and 1650s through a fictional travesty became a response of those who were disillusioned but powerless to reverse their predicament, or that of the nation. For these people, public rhetoric had failed, and their contribution represents a kind of *cul de sac* of persuasive language. So threatened are they, their words often amount to nothing more than a defence of their singular identities: a defence of the limits of their selfhood. Here, in a very real sense, the nonsensical prophet and the obfuscating, eccentric Royalist occupied a similar space. Others felt that rhetoric had achieved too much: the only solution was to acknowledge its power, and see it as a force for social stability. This was to assume that the art of persuasion had a more or less mesmeric power. By contrast, others still, who retained a belief in rhetoric's ancient function, were using it to develop a civic politics during the Commonwealth. In this sense, even the usage of classical rhetoric moved down the social scale.

The rise of the serial newsbook was, as far as we can see, an effect of high politics, but it rapidly became the most visible and readily available evidence of print culture. It sucked literary forms from other kinds of publication into its homogenising single gatherings. Perhaps this was an unjust squashing, but in a broader sense, the newsbook (especially the less extravagant but highly popular productions of the mid-1640s) created an arena of shared meanings in which the politics of the 1640s could be known by the literate populace. The readership may have been largely focused in the metropolis, but the fact remains that the news-book and the pamphlet were servicing and simultaneously creating a public opinion. The proof of that pudding is the Protectorate policy of stifling opposition newsbooks in an attempt to control that public opinion.

That the newsbook and the pamphlet contained so much dramatic material is partly a testimony to the news function of the theatres before 1642. And yet in many ways, we can also say that the Renaissance theatre ended its brilliant career in the ephemeral publications of the 1640s. Pamphlet references to, and uses of, a whole range of playwrights and plays were faithful to the loose integrity of the pre-war stage. The theatre of the 1660s was reborn at a distance, had a habit of vigorous revision of older plays, and took some time to find its way back to the resources of the earlier theatre. It was itself dramatising some of the nondramatic literature of the Interregnum, like the romance.

The exhaustion of forms in the mid-century is also evident in the career of the pulpit. The hold of the spoken sacred word (and a highly emotive one at that), right at the centre of the nation's politics, was never to be so great again. Preaching, and the reading of sermons, was a salient feature of all kinds of religion after 1660, but never again was the public and political influence of the sermon on all kinds of people so great and so telling.

The language of political and religious controversy lends itself to literary analysis because it was so bound by the sphere of the printed pamphlet. Its constituent materials were largely identical with those of 'literature' proper. Writing controversial literature was commonly understood as a kind of warfare, so that authors were imagined to be engaged in a literary heroism. If various kinds of discourse had begun to cause controversy before 1640 by leaping out of their allotted places within institutionally bound frameworks, the 1640s were the time of a rapid cross-fertilisation of rhetorical components. Hostile images of the enemy were developed and traded by all interests. In the domain of discourse, the middle ground was sacrificed to a series of increasingly confident and opposed views and rhetorics – a national epitome of division. The martyrological terms of royalism were in existence long before *Eikon Basilike*, while parliamentarianism evolved into elite republicanism, far more textually sophisticated than the parliamentary apologies of the 1620s. This arena was effectively invaded and disrupted by the special pamphleteering of the Levellers, whose petitioning strategies took the world of popular festivity into high politics. It was in many ways a new kind of voice in politics, although one that spoke in its stress on individual rights for the kind of individualising which is to be seen throughout the religious spectrum. This was true of the most meekly pious devotional treatise, and the prophecies of male and female enthusiasts, which effectively rocked the order of language.

Literary genres suffered similar division and drastic reorganisation but with a complexity indicative not only of social function, but also of axiomatic creativity. The Civil War was inducing entirely new ways of seeing, and forms of representation within which to cast those visions. Thus (and largely within the ruling elite), epic poetry was finally bashed into its Miltonic marriage of puritan interiority and ancient liberty, overcoming Lucanic dissipation, and turning Virgil into a modern voice. Take it or leave it, Milton had fashioned a modern ur-text, as Restoration poets rapidly acknowledged. One could control or expel Milton's enthusiasm, as Dryden did, but the enthusiasm tended to return in the Miltonic line, redolent of the puritan revolution and its aftermath.

Romance was the imaginative space in which courtly and gentile identities were explored, and in which private and public worlds co-existed in a most frankly inter-connected way. National Protestant identity could be said to have been constellated in Sidney's *Arcadia*, its author a hero representing all that was virtuous. The divided nation could not sustain such a confidence, and if Sidneyism continued in the heroes of the Commonwealth, like Sir Henry Vane, those disappointed by *Arcadia* turned more exclusively to French romance, with its highly complicated plotting and its deliberately unfamiliar, yet still historically believable, landscapes. Virtue could be tested outside of a context with national associations, and the implied *salon* readership of the heroic romances encouraged an inward turn. In fact, the doors were being opened to the female romance of the later seventeenth and eighteenth centuries.

Lyric poetry was contaminated by the national conflict, its internal dimensions forced to embody the informational vehicles of the war, the pamphlet and the newsbook. The habit of fragmentation which ensued resulted in a new level of scepticism in the love lyric: love was different after the war. But in a contrary movement, both the elegy and the panegyric were given vital new life; the former through the expense of lives (and one life in particular), the latter through the complications which divided loyalties, or switched loyalties, brought to the form. As was detected long ago, elegy went on to convey regicide to the romantic revolution; it was one of the Civil War's strongest background hums in the eighteenth century. Public poetry favoured the circulation of panegyric as well as satire. In the Restoration, it became a mode of political action, not merely praise or blame. This study has shown the significance of the innovations of the 1640s and 1650s: for too long much of this poetry has been overlooked. The later period, through its inheritance and inevitable transformation of the revolutionary resource, should not blind us to the moment of innovation. Independent wor-ship, in its middle way, between completely de-formalised practice, and its opposite, produced the non-psalmic hymn. It may have seemed a limited affair, but it was a very important moment in the history of the religious lyric.

The 'Augustan Age' was the age of satire, and the Civil War is commonly seen as the root of that practice. In an environment which assumed public attack, it is not surprising to find satire so preferred. But it was not the elitist or purely royalist tool that it is often thought to be in popular literary history. Every group with the power of words had its own means of mockery. In this case, if 'satire' was everywhere, satires faithful to the ancient forms seemed to speak very private kinds of experience in the 1650s: even satire was interiorised.

English historical writing, on the other hand, was finally made. Rather like the case of epic, classical modes were made to articulate the national catastrophe in differently aligned ideological configurations (there was no truly neutralist history). The result was an elevation of national history into classical refinement, and that meant a concomitant meeting of classical narration with the language of vernacular printed reportage. We should not let the republican version of that history be neglected at the expense of better-remembered royalist ones.

Landscapes live in time too, but in a way which is less responsive to volatile change than the affairs of men. Hence the return to the land as an imaginative topos for all kinds of literary endeavour during the 1640s and 1650s. Gerrard Winstanley's turn to the land, after the disappointments of the city, was imagined through what Vico would have recognised as genuine *poesis* – an escape from the vicissitudes of culture into nature (and God). Indeed, we could say that only the landscape provided an environment of sufficient liberty in which civilisation (which, paradoxically, was the war) could be assessed with relative detachment. On the other hand, the inscription of national division into something as apparently innocent as the fishing manual is indicative of the total immersion of national culture in the conflict. The Civil War could never be forgotten, and in an unexpected way, a kind of green politics had begun.

When something as cataclysmic as the English Civil War and Revolution occurs, a massive destabilisation in the order of meaning is engendered. That there were so many words enhanced the sense of this, and it was a time which many acknowledged as a collective loss of reason. When historical analysis properly discovers so many kinds of continuity, pre- as well as post-1640, so that the revolution seems even less than a 'grand rebellion', little more than a constitutional cough, or, in economic history, gradual transformations of ownership and the steady growth of entrepreneurial activity, it is well worth looking at the world of words, which is where the impact of the crisis was most strongly registered. Despairing of his cause, and the plight of the nation, the prophet Thomas Tany claimed that God had given him in dreams all the languages in the world, including the original language, compressed into one primal linguistic atom that sat inside Tany, waiting to be expounded. This seems as good a witness as any to the sense of a need for a return to the origins of language forms, and for a new beginning, which the crisis produced.

Notes

Introduction: Dissent Refracted: Text, Genre and Society 1640–60

1. 12 Car. II, c. 11, para. XXIV, *Statutes of the Realm* (1810–28), Vol. V. See also Paul Seaward, *The Cavalier Parliament and the Reconstruction of the Old Regime, 1661–1667* (Cambridge, 1989), 74.
2. Peter W. Thomas, 'The Impact on Literature', in John Morrill, ed., *The Impact of the English Civil War* (1991), 123–42 (125).
3. John Morrill, 'The Nature of the English Revolution', in *The Nature of the English Revolution* (1993), 19.
4. A view confirmed by Richard Helgerson in his recently published *Forms of Nationhood: The Elizabethan Writing of England* (Chicago, 1992).
5. For the 1790s, see Marilyn Butler, *Romantics, Rebels and Reactionaries: English Literature and its Background 1760–1830* (Oxford, 1981); Nicholas Roe, *Wordsworth and Coleridge: The Radical Years* (Oxford, 1988); Jon Mee, *Dangerous Enthusiasm: William Blake and the Culture of Radicalism in the 1790s* (Oxford, 1992); Peter J. Kitson, '"Sages and Patriots that being dead do not yet speak to us": Readings of the English Revolution in the late Eighteenth Century', in James Holstun, ed., *Pamphlet Wars: Prose in the English Revolution* (1992), 205–30.
6. Mikhail Bakhtin, 'The Problem of Speech Genres', in *Speech Genres and Other Essays* (1986, 1987), 60–102 (70).
7. *Ibid.*, 97. For a parallel theory using structural linguistics, see Maria Corti, *An Introduction to Literary Semiotics* (Bloomington, Indiana, 1978), ch. 5, 115–43.
8. OED gives 1816 as the earliest instance of this use of 'genre'.
9. Barbara Kiefer Lewalski, *Paradise Lost and the Rhetoric of Literary Forms* (Princeton, 1985), ch. 1, esp. 17. See also *idem*, *Protestant Poetics and the Seventeenth-Century Religious Lyric* (Princeton, 1979), ch. 2.
10. On Aristotle, see Alastair Fowler, *Kinds of Literature: An Introduction to the Theory of Genres and Modes* (Oxford, 1982), 28, 38. The weight of supposedly historically-informed criticism has been against the significance of genre in literary interpretation. For a healthy rebuttal of some of these views, see Ralph Cohen, 'History and Genre', *NLH*, 17 (1986), 203–17.
11. See Claude Levi-Strauss, *The Origin of Table Manners: Introduction to a Science of Technology* (1968); Michael McKeon, *The Origins of the English Novel 1600–1740* (1987), 4–11.
12. I am grateful to Professor Jan Assmann of Heidelberg for this information.
13. On the complexity of generic intermixture, see Fowler, *Kinds of Literature*, 45–8, and *idem*, 'Genre and Tradition', in Thomas N. Corns, ed., *The Cambridge Companion to English Poetry: Donne to Marvell* (Cambridge, 1993), 80–100.
14. Helgerson, *Forms of Nationhood*, 7.

15. A view now conceded by Alastair Fowler in 'The Future of Genre Theory: Functions and Constructional Types', in Ralph Cohen, ed., *The Future of Literary Theory* (1989), 291–303.

16. See Thomas Osborne Calhoun, 'Cowley's Verse Satire, 1642–43, and the Beginnings of Party Politics', YES, 21 (1991), 197–206.

17. John Morrill, *Seventeenth-Century Britain 1603–1714* (Folkestone and Hamden, Conn., 1980), 132–3: 'I looked in vain . . . for work on why people wrote poetry, and who for.'

18. See Elaine Hobby, *Virtue of Necessity: English Women's Writing 1646–1688* (1988).

19. Helgerson, *Forms of Nationhood*, 14.

20. McKeon, *The Origins of the English Novel*, 20.

21. Ian Watt, *The Rise of the Novel: Studies in Defoe, Richardson, Fielding* (1957; 1976), 38–54.

22. William Haller's *The Rise of Puritanism* (New York, 1938) and *Liberty and Reformation in the Puritan Revolution* (New York, 1955) draw greatly on sermon literature in their analyses of puritan ideas. For a history of the sermon itself, we shall have to wait upon the research of Arnold Hunt (Trinity College, Cambridge) and James Rigney (Pembroke College, Oxford).

23. On the centrality of the Bible as an ideological weapon and battleground in the period, see Christopher Hill, *The English Bible and the Seventeenth-Century Revolution* (Harmondsworth, 1993).

24. See Nigel Smith, *Perfection Proclaimed: Language and Literature in English Radical Religion 1640–1660* (Oxford, 1989), ch. 8.

25. The translations appeared in the following order: Caxton reprinted (1647), Leonard Willan (1649), R.D. (1650), Sir John Ogilby (1651), *Fables of Aesop in English* (1658). See also *We have fish'd in faine and caught a frog* (5 June 1649).

26. In *Fables of Power: Aesopian Writing and Political History* (Durham, N.C., 1991), Annabel Patterson argues that Ogilby's translations represent a transformation of the genre. I am baffled by this claim; what has changed is the degree of hidden, covert allusion.

27. See Chris Orchard, 'Politics and the Literary Imagination, 1640–1660', (unpublished D.Phil. thesis, University of Oxford, 1994), ch. 3.

28. W.B., *Experiences and Tears* (1652), is the one significant example of a pro-parliamentary fable. See also the anti-Orangist *The Hollandish Catechism*, published in *Mercurius Politicus*, 11 July 1653.

29. Michel Foucault, *The Order of Things: An Archaeology of the Human Sciences* (1966, translation 1970), 17–44.

30. John Saltmarsh, *Dawnings of Light* (1646), 53. The marginal reference here is to Bacon's *Advancement of Learning*.

31. Conal Condren, *George Lawson's Politica and the English Revolution* (Cambridge, 1989).

32. Smith, *Perfection Proclaimed*, 229–67.

33. See J.C. Davis, *Fear, Myth and History: The Ranters and the Historians* (Cambridge, 1986), 76–87.

34. See J.C Davis, 'Cromwell's Religion', in John Morrill, ed., *Oliver Cromwell and the English Revolution* (1990), 181–208.

35. See Glenn Burgess, *The Politics of the Ancient Constitution: An Introduction to English Political Thought, 1603–1642* (1992), 133–7, 173–4; idem, 'The Divine Right of Kings Reconsidered', EHR, CVII (1992), 837–61.

36. See Corinne C. Weston and J.R. Greenburg, *Subjects and Sovereigns: The Grand Controversy over Legal Sovereignty in Stuart England* (Cambridge, 1981); J.P. Sommerville, *Politics and Ideology in England 1603–1640* (1986); Weston, 'England: Ancient Constitution and Common Law', in J.H. Burns, ed., *The Cambridge History of Political Thought*

1450–1700 (Cambridge, 1991), 374–411.

37. A point pleasingly affirmed in the structure of Jonathan Scott's 'The English Republican Imagination', in John Morrill, ed., *Revolution and Restoration* (1992), 35–54 (esp. 49).

38. John Cook, *King Charls His Case* (1649), Sig. c1v.

39. Alfred Harbage, *Cavalier Drama* (New York, 1936, 1964), stresses survival.

40. Nigel Smith, 'The Uses of Hebrew in the English Revolution', in P. Burke and R. Porter, edd., *Language, Self, and Society* (Oxford, 1991), 50–71.

41. Derek Hirst, 'The Politics of Literature in the English Republic', *The Seventeenth Century*, 5 (1990), 133–55.

42. Louis B. Wright, 'The Reading of Plays during the Puritan Revolution', *HLB*, 6 (1934), 73–108.

43. For the poem 'The World is Turned Upside Down', see Hyder E. Rollins, ed., *Cavalier and Puritan: Ballads and Broadsides Illustrating the Period of the Great Rebellion 1640–1660* (New York, 1923), 161–2.

44. George Hickes, *Memoirs of the Life of Mr. John Kettlewell* (1718), 14. I am most grateful to Jeremy Maule for this reference.

45. Henry Ferne, *The Camp at Gilgal* (Oxford, 1643), title-page.

46. Nancy Klein Maguire, 'The Theatrical Mask/Masque of Politics: The Case of Charles I', *JBS*, 28 (1989), 1–22 (2). The following section is indebted to Nancy Maguire's work.

47. [?Robert Wild], *The Bloody Court; or the Fatall Tribunall* (n.p., n.d.; ?1649), Sig. B4v.

48. Anon., 'Caroli' Τῇ Μακαρίτῃ παλιγγενεσία', in [John Cleveland], *Monumentum Regale: Or a Tombe, Erected for the incomparable and Glorious Monarch, Charles I* (1649), 29.

49. See Rebecca Bushnell, *Tragedies of Tyrants: Political Thought and Theater in the English Renaissance* (Ithaca, N.Y., 1990), 76–9.

50. Martin Dzelzainis, 'Milton, *Macbeth*,

and Buchanan', *The Seventeenth Century*, 4 (1989), 55–66.

51. For extensive discussions of the trashing of *Eikon Basilike* by *Eikonoklastes*, see David Loewenstein, *Milton and the Drama of History: Historical Vision, Iconoclasm, and the Literary Imagination* (Cambridge, 1990), ch. 3; Steven N. Zwicker, *Lines of Authority: Politics and English Literary Culture 1649–1689* (Ithaca, N.Y., 1993), ch. 2.

52. *The Tenure of Kings and Magistrates* (1649) in *Political Works*, ed. Martin Dzelzainis (Cambridge, 1991), 17.

53. *First Defence*, ed. Dzelzainis, 171.

54. *The Tenure of Kings and Magistrates*, in Dzelzainis, ed., 12; repeated in *First Defence*, in Dzelzainis, ed., 165.

55. *First Defence*, in Dzelzainis, ed., 179, 165.

56. For incest, see Richard A. MacCabe, *Incest, Drama and Nature's Law, 1550–1700* (Cambridge, 1993). In 'Allegory and the Sublime in *Paradise Lost*' (in *John Milton*, ed. Annabel Patterson (1992), 185–201), Victoria Kahn reads Milton's theological concerns into this passage, and links them with the sublime, but not in terms entirely consistent with Milton's understanding of the sublime (see below, 214–16).

57. See N.I. Matar, 'Aristotelian Tragedy in the Theology of Peter Sterry', *Literature and Theology*, 6 (1992), 310–19.

58. Anon., *A Peece of Ordnance invented by a Jesuite, for Councils, that fight by Whisperings, and raise Iealousie to overthrow both Church and State* (1644).

Chapter 1: Unstable Parameters

1. F.S. Siebert, *Freedom of the Press in England, 1476–1776* (Urbana, Ill., 1952), 165–263; Sheila Lambert, 'The Beginnings of Printing for the House of Commons, 1640–42', *The Library*, 6th ser., 3 (1981), 42–61; Christopher Hill, 'Censorship and English Literature', in *Collected*

Essays. Volume 1. Writing and Revolution in Seventeenth-Century England (Brighton, 1985), 32–71; Annabel Patterson, Censorship and Interpretation: The Conditions of Reading and Writing in Early Modern England (Madison, Wisc., 1984); Blair Worden, 'Literature and Political Censorship in Early Modern England', in Too Mighty to be Free: Censorship and the Press in Britain and the Netherlands (Zutphen, 1987), 45–62; Kevin Sharpe, The Personal Rule of Charles I (New Haven and London, 1992), ch. 11.

2. See Pauline Croft, 'The Reputation of Robert Cecil: Libels, Political Opinion and Popular Awareness in the Early Seventeenth Century', TRHS, 6th ser., 1 (1991), 43–69; Arthur Marotti, 'Manuscript Poetry and the Political World', forthcoming.

3. Tessa Watt, Cheap Print and Popular Piety 1550–1640 (Cambridge, 1991), 178, 219–20; Patrick Collinson, The Birthpangs of Protestant England. Religious and Cultural Change in the Sixteenth and Seventeenth Centuries (1988), 106–12.

4. See Anthony Fletcher, The Outbreak of the English Civil War (1981), esp. 191–227.

5. Nigel Smith, 'The Charge of Atheism and the Language of Radical Speculation, 1640–1660', in Michael Hunter and David Wootton, edd., Atheism from the Reformation to the Enlightenment (Oxford, 1992), 131–58.

6. I am drawing on evidence compiled for the forthcoming A History of the Book in Britain. Vol. IV. 1557–1695, edd. John Barnard and D.F. McKenzie (Cambridge University Press), and I am grateful to its editors for permission to cite from this work.

7. See Richard Rambuss, Spenser's Secret Career (Cambridge, 1993), 30–48.

8. Lois Potter, Secret Rites and Secret Writing: Royalist Literature 1641–1660 (Cambridge, 1989), 59–64; Mercurius Aulicus, 36th week (3 Sept. 1643), 499–500.

9. Francis Freeman, VIII Problems Compounded to the Cavaliers (1646). For Freeman, see BDBR. For a very well selected anthology on this theme, see William Lamont and Sybil Oldfield, edd., Politics, Religion and Literature in the Seventeenth Century (1975).

10. Ibid., Sig. [A1]v.

11. See Sharon Achinstein, 'The Politics of Babel in the English Revolution', in James Holstun, ed., Pamphlet Wars: Prose in the English Revolution (1992), 14–44.

12. See Lucasta Miller, 'The Shattered Violl: Print and Textuality in the 1640s', Essays and Studies (1993), 25–38.

13. I am grateful to Steven Pincus for showing me his work on the First Dutch War in advance of publication.

14. Joseph Hall, An Humble Remonstrance to the High Court of Parliament (1640), 1.

15. Henry Robinson, The Falsehood of Mr. William Pryn's Truth Triumphing (1645), Sig. A2r.

16. Richard Watson, The Panegyric and the Storme (1659), Sig. A4r.

17. A Paralel Between the Proceedings of this Present King And this Present Parliament (1648), 8.

18. Watson, The Panegyricke, Sig. A4r.

19. Ibid., loc. cit.

20. See Joshua Poole, The English Parnassus (1657), q.v. 'libel', 'pamphlet', 'satyre'.

21. Bond was a member of St John's College, Cambridge.

22. Walker and Bray produced popular satires of very different kinds: Walker spoke for the Puritans; Bray against them: see Thomas Bray, The Anatomy of Et Caetera (1641). Harbert remains uncertainly identified, but is probably Thomas Herbert.

23. LJ, 17 Car. 1, 722b.

24. See Lambert, 'The Beginnings of Printing', 56.

25. [Thomas Flatman], Naps upon Parnassus (1658), Sig. A2r.

26. See Edward Browne, *A Meteor. Or, Brief and pleasant Meditations Of the Providence of God toward his CHOSEN: And of the Education of Children* (1640), in *idem*, *A rare Paterne of Iustice and Mercy* (1642).

27. John Hall, *A Serious Epistle to Mr. William Prynne* (1649), 2. Is Hall's evidence on prices accurate? For evidence of book retail prices, see Francis Johnson, 'Notes on English retail book-prices, 1550–1640', *The Library*, 5th ser., 5 (1950), 89–90. For evidence of discounting – which would go against Hall's claim, see Watt, *Cheap Print*, 262 n24; John Blatchly, *The Town Library of Ipswich: A History and Catalogue* (Woodbridge, Suffolk, 1989), 17; Michael Hunter, Giles Mandelbrote and Nigel Smith, edd., *A Radical's Books: The Library Catalogue of Samuel Jeake of Rye* (forthcoming, Boydell and Brewer).

28. See John Harris, *The Accuser Sham'd* (1647).

29. Henry Parker, *Accomodation Cordially Desired* (1642), 3.

30. Anon., *A Paralel Between the Proceedings of this Present King and this Present Parliament* (1648), 1.

31. *Ibid.*, 2; see also Milton, *Areopagitica* (*CPW*, II.503–4).

32. See, for instance, *A Conference between the Pope, the Emperour and the King of Spain. Holden in the Castle of St. Angelo in Rome* (14 July 1642). An edition of this text, and its manuscript recension, prepared by Mark Jenner and Frank Romany, is forthcoming in *ELR*.

33. See Paul Hammond, 'Censorship in the Manuscript Transmission of Restoration Poetry', *Essays and Studies* (1993), 39–62; Harold Love, *Scribal Publication in Seventeenth Century England* (Oxford, 1993).

34. Richard Cust, 'News and Politics in Early Seventeenth-Century England', *Past and Present*, 112 (1986), 60–90.

35. [Richard Overton], *Vox Borealis* (1641), 1.

36. See e.g. Folger MS V.a.170; V.a.322; V.a.282.

37. Harvard University, Houghton Library, fMS Eng. 645.

38. Folger MS V.a.219, fo. 36.

39. See Anthony Cotton, 'London Newsbooks in the Civil War; Their Political Attitudes and Sources of Information' (unpublished D.Phil. thesis, Oxford University, 1971).

40. John Rushworth, *Historical Collections* (1659), Sig. b2v.

41. See R.A. Anselment, *Loyalist Resolve: Patient Fortitude in the English Civil War* (Newark, Delaware, 1988), 46–96.

42. As is the case with Nedham's *The Great Accuser Cast Down* (1657), his attack on John Goodwin.

43. Joseph Frank, *The Beginnings of the English Newspaper 1620–1660* (Camb., Mass., 1961), 346.

44. BL MS Add. 28,002, fo.59., Nedham to Oxenden, 2 Oct., 1648.

45. Cicero, *De Oratore*, Quintilian, *Institutio Oratoria*, [Cicero], *Ad C. Herennium de Ratione Dicendi*.

46. For a sobering account of Athenian rhetoric, see Anna Missiou, *The Subversive Oratory of Andokides. Politics, ideology and decision-making in democratic Athens* (Cambridge, 1992). Andokides, suggests Missiou, spoke in favour of peace with Sparta in order to protect his property. The popular party in Athens wanted war for the purpose of expanding vital food supplies to the city.

47. Thomas Hobbes, *De Cive* (1642, Engl. trans. 1651), X.xi, in English version, *The Clarendon Edition of the Philosophical Works of Thomas Hobbes*, vol. III, ed. Howard Warrender (Oxford, 1983), 137.

48. John Hall, 'To my Lord, the Lord Commissioner Whitelock', in Longinus, Περι Υψους, *Or Dionysius Longinus of the Height of Excellence*, trans. John Hall (1652), Sig. A7v.

49. George Gillespie, *A Late Dialogue Betwixt a Civilian and a Divine* (1644), 1.

50. *De Cive* was published in Paris in Latin in 1642, and in English in London, 1651.

51. Thomas Hobbes, *De Cive*, XII.xiii, in Warrender, ed., 155–6.

52. *Pro Populo Anglicano Defensio Secunda*, CPW, IV.595–6.

53. Robert Mossom, *The Preachers Tripartite* (1657), A3v-4r.

54. John Rushworth, *Historical Collections* (1659), b2v. 'Demagogue' is used here in the neutral sense of a leader of the popular party in the Athenian Assembly, the sense which Milton rescued in *Eikonoklastes*, against the pejorative sense used in *Eikon Basilike* (CPW, III.393).

55. Joseph Caryll, *Englands Plus Ultra* (1646), 29.

56. See Nigel Smith, 'IV', in J.F. McGregor et al., 'Debate: Fear, Myth and Furore, Reappraising the Ranters', *Past & Present*, 140 (1993), 155–210 (174).

57. Sjt Major Generall Brown, *The Lord Digbies Designe to Betray Abingdon* (1644), 13.

58. *Mercurius Britanicus*, 68 (27 Jan.–3 Feb. 1645), 538.

59. [Thomas May], *A Discourse Concerning the Successe of Former Parliaments* (1642), Sig. A2r-v.

60. *An Anti-Remonstrance* (1641), Sig. B3r.

61. *Mercurius Britanicus*, 13 (16–23 Nov. 1643), 99–100.

62. Thomas May, *The History of the Parliament* (1647; Oxford, 1854), 161.

63. J.A.W. Gunn, *Politics and the Public Interest in the Seventeenth Century* (1969), 32.

64. The translation from Euripides' *Suppliants* is on the title page of *Areopagitica* (1644).

65. Keith Stavely, *The Politics of Milton's Prose Style* (New Haven, 1975), ch. 1.

66. See Elizabeth Skerpan, *The Rhetoric of Politics in the English Revolution 1642–1660* (Columbia, Missouri, 1992).

67. Richard Watson, *A Sermon Touching Schisme* (Cambridge, 1642), Sig. B2r.

68. Henry Hammond, *To the Right Honourable, The Lord Fairfax, and His Council of Warre* (1649), 2.

69. James Grantham Turner, 'The Poetics of Engagement', in David Loewenstein and James Grantham Turner, edd., *Politics, Poetics, and Hermeneutics in Milton's Prose* (Cambridge, 1990), 257–75; Lucasta Miller, '"The Shattered *Violl*": Print and Textuality in the 1640s', *Essays and Studies* (1993), 25–38.

70. See J.C. Davis, *Fear, Myth and History: The Ranters and the Historians* (Cambridge, 1986), 76–93.

71. See Sandra Clark, *The Elizabethan Pamphleteers 1580–1640* (1982).

72. Annabel Patterson discusses the place of Cleveland's tract in the history of the representation of peasant uprisings in 'The very name of the game: theories of order and disorder', in Thomas Healy and Jonathan Sawday, edd., *Literature and the English Civil War* (Cambridge, 1990), 21–37 (29–30).

73. See Rosario Villari, 'Massaniello: Contemporary and Recent Interpretations', *Past and Present*, 108 (1985), 117–32, which disagrees with Peter Burke, 'The Virgin of the Carmine and the Revolt of Massaniello', *Past and Present*, 99 (1983), 3–21. See also below, 85.

74. Potter, *Secret Rites*, 108.

75. There is a hint in some of the prefatory poems that Gayton was intending to publish his own translation of *Don Quixote* as well as the notes, but it does seem that Gayton's text was Shelton's translation with some alterations.

76. 'Hectors' were young, bullying, swashbuckling men (OED sb 2). Gayton's text antedates the earliest OED reference by one year.

77. See *The Famous Tragedie of King Charles I, Basely Butchered* (1649).

78. John Hall, *A Serious Epistle to Mr. William Prynne* (1649), 3, 5, 32.

79. The first English translation of Rabelais, made by Sir Thomas Urquhart, was published in 1653. Gayton followed the humorous tradition of Erasmus and Rabelais, and the fragmentation of Thomas Coryat's *Crud-*

ities (1611), as well as Cervantes's picaresque, but he finds in folly and scatalogical excess no ecstasy for his Puritans.

80. [Henry Neville], *The Parliament of Ladies* (1647), 11.

81. [Henry Neville], *Newes from the New Exchange* (1650), 3.

82. See also Susan Wiseman, '"Adam, the Father of all Flesh", Porno-Political Rhetoric, and Political Theory in and After the English Civil War', in James Holstun, ed., *Pamphlet Wars: Prose in the English Revolution* (1992), 134–57.

83. See Thomas Browne (Canon of Winchester), *A Key to the King's Cabinet Opened* (Oxford, 1645), 24, for a royalist attack on the representation of the Queen as a stage she-tyrant.

84. Diane Purkiss, 'Gender, Power and the Body: Symbolic Figurations of Femininity in Milton and Seventeenth-Century Women's Writing', (unpublished D.Phil. thesis, University of Oxford, 1991).

85. See [Henry Neville], *The Isle of Pines* (1668), and associated secondary literature. The most informative edition is Onofrio Nicastro, *Henry Neville e isola di Pines* (Pisa, 1988).

86. *Mercurius Politicus*, 83 (1–8 Jan. 1652), 1320.

87. See Abiezer Coppe, *A Fiery Flying Roll* (1649), in Nigel Smith, ed., *A Collection of Ranter Writings from the Seventeenth Century* (1983); and idem, *Perfection Proclaimed: Language and Literature in English Radical Religion 1640–1660* (Oxford, 1989), 53–66.

88. In *Turned to Account: The Forms and Functions of Criminal Biography in late Seventeenth- and Early Eighteenth-Century England* (Cambridge, 1987), Lincoln B. Faller notes thirteen published accounts of Hind's escapades and punishment in 1651–2. See also Abiezer Coppe, *A Second Fiery Flying Roule* (1649), in Smith, *A Collection of Ranter Writings*, 100.

89. See Sir Thomas Urquhart of Cro-

marty, *The Jewel* (1652), ed. R.D.S. Jack and R.J. Lyall (Edinburgh, 1983).

90. See Smith, *Perfection Proclaimed*, 299–307.

91. See J.C. Davis, 'Formal Utopia/Informal Millennium: The Struggle between Form and Substance as a Context for Seventeenth-Century Utopianism', in Krishan Kumar and Stephen Bann, edd., *Utopias and the Millennium* (1993), 17–32.

92. Sir John Ogilby, *The Relation of His Majestie's Entertainment* (1661). The image is produced in a print in Ogilby, *The Entertainment of His Most Excellent Majestie Charles II* (1662).

93. John Corbet, *An Historicall Relation of the Military Government of Gloucester* (1645), Sig. A2v.

94. *Ibid.*, 2.

95. *Ibid., loc. cit.*

96. [Samuel Turner], *A true Relation Of a late Skirmish at Henley upon Thames* (1643), 5.

97. Epic and heroic it may have been to Parliamentarians, it was derided as mere romance by Royalists.

98. John Ward, *The Christians Incouragement Earnestly to Contend* (1643).

99. [John Haselock], *A true and perfect Relation of the surrender of the strong and impregnable Garrison the Island of Scillie* (1646), Sig. A4v.

Chapter 2: Public Fora

1. See Joseph Frank, *The Beginnings of the English Newspaper 1620–1660* (Camb., Mass., 1961), 1–18. I am also grateful for discussions with Joad Raymond. When Mr Raymond's work on the newsbook is complete, we will have a much fuller account of the newsbook, its contents and its functions. See also Joad Raymond, ed., *Making the News: An Anthology of Newsbooks of Revolutionary England 1641–1660* (Moreton-in-Marsh, 1993).

2. For serials, see Carolyn Nelson and Matthew Seccombe, *British News-*

papers and Periodicals 1641–1700 (New York, 1987).

3. A.N.B. Cotton, 'John Dillingham, Journalist of the Middle Group', EHR, 93 (1978), 817–34.

4. A.N.B. Cotton, 'London Newsbooks in the Civil War: Their Political Attitudes and Sources of Information' (unpublished D.Phil. thesis, University of Oxford, 1971), 104.

5. The Heads of Severall Proceedings (29 Nov.–6 Dec. 1641), [1]–2.

6. See for instance A Perfect Diurnall of the Passages in Parliament, 34 (30 Jan.–6 Feb. 1642).

7. [Richard Overton], Vox Borealis (1641).

8. See Stephen J. Greenberg, 'Dating Civil War Pamphlets, 1641–1644', Albion, 20 (1988), 387–401.

9. Mercurius Britanicus, 63 (23–30 Dec. 1644), 495; 103 (27 Oct.–3 Nov. 1645), 913. The English newsbooks took some of their pattern from earlier continental developments, but they tended not to admit this.

10. Mercurius Britanicus, 112 (29 Dec.– 5 Jan. 1646), 986. Juan de Pineda (1558–1637) was the author of commentaries on the Books of Solomon and Job. Alphonso Tostato was Bishop of Avila.

11. Hermes Stratjcus; Or, A Scourge for Elencticus, 1 (17 Aug. 1648), 1.

12. Ibid., 2. For the politics of Lucianic allusion in the 1640s, see Nigel Smith, 'The Charge of Atheism and the Language of Radical Speculation, 1640–1660', in Michael Hunter and David Wootton, edd., Atheism in Europe from the Reformation to the Enlightenment (Oxford, 1992), 131–58.

13. PRO, SP Dom 46/95.

14. Hermes Stratjcus, 1 (Aug. 1648), 2.

15. Ibid., 1.

16. See [James Howell], Mercurius Hibernicus (Bristol, 1644), Sig. A2r.

17. Such as Cook and Wood's version of the Perfect Diurnall, 38 (27 Feb.–6 March 1643). See Thomason Tracts E246 (37, 38).

18. Mercurius Aulicus, 21st week (week ending 25 May 1644), 987. For Aul-

icus's accuracy, see P.W. Thomas, Sir John Berkenhead 1617–1679: A Royalist Career in Politics and Polemics (Oxford, 1969), 65ff.

19. Mercurius Aulicus, 2nd week (8–14 Jan. 1643), 20.

20. Mercurius Britanicus, 3 (5–12 Sept. 1643), 18.

21. Mercurius Britanicus, 14 (23–30 Nov. 1643), 109.

22. Mercurius Britanicus, 67 (20–27 Jan. 1645), 527.

23. Mercurius Britanicus, 75 (17–24 March 1645), 603.

24. Mercurius Britanicus, 103 (27 Oct.–3 Nov. 1645), 913–14.

25. Mercurius Aulicus, 33rd week (week ending 17 Aug. 1644), 1120 [12 Aug.].

26. 'The Generall of Kent's Answer to the Normans Letter' in Anon., Halesiados. A Message from the Normans (1648), 6–9 (7).

27. Mercurius Insanus, Insanissimus, [4] ([24 April] 1648), 25.

28. Mercurius Militaris, 4 (31 Oct.–8 Nov. 1648), 25.

29. See Nigel Smith, 'The Uses of Hebrew in the English Revolution', in Peter Burke and Roy Porter, edd., Language, Self and Society (Oxford, 1992), 50–71 (62–3).

30. Mercurius Insanus, Insanissimus, 4 ([24 April] 1648), 25. See Jonathan Sawday, '"Mysteriously Divided": Civil War, madness and the divided self', in Thomas Healy and Jonathan Sawday, edd., Literature and the English Civil War (Cambridge, 1990), 127–43.

31. See Sandra Billington, Mock Kings in Medieval Society and Renaissance Drama (Oxford, 1991), 9–29 (especially 23).

32. Cotton, 'London Newsbooks', 133, 136; CJ, iv.664.

33. Until at least the Battle of Roundway Down, Parliamentarians boasted that their commander was another William the Conqueror; the Royalists cock a snook at the defeated general.

34. Mercurius Aulicus, 10th week (3–9 March 1644), 1400.

35. *Mercurius Rusticus*, 10th week (29 July 1643), 73–4.

36. *Mercurius Rusticus*, 18th week (16 Dec. 1643), 142.

37. *Mercurius Britanicus*, 17 (14–21 Dec. 1643), 133. The parallel with another monstrous building with attached organ music, Milton's portrayal of Pandemonium, in *Paradise Lost*, 1.708–30, should not be overlooked.

38. Ryves claims that *Civicus* writes to him making the request on 5 August 1643, some two months after the passing of the Licensing Act.

39. See Cotton, 'London Newsbooks', 165–76.

40. See Franck, *The Beginnings of the English Newspaper*, 154–60.

41. See also *The Royall Diurnall (for King Charles II)*, 1 (beginning Monday, 25 Feb. 1650), Sig. A1v, where Harris is described as an actor once in the 'Company of the Revells', now in the 'Company of the Rebells'.

42. *Ibid., loc. cit.*

43. Possibly by John Taylor.

44. Possibly at the hands of John Streater, republican and publisher (of Harrington's *Oceana*): see below, 296–200.

45. Benne Klaas Faber, 'The Poetics of Subversion and Conservatism: Popular Satire, *c.*1640–*c.*1660' (unpublished D.Phil. thesis, University of Oxford, 1991), goes a long way in rectifying this imbalance.

46. See Smith, 'The Uses of Hebrew', 62–3.

47. Cotton, 'London Newsbooks', 335.

48. See also Samuel Chidley, *The Flying Eagle* (1653).

49. *Mercurius Politicus*, 129 (18–25 Nov. 1652), 2026–8.

50. See M.J. Seymour, 'Pro-Government Propaganda in the Interregnum, 1649–1660' (unpublished D.Phil. thesis, University of Cambridge, 1986), 301–435.

51. David Underdown, 'Popular Politics in Seventeenth-Century England', Ford Lectures, delivered at Examination Schools, Oxford, Feb. 1992.

52. For Elizabeth Poole, see Keith Thomas, 'Women and the Civil War Sects', *Past and Present*, 13 (1958), 46–62; and Maureen Bell, Simon Shepherd, and George Parfitt, *A Biographical Dictionary of Seventeenth-Century Woman Writers* (Brighton, 1991).

53. The palm symbolised military success, so 'vertue' is used more in the sense of *virtus*, or even *virtù*. The laurel stood for poetic achievement – the highest art of peace. For another and very famous treatment of these motifs, see Andrew Marvell, 'The Garden', st. 1.

54. Dorothy Osborne to Sir William Temple, 20 Aug. 1653.

55. *Perfect Occurrences*, 52 (6–13 Aug. 1647), 216.

56. Folger Library, MS V.b.275, Continuation of Stowe's *Survey of London* (1st edn, 1598), *c.* 1658.

57. Edmund Gayton, *Pleasant Notes upon Don Quixot* (1654), 273.

58. See Margot Heineman, *Puritanism and Theatre* (Cambridge, 1980).

59. *Mercurius Britanicus*, 12 (9–16 Nov. 1643), 89.

60. *Diutinus Britanicus*, 2 (2–8 Dec. 1646), 9.

61. *The Oxford Character of the London Diurnall Examined and Answered* ([3 March] 1645), 4.

62. See Judith Milhous and Robert D. Hume, 'New Light on English Acting Companies in 1646, 1648, and 1660', *RES*, new series, 42 (1991), 487–509 (500).

63. Martin Butler, 'A Case Study in Caroline Political Theatre: Brathwaite's "Mercurius Britannicus" (1641)', *HJ*, 27 (1984), 947–53, suggests that Brathwaite's play was performed in Paris in 1637 for the purportedly puritan English ambassador, the Earl of Leicester. A poem entitled 'The Souldier's Counterbuffe to the Cambridge Interludians', which may date from the early 1640s, records the performance of dramatic interludes at Cambridge which criticised the legal profession and the

government, and threatened a punishment for the acting of tragedies showing the fate of princes comparable to the exiling of *Vetus Comoedia* at Rome: Folger Library, MS V.b.303, fo. 254ff.

64. 'it is the lustre and glory of our Nation to have vertue extolled and vice deprodated even upon the publicke Theater, for to no other end an illaborate Comedy or Tragedy ought to be written, ore presented to the view of the vulgar,' *The Parliament Porter*, 4 (18–25 Sept. 1648), 2.

65. Documented interruptions of performances include *Rollo, or the Bloody Brother* (see *Mercurius Elencticus*, 19–26 Dec. 1648); *A King and No King* (1648) (*Perfect Occurrences*, 40 (1–8 Oct. 1647), *Mercurius Pragmaticus*, 4 (5–12 Oct. 1647)); Thomas Killigrew's *Claracella* (1653) and *Mucedorus* (1653). See also Lois Potter, '"True Tragicomedies" of the Civil War and the Commonwealth', in Nancy Klein Maguire, ed., *Renaissance Tragicomedy: Explorations in Genre and Politics* (New York, 1987), 196–217.

66. Folger Library, MS X.d.600, Diary of Sir Humphrey Mildmay.

67. *The Kingdomes Weekly Intelligencer*, 251 (7–14 March 1648), 8 March; *Perfect Occurrences*, 62 (3–10 March 1648), 6 March. The plea was ignored.

68. Cosmo Manuche, *The Just General* (1652), 66; *idem.*, *The Loyal Lovers* (1652), 1. I diverge from Lois Potter here in reading the first scene in the latter play not as a choosing of scurrilous over pious reading, but as an inference towards the need for obscure languages in the context of censorship. See Potter, *Secret Rites and Secret Writing: Royalist Literature 1641–1660* (Cambridge, 1989), 22.

69. Gayton, *Pleasant Notes*, 273.

70. Richard Brome, 'To the Right Noble, Ingenious, and Judicious Gentleman, Thomas Stanley, Esq.', *A Jovial Crew: Or, The Merry Beggars*, ed. Ann Haaker (1968), 4.

71. Robert Greville, Lord Brooke, *A Discourse opening the Nature of that Episcopacie* (1642), 104.

72. See Judith Milhous and Robert D. Hume, 'New Light'.

73. [Marchamont Nedham], *Mercurius Pragmaticus*, 2 (17–24 April 1649), 14.

74. 'The Answer of Mr. Hobbes to Sir Will. Davenant's Preface Before Gondibert', in Sir William Davenant, *Gondibert* (1651), ed. David F. Gladish (Oxford, 1971), 50. See also the valuable discussion in Kevin Sharpe, *Criticism and Compliment: The Politics of Literature in the England of Charles I* (Cambridge, 1987), 101–8.

75. For instance, *A Conference between the Pope, the Emperor and the King of Spain holden in the Castle of St Angelo in Rome* was written and circulated in manuscript in 1631–2, based on an earlier dialogue of 1619–20, and published for the first time in 1642.

76. See D.F. McKenzie, 'The Staple of News and the Late Plays', in William Blissett *et al.*, edd., *A Celebration of Ben Jonson* (Toronto, 1973), 83–128.

77. See Leslie Hotson, *The Commonwealth and Restoration Stage* (Camb., Mass., 1928), 64–5.

78. Albertus Warren, *The Royalist Reformed* (1650; Thomason date 26 Nov. 1649), 15.

79. Lois Potter, 'The Plays and Playwrights, 1642–1660', in Potter, ed., *The Revels History of English Drama*, vol. IV (1981).

80. *Mercurius Britanicus*, 67 (20–27 Jan. 1645), 527–8.

81. O.B., *A Dialogue . . . concerning the Present Government* (1647), 5.

82. Note also the large incidence of Seneca allusion: e.g. Richard Watson, *Regicidium Judaicum* (1649), title page; Anon., *The Princely Pellican* (1649), 37; a reference to Seneca's *Trojans*, interesting because the author is a Royalist. See also the quotation of Seneca's *Hercules Furens* and *Thyestes* in *Good English: Or, Certain Reasons Pointing out the safest*

way of Settlement in this Kingdom (1648), Sig. [A1r], 24.

83. My position on the question of the date for *Samson Agonistes* is that although the text published in 1671 undoubtedly bears the marks of a Restoration context, it may have been a revision of an earlier version produced in the 1647–53 period.

84. See Peter Lake, 'Constitutional Consensus and Puritan Opposition in the 1620s: Thomas Scott and the Spanish Match', *HJ*, 25 (1982), 805–25.

85. Potter, *Secret Rites*, 123.

86. Sheppard, *The Committee-Man Curri'd*, Part 1, Sig. A4r. On the Excise Crisis, see Michael J. Braddick, 'Popular Politics and Public Policy: The Excise Riot at Smithfield in February 1647 and its Aftermath', *HJ*, 34 (1991), 597–626.

87. [Nedham], *Mercurius Pragmaticus*, 12 (30 Nov.–7 Dec. 1647), Sig. M1v.

88. One obvious model here would be John Hacket's Latin play *Loiola* (?1618; published 1648).

89. The commander of Pontefract Castle, from where the sortie which killed Rainborough rode, was in fact the ex-parliamentary renegade Colonel Morrice.

90. In fact, it was the Royalists who used poisoned bullets at Colchester.

91. A widespread rumour fostered by royalist propaganda.

92. John Morrill, 'Charles I, Cromwell and Cicero (A Response to Dale B.J. Randall)', *Connotations*, 1.1 (1991), 96–102, a reply to Dale B.J. Randall, 'The Head and Hands on the Rostra: *Marcus Tullius Cicero* as a Sign of Its Time' in the same issue of the same journal, 34–54. See also Randall, 'Once more to the Rostra (An Answer to John Morrill)', *Connotations*, 1.2 (1991), 204–6.

93. Morrill, 'Charles I, Cromwell and Cicero', 97–8, 100–101.

94. Potter, *Secret Rites*, 34.

95. BL MS Add. 60275, Cosmo Manuche, *The Banished Sheperdess*; MS Add. 60275, *The Cavaliers*; MS

Add. 60277 English translations of Seneca's *Agamemnon* and *Hercules Furens*; MS Add. 60278 Compton, English translation of Machiavelli's *Mandragola* (as *The Mandrake*); MS Add. 60279, Compton, untitled play 'Leontius'; MS Add 60280, *Marianne*; MS Add. 60281, English translation of Plautus, *The Captives* (relating to the fall of Strafford); MS Add. 60282, *The Martird Monarch*.

96. BL MS Add. 60277

97. BL MS Add. 60282, fos. 1r–19r.

98. BL MS Add. 60276, fos. 43rff.

99. BL MS Add. 60282, fos. 4r; 19r.

100. *The Parliament Porter*, 4 (18–25 Sept. 1648).

101. See James R. Jacob and Timothy Raylor, 'Opera and Obedience: Thomas Hobbes and *A Proposition for Advancement of Moralitie* by Sir William Davenant', *The Seventeenth Century*, 6 (1991), 205–50.

102. See Susan J. Wiseman, '"History digested": opera and colonialism in the 1650s', in Healy and Sawday, edd., *Literature and the English Civil War*, 189–204.

103. Jacob and Raylor, 'Opera and Obedience', 210–12, 217–32, stress the indoctrinating nature of education in Davenant (and Hobbes); in his forthcoming edition of Hobbes's correspondence (Oxford University Press) Noel Malcolm challenges this view – in the private sphere, Hobbes supported a very broad toleration of different opinions (see also below, 163).

104. For an adroit reading of the play's performance in 1642, see Martin Butler, *Theatre and Crisis 1632–1642* (Cambridge, 1984), 269–79.

105. See Nigel Smith, ed., *A Collection of Ranter Writings* (1983), 19–20; J.C. Davies, *Fear, Myth and History. The Ranters and the Historians* (Cambridge, 1986), 80, 108–9.

106. Butler, *Theatre and Crisis*, 276.

107. James Harrington, 'The Corollary', *Oceana*, in *Political Works*, ed. J.G.A. Pocock (Cambridge, 1977), 354–5. Harrington stipulates the building of two theatres, one for

tragedy and one for comedy, each placed either side of the 'piazza of the Halo' in Oceana. The 'prelates' are magistrates chosen from the knights, one for each theatre, and their name is clearly meant to cast aspersions on the episcopacy of the *ancien régime*.

108. Deborah C. Payne, 'Patronage and the Dramatic Marketplace under Charles I and II', *YES*, 21 (1991), 137–52 (145–6).

109. For Orrery, see Nancy Klein Maguire, 'Regicide and Reparation: The Autobiographical Drama of Roger Boyle, Earl of Orrery', *ELR*, 21 (1991), 257–82, and below, 244–6.

110. Anon., *Cromwell's Conspiracy* (1661), subtitle.

111. Nancy Klein Maguire, 'The "Whole Truth" of Restoration Tragicomedy', in Maguire, ed., *Renaissance Tragicomedy*, 217–39; *idem*, *Regicide and Restoration: English Tragicomedy, 1660–1671* (Cambridge, 1992).

112. William Clerke, preface to *Marciano; or, The Discovery* (Edinburgh, 1662), Sig. A3r.

113. Maguire, 'The "Whole Truth"', in Maguire, ed., *Renaissance Tragicomedy*, 218–39 (235).

114. For a further consideration, see Sue Owen, 'Drama and the Exclusion Crisis' (unpublished Ph.D. thesis, University of Leeds, 1992).

115. See Nicholas Jose, *Ideas of Restoration in English Literature 1660–71* (1983), 142–63; for a reading of the play as directly reflecting the treatment of the regicides at the Restoration, and particularly Vane, see Blair Worden, '*Samson Agonistes* and the Restoration', forthcoming.

116. *Pace* Jacob and Raylor, 'Opera and Obedience', 208.

117. For an excellent history of the use of Shakespeare after 1660, see Michael Dobson, *The Making of the National Poet: Shakespeare, Adaptation and Authorship, 1660–1769* (Oxford, 1992).

Chapter 3: The Meaning of the Centre

1. Conal Condren, *George Lawson's Politica and the English Revolution* (Cambridge, 1989), 81.

2. Glenn Burgess, *The Politics of the Ancient Constitution: An Introduction to English Political Thought, 1603–1642* (1992), 115–38.

3. See Michael Mendle, *Dangerous Positions: Mixed Government, the Estates of the Realm, and the Making of the Answer to the XIX Propositions* (University, Alabama, 1985). For a general account of the development of these ideas in the 1640s, see John Sanderson, *'But the people's creatures': The Philosophical Basis of the English Civil War* (Manchester, 1989).

4. See Patricia Crawford, 'Charles Stuart, That man of blood', *JBS*, 16 (1977), 41–69; Elizabeth Tuttle, *Religion et idéologie dans la Révolution anglaise* (Paris, 1989), chs 7–12.

5. See Johann P. Sommerville, 'Absolutism and Royalism', in J.H. Burns, ed., *The Cambridge History of Political Thought, 1450–1700* (Cambridge, 1991), 347–73.

6. George Bate, *The Regall Apology* (1648), 46.

7. See Joan E. Hartman, 'Restyling the King: Clarendon Writes Charles I', in James Holstun, ed., *Pamphlet Wars: Prose in the English Revolution* (1992), 45–61.

8. See Michael Mendle, 'Parliamentary Sovereignty: a very English Absolutism', in N. Phillipson and Q. Skinner, edd., *Political Discourse in Early Modern Britain* (Cambridge, 1993), 97–119.

9. Charles Herle, *A Fuller Answer to a Treatise* (1642), 4.

10. See William Bridge, *The Wounded Conscience Cured* (1642), 43.

11. The second edition, entitled *Christus Dei, The Lords Annoynted. Or, A Theological Discourse* (Oxford, 1643), had an additional picture of the King as a frontispiece.

12. William Ball, *A Caveat for Subjects* (1642), 15.

13. J.M., *A Reply to the Answer* (1642), 1.

14. Anon., *A Vindication of the King* (1642), 2.

15. Robert Mossom, *Anti-Paraeus, Or, A Treatise in the Defence of the Royal Right of Kings* (York, 1642), 13.

16. For Parker's use of Cadmus, see Nigel Smith, '*Areopagitica*: Voicing Contexts, 1643–45', in David Loewenstein and James Grantham Turner, edd., *Politics, Poetics and Hermeneutics in Milton's Prose* (Cambridge, 1990), 103–22 (110).

17. On the masque, see Kevin Sharpe, *Criticism and Compliment: The Politics of Literature in the England of Charles I* (Cambridge, 1987), chs 1, 5, 6.

18. For an account of this strand of thinking in royalist theory, and its debt to Grotius, see Richard Tuck, *Philosophy and Government 1572–1651* (Cambridge, 1993), 272–8. For Digges, see Sanderson, '*But the People's Creatures*', ch. 3.

19. Dudley Digges, *The Unlawfulnesse of Subjects taking up Arms Against Their Sovereigne* (1643), 96.

20. *Mercurius Aulicus*, 1st week (1 Jan. 1642), 6.

21. Dudley Digges, *A Review of the Observations* (Oxford, 1643), 13.

22. Robert Mossom, *The King on his Throne* (1642), 8.

23. Folger MS V.b.303, fo. 254.

24. For a similar perception of republican thinking in parliamentary apology, see Henry Hammond, *Of Resisting the Lawfull Magistrate upon Colour of Religion* (1644), 12.

25. Thomas Morton, *The Necessity of Christian Subjection* (Oxford, 1643), 6.

26. Digges, *A Review of the Observations*, 11.

27. Henry Ferne, *Conscience Satisfied* (Oxford, 1643), TP, 76–8.

28. Digges, *The Unlawfulnesse of Subjects*, 142.

29. Digges, *A Review of the Observations* 3–4. For Milton's use of this image in *Areopagitica*, see *CPW*, II.492.

30. No place, printer or publisher is named, although the majority of royalist works printed in these years were produced at Oxford.

31. See Robert Wilcher, 'What was the King's Book for?: The Evolution of *Eikon Basilike*', *YES*, 21 (1991), 218–28; but see also Kevin Sharpe, *The Personal Rule of Charles I* (New Haven and London, 1992), 179.

32. [Edward Symmons], *A Loyall Subjects Beliefe* (Oxford, 1643), 13. A seventeenth-century hand in the Bodleian Library copy of this work annotates these words as 'nonsense most divine'.

33. The dating of *Patriarcha* is controversial, although the weight of evidence seems to be for the first two chapters, c.1628–31, and the third chapter possibly some time later: see Richard Tuck, 'A New Date for Filmer's *Patriarcha*', *HJ*, 29 (1986), 183–6; Sir Robert Filmer, *Patriarcha and Other Writings* (*POW*), ed. Johann P. Sommerville (Cambridge, 1991), xxxii–xxxiv. But part of the earlier section may date from as early as 1614: Tuck, *Philosophy and Government*, 262.

34. *The Anarchy of a Limited or Mixed Monarchy* (1648), in *POW*, 131.

35. *POW*, 142.

36. *The Free-Holders Grand Inquest* (1648), in *POW*, 70, 94.

37. *The Anarchy*, *POW*, 166.

38. *The Anarchy*, in *POW*, 157.

39. *Observations Upon Aristotle's Politiques*, *POW*, 251.

40. *POW*, 253.

41. *POW*, 210–11.

42. *POW*, 237, 243.

43. Filmer's remarks on Milton's use of the Bible in this respect are especially instructive: *Observations Concerning the Originall of Government* (1652), in *POW*, 197–208.

44. *Ibid.*, *POW*, 198–9.

45. *Observations Upon Aristotle's Politiques*, *POW*, 257, 262.

46. For other uses of the Tarquin and

Lucrece story, see below, 197, and for the longer tradition, see Stephanie Jed, *Chaste Thinking: The Rape of Lucretia and the Birth of Humanism* (Bloomington and Indianapolis, 1989). Annabel Patterson, *Reading Between the Lines* (1993), 300–301, raises the possibility of political readings of this topos in the mid- and late-seventeenth century, but finds no examples.

47. *Ibid.*, POW, 259.
48. POW, 260. Filmer's source here is Jean Bodin, *The Six Books of a Commonweale* (1606), 23.
49. POW, 275.
50. These are, properly, [Henry Ireton], *Several Proposals for Peace & Freedom, by an Agreement of the People* (22 Dec. 1648) and 'Verity Victor', *The Royal Project* (1648).
51. See John M. Wallace, *Destiny his Choice: The Loyalism of Andrew Marvell* (Cambridge, 1968), 256.
52. See most recently, Lois Potter, *Secret Rites and Secret Writing: Royalist Literature 1641–1660* (Cambridge, 1989), 160–65, 169–87.
53. See Wilcher, 'What was the King's Book for?'.
54. For an account of metaphor in *Eikon Basilike*, see Thomas N. Corns, *The Development of Milton's Prose Style* (Oxford, 1982), 90, 95, 100.
55. *Eikon Basilike*, ed. Edward Almack (1904), 22–3.
56. See *Anglia Rediviva: Or, England Revived. An Heroick Poem* (1658).
57. Anon., *The Unparalleld Monarch. Or, The Portraiture of a Matchlesse Prince: Exprest in some shadows of His Highness My Lord Protector* (1656), 3, 8, 43. See also Andrew Marvell, 'The First Anniversary of the Government under His Highness the Lord Protector', ll. 13–44, 225–8, 249–56, 387–90; Henry Dawbeny, *Historie & Policie Re-viewed, In the Heroick Transactions of his Most Serene Highnesse, Oliver* (1659).
58. Michael Hawke, *The Right of Dominion and Property of Liberty* (1655), esp. 23, 30.
59. *The Unparalleld Monarch*, 3, 8, 17, 38, 91.
60. See Eamon Duffy, *The Stripping of the Altars* (New Haven and London, 1992).
61. See Julian Davies, *The Caroline Captivity of the Church: Charles I and the Remoulding of Anglicanism 1625–1641* (Oxford, 1992), 5–45.
62. John Morrill, 'The Religious Context of the English Civil War', *TRHS*, 5th ser., 34 (1984), 155–78; *idem*, 'The Church in England, 1642–9', in John Morrill, ed., *Reactions to the English Civil War* (1982); both are now reprinted in *idem*, *The Nature of the English Revolution* (1993), 45–68; 148–75.
63. Joseph Hall, *Fanatick Moderation, Exemplified in Bishop Hall's Hard Measure As it was written by Himself* ([1740]), 11. This passage is dated 29 May 1647 by Hall.
64. *Ibid.*, 16.
65. John Spurr, *The Restoration Church of England, 1646–1689* (New Haven and London, 1991), esp. 2–28.
66. William Nicolson, *An Apology for the Discipline of the Ancient Church* (1659), Sig. A3r.
67. Griffith Williams, *The Discovery of Mysteries* (1643).
68. George Hall, *Gods Appearing for the Tribe of Levi* (1655), 8.
69. *Ibid.*, 17. For Marprelate, see below 297.
70. See William Haller, *The Rise of Puritanism* (New York, 1938); Christopher Hill, *The English Bible and the Seventeenth-Century Revolution* (1992); David Katz, *The Bible in English History* (forthcoming from OUP).
71. See William Parker, *The Late Assembly of Divines Confession of Faith Examined* (1651); *Conway Letters*, ed. M.H. Nicolson (New York, 1930), 109, 275, 280n., 350n.; G.F. Nuttall, 'The Last of James Nayler, Robert Rich and the Church of the First Born', *Friends Quarterly*, 60 (1985), 527–34; Nigel Smith, *Perfection Proclaimed: Language and Litera-*

ture in English Radical Religion, 1640–1660 (Oxford, 1989), 99n.

72. See E.E. Duncan-Jones, 'Who was the recipient of Crashaw's Leyden Letter?', in John R. Roberts, ed., *New Perspectives on the Life and Art of Richard Crashaw* (Columbia, Missouri, 1990), 174–9; for Beaumont, see below, 221–3.

73. Letter from Leiden 1643–4, in *Works*, ed. L.C. Martin (Oxford, 1957), pp. xxx–xxxi.

74. Henry Denne, *The Doctrine and Conversation of John Baptist* (1643), 28–9; source in John Foxe, *Acts and Monuments*, ii.521–2.

75. See Patrick Collinson, *The Religion of Protestants: The Church in English Society, 1559–1625* (Oxford, 1982).

76. Thomas Whitfeld, *A Discourse of Liberty of Conscience* (1649), 11. For the latest general discussion of these matters, see Stephen Baskerville, *Not Peace but a Sword: The Political Theology of the English Revolution* (1993).

77. For Baxter, see G.F. Nuttall, *Richard Baxter* (1965); N.H. Keeble, *Richard Baxter: Puritan Man of Letters* (Oxford, 1982).

78. Robert Greville, Lord Brooke, *A Discourse Opening the Nature of that Episcopacie* (1642), 29.

79. See John Goodwin, *Theomaxia* (1644), 10–11; see also William Haller, *Liberty and Reformation in the Puritan Revolution* (New York, 1955), 249–53.

80. See Edmund S. Morgan, *Roger Williams: The Church and the State* (New York, 1967); W. Clark Gilpin, *The Millenarian Piety of Roger Williams* (Chicago, 1979).

81. Roger Williams, *The Bloudy Tenent of Persecution*, 34.

82. Keith W.F. Stavely, 'Roger Williams: Bible Politics and Bible Art', in James Holstun, ed., *Pamphlet Wars: Prose in the English Revolution* (1992), 76–91.

83. Stavely, 78–9. Neither does this make Williams a 'man without a vision' (*pace* Stavely, 88).

84. See Owen Watkins, *The Puritan Ex-*

perience (1972); Patricia Caldwell, *The Puritan Conversion Narrative* (Cambridge, 1983); Smith, *Perfection Proclaimed*.

85. For example, see Goodwin, *Theomaxia*, 1.

86. Carolyn Polizzotto, 'The Campaign against *The Humble Proposals* of 1652', *JEH*, 38 (1987), 569–81.

87. Sir Henry Vane, *A Needful Corrective or Balance in Popular Government* (1659), 7–8. Vane is controverting Harrington's *Prerogative of Popular Government* (1658). For earlier projections of parliamentary representation onto church government, see Brooke, *A Discourse*, 14.

88. See Smith, *Perfection Proclaimed*, ch. 6.

89. N.I. Matar, 'The Early Prose of Peter Sterry', *PQ*, 71 (1992), 31–46 (43).

90. See, most recently, Phyllis Mack, *Visionary Women: Ecstatic Prophecy in Seventeenth-Century England* (Berkeley and Oxford, 1992).

91. I am grateful to Nicholas Ward-Lowery for this reference, which is related to his forthcoming work 'Patriarchal Negotiations: Women, Writing and Religion in the English Civil War 1640–1660' (unpublished Ph.D. thesis, University of London, 1993).

92. For Mary Pocock, see Smith, *Perfection Proclaimed*, 210–12; Mack, *Visionary Women*, 100, 113, 123, 413.

93. J.C. Davis, 'Religion and the Struggle for Freedom in the English Revolution', *HJ*, 35 (1992), 501–30.

94. *Ibid.*, 516.

95. George Foster, *The Sounding of the Last Trumpet* (1650), 6, 1.

96. See Ann Hughes, 'The Pulpits Guarded: Confrontations between Orthodox and Radicals in Revolutionary England', in Ann Laurence, Stuart Sim and W.B. Owens, edd., *John Bunyan and His World* (1990).

97. Richard Farnworth, *The Pure Language of the Spirit of Truth* (1655), 7.

98. Brian Duppa, *Angels Rejoicing for Sinners Repenting* (1648), 12.

99. *Ibid.*, 3.

100. See Achsah Guibbory, 'A rationall of old Rites: Sir Thomas Browne's *Urue Buriall* and the Conflict over Ceremony', *YES*, 21 (1991), 229–41.

101. See Spurr, *The Restoration Church of England*, 320; Isabel Rivers, *Reason, Grace and Sentiment* (Cambridge, 1991), 89–109.

Chapter 4: Discourse from Below: The Levellers, the City and the Army

1. *The humble Petition of divers wel affected Persons* (1648), in William Haller and Godfrey Davies, edd., *The Leveller Tracts 1647–1653* (New York, 1944; Gloucester, Mass., 1964).

2. Richard Overton, *The Baiting of the Great Bull of Bashan* (1649) in A.L. Morton, ed., *Freedom in Arms: A Selection of Leveller Writings* (1975), 286.

3. Anon., *Match me these two* (1647), 12

4. See H.N. Brailsford, *The Levellers*, ed. Christopher Hill (1961).

5. See Richard Ashcraft, *Revolutionary Politics and Locke's Two Treatise of Government* (Princeton, 1986), 143, 149–50, 152.

6. On the dangers of regarding Leveller philosophy as too consistent, see Mark Kishlansky, 'What Happened at Ware?', *HJ*, 25 (1982), 827–39.

7. See David Wootton, 'Leveller Democracy and the Puritan Revolution', in J.H. Burns, ed., *The Cambridge History of Political Thought, 1450–1700* (Cambridge, 1991), 412–42.

8. Even a supposedly sympathetic recent collection fails to devote an article to them alone: James Holstun, ed., *Pamphlet Wars: Prose in the English Revolution* (1992).

9. For Leveller organisation, see David Underdown, 'The Parliamentary Diary of John Boys, 1647–8', *BIHR*,

39 (1966), 141–64 (157–8), and Norah Carlin, 'The Levellers and the Conquest of Ireland in 1649', *HJ*, 30 (1987), 269–88.

10. I am grateful to Dr Michael Mahony for this point.

11. See Ian Gentles, 'London Levellers in the English Revolution: The Childeys and their Circle', *JEH*, 29 (1978), 281–309.

12. Joan Bennett, *The Eloquent I: Style and Self in Seventeenth-Century Prose* (Madison, 1968), 68–79; John R. Knott, *Discourses of Martyrdom in English Literature, 1563–1694* (Cambridge, 1993), 144–50.

13. See George Bate, *The Royall Apology* (1648), 28, 30, 46.

14. See Nigel Smith, *Perfection Proclaimed: Language and Literature in English Radical Religion 1640–1660* (Oxford, 1989), 96–8, 363.

15. John Lilburne, *Englands Birth-Right Justified* (1645), 10–11.

16. See Norah Carlin, forthcoming article on Levellers and guilds, and Gary De Krey, 'London Radicals and Revolutionary Politics 1675–83', in Tim Harris, Paul Seaward and Mark Goldie, edd., *The Politics of Religion in Restoration England* (Oxford, 1990), 133–62.

17. Gary de Krey, *A Fractured Society: The Politics of London in the First Age of Party, 1688–1715* (Oxford, 1985).

18. Gentles, 'London Levellers', *JEH*, 29 (1982), 281–309.

19. Thomas N. Corns, 'The Freedom of reader-response. Milton's *Of Reformation* and Lilburne's *The Christian Man's Triall*', in R.C. Richardson and G.M. Ridden, edd., *Freedom and the English Revolution* (Manchester, 1986), 93–110.

20. Thomas N. Corns, *Uncloistered Virtue: English Political Literature 1640–1660* (Oxford, 1992), 146.

21. William Larner, *A Vindication of Every Free-Mans Libertie* (1646), 4; for Leveller women, see below, n. 42.

22. Margot Heinemann, *Puritanism and Theatre* (Cambridge, 1980), 237–57.

23. See *England's Miserie, and Remedie. In a Judicious Letter from an Utter-Barrister to his speciall Friend, Concerning Leiutenant Col. LILBURN'S Imprisonment in Newgate* ([14 Sept.] 1645). Reprinted in *DRD*, 276–8.

24. See D.M. Wolfe, ed., *Leveller Manifestoes of the Puritan Revolution* (New York, 1944).

25. *L. Colonel JOHN LILBURNE revived* (1653), 2nd pagination, 1.

26. *Ibid.*, 3.

27. Richard Overton, *The Proceedings of the Councel of State against Richard Overton* (1649 [4 April]), in Morton, ed., *Freedom in Arms*, 204.

28. See David Underdown, *Revel, Riot and Rebellion: Popular Politics and Culture in England 1603–1660* (Oxford, 1985), 209–13, 239–70; *idem*, Ford Lectures, University of Oxford, 1992.

29. Reprinted in Wolfe, ed., *Leveller Manifestoes*, 157.

30. *Ibid.*, 169. See below, 298–302. For a discussion of *An Appeale* in terms of its proximity to those who would support the Rump Parliament, as opposed to those who doubted the supremacy of Parliament, see Richard Tuck, *Philosophy and Government 1572–1651* (Cambridge, 1993), 243.

31. *Ibid.*, 158; taken from Parl. Decl. books.

32. *Ibid.*, 157; see also 179.

33. *Ibid.*, 164.

34. *Ibid.*, 167–8.

35. *Ibid.*, 171–2.

36. *Ibid.*, 186.

37. Quoted in A.S.P. Woodhouse, ed., *Puritanism and Liberty, Being the Army Debates (1647–49)* (1938, 1986) 73.

38. *A Declaration of Some Proceedings* (1648), 95–6.

39. *Ibid.*, 102–4, 117–19.

40. Lilburne, *Englands New Chains Discovered* (1649), in Haller and Davies, edd., *The Leveller Tracts*, 165.

41. In Haller and Davies, edd., *The Leveller Tracts*, 176.

42. See Patricia Higgins, 'The Reactions of Women, with special reference to women petitioners', in Brian Manning, ed., *Politics, Religion and the English Civil War* (1973), 179–97; Ann-Marie McEntee, '"The [Un]Uncivill-Sisterhood of Oranges and Lemons": Female Petitioners and Demonstrators, 1642–53', in Holstun, ed., *Pamphlet Wars*, 92–111.

43. In Haller and Davies, edd., *The Leveller Tracts*, 164.

44. Richard Overton, *The Picture of the Councel of State* (1649), in Haller and Davies, edd., *The Leveller Tracts*, 224.

45. John Wildman, *A Cal To All The Souldiers of the Armie* ([29 Oct.] 1647), 4–5.

46. Was this a symbolic or real representation? Either Lilburne was a very large man indeed, or the copy of Coke looks rather smaller and less weighty than the actual printed editions were. Or was Lilburne using a manuscript digest made from Coke's book? Or was the artist inept?

47. See also later papers like *The Flying Eagle* (Nov. 1652–Jan. 1653), produced by Samuel Chidley. For *The Moderate*, see above, 64.

48. I am grateful to Kate Peters, of Corpus Christi College, Cambridge, for discussing her work on Quaker publication with me.

49. In Haller and Davies, edd., *The Leveller Tracts*, 54.

50. *Ibid.*, 61.

51. *Ibid.*, 68.

52. *Ibid.*, 74.

53. Lilburne's tracts were distributed by Army mutineers in 1649.

54. Richard Overton, *An Appeale from the Degenerate Representative Body*, in Wolfe, ed., *Leveller Manifestoes*, 163.

55. See Richard Tuck, *Natural Rights Theories*, 149–50; also Christopher Hill, *The World Turned Upside Down* (1972), 90, 118, 311, 390–91.

56. See I. Russell-Jones, 'The Relationship between Theology and Politics in the Writings of John Lilburne, Richard Overton and William Walwyn' (unpublished D.Phil. thesis, University of Oxford, 1987).

57. See Nigel Smith, 'The Charge of

Atheism and the Language of Radical Speculation', in Michael Hunter and David Wootton, edd., *Atheism in Europe from the Reformation to the Enlightenment* (Oxford, 1992), 131–58, and Quentin Skinner, 'Thomas Hobbes: Rhetoric and the Construction of Morality', *PBSA*, 76 (1991), 1–61.

58. William Bray, *A Plea for the People's Fundamental Liberties* (1659), 11.

59. See David Wootton, 'From Rebellion to Revolution: The Crisis of the Winter of 1642/3 and the Origins of Civil War Radicalism', *EHR*, 105 (1990), 654–69.

60. Hill, 'Religion of Gerrard Winstanley', *Past and Present*, Supplement No. 5 (1978).

61. See, most recently, R.J. Dalton, 'Gerrard Winstanley: The Experience of Fraud 1641', *HJ*, 34 (1991), 973–84; J.D. Alsop, 'The Origins of a Radical: Gerrard Winstanley 1609–48', *HJ*, forthcoming. See also Ariel Hessayon's important forthcoming study of the prophet Thomas Tany, before and after 1640.

62. Samuel Hartlib, *Ephemerides*, Sheffield University Library, Hartlib MS 31/22/39B.

63. John Taylor, *Crop-Eare Curried or Tom Nash his Ghost* (1644), p.39.

64. In Morton, ed., *Freedom in Arms*, 202.

65. See R.B. Seaburg, 'The Norman Conquest and the Common Law: The Levellers and the Argument from Continuity', *HJ*, 24 (1981), 791–806.

66. L.C. Knights notes in his copy of D.M. Wolfe, *Milton in the Puritan Revolution* (New York, 1941, 153, 158–9; now in the author's possession) that the Levellers are 'simplifiers'.

67. For the fullest account, see Austin Woolrych, *Soldiers and Statesmen: The Army Council and its Debates 1647–8* (Oxford, 1988).

68. Thompson led a mutiny in North Oxfordshire in 1649. After Burford, he was hunted down and fought to the death.

69. G.E. Aylmer, 'Gentlemen Levellers?', *Past and Present*, 49 (1970), 120–26.

70. Wootton, *DRD*, 273.

71. See David Norbrook, 'Levelling Poetry: George Wither and the English Revolution, 1642–1649', *ELR*, 21 (1991), 217–56.

72. William Bray, *A Plea for the Peoples Good Old Cause* (1659), 3. Bray is identifying with the translator of the *Mirror of Justice*. He has further references to Cassiodorus, *A Plea for the Peoples Fundamentall Liberties and Parliaments* (1659), 6.

73. Lilburne refers here to reading the books of his 'old true-hearted, plain and blunt friend Mr. Moyle'. See also Lilburne's letter to Marten, in *The Fairfax Library and Archive* (1993), Sotheby's Sale Catalogue, lot 258 iv.

74. Anon., *A Letter to Lieutenant Collonel John. Lilburn* ([8 Sept.] 1653), esp. 3–4: 'comparing your self to *Titus Flaminius*, whom therefore contrary to all History you will have called the desire and delight of mankind, though you are as farre out in your hystery (it being *Titus* the sone of *Vespasian*, that destroyed *Jerusalem*, who was stiled *Deliciae humani generis*) as comparison'.

75. Lilburne, *A Declaration To the Free-Born People of England* (1654), 4–5.

76. Lilburne, *The Upright Man's Vindication* (2nd edn, [5 Aug.] 1653), esp. 7–9, 15; *idem, As You Were* (?Amsterdam, 1652).

77. *A Letter*, 4.

78. I am grateful to Dr Blair Worden for the suggestion of Nedham's partial authorship of *Vox Plebis*. Other candidates are Marten, Walwyn, Wildman and Sexby.

79. See James Holstun, 'Ehud's Dagger: Patronage, Tyrannicide, and *Killing No Murder*', *Cultural Critique*, 22 (1992).

80. For Milton's 'deradicalization' of his resistance argument between the first and second editions of *The Tenure of Kings and Magistrates*, see M.M. Dzelzainis, 'The Ideological Context of

John Milton's *History of Britain'* (unpublished Ph.D. thesis, University of Cambridge, 1984).

81. *Calendar of Clarendon State Papers*, vol. 3, ed. Rev. W. Dunn MaCray (Oxford, 1876), 297. On 397–8, Clarendon claims he did not know the author of *Killing Noe Murder*, but on 310 he knows how it functioned as anti-Cromwellian propaganda and how Sexby was centrally involved in this business. See also 344.

Chapter 5: Political Theory as Aesthetics: Hobbes, Harrington, Winstanley

1. For considerations of Hobbes and Harrington in these contexts, see J.G.A. Pocock, *The Machiavellian Moment: Florentine Political Thought and the Atlantic Republican Tradition* (Princeton, 1975), 383–400; *idem*, 'Historical Introduction', in James Harrington, *Political Works* (Cambridge, 1977), 1–152; Johann P. Sommerville, *Thomas Hobbes: Political Ideas in Historical Context* (1992).

2. Since Hobbes assumes that human events in the world constitute a history, there arises the question of whether the 'artificiall man' changes if the commonwealth changes over the course of time. There is no space here to discuss this issue. J.G.A. Pocock addresses Hobbes's treatment of time in 'Time, History and Eschatology in the Thought of Thomas Hobbes', *Politics, Language and Time* (New York, 1971), 148–201, but does not consider the rhetorical framework of *Leviathan*. David Johnston, *The Rhetoric of Leviathan: Thomas Hobbes and the Politics of Cultural Transformation* (Princeton, 1986), discusses the concept of rhetoric, but not its practice, in Hobbes.

3. Hobbes mistranslates '*Fiat*'.

4. Howell A. Lloyd, 'Constitutionalism', in J.H. Burns, ed., *The Cambridge History of Political Thought 1450–1700* (Cambridge, 1991), 254–97 (254–5).

5. OED confirms that both 'constitution' (OED 5; 6) and 'state' (OED sb. I 1; 2; IV 28; 29; 32) could refer in the mid-seventeenth century to the individual human frame as well as to a particular polity or form of government.

6. *CPW*, I.572.

7. Far more extensively so than Plato's analogy in *The Republic*, 4.2.

8. Cf. Hobbes's comparison of the structure of *Gondibert* to 'a mans veines, which proceeding from different parts, after the like concourse, insert themselves at last into the two principall veynes of the Body'. 'The Answer of Mr. Hobbes to Sir Will. Davenant's Preface before *Gondibert*', in Sir William Davenant, *Gondibert*, ed. David F. Gladish (Oxford, 1971), 50.

9. Keith Brown, 'The Artist of the *Leviathan* Title-page', *British Library Journal*, 4 (1978), 424–36.

10. I am referring to a lecture by Quentin Skinner on '*Leviathan* and Rhetoric' delivered at Keble College, Oxford, May 1990.

11. George Wither, *Vox Pacifica* (1645), 138.

12. Christopher Pye, 'The Sovereign, the Theater, and the Kingdome of Darknesse: Hobbes and the Spectacle of Power', *Representations*, 8 (1984), 85–106, reprinted in Stephen Greenblatt, ed., *Representing the English Renaissance* (California, 1988), 279–301.

13. Note the contradiction between words as instrumental (in constructing perception) and words as action; it is the way Hobbes *confuses* categories which seems to upset others.

14. Bodl. Rawl. D 753 contains English translations of several Ciceronian texts, attributed to the republican apologist Sir Francis Osborne: Cato the Elder, fo. 46; Oration for Marcus Marcellus, fo. 60; towards the end of the oration for Muraena, fo. 68; Pro Sylla, fo. 73; Familiar Letters, 1, 2 to letter 12, fo. 1.

15. Thomas Hobbes, *Human Nature*

(1640), in *The English Works*, ed. Sir William Molesworth (1840), vol. IV, 40.

16. *Ibid.*, 41.

17. For the political associations of romance, see below, 233–49.

18. *Human Nature*, 75.

19. I am grateful to Dr Ian MacLean for his help with legal language here.

20. The point was first made by J.G.A. Pocock, 'Time, History and Eschatology in the Thought of Thomas Hobbes', in *Politics, Language and Time*, and is reasserted in slightly different terms in Richard Tuck, 'The "Christian Atheism" of Thomas Hobbes', in M. Hunter and D. Wootton, edd., *Atheism from the Reformation to the Enlightenment* (Oxford, 1992), 111–30.

21. A function previously reserved for God in very special circumstances: see Petrus Cunaeus, *Of the Commonwealth of the Hebrews* (1653), 43.

22. In Sir Robert Filmer, *Patriarcha and Other Writings*, ed. Johann P. Sommerville (Cambridge, 1991), 185.

23. Hobbes complains that we have misunderstood him if we presume that suddenly the Roman patricians decided to give their power to a sovereign. Equally puzzling is the paradox, or ironic oxymoron, of the 'state' of nature: how can it be a 'state' if it is a war of everyone against everyone else?

24. See Sommerville, *Thomas Hobbes*.

25. *Ibid.*, 1.

26. A point overlooked by nearly all commentators on Hobbes's use of rhetoric.

27. Charles Cantaloupo, *A Literary Leviathan: Thomas Hobbes's Masterpiece of Language* (Lewisburg, 1991), 96, 108, 133, 175, goes some way towards seeing these two texts interrelate.

28. Usually, this image figures the power of rhetoric. For Hobbes and republicanism, see Mary G. Dietz, 'Hobbes's Subject as Citizen', in Mary G. Dietz, ed., *Thomas Hobbes and Political Theory* (Lawrence, Kansas, 1990), 91–119.

29. I am much indebted to the work of Andrew Ball for information concerning the foundations of Harrington's thought.

30. See Wm Craig Diamond, 'Natural Philosophy in Harrington's Political Thought', *Journal of the History of Philosophy*, 16 (1978), 387–98.

31. See, in this respect, Harrington's quotation of Machiavelli, *Oceana*, ed. Pocock, 332.

32. The king's apologist Henry Ferne, *A Reply unto Severall Treatises* (Oxford, 1643), 14, regarded a superstructure ('Architectonicall power') based on popular consent as building on 'foundations layed in the aire'.

33. See the account of Philautus, *Oceana*, ed. Pocock, 233.

34. See J.C. Davis, *Utopia and the Ideal Society: A Study in English Utopian Writing 1516–1700* (Cambridge, 1981), 205–40; James Holstun, *A Rational Millennium: Puritan Utopias in Seventeenth-Century England and America* (New York, 1986)

35. See also Milton's satirical depiction of Salmasius as a whale: *Defensio Secunda*, CPW, IV.580.

36. James Harrington, *The Stumbling Block of Disobedience and Rebellion* (1658), 574.

37. Note also Harrington's habit of poking fun at himself: 'Her body consists of one order, and her senate is like a rolling stone (as was said) which never did nor, while it continues upon that rotation, ever shall gather the moss of a divided or ambitious interest' (*Oceana*, 276).

38. James Harrington, *The Prerogative of Popular Government* (1658), 391, 403, 412.

39. *Ibid.*, 395.

40. Matthew Wren, *Monarchy Asserted, or the State of Monarchicall and Popular Government in Vindication of the Considerations upon Mr. Harrington's Oceana* (Oxford, 1659), 178.

41. For a fuller account of Harrington and the disputants of *Oceana*, see Anna Strumia, *L'immaginazione repubblicana: Sparta e Israele nel dibattito*

filosofico-politico dell-'età di Cromwell (Turin, 1991).

42. Note the reliance upon Selden's *Titles of Honour* (1614, 2nd edn 1631) here.

43. Jonathan Scott, 'The Rapture of Motion: James Harrington's Republicanism', in N. Phillipson and Q. Skinner, edd., *Political Discourse in Early Modern Britain* (Cambridge, 1993), 139–63.

44. See Harrington, *Oceana*, 262.

45. This subject needs much more detailed exploration, but see also Anna Strummia *L'immaginazione repubblicana*.

46. But see David Armitage, 'The Cromwellian Protectorate and the Languages of Empire', *HJ*, 35 (1992), 531–55.

47. Keith Thomas, 'The Utopian Impulse in Seventeenth-Century England', in Dominic Baker-Smith and C.C. Barfoot, edd., *Between Dream and Nature: Essays on Utopia and Dystopia* (Amsterdam, 1987), 20–46; Davis, *Utopia and the Ideal Society*; Holstun, *A Rational Millennium*.

48. See M.A. Screech, *Erasmus: Ecstasy and the Praise of Folly* (1980), ch 2.

49. Davis, *Utopia and the Ideal Society*, chs 9–11.

50. Nigel Smith, *Perfection Proclaimed: Language and Literature in English Radical Religion 1640–1660* (Oxford, 1989), 258–61.

51. At which point, Hobbes has a civil religion, as well as Harrington. For the influence of 'civil religion', see Justin Champion, *The Pillars of Priestcraft Shaken: The Church of England and its Critics* (Cambridge, 1992).

52. I owe this point to Christopher Kendrick.

53. See Pocock, 'Historical Introduction', in Harrington, *Political Works*, 101, 112, 117–18; Pocock draws on H.F. Russell Smith, *Harrington and his Oceana: A Study of a Seventeenth-Century Utopia and its Influence in America* (Cambridge, 1914).

Chapter 6: The Free State in Letters: Republicanism Comes Out

1. Forthcoming work by David Norbrook explores this matter in greater detail.

2. See, most recently, Jonathan Scott, 'The English Republic Imagination', in John Morrill, *Revolution and Restoration: England in the 1650s* (1992), 35–54.

3. This tract may possibly have had previous MS circulation.

4. Nemesius, trans. George Wither, *The Nature of Man* (1636), Sig. aa6v; George Wither, *Letters of Advice* (1645), 5.

5. Marchamont Nedham, *The Case of the Commonwealth of England, Stated* (1650), ed. Philip A. Knachel (Charlottesville, Va., 1969), 127–8; John Milton, *The Tenure of Kings and Magistrates* (1649), title-page. See also above, 16–18.

6. See Blair Worden, 'The Commonwealth Kidney of Algernon Sidney', *JBS*, 24 (1985), 1–40; Jonathan Scott, *Algernon Sidney and the English Republic 1623–1677* (Cambridge, 1988), 43–8.

7. See C.M. Williams, 'The Political Career of Henry Marten with special reference to the origins of republicanism in the Long Parliament' (unpublished D.Phil. thesis, University of Oxford, 1954); Sarah Barber's forthcoming work presents much new material on Marten and on gentry Republicans.

8. See David Norbrook, 'Levelling Poetry: George Wither and the English Revolution, 1642–1649', *ELR*, 21 (1991), 217–56 (224).

9. Sheffield University, Hartlib Papers 13/50b, 99b, 90a, 127b. See also Johann P. Sommerville, 'Oliver Cromwell and English Political Thought', in John Morrill, ed., *Oliver Cromwell and the English Revolution* (1990), 242.

10. Richard Tuck, *Philosophy and Government 1572–1651* (Cambridge, 1993), 221–40.

11. For Parker's 'theoretical' republicanism, see Michael Mendle, *Dangerous Positions: Mixed Government, the Estates of the Realm and the Answer to the XIX Propositions* (University, Alabama, 1985), 131–2.

12. J.G.A. Pocock, *The Machiavellian Moment: Florentine Political Thought and the Atlantic Republican Tradition* (Princeton, 1975), 269.

13. Tuck, *Philosophy and Government*, 227–32, argues (rightly in my opinion) that Parker was influenced by Tacitus and the theories of interest in Tacitist writers like Virgilio Malvezzi.

14. See above, n. 9.

15. *Ibid., loc. cit.*

16. For details of Ascham's life, see DNB.

17. See Perez Zagorin, *A History of Political Thought in the English Revolution* (1954), 64–7.

18. For a further discussion of this work, see Richard Tuck, *Natural Rights Theories* (Cambridge, 1979), 123–4.

19. Contzen's real intention was to reconcile public and private spheres in a counter-reformed holy, stoical citizenship. See Robert Bireley, *The Counter-Reformation Prince: Anti-Machiavellianism or Catholic Statecraft in Early Modern Europe* (Chapel Hill, 1990), pp. 139–42.

20. For heroic songs and republican identity, see below, 212–13.

21. Anthony Ascham, *A Discourse: Wherein is examined, what is particularly lawfull during the Confusions and Revolutions of Government* (1648), 17.

22. See Marchamont Nedham, *Certain Considerations* (1649). For the significance of Nedham as a new kind of author, see above, 32–5.

23. For similar lexical usage in Harrington, see above, 164, 169–70.

24. See Cynthia Farrar, *The Origins of Democratic Thinking: the Invention of Politics in Classical Athens* (Cambridge, 1988), 30ff. Euripides is the most frequently cited dramatist in this study, *The Suppliants* in particu-

lar. For Milton's use of classical drama, see above 16–18.

25. Unless Nedham participated in the composition of some Leveller tracts.

26. On the rhetorical treatment of '*Isonomia* in ancient Athens, see Anna Missiou, *The Subversive Oratory of Andokides. Politics, ideology and decision-making in democratic Athens* (Cambridge, 1992), 36.

27. For Commonwealth taxation policy, see Michael J. Braddick, 'Popular Politics and Public Policy: The Excise Riot at Smithfield in February 1647 and its Aftermath', *HJ*, 34 (1991) (see above, ch. 2, n.32).

28. Whereas an English commonwealth as an aristocratically-ruled state is maintained by Anthony Ascham, Γενεσις καὶ τελος ἐξουσιας, *The Originall and End of Civil Power* (1649), 34.

29. This repeats Nedham, *The Case of the Commonwealth*, ed. Knachel, 117.

30. *Mercurius Politicus*, 84 (8–15 Jan. 1652), 1335–6.

31. *Ibid.*, 76 (13–20 Nov. 1651), 1206.

32. See Zagorin, *A History of Political Thought*, 127.

33. On the emergence of policy, see Ian MacLean, *From Prudence to Policy: Some Notes on the Prehistory of Policy Sciences* (Nijmegen, 1993).

34. For Hall's place in the educational debate, see Charles Webster, *The Great Instauration. Science, Medicine and Reform 1626–1660* (1975).

35. For Hall's biography, see John Davies of Kidwelly, preface to *Hierocles upon the Golden Verses of Pythagoras* (1657), trans. John Hall; DNB.

36. The image is suggested by Milton's representation of truth in *Areopagitica* (1644), *CPW*, II.549.

37. For further connections between natural philosophy and epic, see below, 226–7.

38. 'To my Lord Commissioner WHITELOCK', Longinus, Περι Υψους, trans. John Hall (1652), A7r-A8v. The context and quality of Hall's translation alongside other trans-

39. *Ibid.*, Sig. B1v.
40. Hall hints at his relationship with Hobbes's writings: 'even Mr. *Hobs* in his *De Civi*, though he assured himself that the rest of his Book (which is principally erected to the assertion of Monarchy) is demonstrated, yet he doubts whether the Arguments which he brings to this business be firm or no; And *Malvezzi* contrarily remonstrates (in his discourses upon *Tacitus*) that Optimacies are clearly better then Monarchies, as to all advantages.' *The Grounds and Reasons of Monarchy* (1651), 20.
41. For the royalist use of fables, see above, 8.
42. Zagorin, *A History of Political Thought*, 149 n.1.
43. Nigel Smith, '*Areopagitica*: Voicing Contexts, 1643–5', in David Loewenstein and James Grantham Turner, edd., *Politics, Poetics and Hermeneutics in Milton's Prose* (Cambridge, 1990), 103–22; on Milton's imbibing of Machiavelli, see Blair Worden, 'Milton's republicanism and the tyranny of heaven', in Gisela Bock, Quentin Skinner and Maurizio Viroli, edd., *Machiavelli and Republicanism* (Cambridge, 1990), 225–46.
44. See Kevin Gilmartin, 'History and Reform in Milton's *Readie and Easie Way*', *Milton Studies*, 24 (1988), 17–41.
45. But for a negative account of Cicero's ideals, see above, 36.
46. See also Sir Anthony Weldon's *A Cat may Look at a King* (1650), a similarly constructed account, and Arthur Wilson, *The Five Years of King James* (1643).
47. See the translations of Cicero attributed to Osborne in Bodl. MS Rawl. D.753.
48. Francis Osborne, *A Perswasive to a Mutuall Compliance under the Present Government. Together with a Plea for a Free State compared with Monarchy* (1652), Sig. A2r.

49. *Ibid.*, 10.
50. *Ibid.*, 12.
51. *Ibid.*, 18; 29.
52. *Ibid.*, 136.
53. Wither quotes widely from Cicero (*De Natura Deorum, De Oratore, Catone, De Officiis, Epistolae Familiares*), Plutarch, Homer, Epictetus, Epicurus, Isocrates, Anaxagoras.
54. In particular, Webster's *The Saints Guide* (1653; 2nd edn, 1654), although Webster's educational platform was more fully expressed in *Academiarum Examen* (1654).
55. See Laura Lunger Knoppers, 'Milton's *Readie and Easie Way* and the English Jeremiad', in Loewenstein and Turner, edd., *Politics, Poetics and Hermeneutics*, 213–25; and Thomas N. Corns, *Uncloistered Virtue: English Political Literature 1640–1660* (Oxford, 1992), 283–4.
56. This is not the sense of authorship given by Hobbes (see above, 161, 166–7).
57. The view that Miltonism led to a faith (always) in inherited nobility as opposed to the original sense of aristocracy – rule by the best, which is what Milton thought the godly elite were – seems exaggerated. See Zagorin, *A History of Political Thought*, 111–20, and now *John Milton: Rebel Aristocrat* (Woodbridge, Suffolk, 1993).
58. See Martin Dzelzainis, 'Milton and The Protectorate in 1658', forthcoming. Milton's involvement in the republication of works attributed to Ralegh is connected with this dissent from the Protectorate.
59. See *An Abridgment of the late Remonstrance Of The Army, With some Marginall Attestations* (1648), 8. John Rushworth signs this tract in his secretarial capacity.
60. See David Armitage, 'John Milton: Poet Against Empire', forthcoming.
61. For Streater, see DNB. More inglorious, according to Ludlow, was Streater's betrayal of the Parliament, when appointed to defend it: Edmund Ludlow, *A Voyce from the*

Watch Tower, ed. Blair Worden (1978), 88, 114.

62. Harrington's influence upon the republican pamphlets of 1659–60 is explored in Zagorin, *A History of Political Thought*, 154–63, and J.C. Davis, *Utopia and the Ideal Society: A Study in English Utopian Writing 1516–1700* (Cambridge, 1981), 241–65.

63. John Streater, *The Continuation of this Session of Parliament* (1659), 5; *idem*, *Clavis ad aperiendum Carceris Ostia* (1654), title-page.

64. John Streater, *The Continuation*, 3, 6. For uses of Dio Cassius (as well as Machiavelli), see *An Oratian of Agrippa to Octavius Caesar Augustus Against Monarchy* (3 March 1659), 'Englished by A.R.'

65. See the full constitutional vision of [John Streater], *Viz. What (Monarchie/Aristocracie/Oligarchie/And/ Democracie) is Together with a brief Model of the Government of the Commonwealth of Ragusa* (1659).

66. John Streater, *A Shield against the Parthian Dart* (1659), 20–21.

67. John Streater, *Secret Reasons* (1659), 18. *Observations* looked forward to the even more demotic but also post-Harringtonian *Faithfull Scout* of 1659.

68. John Streater, *A Glympse of that Jewel, Judicial, Just, Preserving Libertie* (1653), 15.

69. See J.G.A. Pocock, 'Historical Introduction', in *The Political Works of James Harrington* (Cambridge, 1977), 10.

Chapter 7:   Heroic Work

1. For an important account of the relationship between the *Aeneid* and the *Pharsalia*, and the traditions stemming respectively from them, see David Quint, *Epic and Empire: Politics and Form from Virgil to Milton* (Princeton, 1993), chs 1, 2, 4 (131–57).

2. For example, see Thomas Warmstry, *Ramae Olivae; Or, An Humble Motion for Peace* (Oxford, 1644), 7, and

Anon., *Pro-Quiritatio* (1642), Sig. [A1]r, quoting Lucan on the horror of civil war; Francis Blood, *The Souldiers March to Salvation* (1647), 12, quoting Lucan against mercenaries.

3. Edmund Gayton, *Pleasant Notes upon Don Quixot* (1654), 245.

4. Harvard University, Houghton Library, fMS Eng. 645, f.49. These lines imitate those of Walter Ralegh, which prefaced Sir Arthur Gorges's translation of Lucan (1614). Fane sees Lucan as poet of war, Ralegh praises his republican and anti-tyrannical virtue: 'Had Lucan hid the truth to please the time,/He had beene too unworthy of thy Penne:/ Who never sought, noe ever car'd to clime/By flattery, or seeking worthlesse men.'

5. *The Weekly Post*, 187 (11–18 July 1654), in Joad Raymond, ed., *Making the News: An Anthology of the Newsbooks of Revolutionary England 1641–1660* (Moreton-in-Marsh, Gloucs., 1993), 121.

6. James Harrington, *Oceana*, in *Political Works*, ed. J.G.A. Pocock (Cambridge, 1977), 198.

7. The 1626 edition was partial, containing three books. The complete translation appeared in 1627.

8. See: Gerald M. Maclean, *Time's Witness: Historical Representation in English Poetry, 1603–1660* (Madison, Wisc., 1990), 26–46; Colin Burrow, *Epic Romance: Homer to Milton* (Oxford, 1993), 180–99.

9. David Norbrook, Lucan, Thomas May and the Creation of a Republican Literary Culture', in Kevin Sharpe and Peter Lake, edd., *Culture and Politics in Early Stuart England* (1944), 45–66.

10. See R.T. Bruere, 'The Latin and English Versions of Thomas May's *Supplementum Lucani*', *Classical Philology*, 44 (1949), 145–63.

11. BL, MS Sloane 315, fos. 1r, 33. See also fo. 31.

12. 'I have cast away all such pieces as I wrote during the time of the late troubles, with any relation to the dif-

ferences that caused them; as among others, *three Books of the Civil War itself*, reaching as far as the first *Battel of Newbury*, where the succeeding *misfortunes* of the *party* stopt the *work*; for it is so uncustomary, as to become almost *ridiculous*, to make *Lawrells* for the *Conquered.*' Cowley, *Poems* (1657), Sig. a4r.

13. David Trotter, *The Poetry of Abraham Cowley* (1979), 7. For a very valuable, extensive assessment, see MacLean, *Time's Witness*, 177–211.

14. Trotter, *The Poetry of Abraham Cowley*, 21. But see also MacLean, *Time's Witness*, 207–8.

15. See Stephen Orgel, *The Illusion of Power* (1975); Erica Veevers, *Images of Love and Religion: Queen Henrietta Maria and Court Entertainments* (Cambridge, 1989), 113–64; MacLean, *Time's Witness*, 199–201.

16. See notes in *The Collected Works of Abraham Cowley*, 6 vols (Newark, Delaware, 1989–), 1, ed. Thomas O. Calhoun, Laurence Heyworth and Allan Pritchard, 412–3.

17. See below, 224–5. For continental sources of infernal councils in Vida and Tasso, among others, see Quint, *Epic and Empire*, 176, and in Trissino, see Burrow, *Epic Romance*, 266–8.

18. See also *The Civil War*, 3.1–20. Significantly, these passages are very similar to Cowley's published satires, *The Puritans Lecture* (or *A Satyre against Separatists* (1642)), esp. ll. 57–67, and *The Puritan and the Papist* (1643), 6.

19. Allan Pritchard, introduction to Cowley, *The Civil War* (Toronto, 1973), 37, repeated in *Collected Works*, 1. 375.

20. Homer, *Odyssey*, 11.305–20. For a similar perception, see above, 13.

21. Colin Burrow also notes of *The Civil War*: 'Cavalier warriors become the pitifully mortal reincarnations of Virgil's imperial victims, killed by an uncontrolled and devilish *furor*', *Epic Romance*, 238.

22. For the argument that Hobbes's *Leviathan* is an epic, see S. Wolin, *Hobbes and the Epic Tradition of Political Theory* (Los Angeles, 1970) and also above, 163. For further treatment of the *Second Defence* in this way, see David Loewenstein, 'Milton and the Poetics of Defence', in David Loewenstein and James Turner, edd., *Politics, Poetics, and Hermeneutics in Milton's Prose* (Cambridge, 1990), 171–92 (177, 183, 185–7).

23. But for a non-elitist use of Milton's prose, see above, 150.

24. John Hall, *The Grounds and Reasons of Monarchy* (Edinburgh, 1651), 4.

25. See also I.B.'s specifically royalist *Heroick Education* (1657).

26. Hobbes, 'The Answer of Mr. Hobbes to Sir Will. D'Avenant's Preface before Gondibert', in Davenant, *Gondibert*, ed. David Gladish (Oxford, 1971), 49.

27. See above, 157–8, and Cowley's dream vision of Cromwell as gigantic Protector in 'A Discourse by Way of Vision, Concerning the Government of Oliver Cromwell', in *Collected Works*, 2.628–30. For a discussion of this passage in context, see Hans-Dieter Metzger, *Thomas Hobbes und die Englische Revolution 1640–1660* (Stuttgart, 1991), 162.

28. Longinus was translated into Latin as *Dionysii Longini liber de grandi eloquentia* by Gerard Langbaine, Provost of The Queen's College, Oxford, antiquarian and friend of John Selden, and published in 1636 and 1638.

29. Washington, D.C., Folger Shakespeare Library, MS V.A.148, fo. 35v.

30. For further discussion of the circumstances in Cowley's composition of *Davideis*, see Thomas N. Corns, *Uncloistered Virtue: English Political Literature 1640–1660* (Oxford, 1992), 256–9.

31. If Milton was familiar with any sections of *The Civil War*, they would most probably have been the passages redeployed in *Davideis*.

32. See B.S. Capp, *The Fifth Monarchy*

Men: *A Study in Seventeenth-Century English Millenarianism* (1972), 131–576.

33. Corns, *Uncloistered Virtue*, 266–7.

34. See *ibid.*, 267.

35. 'You having from my childhood tuned mine ears to Spencers rhymes, entertaining us on winter nights, with that incomparable Piece of his, *The Fairy Queen*, a Poem as richly fraught with divine Morality as Phansy', 'To his dear Father ALEXANDER MORE, Esquire', *Philosophical Poems* (1647), ed. A.B. Grosart (1878), 1.

36. For Henry More in this context, see Sarah Hutton, 'Henry More and Jacob Boehme', in Sarah Hutton, ed., *Henry More (1614–1687)* (Dordrecht, 1990), 157–71, and for the context more generally, see Nigel Smith, *Perfection Proclaimed: Language and Literature in English Radical Religion, 1640–1660* (Oxford, 1989), 107–225.

37. 'To the reader. Upon this second Edition.', *Psychozoia* in *Philosophical Poems*, 6.

38. *Ibid.*, 6.

39. The animal names, taken from Latin and Italian, point to fabular tradition. The Welsh Independent, Morgan Llwyd's *Llyfr y tri Aderyn* (Book of the Three Birds, 1657) is the nearest example to More's usage in the period.

40. CUL MS Add. 57583.

41. See George Herbert, *The Temple*, 'Mattins', l. 6.

42. For a comparison of Beaumont's account of the Fall of Man with Milton's, see James Grantham Turner, *One Flesh: Paradisal Marriage and Sexual Relations in the Age of Milton* (Oxford, 1987), 251–5, 265, 291, 295–6, 308.

43. See Burrow, *Epic Romance*, 244–89; Charles Martindale, *The Epic of Ideas: Lucan's De bello civili and Paradise Lost, Comparative Criticism*, 3 (1981), 133–56.

44. On Fletcher and Milton, see Quint, *Epic and Empire*, 270–81.

45. See Mary Ann Radzinowicz, *Milton's Epics and the Book of Psalms* (Princeton, 1989).

46. For discussions of puritan theological issues, such as free will, mapped onto the conversation between Adam and Eve, see Joan Bennett, *Reviving Liberty* (Cambridge, Mass., 1989); Quint, *Epic and Empire*, 281–99; David Loewenstein, '*Paradise Regained* and the Culture of Radical Religion', *Literature and History*, forthcoming.

47. See Robert Wiltenburg, 'Damnation in a Roman Dress: Catiline, *Catiline*, and *Paradise Lost*', *Milton Studies*, 25 (1989), 89–108; Blair Worden, 'Milton's republicanism and the tyranny of heaven', in Gisela Bock, Quentin Skinner and Maurizio Viroli, edd., *Machiavelli and Republicanism* (Cambridge, 1990), 225–45.

48. See Kenneth L. Carroll, *John Perrot: Early Quaker Schismatic* (1971); Nigel Smith, 'Exporting Enthusiasm: John Perrot and the Quaker Epic', in Thomas Healy and Jonathan Sawday, edd., *Literature and the English Civil War* (Cambridge, 1990), 248–64.

49. Cf. John Hall, *The Advancement of Learning* (1650), ed. A.K. Croston (Liverpool, 1953), 35: 'whole Landscap of Knowledge'.

50. Compare Perrot's account of crossing the terrifying straits between Euboea and mainland Greece (*A Sea*, 5), and Milton's use of these waters as an image for the state without the control of parliament (*CPW*, IV, 635).

51. Hobbes, 'The Answer of Mr. Hobbes to Sir Will. D'Avenant's Preface before Gondibert', in Davenant, *Gondibert*, 51.

52. [Hezekiah Woodward], *As You Were* (1647), 4.

53. See David Armitage, 'John Milton: Poet against Empire', forthcoming, and see also the flights and orator's journey in Milton, *Second Defence*, *CPW*, IV.551, 555.

54. Louis L. Martz, *Poet of Exile* (New Haven, 1980), 155–68. There is

further political relevance to the translation. Despite outward friendliness towards the Commonwealth, the Portuguese government did assist the Royalists. Matters came to head when, during negotiations for a treaty between the two countries, Cromwell insisted that the brother of the Portuguese ambassador be executed in punishment for murdering a student of Grays Inn.

55. See David Quint, 'The Boat of Romance and Renaissance Epic', in Kevin Brownlee and Marina Scordilis Brownlee, edd., *Romance: Generic Transformation from Chrétien de Troyes to Cervantes* (Hanover, NH, 1985), 178–202.

56. Richard Fanshawe, 'The Translator's POSTSCRIPT', in Luis de Camoens, *The Lusiad* (1654), edited with an introduction by Jeremiah D.M. Ford (Camb., Mass., 1940), [26].

57. 'Out of the Satyr of *Petronius Arbiter*, pag. 48', in Camoens, [7].

58. Escape signals *Gondibert*'s romance affiliations (see above, 239–41). I am not convinced by Prof. Quint's argument that *Paradise Lost* and *Paradise Regained* take similar romance turns (instead, Milton is concerned to create two very different environments); see Quint, *Epic and Empire*, 308–24.

59. See Samuel Sheppard, *The Joviall Crew, or the Devill turn'd Ranter* (1651).

60. Quint, 'The Boat of Romance', 195.

61. Oxford, Christ Church Library. Evelyn Collection, MS Letters 67, John Beale to John Evelyn, 16 Oct. 1667, fo. 1v: 'For . . . Milton, I have no other fondness, than I should have had for Ovid, Martiall, Petronius, and Lucan, which were all four, either lascivious, obscene, dissolute, or traiterous.' In the 1640s and 1650s, all of the Roman poets named here had been in vogue with influential Royalists as well as republicans (see above, 207–12). I am grateful to Professor Nicholas von Maltzahn for this reference.

62. John Boys's translation of *Aeneid* VI, *Aeneas His Descent Into Hell* (1661) is an allegorical account of the Restoration: Aeneas is heroic the personification of Charles II, and Boys intends to praise the King just as Virgil praised Augustus in his epic. It is dedicated to Clarendon and has appended several 'Publick Pieces', including a speech of welcome to Charles II, a letter to Monk and a declaration in favour of the restored Rump Parliament.

63. See Laurence Venuti, *The Destruction of Troy*: Translation and Royalist Cultural Politics in the Interregnum', *JMRS*, 23 (1993), 197–219.

64. Denham, in *Poetical Works*, ed. Theodore Howard Banks (New Haven, 1928), 160. During the act of translation Denham states that 'spirit' evaporates from language; hence the need for expansive translation; *ibid.*, 159.

65. Harrington, *An Essay* (1658), 38.

66. I am grateful to Dr. Paul Hammond for this reference.

67. There have been a number of distinguished attempts to resurrect Wither's reputation. See, most recently, David Norbrook, 'Levelling Poetry: George Wither and the English Revolution, 1642–1649', *ELH*, 21 (1991), 215–56. On 1630s complaint poetry, including Wither's, see MacLean, *Time's Witness*, 96–119.

68. The lines are of course reminiscent of Milton's view of kingship in *Paradise Regained*, 2.458–86.

69. Copy in author's possession.

70. See [John Toland], *Clito: A Poem on the Force of Eloquence* (1700), 10: 'O Glorious LIBERTY for thee I'll prove/The firmest Patron that e'er Tongue did move;/I'll always execute what you decree,/And be the fatal scourge of Slavery.'

71. *Mercurius Britanicus*, 110 (15–22 Dec. 1645), 969.

72. See Annabel M. Patterson, *Censorship and Interpretation* (Madison, Wisc., 1984), 190–202, for a reading of Herbert's *Princess Cloria*.

73. Prof. Patterson is concerned to show how romance evolved in interaction with state censorship. Her mistake is to regard it as a royalist preserve: 'The Royal Romance', *Censorship and Interpretation*, 159–202.

74. Paul Salzman, *English Prose Fiction 1558–1700. A Critical History* (Oxford, 1985), chs 11, 12.

75. See Erica Veevers, *Images of Love and Entertainment: Queen Henrietta Maria and Court Entertainment* (Cambridge, 1989), 16–18, 44–5.

76. BL MS Add. 23,146, f. 7r.

77. Dorothy Osborne to Sir William Temple, September, 1653.

78. The MU copy contains a detailed list of characters with their identities in the real world. Howell's *Dendrologia* was also annotated in this way: see the Bodleian Library copy at J.2.23.Med.

79. I am most grateful to Ian MacLellan of Lincoln College for help with this point; he is producing a far more detailed account of mid-seventeenth-century romance than space allows me here.

80. 'The History of Arcadia, or an Addition to and a Continuance of Sir Phillip Sydney's ARCADIA: Usually Styled The Countesse of Pembrokes ARCADIA', Yale University, Beinecke Library, Osborn MS b.107, 62.

81. Potter, *Secret Rites and Secret Writing: Royalist Literature 1641–1660* (Cambridge, 1989), 93–4.

82. For Sheppard, see P.J. Klemp, ed., *The Faerie King* (Salzburg, 1984), and Potter, *Secret Rites*, 123, 125–8, 135.

83. So David Quint is not quite right to see *Gondibert* as in quest of the ideals of aristocratic retreat against monarchy, although his comparison of *Gondibert* with Marino's *Adone* (and Chapelain's preface to it) is very suggestive: Quint, *Epic and Empire*, 314–17, 321. See also Cornell March Dowlin, *Sir William Davenant's Gondibert, Its Preface, and Hobbes's Answer. A Study in English Neoclassicism* (Philadelphia, 1934).

84. Dorothy Osborne also complained of systematic mistranslation by the Earl of Monmouth (e.g. '*pipeur*' as 'piper' not 'trickster'), possibly implying that libertinism is suppressed in the translations (Letter to Sir William Temple, Sept. 1653). However, comparison of originals with translations reveals a large degree of accuracy, coupled with figurative embellishment very much within the terms of local themes and contexts.

85. See Anna Bryson, 'Concepts of Civility in England, *c.* 1560–1685' (unpublished D.Phil. thesis, University of Oxford, 1984).

86. Madeleine de Scudéry, *Clelia*, trans. John Davies (1656), 2.

87. Just as mock-romance depicted pastoral as an illusion of *bourgeois* characters and readers: see Charles Sorel, *The Extravagant Shepherd*, trans. John Davies (1654). See also above, 45–7.

88. Madeleine de Scudéry, Preface to *Ibrahim*, trans. Henry Cogan (1652), Sig. A4v.

89. Dorothy Osborne to Sir William Temple, 5 March 1653, in *The Letters of Dorothy Osborne to William Temple*, ed. G.C. Moore Smith (Oxford, 1928), 24.

90. See Patricia Caldwell, *The Puritan Conversion Narrative* (Cambridge, 1983); and Nigel Smith, *Perfection Proclaimed*, chs 1, 2.

91. *An Account of Philaretus during his Minority* (1648–9) in *Robert Boyle: Key Biographical Texts*, ed. Michael Hunter (Pickering and Chatto, 1994).

92. Although La Calprenède's *Cassandre* (1642–5; English translation 1652) was also associated with the events of the Fronde, and political resonances were acknowledged by its royalist English translator, Sir Charles Cotterell.

93. See also Richard Wendorf, *The Elements of Life: Biography and Portrait-Painting in Stuart and Georgian England* (Oxford, 1990).

94. For a brilliant analysis, see Annabel

Patterson, 'No meer amatorious novel?', in Loewenstein and Turner, edd., *Politics, Poetics and Hermeneutics*, 85–101.

95. Patterson, *Censorship and Interpretation*, 186–7.
96. Kathleen M. Lynch, *Roger Boyle: First Earl of Orrery* (Knoxville, Tennessee, 1965), 76.
97. Boyle, *Parthenissa* (1655), 3.2.250.
98. Lynch, *Roger Boyle*, 188.
99. *Parthenissa*, 1.4.332.
100. *Parthenissa*, 2.5.492.
101. See Nancy Klein Maguire, 'Regicide and Reparation: The Autobiographical Drama of Roger Boyle, Earl of Orrery', *ELR*, 21 (1991), 257–82.
102. *Oceana*, in *Political Works*, ed. Pocock, 198.
103. *The Prerogative of Popular Government*, *Political Works*, 411.
104. The image connects with Marvell's lyric 'The Unfortunate Lover' (*c.* 1648–9) and related post-regicide royalist iconography.
105. *The Art of Lawgiving* (1659), *Political Works*, 608.
106. *Ibid.*, *loc. cit.*
107. Richard Helgerson's links gothic and romance as a feature of Elizabethan culture in *Forms of Nationhood*, 40–59. Toland's account of Lady Claypole's intercession to her father (the Lord Protector) on Harrington's behalf, to save *Oceana* from suppression, presents her as a romance princess. She is not Elizabeth, but she functions with similar tact to save what Cromwell was told was 'only a kind of Political Romance': Harrington, *Oceana*, ed. John Toland (1700), xix–xx.
108. Gott was an acquaintance of John Selden and the lawyer, Independent and bibliophile, Samuel Jeake. See also J.C. Davis, *Utopia and the Ideal Society. A Study of English Utopian Writing 1516–1700* (Cambridge, 1981), 139–67.
109. Ros Ballaster, *Seductive Forms: Women's Amatory Fiction from 1684–1740* (Oxford, 1992); Donald R. Wehrs, 'Eros, Identity, Royalist Feminism and the Politics of Desire in Aphra Behn's *Love Letters*', *SEL*, 32 (1992), 461–78.

Chapter 8: The Instrumentality of Lyrics

1. Arthur Marotti, *John Donne, Coterie Poet* (Madison, Wisc., 1984); *idem*, 'Manuscript Poetry and the Political World', forthcoming; Gerald Hammond, *Fleeting Things: English Poets and Poems 1616–1660* (Camb., Mass., 1990).
2. John Morrill, *The Revolt of the Provinces: Conservatives and Radicals in the English Civil War 1630–1650* (1976).
3. 'The Argument of his Book', ll. 11–14, *Hesperides* (1648).
4. David Underdown, *Revel, Riot and Rebellion: Popular Politics and Culture in England 1603–1660* (Oxford, 1985); *idem*, *Fire from Heaven* (1992).
5. Clement Barksdale, 'XLI. Upon the Histories of the late Wars', in *Nympha Libethris* (1651), 43. See also Hugh Crompton, Gent., *Pierides or the Muses Mount* (1658).
6. Folger MS V.b.303, fos. 254–6.
7. For another valuable reading, see Thomas N. Corns, *Uncloistered Virtue. English Political Literature 1640–1660* (Oxford, 1992), 64–68, 244–50.
8. See Blair Worden, 'The Commonwealth Kidney of Algernon Sidney', *JBS*, 24 (1985), 1–40; Jonathan Scott, *Algernon Sidney and the English Republic 1623–1677* (Cambridge, 1988); *idem*, *Algernon Sidney and the Restoration Crisis 1677–1683* (Cambridge, 1991).
9. See J.S.A. Adamson, 'The Baronial Context of the English Civil War', *TRHS*, 5th ser., 40 (1990), 93–120.
10. The focus of this publishing activity was the licenser John Bachelor: see Smith, *Perfection Proclaimed*, 138.
11. Gerald Hammond, 'Richard Love-

lace and the Uses of Obscurity', Chatterton Lecture 1985, *PBA*, 71 (1985), 203–34; Corns, *Uncloistered Virtue*, 68–79, 244–50.

12. Ann Baynes Coiro, *Robert Herrick's Hesperides and the Epigram Book Tradition* (Baltimore and London, 1988); Alastair Fowler, 'Georgic and Pastoral: Laws of Genre in the Seventeenth Century', in M. Leslie and T. Raylor, edd., *Culture and Cultivation in Early Modern England* (Leicester, 1992), 81–91.

13. For an account of sectarian language in relation to poetry, see Hugh Ormsby-Lennon, 'The Dialect of those Fanatick Times: Language Communities and English Poetry from 1580–1660' (unpublished Ph.D. thesis, University of Pennsylvania, 1977).

14. See Barbara Kiefer Lewalski, *Writing Women in Jacobean England* (Camb., Mass., 1993).

15. Such as Col. Robert Overton, Governor of Hull, republican and Fifth Monarchist.

16. See Hero Chalmers, 'Constructing the Woman Author' (unpublished D.Phil. thesis, University of Oxford, 1993), ch. 1.

17. See Owen Watkins, *The Puritan Experience* (1972); Patricia Caldwell, *The Puritan Conversion Narrative* (Cambridge, 1983); N.H. Keeble, *The Literary Culture of Nonconformity in the Later Seventeenth Century* (Leicester, 1987); Nigel Smith, *Perfection Proclaimed: Language and Literature in English Radical Religion 1640–1660* (Oxford, 1989).

18. See above, chapter 5, and J.C. Davis, 'Cromwell's Religion', in John Morrill, ed., *Oliver Cromwell and the English Revolution* (1990), 181–208; 'Religion and the Struggle for Freedom in the English Revolution', *HJ*, 35 (1992), 507–30; Ann Kibbey, *The Interpretation of Material Shapes in Puritanism: A Study of Rhetoric, Prejudice and Violence* (Cambridge, 1986), 7–41. These parameters are currently the subject of investigation by Arnold Hunt, of Trinity College, Cambridge.

19. See, for instance, Arthur Pollard, *The English Hymn* (1960). Hymnody was, however, a strong component in Lutheran worship in Europe.

20. John Cotton, *Singing of Psalms* (1650), 32, 60.

21. For the place of hymns in lyric tradition more generally, see Barbara Kiefer Lewalski, *Protestant Poetics and the Seventeenth-Century Religious Lyric* (Princeton, 1979), ch. 2.

22. W[illiam] B[arton], *A Century of Select Hymns* (1659), Sig. A4r.

23. George Wither, *Three Hymns* (1651).

24. Wither's religion and his political republicanism are closely interrelated: see above, 230–32.

25. Corns, *Uncloistered Virtue*, 115–28.

26. Hammond, *Fleeting Things*, 243–5.

27. BL MS Harl. 7019, fos. 71–3.

28. See Thomas F. Healy, *Richard Crashaw* (Leiden, 1986), 88, 136.

29. Shelfmark 4. △.30.

30. 'Made by Dr. Steward.'

31. See Helen Wilcox, 'Something understood: the reputation and influence of George Herbert to 1715' (unpublished D.Phil. thesis, University of Oxford, 1984).

32. See Ann Hughes, 'The Pulpit Guarded: Confrontations between Orthodox and Radicals in Revolutionary England', in Anne Laurence, W.R. Owens, and Stuart Sim, edd., *John Bunyan and His England 1628–1688* (1990), 31–50.

33. See Nigel Smith, 'George Herbert in Defence of Antinomianism', *N & Q*, n.s., 31 (1984), 34–5.

34. Christopher Harvie's poetry was attached to the 1640s edition of Herbert's *The Temple*. For Harvie's treatise against rebellion, see DNB.

35. *Works*, ed. L.C. Martin (2nd edn, Oxford, 1963), 392.

36. See Jeremy Taylor's 'Festival Hymns' in *The Golden Grove* (1655).

37. For Llwyd's biography, see G.F. Nuttall, *The Welsh Saints 1640–1660* (Cardiff, 1957), 37–54; M. Wynn Thomas, *Morgan Llwyd* (Cardiff, 1984).

38. Morgan Llwyd, 'Our Lord is coming once againe', in T.E. Ellis and J.H. Davies, *Gweithiau Morgan Llwyd*, edd., 2 vols (Bangor and Liverpool, 1899, 1908), I.9.

39. Llwyd, 'The Summer', *1648*, in *Gweithiau*, 23–4.

40. See Smith, *Perfection Proclaimed*, 191.

41. See John Webster, *Academiarum Examen* (1654), 26–32.

42. See Alan Rudrum, 'Henry Vaughan, the Liberation of the Creation and Seventeenth-Century English Calvinism', *The Seventeenth Century*, 4 (1989), 33–54.

43. *Gweithiau*, I.302.

44. *Works*, 302.

45. Smith, *Perfection Proclaimed*, 205, n. 56.

46. See also J. Andrew Mendelsohn, 'Alchemy and Politics in England 1649–1665', *Past and Present*, 135 (1992), 30–78, which makes the point that Royalists used alchemical explanations as much as Puritans: not as original as it claims to be, and the article is misleading in that spiritual writers like Boehme are conflated with alchemists proper.

47. See Jonathan Post, *Henry Vaughan: The Unfolding Vision* (1982), 132.

48. Copy seen by the author at Oxford Bookfair, 1988.

49. Post, *Henry Vaughan*, 70–115.

50. Llwyd, 'The Winter', *1648*, in *Gweithiau*, I.20.

51. *Ibid.*, *1648*, in *Gweithiau*, I.19.

52. 'Titts' are horses.

53. 'The Summer', *1648*, in *Gweithiau*, I.25.

54. 'The Harvest', *1648*, in *Gweithiau*, I.31 (wrongly paginated as 30).

55. John Appletree, 'Mr. Appletree's Hymn', in *Three Hymnes* (1650), 10.

56. For Tillam, see David Katz, *Sabbath and Sectarianism in Seventeenth-Century England* (Leiden, 1988), 21–47.

57. Smith, *Perfection Proclaimed*, 332–3.

58. Thomas Willes, Καιροι Χαλεποι. *A Word in Season, For a Warning to England* (1659), 303. For godly ballads, see Tessa Watt, *Cheap Print and Popular Piety 1500–1640* (Cambridge, 1991).

59. A volume of sermons preached as 'lectures' in the Restoration by the sometime Fifth Monarchist Christopher Feake have a large number of hymns appended: possibly they were sung at the lectures, which were meetings of Dissenters designed to avoid the legislation against nonconformist worship. I am indebted to Arnold Hunt for this information. See also 'Mr Feakes Hymne', 11 Aug. 1653, Thomason Tracts, E790 (13).

60. Isaac Watts, 'The Adventurous Muse', reprinted in Roger Lonsdale, ed., *The New Oxford Book of Eighteenth-Century Verse* (Oxford, 1984), 70–2.

61. See David Norbrook, 'Marvell's "Horatian Ode" and the Politics of Genre', in Thomas Healy and Jonathan Sawday, edd., *Literature and the English Civil War* (Cambridge, 1990), 147–69.

62. Published in 1648.

63. For a fuller treatment of verse on Felton, see Hammond, *Fleeting Things: English Poets and Poems 1610–1660* (Camb., Mass., 1990), 51–66; James Holstun, '"God Bless Thee Little David!": John Felton and his Allies', *ELH*, 59 (1992), 513–52.

64. John Corbet, *A Vindication of the Magistrates and Minister of the City of Gloucester* (1646), Sig. A2r.

65. *Ibid.*, A2v.

66. Harvard fMS Eng. 645.

67. Bodl. MS Add. B.5., fo. 68v. 'He prepares weapons, iron and gold more powerful than iron [cf. Ovid, *Metamorphoses*, I.l.141], threatening with religion. There is also a scourge hidden beneath his lacerated heart. The rest are ornaments.' 'Secto' echoes appropriately the English 'sect'.

68. Cf. Henry Vaughan's poem on the same subject, 'The King Disguis'd', '*Written* [said Vaughan afterwards] *about the same time that Mr. John Cleveland wrote his*'.

69. 'An Elegie on the most incomparable Rebell *Oliver Cromwell*' in *A Case for Nol Cromwells Nose* (1648), 3–4.

70. Horace himself is ambivalent: he defended republican liberty, but he also respected monarchs.

71. Milton is reworking the imagery of his earlier poem against Presbyterian intolerance: Sonnet XII. 'On the Detraction which followed upon my Writing Certain Treatises', and 'On the New Forcers of Conscience under the Long Parliament'.

72. Ruth Nevo, *The Dial of Virtue: A Study of Poems on Affairs of State in the Seventeenth Century* (Princeton, 1963), 93–118.

73. See also Waller's sea-battle poetry, and Marvell's parody of it in 'The Last Instructions to a Painter' (1667).

74. No. 1 (3 Feb. 1651); No. 2 (12 Feb. 1651).

75. Adriana MacCrea's 'Reason's Muse: Andrew Marvell, R. Fletcher and the Political Poetry in the Engagement Debate', *Albion*, 23 (1991), 655–80, offers neostoicism in Marvell and R. Fletcher as a system of belief facilitating the public support of different, even opposed political ideals. MacLean, *Time's Witness*, 309–10, nn. 32, 33 denies the connection.

76. See also Roger Pooley, 'The poets' Cromwell', *Critical Survey*, 5 (1993), 223–34 (230–31).

77. W.H., *A Congratulation To our newly restored Parliament* (1659), ssh.

78. *One and Twenty Chester Queries* (1659), 6–7.

79. Payne Fisher, translated by Thomas Manley, *Veni; Vidi; Vici. The Triumphs of the Most Excellent & Illustrious Oliver Cromwell* (1652), 3. MacLean, *Time's Witness*, 226–33 reads this volume as diversified praise of the heroic republic, and gives Manley a greater authorial role than Fisher in the English verse.

80. Fisher, 'To the Most Excellent, The Lord Generall of Great Brittayne, Oliver Cromwell', in *Veni; Vidi; Vici*, Sig. I3r.

81. Fisher, *Veni; Vidi; Vici*, 63–4.

82. I am most grateful to Stella Revard for sharing her thoughts on panegyric.

83. Corns, *Uncloistered Virtue*, 259–65.

84. These, two of four decidedly contentious elegies, were not published in the 1657 edition of King's poems, but were included in the 1664 edition.

85. As Lois Potter (*Secret Rites and Secret Writing: Royalist Literature 1641–1660* (Cambridge, 1989), 123) rightly points out with regard to J.W. Draper's classic study of the elegy, *The Funeral Elegy and the Rise of English Romanticism* (New York, 1929). See also MacLean, *Time's Witness*, 214–19.

86. Royalist sympathiser; executed for his part in Waller's plot, 1643.

87. Isaac Dorislaus (1595–1649) was born in Holland, but came to England under Sir Henry Mildmay's patronage. He developed a formidable academic and legal reputation, and helped draw up the indictments against Charles I. It was this in particular which roused a group of Royalists to assassinate him in Holland when he was representing the Republic.

88. Washington D.C., Folger Shakespeare Library, Richard Washington's copy of Philip Massinger, *The Picture* (1630), Sig. A4v.

89. See Andrew Marvell, *Complete Poems*, ed. Nigel Smith (Longman, forthcoming).

90. Bodl. MS Add. B.5, fols. 43v-42v. Note that the chronological order proceeds backwards through the book.

91. *Eikonoklastes*, CPW, III.342.

92. A similar case can be made for the 'elegies' on the Parliamentarian commander Earl of Essex in the 1640s.

93. Bodl. MS Rawl. poet 116, fo. 75b. See also *The Great Assises holden in Parnassus* (1645).

94. W.G., *In Memorie of that Lively Patterne of true Pietie, and unstain'd Loyaltie, Mris SUSANNA HARRIS* (27 Nov. 1649).

95. See Nicholas Jose, *Ideas of Restoration in English Literature 1660–1671* (1984). MacLean, *Time's Witness*, 264, argues that Restoration panegyrists nonetheless accepted the limited nature of the monarchy.

Chapter 9: Satire: Whose Property?

1. Harold F. Brooks, 'Verse Satire, 1640–1660', *The Seventeenth Century*, 3 (1989), 17–46, continues an older viewpoint in an otherwise important article: 'the Royalists . . . were the immediate predecessors of the Restoration satirists.'
2. Margaret Anne Doody, *The Daring Muse: Augustan Poetry Reconsidered* (Cambridge, 1985), 30–57.
3. Dryden, Preface to *Religio Laici* (1682), in *Poem and Fables*, ed. James Kinsley (Oxford, 1958; 1978), 279–80.
4. See Benne Klaas Faber, 'The Poetics of Subversion and Conservatism: Popular Satire, c.1640–c.1660', unpublished D.Phil. thesis, University of Oxford, 1991.
5. See Leland H. Carlson, *Martin Marprelate, Gentleman. Master Job Throckmorton Laid Open in his Colors* (San Marino, Calif., 1981).
6. See forthcoming work by Patrick Collinson.
7. Keith Thomas, 'The Place of Laughter in Tudor and Stuart England', *TLS*, 21 Jan. 1977, 77–84.
8. Sidrach Simpson, *The Anatomist Anatomis'd* (1644), 3.
9. See Joshua Poole, *The English Parnassus: Or, A Helpe to English Poesie* (1657); Faber, 'The Poetics of Subversion', 111.
10. John Lilburne, *A Worke of the Beast* (1638), 27.
11. Quoted in H.R. Trevor-Roper, *Archbishop Laud, 1573–1645* (1940), 412.
12. For a fuller account, see Nigel Smith, 'Richard Overton's Marpriest Tracts: Towards a History of Leveller Style', *Prose Studies*, 9 (1986), 39–66; and Roger Pooley, *English Prose of the Seventeenth Century 1590–1700* (1992), 159–60. Dr Pooley is currently editing Overton's works.
13. John Taylor, *Crop-Eare Curried, Or, Tom Nash His Ghost* (1644), 18. Calerent: a kind of syllogism. Bocardo: a) another kind of logical proposition b) prison. Fleta: 'weepings' (Latin); also a medieval legal document.
14. Overton, *The Araignment of Mr. Persecution*, 2.
15. For the anti-sectarian image, see *The Picture of an English Persecutor* (1647). The Independent divine John Goodwin was represented in one woodcut as Don Quixote.
16. William Mewe to Richard Baxter, 5 September 1659, in *Calendar and Correspondence of Richard Baxter*, ed. N.H. Keeble and Geoffrey F. Nuttall, 2 vols (Oxford, 1991), I.406.
17. The Roman Emperor, Alexander Severus, was the most famous example. Shakespeare's *Measure for Measure* (1603), and Marston's *The Malcontent* (1603) are the best English dramatic renderings of the topos.
18. Toothless satire is what they were, since they made no *ad hominem* attack (neither did Hall's 'biting satires'), but struck at general human types.
19. Milton talks of Hall as someone whom he thought at first must be 'some sucking Satir, who might have done better to have us'd his corall' (*CPW*, I.915). The coral ring for teething is also used by Overton to describe the petulant infant, Sir John Presbyter. Overton's possible debt to Milton is not usually acknowledged.
20. *The Last Will and Testament of St. James Independent* (1647), 1–2.
21. See Smith, *Perfection Proclaimed*, 94. I am grateful to Ann Geneva for help with astrology.
22. David Underdown, *Revel, Riot, and Rebellion: Popular Politics and Culture*

in England 1603–1660 (Oxford, 1985), illustration 8B.

23. *Mercurius Britanicus*, 70 (10–17 Feb. 1645), 550. Marvell's satire on the Dutch, *The Character of Holland* (Feb. 1653) uses precisely this passage which *Mercurius Britanicus* takes directly from Cleveland.

24. *A Strange Sight to be seen at Westminster* (Oxford, 1643), ssh.

25. M. Bakhtin, *Rabelais and His World* (Camb., Mass., 1968).

26. Despite the continuing closure of the public theatres and bear gardens, puppet theatres did operate in 1650s London. Richard Cromwell is supposed to have been amused by the portrayal of his father as a puppet.

27. Anon., *Light Shining in Buckinghamshire* (1648), in G.H. Sabine, ed., *The Works of Gerrard Winstanley* (New York, 1941, 1965), 618–20.

28. Faber, 'The Poetics of Subversion', 158–76.

29. Potter, *Secret Rites*, 30–31, follows Gimmelfarb-Brack, *Liberté, Egalité, Fraternité, Justice: La Vie et l'oeuvre de Richard Overton, Niveleur* (Bern, 1979), 11, 410, in seeing an interaction between Overton and Crouch, but the comparisons and interconnections go far beyond these two.

30. John Cleveland, 'The Hue and Cry after Sir John Presbyter', in *Poems*, ed. Brian Morris and Eleanor Withington (Oxford, 1967), 45.

31. See Michael P. Parker, 'Satire in Sextodecimo: Davenant, the Dwarf, and the Politics of "Jeffereidos"', in Claude J. Summers and Ted-Larry Pebworth, edd., *'The Muses Common-Weale': Poetry and Politics in the Seventeenth Century* (Columbia, Missouri, 1988), 92–106.

32. *Ibid.*, 46.

33. Cleveland, 'On the Archbishop of Canterbury', ll. 41–3, in Morris and Withington, edd., 39.

34. Doody, *The Daring Muse*, 32.

35. Cleveland, 'A Dialogue between two Zealots, upon the &c. in the Oath', in Morris and Withington, edd., *Poems*, 4.

36. See Thomas Osborne Calhoun, 'Cowley's Verse Satire, 1642–3, and the Beginnings of Party Politics', *YES*, 21 (1991), 197–206.

37. Cleveland, 'A Dialogue', in Morris and Withrington, edd., *Poems*, 5.

38. Cleveland, 'The Kings Disguise', in Morris and Withington, edd., *Poems*, 8.

39. Cleveland, 'The Mixt Assembly', in Morris and Withington, edd., *Poems*, 28.

40. For obvious indebtedness to Cleveland, see the poetry of Andrew Marvell and John Ravenshaw.

41. Bodl. Library, MS Rawl. D 317b, fo. 176v. Note also the contemporary association of the Gunpowder Plot with the Apocalypse.

42. See T.J. Raylor, 'The Achievement of Sir John Mennes and Dr. James Smith' (unpublished D.Phil. thesis, University of Oxford, 1986). On the function of 'wit', see Steven N. Zwicker, *Lines of Authority: Politics and English Literary Culture 1649–1689* (Ithaca, N.Y., 1993), 28–34.

43. Samuel Sheppard, 'To the Parliament of England', *Epigrams* (1651).

44. ?Sir John Mennes, 'Upon Sir John Sucklings most warlike preparations for the Scotish Warre', in Suckling, *Works*, vol. 1, *The Non-Dramatic Works*, ed. Thomas Clayton (Oxford, 1971), 209.

45. ?Sir John Mennes, 'To a friend upon his Marriage', *Musarum Deliciae* (1655), 8–9.

46. Denham's editor, Theodore Howard Banks (*The Poetical Works of Sir John Denham* (New Haven, 1928, 1969), 91–4), does not date the poem, but the allusion to the Pope-converting Irish Quaker, John Perrot, in the second stanza suggests a composition date *c.*1659–61. For Perrot, see above, 225–6.

47. Green the Quaker remains unidentified.

48. Denham, *Works*, ed. Banks, 111.

49. Sir Francis Wortley, *Characters And Elegies* (1646); idem, *Britanicus His Blessing* (Cambridge, 1646).

50. In Hyder E. Rollins, ed., *Cavalier and Puritan: Ballads and Broadsides Illustrating the Period of the Great Rebellion 1640–1660* (New York, 1923), 127.

51. *Rump Songs* (1662), I.17–19.

52. *Rump Songs*, I.291–5.

53. Alexander Brome, Song XXI, 'The Royalists Answer', in *Poems*, ed. Roman R. Dubinski (Toronto, 1982), 1.144.

54. Brome, 'A Satyre on the Rebellion', in Dubinski, ed., 1.283. For the 'turning out' of psalms by hymns, see above, 260–76.

55. In Rollins, ed., *Cavalier and Puritan*, 161–2.

56. See Gerald Hammond, *Fleeting Things: English Poets and Poems 1616–1660* (Camb., Mass., 1990), 246ff.

57. See Andrew Marvell, *Poems*, ed. N. Smith, forthcoming.

58. John Cleveland, 'The Mixt Assembly', in Morris and Withington, edd., 26.

59. John Collop, *The Poems of John Collop*, edited by Conrad Hilberry (Madison, Wisc., 1962), 35.

60. *Ibid.*, 34.

61. *Ibid.*, 46–7.

62. The sociological implications of rumping are considered by Mark Jenner in 'Scatology, Coprophilia and Political Cannibalism: The Rump and the Body Politic in Restoration England', forthcoming.

63. Dryden, *Poems and Fables*, 280, 282.

64. *Rump Songs*, I.289–90.

Chapter 10: Calamity as Narrative

1. See Anthony Low, *The Georgic Revolution* (Princeton, 1985).

2. James Turner, *The Politics of Landscape: Rural Scenery and Society in English Poetry 1630–1660* (Camb., Mass., 1979), 116–85.

3. Low, *The Georgic Revolution*, 201, 228, 251.

4. These lines do not occur in the poem's first draft, but are in every version thereafter. All references to versions of 'Coopers Hill' are taken from Brendan O Hehir, *Expans'd Hieroglyphs: A Critical Edition of Sir John Denham's Coopers Hill* (Berkeley and Los Angeles, 1969).

5. The stork refers of course to Aesop's well-known fable, generally taken to be a warning against tyrants.

6. Denham revives in 1655, in compressed fashion, a simile in the two early drafts (Draft I (?1641), ll. 269–74; Draft II (?1642), ll. 281–6), but which was suppressed in the published version of 1642.

7. The best detailed reading of the poem, in context, is now Derek Hirst and Steven Zwicker, 'High Summer at Nun Appleton: Andrew Marvell and Lord Fairfax's Occasions', *HJ*, 36 (1993), 247–69.

8. For the best accounts, see Gerrard Winstanley, *The Law of Freedom and Other Writings*, ed. Christopher Hill (1973; Cambridge, 1983); Christopher Hill, 'The Religion of Gerrard Winstanley', *Past and Present*, Supplement No. 5 (1978).

9. Sir Walter Scott, Introduction (Edinburgh, 1821), 6.

10. Janus Dubravius, Bishop of Olmutz, was the author of *De piscinis et piscium qui in eis aliter naturis libri quinqui* (?Zurich, 1559).

11. See Nigel Smith, *Perfection Proclaimed: Language and Literature in English Radical Religion 1640–1660* (Oxford, 1989), 185–225.

12. See Lois Potter, *Secret Rites and Secret Writing: Royalist Literature 1641–1660* (Cambridge, 1989), 72–80.

13. For another account of this event, see *Several Proceedings of Parliament*, 24 June–1 July, 1652.

14. See Nathaniel Ingelo, *Bentivolio and Urania* (1660).

15. Other worthies include 'Lord R.', 'Col. Al[gernon] S[idney]', 'Alderman C.'

16. Named as 'Lord R.', 'Col. Al[gernon] S[idney]', 'Alderman C.'

17. This sense of 'harry' as 'hero' or 'worthy' is not in OED.

18. 'Swadling' is also not in OED in this

sense, although the verb may derive from 'swad' (OED sb5 dial.) – 'soldier'. The first recorded usage is 1708. Both 'harry' and 'swadling' might be dialect words picked up by Franck in Scotland.

19. Smith, *Perfection Proclaimed*, 260.
20. Winstanley, *The Law of Freedom*, ed. Hill, 367.
21. William Rabisha, *The whole Body of Cookery Dissected, Taught and Fully Manifested, Methodically, Artificially, and according to the best tradition of the English, French, Italian, Dutch., etc. or a Sympathie of all varieties in Natural Compounds in that Mysterie* (1661).
22. William Rabisha, *Adam Unvailed, And Seen with open Face* (1649), 2.
23. Rabisha, *The whole Body of Cookery Dissected*, 241.
24. Christopher Hill, 'The Mad Hatter', *Puritanism and Revolution* (1958; 1969), 303–10.
25. Robert Everard, *The Creation and Fall of Adam Reviewed* (1649; 2nd edn, 1652), 3, 15–17.
26. See the account in D. R. Woolf, *The Idea of History in Early Stuart England* (Toronto, 1990). The standard work is F. Smith Fussner, *The Historical Revolution: English Historical Writing and Thought, 1580–1640* (1962).
27. John Hall, *A Method of History*, Bodl. MS Rawl. D 152, fo. 4r.
28. Mathias Prideaux, *An Easy and Compendious Introduction For Reading all sorts of Histories* (3rd edn, Oxford, 1654 [1st edn, 1648]), 349.
29. Giovanni Francesco Biondi, *An History of the Civill Warres of England* (1641), trans. Henry Carey, Earl of Monmouth, Sig. c1r.
30. See Francis Bacon, *The Advancement of Learning* (1605), 2.2.
31. See Peter Burke, 'Tacitism' in T.A. Dorey, ed., *Tacitism* (1969), 000–0; *idem*, 'Tacitism, scepticism, and reason of state' in J.H. Burns, ed., *The Cambridge History of Political Thought 1450–1700* (Cambridge, 1991), 479–98.
32. Copy inspected in Worcester College Library.
33. [Clement Walker], *Anarchia Angli-*

cana: Or, The History of Independency, Pt 2 (1649), Sig. A4v.
34. Woolf, *The Idea of History*, 200–242.
35. Martine Watson Brownley, *Clarendon and the Rhetoric of Historical Form* (Philadelphia, 1985), 14.
36. Thomas Hobbes, 'To the Readers', in Thucydides, *The Peloponnesian War*, trans. Thomas Hobbes (1629), ed. David Grene (Chicago, 1959; 1989), xxiii.
37. Brownley, *Clarendon*, 7.
38. Hall, *A Method of History*, fo. 15v.
39. See Hayden White, *Metahistory: The Historical Imagination in Nineteenth-Century Europe* (Baltimore, 1973).
40. F.M. Cornford, *Thucydides Mythos-toricus* (1907; reprinted, New York, 1969). For an account of a pattern of 'double revolution' in Thucydides' translator, Thomas Hobbes, see Hans-Dieter Metzger, *Thomas Hobbes und die Englische Revolution* (Stuttgart, 1991), 176–83.
41. Hobbes, 'To the Readers', xxi–xxii.
42. Thomas Hobbes, 'To the Readers', loc. cit.
43. John Hall, *A Method of History*, fo. 15r.
44. John Hall, *A Method of History*, fos. 4v-5r. Hall refers to the Scottish historian and writer of political romances, John Barclay, *Euphormio-nis Lusininis* (1624), Pt 2 (see above, 235–6).
45. John Rushworth, *Historical Collections of Private Passages of State/Weighty Matters in Law/Remarkable Proceedings in Five Parliaments* (1659), Sig. b1r. Rushworth was later derided by Tories for his reliance upon newsbooks, although, as Joad Raymond has demonstrated (see above, 371 n1), Rushworth was present as scribe to both King, Parliament and Army at crucial points: his written collections can be trusted.
46. See John Vicars, *Jehovah-Jireh. God in the Mount* (1642, 2nd edn, much enlarged 1644); *Gods Arke Overtopping the Worlds Waves* (1646); *Magnalia Dei Anglicana* (1646).

47. See N.H. Keeble, *The Literary Culture of Nonconformity in the Later Seventeenth Century* (Leicester, 1987), 263–82.

48. See, for instance, Thomas Fuller, *The Historie of the Holy Warre* (1st edn, 1639).

49. William Bridge, *The Truth of the Times Vindicated* (1643), 16–17.

50. Folger MS V.a.229.

51. See John C. Coolidge, 'Marvell and Horace', *MP*, 63 (1965), 111–20.

52. On uses of Providence, see Blair Worden, 'Providence and Politics in Cromwellian England', *Past and Present*, 108 (1985), 55–99.

53. But see also Arthur Wilson, *The History of Great Britain* (1653), Sig. A2r.

54. For Lucan's relevance to Ralegh, see above 388 n4.

55. R[ichard] H[awkins], *A Discourse of the Nationall Excellencies of England* (1658), 80.

56. Hobbes, 'On the Life and History of Thucydides', in Grene, ed., 577.

57. Hobbes, 'On the Life and History of Thucydides', quoting Plutarch, *De Gloria Atheniensium*, in Grene, ed., 577.

58. But see the qualifications made in Joan E. Hartman, 'Restyling the King: Clarendon Writes Charles I', in James Holstun, *Pamphlet Wars: Prose in the English Revolution* (1992), 45–59.

59. Calendar of Clarendon State Papers, 2620.

60. Letter to Sir Edward Nicholas, 15 Nov. 1646, Calendar of Clarendon State Papers, 2354, 342.

61. Clarendon's notion of Buckingham's inexperience of Parliaments is open to serious question.

62. Thomas May, *History of the Parliament* (1647), 173–4.

63. Brownley, *Clarendon*, 30.

64. Nicholas Von Maltzahn, *Milton's History of Britain. Republican Historiography in the English Revolution* (Oxford, 1991). Austen Woolrych's argument for a later dating of the *History* also carries much force: 'The

Date of the Digression in Milton's History of Britain', in R. Ollard and P. Tudor-Craig, *For Veronica Wedgwood These: Studies in Seventeenth-Century History* (1986), 217–46.

65. The classic work on this aspect of English historiography is J.G.A. Pocock, *The Ancient Constitution and the Feudal Law* (Cambridge, 1957; 2nd edn, 1987), but see also Richard Tuck, *Philosophy and Government 1572–1651* (Cambridge, 1993), 209–11, 235–40.

66. George Lawson, *An Examination of the Political Part of Mr. Hobbs his Leviathan* (1657), 43.

67. See Peter Heylyn, *Observations on the Historie of the Reign of King Charles* (1656); idem, *Extraneus Vapulans: or the Observator Rescued* (1656).

68. Although Ludlow's text was classicised by Toland in the 1690s, and the millennial content reduced. See Edmund Ludlow, *Memoirs*, ed. C.H. Firth, 2 vols (Oxford, 1894); idem, *A Voyce from the Watch Tower: Part Five 1660–1662*, ed. A.B. Worden, Camden Fourth Series, vol. 21 (1978); Lucy Hutchinson, *Memoirs of the Life of Colonel Hutchinson*, ed. James Sutherland (1806); Bulstrode Whitelocke, *Memorials of the English Affairs* (1682); N.H. Keeble, '"The Colonel's Shadow": Lucy Hutchinson, Women's Writing and the Civil War', in Thomas Healy and Jonathan Sawday, edd., *Literature and the English Civil War* (Cambridge, 1990), 227–47.

Conclusion

1. For other modern interpretations of the period, see Caryl Churchill, *Light Shining in Buckinghamshire* (1976); Howard Barker, *Restoration* (1981). The Army debates have been dramatised in two different versions by Lesley Montgomery (now Le Claire) and Jack Emery, who has also dramatised the trial of Charles I and one of Lilburne's trials.

2. For an impressive argument for the continuing importance of manuscripts, see Harold Love, *Scribal Publication in Seventeenth-Century England* (Oxford, 1993).

Index